MW01181448

MARRIAGE AND FAMILY 94/95

Twentieth Edition

Editor

Ollie Pocs
Illinois State University

Ollie Pocs is a professor in the Department of Sociology, Anthropology, and Social Work at Illinois State University. He received his B.A. and M.A. in sociology from the University of Illinois. His Ph.D. in family studies is from Purdue University. His primary areas of interest are marriage and family, human sexuality and sexuality education, sex roles, and counseling/therapy. He has published several books and articles in these areas.

A Library of Information from the Public Press

Cover illustration by Mike Eagle

The Dushkin Publishing Group, Inc.
Sluice Dock, Guilford, Connecticut 06437

The Annual Editions Series

Annual Editions is a series of over 60 volumes designed to provide the reader with convenient, low-cost access to a wide range of current, carefully selected articles from some of the most important magazines, newspapers, and journals published today. Annual Editions are updated on an annual basis through a continuous monitoring of over 300 periodical sources. All Annual Editions have a number of features designed to make them particularly useful, including topic guides, annotated tables of contents, unit overviews, and indexes. For the teacher using Annual Editions in the classroom, an Instructor's Resource Guide with test questions is available for each volume.

VOLUMES AVAILABLE

Africa
Aging
American Foreign Policy
American Government
American History, Pre-Civil War
American History, Post-Civil War
Anthropology
Biology
Business Ethics
Canadian Politics
Child Growth and Development
China
Comparative Politics
Computers in Education
Computers in Business
Computers in Society
Criminal Justice
Drugs, Society, and Behavior
Dying, Death, and Bereavement
Early Childhood Education
Economics
Educating Exceptional Children
Education
Educational Psychology
Environment
Geography
Global Issues
Health
Human Development
Human Resources
Human Sexuality
India and South Asia
International Business
Japan and the Pacific Rim

Latin America
Life Management
Macroeconomics
Management
Marketing
Marriage and Family
Mass Media
Microeconomics
Middle East and the Islamic World
Money and Banking
Multicultural Education
Nutrition
Personal Growth and Behavior
Physical Anthropology
Psychology
Public Administration
Race and Ethnic Relations
Russia, Eurasia, and Central/Eastern Europe
Social Problems
Sociology
State and Local Government
Third World
Urban Society
Violence and Terrorism
Western Civilization, Pre-Reformation
Western Civilization, Post-Reformation
Western Europe
World History, Pre-Modern
World History, Modern
World Politics

Library of Congress Cataloging in Publication Data
Annual Editions: Marriage and Family. 1994/95.
        1. Family—United States—Periodicals. 2. Marriage—United States—Periodicals. I. Pocs, Ollie, *comp.* II. Title: Marriage and Family.
ISBN 1–56134–283–1   301.42'05   74–84596
HQ 536.A57

Twentieth Edition

Printed in the United States of America

Editors/ Advisory Board

EDITOR

Ollie Pocs
Illinois State University

ADVISORY BOARD

Members of the Advisory Board are instrumental in the final selection of articles for each edition of Annual Editions. Their review of articles for content, level, currentness, and appropriateness provides critical direction to the editor and staff. We think you'll find their careful consideration well reflected in this volume.

STAFF

Ian A. Nielsen, Publisher
Brenda S. Filley, Production Manager
Roberta Monaco, Editor
Addie Raucci, Administrative Editor
Cheryl Greenleaf, Permissions Editor
Diane Barker, Editorial Assistant
Lisa Holmes-Doebrick, Administrative Coordinator
Charles Vitelli, Designer
Shawn Callahan, Graphics
Steve Shumaker, Graphics
Lara M. Johnson, Graphics
Libra A. Cusack, Typesetting Supervisor
Juliana Arbo, Typesetter

To the Reader

In publishing ANNUAL EDITIONS we recognize the enormous role played by the magazines, newspapers, and journals of the *public press* in providing current, first-rate educational information in a broad spectrum of interest areas. Within the articles, the best scientists, practitioners, researchers, and commentators draw issues into new perspective as accepted theories and viewpoints are called into account by new events, recent discoveries change old facts, and fresh debate breaks out over important controversies.

Many of the articles resulting from this enormous editorial effort are appropriate for students, researchers, and professionals seeking accurate, current material to help bridge the gap between principles and theories and the real world. These articles, however, become more useful for study when those of lasting value are carefully *collected, organized, indexed,* and *reproduced* in a *low-cost format,* which provides easy and permanent access when the material is needed. That is the role played by *Annual Editions.* Under the direction of each volume's *Editor,* who is an expert in the subject area, and with the guidance of an *Advisory Board,* we seek each year to provide in each *ANNUAL EDITION* a current, well-balanced, carefully selected collection of the best of the public press for your study and enjoyment. We think you'll find this volume useful, and we hope you'll take a moment to let us know what you think.

> I have made a ceaseless effort, not to ridicule, not to bewail, nor to scorn human actions, but to understand them.
>
> —Spinoza

The above quotation expresses the focus of this anthology—the intimate relationships of marriage and family. The purpose of *Annual Editions: Marriage and Family 94/95* is to make you aware of the latest thinking, trends in behavior, concerns, and problems regarding these important social institutions. The anthology also attempts to counteract some of the misleading information provided by the mass media.

The institutions of marriage and family remain popular despite reports to the contrary. Over 90 percent of the population continues to marry. Though it is true that over a third of the couples who marry terminate their marriages by divorce, the majority of divorced people remarry rather quickly. The family remains popular as well, although many couples are having fewer children and are spacing them farther apart than in previous generations.

The articles in this volume are taken from professional publications, semiprofessional journals, and popular lay publications aimed at both special populations and a general readership. The selections are carefully reviewed for their currency and, especially, their accuracy. Not only the publication date but the data must be recent.

This anthology is organized to cover many of the important aspects of marriage and family. The first unit looks at historical and cross-cultural changes in marriage and family patterns. In the second unit, the articles deal with the formation of relationships. The third unit concerns relationship maintenance after a relationship has been established. Relationships in transition are considered in the fourth unit; topics include parenting, divorce and remarriage, and the later years. The fifth unit covers emerging family styles and the future of the family. A special section is devoted to articles on finding happiness in intimate relationships and today's happy and healthy families.

This book can be used as a primary text for marriage and family classes when instructors relate some basic information about these institutions to the views expressed in the articles. It can also be used as a supplement to update and/or emphasize certain selected areas or chapters of regular marriage and family textbooks. In addition, this volume works especially well as a source or basis for class discussion about various aspects of marriage and family relationships.

Satisfying relationships are secured through the active processes of study, thought, and verbal communication. This book can provide stimulation for communicating feelings, thoughts, and values by teaching you how to convey them to people who are important to you—your significant others.

Special thanks go to Susan J. Bunting for her contributions to the editing process. Also, I wish to express appreciation to those who sent in article rating forms with their comments about the previous edition and/or suggestions of articles to consider for this edition. Several of the opinions are reflected in this volume. Readers can have input into future editions of *Annual Editions: Marriage and Family* by completing and returning the article rating form at the end of this book. Any anthology can be improved. This one will continue to be—annually.

Ollie Pocs
Editor

Contents

Unit 1

Historical and Cross-Cultural Patterns

Four articles consider marriage and the family as they have changed over the years, and analyze trends among societies.

Unit 2

Formation of Relationships

Six selections discuss the important elements in the formation of relationships. Topics include romance, jealousy, trust, the single life, and the dynamics of married life.

The concepts in bold italics are developed in the article. For further expansion please refer to the Topic Guide and the Index.

Unit 3

Relationship Maintenance

Eleven articles examine what is involved in maintaining
relationships when they are challenged by some of
today's economic and social demands.

The concepts in bold italics are developed in the article. For further expansion please refer to the Topic Guide and the Index.

Unit 4

Relationships in Transition

Nineteen articles discuss the transition from marriage to family, the dynamics of parenting, the consequences of divorce and remarriage, and the individual in the later years of life.

The concepts in bold italics are developed in the article. For further expansion please refer to the Topic Guide and the Index.

The concepts in bold italics are developed in the article. For further expansion please refer to the Topic Guide and the Index.

Unit 5

New Styles and the Future

Ten articles examine emerging patterns in American family life and predict future trends.

The concepts in bold italics are developed in the article. For further expansion please refer to the Topic Guide and the Index.

Topic Guide

This topic guide suggests how the selections in this book relate to topics of traditional concern to students and professionals involved with the study of marriage and family. It is useful for locating articles that relate to each other for reading and research. The guide is arranged alphabetically according to topic. Articles may, of course, treat topics that do not appear in the topic guide. In turn, entries in the topic guide do not necessarily constitute a comprehensive listing of all the contents of each selection.

TOPIC AREA	TREATED IN:	TOPIC AREA	TREATED IN:
Abortion	1. Prophets of Doom 25. "She Died Because of a Law" 45. Single Parents and Damaged Children	**Communication (cont.)**	19. Sex and the Female Agenda 20. Sexual Desire 27. Sanity Savers 33. "Will the Kids Ever Adjust to Our Divorce?" 36. Remarriage Education 39. What Women Want Men to Know about Menopause 47. Marriage and Romantic Relationships 48. How Our Marriage Was Saved 49. Happy Families 50. Happy Families Are Not All Alike
Abuse	15. Inside the Heart of Marital Violence 16. After He Hits Her		
Adolescence	8. Choosing Mates—The American Way 17. Crisis of the Absent Father 25. "She Died Because of a Law" 30. Fathers and Families 42. New Family 45. Single Parents and Damaged Children		
Adultery	*See* Infidelity	**Dating**	8. Choosing Mates 9. Love and Mate Selection
Aging	4. Generalized Extended Family Exchange 13. Receipts from a Marriage 34. Second Time Around 38. Divorce after 50 39. What Women Want Men to Know about Menopause 40. Grandparent Bond	**Divorce**	1. Prophets of Doom 12. What's Happening to American Marriage? 17. Crisis of the Absent Father 21. Beyond Betrayal 31. Father Figures 32. Family Values 33. "Will the Kids Ever Adjust to Our Divorce?" 37. After My Son's Divorce 38. Divorce after 50 41. Terms of Endearment
Childbirth	22. Ultrasound 23. Home Delivery 24. Unnecessary Cesarean Sections		
Children and Child Care	4. Generalized Extended Family Exchange 15. Inside the Heart of Marital Violence 17. Crisis of the Absent Father 18. How Kids Grieve 26. When Your Child Is Choking 27. Sanity Savers 28. Who's Minding America's Kids 29. Child Care 30. Fathers and Families 31. Father Figures 33. "Will the Kids Ever Adjust to Our Divorce?" 35. Stepmother Identity 37. After My Son's Divorce 40. Grandparent Bond 42. New Family 44. "Stop the World So I Can Get Off for a While" 45. Single Parents and Damaged Children 46. Pessimistic Views about U.S. Families 49. Happy Families 50. Happy Families Are Not All Alike	**Family/Families— Traditional/ Nontraditional**	4. Generalized Extended Family Exchange 27. Sanity Savers 31. Father Figures 34. Second Time Around 35. Stepmother Identity 37. After My Son's Divorce 42. New Family 43. New Family Values 44. "Stop the World So I Can Get Off for a While" 45. Single Parents and Damaged Children 46. Pessimistic Views about U.S. Families 49. Happy Families 50. Happy Families Are Not All Alike
		Finances	4. Generalized Extended Family Exchange 13. Receipts from a Marriage 32. Family Values 34. Second Time Around 41. Terms of Endearment 42. New Family
Communication	2. What Is Love? 3. Right Chemistry 6. Intimacy 7. Relationships on Campus 10. Mating Game 11. When Parents Disagree 14. Saving Relationships 18. How Kids Grieve	**Gender Roles**	1. Prophets of Doom 2. What Is Love? 3. Right Chemistry 4. Generalized Extended Family Exchange 5. Sizing Up the Sexes 7. Relationships on Campus 8. Choosing Mates

TOPIC AREA	TREATED IN:	TOPIC AREA	TREATED IN:
Gender Roles (cont.)	9. Love and Mate Selection 10. Mating Game 14. Saving Relationships 15. Inside the Heart of Marital Violence 16. After He Hits Her 17. Crisis of the Absent Father 19. Sex and the Female Agenda 30. Fathers and Families 31. Father Figures 32. Family Values 35. Stepmother Identity 39. What Women Want Men to Know about Menopause 43. New Family Values	Marriage	1. Prophets of Doom 8. Choosing Mates 9. Love and Mate Selection 12. What's Happening to American Marriage? 13. Receipts from a Marriage 32. Family Values 34. Second Time Around 41. Terms of Endearment 43. New Family Values 47. Marriage and Romantic Relationships 48. How Our Marriage Was Saved 49. Happy Families 50. Happy Families Are Not All Alike
Health Concerns	19. Sex and the Female Agenda 22. Ultrasound 23. Home Delivery 24. Unnecessary Cesarean Sections 25. "She Died Because of a Law" 39. What Women Want Men to Know about Menopause	Parents/Parenting	4. Generalized Extended Family Exchange 11. When Parents Disagree 13. Receipts from a Marriage 17. Crisis of the Absent Father 25. "She Died Because of a Law" 27. Sanity Savers 30. Fathers and Families 31. Father Figures 33. "Will the Kids Ever Adjust to Our Divorce?" 34. Second Time Around 35. Stepmother Identity 37. After My Son's Divorce 40. Grandparent Bond 42. New Family 43. New Family Values 44. "Stop the World So I Can Get Off for a While" 45. Single Parents and Damaged Children 46. Pessimistic Views about U.S. Families 49. Happy Families 50. Happy Families Are Not All Alike
Infidelity	3. Right Chemistry 10. Mating Game 19. Sex and the Female Agenda 20. Sexual Desire 21. Beyond Betrayal 38. Divorce after 50 43. New Family Values		
Intimacy/Love	2. What Is Love? 3. Right Chemistry 5. Sizing Up the Sexes 6. Intimacy 8. Choosing Mates 9. Love and Mate Selection 10. Mating Game 12. What's Happening to American Marriage? 14. Saving Relationships 15. Inside the Heart of Marital Violence 19. Sex and the Female Agenda 20. Sexual Desire 21. Beyond Betrayal 27. Sanity Savers 32. Family Values 34. Second Time Around 36. Remarriage Education 38. Divorce after 50 43. New Family Values 47. Marriage and Romantic Relationships 48. How Our Marriage Was Saved 49. Happy Families 50. Happy Families Are Not All Alike	Sex/Sexuality	2. What Is Love? 3. Right Chemistry 5. Sizing Up the Sexes 10. Mating Game 14. Saving Relationships 19. Sex and the Female Agenda 20. Sexual Desire 21. Beyond Betrayal 39. What Women Want Men to Know about Menopause 43. New Family Values 45. Single Parents and Damaged Children 47. Marriage and Romantic Relationships
		Values	2. What Is Love? 6. Intimacy 7. Relationships on Campus 8. Choosing Mates 9. Love and Mate Selection 11. When Parents Disagree 12. What's Happening to American Marriage? 21. Beyond Betrayal 31. Father Figures 32. Family Values 36. Remarriage Education 43. New Family Values 45. Single Parents and Damaged Children 49. Happy Families 50. Happy Families Are Not All Alike
Laws/Legislation/ Governmental Roles	1. Prophets of Doom 17. Crisis of the Absent Father 25. "She Died Because of a Law" 28. Who's Minding America's Kids 29. Child Care 32. Family Values 41. Terms of Endearment 42. New Family 45. Single Parents and Damaged Children		

Historical and Cross-Cultural Patterns

When we shut all the world out, we find that we have shut ourselves in.

—W. G. Sumner

This statement holds true both culturally and historically. It has been said that in order to properly understand the present and plan for the future, it is necessary to have some understanding of the past. This understanding encompasses many areas, including marriage and family. As social historian John Demos said, "Much of what we expect from family life bears the stamp of an earlier time." How often have you heard people talk of "the good old days"? Have you wondered if things were really as they are remembered? It is only through careful historical and cross-cultural study that family patterns today can be understood or compared with those of times past or those characteristic of other cultures.

In order to establish a historical and cross-cultural perspective on marriage and family, this first unit will endeavor to meet several goals. These include: (1) to assist readers in distinguishing nostalgia from history pertaining to marriage and family patterns in the past and present; (2) to assist readers in separating facts from opinions pertaining to marriage and family patterns; and (3) to broaden readers' knowledge about the range of current and emerging marriage and family forms and styles in this and other cultures.

The first article, "Prophets of Doom," exposes the popular practice of decrying today's family while romanticizing the good old days. This opening chapter of a new family text, The Myth of Family Decline, places today's family life within a broader and more factual historical context.

The next two articles focus on love and its historical and cross-cultural meanings, experiences, and functions. Customs for attracting a mate, showing one's love, or keeping the romantic fires burning vary from China to Africa to Russia or the United States. This amazing diversity, however, involves the way these humans choose to express love. Science has come to firmly believe that humankind is biologically and genetically made to love.

The last article focuses on extended-family functions, members, and customs in an Asian setting: the Philippines. "Generalized Extended Family Exchange: A Case from the Philippines" describes the relationships and interdependence between households within extended families. This article suggests national and international applications relative to both family needs and governmental supporters and programs to address them.

Looking Ahead: Challenge Questions

Why do people put on rose-colored glasses about the families of the past? How does this practice affect today's families?

What is your definition of love? How do you "know" you are in love? How do you show you love someone? What does it take for you to believe someone loves you? What can you do when love fades?

As science investigates love, attracting, and mating, a biological, genetic, evolutionary basis is becoming very clear. How do you react to these findings and why?

How often do you interact with family members other than those with whom you have lived? How would you describe your relationship with your aunts, uncles, cousins, grandparents, nieces, nephews? Do you think families with ongoing ties to these extended-family members are strengthened? Why or why not?

Has your family cared for an aging grandparent or other relative? Do you expect to do so for your parents? Do you expect your children to care for you? Describe your feelings and reactions to these three questions about your norms and expectations for family elderly care.

Prophets of Doom

Edward L. Kain

Almost daily, the headlines scream out yet another message that seems to indicate the family is on its deathbed in modern America. News magazines include stories on unprecedented rates of divorce, frightening reports of elderly Americans (seemingly forgotten by their family and society) being mistreated and neglected in nursing homes, and children being raised in single-parent families. The evening news talks about the majority of mothers working outside the home and of social movements supporting concerns as diverse as abortion rights and homosexual freedom. All these issues seem to signal that the basic institution in our society is threatened.

These challenges to the family have been met sometimes with dismay and sometimes with resignation, but in recent years they have also been met with counterattacks led by groups rallying around a battle cry for a return to the traditional family of the past. It appears that the war has begun. Those fighting in the trenches, however, are not at all certain of the outcome because there are many separate battles being waged at once.

This . . . is an attempt to step back from the apparent battleground of the closing decades of the twentieth century and evaluate the health of the family in the United States from a broader perspective—one that places current family life within the context of social change. Families do not exist in a vacuum, and we cannot begin to understand the quality of family life in the last decade of the twentieth century unless it is placed within historical and social context. What were American families like in the past? How have families been changing over the past century? What types of family patterns can we expect to see over the next several decades?

Unfortunately, the task of placing family life within a broader context is an assignment with many dangers.

Because most of us were born into families and have spent most of our lives in the context of our own family structures, we all have some sense that we are knowledgeable on the topic of family life. It is somewhat difficult to step back from our personal experience and evaluate the institution of the family with objectivity.

To understand families in the present or the future, we must understand families in the past. We cannot possibly assess the health of family life as we near the twenty-first century unless we place it within a broader span of historical time. As individuals and as a culture, however, Americans tend not to think of contemporary issues in historical perspective. This is true not only of popular accounts of family life, but also of the work done by many family scholars as well. Like Rip Van Winkle who awoke to a world vastly different than that to which he was accustomed, we often look upon contemporary family life with dismay. Our world is changing rapidly, and many of these changes seem to challenge our very conception of family life. We long for a return to traditional values and the traditional family structure that we remember from the past.

This dismay at the current state of affairs and desire to return to the past is what I have come to label the "myth of family decline." Our image of families in the past is often based on myth rather than reality. For the past three decades, work by historians, demographers, and sociologists has begun to paint a new picture of the history of family life. Using innovative methods to explore church, family, and civil records, these researchers have discovered patterns of family experience that stand in stark contrast to the images many of us have held about the traditional family.[1]

As an illustration of this point, take the following quiz, which asks a few basic questions about family life both in the past and the present.

A Brief Quiz on Families and Change in the United States

1. Which of the following years had the highest divorce rate in the United States?
   - A) 1935
   - B) 1945
   - C) 1955
   - D) 1965

2. T F Because of the rapid rise in the divorce rate, children are much more likely to live in a single-parent household than they were a century ago.

3. T F In the past, most families lived in three-generation households. It is now much less likely for this to occur, since grandparents are put into nursing homes instead of cared for in the home.

4. What proportion of women worked outside the home in 1900?
   - A) one in fifty
   - B) one in twenty
   - C) one in ten
   - D) one in five

5. T F Over the past one hundred years, fewer and fewer people have been getting married, so the number of single people has been increasing.

6. T F The high incidence of female-headed households among black families today can be traced to the impact of slavery on family life as well as to the disruption of two-parent, nuclear families among black Americans during the time of Emancipation.

7. What is the most common household type in the United States today?
   - A) a single-parent family with one adult wage earner
   - B) a two-parent family with one adult male wage earner
   - C) a two-parent family with two adult wage earners

8. T F Very few families live below the poverty line (as officially defined by the federal government) for extended periods of time (five consecutive years).

Before I give the results to this quiz, there are two things to keep in mind: First, don't be upset if you did not score very well. I have given this quiz to hundreds of students and professionals, and the typical result is that scores are extremely low. In fact, when I gave the quiz at a conference attended only by professionals who specialize in working with and teaching about family life, most of the questions were answered incorrectly by a majority of the group! Rather than being a statement about the quality of professionals in the area of family, this reflects the tendency of our culture to ignore the past and to base opinions about our basic social institutions (family, education, economy, religion, and government) on a cultural image that often is greatly at variance with reality.

Second, I want to suggest that each of these questions illustrates a basic point. . . . Now, for the answers to the quiz:

Question 1. Which of the following years had the highest divorce rate in the United States?: A) 1935; B) 1945; C) 1955; D) 1965. The correct answer to this question is B. No, that is not a typographical error in the book; the correct answer is 1945. Most people are very surprised that the correct answer is not 1965. "Isn't it true that divorce rates have been rising throughout the century?", they ask. This response clearly illustrates one of the first central points . . .: *We seldom have a historical understanding of family life or of the impact of specific historical events on the functioning of families.* The divorce rates in this country reached a historical peak at the end of World War II. Several explanations have been given for this: First, it is likely that a number of couples married hurriedly after relatively short courtships when the man was about to be sent off to war. Second, the stress of separation may have resulted in the development of other relationships for both the women at home and the men who were away. Third, both spouses may have changed considerably during the war years. The man who returned home from the battlefields may not have been the boy who left, and the woman at home may not have been the same girl whom he had courted and married. While it is true that divorce rates in this country consistently increased from 1950 through 1980, they did not match the peak of 1945 until the mid-1970s.[2]

Question 2. (True or False) Because of the rapid rise in the divorce rate, children are much more likely to live in a single-parent household than they were a century ago. This statement is false. Most people do not realize the profound effects on family life that have resulted from rapid declines in the mortality rate since the turn of the century. While divorce has increased throughout this century, the drastic decline in the number of parents who die at an early age (leaving widows, widowers, and orphans behind) more than offsets the increase in single-parent households that results from marital disruption caused by divorce.[3] This question reflects a second basic principle . . .: *If an adequate understanding of family change is to be developed, we must look not only at data from the past but also at the relationships between different types of changes affecting family life.*

Question 3. (True or False) In the past, most families lived in three-generation households. It is now much less likely for this to occur, since grandparents are put into nursing homes instead of cared for in the home. This statement is false for a number of reasons. One of the most important findings of the new family history has been a challenge to the idea that the rise of the modern nuclear family (the family including only two parents and their children) is linked to industrialization and is a result of that process. Peter Laslett[4] and others have demonstrated that, at least in England, the nuclear family was the dominant form of household long before the advent of industrialization. Laslett makes a strong argument for the continuity of family life over time, and suggests that in a number of ways the family in the "world we have lost" was much as it is today. This illustrates a third central point . . .: *When we have actual data about family life in the past, it often presents a picture of family life that is drastically different from the image that is common in popular mythology.*

In fairness, I must say that Laslett's work is a reaction to most contemporary theories of the family, which ignore the importance of historical time. Unfortunately Laslett's approach has been criticized for ignoring the dynamic nature of the family as a group. Just as the institution of the family has changed over historical time, individual families change over the family cycle. Subsequent work has suggested that while at any point in time most families in preindustrial Europe may have been nuclear in structure, if families are traced over their development cycle, many of them are extended for brief periods while the elder parents are still alive.[5]

Even if everyone wanted to spend part of their family cycle in a three-generation household, however, it still would not be possible for many families. First, only *one* of the children and his or her family typically lived with the elderly parents, so in every family there would be a number of siblings who would live in nuclear households. In addition, the elder generation seldom survived long enough to spend much time in a three-generation household.

Question 4. What proportion of women worked outside the home in 1900?: A) one in fifty; B) one in twenty; C) one in ten; D) one in five. If you chose answer D, you are right. Yes, fully one in five women worked outside the home in paid occupations at the turn of the century.[6] Many were employed as domestic servants and in agriculture. Others worked in textile mills and in teaching positions. Still others were employed in the new clerical sector, which was expanding as our country moved further into the industrial age. . . .

Most people are surprised that the female labor force participation rate was that high. We tend to have an image that women only started working outside the home during World War II, and that they returned home when the war ended. The rise of female labor force participation is often seen as a recent event linked to the women's movement of the 1960s. Certainly there has been an increase in the number of women working outside the home since 1950. In real-

ity, however, the rate of female labor force participation has been rising relatively consistently since the late nineteenth century. This points to a fourth principle . . .: *Most of the changes occurring in families in the United States are not revolutionary but evolutionary—they are changes that have been happening gradually over a long period of time, and they do not represent a radical change from patterns in the past.*

Question 5. (True or False) Over the past one hundred years, fewer and fewer people have been getting married, so the number of single people has been increasing. The correct answer to this question is false. (By now you are probably catching on to the idea that your first guess may have been wrong.) Both the popular press and sociological research in recent years has focused on the increase in singlehood.[7] This increase, however, has only been happening since 1950, a period when more people married than any other time in all of American history. In essence, there was no place for the rate of singlehood to go but up. If a longer historical view is taken, it becomes clear that the rates of singlehood today are still lower than they were a century ago. This reflects a fifth basic point . . .: *When we do include history in our conceptions of family life, we tend to focus only on recent history and remain blind to the broader picture of social change and continuity in family life.*

Question 6. (True or False) The high incidence of female-headed households among black families today can be traced to the impact of slavery on family life as well as to the disruption of two-parent, nuclear families among black Americans during the time of Emancipation. This statement is false. While the reasons for the high incidence of single-parent, female-headed households among black Americans today may be complex, they cannot be traced to a legacy developed from the period of slavery and Emancipation. In a series of careful studies, Herbert G. Gutman[8] shows that between 1855 and 1880 as many as 90 percent of black households contained both a husband and wife or just a father with children. The matriarchal household was common neither among antebellum free blacks, nor among black families after Emancipation. The continuing myths about the causes and implications of the structure of black families illustrate another central point . . .: *Historical causes may be built into current explanation of family life, but unless data are used to examine the validity of these historical explanations, our understanding of the relationship between historical events and family life may be seriously flawed.* I might add to this statement the general observation that when groups that are not white, male, or middle-class are concerned, our historical understanding is usually less sophisticated and more often incorrect. The new family history has involved more attention to issues of race, class, and gender—much to the benefit of our understanding of family life in the past.

Question 7. What is the most common household type in the United States today?: A) a single-parent family with one adult wage earner; B) a two-parent family with one adult male wage earner; C) a two-parent family with two adult wage earners. This question turns from the history of family life to the contemporary family in the United States. Like the questions on the history of the family, it illustrates that we may have misconceptions about families in contemporary America. The correct answer is C. By far the most common type of household in the United States today is one in which both adults work outside the home.[9] This illustrates that *no matter what family life was like in the past, in the contemporary United States the so-called traditional family is in a distinct minority.*

Question 8. (True or False) Very few families live below the poverty line (as officially defined by the federal government) for extended periods of time (five consecutive years). The statement in question 8 is true. Research using data from the Panel Study of Income Dynamics at the University of Michigan illustrates clearly that a very small percentage of families remain consistently below the poverty line (approximately 4 percent).[10] Rather, families move in and out of poverty as wage earners lose a job, are rehired, a divorce occurs, or additional children are born, changing the stresses upon the family budget. This clearly points to the fact that *our conceptions of the family as a static institution are inadequate, and we must think of families as dynamic groups that change over the lifetimes of the individuals who are involved.*

. . . Many of these new findings in family history and family sociology have taken quite some time to find their way into textbooks in the social sciences—and even longer to reach the popular consciousness. Most of us still carry images of a mythic extended family of domestic bliss within our minds. It is important, however, to base our decisions about political issues related to families on reality rather than myth.

Partly because of the American tendency to romanticize the past, and partly because of the many changes in family life that seem so evident during the past several decades, it is common for social analysts to conclude that the family is, indeed, in trouble. Analyses that predict the demise of the family have come from both ends of the political spectrum. On the radical side, Christopher Lasch has suggested that the family is a failure as a "haven in the heartless world" of industrial capitalism, and he paints a gloomy picture about the future prospects of any improvement.[11] According to Lasch, the family is supposed to shield its members from the harsh realities of working life in modern society, and it has failed in this task.

Similarly, the New Evangelical Right fears that the traditional family is in serious danger. Groups like the Moral Majority preach against the sins of modern times and demand that we return to the core American values of the traditional family. The forces of the New Right have supported a variety of types of legislation that attempt to embody these so-called traditional values into the legal structure. Most notable among these attempts was the Family Protection Act, first introduced in September of 1979 by Senator Paul Laxalt. Later versions of the Family Protection Act were introduced to the House by Representative Hansen of Idaho and Representative Smith of Alabama in 1981, and Senator Jepsen of Iowa introduced a revised version to the Senate in June of the same year.[12] I have more fully discussed some of the provisions of the Family Protection Act elsewhere, and a full explication is not necessary here.[13] In essence, the goal of the legislation was to reinforce what is defined as the traditional family—based upon a mythical vision of peaceful family life under patriarchal rule, in which the husband is the breadwinner and the wife is in the home raising the children.

While certainly the most comprehensive in scope, the Family Protection Act is not the only example of attempts in the 1980s to enshrine what is perceived as the traditional family in the laws of the land. Perhaps the most visible example has been the introduction of various versions of a Human Life Amendment, which would ban or limit legal abortion. All these measures can be seen as an attempt to shore up what is perceived as the crumbling foundation of the central institution of any society—the family.

Not everyone, however, agrees with the assessment that the modern family is in trouble. Some, such as Harvard sociologist Mary Jo Bane, argue that while families are changing, they are still vigorous and "here to stay."[14] Bane provides convincing evidence that ties between grandparents and grandchildren and between parents and children have, if anything, become stronger in recent times, rather than weaker.

One reason that the debate about the health of the family is such an important concern is the rapid rate of social change in our society. Changes in our culture create many social problems, as adjustments in some parts of the culture lag behind. William F. Ogburn's concept of cultural lag provides a useful tool for evaluating this problem.[15] As we have moved in the space of a century from an agricultural economy to a post-industrial society, our social institutions have had difficulty keeping up with the massive shifts generated by technological change. The resulting social problems are at the core of many of the political controversies seen today at the national level, including civil rights for people of color, women's rights, and homosexual rights.

Not surprisingly, many of these controversies center on the family: abortion and reproductive rights; homosexuality; the changing roles of women and men; day-care; and comparable worth (the idea that men and women should receive equal pay for jobs that are similar in content, not only for jobs that have the same job title). Because the family is a key institution in any society, and because the transition from agriculture to industry transforms the basic relationships between economic production and family life, many of the cultural lags demanding attention today are reflected in these national political issues.

Unfortunately, as is clear . . ., we are often blind to the realities of family life in the past. Our cultural images of family life in past times are difficult to change, even when data indicate the images are much more myth than reality. Like Rip Van Winkle, we long for a return to the good old days, when life was much simpler and times were happier. . . .

NOTES

1. See, for example, John Demos, *A Little Commonwealth: Family Life in Plymouth Colony* (New York: Oxford University Press, 1970); John Demos and Sarane Spence Boocock (eds.), *Turning Points: Historical and Sociological Essays on the Family* (Chicago: The University of Chicago Press, 1978); Michael Gorden (ed.), *The American Family in Social-Historical Perspective*, 3rd ed. (New York: St. Martin's Press, 1983); Philip Greven, *Four Generations: Population, Land, and Family in Colonial Andover, Massachusetts* (Ithaca: Cornell University Press, 1970); Herbert Gutman, *The Black Family in Slavery and Freedom*, (New York: Pantheon, 1976); Kenneth A. Lockridge, *A New England Town: The First Hundred Years*, (New York: W. W. Norton & Company, 1970); and Theodore K. Rabb and Robert I. Rotberg (eds.), *The Family in History: Interdisciplinary Essays* (New York: Harper & Row, 1970).

2. For more complete data on trends in marriage, divorce, and remarriage, see Andrew Cherlin, *Marriage, Divorce, Remarriage* (Cambridge, MA: Harvard University Press, 1981).

3. See Peter Uhlenberg, "Death and the Family," *Journal of Family History* 5 (1980):313–320.

4. See Peter Laslett, *The World We Have Lost*, 2nd ed. (New York: Charles Scribner's Sons, 1971).

5. See Lutz Berkner, "The Stem Family and the Developmental Cycle of the Peasant Household: An 18th-Century Austrian Example," *American Historical Review* LXXVII (1972):398–418.

6. Historical data on female labor force participation in the United States can be found in a number of sources. See, for example, *The Statistical History of the United States from Colonial Times to the Present* (New York: Basic Books, 1976) and United States Bureau of the Census, *The Historical Statistics of the United States from Colonial Times to 1970, Bicentennial Edition* (Washington, DC: Government Printing Office, 1975).

7. See, for example, Peter Stein, *Single* (Englewood Cliffs, NJ: Prentice-Hall, 1976). The best example of media coverage on singlehood is the flurry of popular articles that quickly appeared after a 1986 study was released projecting the rate of marriage among college-educated women. Both *Newsweek* ("The Marriage Crunch: If You're a Single Woman, Here Are Your Chances of Getting Married," June 2, 1986) and *People* ("Are These Old Maids? A Harvard-Yale Study Says that Most Single Women Over 35 Can Forget About Marriage," March 31, 1986) carried extensive cover stories examining the plight of single women. Little mention is made of where these patterns fit in historical perspective.

8. See Herbert G. Gutman, *The Black Family in Slavery and Freedom* (New York: Pantheon, 1976).

9. See George Masnick and Mary Jo Bane, *The Nation's Families: 1960–1990* (Boston: Auburn Publishing, 1980).

10. Data from the important research resulting from the Michigan Panel of Income Dynamics can be found in a number of volumes, such as Greg J. Duncan and James N. Morgan (eds.), *Five Thousand American Families—Patterns of Economic Progress* (Ann Arbor, MI: Institute for Social Research, 1979).

11. See Christopher Lasch, *Haven in a Heartless World: The Family Besieged* (New York: Basic Books, 1977).

12. For different versions of this legislation, see The Family Protection Act bill H.R. 311. 1981; The Family Protection Act bill H.R. 3955. 1981; The Family Protection Act bill S. 1378. 1981; and The Family Protection Act bill S. 1808. 1979.

13. See Edward L. Kain, "The Federal Government Should Not Foster Legislation Relating to the Family," in Harold Feldman and Andrea Purrot, *Human Sexuality: Contemporary Controversies* (Beverly Hills: Sage, 1984).

14. See Mary Jo Bane, *Here to Stay: American Families in the Twentieth Century* (New York: Basic Books, 1976).

15. See William F. Ogburn, "Cultural Lag as Theory" in Otis Dudley Duncan, *William F. Ogburn on Culture and Social Change* (Chicago: University of Chicago Press, 1964).

What Is LOVE?

After centuries of ignoring the subject as too vague and mushy, science has undergone a change of heart about the tender passion

By PAUL GRAY

What is this thing called love? What? Is this thing called love? What is this thing called? Love.

HOWEVER PUNCTUATED, COLE Porter's simple question begs an answer. Love's symptoms are familiar enough: a drifting mooniness in thought and behavior, the mad conceit that the entire universe has rolled itself up into the person of the beloved, a conviction that no one on earth has ever felt so torrentially about a fellow creature before. Love is ecstasy and torment, freedom and slavery. Poets and songwriters would be in a fine mess without it. Plus, it makes the world go round.

Until recently, scientists wanted no part of it.

The reason for this avoidance, this reluctance to study what is probably life's most intense emotion, is not difficult to track down. Love is mushy; science is hard. Anger and fear, feelings that have been considerably researched in the field and the lab, can be quantified through measurements: pulse and breathing rates, muscle contractions, a whole spider web of involuntary responses. Love does not register as definitively on the instruments; it leaves a blurred fingerprint that could be mistaken for anything from indigestion to a manic attack. Anger and fear have direct roles—fighting or running—in the survival of the species. Since it is possible (a cynic would say common-place) for humans to mate and reproduce without love, all the attendant sighing and swooning and sonnet writing have struck many pragmatic investigators as beside the evolutionary point.

So biologists and anthropologists assumed that it would be fruitless, even frivolous, to study love's evolutionary origins, the way it was encoded in our genes or imprinted in our brains. Serious scientists simply assumed that love—and especially Romantic Love—was really all in the head, put there five or six centuries ago when civilized societies first found enough spare time to indulge in flowery prose. The task of writing the book of love was ceded to playwrights, poets and pulp novelists.

But during the past decade, scientists across a broad range of disciplines have had a change of heart about love. The amount of research expended on the tender passion has never been more intense. Explanations for this rise in interest vary. Some cite the spreading threat of AIDS; with casual sex carrying mortal risks, it seems important to know more about a force that binds couples faithfully together. Others point to the growing number of women scientists and suggest that they may be more willing than their male colleagues to take love seriously. Says Elaine Hatfield, the author of *Love, Sex, and Intimacy: Their Psychology, Biology, and History:* "When I was back at Stanford in the 1960s, they said studying love and human relationships was a quick way to ruin my career. Why not go where

1. HISTORICAL AND CROSS-CULTURAL PATTERNS

MEXICO
Shawls in the Marketplace
In the highlands of Chiapas, weaving skills are treasured, and a colorful, well-made shawl advises potential husbands of its wearer's dexterity.

CHINA
Courtship on Horseback
On the plains of Xinjiang, mounted Kazakh suitors play Catch the Maiden. He chases her in pursuit of a kiss. If he succeeds, she goes after him with a riding crop.

INDIA
A Bed of Roses
Many hotels offer newlyweds lavishly flowered honeymoon suites. In Bombay a couple on their wedding night relax amid and upon a floral panoply.

the real work was being done: on how fast rats could run?" Whatever the reasons, science seems to have come around to a view that nearly everyone else has always taken for granted: romance is real. It is not merely a conceit; it is bred into our biology.

Getting to this point logically is harder than it sounds. The love-as-cultural-delusion argument has long seemed unassailable. What actually accounts for the emotion, according to this scenario, is that people long ago made the mistake of taking fanciful literary tropes seriously. Ovid's *Ars Amatoria* is often cited as a major source of misreadings, its instructions followed, its ironies ignored. Other prime suspects include the 12th century troubadours in Provence who more or less invented the Art of Courtly Love, an elaborate, etiolated ritual for idle noblewomen and aspiring swains that would have been broken to bits by any hint of physical consummation.

Ever since then, the injunction to love and to be loved has hummed nonstop through popular culture; it is a dominant theme in music, films, novels, magazines and nearly everything shown on TV. Love is a formidable and thoroughly proved commercial engine; people will buy and do almost anything that promises them a chance at the bliss of romance.

But does all this mean that love is merely a phony emotion that we picked up because our culture celebrates it? Psychologist Lawrence Casler, author of *Is Marriage Necessary?*, forcefully thinks so, at least at first: "I don't believe love is part of human nature, not for a minute. There are social pressures at work." Then falls a shadow over this certainty. "Even if it is a part of human nature, like crime or violence, it's not necessarily desirable."

Well, love either is or is not intrinsic to our species; having it both ways leads nowhere. And the contention that romance is an entirely acquired trait—overly imaginative troubadours' revenge on muddled literalists—has always rested on some teetery premises.

For one thing, there is the chicken/egg dilemma. Which came first, sex or love? If

the reproductive imperative was as dominant as Darwinians maintain, sex probably led the way. But why was love hatched in the process, since it was presumably unnecessary to get things started in the first place? Furthermore, what has sustained romance—that odd collection of tics and impulses—over the centuries? Most mass hallucinations, such as the 17th century tulip mania in Holland, flame out fairly rapidly when people realize the absurdity of what they have been doing and, as the common saying goes, come to their senses. When people in love come to their senses, they tend to orbit with added energy around each other and look more helplessly loopy and self-besotted. If romance were purely a figment, unsupported by any rational or sensible evidence, then surely most folks would be immune to it by now. Look around. It hasn't happened. Love is still in the air.

And it may be far more widespread than even romantics imagined. Those who argue that love is a cultural fantasy have tended to do so from a Eurocentric and class-driven point of view. Romance, they say, arose thanks to amenities peculiar to the West: leisure time, a modicum of creature comforts, a certain level of refinement in the arts and letters. When these trappings are absent, so is romance. Peasants mated; aristocrats fell in love.

But last year a study conducted by anthropologists William Jankowiak of the University of Nevada–Las Vegas and Edward Fischer of Tulane University found evidence of romantic love in at least 147 of the 166 cultures they studied. This discovery, if borne out, should pretty well wipe out the idea that love is an invention of the Western mind rather than a biological fact. Says Jankowiak: "It is, instead, a universal phenomenon, a panhuman characteristic that stretches across cultures. Societies like ours have the resources to show love through candy and flowers, but that does not mean that the lack of resources in other cultures indicates the absence of love."

Some scientists are not startled by this contention. One of them is anthropologist Helen Fisher, a research associate at the American Museum of Natural History and the author of *Anatomy of Love: The Natural History of Monogamy, Adultery and Divorce*, a recent book that is making waves among scientists and the general reading public. Says Fisher: "I've never *not* thought that love was a very primitive, basic human emotion, as basic as fear, anger or joy. It is so evident. I guess anthropologists have just been busy doing other things."

Among the things anthropologists—often knobby-kneed gents in safari shorts—tended to do in the past was ask questions about courtship and marriage rituals. This now seems a classic example, as the old song has it, of looking for love in all the wrong places. In many cultures, love and marriage do not go together. Weddings can have all the romance of corporate mergers, signed and sealed for family or territorial interests. This does not mean, Jankowiak insists, that love does not exist in such cultures; it erupts in clandestine forms, "a phenomenon to be dealt with."

Somewhere about this point, the specter of determinism begins once again to flap and cackle. If science is going to probe and prod and then announce that we are all scientifically fated to love—and to love preprogrammed types—by our genes and chemicals, then a lot of people would just as soon not know. If there truly is a biological predisposition to love, as more and more scientists are coming to believe, what follows is a recognition of the amazing diversity in the ways humans have chosen to express the feeling. The cartoon images of cavemen bopping cavewomen over the head and dragging them home by their hair? Love. Helen of Troy, subjecting her adopted city to 10 years of ruinous siege? Love. Romeo and Juliet? Ditto. Joe in Accounting making a fool of himself around the water cooler over Susan in Sales? Love. Like the universe, the more we learn about love, the more preposterous and mysterious it is likely to appear. —***Reported by Hannah Bloch/ New York and Sally B. Donnelly/Los Angeles***

The Right Chemistry

Evolutionary roots, brain imprints, biological secretions. That's the story of love.

ANASTASIA TOUFEXIS

O.K., LET'S CUT OUT ALL THIS nonsense about romantic love. Let's bring some scientific precision to the party. Let's put love under a microscope.

When rigorous people with Ph.D.s after their names do that, what they see is not some silly, senseless thing. No, their probe reveals that love rests firmly on the foundations of evolution, biology and chemistry. What seems on the surface to be irrational, intoxicated behavior is in fact part of nature's master strategy—a vital force that has helped humans survive, thrive and multiply through thousands of years. Says Michael Mills, a psychology professor at Loyola Marymount University in Los Angeles: "Love is our ancestors whispering in our ears."

It was on the plains of Africa about 4 million years ago, in the early days of the human species, that the notion of romantic love probably first began to blossom—or at least that the first cascades of neurochemicals began flowing from the brain to the bloodstream to produce goofy grins and sweaty palms as men and women gazed deeply into each other's eyes. When mankind graduated from scuttling around on all fours to walking on two legs, this change made the whole person visible to fellow human beings for the first time. Sexual organs were in full display, as were other characteristics, from the color of eyes to the span of shoulders. As never before, each individual had a unique allure.

When the sparks flew, new ways of making love enabled sex to become a romantic encounter, not just a reproductive act. Although mounting mates from the rear was, and still is, the method favored among most animals, humans began to enjoy face-to-face couplings; both looks and personal attraction became a much greater part of the equation.

Romance served the evolutionary purpose of pulling males and females into long-term partnership, which was essential to child rearing. On open grasslands, one parent would have a hard—and dangerous—time handling a child while foraging for food. "If a woman was carrying the equivalent of a 20-lb. bowling ball in one arm and a pile of sticks in the other, it was ecologically critical to pair up with a mate to rear the young," explains anthropologist Helen Fisher, author of *Anatomy of Love.*

While Western culture holds fast to the idea that true love flames forever (the movie *Bram Stoker's Dracula* has the Count carrying the torch beyond the grave), nature apparently meant passions to sputter out in something like four years. Primitive pairs stayed together just "long enough to rear one child through infancy," says Fisher. Then each would find a new partner and start all over again.

WHAT FISHER CALLS THE "four-year itch" shows up unmistakably in today's divorce statistics. In most of the 62 cultures she has studied, divorce rates peak around the fourth year of marriage. Additional youngsters help keep pairs together longer. If, say, a couple have another child three years after the first, as often occurs, then their union can be expected to last about four more years. That makes them ripe for the more familiar phenomenon portrayed in the Marilyn Monroe classic *The Seven-Year Itch.*

If, in nature's design, romantic love is not eternal, neither is it exclusive. Less than 5% of mammals form rigorously faithful pairs. From the earliest days, contends Fisher, the human pattern has been "monogamy with clandestine adultery." Occasional flings upped the chances that new combinations of genes would be passed on to the next generation. Men who sought new partners had more children. Contrary to common assumptions, women were just as likely to stray. "As long as prehistoric females were secretive about their extramarital affairs," argues Fisher, "they could garner extra resources, life insurance, better genes and more varied DNA for their biological futures. Hence those who sneaked into the bushes with secret lovers lived on—unconsciously passing on through the centuries whatever it is in the female spirit that motivates modern women to philander."

Love is a romantic designation for a most ordinary biological—or, shall we say, chemical?—process. A lot of nonsense is talked and written about it.
—Greta Garbo to Melvyn Douglas in *Ninotchka*

Lovers often claim that they feel as if they are being swept away. They're not mistaken; they are literally flooded by chemicals, research suggests. A meeting of eyes, a touch of hands or a whiff of scent sets off a flood that starts in the brain and races along the nerves and through the blood. The results are familiar: flushed skin, sweaty palms, heavy breathing. If love looks suspiciously like stress, the reason is simple: the chemical pathways are identical.

Above all, there is the sheer euphoria of falling in love—a not-so-surprising reaction, considering that many of the substances swamping the newly smitten are chemical cousins of amphetamines. They include dopamine, norepinephrine and especially phenylethylamine (PEA). Cole Porter knew what he was talking about when he wrote "I get a kick out of you." "Love is a natural high," observes Anthony Walsh, author of *The Science of Love: Understanding Love and Its Effects on Mind and Body*. "PEA gives you that silly smile that you flash at strangers. When we meet someone who is attractive to us, the whistle blows at the PEA factory."

But phenylethylamine highs don't last forever, a fact that lends support to arguments that passionate romantic love is short-lived. As with any amphetamine, the body builds up a tolerance to PEA; thus it takes more and more of the substance to produce love's special kick. After two to three years, the body simply can't crank up the needed amount of PEA. And chewing on chocolate doesn't help, despite popular belief. The candy is high in PEA, but it fails to boost the body's supply.

Fizzling chemicals spell the end of delirious passion; for many people that marks the end of the liaison as well. It is particularly true for those whom Dr. Michael Liebowitz of the New York State Psychiatric Institute terms "attraction junkies." They crave the intoxication of falling in love so much that they move frantically from affair to affair just as soon as the first rush of infatuation fades.

Still, many romances clearly endure beyond the first years. What accounts for that? Another set of chemicals, of course. The continued presence of a partner gradually steps up production in the brain of endorphins. Unlike the fizzy amphetamines, these are soothing substances. Natural pain-killers, they give lovers a sense of security, peace and calm. "That is one reason why it feels so horrible when we're abandoned or a lover dies," notes Fisher. "We don't have our daily hit of narcotics."

Researchers see a contrast between the heated infatuation induced by PEA, along with other amphetamine-like chemicals, and the more intimate attachment fostered and prolonged by endorphins. "Early love is when you love the way the other person makes you feel," explains psychiatrist Mark Goulston of

the University of California, Los Angeles. "Mature love is when you love the person as he or she is." It is the difference between passionate and compassionate love, observes Walsh, a psychobiologist at Boise State University in Idaho. "It's Bon Jovi vs. Beethoven."

Oxytocin is another chemical that has recently been implicated in love. Produced by the brain, it sensitizes nerves and stimulates muscle contraction. In women it helps uterine contractions during childbirth as well as production of breast milk, and seems to inspire mothers to nuzzle their infants. Scientists speculate that oxytocin might encourage similar cuddling between adult women and men. The versatile chemical may also enhance orgasms. In one study of men, oxytocin increased to three to five times its normal level during climax, and it may soar even higher in women.

One mystery is the prevalence of homosexual love. Although it would seem to have no evolutionary purpose, since no children are produced, there is no denying that gays and lesbians can be as romantic as anyone else. Some researchers speculate that homosexuality results from a biochemical anomaly that occurs during fetal development. But that doesn't make ro-

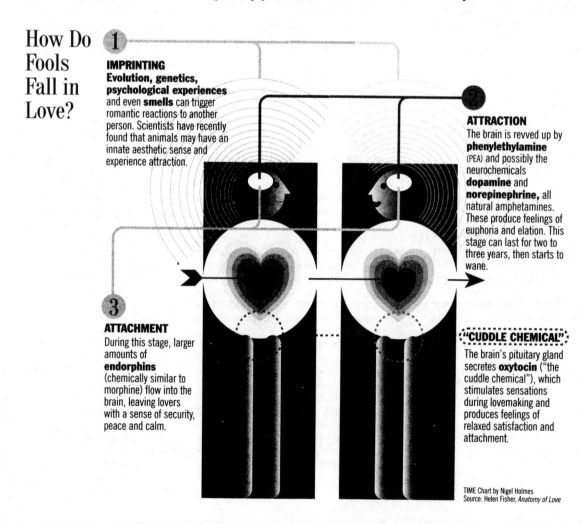

How Do Fools Fall in Love?

1 IMPRINTING
Evolution, genetics, psychological experiences and even **smells** can trigger romantic reactions to another person. Scientists have recently found that animals may have an innate aesthetic sense and experience attraction.

2 ATTRACTION
The brain is revved up by **phenylethylamine** (PEA) and possibly the neurochemicals **dopamine** and **norepinephrine,** all natural amphetamines. These produce feelings of euphoria and elation. This stage can last for two to three years, then starts to wane.

3 ATTACHMENT
During this stage, larger amounts of **endorphins** (chemically similar to morphine) flow into the brain, leaving lovers with a sense of security, peace and calm.

"CUDDLE CHEMICAL"
The brain's pituitary gland secretes **oxytocin** ("the cuddle chemical"), which stimulates sensations during lovemaking and produces feelings of relaxed satisfaction and attachment.

TIME Chart by Nigel Holmes
Source: Helen Fisher, *Anatomy of Love*

mance among gays any less real. "That they direct this love toward their own sex," says Walsh, "does not diminish the value of that love one iota."

A certain smile, a certain face
—Johnny Mathis

Chemicals may help explain (at least to scientists) the feelings of passion and compassion, but why do people tend to fall in love with one partner rather than a myriad of others? Once again, it's partly a function of evolution and biology. "Men are looking for maximal fertility in a mate," says Loyola Marymount's Mills. "That is in large part why females in the prime childbearing ages of 17 to 28 are so desirable." Men can size up youth and vitality in a glance, and studies indeed show that men fall in love quite rapidly. Women tumble more slowly, to a large degree because their requirements are more complex; they need more time to

check the guy out. "Age is not vital," notes Mills, "but the ability to provide security, father children, share resources and hold a high status in society are all key factors."

Still, that does not explain why the way Mary walks and laughs makes Bill dizzy with desire while Marcia's gait and giggle leave him cold. "Nature has wired us for one special person," suggests Walsh, romantically. He rejects the idea that a woman or a man can be in love with two people at the same time. Each person carries in his or her mind a unique subliminal guide to the ideal partner, a "love map," to borrow a term coined by sexologist John Money of Johns Hopkins University.

Drawn from the people and experiences of childhood, the map is a record of whatever we found enticing and exciting—or disturbing and disgusting. Small feet, curly hair. The way our mothers patted our head or how our fathers told a joke. A fireman's uniform, a doctor's

stethoscope. All the information gathered while growing up is imprinted in the brain's circuitry by adolescence. Partners never meet each and every requirement, but a sufficient number of matches can light up the wires and signal, "It's love." Not every partner will be like the last one, since lovers may have different combinations of the characteristics favored by the map.

O.K., that's the scientific point of view. Satisfied? Probably not. To most people—with or without Ph.D.s—love will always be more than the sum of its natural parts. It's a commingling of body and soul, reality and imagination, poetry and phenylethylamine. In our deepest hearts, most of us harbor the hope that love will never fully yield up its secrets, that it will always elude our grasp. —*Reported by Hannah Bloch/ New York and Sally B. Donnelly/Los Angeles*

Generalized Extended Family Exchange:

A Case from the Philippines

JEAN TRELOGGEN PETERSON

Division of Human Development and Family Studies, and Women's Studies Program, University of Illinois, Urbana, IL 61801.

This article distinguishes between concepts of household and family, and explores generalized exchange between households within extended families. Conceptions of essential structural differences between generalized and dyadic exchange are adapted from Levi-Strauss to evaluate implications of exchange within these extended family networks. Qualitative and quantative data from three highland Philippine communities are presented to illustrate these conceptions, and to demonstrate the interaction of lateral and intergenerational exchange within extended families. Cooperation, diversification of economic endeavor, fosterage, and family size are all pertinent to generalized exchange. Examples are offered of the application of this perspective to examination of low-income families in the United States, especially in meeting the needs of dependent elderly and female-headed households, and to issues of family planning and economic development internationally.

Generalized exchange among households within the extended family is often central to the welfare of the family. This article explores this premise using three conceptual frameworks. First, I differentiate between *household* and *family,* and suggest that, by failing to distinguish adequately between these two concepts, much of family studies in the United States has tended to focus on coresidential arrangements to define and study the family. Second, I adapt from Levi-Strauss (1949) a conception of generalized, as opposed to dyadic or restricted, exchange to argue that generalized exchange is often typical of extended families, and may be crucial to family welfare. Much of our analysis of families, however, has focussed on dyadic exchange and particularly the coresidential marital dyad, and thus has overlooked important sources of family support for some populations.

With these first two conceptual issues in mind, I offer data from the Philippines to demonstrate how interhousehold, generalized exchange operates—both laterally and intergenerationally—and how examination of this phenomenon can enhance our understanding of family organization as a means of assuring family welfare. Specifically, I find that these Filipino families rely on cooperation and diversification of endeavor among individual members, family size, and fosterage to maintain an active, lateral, and intergenerational network of generalized exchange. I suggest that this approach is useful both in the United States and internationally in addressing a range of contemporary social issues. Finally, I suggest that, by examining the family in its cultural and economic contexts from a cross-cultural comparative perspective, and by remaining attentive to the possibility of generalized exchange between households, we may better understand diversity of family organization.

THE FAMILY AND THE HOUSEHOLD

The relationship between the family and the household is basic to our understanding of extended family networks. Much of the research on the family assumes implicitly that *family* equals *household* equals *coresidence.* Given that household and family are conceptually and actually different units, it is clear that failure to maintain the distinction obscures adequate descriptions of the family, and identification of what is, in fact, happening to that social institution. Consider, for example, the observation by Mary Grace Kovar, a statistician for the National Center for Health Statistics, that there is justifiable concern about

From *Journal of Marriage and the Family,* Vol. 55, No. 3, August 1993, pp. 570-584. © 1993 by the National Council on Family Relations, 3989 Central Ave., NE, Suite 550, Minneapolis, MN 55421. Reprinted by permission of the author.

"what constitutes a family" (Stanfield, 1992). She explains,

> The Census Bureau—and by default everybody else—defines family as "people related by blood or marriage living in the same household" and household is defined by separate entrance and cooking facilities. So you could have children living with unmarried parents but [the statistics] don't pick it up appropriately. Or a woman lives next door to her kids and sees them all the time, but we interview that woman and say she is living alone (p. 1564).

A separate literature has focussed on households exclusively, essentially neglecting the family (e.g., Binswanger, Evenson, Florencio, & White, 1980; Wilk & Netting, 1984). In this approach, any interaction among households—for example, within the extended family—is ignored, and the household is discussed as if it were a rigidly bounded unit. Within this literature, there is further confusion between those who define household in terms of function (pooling resources, child care, etc.; Wilk & Netting, 1984), and those, including the national census, who assume that *household* may be defined adequately in terms of coresidence. This distinction—between a functionally defined household based on pooling of labor and resources, and household defined in terms of coresidence—is pertinent to the argument I present here, as well. Functional definitions recognize that resource flows, especially the pooling of resources—that is, holding and managing resources in common—yield a distinct picture of the household, one that may vary from that developed out of coresidential definitions. Pooling, as used in functional definitions of the household, may occur among two or more coresidential units, or we may identify two or more functionally distinct subgroups (households) within a single dwelling unit. Support of the sort so frequently discussed in studies of African American extended family networks, for example, may occur both within households and among households.

A recent article from The Population Council (Bruce & Lloyd, 1993) suggests that the household may be an insufficient unit of study given the relevance of resource flows among coresidential units. That study re-evaluates recent work on female-headed households to suggest that approaching the household as a bounded unit and addressing household "headship" alone, a prevalent practice in research on women in development and much of the literature on African American families, do not provide adequate "policy tool(s) for identifying vulnerable households,

women, and children" (p. 2). Bruce and Lloyd (1993) recognize that "family necessarily transcends the boundaries of the household" (p. 3), and may be more important than coresidential arrangements or parents' marital status in affecting the welfare of vulnerable populations (p. 30). They call for "a new research focus on the family that transcends the physical and temporal boundaries of the household, and for a policy focus that inquires into meaningful family relationships" (pp. 3-4).

While most treatments of the extended family identify whether they are addressing extended family support within or beyond the household, they fail to recognize any essential difference between the two. The perspectives summarized above clarify that there are, indeed, differences in how extended family support within and beyond the household function (cf. Hofferth, 1984). The following are advantages of extended family, or other support organized within households: (a) ability to coordinate short-term, recurring labor needs; (b) ability to organize short-term, recurring child-care needs, or needs of other dependents; (c) flexibility, that is, ability to change membership and organization almost literally overnight; and (d) ability to pool resources, to draw on those pooled resources on a daily and recurring basis, and, consequently, to achieve some economies of scale. This economy is most salient in terms of housing. Disadvantages of household level organization include the following: (a) while individuals are producing for the household, they are also calling upon and consuming the resources of that household; (b) shared endeavor and pooling leave the household vulnerable to shared failure, or hardship, with little potential, as an isolated unit, to recover; (c) members lose autonomy over the products of their labors, and some may contribute more than they receive; and (d) incompatibility in interpersonal relations cannot be easily tolerated. We can imagine some optimal size and organization of individual households under varying circumstances of context and need, and a considerable literature addresses this kind of variation among households (e.g., Wilk, 1984; Wilk & Netting, 1984).

Extended family support beyond the household offers a different set of advantages. By managing diversity of economic activity, complementarity of those activities, and sustaining cooperative relations within the extended family, extra household extended families are able to effectively respond to crises in ways that households alone cannot. In part, this is true because the extra household extended family, unlike household members, can contribute to a given household, without drawing upon its resources. Through these various mechanisms, the extended family beyond the household can be seen as providing a source of stability that is lacking in the isolated household. Although the extrahousehold extended family provides stability, it is less flexible than the household; typically, there are relatively few formal means of modifying family membership, including birth, adoption, marriage, and divorce.

Understanding differences between the household and the family or, more specifically, the extended family, can improve our understanding of adjustments to short-term needs at a household level, as opposed to much more basic social change, or change in family values. It can also help us appreciate how families operate and what affects variation among families in diverse circumstances, independent of any specific cultural expectations of appropriate family form. Finally, recognizing these distinctions can help us better evaluate social needs and plan to meet them.

STRUCTURE OF EXTENDED FAMILY EXCHANGE

To borrow a set of terms from Levi-Strauss' discussion of Australian marriage (1949), we can think of the structure of family networks as involving both *restricted* and *generalized* exchanges. Levi-Strauss characterized restricted exchanges (of wives, in his analysis) as reciprocal exchanges between two groups or lineages. Thus, A gives to B, and B gives to A. These are comparable to dyadic exchanges as described for some extended family networks (see Johnson & Catalano, 1981). Generalized exchanges are those in which A gives to B, B gives to C, C gives to a D, and D gives to A. Generalized exchanges, as discussed by Levi-Strauss, need not be completed within a single generation or in the strictly circular pattern I have described.

Participation in generalized exchange represents an investment in collective future welfare and prosperity. Calls upon kin and responses to kin simultaneously strengthen and reinforce social ties (Peterson, 1989). The importance of the Levi-Straussian distinction lies in his observation that generalized exchange, more than restricted exchange, promotes interdependence and social solidarity. It is a firmer sort of social "glue" (cf. Johnson, 1982). Applied to resource flows within the extended family, one must, of course, acknowledge that restricted exchange does occur within dyads, but it is important to recognize, as well, that generalized exchange is pervasive, and important to the resilience of extended family networks over time.

THE PHILIPPINE STUDY

The Philippine data presented here demonstrate the structure and management of extrahousehold, extended family exchange, and emphasize the achievements that generalized exchange can support.

Methods

Primarily two types of interview data were utilized in the research presented here. Quantitative data were collected by surveying a random sample of dwelling units in each community. In Communities A and B, no household lists were available, so sketch maps were developed showing residences, and one-third of these dwellings were randomly selected for interview. In Community C, this random selection was made from household lists generated by a census completed by the local government a few months before this research was initiated. These interviews typically required 2 or more hours each and, whenever possible, were administered with both male and female household heads present. The data presented here are based on questions about children and siblings of male and female household heads living in other houses. These data, therefore, reflect two avenues of interhousehold, intrafamilial exchange, but do not address the intense exchange or pooling of resources among siblings or parents and adult children who share the same household (see Peterson, 1992, for a discussion of this). The interview consisted of structured questions, often eliciting strictly quantitative data. A wide range of questions was asked, covering subjects' residence histories (where they lived, the dates of residence, reasons for moving) and collecting similar data on employment history, educational background, and other demographics of household members. Names of children and siblings residing in other houses were elicited, household inventory was taken, and farm land was inventoried, and, for a subsample, measured. The quantitative data presented here were drawn from questions on the survey regarding demographic attributes of children and siblings residing in other houses, and from questions that asked, "How do you help them?" and "How do they help you?" The responses were organized into four categories for statistical analysis.

In addition to these interviews, individuals were selected in each community for reconstruction of family histories. These individuals were selected for their ability to recall details and their willingness to give time and thought to the project. Whenever possible, selected members of their kin networks were interviewed, as well, in order to provide additional perspectives on the family history. Whenever possible, both males and females and representatives of different generations were interviewed. These interviews required from 2 to 8 hours with each individual. Each respondent was asked to recall his or her own life history. To stimulate further recollections, respondents were asked, for example, to recall what life was like in childhood, major turning points in life, and happiest and saddest events. Probes were employed to clarify reasons and circumstances surrounding life events. In addition, a genealogy was elicited from each respondent in the life history component of the project, and, within each geneology, information was elicited regarding patterns of coresidence, circumstances of marriages, reasons for changes in residence or employment, and so forth. Most of these interviews were formally scheduled, but participant observation was used, as well; my assistants and I lived with these people as neighbors, attended ritual events, participated in market days, and so forth. There were many informal opportunities for observation of actual interactions and exchanges.

All formal interviews were taped and transcribed, and comparisons were made with data elicited from other respondents about similar events or individuals. These data were also compared with the resident histories and employment histories from the survey interviews. A time line was developed for each extended family, discrepancies were identified and rectified, and gaps were filled in until a coherent history could be developed.

The Social and Economic Context

Benguet Province in the Philippines is a rugged mountainous area that experienced its first significant commercial economic development in this century. With a majority of residents living below the poverty line, this area offers, at best, a precarious and economically marginal existence to most inhabitants, and, throughout the region, organization of the extended family is an essential feature of domestic and extended family welfare (Peterson, 1989, 1990, 1991). Traditionally, the Kankana-ey and Ibaloi peoples of this province made their livings by growing irrigated rice in high valleys and along the lower slopes of the mountains, or by growing yams and tree crops on the higher slopes of the mountains. They also dug gold from the mountains and panned for it in their rivers, carrying these treasures down to the lowlands to trade for Chinese porcelains and beads;

but significant economic development did not occur until this century, most dramatically following World War II and national independence. The traditional culture persists and is expressed in technology, kinship, and religious practice, even among Christians. Benguet is now a busy commercial farming, mining, logging, and tourist area, which has experienced expanding industrial prospects in recent years; nonetheless, the majority of residents continue to live below the poverty line, and most communities lie far from roads, schools, salaried or wage employment, health care, and other amenities of modern life. Given the lack of economic opportunity, Benguet residents survive largely because of their ability to organize their social environment effectively. Specifically, they rely on interhousehold, extended family cooperation and on diversification of economic endeavor to see them through crises and to promote economic advancement whenever possible. The specific nature of economic challenge varies from one community to another, and the content and specific strategies of extended family exchange vary to meet it.

Three communities were selected for study on the basis of their primary economic orientations in order to explore their responses to economic circumstance. Community A is the most traditional of these three, and its lack of access to participation in the commercial economy is a primary difficulty. Access to commercial farming is limited principally by altitude, inadequate roads and transportation, and lack of credit and appropriate technology. Farmers there continue to cultivate rice along the valley floor with traditional plows and draft animals, and to cultivate yams and tree crops on the upper slopes with simple tools and arduous human labor, raising enough for home consumption and, with luck, sometimes a small surplus to sell locally. A few families with fields at higher altitudes and access to roads grow one or more crops of temperate climate vegetables each year for a commercial market. Market access is limited to a narrow dirt road that winds along the mountainside to this community, but does not extend beyond, and that is blocked by landslides every rainy season. None of these farmers own vehicles and all are dependent on the daily bus, or on vegetable dealers, to transport produce to market.

Community B stretches along the upper slopes of a nearby mountain, reaching at some points down into higher valleys. It is almost wholly dependent on commercial production of temperate climate vegetables, which were introduced to the area in this century. All cultivation is done by hand, and all produce is carried up steep mountain slopes to the road on human backs. Although residents of Community B enjoy better access to schools, a road, and health care than do their counterparts in Community A, this form of production, dependent as it now is on imported seeds, fertilizers, pesticides, herbicides, and on rainfall or costly irrigation, is risky, and capital and labor intensive. Commercial vegetable production promises potentially substantial gains, but often generates staggering losses.

Community C is a neighborhood in Baguio City. Residents, some of whom grow flowers for a commercial market, enjoy access to jobs in the city, principally as skilled and unskilled laborers and as domestic helpers, or in small-scale buying and selling. Although this community benefits from a support infrastructure lacking in the other two communities, economic impediments still limit access to educational participation and health care in this community. Like residents of the other two communities, they are poor.

A Family History

Family histories from Benguet Province illustrate the complexity and economic value of extended family support networks. One example of such a history will demonstrate the dynamic of the exchanges that typically occur.

Hector and Zenaida married in 1910, initially living with her family and pooling resources with them. Both Hector and Zenaida had been employees of an American who taught them how to plant temperate climate vegetables. By 1913, they had two children and established a home independent of Zenaida's parents. Eventually eight more children were born. When their first-born was six they began farming their own land. Of the first five children, only the fourth, Ester, finished high school. Ester completed a teacher training course in Baguio City, and returned home to teach elementary school. She encouraged the education of five younger siblings and helped support their school expenses. She also took in and reared her sister's daughter, a brother's two sons, and two children from an indigent family. Ester married in 1967 when her foster children, with the exception of one widowed foster daughter, Linda, who continued to live with her, were grown and on their own. This widowed foster daughter and her three children continue to live with Ester from time to time when they encounter particularly difficult economic periods.

Hector and Zenaida's fifth-born child, Victor, finished high school with support from Ester and married Joanna in 1945. Victor and Joanna's first child died, and a daughter, Selma, was born in 1947. Victor worked as a farm manager for a wealthy farmer until 1957, when, by borrowing money from his siblings, he was able to begin farming on his own. He and Joanna had eight children at this time. From 1957 to 1962, Victor and Joanna worked hard to extend their farming operation; they acquired land and learned to fertilize. During this period they planted as many as four crops a year. This effort was aimed at sending Selma to college and, with additional support from their siblings, especially Joanna's younger brother and sister, both of whom had finished high school, they were able to do so. By 1967, Victor found himself always in debt for farming expenses and decided to cut back on farm inputs and, as he expresses it, "do with less." Although he and Joanna still had nine children at home, Selma, who had graduated from college and was working in the city, sent a majority of her paycheck home to her parents.

It was during this period that Hector's younger sister had an opportunity to sell 2 hectares of family land and to buy 50 hectares of pasture and orchard land at a lower altitude. She sought the council of her siblings, who agreed that she should accept the opportunity. Hector explained the value of this move by pointing out that when his sister needs produce or a small cash loan, those siblings who are vegetable farmers can provide it, and if the vegetable-farming siblings are in need of capital when crops or market prices fail, this sister may be able to make a loan. It was also during this period that a younger brother left farming to become a small-scale merchant in the Baguio market, a move Hector explicitly sees as offering further risk reduction to the extended family.

Once Selma was established in her new job in 1967, her younger brother, James, started college, with Selma paying his tuition and living costs. In 1968, Selma married a farmer, George, but continued to live and work in the city. In 1969, their first child was born, and George's eldest sister, Lourdes, a single woman who was a travelling buyer and seller of farm produce and inputs, abandoned her business for a time to take up farming and, with her new sedentary lifestyle, provide care for this child. In 1971, James finished college and began supporting his younger sister, Juliet, in college. Three intervening siblings, two girls and a boy, completed high school, but did not go on to college. Also in 1971, Selma's second child was born and Selma gave up her job to join George on his farm. A third child was born in 1973 and, in 1974, George and Selma retrieved their first-born from Lourdes, who returned to her business.

In 1977, George and Selma moved to Community B, where they could be near Selma's parents and Selma's new job in a municipal office. George turned his farm over to his brother. Selma's father provided farm inputs, tools, and land to help George and Selma get established in their new community. Selma and George began paying school expenses for Selma's three youngest siblings, two boys and a girl, and provided substantial financial help to the widowed Linda and her three children, as well. In 1977, the eldest of Selma's younger siblings started college, followed by the next in 1979. In 1980, Juliet finished college, and she and James helped Selma and George with the expenses of these three younger children. Selma, out of her salary, paid their tuition, fees, and room and board. In 1981, George's brother's son came to live with George and Selma in order to attend high school and help on the farm weekends and after school. He returned home during holidays and worked for his parents. By 1983, Hector and Joanna had only one child still at home, and George was relieving Hector of many of his heavier farm chores.

This family history is very like others I collected in its evidence of cooperation in parent-child, sibling, and affinal relations, in the mechanisms utilized to establish and maintain cooperation, and in the importance of both cooperation and economic diversification to family welfare. These histories vary principally in the specific choice of economic strategy emphasized by different families and in the degree of success achieved. This family successfully combined principally commercial farming and education as avenues to assured material welfare, with some dependence on emigration to different environmental zones for agricultural diversification, and on occasional exploitation of urban employment and business enterprise. Other families rely more heavily on emigration to the city, or invest substantial resources in the development of farming enterprises in the lowlands. Roberto, for example, describes how his father acquired a large tract of land in the Cagayan Valley that was developed by a series of Roberto's cousins to provide a hedge against crop failure in the highlands. Angela, who manages both a business and a flower farm in Community C, persuaded her ex-husband and his new wife to maintain her family land in the country, and she took in her brother's son, his wife, and their infant son when they immigrated to the city to find work. Some families offer support for foreign migration, and Primo, for example, is explicit about his expectation that, having contributed to airfare to send his wife's brother and sister to the United States, they will send him money when he needs it. Not every family is as successful as the one described in this history. Some cannot sustain the resources necessary to establish an independent commercial farming enterprise or ed-

ucation, and some fail because of an inability to maintain cooperative relations in the extended family.

The mutual support described here serves two basic purposes. On the one hand, it cushions against crisis and sustains during difficult transitions or periods of dependency. For example, the fosterage of children relieves vulnerable households of some responsibility, or it provides labor or some forms of support to households receiving children. The widow, Linda, and her children can and do draw heavily on support from the extended family whenever they need it. Other analyses of this population fully address the frequent role of these exchanges in meeting need (Peterson, 1989; cf. Taylor, 1990). On the other hand, these networks can promote increasing prosperity, for example, by providing support for children's education. It is significant in this case that, although these people are poor, substantial numbers of children receive secondary, and even higher, education (Peterson & Paranjape, in press). Prosperity is promoted, as well, when network members farm collaboratively, cooperate in land acquisition or participation in new technologies, or support foreign migration. In this respect, it is not surprising that the literature on extended family networks reports actively functioning networks among both the very poor and the very rich (cf. Hofferth, 1984).

The complexity of this exchange could not be captured by approaching the family as a coresidential unit, by examining only single dyadic relationships, or by focussing only on relationships most culturally relevant in a Euro-American context, such as marriage or the parent-child relationship. Such an approach could not, for example, explain how Victor and Joanna were able to establish an independent farming operation in 1957 or how very poor farmers are able to provide college education for their children, or explain the advantages of Hector's younger brother becoming a merchant or the benefits of Lourdes abandoning her business. It could not recognize the female-headed households in this family history as examples of positive, productive, coping strategies. Without information about the social and economic context, many strategic activities of this network, and the generalized exchange they practice, would be overlooked.

The network of exchanges described in the family history above, illustrates generalized exchange, as defined by Levi-Strauss, in that the principal contributions recalled are not strictly dyadic (cf. Hill, Foote, Aldous, Carlson, & MacDonald, 1970). Contributions are made in one generation and returned in the next, or made to one sibling and received from another. Thus, Joanna's brother and sister provided principal support for Selma's education. Selma supported James' education, and James, in turn, supported Juliet. Similarly, George's sister, Lourdes, made a significant life readjustment to care for George and Selma's oldest son in a foster relationship, and George and Selma fostered George's brother's son. While Ester received support from her parents, she gave support to her younger siblings and siblings' children and to unrelated children, as well. It is significant, also, that none of these exchanges represents what economic anthropologists call *measured reciprocity*; that is, no accounts were kept. Rather, generosity was assumed to serve the collective well-being of the group and need directed the flow of exchange (Peterson, 1989; Sahlins, 1965). It is important to note that restricted exchange and measured reciprocity require some equality of support ability and some degree of complementary needs. Generalized exchange does not and, therefore, offers a more flexible response to both crisis and opportunity.

It is also significant that these exchanges are both lateral and intergenerational. The quantitative data collected for the Philippine study demonstrate the structure of these lateral and intergenerational exchanges more clearly, perhaps, than do the family histories, and demonstrate how these exchanges are activated at different points in individual life cycles. They also demonstrate the importance of locating analysis in the context of specific communities to appreciate variation as a response to local conditions.

The Survey

The survey data illustrate the structure of lateral and intergenerational linkages. Elsewhere (Peterson, 1990), I have demonstrated active exchange of goods and services within sets of adult siblings who are members of different households, and interpreted these data as representing a flow of support among siblings to those experiencing greatest need, specifically, those who are rearing children (Peterson, 1990; cf. Turke, 1989). These exchanges among siblings are examples of lateral exchanges, and examination of sibling relationships alone, independent of the broader family network, might suggest neglect of the elderly. The survey data presented here, however, demonstrate that these elders, as parents, receive more contributions from children than do parents in other age categories. For them, intergenerational linkages are particularly important. They, of course, have more children and more

mature children to provide various forms of support, and, if they are among the few survivors of a once-large sibling set, they may have fewer living siblings than do younger persons. Nonetheless, these patterns of children's support to parents, and of support among siblings, suggest complementarity not only among roles (Peterson, 1990), but also among lateral and intergenerational sets of relationships within the extended family. In short, this provides additional evidence of the efficacy and significance of broad-based, interhousehold support.

In Communities A and C, those over the age of 50 receive assistance from their children more often than younger parents do, and most of that help is given in the form of labor and money (see Table 1). This, in contrast to the low rates of support from siblings, suggests a shift from greater dependence on siblings, and probably on parents, in young adulthood, to equal dependence on siblings and children in middle age, and to greater dependence on children among those over 50 (cf. Chatters, Taylor & Jackson, 1985).

Only in Community B, the labor-intensive commercial farming community, do younger parents receive more substantial support from their children than older parents do. In that community, parents between 36 and 50 years of age ($n = 23$) receive the most contributions in every category, and labor is the most common form of support (95.6% of all contributions to this age category). In this community, those in the ages 36 to 50 category make heavy claims on both children and siblings in every category.

While the shifts in sources of support found in Communities A and C are perhaps a self-evident product of family maturation, they nonetheless reflect complementarity of kin relationships in meeting needs differentially over the life cycle (cf. Taylor, 1986). The anomaly of Community B can be accounted for in terms of its unique economic orientation and it demonstates the importance of examining family relationships relative to economic context. As I have observed above, persons in the middle years must make especially heavy claims on resources from the entire extended family, and this is most evident in the costly and labor intensive economic context of Community C. Like other communities, the demands of dependent children are greatest during this midlife period, but these farmers, more than residents of Communities A or C, meet this need with substantial intensification of the farming operation by multiple cropping and by increasing the use of labor-intensive farm inputs. This intensification is evident in the fact that, in Community C, the majority of total contributions

TABLE 1. KINDS OF HELP PROVIDED TO PARENTS BY PARENTS' AGES IN THREE COMMUNITIES

	Community A		Community B		Community C	
	Age 36-50	Over 50	Age 36-50	Over 50	Age 35-50	Over 50
No help						
Percentage by age group	52.9	47.1	100	0	14.3	85.7
n	9	8	2	0	2	12
Labor						
Percentage by age group	15.4	84.6	82.1	17.9	0	100
n	2	11	23	5	0	11
Goods						
Percentage by age group	0	100	100	0	0	100
n	0	12	1	0	0	3
Money						
Percentage by age group	15.4	84.6	0	0	0	100
n	4	22	0	0	0	10

Note: The analysis of Community A yields significance of less than .004. Statistical analyses of the other communities in this set of variables do not yield significance, probably because of the preponderance of contributions, in both cases, to a single age category and the resulting number of empty cells.

among siblings, and 45.8% of children's total contributions to the group in this age category, are in the form of labor.

Strategies and Mechanisms of Extended Family Exchange

Clearly, the family exchanges described for Benguet Province meet human needs effectively, and we need to understand better the strategies and mechanisms which promote their effectiveness. The approach taken here to studying family life in context demonstrates four features of this exchange. They are cooperation, diversification of activity within the sibling set, fosterage, and family size.

Cooperation. The importance of cooperation is discussed repeatedly in the family histories collected. As one old man put it:

> With help from parents-in-law a young farmer will not need so many inputs, for example, farm implements. He utilizes the farm implements of his parents-in-law. It is the family that helps him start to farming now . . . . Otherwise he could do it only if he had the capital . . . . In the starting most must have capital, they live with their parents-in-law so they get to utilize the land of their parents-in-law.

One married couple expressed the importance of cooperation as follows:

WIFE: For me, if it were always the bank and there were no other individuals helping us out, I don't think it [the farm] would survive, because if they [the bank] gave them [the farmers] a loan and they [the farmers] won't be able to repay them, they [the bank] won't lend again. And they

might take the land. Farmers become tenants on their own land. If all the members of the family will be cooperative in helping each other, so that if possible they will avoid borrowing from the bank, then that will preserve the land and the members of the family.

HUSBAND: Brothers and sisters lend the equipment, money. I lend them money when I have it. Whoever has the money just gives it. When you need to borrow you go to the family.

JTP: Who do you go to first?

HUSBAND: Brothers and sisters, then cousins. You might go to parents if they have the money, but parents can't really afford it. Maybe they are still taking care of the family and maybe they are old. Older children might get help from parents, but then they help the younger ones.

WIFE: Whenever family needs, also, they will ask for it, and sometimes they will need help for harvest. We supply. Sometimes we have a good harvest and we check if they are in need.

HUSBAND: Some families are more successful than others because of the location and quality of the land.

WIFE: The water system and sometimes the personality of the family. They don't like to work. They don't help each other.

HUSBAND: They are lazy.

WIFE: And especially some are very selfish with each other.

HUSBAND: They will have a harder time because they must all help each other.

WIFE: I think there is no farmer here who made good in farming without the help of the family.

They can't farm on their own. They must have some help. All in the family are working.

HUSBAND: If we cooperate we can help each other.

Economic complementarity and diversification. One woman discussed the need for diversification to assure the welfare of farmers by saying:

That's why some of these families are sending their children to school, so that in case they would not have anything to get from farming there are some children who can help.

A man described this strategy as follows:

My parents tried to sacrifice to keep us in school. Because the parents are hard up those children who are already established will help out. . . . Now some people will want the college education for their children, because farming is a hit or miss proposition. There is a drought, or calamities, or [you] have a very good crop, but no price. So sometimes it seems that it would not be very good to encourage the children to go to farming because of the risk. Some are forcing their children to go to a profession. They can always predict an income. Farming is so much hit or miss, and if we all go into farming there is not any way to deal with that.

Another man commented:

I really encouraged my children to get an education because I come from a poor family. It is good for some children to be professionals, then they can have work even if there is no more land, and they can help each other.

Clearly education is attractive because an educated child can be called upon in times of acute economic need or when parents are old and in need of assistance. The specific skills acquired through education may be attractive, too. I asked one man why his daughter went to college, and he replied:

It happens in business farming that we are required by the BIR [Bureau of Internal Revenue] to have accounts. So I have to hire always the bookkeeper to do our books. So I thought of asking her to take up bookkeeping. So she took that course. . . [and] is our bookkeeper. Even most of the farmers, the relations of her husband, use her.

Education is a family matter and not simply an individual's choice, as reflected in this daughter's response when I asked her to recall the happiest time in her life. Now married, gainfully employed and the mother of three healthy, competent, attractive children she responded:

Probably when I finished college, [when] I finished my education. I made my parents happy.

The employment of educated members is also seen as an important means of supplementing household income from the farm, and of obtaining fringe benefits, such as insurance and retirement, which may be provided.

Education, although gaining importance as a means of providing access to off-farm employment, is not the only avenue to diversification. Thus, Victor supported his sister's purchase of land at a lower altitude and a brother's retailing activities for the complementarity they provided to his own farming effort. Similarly, Roberto's family and Angela developed deliberate strategies to achieve diversity of economic endeavor within the extended family. Cooperation and diversification go hand-in-hand. While cooperation, especially through exchange, enhances extended family endeavor to promote well-being, it is especially effective when combined with diversification of economic endeavor.

Fosterage and extended family linkages. Fosterage appears to be especially relevant to the development of the family networks described here (cf. Stack, 1974; Taylor, Chatters, Tucker, & Lewis, 1990). In the data discussed here, Ester, Lourdes, Angela, and George and Selma all provided foster care for younger kin at one time or another. Elsewhere (Carroll, 1970), fosterage is seen as a mechanism that provides children to those who have none, provides nurturance to children who lack parents, or adjusts gender ratios within families. It is evident from the Philippine data that fosterage also plays an important role in the development of intergenerational bonds and extended family linkages. Family histories reveal numerous cases of children fostered so that a mother may be free to work in the city, because the parents lack the resources for caring for all of their children, or in order to give children easier access to schools. The child who spends a period of time in another household away from parents often forms exceptionally close bonds with those members of the extended family. These particularly tight linkages become especially important in the formation of the extended family network across generations.

Family size. The developmental organization of extended family exchange suggested by the survey data is supported by the family histories, and it is shown to be far more complex than the survey data alone suggest. Fosterage, affinal relations, cousin relationships, and diverse cross-generational bonds combine to produce a highly effective support network capable of achieving economic diversity to meet crises and expand economic options. Family size is crucial to the development of an effective intergenerational kin support network like the ones described here. While large sibling sets—for example, those with five or more children spaced 2 or more years apart—offer substantial potential for this intergenerational bonding and cooperation, small sibling sets do not. The eldest of five children may be 10 years older than the youngest, and, therefore, sufficiently independent and prosperous to lend significant support to his or her younger siblings as they mature. Reciprocally, his or her children may receive support from younger aunts or uncles who are not yet parents themselves. Together, these exchanges promote bonds that endure across generations. On the other hand, smaller sibling sets—those with only two or three children all within the same family developmental range as they mature and establish their own households, are somewhat limited in their ability to meet each others' needs. Three children, for example, born within 4 or 5 years, experience similar needs at about the same time as they enter adulthood; their children will be of about the same age, and, although helpful mutual exchange may occur, the potential for intense, reciprocal, complementary exchange will be more limited than within the larger sibling set. It is not surprising, therefore, that although other research (e.g., Sussman & Burchinal, 1962) demonstrates the existence of extended family exchanges in industrialized countries, these networks are less active and more focussed on affective relations than in the Philippine case described here.

Large sibling sets serve parents well, too. There are more children to make returns to aging parents, and at least some of those children, because of the age span in a large sibling set, are likely to be able to assist parents when others cannot. Thus a 70-year-old parent whose health is failing may receive little from the 42-year-old offspring who is struggling to launch his or her own family, while still meeting the needs of young children at home, but the 23-year-old, still single, may be able to provide quite ample support. Fewer children, more closely spaced, may have difficulty meeting the needs of both their parents and their children. Economic cooperation among larger sibling sets, therefore, alleviates some of the stresses of what is referred to in the United States as the "sandwich generation," and of what Oppenheimer (1974) has referred to as "life cycle squeeze."

DISCUSSION

Understanding extended family organization from a global perspective, I believe, is crucial to development of a theoretical framework applicable to diverse cultural contexts, and to several areas of effective policy development in the United States and internationally. I address four areas of theoretical and applied interest.

Family Support for Dependent Elderly

The survey data on support received by the elderly, and the structural attributes of that support in the Philippine highlands, invite comparison with attributes of family support of dependent elderly in the United States. Before embarking on this comparison, I must call attention to some of the limitations in such a comparison. First, the United States studies I cite refer, in most cases, to dependent elderly, those who suffer poor health and are in need of support services including assistance with bathing, dressing, and so forth. The Filipino population described in the survey is younger, and certainly some of them are more able-bodied. Second, health care in the United States provides for survival of elderly to a dependent age; in the rural Philippines, some of these ailing elderly would not survive so long. Third, the formal support services available in the United States, attenuated as they are compared to other industrialized countries, are not found at all in the Philippines; if the family or community cannot meet the needs of their elderly members, those needs will not be met. Finally, the family histories from the Philippines offer a diachronic perspective on family support, while the studies cited from this country are based on data which do not explore family history, and, therefore, do not capture a diachronic perspective. Given the addition of time depth, it is possible that the picture of these American families would look somewhat different, as well.

The literature on family care of dependent elderly in the United States distinguishes between dyadic support and support from the family as a functional unit (Johnson, 1983). Dyadic support refers to support received within a single relationship, that is from a spouse, child, sibling, or friend. Dyadic support is found to operate according to what Shanas (1979) has called the "principle of substitution." According to this principle, certain relationships are called on first in eliciting help and, if no individual exists within that relationship, a substitute will be found within another relationship. Thus, among Euro-American samples, married elderly will turn principally to the spouse for assistance, but unmarried or widowed elderly will turn to a child. One principal relationship is activated at any given time. There are two types of dyadic relationships, those with peers (spouse or siblings) and those with a younger person (a child). Each is characterized by certain limitations. In the case of peers, the elderly peer is often in poor health, as well, and it may be difficult to provide the necessary care (Johnson, 1983; Johnson & Catalano, 1981). Younger persons may encounter difficulty in meeting the needs of dependent elderly family members because of competing demands from their own nuclear families (Johnson, 1983). Moreover, reciprocity, or lack thereof, can be a source of conflict or stress in these relationships (Johnson, 1983). These dyadic relationships can be characterized in Levi-Straussian terms, as examples of restricted exchange. LeviStrauss (1949) argues that such exchanges are "not capable of attaining any other form than a multitude of little closed systems . . . without ever realizing a global structure" (p. 553). Seen from this perspective, dyadic exchange might produce a less well-integrated, and less flexible, extended family system.

Elderly assistance from the family as a functional unit is an example of generalized exchange, on the other hand, with greater potential for what Levi-Strauss (1949) calls "organic solidarity" (p. 548). It is more likely characterized by complementarity than substitutability. Thus, a child in the middle years of life, who is supporting young children, may be unable to provide much support, but an elder grandchild can live with the dependent grandparent to help out, while the youngest unmarried child of the dependent elder provides financial aid, and a nephew helps by contributing his labor to growing a few food crops (see Peterson, 1989, 1990, 1991). Comparison of survey data on sibling help, as opposed to child-to-parent assistance, as well as the qualitative data on family histories, suggest just this sort of complementarity. Chatters, Taylor, and Jackson (1985) refer to this pattern, which, significantly, they find among African Americans, as the "sharing of support duties across several helpers" (p. 613). Presumably this kind of sharing reduces the stress of support which falls on one or two relationships in the case of dyadic support. On the whole, although Chatters and associates suggest that their data on African American elderly "highlight the possible operation of a hierarchy of support resources" (p. 611), they emphasize the greater breadth of support among African Americans.

They also identify attributes of elderly African Americans which distinguish them from Euro-American elderly, and which are similar to the attributes of the Philippine populations described here. Older African Americans represent one of our country's most severely disadvantaged groups, limited by inadequate housing, incomes below poverty level, and little formal education. These difficulties are exacerbated by "limited access to formal societal supports due to discrimination in the areas of education, health care, and the labor market" (p. 606). These conditions are remarkably similar to the conditions of the Philippines and other less developed countries, where limited services, limited educational participation, limited health care, and general poverty create a context quite different from that experienced by most Euro-Americans. This supports the position that social and economic disadvantage promote extended family exchange.

A final point of comparison between American and Filipino elderly support draws on my discussion earlier in this article of the household and the family. Shanas (1979) and Johnson and Catalano (1981) find that spouses offer the principle support if they are living. Given my discussion of the benefits of intrahousehold support as opposed to interhousehold support, this is not surprising; daily, recurring needs can be met most effectively within the household and spouses are likely to be coresidential.

Extended Families and Female Household Heads

The literature on female-headed households typically operationalizes family as a coresidential unit (Dressler, Hoffner & Pitts, 1985; Hofferth, 1984), operationalizes the household as a coresidential unit (Dressler et al., 1985; Hofferth, 1984; McLanahan, 1985; Taylor, 1986), and, therefore, implicitly assumes that *household* equals *family*. This tendency persists, sometimes to the extent of overlooking cultural differences or ignoring the extended kin network altogether (McLanahan, 1985). As Dressler and his associates (1985) observe, for example, among African Americans, "family and household are not coterminous" (p. 861). (See Gonzalez, 1969, on the need for "rigid distinctions" between household and family among New World Africans.) Research often does not distinguish between them (see Dressler et al., 1985; cf. Hofferth, 1984; McLanahan, 1985; Taylor, 1986, 1990). Further, this literature appears to be particularly concerned with the presence or absence of a marital dyad within the coresidential unit. This preoccupation introduces a cultural bias that fails to address other highly relevant relationships and sources of support, such as those between grandparents and grandchildren, siblings, and so forth, within and among households (see Dressler et al., 1985, for an example).

Bruce and Lloyd (1992), as noted above, have recognized the importance of what I have identified as interhousehold, generalized support in relation to variation among female-headed households internationally. From this international work we know that exclusively female-headed households (those in which there are no adult males) are different in two important respects from households that include adult males. Some studies report that in some female-headed households, in spite of poverty, a greater proportion of household budget goes to children and to overall nutritional quality (see Thomas, 1992), as opposed to alcohol and other luxury items (Hoddinott & Haddad, 1991). Children in this type of household have also been found to be healthier (Kennedy & Peters, in press). On the other hand, we know that these households are likely to be among the very poorest of the poor (Buvinic, Valenzuela, Molina, & Gonzales 1992; Taylor et al., 1990). Apparent discrepancies of this magnitude demand clarification, and may be explained by recognizing the relationships among households and families, and between dyadic or restricted responses and generalized exchange. These observations are not new, but recent literature—especially on African American families and on female-headed households—suggest that we need to be reminded of them.

Examination of these two areas of social concern in the United States, and comparisons with the Philippines, suggest the possibility of two very basically different structures of family support—one restricted or dyadic, and heavily dependent on single (spousal, parent-child) relationships, and the other, broad-based, generalized, and flexible. Research has tended to evaluate all support relationships relative to Euro-American or middle-class expectations of dependence on specific dyads.

Family Planning

Turke (1989), writing about international development and Third World families, identifies advantages of generalized extended family organization, including "that they provide opportunities to disperse the costs of childrearing from parents who are in their reproductive prime of life to close relatives with diminished ability to produce children of their own" (p. 66). Sibling relationships, in particular, have bearing on the effectiveness of the kinship networks in that "in traditional societies siblings are likely to somewhat (or in some cases completely) offset the negative effects they have on each other while young through the assistance they provide to each other as adults" (p. 88).

Kin support, and especially sibling support, are among considerations that prompt Turke (1989) to challenge Caldwell's (1981) theory of fertility decline. Given that parents may be simultaneously receiving support from some children and giving support to others, the issue of the direction of net wealth flow between parents and children may be more complex than what has been previously suggested. While net wealth flow is important to macrolevel demographic change, especially to fertility decisions, for the poor any wealth flow may be critical to survival. It is possible to conceive, not of a life-time balance sheet expressed as net wealth flow, but of certain exchanges which are critical to survival or opportunity at a given time. The Philippine data, seen from the approach taken here, support this perspective. These perspectives on extended family exchange clearly have implications for family planning decisions and resulting family size that may be applicable in the United States, as well, particularly in studying support networks of adolescent mothers.

Planned Change

The kin support network represents an essential form of human collateral which needs to be considered in economic development planning, and the value of that collateral and the form it takes vary with stage of family development. For example, very mature households or young persons with no dependents may be better able to take risks or to invest labor than midlife households or young independent couples with young children. A range of technological packages, targeting a range of family capital and labor capability, may promote more effective agricultural development efforts, as opposed to a single package which may be infeasible for many families or households, given the human resources available to them at a given stage of family development. Moreover, "innovative" farmers, in the parlance of agriculture extension, may be those who have the wherewithal in terms of human capital to accept innovation, and "conservative" or "traditional" or "backward" nonadopters of new technologies may only be those who, at a given point in time, do not have the human resources to adopt the technology offered, but who might be able to adopt a less capital- or labor-intensive technology. Human resources within the extended family will affect a family's capacity to make good use of credit and to repay loans, as well.

While recognition of the complexity and efficacy of the family support network can enhance development efforts, failure to do so can jeopardize family welfare (cf. Taylor, 1990). Limitation of family bonds or encouragement of nuclearization of the family anywhere in the world, for example, through resettlement, urban zoning, or family policies, without concomitant development of alternative support structures or assured economic well-being, could adversely affect family welfare.

I cannot leave this discussion without addressing a tendency among anthropologists to view the difference between what I have called restricted and generalized social and economic exchange in terms of evolutionary change or "modernization." Turke (1989) argues that sibling dispersal—that is, geographic dispersal—is characteristic of "modern" societies and, therefore, that the support among siblings that I have identified as generalized exchange, is typical of "traditional" societies. A similar line of reasoning is offered by LeVine and White (1992), who identify greater investment in each of fewer children as an attribute of "modern" societies. If, as I argue here, generalized support of dependent family members is characteristic of African Americans and other populations in the United States, these discussions of modernity would imply that large numbers of Americans are not "modern," or that their cultures have constrained their progress. This, indeed, is the tone of many discussions of African American families or of "familism" among Hispanics (see Vega, 1990). I suggest that dyadic exchange and intense dyadic relationships serve well for those populations for whom upward mobility is unimpeded, but less well for those whose access to prosperity is limited by social and economic discrimination. Coontz (1989) provides an insightful analysis of the deterioration of the face-to-face community in the United States, and concomitant class mobility, especially during the nineteenth century. Families who were able to restructure themselves so as to invest heavily in few children—and, I would add, limit claims on their resources by extended family members—could, indeed, achieve upward mobility. Many could not.

I have suggested that there is a dynamic interaction between family form, household organization, and a larger social and economic context. This perspective is contrary to the position that family form causes social outcomes (see Hofferth, 1984; McLanahan, 1985; Zinn, 1989). This examination of different structures of exchange within and among households may suggest future directions for improving our understanding of the relationships among culture, family, and economy.

NOTE

This work was supported by a Fulbright-Hayes Fellowship, by the Research Board of the University of Illinois, and by a Hewlett Foundation Fellowship.

REFERENCES

Binswanger, H. P., Evenson, R. E., Florencio, C., & White, B. N. F. (Eds.). (1980). *Rural household studies in Asia*. Singapore: Singapore University Press.

Bruce, J., & Lloyd, C. B. (1993). *Finding the ties that bind: Beyond headship and household*. New York: Population Council.

Buvinic, M., Valenzuela, J. P., Molina, T., & Gonzales, E. (1992). The fortunes of adolescent mothers and their children: The transmission of poverty in Santiago, Chile. *Population and Development Review, 18*(2), 269-298.

Caldwell, J. (1981). *The theory of fertility decline*. Homewood, IL: Irwin Publishers.

Carroll, V. (Ed.). (1970). *Adoption in eastern Oceania*. Honolulu: University of Hawaii Press.

Chatters, L. M., Taylor, R. J., & Jackson, J. S. (1985). Size and composition of the informal helper networks of elderly blacks. *Journal of Gerontology, 40*, 605-614.

Coontz, S. (1988). *The social origins of private life: A history of American families 1600-1900*. New York: Verso.

Dressler, W., Hoffner, S., & Pitts, B. (1985). Household structure in a Southern Black community. *American Anthropologist, 87*, 853-862.

Gonzalez, N. S. (1969). *Black Carib household structure: A study of migration and modernization*. Seattle: University of Washington Press.

Hill, R., Foote, N., Aldous, J., Carlson, R., & MacDonald, R. (1970). *Family development in three generations*. Cambridge, MA: Schenkman.

Hoddinott, J., & Haddad, L. (1991). *Household expenditures, child anthropomorphic status and the intrahousehold division of income: Evidence from the Côte d'Ivoire*. Oxford: Oxford University, Unit for the Study of African Economics.

Hofferth, S. L. (1984). Kin networks, race and family structures. *Journal of Marriage and the Family, 46*, 791-806.

Johnson, C. L. (1982). Sibling solidarity: Its origin and functioning in Italian-American families. *Journal of Marriage and the Family, 44*, 155-167.

Johnson, C. L. (1983). Dyadic family relations and social support. *The Gerontologist, 23*, 377-383.

Johnson, C. L., & Catalano, D. J. (1981). Childless elderly and their family support. *The Gerontologist, 21*, 610-618.

Kennedy, E., & Peters, P. (in press). Household food

security and child nutrition: The interaction of income and gender of household head. *World Development*.

LeVine, R. A., & White, M. (1992). The social transformation of childhood. In A. S. Skolnick & J. H. Skolnick (Eds.), *Family in transition* (295-315). New York: Harper Collins.

Levi-Strauss, C. (1949). *Les structures élémentaires de la parenté*. Paris: Presses Universitaire de France.

McLanahan, S. (1985). Family structure and the reproduction of poverty. *American Journal of Sociology*, *90*, 873-901.

Oppenheimer, V. K. (1974). The life cycle squeeze: The interaction of men's occupational and family life cycles. *Demography*, *11*, 227-245.

Peterson, J. T. (1989). Interhousehold exchange and the public economy. In B. L. Isaac (Ed.), *Research in Economic Anthropology* (Vol. 11, pp. 123-142). Greenwich, CT: JAI Press.

Peterson, J. T. (1990). Sibling exchanges and complementarity in the Philippine highlands. *Journal of Marriage and the Family*, *52*, 441-451.

Peterson, J. T. (1991). Returns to parental investment in children in Benguet Province, Philippines. *Journal of Comparative Family Studies*, *22*, 313-328.

Peterson, J. T. (1992). *Household dependency ratios and production in highland Philippines*. Unpublished manuscript.

Peterson, J. T. (in press). Anthropological approaches to the household. In R. Borooah, K. Cloud, J. T. Peterson, T. S. Saraswathi, S. Seshadri, & A. Verma (Eds.), *Capturing complexity: Women, households, and development*. New Delhi: Sage Publishers.

Peterson, J. T., & Paranjape, S. (in press). Education in the Philippine highlands. In J. T. Peterson, L. Pavia-Ticson, & J. Franciso (Eds.), *Women in the Philippines*.

Sahlins, M. (1965). On the sociology of primitive exchange. In M. Banton (Ed.), *The Relevance of Models for Social Anthropology* (pp. 139-236). London: Tavistock Publications.

Shanas, E. (1979). The family as a social support system in old age. *The Gerontologist*, *19*, 169-174.

Stack, C. B. (1974). *All our kin: Strategies for survival in a black community*. New York: Harper & Row.

Stanfield, R. (1992). Valuing the family. *National Journal*, *27*, 1562-1566.

Sussman, M. B., & Burchinal, L. (1962). Kin family network: Unheralded structure in current conceptualizations of family functioning. *Marriage and Family Living*, *24*, 231-240.

Taylor, R. J. (1986). Receipt of support from family among Black Americans: Demographic and familial differences. *Journal of Marriage and the Family*, *48*, 67-77.

Taylor, R. J. (1990). Need for support and family involvement among black Americans. *Journal of Marriage and the Family*, *52*, 584-590.

Taylor, R. J., Chatters, L. M., Tucker, M. B., & Lewis, E. (1990). Developments in research on black families: A decade review. *Journal of Marriage and the Family*, *52*, 993-1014.

Thomas, D. (February 1992). *The distribution of income and expenditure within the household*. Paper presented at the International Food Policy Research Group/World Bank Conference on Intrahousehold Resource Allocation, Washington, DC.

Turke, P. W. (1989). Evolution and the demand for children. *Population and Development Review*, *15*, 61-90.

Vega, W. A. (1990). Hispanic families in the 1980s: A decade of research. *Journal of Marriage and the Family*, *52*, 1015-1024.

Wilk, R. R. (1984). Households in process: Agricultural change and domestic group transformation among the Kekchi Maya of Belize. In R. M. Netting, R. Wilk, & E. J. Arnould (Eds.), *Households: Comparative and historical studies of the domestic group* (pp. 217-244). Berkeley: University of California Press.

Wilk, R. R., & Netting, R. M. (1984). Households: Changing forms and functions. In R. M. Netting, R. Wilk, & E. J. Arnould (Eds.), *Households: Comparative and Historical Studies of the Domestic Group* (pp. 1-28). Berkeley: University of California Press.

Zinn, M. B. (1989). Family, race, and poverty in the eighties. *Signs: Journal of Women in Culture and Society*, *14*, 856-874.

Formation of Relationships

- **Emotions and Relating (Articles 5–7)**
- **From Singlehood to Marriage (Articles 8–10)**

Men have willingly chosen to die at their own hands rather than undergo the suffering of loneliness.
—B. L. Mijuskovic

Since humans are basically social beings, few people thrive in social isolation. Most men and women search and strive for meaningful human interaction. Keys to the attainment of meaningful human interaction include understanding one's emotions and being able to relate them to others. These issues are considered in this section.

Emotions and the relating of emotions play an important part in the establishment and maintenance of any meaningful relationship. Between individuals, communication is both an essential and complex form of relating thoughts and emotions, needs, and desires. Verbal or body language does not actually become communication until the message has been taken in and interpreted by the receiver of that message. Any message that is not perceived or understood as it was intended is considered an example of miscommunication. Frequently, the intensity of the message interferes with the adequate signaling of the message, hindering the reception of the intended communication. This is a common occurrence in relationships, and it often leads to painful misunderstandings.

People bring themselves, their history, especially how they were socialized, their feelings, needs, experiences, and a certain level of skills into any communication situation. Because in this society people are not socialized identically, nor do we have matching expectations or roles for all, we may bring profound differences to interaction and communication settings. Differences are particularly still evident between the genders, between and among certain racial and/or ethnic groups, and may also be significant between people of different socioeconomic levels and/or religious persuasion. Confusion or misunderstanding in interpersonal communication can lead to anger, hurt, fear, or other strong emotions. Add to this the possibility of increased vulnerability in the face of attraction or love, and/or the chemistry of physical or sexual arousal, and the process of relating to others can seem a dangerous endeavor.

How do people today find companions or mates? The formal courting system of earlier times has been replaced for the most part by informal, even casual, dating. This newer style does not seem to be meeting the needs of all who look for mates or companions, however. In this time of numerous divorces, fast-track careers, AIDS, and other realities, professional dating services, the matchmakers of the 1980s and 1990s, have become a booming business.

Although over 90 percent of individuals will marry (and the majority of those who divorce will remarry), people appear to be looking for and considering different things in mates and marriage partners than has been the case historically. There is also a great deal of variation in what is perceived as desirable across groups today. What is perceived as an ideal mate by one person may not be even minimally acceptable to another. While many men and women today are waiting longer before making the transition from singlehood to marriage, some choose a period of living together either as an alternative or a trial period. While these changes may be the result of social, psychological, and/or economic factors, they may also be due to a combination of influences that bring about a certain zeitgeist, or "spirit of the times."

Although in today's world few people still endeavor to keep women (and men) "in their place"—we support making both wider and more overlapping choices—men and women are not the same. The first article, "Sizing Up the Sexes," focuses on the male-female differences that often affect, even capsize, communication and relating.

The second article, "Intimacy: The Art of Working Out Your Relationships," attributes "much of what goes wrong in relationships" to feelings, especially hurt ones, confusion, disillusionment, and silence. It offers a variety of preventive and remediation techniques for working out problems, maintaining an atmosphere where hurts, fears, hopes, and needs can be shared, and couples can strengthen their relationships.

The final article in the first subsection focuses on male-female relationships on campuses. It acknowledges "differences in experiences, perceptions and power" while advocating a breaking down of stereotypes and examining how campuses can facilitate a "climate of mutuality between men and women."

The second subsection addresses the transition from singlehood to marriage. The first two articles trace the history of mate selection, contrasting the qualities considered desirable 50 years ago with those considered so today. It may surprise many readers that being in love is a relatively new requirement, which some people mindful of the soaring divorce rates are beginning to question. The final article focuses on the physical and sexual components of "The Mating Game." Readers may be surprised to find that many of the patterns of attraction, seduction, and sexual interaction have changed little since the Stone Age.

Looking Ahead: Challenge Questions

Do you still find it hard to understand and communicate with "the opposite sex"? What still confuses or frustrates you? Why?

When have you felt hurt or disillusioned in a relationship? What did you do or not do to try to deal with your feelings? How hard is it for you to talk about your feelings and needs with a partner?

What has made it hard for you to talk to and feel comfortable when interacting with the opposite sex? Why? If you had the opportunity to be the opposite sex for a week, what do you expect you would like and not like?

Under what circumstances would you use (or have you considered using) a dating service?

Are you looking for Mr. or Ms. Right? Why or why not? Has someone you thought was this person turned out not to be? Why or how?

What five characteristics do you feel are desirable in a mate or marriage partner? How does being in love fit in for you? If your top characteristics did not include love, would you consider marriage?

What do you consider attractive? Do these characteristics have logical reasons, or do they seem to be inborn or instinctual?

Sizing Up The Sexes

**Scientists are discovering
that gender differences
have as much to do with
the biology of the brain as with
the way we are raised**

CHRISTINE GORMAN

What are little boys made of?
What are little boys made of?
Frogs and snails
And puppy dogs' tails,
That's what little boys are made of.

What are little girls made of?
What are little girls made of?
Sugar and spice
And all that's nice,
That's what little girls are made of.
—Anonymous

Many scientists rely on elaborately complex and costly equipment to probe the mysteries confronting humankind. Not Melissa Hines. The UCLA behavioral scientist is hoping to solve one of life's oldest riddles with a toybox full of police cars, Lincoln Logs and Barbie dolls. For the past two years, Hines and her colleagues have tried to determine the origins of gender differences by capturing on videotape the squeals of delight, furrows of concentration and myriad decisions that children from 2 1/2 to 8 make while playing. Although both sexes play with all the toys available in Hines' laboratory, her work confirms what most parents (and more than a few aunts, uncles and nursery-school teachers) already know. As a group, the boys favor sports cars, fire trucks and Lincoln Logs, while the girls are drawn more often to dolls and kitchen toys.

But one batch of girls defies expectations and consistently prefers the boy toys. These youngsters have a rare genetic abnormality that caused them to produce elevated levels of testosterone, among other hormones, during their embryonic development. On average, they play with the same toys as the boys in the same ways and just as often. Could it be that the high levels of testosterone present in their bodies before birth have left a permanent imprint on their brains, affecting their later behavior? Or did their parents, knowing of their disorder, somehow subtly influence their choices? If the first explanation is true and biology determines the choice, Hines wonders, "Why would you evolve to want to play with a truck?"

Not so long ago, any career-minded researcher would have hesitated to ask such questions. During the feminist revolution of the 1970s, talk of inborn differences in the behavior of men and women was distinctly unfashionable, even taboo. Men dominated fields like architecture and engineering, it was argued, because of social, not hormonal, pressures. Women did the vast majority of society's child rearing because few other options were available to them. Once sexism was abolished, so the argument ran, the world would become a perfectly equitable, androgynous place, aside from a few anatomical details.

But biology has a funny way of confounding expectations. Rather than disappear, the evidence for innate sexual differences only began to mount. In medicine, researchers documented that heart disease strikes men at a younger age than it does women and that women have a more moderate physiological response to stress. Researchers found subtle neurological differences between the sexes both in the brain's structure and in its functioning. In addition, another generation of parents discovered that, despite their best efforts to give baseballs to their daughters and sewing kits to their sons, girls still flocked to dollhouses while boys clambered into tree forts. Perhaps nature is more important than nurture after all.

Even professional skeptics have been converted. "When I was younger, I believed that 100% of sex differences were due to the environment," says Jerre Levy, professor of psychology at the University of Chicago. Her own toddler toppled that utopian notion. "My daughter was 15 months old, and I had just dressed her in her teeny little nightie. Some guests arrived, and she came into the room, knowing full well that she looked adorable. She came in with this saucy little walk, cocking her head, blinking her eyes, especially at the men. You never saw such flirtation in your life." After 20 years spent studying the brain, Levy is convinced: "I'm sure there are biologically based differences in our behavior."

Now that it is O.K. to admit the possibility, the search for sexual differences has expanded into nearly every branch of the life sciences. Anthropologists have debunked Margaret Mead's work on the extreme variability of gender roles in New Guinea. Psychologists are untangling the complex interplay between hormones and aggression. But the most provocative, if as yet inconclusive, discoveries of all stem from the pioneering exploration of a tiny 3-lb. universe: the human brain. In fact, some researchers predict that the confirmation of innate differences in behavior could lead to an unprecedented understanding of the mind.

Some of the findings seem merely curious. For example, more men than women are lefthanded, reflecting the dominance of the brain's right hemisphere. By contrast, more women listen equally with both ears while men favor the right one.

Other revelations are bound to provoke more controversy. Psychology tests, for instance, consistently support the notion that men and women perceive the world in subtly different ways. Males excel at rotating three-dimensional objects in their head. Females prove better at reading emotions of people in photographs. A growing number of scientists believe the discrepancies reflect functional differences in the brains of men and women. If true, then some misunderstandings between the sexes may have more to do with crossed wiring than cross-purposes.

Most of the gender differences that have been uncovered so far are, statistically speaking, quite small. "Even the largest differences in cognitive function are not as large as the difference in male and female height," Hines notes. "You still see a lot of overlap." Otherwise, women could never read maps and men would always be lefthanded. That kind of flexibility within

EMOTIONS

FEMALE INTUITION: THERE MAY BE SOMETHING TO IT

Do women really possess an ability to read other people's hidden motives and meanings? To some degree, they do. When shown pictures of actors portraying various feelings, women outscore men in identifying the correct emotion. They also surpass men in determining the emotional content of taped conversation in which the words have been garbled. This ability may result from society's emphasis on raising girls to be sensitive. But some researchers speculate that it has arisen to give women greater skill in interpreting the cues of toddlers before they are able to speak.

MALE INSENSITIVITY: IT'S A CULTURAL RELIC

If men seem less adept at deciphering emotions, it is a "trained incompetence," says Harvard psychologist Ronald Levant. Young boys are told to ignore pain and not to cry. Some anthropologists argue that this psychic wound is inflicted to separate boys from their mothers and prepare them for warfare. Many men, says Levant, can recognize their emotions only as a physical buzz or tightness in the throat—a situation that can be reversed, he insists, with training.

the sexes reveals just how complex a puzzle gender actually is, requiring pieces from biology, sociology and culture.

Ironically, researchers are not entirely sure how or even why humans produce two sexes in the first place. (Why not just one—or even three—as in some species?) What is clear is that the two sexes originate with two distinct chromosomes. Women bear a double dose of the large X chromosome, while men usually possess a single X and a short, stumpy Y chromosome. In 1990 British scientists reported they had identified a single gene on the Y chromosome that determines maleness. Like some kind of biomolecular Paul Revere, this master gene rouses a host of its compatriots to the complex task of turning a fetus into a boy. Without such a signal, all human embryos would develop into girls. "I have all the genes for being male except this one, and my husband has all the genes for being female," marvels evolutionary psychologist Leda Cosmides,

of the University of California at Santa Barbara. "The only difference is which genes got turned on."

Yet even this snippet of DNA is not enough to ensure a masculine result. An elevated level of the hormone testosterone is also required during the pregnancy. Where does it come from? The fetus' own undescended testes. In those rare cases in which the tiny body does not respond to the hormone, a genetically male fetus develops sex organs that look like a clitoris and vagina rather than a penis. Such people look and act female. The majority marry and adopt children.

The influence of the sex hormones extends into the nervous system. Both males and females produce androgens, such as testosterone, and estrogens—although in different amounts. (Men and women who make no testosterone generally lack a libido.) Researchers suspect that an excess of testosterone before birth enables the right hemisphere to dominate the brain, resulting in lefthandedness. Since testosterone levels are higher in boys than in girls, that would explain why more boys are southpaws.

Subtle sex-linked preferences have been detected as early as 52 hours after birth. In studies of 72 newborns, University of Chicago psychologist Martha McClintock and her students found that a toe-fanning reflex was stronger in the left foot for 60% of the males, while all the females favored their right. However, apart from such reflexes in the hands, legs and feet, the team could find no other differences in the babies' responses.

One obvious place to look for gender differences is in the hypothalamus, a lusty little organ perched over the brain stem that, when sufficiently provoked, consumes a person with rage, thirst, hunger or desire. In animals, a region at the front of the organ controls sexual function and is somewhat larger in males than in females. But its size need not remain constant. Studies of tropical fish by Stanford University neurobiologist Russell Fernald reveal that certain cells in this tiny region of the brain swell markedly in an individual male whenever he comes to dominate a school. Unfortunately for the piscine pasha, the cells will also shrink if he loses control of his harem to another male.

Many researchers suspect that, in humans too, sexual preferences are controlled by the hypothalamus. Based on a study of 41 autopsied brains, Simon LeVay of the Salk Institute for Biological Studies announced last summer that he had found a region in the hypothalamus that was on average twice as large in heterosexual men as in either women or homosexual men. LeVay's findings support the idea that varying hormone levels before birth may immutably stamp the developing brain in one erotic direction or another.

These prenatal fluctuations may also steer boys toward more rambunctious behavior than girls. June Reinisch, director of the Kinsey Institute for Research in Sex, Gender and Reproduction at Indiana University, in a pioneering study of eight pairs of brothers and 17 pairs of sisters ages 6 to 18 uncovered a complex interplay between hormones and aggression. As a group, the young males gave more belligerent answers than did the females on a multiple-choice test in which they had to imagine their response to stressful situations. But siblings who had been exposed in utero to synthetic antimiscarriage hormones that mimic testosterone were the most combative of all. The affected boys proved significantly more aggressive than their unaffected brothers, and the drug-exposed girls were much more contentious than their unexposed sisters. Reinisch could not determine, however, whether this childhood aggression would translate into greater ambition or competitiveness in the adult world.

While most of the gender differences uncovered so far seem to fall under the purview of the hypothalamus, researchers have begun noting discrepancies in other parts of the brain as well. For the past nine years, neuroscientists have debated whether the corpus callosum, a thick bundle of nerves that allows the right half of the brain to communicate with the left, is larger in women than in men. If it is, and if size corresponds to function, then the greater crosstalk between the hemispheres might explain enigmatic phenomena like female intuition, which is supposed to accord women greater ability to read emotional clues.

These conjectures about the corpus callosum have been hard to prove because the structure's girth varies dramatically with both age and health. Studies of autopsied material are of little use because brain tissue undergoes such dramatic changes in the hours after death. Neuroanatomist Laura Allen and neuroendocrinologist Roger Gorski of UCLA decided to try to circumvent some of these problems by obtaining brain scans from live, apparently healthy people. In their investigation of 146 subjects, published in April, they confirmed that parts of the corpus callosum were up to 23% wider in women than in men. They also measured thicker connections between the two hemispheres in other parts of women's brains.

Encouraged by the discovery of such structural differences, many researchers have begun looking for dichotomies of function as well. At the Bowman Gray Medical School in Winston-Salem, N.C., Cecile Naylor has determined that men and women enlist widely varying parts of their brain when asked to spell words. By monitoring increases in blood flow, the neuropsychologist found that women use both sides of their head when spelling

PERCEPTION

HE CAN READ A MAP BLINDFOLDED, BUT CAN HE FIND HIS SOCKS?

It's a classic scene of marital discord on the road. Husband: "Do I turn right?" Wife, madly rotating the map: "I'm not sure where we are." Whether men read maps better is unclear, but they do excel at thinking in three dimensions. This may be due to ancient evolutionary pressures related to hunting, which requires orienting oneself while pursuing prey.

IF LOST IN A FOREST, WOMEN WILL NOTICE THE TREES

Such prehistoric pursuits may have conferred a comparable advantage on women. In experiments in mock offices, women proved 70% better than men at remembering the location of items found on a desktop—perhaps reflecting evolutionary pressure on generations of women who foraged for their food. Foragers must recall complex patterns formed of apparently unconnected items.

while men use primarily their left side. Because the area activated on the right side is used in understanding emotions, the women apparently tap a wider range of experience for their task. Intriguingly, the effect occurred only with spelling and not during a memory test.

Researchers speculate that the greater communication between the two sides of the brain could impair a woman's performance of certain highly specialized visual-spatial tasks. For example, the ability to tell directions on a map without physically having to rotate it appears stronger in those individuals whose brains restrict the process to the right hemisphere. Any crosstalk between the two sides apparently distracts the brain from its job. Sure enough, several studies have shown that this mental-rotation skill is indeed more tightly focused in men's brains than in women's.

But how did it get to be that way? So far, none of the gender scientists have figured out whether nature or nurture is more important. "Nothing is ever equal, even in the beginning," observes Janice Juraska, a biopsychologist at the University of Illinois at Urbana-Champaign. She points out, for instance, that mother rats lick their male offspring more frequently than they do their daughters. However, Juraska has demonstrated that it is possible to reverse some inequities by manipulating environmental factors. Female rats have fewer nerve connections than males into the hippocampus, a brain region associated with spatial relations and memory. But when Juraska "enriched" the cages of the females with

stimulating toys, the females developed more of these neuronal connections. "Hormones do affect things—it's crazy to deny that," says the researcher. "But there's no telling which way sex differences might go if we completely changed the environment." For humans, educational enrichment could perhaps enhance a woman's ability to work in three dimensions and a man's ability to interpret emotions. Says Juraska: "There's nothing about human brains that is so stuck that a different way of doing things couldn't change it enormously."

Nowhere is this complex interaction between nature and nurture more apparent than in the unique human abilities of speaking, reading and writing. No one is born knowing French, for example; it must be learned, changing the brain forever. Even so, language skills are linked to specific cerebral centers. In a remarkable series of experiments, neurosurgeon George Ojemann of the University of Washington has produced scores of detailed maps of people's individual language centers.

First, Ojemann tested his patients' verbal intelligence using a written exam. Then, during neurosurgery—which was performed under a local anesthetic—he asked them to name aloud a series of objects found in a steady stream of black-and-white photos. Periodically, he touched different parts of the brain with an electrode that temporarily blocked the activity of that region. (This does not hurt because the brain has no sense of pain.) By noting when his patients made mistakes, the surgeon was able to determine which sites were essential to naming.

Several complex sexual differences emerged. Men with lower verbal IQs were more likely to have their language skills located toward the back of the brain. In a number of women, regardless of IQ, the naming ability was restricted to the frontal lobe. This disparity could help explain why strokes that affect the rear of the brain seem to be more devastating to men than to women.

Intriguingly, the sexual differences are far less significant in people with higher verbal IQs. Their language skills developed in a more intermediate part of the brain. And yet, no two patterns were ever identical. "That to me is the most important finding," Ojemann says. "Instead of these sites being laid down more or less the same in everyone, they're laid down in subtly different places." Language is scattered randomly across these cerebral centers, he hypothesizes, because the skills evolved so recently.

What no one knows for sure is just how hardwired the brain is. How far and at what stage can the brain's extraordinary flexibility be pushed? Several studies suggest that the junior high years are key. Girls show the same aptitudes for math as

LANGUAGE

IN CHOOSING HER WORDS, A WOMAN REALLY USES HER HEAD

For both sexes, the principal language centers of the brain are usually concentrated in the left hemisphere. But preliminary neurological studies show that women make use of both sides of their brain during even the simplest verbal tasks, like spelling. As a result, a woman's appreciation of everyday speech appears to be enhanced by input from various cerebral regions, including those that control vision and feelings. This greater access to the brain's imagery and depth may help explain why girls often begin speaking earlier than boys, enunciate more clearly as tots and develop a larger vocabulary.

IF JOHNNY CAN'T READ, IS IT BECAUSE HE IS A BOY?

Visit a typical remedial-reading class, and you'll find that the boys outnumber the girls 3 to 1. Stuttering affects four times as many boys as girls. Many researchers have used these and other lopsided ratios to support the argument that males, on average, are less verbally fluent than females. However, the discrepancy could also reflect less effort by teachers or parents to find reading-impaired girls. Whatever the case, boys often catch up with their female peers in high school. In the past few years, boys have even begun outscoring girls on the verbal portion of the Scholastic Aptitude Test.

Is Sex Really Necessary?

Birds do it. Bees do it. But dandelions don't. The prodigious spread of these winsome weeds underscores a little-appreciated biological fact. Contrary to human experience, sex is not essential to reproduction. "Quite the opposite," exclaims anthropologist John Tooby of the University of California at Santa Barbara. "From an engineer's standpoint, sexual reproduction is insane. It's like trying to build an automobile by randomly taking parts out of two older models and piecing them together to make a brand-new car." In the time that process takes, asexual organisms can often churn out multiple generations of clones, gaining a distinct edge in the evolutionary numbers game. And therein lies the puzzle: If sex is such an inefficient way to reproduce, why is it so widespread?

Sex almost certainly originated nearly 3.5 billion years ago as a mechanism for repairing the DNA of bacteria. Because ancient earth was such a violent place, the genes of these unicellular organisms would have been frequently damaged by intense heat and ultraviolet radiation. "Conjugation"—the intricate process in which one bacterium infuses genetic material into another—provided an ingenious, if cumbersome, solution to this problem, although bacteria continued to rely on asexual reproduction to increase their numbers.

Animal sex, however, is a more recent invention. Biologist Lynn Margulis of the University of Massachusetts at Amherst believes the evolutionary roots of egg and sperm cells can be traced back to a group of organisms known as protists that first appeared some 1.5 billion years ago. (Modern examples include protozoa, giant kelp and malaria parasites.) During periods of starvation, Margulis conjectures, one protist was driven to devour another. Sometimes this cannibalistic meal was incompletely digested, and the nuclei of prey and predator fused. By joining forces, the fused cells were better able to survive adversity, and because they survived, their penchant for union was passed on to their distant descendants.

From this vantage point, human sexuality seems little more than a wondrous accident, born of a kind of original sin among protozoa. Most population biologists, however, believe sex was maintained over evolutionary time because it somehow enhanced survival. The mixing and matching of parental genes, they argue, provide organisms with a novel mechanism for generating genetically different offspring, thereby increasing the odds that their progeny could exploit new niches in a changing environment and, by virtue of their diversity, have a better chance of surviving the assaults of bacteria and other tiny germs that rapidly evolve tricks for eluding their hosts' defenses.

However sex came about, it is clearly responsible for many of the most remarkable features of the world around us, from the curvaceousness of human females to the shimmering tails of peacocks to a lion's majestic mane. For the appearance of sex necessitated the evolution of a kaleidoscope of secondary characteristics that enabled males and females of each species to recognize one another and connect.

The influence of sex extends far beyond the realm of physical traits. For instance, the inescapable fact that women have eggs and men sperm has spurred the development of separate and often conflicting reproductive strategies. University of Michigan psychologist David Buss has found that men and women react very differently to questions about infidelity. Men tend to be far more upset by a lover's sexual infidelity than do women: just imagining their partner in bed with another man sends their heart rate soaring by almost five beats a minute. Says Buss: "That's the equivalent of drinking three cups of coffee at one time." Why is this so? Because, Buss explains, human egg fertilization occurs internally, and thus a man can never be certain that a child borne by his mate is really his. On the other hand, because women invest more time and energy in bearing and caring for children, they react more strongly to a threat of emotional infidelity. What women fear most is the loss of their mates' long-term commitment and support.

The celebrated war between the sexes, in other words, is not a figment of the imagination but derives from the evolutionary history of sex—from that magic moment long, long ago when our unicellular ancestors entwined in immortal embrace.
—*By J. Madeleine Nash/Chicago*

HOW OTHER SPECIES DO IT

Humans think there's nothing more natural than males and females in mutual pursuit of the urge to be fruitful and multiply. But nature follows more than one script. Not every species has two sexes, for example. And even when it does, neither their behavior nor their origin necessarily conforms to human notions of propriety. Some of the more bizarre cases in point:

TURTLES
Among most reptiles, males are literally made in the shade. The gender of a turtle hatchling, for instance, is determined not by sex chromosomes but by the temperature at which it was incubated. Eggs that develop in nests located in sunny areas, where it is warm and toasty, give rise to females. Eggs nestled in shady places, where it may be 5°C (10°F) cooler, will yield a crop of males.

WHIPTAIL LIZARDS
For some varieties of these lizards there's no such thing as a battle of the sexes. All of them are female. In a process known as parthenogenesis, they produce eggs that hatch without ever being fertilized. Yet, because they evolved from lizards that come in two sexes, pairs of these single-minded creatures will take turns imitating males and mount each other. The act apparently stimulates greater egg production.

JACANA BIRDS
Females usually rule the roost on every shore, marsh and rice field where these long-legged "lily trotters" abound. They are generally larger than the males, which are saddled with the duties of building the nest, incubating the eggs and raising the chicks. In fact in some varieties, female Casanovas regularly jilt their domestic-minded mates and search for more sexually available males.

CICHLIDS
These fish come in three sexes: brightly hued macho males, paler females, and male wimps that look and act like females. There are only a few sexually active males in a school. But the minute a piscine Lothario dies, an ambitious wimp rises to the occasion. His brain unleashes sex hormones that bring color to his scales and make him feisty, but he can revert to pallid impotence if challenged by a more macho fish.

boys until about the seventh grade, when more and more girls develop math phobia. Coincidentally, that is the age at which boys start to shine and catch up to girls in reading.

By one account, the gap between men and women for at least some mental skills has actually started to shrink. By looking at 25 years' worth of data from academic tests, Janet Hyde, professor of psychology and women's studies at the University of Wisconsin at Madison, discovered that overall gender differences for verbal and mathematical skills dramatically decreased after 1974. One possible explanation, Hyde notes, is that "Americans have changed their socialization and educational patterns over the past few decades. They are treating males and females with greater similarity."

Even so, women still have not caught up with men on the mental-rotation test. Fascinated by the persistence of that gap, psychologists Irwin Silverman and Marion Eals of York University in Ontario wondered if there were any spatial tasks at which women outperformed men. Looking at it from the point of view of human evolution, Silverman and Eals reasoned that while men may have developed strong spatial skills in response to evolutionary pressures to be successful hunters, women would have needed other types of visual skills to excel as gatherers and foragers of food.

The psychologists therefore designed a test focused on the ability to discern and later recall the location of objects in a complex, random pattern. In series of tests, student volunteers were given a minute to study a drawing that contained such unrelated objects as an elephant, a guitar and a cat. Then Silverman and Eals presented their subjects with a second drawing containing additional objects and told them to cross out those items that had been added

and circle any that had moved. Sure enough, the women consistently surpassed the men in giving correct answers.

What made the psychologists really sit up and take notice, however, was the fact that the women scored much better on the mental-rotation test while they were menstruating. Specifically, they improved their scores by 50% to 100% whenever their estrogen levels were at their lowest. It is not clear why this should be. However, Silverman and Eals are trying to find out if women exhibit a similar hormonal effect for any other visual tasks.

Oddly enough, men may possess a similar hormonal response, according to new research reported in November by Doreen Kimura, a psychologist at the University of Western Ontario. In her study of 138 adults, Kimura found that males perform better on mental-rotation tests in the spring, when their testosterone levels are low, rather than in the fall, when they are higher. Men are also subject to a daily cycle, with testosterone levels lowest around 8 p.m. and peaking around 4 a.m. Thus, says June Reinisch of the Kinsey Institute: "When people say women can't be trusted because they cycle every month, my response is that men cycle every day, so they should only be allowed to negotiate peace treaties in the evening."

Far from strengthening stereotypes about who women and men truly are or how they should behave, research into innate sexual differences only underscores humanity's awesome adaptability. "Gender is really a complex business," says Reinisch. "There's no question that hormones have an effect. But what does that have to do with the fact that I like to wear pink ribbons and you like to wear baseball gloves? Probably something, but we don't know what."

Even the concept of what an innate difference represents is changing. The physical and chemical differences between the brains of the two sexes may be malleable and subject to change by experience: certainly an event or act of learning can directly affect the brain's biochemistry and physiology. And so, in the final analysis, it may be impossible to say where nature ends and nurture begins because the two are so intimately linked.

—Reported by
J. Madeleine Nash/Los Angeles

Intimacy: The Art of Working Out Your Relationships

Most of what goes wrong in relationships can be traced to hurt feelings, miscommunication, and disillusionment—leading partners to erect defenses against one another.

Lori H. Gordon, Ph.D.

Confusion. Hurt. Silence. Missed opportunity. It is one of the ironies of modern life that many couples today are living together as complete strangers. Or worse, in great unhappiness. The data on divorce lead us to conclude that intimate relationships have been falling apart for the last 20 years or so. The truth is that couples have never learned reliably how to sustain pleasure in intimate relationships. The difference is it never mattered so much before.

Here at the close of the 20th century we have the luxury of living in splendid isolation. Unlike in more "primitive" cultures, most Americans no longer live as part of a large family or community where we develop a sense of comfort and safety, a network of people to confide in, to feel at home with. This, I have come to believe, is what has drawn many people into cults—the need to feel part of a bonded community, where there is a sense of being at home emotionally as well as physically. Our culture provides for meeting all other needs, especially the need for autonomy, but not for intimacy. Within this framework, couples today must provide for each other more of the emotional needs that a larger community used to furnish.

Compounding the wide-scale deprivation of intimacy we actually experience, our cultural talent for commercialization has separated out sex from intimacy. In fact, intimacy involves both emotional and physical closeness and openness. But we wind up confusing the two and end up feeling betrayed or used when, as often happens, we fail to satisfy our need for closeness in sex.

Shifts in our general views about what makes life worth living have also contributed to a new demand for intimacy. For many generations the answer lay in a productive life of work and service in which the reward of happiness would be ours, in Heaven. That belief has broken down. People want happiness here and now. And they want it most in their intimate relationships.

Here, it's clear, we are unlikely to find it easily. Couples today are struggling with something new—to build relationships based on genuine feelings of equality. As a result, we are without role models for the very relationships we need. And rare were the parents who modeled intimacy for us; most were too busy struggling with survival requirements. Yet the quality of our closest relationships is often what gives life its primary meaning.

Intimacy, I have come to believe, is not just a psychological fad, a rallying cry of contemporary couples. It is based on a deep biological need. Shortly after I began my career as a family therapist I was working in a residential treatment center where troubled teenage boys were sent by the courts. Through my work I began to discover what had been missing for these kids: They needed support and affection, the opportunity to express the range and intensity of their emotions. It was remarkable to discover their depth of need, their depth of pain over the lack of empathy from significant people in their lives.

It is only in the last 20 years that we recognize that infants need to be held and touched. We know that they cannot grow—they literally fail to thrive—unless they experience physical and emotional closeness with another human being. What we often don't realize is that that need for connection never goes away. It goes on throughout life. And in its absence, symptoms develop—from the angry acting out of the adolescent boys I saw, to depression, addiction, and illness. In fact, researchers are just at the very beginning of understanding the relationship of widespread depression among women to problems in their marriages.

When I brought the boys together with their families, through processes I had not learned about in graduate school, it transformed the therapy. There was change. For the adolescent boys, their problems were typically rooted in the often-troubled relationships between their parents. They lacked the nurturing environment they needed for healthy growth. What I realized was that to help the children I first had to help their parents. So I began to shift my focus to adults.

From my work in closely observing the interactions of hundreds of couples, I have come to recognize that most of what goes wrong in a relationship stems from hurt feelings. The disappointment couples experience is based on misunderstanding and misperception. We choose a partner hoping for a source of affection, love, and support, and, more than ever, a best friend. Finding such a partner is a wonderful and ecstatic experience—the stage of illusion in relationships, it has been called.

From *Psychology Today,* September/October 1993, pp. 40-42, 79-80, 82-83, 87, 90. © 1993 by Sussex Publishers, Inc. Reprinted by permission.

To use this conceit, there then sets in the state of disillusion. We somehow don't get all that we had hoped for. He didn't do it just right. She didn't welcome you home; she was too busy with something else; maybe she didn't even look up. But we don't have the skills to work out the disappointments that occur. The disappointments big and little then determine the future course of the relationship.

If first there is illusion, and then disillusion, what follows is confusion. There is a great deal of unhappiness as each partner struggles to get the relationship to be what each of them needs or wants it to be. One partner will be telling the other what to do. One may be placating—in the expectation that he or she will eventually be rewarded by the other. Each partner uses his or her own familiar personal communication style.

Over the disappointment, the partners erect defenses against each other. They become guarded with each other. They stop confiding in each other. They wall off parts of themselves and withdraw emotionally from the relationship, often into other activities—or other relationships. They can't talk without blaming, so they stop listening. They may be afraid that the relationship will never change but may not even know what they are afraid of. There is so much chaos that there is usually despair and depression. One partner may actually leave. Both may decide to stay with it but can't function. They live together in an emotional divorce.

Distractors need to know that they're safe, not helpless, that problems can be solved, conflicts resolved.

Over the years of working with couples, I have developed an effective way to help them arrive at a relationship they can both be happy with. I may not offer them therapy. I find that what couples need is part education in a set of skills and part exploration of experience that aims to resolve the difficulties couples trip over in their private lives.

Experience has demonstrated to me that the causes of behavior and human experience are complex and include elements that are biological, psychological, social, contextual, and even spiritual. No single theory explains the intricate dynamics of two individuals interacting over time to meet all their needs as individuals and as a couple. So without respect to theoretical coherence I have drawn from almost every perspective in the realm of psychology—from psychodynamics to family systems, communication theory and social learning theory, from behavior therapy to object relations. Over the past 25 years I have gradually built a program of training in the processes of intimacy now known as Practical Application of Intimate Relationship Skills (PAIRS). It is taught to small groups of couples in a four-month-long course in various parts of the United States and now in 13 countries.

There are no specific theories to explain why the course works. In time that will come, as researchers pinpoint exactly which cognitive, behavioral, and experiential elements (and when and for whom) are most responsible for which types of change. Nevertheless I, my associates, and increasing numbers of graduate students have gathered, and are gathering, evidence that it powerfully, positively influences marital interaction and satisfaction.

Studies of men and women before and after taking the course show that it reduces anger and anxiety, two of the most actively subversive forces in relationships. Judging from the hundreds of couples who have taken the PAIRS course,

The Daily Temperature Reading

Confiding—the ability to reveal yourself fully, honestly, and directly—is the lifeblood of intimacy. To live together with satisfaction, couples need clear, regular communication. The great intuitive family therapist Virginia Satir developed a technique for partners and families to maintain an easy flow about the big and little things going on in their lives. I have adapted it. Called the Daily Temperature Reading, it is very simple (and works for many other kinds of relationships as well).

Do it daily, perhaps as you sit down to breakfast. At first it will seem artificial—hokey, even. In time you'll evolve your own style. Couples routinely report it is invaluable for staying close—even if they let it slide for a day or two when they get busy. It teaches partners how to listen nondefensively and to talk as a way to give information rather than to stir a reaction. Here are the basics:

Sit close, perhaps even knee-to-knee, facing your partner, holding each other's hands. This simple touching creates an atmosphere of acceptance for both.

1. APPRECIATION. Take turns expressing appreciation for something your partner has done—and thanking each other.

2. NEW INFORMATION. In the absence of information, assumptions—often false ones—rush in. Tell your partner something ("I'm not looking forward to the monthly planning meeting this morning") to keep contact alive and let your partner in on your mood, your experiences—your life. And then listen to your partner.

3. PUZZLES. Take turns asking each other something you don't understand and your partner can explain: "Why were you so down last night?" Or voice a question about yourself: "I don't know why I got so angry while we were figuring out expenses." You might not find answers, but you will be giving your partner some insight about yourself. Besides, your partner may have insights about your experiences.

4. COMPLAINT WITH REQUEST FOR CHANGE. Without placing blame or being judgmental, cite a specific behavior that bothers you and state the behavior you are asking for instead. "If you're going to be late for dinner tonight, please call me. That way the kids and I can make our own plans and won't be waiting for you."

5. HOPES. Sharing hopes and dreams is integral to a relationship. Hopes can range from the mundane ("I hope you don't have to work this weekend") to the grandiose ("I'd really love to spend a month in Europe with you"). But the more the two of you bring dreams into immediate awareness, the more likely you'll find a way to realize them.

Bonding Exercise

Most people put a lid on the hurts or fears of the past: "It doesn't bother me anymore"; "It isn't that important." But I find that it is essential to lift that lid—in the context of the current relationship—to close the revolving ledger.

- Choose a time when you are feeling somewhat edgy.
- Put on some soft music in the background.
- Lie down with your partner. Lie on your sides cradled into each other, both facing the same direction.

While your partner is holding you, quietly reveal something he or she does that triggers a full-blown intense emotional reaction in you. It might be that she doesn't listen to you. Or he interrupts you constantly. Or doesn't call

when he's away. Or rejects whatever you suggest. "When you do this, I am very upset." As you are speaking, your partner is holding you and listening.

Now tell your partner what experience out of your history your reaction connects to. Perhaps his not calling infuriates you because it arouses the fear you felt when a parent left or died. Or your first husband walked out.

Now comes the remarkable part. Tell your partner what you would have needed to happen in your history that would have helped. What actions would you have preferred to have happen? What words would you have needed to hear?

Now let your partner tell you what you needed to hear, while you take it in. Your partner is free to say it in his or her own

way: "I'm sorry that happened to you"; "I wish I had been there."

And now discuss the price you are paying in your current relationship for having this emotional reaction to events of the past. Perhaps it is that you don't talk to your partner, you withdraw, withhold, get even.

What you talk about next is what you can then do to help yourself. "How can I signal you neutrally to let you know when you trigger this response in me."

At this point you are talking about what will help you in the future. You are jointly and consciously outlining useful behaviors, constructing a relationship in which actions and experiences have the same meaning and same effect for both of you. This is essential for happiness to occur in a relationship.

---

partners in distressed relationships tend to have more anxiety and anger than does the general population. Once they have taken the course there is a marked reduction in this state of anger and anxiety. What is most notable is that there is also a reduction in the personality trait of anger, which is ordinarily considered resistant to change. Learning the skills of intimacy—of emotional and physical closeness—has a truly powerful effect on people.

We also see change in measurements of marital happiness, such as the Dyadic Adjustment Scale. Tests administered before the course show that we are seeing a range of couples from the least to the most distressed. And we are getting significant levels of change among every category of couple. It is no secret that most attempts at therapy produce little or no change among the most distressed couples. Perhaps it's because what we are doing is not in the form of therapy at all, although its effects are therapeutic. In addition to improvement in many dimensions of the relationship, achieving intimacy bolsters the self-worth of both partners.

Love is a feeling. Marriage, on the other hand, is a contract—an invisible contract. Both partners bring to it expectations about what they want and don't want, what they're willing to give and not willing to give. Most often, those are out of awareness. Most marriage part-

ners don't even know they expected something until they realize that they're not getting it.

The past is very much present in all relationships. All expectations in relationships are conditioned by our previous experience. It may simply be the nature of learning, but things that happen in the present are assimilated by means of what has happened in the past. This is especially true of our emotions: every time we have an experience in the present we also are experiencing it in the past. Emotional memory exists outside of time. It is obvious that two partners are conditioned by two different pasts. But inside the relationship it is less obvious. And that leads to all kinds of misunderstanding, disagreement, disappointment, and anger that things are not going exactly as expected.

The upshot is statements like "I can't understand women," "who knows what a woman wants," and "you can never please a man." All of the classic complaints reflect hidden expectations that have never surfaced to the point where they could be discussed, examined, kept, or discarded.

To add insult to injury, when one partner is upset, the other often compounds it unintentionally. When, for example, a woman is unhappy, men often feel they are expected to charge out and fix something. But what she really wants is for

her partner to put his arms around her and hold her, to soothe her, to say simply, "I'm sorry you feel bad." It is a simple and basic longing. But instead of moving toward her, he moves away. And if when you are upset you don't get what you want from the person you are closest to, then you are not going to feel loved. Men, too, I hasten to say, have the same basic need. But they erect defenses against it for fear it will return them to a state of helplessness such as they experienced as children.

Much unhappiness in relationships can be traced to a partner who learned never to express anger.

At the heart of intimacy, then, is empathy, understanding, and compassion; these are the humanizing feelings. It is bad enough that they are in short supply among distressed couples. Yet I have observed that certain careers pose substantial roadblocks to intimacy because the training involves education not in humanization but in dehumanization. At the top of the list is law. Built primarily on the adversarial process, it actively discourages understanding and compassion in favor of destroying an opponent. Careers in the military and in engineering also are dismissive of feelings and emotions. Men and women who bring what they learn from such work into a love relationship may find that it can't survive.

An understanding of intimacy has its own logic. But it runs counter to conventional wisdom and most brands of psychology. They hold that to understand the nature of, and to improve, relationships, the proper place to start is the self. The thinking is that you need to understand yourself before you can confide in a partner. But I have found just the opposite to be true.

An exploration of the self is indeed absolutely essential to attaining or rebuilding a sense of intimacy. Most of the disappointments that drive our actions and reactions in relationships are constructed with expectations that are not only hidden from our partners but also ourselves. From our families of origin and past relationship experiences, we acquire systems of belief that direct our behavior outside of our own awareness. It is not possible to change a relationship without bringing this belief system into our awareness.

But a man or a woman exploring their personal history experiences some powerful feelings that, in the absence of a partner to talk to, may make one feel worse rather than better. So the very first step a couple must take to rebuild intimacy is to learn to express their own thoughts and feelings and carefully listen to each other. A partner who knows how to listen to you can then be on hand when you open up your past.

Exploration of the self is an activity often relegated to psychotherapy; in that case a psychotherapist knows how to listen with empathy. But that is not necessarily the only way and at best is a luxury affordable only by a few. It is not only possible but desirable for couples of all economic strata to choose to confide in each other and build a relationship with a life partner rather than with a paid confidant. Both partners have an ongoing need to open up the past as well as share the present. But there are skills that have to be learned so that such interaction can be safe. Both partners need to learn how to listen without judging or giving unwanted advice. Disappointment in a partner's ability to hear is what often sends people to a psychotherapist in the first place.

All of us bring to our intimate relationships certain expectations that we have of no one else. On the positive side they usually involve undivided attention—words and gestures of love and caring, loyalty, constancy, sex, companionship, agreement, encouragement, friendship, fidelity, honesty, trust, respect, and acceptance. We are all too alert to the possibility that we will instead find their exact opposites. yeah

If we are not aware of our own expectations (and how they are affected by our history), there is no hope of expressing them to a partner so that he or she has a shot at meeting them. More often than not, we engage instead in mind reading. Mind reading is often related to a past disappointing relationship experience. We tend to expect what we previously had the opportunity to learn; we make assumptions based on our history. And when in personal history there are people or situations that were the source of heartache, resentment, or anxiety, then any action by a partner in the present that is similar in some way often serves as a reminder—and triggers an intense emotional reaction. I call this "emotional allergy." As with other forms of prior sensitization, the result tends to be an explosive reaction—withdrawal, counterattack—and it is typically incomprehensible to a current partner.

If I had to summarize how to change the hidden expectations that work to distort a relationship, I would boil it all down to a few basic rules:

If you expect a partner to understand what you need, then you have to tell him or her. That of course means you have to figure out for yourself what you really need.

You cannot expect your partner to be sensitive and understand exactly how you feel about something unless you're able to communicate to him or her how you feel in the first place.

If you don't understand or like what your partner is doing, ask about it and why he or she is doing it. And vice versa. Explore. Talk. Don't assume.

Expressing your feelings about a given situation and asking for your partner's honesty in return is the most significant way to discover truth in your relationship. Instead, most communication between intimates is nonverbal and leans heavily on mind reading. The only thing you have to go on is your own internal information, which could easily be skewed by any number of factors. This is also

why genuine responses are so important. Telling your partner what you think he or she wants to hear, instead of what is really going on, complicates and postpones a useful solution to the problem.

Confiding is much more than being able to reveal yourself to another. It is knowing with absolute certainty that what you think and feel is being heard and understood by your partner. Instead, we tend to be passive listeners, picking up only those messages that have a direct bearing on ourselves, rather than listening for how things are for our partner.

Men discover that bonding is a valid need in its own right. It doesn't weaken you, it strengthens you.

Listening with empathy is a learned skill. It has two crucial ingredients: undivided attention and feeling what your partner feels. Never assume that you know something unless it is clearly stated by your partner. And you need to understand fully what your partner's thoughts and feelings mean to him or her. Instead of focusing on the effects of your partner's words on you, pay attention instead to your partner's emotions, facial expression, and levels of tension. The single biggest barrier to such empathic listening is our self-interest and self-protective mechanisms. We anticipate and fill in the blanks. One of the simple truths of relationships is that often enough, all we need to do to resolve a problem is to listen to our partner—not just passively listen but truly hear what is in the mind and in the heart.

What more often happens is that, when we experience threats to our self-esteem or feel stressed, we resort to styles of communication that usually lead to more of a problem than the problem itself. The styles of communication that we resort to during stress then often prevent real contact from happening. If your partner tends to be a blamer, you will distance yourself. You develop a rational style of relating, but no feelings are ever dealt with. Not only is no love experienced, but at the emotional level nothing can get resolved.

Most people tend to react to stress with one or more of four communication styles:

●PLACATING. The placater is ingratiating, eager to please, apologetic, and a "yes" man or woman. The placater says things like "whatever you want" or "never mind about me, it's okay." It's a case of peace at any price. The price, for the placater, is worthlessness. Because the placater has difficulty expressing anger and holds so many feelings inside, he or she tends toward depression and, as studies show, may be prone to illness. Placaters need to know it is okay to express anger.

●BLAMING. The blamer is a fault-finder who criticizes relentlessly and speaks in generalizations: "You never do anything right." "You're just like your mother/father." Inside, the blamer feels unworthy or unlovable, angry at the anticipation he or she will not be getting what is wanted. Given a problem, the best defense is a good offense. The blamer is unable to deal with or express pain or fear. Blamers need to be able to speak on their own behalf without indicting others in the process. *So True*

●COMPUTING. The computer is super reasonable, calm and collected, never admits mistakes, and expects people to conform and perform. The computer says things like, "Upset? I'm not upset. Why do you say I'm upset?" Afraid of emotion, he or she prefers facts and statistics. "I don't reveal my emotions and I'm not interested in anyone else's." Computers need someone to ask how they feel about specific things.

Disappointment in a partner's ability to hear is what sends people to a psychotherapist in the first place.

●DISTRACTING. The distractor resorts to irrelevancies under stress, avoids direct eye contact and direct answers. Quick to change the subject, he or she will say, "What problem? Let's have Sam and Bridget over." Confronting the problem might lead to a fight, which could be dangerous. Distractors need to know that they are safe, not helpless, that problems can be solved and conflicts resolved.

Each style is a unique response to pain, anger, or fear, which keeps us from understanding each other. Knowing that,

the next time you find yourself resorting to blame, you can conclude there is something painful or scary bothering you and try to figure out what it is. If it's your partner who is blaming, you can conclude he or she is possibly not intending to be aggressive or mean but probably afraid of some development. What's needed is to find a way to make it safe to talk about the worry; find out what is bothering him or her.

How, then, can you say what is bothering you, or express what you really need, in a way that your partner can hear it, so that your message can be understood? This is a basic step in building the relationship you want. For this, the Daily Temperature Reading is particularly helpful [See box].

After partners have been heard and understood, they may need to work on forgiveness. Of course, some things are unforgivable, and each partner has to decide if that line has been crossed and the relationship is worth continuing. If it is, there has to be a recognition that you can't change the past. No relationship can recover from past disappointments and mature unless both partners can find a way to let go of grudges. This is one of the most important relationship skills couples can develop.

In a relationship, letting go of grudges is something you do for yourself, not just to make your partner feel better. It is done by making simple statements of facts, not statements of blame. "You took me to your office party and you got so busy with everyone else you didn't introduce me to anyone to talk to me all night. You acted like I didn't matter and that your boss was the most important man in your life."

In the beginning, the course works best in the safety of a group, which prevents the isolation of couples and keeps partners from getting defensive and negative. But once they've practiced this, and it's a simple act of confiding, couples continue it on their own far more easily.

This is not just an exercise of the emotions. There is a cognitive restructuring taking place during these exercises. What is really going on is that one partner is, probably for the first time, learning the meaning of another's experience. That by itself enhances their closeness. All it requires is listening with empathy, and the experience becomes a source of pleasure for both of them. At the same time, there is conceptual under-

standing of what each is doing that deprives the relationship of pleasure and what they need to do to make it better.

Because the past continually asserts itself in present experience, both partners in a relationship are obligated to explore themselves, their beliefs, needs, and hopes, and even uniqueness of personality through their family's emotional history. Most people operate in the present, using messages and beliefs silently transmitted to them in their family of origin. Or they may be living out invisible loyalties, making decisions based not on the needs of their partner or present relationship, or even their own needs, but on some indebtedness that was incurred sometime in the past.

Particularly at issue are messages we acquire about ourselves, about life and love, trust, confiding, and closeness. Those things we take as truths about love, life, and trust are beliefs we had the chance to learn from specific people and situations in the past. It is on this information that we make the private decision to ourselves: "Nobody cares." "It doesn't matter what I think or say, you're not interested in me." If, for example, you grew up in a family where your mother or father drank or was depressed, or was otherwise emotionally unavailable, you may have drawn the conclusion that no one was really interested in you.

It is vital to know the lineage of our beliefs because we transfer onto our partners what we were dealt in the past. One of the decisions often made unwittingly is, "I don't trust that anybody is really going to be any better to me." It can become a way of saying, "I'm going to get even for the way I was treated." You wind up punishing your partner for what someone else actually did. *Not Always*

When you displace the blame for past hurts onto your present partner, you are activating a dynamic that psychiatrist Ivan Boszormenyi-Nagy, M.D., describes as "the revolving ledger." At certain periods in your life, important people, or even life itself, through events that affected you, ran up a series of debits or credits in terms of what you needed. Time passed. You walked through life's revolving door. And now you hand me the bill. And you hold two hidden expectations. "Prove to me you are not the person who hurt me." In other words, "make up to me for the past." "Pay me back." And, "if you don't, if you do one thing that reminds me of that, I will punish you." The emotional transfer is accomplished.

Freud described this as transference and identified it as a crucial part of the therapeutic relationship. In fact, it is part of our everyday transactions in relationships. It is crucial to understand that this emotional transfer often does not take place early in a relationship. It sets in after a couple has been married for some time—when you are disappointed and discover what you expected or hoped to happen isn't happening.

That is the point when we transfer the hidden expectations, especially the negative ones, from our history, from any or

---

The thinking is that you need to understand yourself before confiding in a partner. Just the opposite is true.

---

all of our previous close relationships, whether to parents, siblings, former spouses, lovers, or friends. It is one of the core emotional transactions of marriage. And making it explicit is one of the psychological tasks of achieving intimacy.

The problem is, the person to whom you hand the bill is unaware of the account books in your head. The result is endless misunderstanding and disturbance. In fact, the attitudes you hold tend to be outside of your own awareness. I believe that they can be found through personal exploration.

Otherwise, you find yourself thinking of your partner as the enemy, someone to hurt, someone to get even with, to punish. And because you don't recognize the ledger as the motivating power behind your behavior, you rationalize. You seek reasons to treat your partner as the enemy. You are really just evening up the balance on someone else's account.

Roger called his wife Jenny at work. She was in the middle of a staff meeting and so she was particularly abrupt with him. When she got home, she found a note from him. He was gone. From somewhere in his past experience he was so sensitized to demonstrations of lack of interest in him that her behavior constituted absolute proof. One misstep—one

hint that she was anything like whoever ran up the debit—was all she was allowed. This is a common pattern in relationships. And the "proof" of disinterest could be anything. Perhaps she didn't look at him. Perhaps she was tired. Perhaps she was sick. One reason men are often intolerant of a wife who gets sick is that she isn't there for them. It is a painful reminder of other accounts from the past.

Not only do couples maintain revolving ledgers, but they also carry over feelings of indebtedness and entitlement from one generation to the next. Invisible loyalties thus accrue in a family over the generations, whether or not we end up acknowledging them. An artistic man buries his creative longing because his family legacy calls for being a success in business. For each of us, behavior is greatly affected by the family ledger of entitlement and indebtedness.

Every couple needs to trace the source of behaviors and attitudes, many of which turn out to have been handed down through their families of origin. Much unhappiness in relationships can be traced to the fact that one partner learned as a family rule never to express anger, or even perhaps happiness. Many people grow up learning to subjugate their own needs and feelings to those of others. Still the feelings influence present relationships, and until they can be brought into awareness and spoken, it is very difficult to improve current relationships.

Once a couple has done this and discovers where their beliefs come from, they can review them together and decide which legacies they want to keep, which they'd rather discard. They each work out their personal history so they do not punish the one who's here now.

At this point I find that couples do well if I introduce an experience in bonding that is usually very emotionally powerful.

For men, these experiences are revelatory. Men, because they are often cut off from the emotional part of themselves, are especially often forced to piggyback their need for intimacy on sex. They have no less need for intimacy than women, but it usually gets suppressed and denied. Or they attempt to satisfy their need for closeness through contact sports and roughhousing. They don't know how to work things out in man-woman intimate relation-

ships. But when they learn, they almost always feel an enormous sense of wholeness and relief.

In growing up men have learned that the only thing they are supposed to need to be close to a woman is sex. They discover that bonding is a valid need in its own right, and needing physical closeness doesn't mean they are going to regress into helplessness and never function again. It doesn't weaken you, it strengthens you.

But this is not learnable merely by cognitive statement. Having the experience illuminates the point and changes the thinking. The exercises are important because they integrate the emotional acceptance, the behavioral change, and the cognitive understanding that occur.

It is no news that sexual problems in a relationship are frequently the by-product of personal and relational conflicts and anxieties. For too many couples, sex has become a substitute for intimacy and a defense against closeness. Most poor sex stems from poor communication, from misunderstandings of what one's mate actually wants—not from unwillingness or inability to give it.

In the realm of sex as in other domains of the relationship, you cannot expect your partner to guess what pleases you. You are obligated to figure out for yourself what stimulates, delights, and satisfies you—and acknowledge it. It is not enough to give and receive, you also have to be able to speak up or reach out on your own behalf and take. Ideally, sexual love will be a flow of this give and take, but it has to go both ways to keep desire alive.

Before sex can be rewarding for both partners, they have to first restore the ability to confide and reestablish emotional openness, to establish a sense of camaraderie. Then physical closeness has meaning, and the meaning serves only to heighten the pleasure of the physical experience even more.

Of course, intercourse is not the only avenue to physical pleasure. There is a whole range of physical closeness couples can learn to offer each other. Being together. Hugging. Holding each other. Caressing each other's face. Massaging your partner's body. In fact, taking pleasure in each other is a habit that some couples actually have to acquire. But taking pleasure in your partner is the very thing your partner needs most from you.

The Changing Nature of Relationships on Campus:

Impasses and Possibilities

STEPHEN J. BERGMAN
JANET SURREY

Stephen J. Bergman and Janet Surrey are on the faculty of Harvard Medical School and the Stone Center, Wellesley College.

Old models of male-female relationships are breaking down. In the past, role differentiation helped define what was "male" and "female" and helped shape the male-female relationship. Although it was important for women to be educated, often a woman's "role" was to support a man's self-development and career. Healthy development was defined primarily as "male" development: a strong, independent "self" that could connect with others only after achieving a degree of separation and maturity. (The epitome of this was the Freudian model of development.) Deviation from this "separate self" model, by man or woman, was seen as pathology. Campus counseling centers by and large endorsed this model. "Relationship" was seen as the coming together, in role-defined ways, of two separate "selves."

But this model will no longer serve. In society and on campus, the old paradigms of roles and identities tied to gender are no longer the reality. In all aspects of society, male-centered models are being challenged. Campuses are at the forefront of these challenges as many young adults struggle to create and develop new forms of relationships.

In her 1976 book, *Toward a New Psychology of Women*, Jean Baker Miller challenged whether the male model fit women's experience. For the past 15 years, we and others at the Stone Center (Wellesley College) have been developing a new paradigm of psychological development, shifting from a "self-centered" model of healthy development to a "relationship-centered" model. The work has focused primarily on shaping an accurate description of women's psychological development.[1] Recently, the relational paradigm has been applied to male development.[2] Gilligan and Belenky have also developed this model.[3]

2. FORMATION OF RELATIONSHIPS: Emotions and Relating

The Stone Center model

The relational model differs markedly from old models of development. First, it suggests that the primary motivation for all humans is not Freud's "sex and aggression," but rather a desire for connection. Second, it suggests that healthy growth takes place "through and toward connection," rather than in isolation or in the fashioning of a separate isolated self. And finally, in a paradigm shift, it suggests the existence of a third element, "the relationship," a process that encompasses the sense of "self" and "other." "The relationship" reflects and informs all participants. Each person's reality can be seen in a "relational context," the field of connection between and among people, which extends to the greater community and society.

We have come to believe that to work on gender issues within relationship, it is useful for men and women to work on these issues not only individually, but also in groups. In groups of men and women discussing cross-gender relationship, it soon becomes apparent that an individual concern — which may have been thought of as "pathological" and therefore kept hidden — is in fact a concern shared by other men and women; further, what were thought to be an individual couple's difficulties in relationship are found to be difficulties inherent in all cross-gender relationships. Once these difficulties can be seen as shared, they can be "de-pathologized," and dialogue can begin. We feel strongly that to look at these issues, men and women on campus must work together, and we have found that once a climate of mutuality between men and women has been created, diffi-

> **Each person's reality can be seen in a "relational context," the field of connection between and among people, which extends to the greater community and society.**

cult issues — among them, sexuality and violence — can be addressed.

The male-female workshop

Using the Stone Center model, we have worked for the last ten years to bring the genders together, offering workshops on "The Woman/Man Relationship: Creating Mutuality."[4] (Our work thus far has focused particularly on the obstacles to mutuality in heterosexual relationships.) We offer a vision of "relational mutuality," a model of engagement around gender differences. Each time we hold this workshop, we find that almost without exception, it is the first time that men and women have been brought together for the specific purpose of attending to gender differ-

ences and working through the conflicts around difference toward mutual understanding and action.

First, in a brief didactic session, we describe the Stone Center paradigm, which helps participants shift their focus to "the relationship." We try to enhance attention to and awareness of the relationship and the qualities of connection or disconnection in the relationship. For example, we ask each person to think of an important relationship and imagine its color, texture, sound, and climate, as well as animal that might be a metaphor for it. This shift of focus from the individual to the relationship is very new for most people who have grown up in western industrialized cultures like the United States'.

Next we separate the men and women in different rooms, and in small groups of three or four they come up with consensus answers to three questions:

1. Name three strengths the other gender group brings to relationships.
2. What do you most want to understand about the other gender group?
3. What do you most want the other gender group to understand about you?

After separate group discussions about the questions, the men and women come back together. Without having told them in advance, we seat the men and women in two semicircles facing each other. We then ask them to discuss their answers.

Immediately, things get heated. The men are often fearful; the women are usually curious. We asked one male college

Once a climate of mutuality between men and women has been created, difficult issues – among them, sexuality and violence – can be addressed.

While it is crucial to begin the discussion about breaking down stereotypes, it is equally crucial to acknowledge differences in experience, perceptions, and power.

student who looked particularly anxious to describe what was going on. He said, "I'm afraid that something might happen." A woman responded enthusiastically, "I'm *hoping* that something might happen!" Thus, some familiar and important differences begin to emerge as men and women try to engage in relationship. The men start to feel what we have called "relational dread," and they start to withdraw; the women start to feel angry, and they either pursue or give up. This impasse is familiar to participants from their own relationships, where things spiral out of control and get stuck in a hostile standoff. We have termed this a "relational impasse": it exists not in the man or in the woman, but in the relational space in which they meet.

We have called the three im-passes we have identified Dread/Anger, Product/Process (where the men are trying to complete the task, while the women want to keep opening up the process), and Power-Over/Power-With (where the men experience conflict as a threat or as an attempt to control and as something that should be resolved through some rule or criterion, while the women want everyone's voice to be attended to and retreat from what seem like definitive stands). Any or all of these impasses may occur in any particular aspect of relationship. Think, for example, of how Dread/Anger, Product/Process, and Power-Over/Power-With might get played out around sex. For example, a man may approach a woman sexually:

Woman: "I can't just go right into something physical – I need to feel connected to you first."
Man: "That's what I'm trying to do – making love is how I connect."
Woman: "But I need to connect with you in order to make love."

We have held these workshops on various campuses, ranging from a liberal eastern school where the group started out fragmented along ethnic, racial, gender, sexual, and class lines and was embroiled in an ongoing debate about "political correctness," to a conservative midwestern school where the concerns were less political. In each workshop, strong feelings are generated – fear, anger, confusion, hopelessness – and yet there is a sense of freshness and newness in actually talking together about these feelings, especially when the students begin to discuss their responses to the question, "What do you most want to understand about the other gender group?"

Some of the responses of these college students are as follows:

Men's questions to the women:
"Why are you so angry?"
"How often do women feel threatened by the presence of a man? Or a group of men?"
"What is your intense need to talk about feelings?"
"Do I need to prove myself to you?"
"Do women feel they are holding up the emotional end of relationships, and do they want to?"
"How does your emotion affect connections?"
"Why are you more curious than we are? Why do you value means over ends?"
"Can you really accept vulnerability in a man?"

**Women's questions
to the men:**

"How can you compartmentalize your thoughts?"

"How deep does male bonding go? How close are male-male relationships?"

"Are you ever conscious of being a member of the dominant sex?"

"Do you go through the same self-questioning that we do and that we think you don't? Do you depend at all on outside approval and affirmation for your confidence?"

"Why is it hard for men to express their emotions?"

"Why is it so hard for men to deal with other people's emotions?"

"Why – if men have a need for connection – do they act directly against their primary need?"

"What is the meaning of men's silence?"

"How do we get your attention?"

Out of the dialogue around these questions, several main areas of conflict between male and female college students become apparent.

Stereotypes and political correctness ("PC")

Political correctness has been well discussed. (See, for example, *Educational Record*, Winter 1992.) One solution to the conflict is to try to equalize everything and deny any differences in experience. (This may be a reaction to the history of inequality, where difference was used hierarchically and the dominant race or gender or class exerted power over the subordinate.)

While it is crucial to begin the discussion about breaking down stereotypes, it is equally crucial to acknowledge differences in experience, perceptions, and power.

In American culture and on campus, there seems to be an unspoken fear that addressing difference will lead to stereotyping.

Denial interferes with dialogue, engagement, and real understanding. The problem is not "diversity" versus "PC," but rather how to open the dialogue about difference. It is essential to begin to distinguish "stereotype" from "difference."

In our workshops, issues of stereotype are raised immediately. Often, women will ask questions such as:

"Are you men ever conscious of being a member of the dominant sex?"

"Why is it hard for men to express their emotions?"

"Why do men separate love and sex?"

"When are you men going to *wake up*?"

These questions from the women often evoke anger in the men, who answer:

"Don't stereotype me – I'm not into that macho thing."

"Don't blame *me* for the things that other men do."

Often, when the men list women's "strengths," they say things like "women are nurturant" and "women take care of the details of the relationship"; this tends to make women angry because they are unwilling to be thought of mainly in these traditional "female-role" ways.

In this atmosphere, we find that it is difficult to ask about each others' experiences and listen to the answers. It becomes clear why stereotypes tend to prevail when men and women are placed in situations where there is no chance for dialogue, no opportunity for the movement of relationship – that is, when there are disconnections between men and women. In disconnection, stereotypes become more powerful; if there is an opportunity for mutual connection, stereotypic thinking and language become less evident. This is certainly true of gender/sexual stereotypes, and it probably is true of others. In American culture and on campus, there seems to be an unspoken fear that addressing difference will lead to stereotyping. In fact, our workshops suggest that it may be just the reverse: *exploring* difference together breaks through stereotypes. As we help students pursue the dialogue, they begin to discuss the deeper roots and effects of these images of being "nurturers" or "macho."

Violence and date rape

There is an increasing incidence of alleged violence and date rape on campus, and a sense that more women are beginning to speak out about rape, harassment, and abuse. But women still feel that it is risky to speak out – and with good rea-

It became clear to the students how the power of the dominant group (men) over the subordinate group (women) can often be invisible to the dominant group.

son. The Anita Hill phenomenon showed just how difficult it is for a victim to be believed, and how the victim who speaks out may find herself the target of anger. A woman may conclude: "It's all right to speak out, but it can get you in a lot of trouble – you may not be believed."

Men, too, are placed in a difficult position. They are confused and annoyed about this issue: on the one hand, they feel accused, and on the other, they feel that it is difficult to take a moral stand against the problem without dissociating from their gender: "Yeah, some men do that stuff, but not *me*."

In one workshop, at a point when the men and women were caught in an impasse around this issue of violence, one man helped break through the impasse by frankly relating a dilemma he had recently experienced:

Man: "I was walking behind a woman student at night on a dark path, and I didn't want to scare her. But I didn't know whether to stop and let her go ahead so that I wouldn't frighten her, to walk up to her to make her feel more safe, or just to walk normally and let what would happen happen. She heard me. When she turned around, I saw on her face a look of real terror. I thought to myself – What? She's scared of *me*? And then, for the first time, I really got it. I mean, I realized how much fear of physical violence women carry around with them all the time."
Woman: "You mean you didn't *know?*"
Man: "Not 'til that night, no."

Responding to the man's gentle authenticity, the other students raised similar concerns. The men identified with the dilemma. The women, feeling understood, were able both to hold to their experience and to empathize with the men's experience. Together, they discussed aspects of this difficult issue, moving back and forth between individual and societal arenas. It became clear to the students how the power of the dominant group (men) over the subordinate group (women) can often be invisible to the dominant group. The extension to racial, ethnic, sex, and class divisions was apparent. The discussion led to a listing of proposals to deal with violence and date rape on campus: men offering to escort women, initiating discussion groups to further explore the issue, etc.

Our workshops have also shown us how infrequently men and women discuss sexuality. Each gender is curious about the other's

If asking men to be more "relational" is called "feminization," we are all in big trouble. We are bringing men and women together to work on the "relationalization" of all.

sexual style, and sometimes the facts are at odds with the stereotypes. One men's group asked the women, "Do you like to flirt? What is a sure sign [that you are interested in a man]?" "What are your signals and standards of attractiveness?" "How do you feel about taking an active role in initiating relationships and sex?" One man said, "The big lie is that we men are the pursuers, but the fact is, the woman's the one who opens the door." A women's group asked, "Why are men intimidated by women when we're expressing our sexuality?" "What's with this breast fetish?" "Why are male bodily functions so important to you?"

"Why do men separate love and sex?"

Given this basic level of uncertainty about the other gender's sexuality, it is not surprising that impasses arise. And when a man feels trapped in an impasse, especially if alcohol or drugs are involved, violence can arise. (Violence could, in fact, be reframed as the ultimate disconnection.) In the workshops, the exchange of questions and answers between genders can result in remarkable movement toward mutuality in a short period of time. It is astonishing to see just how far a simple exchange of previously "hidden" information or "secrets" about the other gender can go. For example, the men asked the women: "How often do you feel like a sexual being?" A woman answered: "We are multifaceted, changing creatures, and our sexuality is different from yours – we can be highly sensual and sexual, but we're not necessarily pleased in the same ways, nor do we have the same appetites, as men. For us, sex is not a linear activity." From this interchange, the group had a fascinating discussion about how to understand the other gender's sensuality and sexuality.

Backlash

Over the past 12 years, as American society has fragmented along lines of income, race, ethnicity, and class, there has been a violent increase in hostility toward women, described in Susan Faludi's prize-winning book, *Backlash.*[5] A reciprocal backlash against men was fired up by the Anita Hill-Clarence Thomas hearings: "Men just don't get it." The economic climate has increased pressures on students, promoting an atmosphere of every person for him or herself and fueled by anxiety about getting a job.

The isolation of both genders is intense, as is the private devaluation of genders in stereotypical ways. Groups of men, in particular, "get into" this devaluation of women. Recently, in a college workshop, a woman asked her boyfriend, "Why do you get so different, so weird, so unaffectionate toward me, when you're with your friends?" Other women asked, "How do you feel about status differences with women partners?" and "Do you know what it feels like to make 67 cents on the dollar?" At another college workshop, we heard about a hidden microphone at a college fraternity that picked up incredibly sexist language and hateful remarks. Once again, disconnection inflames isolation and backlash.

The way to "reconnect" is to express the anger and fear and to work to understand the other gender's experience and perceptions. It is increasingly clear that the way through is *not* to further solidify gender identity – to become "more female" or "more male" – but to value and learn how to make mutually empowering connections, not only within gender, but across gender.

Often, both women and men will raise the question, "But we don't want men to become more like women – are you talking about the 'feminization' of men?" If asking men to be more "relational" is called "feminization," we are all in big trouble. We are bringing men and women together to work on the "relationalization" of all.

The economy, commitment, and identity

The past decade has seen a dramatic worsening of the economic climate. For college students, this means increased pressure to get a good job, which in turn promotes an atmosphere of competitiveness rather than cooperation. There is tremendous anxiety, in both college and graduate school, about being able to make a "good living."

These tensions have profound effects on the qualities of relationships. College is a transition period, in which relationships are based on work identity, concerns about personal identity, and the formation of the so-called "adult" identity. We would reframe these concerns not only in "self" terms, but in "self-in-relationship" terms. As they set the stage for adult growth, college students both absorb the current culture and are the creators of it.

The Reagan-Bush era focused on the old notion of "self." At best, it fostered a kind of heightened individual achievement; at worst, it fostered a greedy discounting of the value of personal relationships. In individual relationships on campus, both women and men express a terrible fear of "getting involved." One man asked, "Why do you have such lofty expectations about relationships?" Another asked, "If you had on your tombstone: 'She was wonderful at relationships,' would you be satisfied?" A woman answered: "It would be great – but I'd like a second line: 'She pitched in the World Series.'" A woman asked, "What are your needs in a relationship? Does a relationship ever matter as much as a career?"

In college, as in society, pressures abound, competition is fierce, and the ethos is "do it for yourself," for your own development. But how can these be reconciled with commitment? Most college students want to be committed to a person – in fact, they want to be committed not only to a person, but to a relationship – and yet they are truly afraid of making the commitment.

Women in particular have been struggling long and hard for "self-hood," which often is based on the male model of success. In an eastern women's college, women are expected to put their own careers first: "If you are going with somebody, and you both get into grad school in different parts of the country, there are no more of the old rules, which said that women were supposed to follow the men's careers. But there's no new model of relationship. It's everyone for herself." This leaves students with a terrible fear and doubt about whether to get involved and committed. Women and men want relationships badly, but they are told to put their own careers first.

Again, we might reframe this by teaching men and women how to enter into a dialogue that includes but transcends "self" and reframes "identity" in terms of "what will make this relationship truly mutual and foster the healthy growth of both participants."

The shift toward mutuality

In the workshops, once the work begins and the impasses develop, when the male and female students persist in a dialogue around their differences, a shift in the "sense" of the group invariably occurs. Suddenly, the men and women are working *together* on the questions, helping each to find out about the other's experience. We have called this a "shift toward mutuality." Men and women have described this ex-

In an atmosphere of mutual endeavor, almost any topic can be discussed productively, including sexuality, violence, stereotype, backlash, and commitment.

perience of mutuality in these words:

Release, comfort, caring, safety, sharing, peaceful, easy, enjoyment of different styles, hopefulness, mutual nurturance, energizing, movement, insight, softening, appropriate confrontation, dynamic process, clearer recognition of others' experience.[6]

Even in groups that start out angry and fragmented, this shift occurs. There is a great sense of relief, movement out of the impasses and stuck places, away from shame and blame, and toward a new sense of possibility.

In an atmosphere of mutual endeavor, almost any topic can be discussed productively, including sexuality, violence, stereotype, backlash, and commitment. In this atmosphere of mutual

connection, stereotypes fade. In their place we see mutual inquiry, authenticity, and empowerment. Often, this results in men and women working together to take action on campus.

We have found that the possibility of moving from separation to mutuality is always present when men and women get together. The openness, the desire to work together, the strong feelings, and the vitality of college students make them an excellent group in which to begin the work of redefining the nature of cross-gender relationships.

[1] Jordan, J., A. Kaplan, J. Miller, I. Stiver, and J. Surrey, *Women's Growth in Connection*. New York: Guilford, 1991.

[2] Bergman, Stephen. "Men's Psychological Development: A Relational Perspective." *Work in Progress*, No. 48. Wellesley, MA: Stone Center Working Paper Series, 1990.

[3] Gilligan, Carol. *In A Different Voice*. Cambridge: Harvard University Press, 1982; Belenky, M., et al. *Women's Ways of Knowing*. New York: Basic Books, 1986.

[4] Bergman, Stephen and Janet Surrey. "The Woman/Man Relationship: Impasses and Possibilities." *Work in Progress*, No. 55. Wellesley, MA: Stone Center Working Paper Series, 1992.

[5] Faludi, Susan. *Backlash*. New York: Crown, 1991.

[6] Bergman, Stephen and Janet Surrey, Ibid.

Choosing Mates—The American Way

Martin King Whyte

Martin King Whyte is professor of sociology and faculty associate in the Center for Chinese Studies at the University of Michigan. He has published numerous works on family sociology and contemporary Chinese social organization. His is currently involved in a comparative study of mate choice and marital relations in China and the United States. His latest book is Dating, Mating, and Marriage.

As America's divorce rate has been soaring, popular anxieties about marriage have multiplied. Is it still possible to "live happily ever after," and if so, how can this be accomplished? How can you tell whether a partner who leaves you breathless with yearning will, as your spouse, drive you to distraction? Does "living together" prior to marriage provide a realistic assessment of how compatible you and your partner might be as husband and wife? Questions such as these suggest a need to examine our American way of mate choice. How do we go about selecting the person we marry, and is there something wrong with the entire process?

For most twentieth-century Americans choosing a mate is the culmination of a process of dating. Examination of how we go about selecting mates thus requires us to consider the American dating culture. Dating is a curious institution. By definition it is an activity that is supposed to be separate from selecting a spouse. Yet, dating is expected to provide valuable experience that will help in making a "wise" choice of a marital partner. Does this combination work?

How well dating "works" may be considered in a number of senses of this term. Is it easy or difficult to find somebody to go out with? Do dates mostly lead to enjoyable or painful evenings? However, these are not the aspects of dating I wish to consider. The issue here is whether dating works in the sense of providing useful experience that helps pave the way for a successful marriage.

Dating is a relatively new institution. The term, and the various practices associated with it, first emerged around the turn of the century. By the 1920s dating had more or less completely displaced earlier patterns of relations among unmarried Americans. Contrary to popular assumptions, even in colonial times marriages were not arranged in America. Parents were expected to give their approval to their children's nuptial plans, a practice captured in our image of a suitor asking his beloved's father for her hand in marriage. Parental approval, especially among merchants and other prosperous classes, put some constraint on the marriages of the young. For example, through the eighteenth century, children in such families tended to marry in birth order and marriage to cousins was not uncommon. (Both practices had declined sharply by the nineteenth century.) However, parents rarely directly arranged the marriages of their children. America has always exhibited "youth-driven" patterns of courtship. Eligible males and females took the initiative to get to know each other, and the decision to marry was made by them, even if that decision was to some degree contingent on parental approval. (Of course, substantial proportions of later immigrant groups from Southern and Eastern Europe, Asia, and elsewhere brought with them arranged marriage traditions, and contention for control over marriage decisions was often a great source of tension in such families.)

How did young people get to know one another well enough to decide to marry in the era before dating? A set of customs, dominant for the two centuries, preceded the rise of the dating culture. These activities came to be referred to as "calling" and "keeping company." Young people might meet in a variety of ways— through community and church socials, informally in shops or on the street, on boat and train trips, or through introductions from friends or relatives. (America never developed a system of chaperoning young women in public, and foreign observers often commented on the freedom unmarried women had to travel and mix socially on their own.) Usually young people would go to church fairs, local dances, and other such activities with family, siblings, or friends, rather than paired off with a partner. Most activities would involve a substantial degree of adult and community supervision. Nonetheless, these gatherings did encourage some pairing off and led to hand holding, moonlit walks home, and other romantic exploration.

By late nineteenth century, a formal pattern of "calling" developed among the upper and middle classes.

As relationships developed beyond the platonic level, the suitor would pay visits to the home of the young woman. By the latter part of the nineteenth century, particularly among the middle and upper classes, this activity assumed a formal pattern referred to as "calling." Males would be invited to call on the female at her home, and they were expected to do so only if invited. (A bold male could, however, request an invitation to call.) Invitations might be extended by the mother of a very young woman, but eventually they would come from the young woman herself. Often a woman would designate certain days on which she would receive callers. She might have several suitors at one time, and thus a number of men might be paying such calls. A man might be told that the woman was not at home to receive him, and he would then be expected to leave his calling card. If this happened repeatedly, he was expected to get the message that his visits were no longer welcome.

Initiative and control in regard to calling were in the hands of women (the eligible female and her mother). Although some variety in suitors was possible, even in initial stages the role of calling in examining potential marriage partners was very clear to all involved. The relatively constrained and supervised nature of calling make it certain that enjoyment cannot have been a primary goal of this activity. (During the initial visits the mother was expected to remain present; in later visits she often hovered in an adjacent room.) If dating is defined as recreational and romantic pairing off between a man and a woman, away from parental supervision and without immediate consideration of marriage, then calling was definitely not dating.

The supervised and controlled nature of calling should not, however, lead us to suppose that propriety and chastity were always maintained until marriage. If the relationship had deepened sufficiently, the couple might progress from calling to "keeping company," a precursor of the twentieth-century custom of "going steady." At this stage, the primary activity would still consist of visits by the suitor to the woman's home. However, now she would only welcome calls from one man, and he would visit her home on a regular basis. Visits late into the evening would increasingly replace afternoon calls. As the relationship became more serious, parents would often leave the couple alone. Nineteenth-century accounts mention parents going off to bed and leaving the young couple on the couch or by the fireplace, there to wrestle with, and not infrequently give in to, sexual temptation.

Even though some women who headed to the altar toward the end of the nineteenth century had lost their virginity prior to marriage, premarital intimacy was less common than during the dating era. (The double standard of the Victorian era made it possible for many more grooms to be non-virgins at marriage than brides. Perhaps 50 percent or more of men had lost their virginity prior to marriage, as opposed to 15 to 20 percent of women, with prostitutes and "fallen women" helping to explain the differential.) What is less often realized is that the formalization of the calling pattern toward the end of the nineteenth century contributed to a decline in premarital sexual intimacy compared to earlier times. America experienced not one but two sexual revolutions—one toward the end of the eighteenth century, at the time of the American Revolution, and the other in the latter part of the twentieth century.

The causes of the first sexual revolution are subject to some debate. An influx of settlers to America who did not share the evangelical puritanism of many early colonists, the expansion of the population into the unsettled (and "unchurched") frontier, the growth of towns, and the individualistic and freedom-loving spirit of the American revolution may have contributed to a retreat from the fairly strict emphasis on premarital chastity of the early colonial period. Historians debate the extent to which the archetypal custom of this first sexual revolution, bundling, (which allowed an unmarried couple to sleep together, although theoretically fully clothed and separated by a "bundling board") was widespread or largely mythical. Whatever the case, other evidence is found in studies of communities, such as those by Daniel Scott Smith and Michael Hindus, which found that the percentage of married couples whose first births were conceived premaritally increased from about 11 percent before 1700 to over 33 percent in the last decades of the eighteenth century.

This first sexual revolution was reversed in the nineteenth century. The reasons for its demise are also not clear. The closing of the frontier, the rise of the middle class, the defensive reactions of that new middle class to new waves of immigrants, the growth of Christian revivalism and reform movements, and the spread of models of propriety from Victorian England (which were in turn influenced by fear of the chaos of the French Revolution)—all these have been suggested as having contributed to a new sexual puritanism in the nineteenth century. According to Smith and Hindus, premarital conceptions decreased once again to about 15 percent of first births between 1841 and 1880.

It was in the latter time period that the customs of calling and keeping company reached their most formal elaboration—calling, in less ritualized forms, can be traced back to the earliest colonial period. Not long after reaching the formal patterns described, calling largely disappeared. In little more than a generation, dating replaced calling as the dominant custom.

Dating involved pairing off of couples in activities not supervised by parents, with pleasure rather than marriage as the primary goal. The rules governing dating were defined by peers rather than by adults. The initiative, and much of the control, shifted from the female to the male. The man asked the woman out, rather than waiting for her invitation to call. The finances and transportation for the date were also his responsibility. The woman was expected to provide, in turn, the pleasure of her company and perhaps some degree of romantic and physical intimacy. By giving or withholding her affection and access to her body, she exercised considerable control over the man and the date as an event. Nonetheless, the absence of parental oversight and the pressure to respond to a man's initiatives placed a woman in a weaker position than she was in the era of calling.

The man might pick up the woman at her home, but parents who tried to dictate whom their daughters dated and what they did on dates generally found such efforts rejected and evaded. Parents of a son might not even know where junior was going or whom he was dating. Dates were conducted mostly in the public arena, and in some cases—such as at sporting events or school dances—adults might be present. But dates often involved activities and venues where no adults were present or where young people predominated—as at private parties or at local dance halls. Or in other cases the presence of adults would have little inhibiting effect, as in the darkened balconies of movie theaters. American youths also developed substantial ingenuity in finding secluded "lovers' lanes" where they could escape the supervision of even peers. (Localities varied in the places used for this purpose and how they were referred to. In locales near bodies of water young people spoke of "watching submarine races;" in the rural area of upstate New York where I grew up the phrase was "exploring tractor roads.") Community dances and gatherings for all generations and ages practically disappeared in the dating era.

Greater privacy and autonomy of youths promoted romantic and physical experimentation. Not only kissing but petting was increasingly accepted and widespread. Going beyond petting to sexual intercourse, however, involved substantial risks, especially for the female. This was not simply the risk of pregnancy in the pre-pill era. Dating perpetuated the sexual double standard. Men were expected to be the sexual aggressors and to try to achieve as much intimacy as their dates would allow. But women who "went too far" risked harming their reputations and their ability to keep desirable men interested in them for long. Women were expected to set the limits, and they had to walk a careful line between being too unfriendly (and not having males wanting to date them at all) and being too friendly (and being dated for the "wrong reasons").

Rules governing dating were defined by peers rather than adults.

During the initial decades of the dating era, premarital intimacy increased in comparison with the age of calling, but still a majority of women entered marriage as virgins. In a survey in the greater Detroit metropolitan area, I found that of the oldest women interviewed (those who dated and married prior to 1945), about one in four had lost her virginity prior to marriage. (By the 1980s, according to my survey, the figure was closer to 90 percent.) Escape from parental supervision provided by dating weakened, but did not immediately destroy, the restraints on premarital intimacy.

When Americans began dating, they were primarily concerned with enjoyment, rather than with choosing a spouse. Indeed, "playing the field" was the ideal pursued by many. Dates were not suitors or prospects. Seeing different people on successive nights in a hectic round of dating activity earned one popularity among peers. One of the early students and critics of the dating culture, Willard Waller, coined the term "rating and dating complex" to refer to this pattern. After observing dating among students at Pennsylvania State University in the 1930s, Waller charged that concern for impressing friends and gaining status on campus led to superficial thrill-seeking and competition for popularity, and eliminated genuine romance or sincere communication. However, Waller has been accused of both stereotyping and exaggerating the influence of this pattern. Dating was not always so exploitative and superficial as he charged.

Dating was never viewed as an endless stage or an alternative to courtship. Even if dates were initially seen as quite separate from mate selection, they were always viewed as only the first step in a progression that would lead to marriage. By the 1930s, the stage of "going steady" was clearly recognized, entailing a commitment by both partners to date each other exclusively, if only for the moment. A variety of ritual markers emerged to symbolize the increased commitment of this stage and of further steps toward engagement and marriage, such as wearing the partner's high school ring, being lavaliered, and getting pinned.

Growing affluence fueled new industries designed to entertain and fill leisure time.

Going steady was a way-station between casual dating and engagement. Steadies pledged not to date others, and they were likely to become more deeply involved romantically and physically than casual daters. They were not expected explicitly to contemplate marriage, and the majority of women in our Detroit survey had several steady boyfriends before the relationships that led to their marriages. If a couple was of a "suitable age," though, and if the steady relationship lasted more than a few months, the likelihood increased of explicit talk about marriage. Couples would then symbolize their escalated commitment by getting engaged. Dating arose first among middle and upper middle class students in urban areas, and roughly simultaneously at the college and high school levels. The practice then spread to other groups—rural young people, working class youths, to the upper class, and to employed young people. But what triggered the rapid demise of calling and the rise of dating?

One important trend was prolonged school attendance, particularly in public, co-educational high schools and colleges. Schools provided an arena in which females and males could get to know one another informally over many years. Schools also organized athletic, social, and other activities in which adult supervision was minimal. College campuses generally allowed a more total escape from parental supervision than high schools.

Another important influence was growing affluence in America. More and more young people were freed from a need to contribute to the family economy and had more leisure time in which to date. Fewer young people worked under parental supervision, and more

and more fathers worked far from home, leaving mothers as the primary monitors of their children's daily activities. These trends also coincided with a rise in part-time and after-school employment for students, employment that provided pocket money that did not have to be turned over to parents and could be spent on clothing, makeup, movie tickets, and other requirements of the dating culture. Rising affluence also fueled the growth of entire new industries designed to entertain and fill leisure time—movies, popular music recording, ice cream parlors, amusement parks, and so on. Increasingly, young people who wanted to escape from supervision of their parents found a range of venues, many of them catering primarily to youth and to dating activities.

Technology also played a role, and some analysts suggest that one particular invention, the automobile, deserves a lion's share of the credit. Automobiles were not only a means to escape the home and reach a wider range of recreation spots. They also provided a semi-private space with abundant romantic and sexual possibilities. New institutions, such as the drive-in movie theater, arose to take advantage of those possibilities. As decades passed and affluence increased, the borrowed family car was more and more replaced by cars owned by young people, advancing youth autonomy still further.

All this was part of a larger trend: the transformation of America into a mass consumption society. As this happened, people shifted their attention partially from thinking about how to work and earn to pondering how to spend and consume. Marketplace thinking became more and more influential. The image of the individual as *homo economicus* and of modern life typified by the rational application of scientific knowledge to all decisions became pervasive. The new ideological framework undermined previous customs and moral standards and extended to the dating culture.

Dating had several goals. Most obviously and explicitly, dates were expected to lead to pleasure and possibly to romance. It was also important, as Waller and others have observed, in competition for popularity. But a central purpose of dating was to gain valuable learning experience that would be useful later in selecting a spouse. Through dating young people would learn how to relate to the opposite sex. Dating would increase awareness of one's own feelings and understanding of which type of partner was appealing and which not. Through crushes and disappointments, one would learn to judge the character of people. And by dating a variety of partners and by increasingly intimate involvement with some of them, one would learn what sort of person one would be happy with as a marital partner. When it came time to marry one would be in a good position to select "Mr. Right" or "Miss Right." Calling, which limited the possibilities of romantic experimentation, often to only one partner, did not provide an adequate basis for such an informed choice.

What emerged was a "marketplace learning viewpoint." Selecting a spouse is not quite the same as buying a car or breakfast cereal, but the process was seen as analogous. The assumptions involved in shopping around and test driving various cars or buying and tasting Wheaties, Cheerios, and Fruit Loops were transferred to popular thinking about how to select a spouse.

According to this marketplace learning viewpoint, getting married very young and without having acquired much dating experience was risky, in terms of marital happiness. Similarly, marrying your first and only sweetheart was not a good idea. Neither was meeting someone, falling head over heels in love, and marrying, all within the course of a month. While Americans recognized that in some cases such beginnings could lead to good marriages, the rationale of our dating culture was that having had a variety of dating partners and then getting to know one or more serious prospects over a longer period time and on fairly intimate terms were experiences more likely to lead to marital success.

Eventually, this marketplace psychology helped to undermine America's premarital puritanism, and with it the sexual double standard. The way was paved for acceptance of new customs, and particularly for premarital cohabitation. Parents and other moral guardians found it increasingly difficult to argue against the premise that, if sexual enjoyment and compatibility were central to marital happiness, it was important to test that compatibility before marrying. Similarly, if marriage involved not just hearts and flowers, but also dirty laundry and keeping a budget, did it not make sense for a couple to live together prior to marriage to see how they got along on a day-to-day basis? Such arguments on behalf of premarital sex and cohabitation have swept into popular consciousness in the United States, and it is obvious that they are logical corollaries of the marketplace learning viewpoint.

Our dating culture thus is based upon the premise that dating provides valuable experience that will help individuals select mates and achieve happy marriages. But is this premise correct? Does dating really work? What evidence shows that individuals with longer dating experience, dates with more partners, or longer and more intimate acquaintances with the individuals they intend to marry end up with happier marriages?

Surprisingly, social scientists have never systematially addressed this question. Perhaps this is one of those cherished beliefs people would prefer not to examine too closely. When I could find little evidence on the connection between dating and other premarital experiences and marital success in previous studies, I decided to conduct my own inquiry.

Dating was to give valuable experience to help in future mate selection.

My desire to know whether dating experiences affected marriages was the basis for my 1984 survey in the Detroit area. A representative sample of 459 women was interviewed in three counties in the Detroit metropolitan area (a diverse, multi-racial and multi-ethnic area of city and suburbs containing about 4 million people in 1980). The women ranged in ages from 18 to 75, and all had been married at least once. (I was unable to interview their husbands, so unfortunately marriages in this study are viewed only through the eyes of women.) The interviewees had first married over a sixty year span of time, between 1925 and 1984. They were asked to recall a variety of things about their dating and premarital experiences. They were also asked a range of questions about their marital histories and (if currently married) about the positive and negative features of their relations with their husbands. The questionnaire enabled us to test whether premarital experiences of various types were related to marital success, a concept which in turn was measured in several different ways. (Measures of divorce and of both positive and negative qualities in intact marriages were used.)

The conclusions were a surprise. It appears that dating does not work and that the "marketplace learning viewpoint" is misguided. Marrying very young tended to produce unsuccessful marriages. Premarital pregnancy was associated with problems in marriage. However, once the age of marriage is taken into account, none of the other measures—dating variety, length of dating, length of courtship or engagement, or degree of premarital intimacy with the future husband or others—was clearly related to measures of marital success. A few weak tendencies in the results were contrary to predictions drawn from the marketplace learning viewpoint. Women who had dated more partners or who had engaged in premarital sex or cohabited were slightly less likely to have successful marriages. This might be seen as evidence of quite a different logic.

Perhaps there is a "grass is greener" effect. Women who have been led less sheltered and conventional lives prior to marriage may not be as easily satisfied afterward. Several other researchers have found a similar pattern with regard to premarital cohabitation. Individuals who had been living together prior to marriage were significantly less likely to have successful marriages than those who did not.

Individuals who had been living together were less likely to have successful marriages.

In the Detroit survey, these "grass is greener" patterns were not consistent or statistically significant. It was not that women with more dating experience and greater premarital intimacy had less successful marriages; rather, the amount and type of dating experience did not make a clear difference one way or the other.

Women who had married their first sweethearts were just as likely to have enduring and satisfying marriages as women who had married only after considering many alternatives. Similarly, women who had married after only a brief acquaintance were no more (nor less) likely to have a successful marriage than those who knew their husbands-to-be for years. And there was no clear difference between the marriages of women who were virgins at marriage and those who had had a variety of sexual partners and who had lived together with their husbands before the wedding.

Dating obviously does not provide useful learning that promotes marital success. Although our dating culture is based upon an analogy with consumer purchases in the marketplace, it is clear that in real life selecting a spouse is quite different from buying a car or a breakfast cereal. You cannot actively consider several prospects at the same time without getting your neck broken and being deserted by all of them. Even if you find Ms. Right or Mr. Right, you may be told to drop dead. By the time you are ready to marry, this special someone you were involved with earlier may no longer be available, and you may not see anyone on the horizon who comes close to being as desirable. In addition, someone who is well suited at marriage may grow apart from you or find someone else to be with later. Dating experience might facilitate marital success if deciding whom to marry was like deciding what to eat for breakfast (although even in the latter regard tastes change, and toast and black coffee may replace bacon and eggs). But these realms are quite different,

and mate selection looks more like a crap-shoot than a rational choice.

Is there a better way? Traditionalists in some societies would argue that arranged marriages are preferable. However, in addition to the improbability that America's young people will leave this decision to their parents, there is the problem of evidence. The few studies of this topic, including one I have been collaborating on in China, indicate that women who had arranged marriages were less satisfied than women who made the choice themselves. So having Mom and Dad take charge is not the answer. Turning the matter over to computerized matchmaking also does not seem advisable. Despite the growing sophistication of computers, real intelligence seems preferable to artificial intelligence. As the Tin Woodman in *The Wizard of Oz* discovered, to have a brain but no heart is to be missing something important.

Perhaps dating is evolving into new patterns in which premarital experience will contribute to marital success. Critics from Waller onward have claimed that dating promotes artificiality, rather than realistic assessment of compatibility. Some observers suggest that the sort of superficial dating Waller and others wrote about has become less common of late. Dating certainly has changed significantly since the pre-Second World War era. Many of the rigid rules of dating have broken down. The male no longer always takes the initiative; neither does he always pay. The sexual double standard has also weakened substantially, so that increasingly Americans feel that whatever a man can do a woman should be able to do. Some writers even suggest that dating is going out of style, replaced by informal pairing off in larger groups, often without the prearrangement of "asking someone out." Certainly the terminology is changing, with "seeing" and "being with" increasingly preferred to "dating" and "going steady." To many young people the latter terms have the old fashioned ring that "courting" and "suitor" had when I was young.

My daughter and other young adults argue that current styles are more natural and healthier than the dating experienced by my generation and the generation of my parents. Implicit in this argument is the view that, with formal rules and the "rating and dating" complex in decline, it should be possible to use dating (or whatever you call it) to realistically assess compatibility and romantic chemistry. These arguments may seem plausible, but I see no evidence that bears them out. The youngest women we interviewed in the Detroit survey should have experienced these more informal styles of romantic exploration. However, for them dating and premarital intimacy were, if anything, less closely related to marital success than was the case for the older women. The changes in premarital relations do not seem to make experience a better teacher.

While these conclusions are for the most part quite negative, my study leads to two more positive observations. First, marital success is not totally unpredictable. A wide range of features of how couples structure their day-to-day marital relations promote success—sharing in power and decision-making, pooling incomes, enjoying similar leisure time activities, having similar values, having mutual friends and an active social life, and other related qualities. Couples are not "doomed" by their past histories, including their dating histories, and they can increase their mutual happiness through the way they structure their marriages.

Second, there is something else about premarital experience besides dating history that may promote marital success. We have in America not one, but two widely shared, but quite contradictory, theories about how individuals should select a spouse: one based on the marketplace learning viewpoint and another based on love. One viewpoint sees selecting a spouse as a rational process, perhaps even with lists of criteria by which various prospects can be judged. The other, as song writers tell us, is based on the view that love conquers all and that "all you need is love." Love is a matter of the heart (perhaps with some help from the hormonal system) and not the head, and love may blossom unpredictably, on short notice or more gradually. Might it not be the case, then, that those couples who are most deeply in love at the time of their weddings will have the most successful marriages? We have centuries of poetry and novels, as well as love songs, that tell us that this is the case.

In the Detroit study, we did, in fact, ask women how much they had been in love when they first married. And we did find that those who recalled being "head over heels in love" then, had more successful mar-

riages. However, there is a major problem with this finding. Since we were asking our interviewees to recall their feelings prior to their weddings—in many cases weddings that took place years or even decades earlier—it is quite possible and even likely that their answers are biased. Perhaps whether or not their marriage worked out influenced these "love reports" from earlier times, rather than having the level of romantic love then explain marital success later. Without either a time machine or funds to interview couples prior to marriage and then follow them up years later, it is impossible to be sure that more intense feelings of love lead to more successful marriages. Still, the evidence available does not question the wisdom of poets and songwriters when it comes to love. Mate selection may not be a total crap-shoot after all, and even if dating does not work, love perhaps does.

READINGS SUGGESTED BY THE AUTHOR:

Bailey, Beth. *From Front Porch to Back Seat.* Baltimore: Johns Hopkins University Press, 1988.

Burgess, Ernest W. and Paul Wallin. *Engagement and Marriage.* Chicago: Lippincott, 1953.

Modell, John. "Dating Becomes the Way of American Youth," in *Essays on the Family and Historical Change,* Leslie P. Moch and Gary Stark (eds.). College Station, Tex.: Texas A&M University Press, 1983.

Rothman, Ellen K. *Hands and Hearts: A History of Courtship.* New York: Basic Books, 1984.

Smith, Daniel S. and Michael Hindus. "Premarital Pregnancy in America, 1640-1971: An Overview and Interpretation," *Journal of Interdisciplinary History,* 4 (1975), 537-570.

Waller, Willard, "Rating and Dating Complex," *American Sociological Review,* (1937), 2:737-739.

Whyte, Martin King. *Dating, Mating, and Marriage.* New York: Aldine de Gruyter, 1990.

Love and Mate Selection in the 1990s

Elizabeth Rice Allgeier and Michael W. Wiederman

Elizabeth Rice Allgeier is professor of psychology at Bowling Green State University, and researches many aspects of human sexuality and social interaction. She has just completed the third edition of the human sexuality text, Sexual Interactions, *with her husband Richard Allgeier. She is editor-elect of* The Journal of Sex Research.

Michael W. Wiederman is a graduate student in clinical psychology at Bowling Green State University where his research interests include love, mate selection, and premarital sexuality.

Would you marry someone who had all the qualities you desired in a mate if you were not in love with him or her? During other points in history and in cultures other than our own, love has played either a small or nonexistent role in the selection of a marriage partner. Also, the other qualities that we value in selecting a mate are not necessarily the same ones most valued by our ancestors, nor the ones valued most by people in other cultures.

In contemporary industrialized societies, however, love is seen as the primary basis for marriage. What qualities would you seek in a mate? Presumably people have wondered about this question ever since humans began forming lasting bonds, but researchers have only begun empirical investigation of this issue in the past half-century.

Fifty years ago, Rubin Hill (1945) developed the following list of eighteen characteristics to conduct a study of the qualities that were most valued in a mate:

Dependable Character 7	Good Health 6
Mutual Attraction 7	Similar Political Background 7
Education/Intelligence 7	Ambition/Industriousness 6
Similar Educational Background 1	Pleasing Disposition 7
Desire for Home/Children 7	Sexual Chastity 7
Favorable Social Status 5	Good Financial Prospect 7
Emotional Stability 7	Sociability 5
Refinement/Neatness 7	Good Cook/Housekeeper 5
Similar Religious Background 5	Good Looks 7

Before reading further you may want to consider how important each of these characteristics would be to you if you were seeking a marriage partner by rating each on a scale from 1 (not at all important) to 7 (extremely important).

The importance of these qualities in a potential mate was rated by samples of college students in 1939, 1956, and 1967. In that three-decade period, the qualities most valued by respondents were remarkably consistent. Both men and women assigned the most importance to the qualities Dependable Character and Emotional Stability.

Although many researchers have been interested in the area of mate selection, they do not all share the same theoretical perspective. Sociobiologists rely on the principles of evolution and natural selection to explain humans' mate selection preferences (Buss 1989; Symons 1979). As physical attractiveness may be an indication of health and reproductive fitness, they hypothesize that males who highly valued factors related to a potential mate's physical attractiveness were more likely to be successful in passing their genes to future generations than were males who placed less value on the physical attractiveness of a potential mate. In contrast, they predict that females have been selected to place more importance on factors that relate to their potential partners' ability to be good providers, and thus contribute to the well-being of the offspring. During the period in which humans were physically evolving, those children who were fathered by a male who could provide food and protection were probably more likely to live long enough to reproduce. Thus, those females who valued males who could provide resources would be more successful in passing along their genes than females who did not value those qualities in a mate. Evolutionary theory asserts that these tendencies for males and females to value different qualities in a potential mate have been passed on to contemporary humans.

David Buss (1989) set out to test these hypotheses using Hill's list of eighteen characteristics. He organized a study involving the collection of data from more than ten thousand respondents, from thirty-three societies around the world. The quality of physical attractiveness is similar to the item Good Looks in Hill's list, and the ability to provide resources corresponds to such listed characteristics as Good Financial Prospect and Ambition/Industriousness. In the study conducted by Buss, the evolutionary hypotheses were supported. Significant gender differences on these three items were found in almost all the cultures surveyed. That is, men placed significantly more emphasis on physical attractiveness in a potential mate than did women, whereas women valued financial prospects and ambition much more highly in a mate than did men. These same differences have also emerged in the studies surveying college students over the past fifty years.

> **"Very few young people today would consider marrying a person with whom they were not in love, regardless of the qualities that person possessed. However, although about 90 percent of students surveyed would not marry without love, only about half agreed that the disappearance of love is sufficient reason for divorce."**

You may have noticed that the list of eighteen characteristics lacks an explicit reference to love. It seems, however, that love has become an important requirement for marriage in the United States for both men and women. Such hasn't always been the case. In the mid-1960s, Kephart (1967) asked a thousand college students "If a man or woman had all the other qualities you desired, would you marry this person if you were not in love with him or her?" Two-thirds of the men said "No," whereas only a quarter of the women said that they would not. Simpson, Campbell, and Berscheid (1986) asked the same question of large samples of college students in 1976 and 1984. By 1976 students' ratings of the importance of love had changed dramatically from the ratings given in the mid-1960s. At that time, 86 percent of the men and 80 percent of the women said that they would not marry someone if they were not in love with them. Over the period of a decade, a greater number of both men and women rated love as a prerequisite for marriage, but the relative increase was considerably larger for women. That is, from the mid-1960s to the mid-1970s, the number of women who said that they would not marry a man with whom they were not in love more than tripled. By 1984, the percentages of men and women

responding "No" to the question were equal at about 85 percent. We were interested in exploring possible reasons for the profound jump from the mid-1960s to the mid-1970s in the number of women who said that they required love for marriage.

Simpson and his colleagues, who conducted the love studies, used a sociological explanation for their findings. Specifically, they speculated that, as women became more economically independent, there was a decrease in the likelihood of a woman settling for a man who was a good provider but with whom she was not in love. Such an explanation sounded reasonable to us, so we tested this hypothesis by surveying a thousand undergraduate students at Bowling Green State University regarding their values concerning the importance of love in choosing a mate, and the relative weight they placed on the eighteen qualities listed by Hill. Besides asking the question about love cited above, we also asked the students to indicate how much annual income they expected to earn three to four years after graduating from college. In this way, we crudely measured how economically independent the women in our sample expected themselves to be after college graduation. Based on the explanation given by Simpson and his colleagues, we hypothesized that the less a woman expected to earn, the more she would be economically dependent on her mate, and thus the less she would require love in a marriage partner. That is, a woman who does not expect to earn much money may not be able to afford turning away a man who is a good provider simply because she is not in love with him. Similarly, we hypothesized that the more a woman expected to earn, the more economically independent she expected to be, and the more she could afford to require love in her marriage.

How important is love as a basis for marriage today? In our study, 87 percent of the men and 91 percent of the women said that they would not marry someone unless they were in love with that person, regardless of whether that person had all the other qualities that they desired in a mate. Was expected annual income after graduation from college related to women's responses to the "Love" question? The answer is yes, but to our surprise the results of our study were in the opposite direction from those we hypothesized. That is, the more the women in our sample expected to earn after college, the less they required love. Those women who indicated that they expected to earn the most money after graduation were the ones most likely to consider marrying a man with whom they were not in love, provided he had all the other qualities they desired in a mate. For the men in our study, there was no relationship between how much money they expected to earn and their responses to the "Love" question.

In addition to the "Love" question, Simpson and his colleagues had also included two questions that had to do with the disappearance of love in marriage. We included the same questions in our survey. Specifically, we asked students to indicate the extent to which they agreed or disagreed with the statement, "If love has completely disappeared from a marriage, I think it is probably best for the couple to make a clean break and start new lives." About half of the thousand students agreed with the statement, about a third disagreed, and the rest indicated that they were neutral. Respondents also indicated the extent of their agreement or disagreement with the statement, "In my opinion, the disappearance of love is not a sufficient reason for ending a marriage, and should not be viewed as such." About half of the students disagreed, about a third agreed, and the rest said that they were neutral on the issue. These results were very similar to those obtained by Simpson and his colleagues. It seems that most contemporary young men and women are very reluctant to marry someone with whom they are not in love, but are less sure that the disappearance of love in marriage is a sufficient reason for dissolving the marital contract.

How do today's youth compare to their counterparts of the past fifty years in the relative emphasis they place on each of the eighteen listed desirable characteristics in a potential mate? In our sample surveyed in 1990, men and women were alike in the three characteristics rated most important, but Mutual Attraction supplanted all other qualities in ranked importance. The top three qualities, in order, were Mutual Attraction, Dependable Character, and Emotional Stability. The least important, for both men and women, was Similar Political Background, and that generally characterized the earlier studies as well. Other qualities that were rated as relatively unimportant included Similar Religious Background (seventeenth for men, sixteenth for women); Good Cook/Housekeeper (seventeenth for women, fifteenth for men); and Favorable Social Status (fourteenth for women, thirteenth for men). When compared to past ratings of the eighteen characteristics, some differences over time are apparent. In the past, similarity in religious background was valued more highly in a potential mate, especially by women, and cooking and housekeeping were much more highly valued by men in decades past than they are now. Also, both men and women now place greater emphasis on the sociability and physical attractiveness in a potential mate than did their counterparts of the past fifty years. What about the gender differences reported by Buss? In our sample of college students, the findings were consistent with past research; that is, the largest gender differences were apparent on the items dealing with physical attractiveness, financial prospects, and ambition. Men placed more emphasis on the former quality, whereas women emphasized the latter two.

We also explored relationships between expected income and the value placed on the qualities of a potential mate. There were associations, at least for women, between how much money the respondents expected to earn after college and how they rated certain characteristics in a potential husband. As stated earlier, one might think that the less a woman expects to earn herself, the more she would value the financial prospects of a mate, but such was not the case. Actually the reverse was true in our study. That is, it was the women who expected to earn the most after college who placed the most value on financial prospects. There was not a relationship between how much men expected to earn and

how they rated any of the characteristics in a potential mate.

In summary, it seems that very few young people today would consider marrying a person with whom they were not in love, regardless of the qualities that person possessed. However, although about 90 percent of students surveyed would not marry without love, only about half agreed that the disappearance of love is sufficient reason for divorce. Men and women do agree on the three most important characteristics in a potential mate, but there are clear gender differences as to the relative emphasis placed on certain other qualities. Specifically, men value physical attractiveness more than do women, whereas women place more emphasis on the financial prospects and ambitiousness and industriousness in a potential marriage partner.

Would our findings be true of North Americans in general, or are they limited to today's college students? We are currently in the process of exploring that question by surveying the general public and asking adults, of all ages, the same questions we posed to the student sample. Perhaps we will find that people answer these questions differently depending on the generation to which they belong. For example, someone born in 1942 is of the same generation as those students Kephart surveyed in the mid-1960s, and we may find their attitudes regarding love and marriage to be more consistent with Kephart's findings than with our own. On the other hand, if the changes we have seen in the emphasis of certain qualities in a mate and the increased value of love as a basis for marriage have permeated the culture, we may find contemporary adults across the age-span responding in the same way as our 1990 sample of college students.

Regardless of what we find in our community sample, our results with the college students did not support Simpson et al.'s (1986) speculation that, in selecting a marital partner, love has become more important in women's choices as a function of their increased independence from men for financial support. Why do women who expect to earn more money place less emphasis on love as a requirement for marriage? What do you think the answer is? We encourage you to test your hypothesis, and relay your ideas to us. Eventually, we may be able to explain this puzzling link between a woman's expected income and her requirements for marriage.

References

Buss, D. M. 1989. Sex differences in human mate preference. Evolutionary hypothesis tested in 37 cultures. *Behavioral and Brain Sciences,* 12: 1–49.

Hill, R. 1945. Campus Values in Mate Selection. *Journal of Home Economics,* 37:554–558.

Hudson, J. W., and L. F., Henze. 1969. Campus values in mate selection: A replication. *Journal of Marriage and the Family,* 31:772–775.

Kephart, W. M. 1967. Some correlates of romantic love. *Journal of Marriage and the Family,* 29:470–474.

Simpson, J. A., B. Campbell, and E. Berscheid. 1986. The association between romantic love and marriage: Kephart (1967) twice revisited. *Personality and Social Psychology Bulletin,* 12:363–372.

Symons, D. 1979. *The Evolution of Human Sexuality.* New York: Oxford University Press.

THE

Mating

GAME

The sophisticated sexual strategies of modern men and women are shaped by a powerful Stone Age psychology.

It's a dance as old as the human race. At cocktail lounges and church socials, during office coffee breaks and dinner parties—and most blatantly, perhaps, in the personal ads in newspapers and magazines—men and women perform the elaborate ritual of advertisement and assessment that precedes an essential part of nearly every life: mating. More than 90 percent of the world's people marry at some point in their lives, and it is estimated that a similarly large number of people engage in affairs, liaisons, flings or one-night stands. The who, what, when and where of love, sex and romance are a cultural obsession that is reflected in everything from Shakespeare to soap operas and from Tristram and Isolde to 2 Live Crew, fueling archetypes like the coy ingénue, the rakish cad, the trophy bride, Mrs. Robinson, Casanova and lovers both star-crossed and blessed.

It all may seem very modern, but a new group of researchers argues that love, American style, is in fact part of a universal human behavior with roots stretching back to the dawn of humankind. These scientists contend that, in stark contrast to the old image of brute cavemen dragging their mates by the hair to their dens, our ancient ancestors—men and women alike—engaged in a sophisticated mating dance of sexual intrigue, shrewd strategizing and savvy negotiating that has left its stamp on human psychology. People may live in a thoroughly modern world, these researchers say, but within the human skull is a Stone Age mind that was shaped by the mating concerns of our ancient ancestors and continues to have a profound influence on behavior today. Indeed, this ancient psychological legacy

———— HOW WE CHOOSE ————

Women are more concerned about whether mates will invest time and resources in a relationship; men care more about a woman's physical attractiveness, which in ancient times reflected her fertility and health.

influences everything from sexual attraction to infidelity and jealousy—and, as remarkable new research reveals, even extends its reach all the way down to the microscopic level of egg and sperm.

These new researchers call themselves evolutionary psychologists. In a host of recent scientific papers and at a major conference last month at the London School of Economics, they are arguing that the key to understanding modern sexual behavior lies not solely in culture, as some anthropologists contend, nor purely in the genes, as some sociobiologists believe. Rather, they argue, understanding human nature is possible only if scientists begin to understand the evolution of the human mind. Just as humans have evolved

specialized biological organs to deal with the intricacies of sex, they say, the mind, too, has evolved customized mental mechanisms for coping with this most fundamental aspect of human existence.

Gender and mind. When it comes to sexuality and mating, evolutionary psychologists say, men and women often are as different psychologically as they are physically. Scientists have long known that people typically choose mates who closely resemble themselves in terms of weight, height, intelligence and even earlobe length. But a survey of more than 10,000 people in 37 cultures on six continents, conducted by University of Michigan psychologist David Buss, reveals that men consistently value physical attractiveness and youth in a mate more than women do; women, equally as consistently, are more concerned than men with a prospective mate's ambition, status and resources. If such preferences were merely arbitrary products of culture, says Buss, one might expect to find at least one society somewhere where men's and women's mating preferences were reversed; the fact that attitudes are uniform across cultures suggests they are a fundamental part of human psychology.

Evolutionary psychologists think many of these mating preferences evolved in response to the different biological challenges faced by men and women in producing children—the definition of success in evolutionary terms. In a seminal paper, evolutionary biologist Robert Trivers of the University of California at Santa Cruz points out that in most mammals, females invest far

From *U.S. News & World Report*, July 19, 1993, pp. 57-63. © 1993 by U.S. News & World Report. Reprinted by permission.

more time and energy in reproduction and child rearing than do males. Not only must females go through a long gestation and weaning of their offspring, but childbirth itself is relatively dangerous. Males, on the other hand, potentially can get away with a very small biological investment in a child.

Human infants require the greatest amount of care and nurturing of any animal on Earth, and so over the eons women have evolved a psychology that is particularly concerned with a father's ability to help out with this enormous task—with his clout, protection and access to resources. So powerful is this psychological legacy that nowadays women size up a man's finances even when, as a practical matter, they may not have to. A recent study of the mating preferences of a group of medical students, for instance, found that these women, though anticipating financial success, were nevertheless most interested in men whose earning capacity was equal to or greater than their own.

Healthy genes. For men, on the other hand, reproductive success is ultimately dependent on the fertility of their mates. Thus males have evolved a mind-set that homes in on signs of a woman's health and youth, signs that, in the absence of medical records and birth certificates long ago, were primarily visual. Modern man's sense of feminine beauty—clear skin, bright eyes and youthful appearance—is, in effect, the legacy of eons spent diagnosing the health and fertility of potential mates.

This concern with women's reproductive health also helps explain why men value curvaceous figures. An upcoming paper by Devendra Singh of the University of Texas at Austin reveals that people consistently judge a woman's figure not by whether she is slim or fat but by the ratio of waist to hips. The ideal proportion—the hips roughly a third larger than the waist—reflects a hormonal balance that results in women's preferentially storing fat on their hips as opposed to their waists, a condition that correlates with higher fertility and resistance to disease. Western society's modern-day obsession with being slim has not changed this equation. Singh found, for instance, that while the winning Miss America has become 30 percent thinner over the past several decades, her waist-to-hip ratio has remained close to this ancient ideal.

Women also appreciate a fair face and figure, of course. And what they look for in a male's physique can also be explained as an evolved mentality that links good looks with good genes. A number of studies have shown that both men and women rate as most attractive

WHOM WE MARRY

More than 90 percent of all people marry and, they typically choose mates who closely resemble themselves, from weight and height, to intelligence and values, to nose breadth and even earlobe length.

faces that are near the average; this is true in societies as diverse as those of Brazil, Russia and several hunting and gathering tribes. The average face tends to be more symmetrical, and, according to psychologist Steven Gangestad and biologist Randy Thornhill, both of the University of New Mexico, this symmetry may reflect a person's genetic resistance to disease.

People have two versions of each of their genes—one from each parent—within every cell. Sometimes the copies are slightly different, though typically each version works just as effectively. The advantage to having two slightly different copies of the same gene, the researchers argue, is that it is harder for a disease to knock out the function of both copies, and this biological redundancy is reflected in the symmetry in people's bodies, including their faces. Further evidence for a psychological mechanism that links attractiveness with health comes from Buss's worldwide study of mating preferences: In those parts of the world where the incidence of parasites and infectious diseases is highest, both men and women place a greater value on attractive mates.

Some feminists reject the notion that women should alter physical appearance to gain advantage in the mating game. But archaeological finds suggest that the "beauty myth" has been very much a part of the human mating psychology since the times of our ancient ancestors—and that it applies equally to men. Some of the very first signs of human artistry are carved body ornaments that date back more than 30,000 years, and findings of worn nubs of ochre suggest that ancient humans may have used the red and black chalklike

substance as makeup. These artifacts probably served as social signs that, like lipstick or a Rolex watch today, advertised a person's physical appearance and status. In one grave dating back some 20,000 years, a male skeleton was found bedecked with a tunic made from thousands of tiny ivory beads—the Stone Age equivalent of an Armani suit.

Far from being immutable, biological mandates, these evolved mating mechanisms in the mind are flexible, culturally influenced aspects of human psychology that are similar to people's tastes for certain kinds of food. The human sweet tooth is a legacy from a time when the only sweet things in the environment were nutritious ripe fruit and honey, says Buss, whose book "The Evolution of Desire" is due out next year. Today, this ancient taste for sweets is susceptible to modern-day temptation by candy bars and such, though people have the free will to refrain from indulging it. Likewise, the mind's mating mechanisms can be strongly swayed by cultural influences such as religious and moral beliefs.

Playing the field. Both men and women display different mating psychologies when they are just playing around as opposed to searching for a lifelong partner, and these mental mechanisms are also a legacy from ancient times. A new survey by Buss and his colleague David Schmitt found that when women are looking for "short term" mates, their preference for attractive men increases substantially. In a study released last month, Doug Kenrick and Gary Groth of Arizona State University found that while men, too, desire attractive mates when they're playing the field, they will actually settle for a lot less.

Men's diminished concern about beauty in short-term mates reflects the fact that throughout human evolution, men have often pursued a dual mating strategy. The most successful strategy for most men was to find a healthy, fertile, long-term mate. But it also didn't hurt to take advantage of any low-risk opportunity to sire as many kin as possible outside the relationship, just to hedge the evolutionary bet. The result is an evolved psychology that allows a man to be sexually excited by a wide variety of women even while committed to a partner. This predilection shows up in studies of men's and women's sexual fantasies today. A study by Don Symons of the University of California at Santa Barbara and Bruce Ellis of the University of Michigan found that while both men and women actively engage in sexual fantasy, men typically have more fantasies about anonymous partners.

Surveys in the United States show

that at least 30 percent of married women have extramarital affairs, suggesting that, like men, women also harbor a drive for short-term mating. But they have different evolutionary reasons for doing so. Throughout human existence, short-term flings have offered women an opportunity to exchange sex for resources. In Buss and Schmitt's study, women value an "extravagant lifestyle" three times more highly when they are searching for a brief affair than when they are seeking a long-term mate. Women who are secure in a relationship with a committed male might still seek out attractive men to secure healthier genes for their offspring. Outside affairs also allow women to shop for better partners.

Sperm warfare. A woman may engage the sexual interest of several men simultaneously in order to foster a microscopic battle known as sperm competition. Sperm can survive in a woman's reproductive tract for nearly a week, note biologists Robin Baker and Mark Bellis of the University of Manchester, and by mating with more than one man within a short period of time, a woman sets the stage for their sperm to com-

---

JEALOUS PSYCHE

Men are most disturbed by sexual infidelity in their mates, a result of uncertainty about paternity. Women are more disturbed by emotional infidelity, because they risk losing their mate's time and resources.

pete to sire a child — passing this winning trait on to her male offspring as well. In a confidential survey tracking the sexual behavior and menstrual cycles of more than 2,000 women who

said they had steady mates, Baker and Bellis found that while there was no pattern to when women had sex with their steady partners, having sex on the side peaked at the height of the women's monthly fertility cycles.

Since in ancient times a man paid a dear evolutionary price for being cuckolded, the male psychology produces a physiological counterstrategy for dealing with a woman's infidelity. Studying the sexual behavior of a group of couples, Baker and Bellis found that the more time a couple spend apart, the more sperm the man ejaculates upon their sexual reunion — as much as three times higher than average.

This increase in sperm count is unrelated to when the man last ejaculated through nocturnal emission or masturbation, and Baker and Bellis argue that it is a result of a man's evolved psychological mechanism that bolsters his chances in sperm competition in the event that his mate has been unfaithful during their separation. As was no doubt the case in the times of our ancient ancestors, these concerns are not unfounded: Studies of blood typings show that as many as 1 of every 10 babies born to couples in North America is not the offspring of the mother's husband.

Despite men's efforts at sexual subterfuge, women still have the last word on the fate of a man's sperm in her reproductive tract — thanks to the physiological effects of the female orgasm. In a new study, Baker and Bellis reveal that if a woman experiences an orgasm soon after her mate's, the amount of sperm retained in her reproductive tract is far higher than if she has an earlier orgasm or none at all. Apparently a woman's arousal, fueled by her feelings as well as her mate's solicitous attentions, results in an evolutionary payoff for both.

Cads and dads. Whether people pursue committed relationships or one-night stands depends on their perceptions of what kind of mates are in the surrounding sexual environment. Anthropologist Elizabeth Cashdan of the University of Utah surveyed hundreds of men and women on whether they thought the members of their "pool" of potential mates were in general trustworthy, honest and capable of commitment. She also asked them what kinds of tactics they used to attract mates. Cashdan found that the less committed people thought their potential mates would be, the more they themselves pursued short-term mating tactics. For example, if women considered their world to be full of "cads," they tended to dress more provocatively and to be more promiscuous; if they thought that the world was populated

---

BEAUTY QUEST

the most attractive men and women are in fact those whose faces are most average, a signal that they are near the genetic average of the population and are perhaps more resistant to disease.

by potential "dads" — that is, committed and nurturing men — they tended to emphasize their chastity and fidelity. Similarly, "cads" tended to emphasize their sexuality and "dads" said they relied more on advertising their resources and desire for long-term commitment.

These perceptions of what to expect from the opposite sex may be influenced by the kind of home life an individual knew as a child. Social scientists have long known that children from homes where the father is chronically absent or abusive tend to mature faster physically and to have sexual relations earlier in life. Psychologist Jay Belsky of Pennsylvania State University argues that this behavior is an evolved psychological mechanism, triggered by early childhood experiences, that enables a child to come of age earlier and leave the distressing situation. This psychological mechanism may also lead to a mating strategy that focuses on short-term affairs.

The green monster. Whether in modern or ancient times, infidelities can breed anger and hurt, and new research suggests subtle differences in male and female jealousy with roots in the ancient past. In one study, for example, Buss asked males and females to imagine that their mates were having sex with someone else or that their mates were engaged in a deep emotional commitment with another person. Monitoring his subjects' heart rates, frowning and stress responses, he found that the stereotypical double standard cuts both ways. Men reacted far more strongly than

EVOLVED FANTASIES

Eroticism and gender

For insights into the subtle differences between men's and women's mating psychologies, one need look no further than the local bookstore. On one rack may be magazines featuring scantily clad women in poses of sexual invitation — a testimony to the ancient legacy of a male psychology that is acutely attuned to visual stimulus and easily aroused by the prospect of anonymous sex. Around the corner is likely to be a staple of women's erotic fantasy: romance novels.

Harlequin Enterprises Ltd., the leading publisher in the field, sells more than 200 million books annually and pro-duces about 70 titles a month. Dedicated romance fans may read several books a week. "Our books give women every-thing," says Harlequin's Kath-leen Abels, "a loving relation-ship, commitment and having sex with someone they care about." Some romance novels contain scenes steamy enough to make a sailor blush, and studies show that women who read romances typically have more sexual fantasies and en-gage in sexual intercourse more frequently than nonread-ers do.

Sexual caricature. Since sex-ual fantasy frees people of the complications of love and mat-ing in the real world, argue psychologists Bruce Ellis and Don Symons, it is perhaps not surprising that in erotic mate-rials for both men and women, sexual partners are typically caricatures of the consumer's own evolved mating psycholo-gy. In male-oriented erotica, for instance, women are de-picted as being lust driven, ever willing and unencum-bered by the need for emo-tional attachment. In romance novels, the male lead in the book is typically tender, emo-tional and consumed by pas-sion for the heroine, thus en-suring his lifelong fidelity and dependence. In other words, say Ellis and Symons, the ro-mance novel is "an erotic, uto-pian, female counterfantasy" to male erotica.

Of course, most men also en-joy stories of passion and ro-mance, and women can be as easily aroused as men by sexu-ally explicit films. Indeed, sev-eral new entertainment ven-tures, including the magazine *Future Sex* and a video compa-ny, Femme Productions, are creating erotic materials using realistic models in more sensual settings in an attempt to appeal to both sexes. Still, the new re-search into evolutionary psy-chology suggests that men and women derive subtly different pleasures from sexual fantasy — something that even writing un-der a ghost name can't hide. According to Abels, a Harle-quin romance is occasionally penned by a man using a female pseudonym, but "our avid read-ers can always tell."

---

women to the idea that their mates were having sex with other men. But women reacted far more strongly to the thought that their mates were developing strong emotional attachments to someone else.

As with our evolved mating prefer-ences, these triggers for jealousy ulti-mately stem from men's and women's biology, says Buss. A woman, of course, has no doubt that she is the mother of her children. For a man, however, paternity is never more than conjecture, and so men have evolved psychologies with a height-ened concern about a mate's sexual infi-delity. Since women make the greater biological investment in offspring, their psychologies are more concerned about a mate's reneging on his commitment, and, therefore, they are more attentive to signs that their mates might be attaching them-selves emotionally to other women.

Sexual monopoly. The male preoccu-pation with monopolizing a woman's sexual reproduction has led to the op-pression and abuse of women world-wide, including, at its extremes, confine-ment, domestic violence and ritual mutilation such as clitoridectomy. Yet the new research into the mating game also reveals that throughout human evolution, women have not passively ac-quiesced to men's sexual wishes. Rath-

DUELING SPERM

*I*f a couple has been apart for some time, the man's sperm count goes up during sex at their reunion — an ancient, evolved strategy against a female's possible infidelities while away.

er, they have long employed a host of behavioral and biological tactics to fol-low their own sexual agenda — behaviors that have a huge impact on men's be-havior as well. As Buss points out, if all women suddenly began preferring to have sex with men who walked on their hands, in a very short time half the hu-man race would be upside down.

With its emphasis on how both men and women are active players in the mating game, evolutionary psychology holds out the promise of helping negoti-ate a truce of sorts in the battle of the sexes — not by declaring a winner but by pointing out that the essence of the mating game is compromise, not vic-tory. The exhortations of radical femi-nists, dyed-in-the-wool chauvinists and everyone in between are all spices for a sexual stew that has been on a slow boil for millions of years. It is no accident that consistently, the top two mating preferences in Buss's survey — expressed equally by males and females world-wide — were not great looks, fame, youth, wealth or status, but *kindness* and *intelligence*. In the rough-and-tum-ble of the human mating game, they are love's greatest allies.

WILLIAM F. ALLMAN

Relationship Maintenance

- Marital Challenges (Articles 11–14)
- Potential Crisis Situations (Articles 15–18)
- Relating Sexually (Articles 19–21)

Coming together is a beginning; keeping together is a process; working together is a success.

—Henry Ford

A good relationship does not just happen—it takes work. As couples establish relationships, they generally hold dreams of the future and ambitions of their relationship's success. However, "success" in a relationship depends largely on the couple's definition of the word. Once a relationship has been formed, it is up to the couple to make the aspirations become real. A continuous expenditure of energy on the part of both partners is necessary to keep these aspirations, as well as the relationship, alive, well, and growing. Disappointment and frustration can result when reality does not measure up to expectations.

Most marriages have problems. Unrealistic expectations and incompatible goals are usually contributing factors to marital conflict. Certain areas of marriage are especially prone to conflict. These include sex, money, jobs, leisure time, religion, and communication. Realizing that no marriage is perfect, anticipating problems, facing them, and learning to work toward positive solutions will inevitably help in overcoming marital difficulties.

The first subsection addresses marital challenges. It contains four articles that focus on the multiple and often competing roles played by today's couples. Work and home are nearly impossible to separate for many of them. They expect to fulfill individual as well as couple needs, which can be a difficult balancing act. Figuring out how they can cope with the expectations and pressures of work, home, and child care and still have time for each other may be the most important way today's couples can prevent the problems and crises that often lead to dissatisfaction.

The next subsection highlights some special problems that can affect marriages and families. The first two articles address the marital crisis of domestic violence. Both explore the relationship dynamics involved that can be at the core of a continuing cycle of trauma and pain or help to begin the slow process of change. "The Crisis of the Absent Father" focuses on the quarter of American children who have little or no contact with their fathers. It discusses the personal and societal consequences—emotional through financial—of this deprivation. The final article deals with another type of loss: death. Sometimes in the midst of dealing with the loss of a loved one, adults forget that children are also affected and need help in understanding and coping with what has happened, their feelings, and fears.

The final subsection focuses on relating to others sexually. "Sex and the Female Agenda" compares female human and animal patterns of telling their partners when it is time to have sex. "Sexual Desire" addresses the most significant sexual dysfunction or complaint among couples of the 1990s: that their individual and mutual desire level is too high, too low, too variable—something other than the preferred "just right." The final article in the subsection examines infidelity and its aftermath. From the accidental liaison—often under the influence—to the philanderer's ongoing string of affairs, Frank Pittman, author of the popular book *Private Lies: Infidelity and the Betrayal of Intimacy* (Norton, 1989), recounts the emotional and practical wreckage that results from extramarital sex.

Looking Ahead: Challenge Questions

Do you feel the stresses and difficulties of dual-career marriages are worth it? Why or why not? In conflict situations, should couples compromise, take turns compromising, or should a spouse's career be subordinate? Why?

What share of household and child-care responsibilities do you expect to be responsible for in your marriage or family? Is this a traditional gender-role split or a division of labor, based on your own work, home, or family situation? How does it compare to your mother's and father's division of labor?

To what extent did your parents allow you to see their disagreements? What are the advantages and disadvantages in your opinion of presenting a united front to children?

How would you rate your own level of jealously on a scale from mild to enraged? Has it ever been problematic for you or someone else?

What role has your father played in your life? If you or someone you know has had little contact with your/their father for an extended period of time, what have been the effects?

When you were a child, did anyone close to you die? If so, can you remember how you felt?

How comfortable do you feel talking openly to your partner about sexuality? What hinders your openly talking about feelings, needs, and desires?

How would you feel or react if your spouse were unfaithful? Under what, if any, circumstances might you consider extramarital sex? Why do you think so many people are unfaithful?

Unit 3

When Parents Disagree

Two partners, two approaches to discipline—here's how to make it work.

Nancy Samalin with Patricia McCormick

Nancy Samalin is the author of Loving Your Child Is Not Enough *(Penguin) and* Love and Anger: The Parental Dilemma *(Viking).*

Patricia McCormick is an associate editor at Parents *Magazine.*

If you and your spouse have been married long enough to have a child, then you probably already know how to negotiate the finer points of squeezing the toothpaste and finding where to put the dirty socks. You may even successfully manage having a joint checking account with two cash cards.

Enter one small child and that hard-won harmony is threatened. "Honey, you know one soda is the limit," you might tell your child. To which your spouse replies, "Ah, let her have another one." To which your child responds, "Pleease, Mom. Dad says I can." At which point you do something very mature, such as putting your hands on your hips, rolling your eyes, and saying "Fine, then *you* take her to the dentist for the next appointment."

Meanwhile, in the rational part of your brain, there is the voice of an "expert" reminding you that parents should always present a united front when disciplining their children.

All spouses disagree. The key is to respect each other's differences and to fight fair.

As commendable a goal as that may be, it isn't always possible. All spouses disagree; they were brought up in two different households by different parents. When a child comes along, an occasional clash of opinions is inevitable.

A more realistic goal would be to accept the fact that you will have disagreements with your spouse over discipline; you will even, on occasion, fight in front of your children. The key is to respect each other's differences and to fight fair when you fight.

It is 3:00 A.M. Two-year-old Sam is awake—as he has been every night for the past two weeks—crying. Cathy, his mother, wearily throws off the covers and gets up. "Why don't you just let him cry it out?" says Andrew, her husband.

"You know you're just reinforcing this whole crying thing by going in there and rocking him back to sleep every night. I think you're spoiling him," he adds.

"You just don't understand," Cathy replies. "He must be scared or lonely. I think you're too tough on him."

Mr. Softy vs. Mrs. Bad Guy.

Because we are not carbon copies of our mates, we often have different takes on the same situation. If, for instance, your spouse was brought up in a strict home, he or she may be most comfortable with a firm approach to discipline.

If you were raised in a more relaxed environment, you may feel comfortable using an easygoing approach—or the reverse might be true.

The seeds of conflict—planted long ago—are ready to flower with your child's first midnight squall.

The art of compromise.

Instead of trying to present a united front that is sure to crumble, try to accept your differences. When you and your spouse have some time alone, discuss the situations that have put you at odds with each other. You will soon find that one parent has stronger feelings than the other over certain issues—junk food, bedtimes, or homework.

In the interest of harmony, you and your spouse might agree to abide by the wishes of the person whose feelings are stronger. If, for instance, you are strenuously opposed to spanking and your spouse is neutral about it, both parents should agree not to spank. Or, if your spouse wants to take a firm line on junk food, you could agree to go along with his wishes when that issue comes up.

The next step would be for both of you to agree that one parent (usually the one with the stronger feelings) will deal with the child on that issue and the other will stay on the sidelines. And, most important, you should agree to back each other up. This means that you won't intervene when your spouse is carrying out a policy that you may not like but have agreed to abide by.

For example, Cathy might tell Andrew, "I wish I felt as comfortable as you do about letting him cry, because if I did, I'd go back to sleep too. But I can't listen to him cry, so I'm going to get up. I'm not going to try to make you get up, though, because I know that you don't believe in it."

For his part, Andrew might pledge not to interfere or to criticize Cathy. Although this approach will work, it's not always easy; compromise often takes effort and restraint.

The gentle art of compromise works well when you have had a chance to come up with a party line in advance. But it is also an effective policy when a divisive discipline issue crops up without warning. If, for example, your child's request for a second soda triggers a strong reaction in you, you may want to tell your spouse, "I really don't want her to have another soda. I'd like to handle this one."

Hopefully your spouse will oblige and let you manage the situation. It would be even better if he supported you by telling your child, "This is between you and Mommy."

Naturally there will be times when you will feel too angry to handle a disciplinary issue effectively. Such instances would be a good time to say, "I'm too upset about this; will you handle it?" On the other hand, if you are lukewarm about an issue but your spouse is not, you might want to say, "I really don't feel too strongly about this. Why don't you handle it?" or, "You'd probably prefer to handle this since you obviously have strong feelings about it."

You may sometimes find that no matter how accommodating you and your partner try to be, there are situations in which you are still at loggerheads. You may never be able to con-

Ground Rules For Fighting Fair

● Avoid name-calling and sarcasm. Comments such as "How stupid can you be?" and "Oh, great. I married a real genius" are not conducive to compromise or harmony.
● Try not to lapse into angry silences. They don't bring you any closer to a resolution and can be scary for children to observe.
● Try not to use words such as "always" and "never," as in "You always let him have his way" and "You never back me up when I'm disciplining him."
● Try not to "futurize" by saying things such as, "If you keep letting him eat all that junk food, he's going to be the size of a barn."
● Give yourself time to cool off before you approach your spouse about his or disciplinary techniques.
● Reassure your children that your disagreements are not their fault.
—N.S. and P.M.

Children need not be shielded from everyday conflicts. They can learn a lot from how parents resolve disagreements.

vince each other of the merits of your different approaches.

Unless disciplining becomes damaging or abusive, resist the urge to lecture or to try to reform each other. (It won't work anyway.) If you really want to win your partner over, try demonstrating your approach. The next time a divisive issue comes up, tell your spouse that you'd like to try to handle it your way, and let him see the results. (No gloating allowed!)

Divide and conquer.

Ann is busily raking leaves while Joe, her husband, is inside paying the bills. Four-year-old Kate makes a beeline across the front yard and dives into Ann's neatly raked pile. "Don't jump in the leaves, Kate," she says.

"I'm trying to gather them, not scatter them." Kate begs her to change her mind, to no avail.

Kate stomps away into the house. "Dad, can I jump in the leaves?"

Joe, in the middle of adding up a long string of figures, responds without looking up. "Sure," he says absentmindedly. Kate flies out the door and into the pile of leaves.

Her mother, who had just repaired the damage from Kate's first dive into the leaves, yanks her off the ground. "I told you not to jump in the leaves," she says.

"You're so mean! Dad said I could," Kate whines.

There are two rules for family living that can prevent this kind of situation. For children: If one parent says no, it is not acceptable to go to the other one on appeal. The corollary rule for parents: If one parent says no, the other must agree to back him or her up. It is not acceptable to undermine your spouse's decision.

In this example, Joe was an innocent participant in Kate's divide-and-conquer strategy. But children often take advantage of one parent's tendency to say yes when the other has already said no.

Although this strategy can be effective in the short run—Kate got her wish, to jump in the leaves—children need to understand that ultimately it will backfire, that they will get caught when they try to make an end run around one parent. If the child succeeds in igniting fireworks between her parents, the attention is diverted from her misdeed and she has achieved her goal.

To avoid a similar occurrence in the future, Ann might tell Kate, "Daddy and I know that you went behind my back to get him to go along with your wishes, and we don't like it." Joe could add, "When your mother says no, I don't want you to ask me for something that you know she doesn't want you to do." They could then tell Kate that she has to help rake up the scattered leaves.

Another method children use to divide and conquer is to complain to one parent about the other. "Mom was mean to me," so goes the lament. "She made me go to bed when I wasn't tired, and she told me that I couldn't read." How tempting it is to be the nice, understanding parent and come to your poor, "wronged" child's rescue by telling your spouse something along the lines of, "I think you were too hard on Julie. You hurt her feelings." The parents end up pitted against each other, and the spotlight is deflected from whatever Julie did in the first place that prompted Mom to issue such an order.

A more effective and just approach might be to say, "I think you should tell Mom that you're mad at her." If your child says that Mom won't listen, you can encourage her to work out the dispute. "It's between you and your mother—not you and me. I'm sure you can talk to her."

Fight fair.

Ben, three, is in the midst of a full-blown tantrum while the entire extended family, gathered for a family reunion, looks on. "Make him stop," says Paul, his father.

"*You* handle it," replies Jane. "You started it by telling him that he had to take a nap. That was a brilliant move when all of his cousins were going outside to play."

Paul's frown turns into a scowl. "*You're* the expert. *You're* the one reading all the child-rearing books. *You* handle it."

The above scene is understandable; however, it's not good for either the child or the marriage. Although it is very tempting to blame your partner when something goes wrong, this sends kids the message that they are responsible for their parents' disagreements.

What We Fight About

What's there to fight about? Plenty. Here are some common grounds for disagreement between even harmonious couples:

- Junk food
- Bedtimes
- Homework
- Spanking and other punishments
- Mealtime behavior
- Public misbehavior
- Neatness
- Sibling disputes
- Dealing with "the gimmes"
- Allowances
- Chores
- Forgetfulness
- Television

If you feel your temper beginning to rise when your spouse disagrees on how to handle one of these issues, take five. Tell your spouse that you feel strongly about the situation and want to handle it without his or her involvement. Likewise, if your spouse feels strongly and you don't, then step aside.   —N.S. and P.M.

If you and your spouse can manage to fight fair, your children can learn from such everyday arguments. When they see you argue and then resolve the disagreement, they learn that it is possible to become angry with someone you love and to reconcile your differences.

Fighting about everyday issues is a normal part of home life. Children do not need to be shielded from these conflicts; indeed, they can actually learn a lot from how you and your spouse arrive at an agreeable resolution. But discussions about larger, more divisive issues, such as sex, money, and relatives, are better handled in private. It may also be better to wait and discuss especially difficult situations after the smoke has cleared from the immediate battle.

It takes enormous self-control to hold your tongue when you see your spouse handling a disciplinary matter in a way that bothers you. Later on you can acknowledge how difficult the situation was by saying something like, "I know how frustrating it can be when Julie fights going to bed. I didn't want to interfere, but I don't think threats are the best way to handle this situation. Let's talk about another approach."

If, however, you lose your cool and you and your spouse have a noisy brawl that is witnessed or overheard by your children, you need to reassure them, after you've cooled off, that everything is okay. Tell them that you and your spouse are no longer angry at each other. Reassure them that, yes, it can be frightening to hear their parents lose their temper and fight but that it's okay because they can work things out and make up.

What's Happening to

AMERICAN MARRIAGE?

Demands for intimacy, emotional support, companionship, and sexual gratification have increased, although there has been a decline in what individuals are willing to sacrifice for a relationship.

Norval D. Glenn

Dr. Glenn is Ashbel Smith Professor of Sociology and Stiles Professor in American Studies, University of Texas at Austin.

VER THE PAST three decades, there has been a period of substantial changes in the institution of marriage in the U.S. The divorce rate doubled from 1965 to 1975, increased more slowly through the late 1970s, and leveled off in the 1980s, but at such a high level that almost two-thirds of the marriages entered into in recent years are expected to end in divorce or separation. The increase in divorce, a decrease in remarriage after divorce, and a higher average age at first marriage have lowered the proportion of adults who are married. Out-of-wedlock births have increased substantially, so that one-fourth of all births now are to unmarried mothers. The proportion of married women who work outside the home has risen steadily, the increase being especially great among those with pre-school-age children.

Everyone agrees that these changes are important, but different authorities and commentators disagree as to what they mean for the health and future of the institution of marriage. One point of view is that marriage is in serious trouble—that it may disappear or lose its status as the preferred way of life for adult Americans. For example, a recent book is titled *The Retreat from Marriage,* and numerous books and articles refer to a decline or deinstitutionalization of marriage.

An opposing view, held until recently by most social scientific students of marriage, is that recent changes do not indicate decline or decay, but, rather, are adaptive and have kept the institution viable and healthy. These observers point out, for instance, that the increase in divorce has come about because people are rejecting particular marriages, rather than the institution of marriage—that most divorced persons want to remarry, and about three-fourths of them do so. Some of these commentators even view the increase in divorce positively, claiming that it reflects an increased importance people place on having good marriages and a decreased willingness to endure unsatisfactory ones. Divorce and remarriage, according to this view, are mechanisms for replacing poor relationships with better ones and keeping the overall quality of marriages high.

The evidence doesn't support consistently either the most negative or most positive views of what is happening to American marriage. For instance, the notion that it is a moribund or dying institution is inconsistent with the fact that a large percentage of Americans say that having a happy marriage is one of the most important, if not *the* most important, goal in their lives.

About two-fifths of the respondents to the 1989 Massachusetts Mutual American Family Values Study indicated this was one of their most important values, and more than 90% said it was one of the most important or very important. Approximately three-fourths of the high school seniors studied by the Monitoring the Future Project at the University of Michigan in recent years have stated they definitely will marry, and the proportion has not declined. When adults are asked what kind of lifestyle they prefer, a very large majority select one involving wedlock, and a substantial minority (more than one-third) choose a traditional marriage in which the husband is the bread-winner and the wife a homemaker.

Even when one takes into account that what people say in response to survey questions may not always reflect accurately what they think and feel, these survey data clearly demonstrate that Americans in general have not given up on matrimony. However, there is even more compelling evidence against the most extremely positive assessments of recent changes. Although having good marriages may be as important to people as ever, or may have become even more important in recent years, my research indicates that the probability of attaining them has declined to a large extent.

Those who argue that marriages in this country in general are doing quite well often cite data showing that a high and rather stable percentage of married persons give positive responses when they are asked

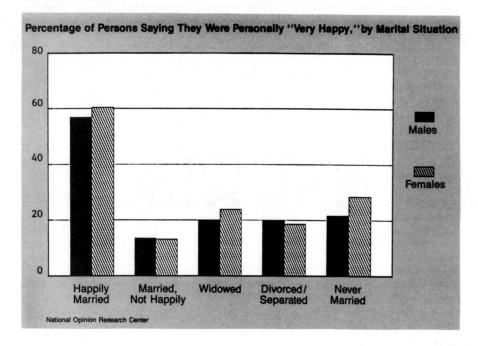

Percentage of Persons Saying They Were Personally "Very Happy," by Marital Situation

National Opinion Research Center

about the quality of their unions. In fact, since the early 1970s, the reported quality of marriages has gone down, though not very much. Most years since 1973, the General Social Survey conducted by the National Opinion Research Center at the University of Chicago has asked people to rate their marriages as very happy, pretty happy, or not too happy. The percentage of those who cited "very happy" fell by five percentage points from 1973-76 to 1988-91, dropping from 68 to 63%.

The indicated over-all happiness quality of American marriages still would be quite high if these ratings were to be taken at their face value, but they should not be interpreted that way. Many people are reluctant to admit to an interviewer—and perhaps even to themselves—that their marriages are less than satisfactory. Therefore, an unknown, but possibly substantial, proportion of the marriages reported to be "very happy" are not of very high quality, whereas virtually all those reported to be less than very happy are seriously deficient.

What is important about the indicated trend in marital quality is not that it has been slightly downward, but that it has not been steeply upward. If, as some commentators have claimed, the increase in divorce resulted only from people becoming less willing to stay in unsatisfactory marriages, the average quality of intact marriages should have climbed in tandem with the divorce rate. The fact that it didn't means that the probability of marriages remaining satisfactory must have declined substantially.

During 1973-76, about 60% of the persons who had first married three-five years earlier were still in their first marriages and

reported them to be "very happy." By 1988-91, it had declined to about 54%. For persons who first married 12-14 years earlier, the decline was greater, from 54 to 38%, while for those who married 20-24 years earlier, it dropped from 50 to 36%. There were declines of around 10 or more percentage points at most other lengths of time since the first marriage.

Those who view recent changes in American marriage positively may not find these data very alarming. To them, what is important is the kind of marriage a person eventually attains, not the success of his or her first union. From this perspective, the percentages of ever-married persons who were in marriages of any order (first, second, or subsequent) that they reported to be "very happy" are even more significant.

The changes from 1973-76 to 1988-91 show a distinct downward trend in the probability of being in a successful marriage. Among persons who have sought marital happiness by marrying at least once, a decreased proportion seem to be experiencing it. This indicates that the increase in divorce and the other changes in marriage during the past three decades have not been solely or primarily a matter of people becoming more willing and able to go from poor marriages to better ones.

Still, one might suspect that there has been one positive aspect of the changes of the past few years—namely, a decreased tendency for people to be in poor marriages. However, the proportion of ever-married persons who were in marriages they reported to be less than "very happy" increased from 1973-76 to 1988-91 at all lengths of time after the first marriage up to 20 years—the changes being in the range

of three to five percentage points. Only among persons who married 20-29 years earlier was there a slight decrease in the percentage of persons in the less satisfactory unions.

Most of the decrease in the probability of being in a very happy marriage resulted from an increase in the probability of being divorced or separated. For instance, at 12-14 years after the first marriage, the percentage divorced or separated at the time of the surveys went from eight to 18%, and at 20-24 years, it rose from eight to 19%.

The most important consequences of the increase in marital failure have been on the offspring. An enormous amount of evidence, from sources varying from in-depth clinical studies to large-scale surveys, indicates moderate to severe short-term negative effects on the well-being and development of most of the children of divorce. Although the causal link is less well-established, there also apparently are some important long-term effects on a substantial minority of those whose parents divorce, including difficulty in making commitments in relationships and an increased probability of various mental health problems. Equally important is evidence for harmful effects from failed parental marriages that do not end in divorce—especially from those unions characterized by high levels of tension and conflict.

The changes in matrimony also have tended to lower the well-being of adults. Although there are exceptions, in general, those who are the happiest and most fulfilled and who function the best are those in successful marriages. On average, the happily married are the happiest, by a large margin, and the less than happily married are the least happy. In other words, to be in a good marriage is the best situation, but a poor marriage is not better than no marriage at all.

The causal relationship between marital situation and well-being is not entirely clear. Happily married individuals may do best partly because those who are the happiest and best-adjusted, for whatever reasons, are more likely than others to marry and to succeed at marriage. However, most researchers who have studied the relationship between marital situation and well-being believe that it primarily is the former that affects the latter. If so, and if the strength of the effects has not diminished markedly in recent years, the decline in the percentage of persons at various stages of adulthood who are happily married has been distinctly detrimental to their welfare.

Why the decline in marital success?

One of the most likely reasons for the decline in marital success is the well-documented increase in what persons expect of marriage. The levels of intimacy, emotional support, companionship, and sexual gratification that people believe they should get from marriage have increased, while what they are willing to give very likely has declined. In other words, the motivation for marriage has become more purely hedonistic, or more selfish. This is just one aspect of a general increase in individualism in America and throughout most of the modern world.

Another likely reason is the breakdown in the consensus of what it means to be a husband or wife. Whereas, until recently, the rights and obligations of spouses were prescribed culturally and fairly well understood by just about everyone, they have become a matter for negotiation in individual marriages. This increased flexibility in marital roles, according to its advocates, should have increased the quality of matrimony or at least the quality of the lives of married persons, and for many persons it may have done so. For others, however, it has led to discord and disappointment. The optimistic view is that we eventually will learn to deal more effectively with the new freedom and flexibility in marriage, but that remains to be seen.

Another change that was supposed to have had unambiguously positive effects, but that may not have done so, is the easing of moral, religious, and legal barriers to divorce. The reasoning of those who advocated this was that making it easier for persons to correct marital mistakes—to escape from unsatisfying, stultifying, or dehumanizing marriages—would have

positive effects on human welfare. Indeed, if one concentrates only on individual cases, as therapists and marriage counselors do, one readily can see how diminishing the guilt, social disapproval, and legal penalties of divorce has improved the quality of many lives.

However, the changes that resulted in short-term benefits to many individuals may have lessened the probability of marital success and resulted in long-term losses in the well-being of the population as a whole. One spouse's freedom—to leave the marriage, to change the terms of the marital contract—is the other spouse's insecurity. That insecurity tends to inhibit the strong commitment and investment of time, energy, and lost opportunities that are conducive to marital success. The decline in the ideal of marital permanence—one of the most well-documented value changes among Americans in recent decades—also has tended to make persons less willing and able to make the needed commitments to and investments in marriage. To the extent that a person constantly compares the existing marriage with real or imagined alternatives to it, that marriage inevitably will compare unfavorably in some respects. People are hardly aware of needs currently being well-served, but tend to be keenly attuned to them not being well-satisfied. Since attention tends to center on needs not being especially well-met in one's marriage (and there always are some), the grass will tend to look greener on the other side of the marital fence. Therefore, merely contemplating alternatives to one's marriage may engender discontent.

Those authorities who have come to recognize the negative aspects of recent changes in American marriage are dividing into two camps—those who believe that the negative changes are inevitable and irreversible and that the best we can do is to try to lessen their impact, and those who believe that at least some of the changes can be reversed. The pessimists give strong arguments for their position, pointing out, for instance, that the trend to individualism that underlies many of the changes has occurred in most parts of the modern world and may characterize an advanced stage of economic development. Furthermore, the insecurity that inhibits commitment in marriage is likely to be self-perpetuating, as it leads to marital instability, which in turn leads to further insecurity.

There are signs, however, that a reversal in some of the changes already may be occurring. In recent years, there has been a strong reaction against radical individualism among many intellectuals in this country, and attitudinal survey data indicate that a similar reaction may be beginning in the general public. Marriage is just as crucial an institution as ever, and most Americans seem to know that. What has been missing is sufficient awareness of the costs of maintaining the health of the institution. It is to be hoped that Americans will recognize that the loss of personal freedom, renunciation of pleasure seeking, and acceptance of greater responsibility necessary for good marriages will benefit themselves, their children, and the entire society.

Receipts from

A Marriage

SUMMARY   Married-couple families are America's largest and most powerful consumer segment. These traditional households experience life as a roller coaster of child-rearing and spending. As married couples advance through various lifestages— from childless couples to new parents, prime-time families, mature families, and empty nesters—their spending waxes, wanes, and shifts in important ways.

Margaret K. Ambry

Margaret K. Ambry is director of consulting services at New Strategist Publications & Consulting in Ithaca, New York.

While single parents and alternative lifestyles get a lot of media attention, business's best customers are still "traditional" families. Married-couple families account for 55 percent of all U.S. households, and seven in ten Americans live in them. Married-couple families also account for 70 percent of total consumer spending. The biggest spenders—married couples with children under 18—comprise just 27 percent of all households, but the number of such households is projected to grow 12 percent during the 1990s.

Blame it on the baby boomlet. There is nothing like a child to change a couple's spending priorities, and baby-boomer par-ents have been making a lot of changes since the mid-1980s. Having a child doesn't mean getting an automatic raise, however. When the average young married couple makes the transition from childless couple to new parents (oldest child under age 6), their total expenditures increase less than 1 percent. Yet their spending patterns shift considerably: they spend more than their childless counterparts on health care, clothing, housing, and food, and much less on alcohol, education, and transportation. They also spend more on cigarettes and less on personal care and entertainment.

As parents and children get older, income and spending increase in nearly every category of household products and services. Married couples who make the transition to prime-time families (oldest child aged 6 to 17) spend 11 percent more overall than new parents. They spend more on virtually all products and services, although they spend less on alcohol and housing.

Mature families are couples with children aged 18 or older at home. They spend 9 percent more than prime-time families, and they generally have the highest incomes. But when children finally leave home, household spending falls by almost 30 percent. Empty-nester couples spend less than mature families on everything except health care and cash contributions.

Our analysis of the 1989-90 Consumer Expenditure Survey (CEX) shows how the birth, growth, and departure of children affect a married couple's spending. It shows that a couple's lifestage is at least as important as their ages in determining consumer behavior.

CHILDLESS COUPLES

Childless couples with a householder aged 25 to 34 have an average annual before-tax income of nearly $46,000. Each year, they spend an average of $34,000, 22 percent more than the average for all American households. The biggest chunk of a childless young couple's budget (32 per-

Parents' Progress

As married couples move through life, their spending patterns change. New parents spend less on alcoholic beverages than young childless couples. As children age, couples spend more on education. When children leave, couples reduce their spending on almost everything.

(percent change in average annual expenditures of married couples by lifestage change and expenditure category)

	childless couples to new parents	new parents to prime-time families	prime-time families to mature families	mature families to empty nesters
TOTAL EXPENDITURES	0.3%	11.0%	8.8%	-29.0%
Food	2.4	29.8	8.6	-33.5
Alcoholic beverages	-33.8	-6.2	17.5	-21.8
Housing	9.5	-5.0	-6.2	-18.8
Apparel and services	10.8	20.4	-0.2	-32.7
Transportation	-10.1	12.6	24.7	-40.1
Health care	49.3	9.2	18.9	28.1
Entertainment	-5.6	25.2	1.8	-34.6
Personal-care products	-7.3	21.7	16.6	-28.6
Reading	-7.4	9.7	4.7	-3.8
Education	-28.9	178.7	101.1	-86.4
Tobacco products	12.4	26.0	25.3	-39.3
Cash contributions*	-32.1	62.8	54.6	5.7
Personal insurance, pensions, Social Security ...	-8.3	6.2	4.3	-41.7
Miscellaneous	-13.3	29.7	5.9	-32.9

Cash contributions include alimony, child support, cash gifts to nonhousehold members, and charitable contributions.

Note: A prime-time family may have both preschool and school-aged children, while a mature family may have both adult children and children aged 0 to 17.

Source: Author's calculations based on 1989-90 Consumer Expenditure Survey data

cent) is devoted to housing. One-fifth of their spending (20 percent) goes directly into dwellings, and another 5 percent is spent on furnishings; both are higher-than-average shares. Yet childless couples spend very little on household operations. With fewer people to care for, their average annual tab for housekeeping supplies—about $400—is less than their liquor bill.

Like other households, childless couples devote the second-largest share of their spending to transportation. Although they spend an average amount on used cars, they spend 72 percent more than the average household on new cars. Spending on new cars drops off once there are young children in the household, then bounces back. It peaks among mature families and young empty nesters.

When children finally leave home, household spending falls by almost 30 percent.

Just 13 percent of a childless couple's spending goes to food, but more than half of those dollars are given to restaurants and carry-out places. In all other lifestages, couples spend the majority of their food dollars on groceries. Childless couples spend an average of $440 a year on alcohol, more than 1 percent of their average annual budget.

Payments to personal insurance, pensions, and Social Security account for nearly 12 percent of a young childless couple's budget, about $4,000 a year. Because most are two-earner households, childless couples spend 70 percent more than average on pensions and Social Security.

Childless couples devote 5 percent of their spending to clothing, a smaller share than other couples. Another 5 percent goes to entertainment, with equal shares devoted to tickets for movies, theater, sports, and other events; TV, radio, and sound equipment; and other entertainment products and services such as sports equipment and boats. Although they have no children, childless couples also spend more than average on pets and toys.

They're young and don't have children to take to the doctor, so childless couples spend 34 percent less than the average household on out-of-pocket health-care expenses. Health care accounts for only about 3 percent of their budgets. They also spend less than average on tobacco products, education, and cash contributions (perhaps because the latter category includes alimony and child support). They spend less than 1 percent of their money on reading materials, although the $190 spent is 22 percent more than average. Young childless couples' trips to the hairdresser, cosmetics, shampoo, and other personal-care products and services take up another 1 percent of their household spending. This share doesn't vary much from lifestage to lifestage.

NEW PARENTS

New parents are couples whose oldest child is under the age of 6. They break down into two groups—younger parents (householders aged 25 to 34) and older new parents (householders aged 35 to 54). Although both types of households average 3.5 people, the older group's average income is just over $15,000 higher. Conse-

3. RELATIONSHIP MAINTENANCE: Marital Challenges

quently, older new parents spend more on all major categories of products and services. They also allocate their funds differently than younger new parents do.

Both younger and older new parents devote a larger-than-average share of spending to housing—35 percent and 37 percent, respectively. Younger parents' housing expenditures are boosted by the 4 percent share that goes to household operations, mostly child care. But older parents of preschoolers outspend all other households on child care, mortgage payments, home maintenance, and other household services such as housekeeping, lawn-and-garden work, and household furnishings.

> **The average childless couple spends more than 1 percent of their entire budget on alcoholic beverages.**

Older new parents also spend more than younger new parents on transportation, although getting around consumes a smaller share of their total spending (15 percent versus 19 percent). Younger new parents outspend their older counterparts on cars, trucks, and other vehicles, while older new parents spend more on operating costs and public transportation.

Because of their higher incomes, older new parents are free to spend more on food and alcohol, although they allocate a smaller share of income to those categories. Food accounts for nearly 14 percent of young new parents' budgets, compared with 12 percent for older new parents. But older parents channel a larger share of funds to personal insurance, pensions, Social Security, entertainment, and cash contributions.

Older new parents outspend younger ones on all other major products and service categories, but the share they spend is similar. For example, both kinds of couples devote about 0.5 percent of their spending to reading materials. But younger couples spend an average amount, while older couples spend 81 percent more than the average household.

PRIME-TIME FAMILIES

Once the oldest child reaches school age, a family's lifestyles and spending patterns shift again. Like Ozzie and Harriet's family, the average household in the prime-time lifestage has two parents and two children, the oldest of whom is aged 6 to 17. Yet householders in this stage range

Doling Out

	ALL HOUSEHOLDS	CHILDLESS COUPLES	
		25 to 34	25 to 34
NUMBER OF HOUSEHOLDS (in thousands)	96,393	3,020	4,038
AVERAGE INCOME BEFORE TAXES	$31,600	$45,835	$37,846
AVERAGE HOUSEHOLD SIZE	2.6	2.0	3.5
AVERAGE TOTAL EXPENDITURES	$28,090	$34,323	$32,793
FOOD	4,224	4,533	4,492
At home	2,438	2,126	2,826
Away from home	1,787	2,407	1,666
ALCOHOLIC BEVERAGES	289	441	288
HOUSING	8,748	11,119	11,589
Shelter	4,934	7,024	6,279
Owned dwellings	2,902	4,132	4,051
Rented dwellings	1,517	2,390	1,933
Utilities, fuels, public services	1,863	1,746	1,966
Household operations	453	178	1,435
Housekeeping supplies	400	407	495
Household furnishings	1,099	1,763	1,426
APPAREL AND SERVICES	1,600	1,725	1,786
Men and boys	395	449	436
Women and girls	665	658	509
Children younger than age 2	71	38	384
Footwear	207	170	214
Other apparel products and services	262	409	249
TRANSPORTATION	5,154	6,989	6,253
Vehicle purchases	2,209	3,095	2,984
Cars and trucks, new	1,188	2,046	1,436
Cars and trucks, used	999	998	1,533
Gas and motor oil	1,016	1,216	1,149
Other vehicle expenses	1,636	2,286	1,934
Public transportation	293	392	184
HEALTH CARE	1,444	970	1,453
ENTERTAINMENT	1,423	1,867	1,594
Fees and admissions	374	485	294
TV, radios, sound equipment	441	525	484
Pets, toys, playground	263	312	394
Other products and services	345	545	422
PERSONAL-CARE PRODUCTS AND SERVICES	365	427	394
READING	155	189	154
EDUCATION	386	284	194
TOBACCO PRODUCTS	68	226	224
CASH CONTRIBUTIONS	858	791	474
PERSONAL INSURANCE, PENSIONS, SOCIAL SECURITY	2,532	4,026	3,342
MISCELLANEOUS	644	737	564

Cash contributions include alimony, child support, cash gifts to nonhousehold members, and charitable contributions.

in age from 25 to 54, and their average before-tax household income ranges from $35,000 for households with a head aged 25 to 34 to just over $49,000 for households with a head aged 45 to 54. Their total spending ranges from 12 percent above average for prime-time families headed by 25-to-34-year-olds to 49 percent above average for those headed by 45-to-54-year-olds.

Housing accounts for a smaller share of spending for prime-time families than for

Dollars

Older families with children have the highest incomes among married couples, but new parents and mature families spend the most.

(average total income before taxes, average household size, and average annual expenditures by expenditure category and by married-couple lifestage and age of householder)

...RENTS	PRIME-TIME FAMILIES			MATURE FAMILIES			EMPTY NESTERS		
35 to 54	25 to 34	35 to 44	45 to 54	35 to 44	45 to 54	55 to 64	45 to 54	55 to 64	65 and older
1,466	3,952	7,334	2,011	1,857	3,455	1,819	2,796	4,718	7,601
53,270	$35,251	$47,845	$49,374	$49,214	$51,948	$55,216	$52,736	$38,701	$24,477
3.5	4.3	4.2	3.9	4.5	3.9	3.5	2.0	2.0	2.0
44,839	$31,500	$41,144	$41,816	$43,149	$45,163	$40,730	$40,778	$31,534	$24,136
5,424	4,993	6,403	6,820	6,634	7,015	6,508	5,252	4,685	3,809
3,350	3,175	3,742	3,724	3,993	3,854	3,830	2,674	2,668	2,399
2,074	1,818	2,661	3,096	2,640	3,160	2,677	2,579	2,017	1,411
371	250	295	271	248	343	407	348	291	192
16,539	9,861	12,518	11,986	11,244	12,052	10,264	12,263	9,034	7,407
9,005	5,397	6,946	6,829	6,176	6,584	5,079	7,179	4,496	3,524
7,003	3,296	5,423	4,604	4,803	4,763	3,848	4,939	3,250	2,335
1,029	1,716	858	1,067	728	683	582	881	390	562
2,366	2,075	2,428	2,513	2,703	2,832	2,674	2,242	2,180	1,959
2,357	760	699	638	322	345	334	301	419	512
637	463	593	596	623	574	687	579	508	482
2,174	1,166	1,852	1,411	1,419	1,717	1,490	1,962	1,432	930
2,490	1,726	2,515	2,815	2,844	2,385	2,119	2,300	1,808	1,108
600	447	704	845	846	721	517	561	457	266
882	679	1,041	1,142	1,202	966	852	1,028	887	511
385	123	53	37	41	65	64	57	39	24
225	240	343	397	315	253	293	215	205	171
399	236	373	393	440	380	393	439	220	137
6,737	6,362	7,366	7,469	9,598	9,655	8,251	7,789	5,585	4,188
2,694	3,104	3,516	3,107	4,300	4,261	3,614	3,518	2,151	1,718
1,441	1,512	1,968	1,790	2,099	2,358	2,089	1,802	1,347	1,078
1,253	1,576	1,504	1,283	2,166	1,868	1,443	1,700	788	640
1,249	1,378	1,414	1,503	1,965	1,886	1,615	1,424	1,194	883
2,387	1,769	2,127	2,468	3,070	3,035	2,607	2,424	1,808	1,307
407	111	309	391	263	473	416	423	432	330
1,862	1,262	1,699	1,794	1,518	1,736	2,123	1,705	2,154	2,824
2,478	1,741	2,486	2,216	2,923	2,358	1,974	2,059	1,765	1,069
541	363	745	621	566	588	566	449	437	428
674	610	680	746	675	644	464	534	402	306
550	401	454	425	360	306	367	407	253	199
713	368	607	424	1,322	820	578	668	673	136
453	372	521	583	562	606	592	462	410	374
281	154	209	208	174	209	216	222	198	180
298	314	633	812	1,125	1,437	1,022	573	99	35
253	353	306	300	401	404	384	321	327	163
921	458	880	1,372	1,197	1,509	1,397	1,721	1,265	1,421
5,734	2,961	4,407	4,333	3,877	4,523	4,472	4,877	3,328	882
997	692	908	837	806	931	1,001	887	585	483

Source: 1989-90 Consumer Expenditure Survey

childless couples or new parents. Prime-time households headed by 45-to-54-year-olds spend just 29 percent of their budget on housing, compared with the 35 to 37 percent allocated by younger householders. With larger households and older children, however, prime-timers devote 16 percent of their budgets to food. They don't allocate more than half of their food budget to restaurants and carry-out food as childless couples do, but they tend to outspend new parents on food away from home.

Transportation claims 18 to 20 percent of a prime-time family's spending. This group outspends new parents on new vehicles, and they drive a lot more. Their tab for gas and oil is 36 percent more than the average household's.

Prime-time families have a lot to protect. That's why they spend 74 percent more than the average household on personal insurance and pensions, allocating 9 to 11 percent of their budgets to this

---

CINCINNATI, OHIO

DEMOGRAM

Tom Parker

Giving birth to twins in America isn't a big deal—it happens about 1,600 times a week. Quadruplet births, on the other hand, only happen four times a week. Quads make the evening news. But what about the 40 mothers a week who give birth to triplets? They get big guts, but what about the glory?

Janet Davis, 25, didn't even think she was pregnant. She went to the doctor for a routine exam. Later, when she gained weight faster than expected, her doctors thought her due date was wrong. So they scheduled a sonogram. "There's a very good reason you're getting so big," said the sonogram technician. "You have three babies in there." Janet, already the mother of two kids, ages 8 and 6, just sat in shock. Her mother said, "Oh, my God! I'm leaving town!" Her husband Pat got the news while at his job moving office furniture. He said he would have fainted if he hadn't been wedged into a phone booth.

That's where the fireworks ended. Janet didn't even discuss the triplets with her doctor until her next appointment a week later. Luckily, she stopped at a garage sale to look at a carseat. When she mentioned needing two more seats, the lady at the sale told her about a woman who lived just up the street with three newborn baby boys. Janet stopped and left a note on the woman's door. That's how she found The Triplet Connection.

The Triplet Connection is a nonprofit information clearinghouse and network for multiple-birth families based in Stockton, California. It was founded by Janet Bleyl, mother of ten, after a particularly difficult triplet pregnancy in 1982. According to Bleyl, the organization now has the largest database of multiple-birth information in the world. "We are in contact with more than 7,000 families of triplets and larger multiple births," she says. "And we currently work with over 1,250 expectant mothers per year."

Bleyl says that because triplets are not very common, most doctors have little experience in the special problems of large multiple pregnancies. And she adds that many doctors lack the nutritional training that is critical for these births. "We've found that the most important factor in large multiple pregnancies is keeping close track of nutrition and weight gain," says Bleyl. "As a rule, a mother hoping to walk out of the hospital with healthy triplets should plan on walking in with a weight gain of 50 to 70 pounds.

"We are also very concerned with the insidious nature of early contractions and preterm labor. In large multiple pregnancies, the uterus becomes so distended that it doesn't behave normally. Unless you take some extraordinary measures, it is often quite difficult to know if you are in premature labor. I had six kids before my triplets, but I didn't know!"

Bleyl's organization relies on two sources: a panel of medical advisors, and what she calls the "fabulous networking abilities of mothers" to help expectant parents and inexperienced physicians.

The Triplet Connection sent Janet Davis a packet of information, a medical questionnaire, an audiotape, and a quarterly newsletter. She says the material helped her check the quality of her doctor's advice. Janet's pregnancy was far from easy. Twice, she went to the hospital with premature contractions. Her doctors sent her home hooked to a Terbutaline pump to help prevent early labor. They kept track of Janet's progress with a fetal monitor hooked to a modem. The identical boys, Andrew, Adam, and Anthony, were delivered at 31 weeks—6 weeks early—by emergency C-section. Pat spent the last hour waiting at the hospital while Janet and her dad sat stuck in Cincinnati traffic.

I met the triplets at age 10 weeks. All three seemed healthy and as hard to tell apart as matching spoons. "Thanks to the good medical care, the boys were in the hospital for less than three weeks," Janet says. "The bill came to $90,000. Luckily, Pat's insurance paid most of it. Since then, Andrew and Anthony have had bouts with viral meningitis, we've moved to a different house, our car died, and our plumbing went out.

"Other than that, my biggest problem is simply getting the babies from one place to the next. Just to get into the doctor's office, I have to call ahead and ask the nurse to watch the parking lot for my arrival. Believe it or not, some mothers have figured out how to nurse triplets. Nursing is one thing, but lifting three babies is a different story. When your babies outnumber your arms, you've got problems."

If life's changes didn't throw us for a few loops, they wouldn't be changes at all. At first, most people respond with their own versions of, "Oh my God! I'm leaving town." But few of us ever really leave. We just gather our wits and do the best we can. And that's what Janet Davis is doing. She's got three bedrooms, one bath, two arms—and she's doing her best to hold seven people together. For more information: The Triplet Connection, P.O. Box 99571, Stockton, CA 95209; telephone (209) 474-0885.

spending category. Clothing and entertainment account for another 5 to 7 percent of their total spending. The amount spent on clothing is highest among prime-timers with householders aged 45 to 54. Households headed by 35-to-44-year-olds spend more on entertainment than others in this lifestage. Prime-time families are also among the biggest spenders on pets and toys.

MATURE FAMILIES

Mature families are couples whose oldest child at home is aged 18 or older. They have consistently above-average spending levels for food, transportation, entertainment, personal-care products and services, and education. Parents in mature families tend to be in their peak earning years, and many adult children also contribute to the family income. Average incomes in this lifestage range from a high of $55,000 for households headed by someone aged 55 to 64 to a low of $49,000 for those headed by someone aged 35 to 44. Mature families also shrink as householders age, from an average of 4.5 persons in families headed by 35-to-44-year-olds to 3.5 persons among those headed by 55-to-64-year-olds.

Compared with families in other lifestages, mature families allocate the smallest share of their budgets (25 to 27 percent) to housing, although they spend more than average on everything except rent, personal services, clothing for children younger than age 2, and household operations. What they save on housing prob-

ably goes to automobiles. Mature families spend 64 to 95 percent more than the average household on vehicles. They also spend above-average amounts on related items such as fuel and maintenance.

Because mature families support ravenous college-age youths, they spend more than other households on food and education. Their expenditures on food are at least 54 percent greater than average, and they allocate 15 to 16 percent of their budgets to food. Education eats up about 3 percent of the average mature family's spending dollar, triple the average amount.

EMPTY NESTERS

Couples' spending doesn't necessarily drop off as soon as the children leave the nest, especially if both spouses are still working. The average before-tax income of empty-nest households headed by people aged 45 to 54 is 67 percent greater than average, and their spending is 45 percent higher than average.

Income and spending do fall off among older couples. But the average income for empty nesters aged 55 to 64 is still 22 percent above the average for all households, and their spending is 12 percent above average. Among empty nesters aged 65 and older, both income and spending are below average (by 23 percent and 14 percent, respectively).

Not surprisingly, empty nesters spend more than younger couples on health care. Young empty nesters spend 18 percent more than average on health care, and their counterparts aged 65 or older spend almost twice as much as the average U.S. household. The share of spending devoted to health care by empty nesters climbs from 4 percent for pre-retirees to 12 percent among the elderly. As empty nesters age and their incomes decline, they also spend higher shares of income on food, personal-care products and services, reading, and cash contributions.

Young empty nesters spend nearly 60 percent more than the average household on vehicles, while the oldest empty nesters spend 22 percent less than average. Aging empty nesters also spend increasingly smaller budget shares on clothing, education, personal insurance, pensions, and Social Security.

Spending patterns change as children arrive and grow up. Children born to baby boomers during the 1980s and early 1990s will determine the lion's share of household spending for the rest of the decade. As they grow, their family's budget will almost certainly expand. For businesses that have struggled through the recession, this is something to look forward to.

Behind the Numbers This analysis is derived from the Bureau of Labor Statistics' annual Consumer Expenditure Survey (CEX). The unit of analysis in the CEX is a consumer unit, referred to in this article as a household. The analysis is based on a cross-tabulation of age of consumer unit head by composition of consumer unit. In order to obtain a large enough sample, data for the survey years 1989 and 1990 were combined. Because of low frequency counts, spending data could not be tabulated for all types of consumer units for all age groups. The lifestage called childless couples, for example, includes only those headed by someone aged 25 to 34 because there are so few couples headed by a person under age 25. Likewise, most couples aged 35 to 44 have children; the small number who do not are also excluded from the analysis. For more information about the CEX, contact the Bureau of Labor Statistics at (202) 272-5060. Margaret Ambry is co-author of *The Official Guide to American Incomes* and *The Official Guide to Household Spending*, to be published by New Strategist in spring 1993. Some of the data in this article come from these books.

SAVING RELATIONSHIPS:
THE POWER OF THE UNPREDICTABLE

When one partner silently switches the "rules," both partners can benefit. Welcome to the surprising world systems thinking.

Barry L. Duncan, Psy.D., and Joseph W. Rock, Psy.D.

Sharon, 30, and Jeff, 35, have been married for nine years. Since the recent birth of their first child, Sharon has become increasingly aware of Jeff's propensity for giving instructions and pointing out imperfections in her methods of doing things. She knows that he is usually just trying to help.

The first thing Sharon does to address the problem is mention it to Jeff. She explains that when they were first married she needed and appreciated his knowledge and experience but now sometimes feels he is treating her like a child. She asks him to please hold his comments and advice until she asks for them. Jeff agrees to make every effort to treat her like the mature, independent woman she has become.

But before long, Jeff resumes sharing his observations of the way Sharon does things and making suggestions about better ways of doing them. When Sharon points this out to him, he becomes defensive and accuses her of overreacting and not being able to accept constructive criticism.

Sharon continues to make Jeff aware of his now "critical, paternalistic, and sexist nature." She takes every opportunity to point out his need to dominate and keep her in her place. Jeff responds by defensively backing off and withdrawing from conversation in general. When conversa-

tion does occur, he seems more apt to criticize Sharon about her "crazy, feminist" ideas as well as her way of doing almost everything. Their latest interactions seem to be best characterized by an unspoken tension.

Sharon decides to try a different approach. She goes "on strike," discontinuing to do anything Jeff criticizes. When he comments that the spaghetti sauce needs more garlic, she announces she's no longer cooking. When he criticizes how the grass is cut, she blows up in anger, and both Sharon and he say many things that they later regret. Jeff decides not only to stop commenting and suggesting but to stop talking altogether. Now an unspoken hostility hovers over their relationship.

Sharon and Jeff illustrate three ways in which people get stuck in their relationships and sabotage their own attempts to improve them. First Sharon believes she is trying different strategies to improve her relationship when in reality she is trying only slight variations on a single theme: "I will make my dissatisfaction apparent to him, and he will respond with less criticism." People get stuck by trying the same basic approach over and over, even though it might not be obvious to them that they are doing so.

Further, when her first method makes things worse, she tries more of the same. A well-intentioned attempt to resolve a

small difficulty ends up turning it into a serious conflict despite good intentions. Sharon wound up with increased criticism and an overly sensitive, defensive, withdrawn husband.

Third, Sharon recognized the problem but did not succeed in getting Jeff to help solve it. Almost always, one partner notices a joint problem first. That person mentions it to the other and then proceeds to try to solve the problem, while assuming the other person is motivated and cooperative. This can be a faulty assumption even if both people agree on how serious it is or how to solve it.

A widely shared belief is that in order for a relationship to change, both partners have to actively participate in changing it. As family therapists, we disagree. We subscribe to a "systems" approach with couples. In a relationship system, a noticeable change in one person can set in motion a change in the whole system, that is, the couple.

Early in relationships, rules begin to form that grow out of patterns of ways people to relate to each other. Rules can be simple and straightforward—one partner initiates sex, one partner does the dishes; or they can be more subtle—when both partners are angry they don't yell. Sometimes the rules are talked about openly, but typically they are assumed rather than discussed, and those involved

From *Psychology Today*, January/February 1993, pp. 46-51, 86, 95. Adapted from *Overcoming Relationship Impasses* by Barry L. Duncan and Joseph W. Rock. © 1991 by Plenum Publishing Corporation. Reprinted by permission.

may not even be consciously aware of the assumed rules. This non-awareness causes the most difficulty when problems arise.

Rules have their uses; in recurring situations, we don't have to figure out what to do from scratch. But because rules are based on previous experience, they also maintain the status quo. The very qualities that make rules useful day-to-day can render them harmful when a relationship problem needs to be resolved. Rules simplify life by limiting options to an acceptable few. But when we get stuck in solving a problem, we need *more* options, not fewer. The assumed rules we carry into a situation prevent us from exploring potentially helpful options and limit our flexibility. They discourage change—even helpful, necessary change.

Beyond Blame: Systems Thinking

Most theories of human behavior are couched in linear cause-effect terms and offer either historical (unhappy childhood) or physical (bad nerves) explanations for behavior. Both the medical and Freudian perspectives on problem behaviors or emotional stress consider only the individual, apart from his or her relationships.

Systems theory is evolving to explain the complexities of relationships and to help resolve the problems and distress in-

> In a relationship, you are not acting completely of your own free will. You are constantly influenced by your partner, and vice versa.

herent in relationships. It offers a refreshing, illness-free lens through which to observe human behavior—the focus of study shifts from what goes on inside a person to what takes place between people.

When two individuals come together in a relationship, something is created that is different from, larger, and more complex than those two individuals apart—a system. The most important feature of such a relationship is communication. Relationships are established, maintained, and changed by communicative interaction among members.

As relationships endure, communication sequences form patterns over time, and it is the patterning over time that is the essence of a couple system. Sometimes the enduring patterns begin to create difficulties for couples, and new patterns are need-

ed. With Jeff and Sharon, the pattern concerning the giving and receiving of advice was at the heart of their relationship problems.

In a system, all elements are mutually dependent. What one person does depends on what the other person does. In the context of a relationship, you are not acting completely of your own free will. You are constantly being influenced by your partner, and vice versa. When Sharon attempted to get less criticism, Jeff responded by criticizing more and pulling away. Each person's actions helped determine what the other did, and each person's actions affected the relationship as a whole.

A marriage, then, is not a static and fixed relationship. No matter how entrenched one's behavior or how strong one's personality, each individual is influenced by the other on an ongoing basis. *Once you recognize your partner's dependence upon your pattern of behavior, you can consciously plan and change your own behavior, thereby influencing your partner and the relationship in a constructive manner.*

Virtually every couple we see in therapy is interested in what, or who, caused their problems; they look for guilt, blame, or responsibility. But influence among people in relationships is reciprocal and mutually dependent, causality is circular. Choosing the point at which the causal chain begins is pointless and arbitrary.

One implication is that the circle can be broken or interrupted at any point, regardless of how the problem started or how long it has existed. If one person in a couple changes behavior noticeably and consistently, the other person's reactions will change, which will change the first person's reactions. In this way, one person can positively impact a troubled relationship; the partner's cooperation is not required.

Does Sharon have a problem with constructive criticism, or does Jeff have a problem with control and sexism? One partner, either partner, can interrupt the causal circle and move the relationship in another direction.

In much the same way that a stone thrown into a pond affects the surface well beyond the small point at which it enters, a small change in a specific area can lead to a positive ripple effect on the entire relationship. When there are many problems in a relationship, people assume that a major overhaul is required. Many times, however, a small adjustment, strategically employed, is all that is needed.

Communication: The Sound of Silence

Communication theory is crucial in systems thinking. Gestures, tone of voice, and facial expressions are important in understanding what someone is saying. Much has been written about body language, addressing what people "say" by their posture. What gets lost is that *all behavior is communicative.* Even silence conveys some message. There is no such thing as *not* communicating.

A spouse who routinely comes home late for dinner without calling may be saying, "Your inconvenience is unimportant compared to what happens at work" or "Your feelings are not a priority to me." The spouse who prepares dinner may not comment to the late spouse. Yet the silence may be a worse indictment than a verbal scolding.

Viewing behavior itself as a powerful means of communication significantly increases your options when verbal com-

> What gets lost is that all behavior is communicative. Even silence conveys some message. There is no such thing as *not* communicating.

munication is not working. If, like Sharon, you have tried to fix your relationship problems by talking ad nauseam, then behavioral options may provide a more powerful way.

Communication occurs at different levels, even though most of us focus our attention on only one—the content, or the literal meaning of the words. Most important, but less obvious, is the relationship level. It indicates how the sender of the message is attempting to influence the receiver. It conveys a command or directive concerning the sender's needs and is an implicit attempt to influence the receiver. "My back itches" may mean "Scratch my back." "I had a rough day" may mean "Leave me alone," "I need your support," or "Fix me a drink." Even "I love you" can be an implicit command, depending upon the circumstances. It may mean "Tell me that you love me."

Influence is unavoidable in communication; it is inherent in how we interact. Just as one cannot *not* communicate, one cannot *not* influence when communicating. Implicit directives also define the nature of the relationship. The statement, "The garbage can is overflowing," not only conveys the obvious, but may also contain

Relationship Myths

Myth #1: What people say is very important and has a big impact on what they do.

Words often fall short of accurately depicting someone's intentions and we can't really guess at times what someone else really means. In the long term, behavior is what gives evidence of our true intentions.

Myth #2: People can and should understand and explain their own and others' motives.

Behavior is the result of a tremendous number of interacting influences: biological, psychological, interpersonal, situational. We never get answers to "why," only plausible-sounding guesses. Knowing "why" seldom produces a solution. *Understanding* a behavior pattern and *changing* it are often completely different. Consider *what* is happening now between you and your partner and *how* that pattern can be changed.

Myth #3: In close relationships being completely open and honest is critical if the relationship is to work.

If the person with whom you are communicating is unable or unwilling to respond honestly and openly, honesty and openness may well be a bad idea at times. Being open with someone who will use the information to manipulate you or gain power over you is like playing poker and showing your cards before you bet. An open and honest expression must be interpreted as such by the receiver of the message for it to be truly open and honest. Openness is not the only way, and, in some situations, not the best way.

Myth #4: A good relationship is one in which both people give unselfishly.

Unselfish giving is not a prerequisite for a good relationship. In fact, attempts to do so usually create more problems than they solve. Giving is an important part of any relationship. However, all of us expect something back; it helps to let the other person know what that is. Balance is also important. Rather than expecting to meet all of each other's needs, stay in practice at meeting some of your own. It adds stability to a relationship and reduces the risk of resentment. Complete selfishness certainly does not lend itself to healthy relationships, but it turns out that neither does utter unselfishness.

Myth #5: In any situation there is only one reality or one truth.

Reality is entirely dependent upon who is observing and describing it, especially in complex situations such as interactions in relationships. When two people have very different stories to tell about the same situation, it does not mean that one is lying, although each partner usually believes that about the other. Rather, each is describing reality from his or her frame of reference. A lot of time usually is wasted trying to convince your partner that you are right. This time could be better spent trying to understand the others' point of view and using that understanding to change your own behavior in a way that will help the relationship.

---

the implicit directive, "Take the garbage out." The statement defines the relationship as one in which the sender has the right to comment on the state of garbage and expect the receiver to follow the (implicit) directive.

Implicit commands are largely automatic and occur outside of awareness. As a result, we often address the most important parts of our lives, our relationships, in an extremely haphazard fashion. By becoming aware of the implicit influence in communication we can deliberately use it in improving relationships.

When we think about communication, we usually think of a speaker actively conveying a message and a listener passively receiving it. This, however, is a very inaccurate perception. Listening is an active process. We have to make sense of the speaker's words; we compare their ideas to beliefs and attitudes we hold and to perceptions about the speakers we've already formed. We consider gestures, tone of voice, and facial expressions, and the circumstances. In addition, our needs influence what we hear.

The conclusion is inescapable—the listener helps create meaning. Much of this process tends to be automatic and outside of awareness. We're seldom aware of how our beliefs and attitudes affect how we hear, or the ways we interpret nonverbal communication, much less how our own needs affect our perceptions. By paying attention to these factors, however, we can make them conscious, then control them.

The upshot is, we can choose how to interpret a given communication. Words

Words that hurt us before no longer have to have power. We can choose to interpret a message differently from the way the sender intended.

or behaviors that have hurt us before no longer have to have this power. Further, we can choose to interpret a message differently from the way the sender intended. Just because people intend to hurt or manipulate us doesn't mean we have to cooperate by giving their messages the meanings they want us to get.

Often, the listener's understanding of a message is *already* different from the sender's. If a woman believes her husband is stressed out and needs time away, she might suggest he go away for a week. If he interprets this as "She's trying to get rid of me," the whole point of her message is twisted, and caring is perceived as rejection. This may be the most common problem seen in couples: The message sent is not the message received. Finding ways to understand and express your partner's view of a situation can reduce defensiveness and change old, conflictual patterns in a relationship.

Guidelines for Change

The ideas that one person can produce meaningful change in a relationship, and that a small change can and will lead to a ripple of other changes, are not part of conventional wisdom. Nor are the implications that change can occur quickly and that it can happen without the knowledge or cooperation of one member of the couple. But strategies developed from systems concepts do work, even when both partners aren't equally motivated to change. Here, then, are some very practical guidelines for creating change in a troubled relationship where the partners are stuck at an impasse:

• Create confusion. Change the rules by which you've been playing. Be unpredictable. That encourages your partner to find new ways to react.

•Do not be completely honest and open at all times. If your partner tends to manipulate or use power plays, openness just tips your hand and makes you more vulnerable.

•"Give up" power, or "lose" by telling your partner that you agree that he or she is "right," but continue to do whatever you think is best. Allow yourself to give up power verbally, to gain control behaviorally.

•Recognize that words and behaviors are not consistent. People often say one thing but do another. Believe what your partner does, not what he or she says.

•Do things that are truly different, not just variations on a theme. Allow yourself to change 180 degrees in how you approach a problem. That alteration can loosen things up and produce real change in your partner's response.

•Stay off the defensive. If you spend all your time justifying what you are doing, you become reactive and lose track of what you are trying to accomplish. Most people are too busy trying to defend themselves to see other ways of approaching a problem. Relationships are very complex and much creativity is needed.

•If your partner openly resists change, don't push. Finding a different, less confrontational path the change can be much more effective—and less frustrating.

•Go with the flow whenever possible and recognize the disadvantages of change. Things are rarely black and white; consider the advantages of maintaining the problem. This form of creative interpretation directly addresses the ambivalence people have about changing their behavior and aligns with that part of the individual that may be reluctant to change. It helps clarify the feared consequences of change in the hope of motivating the person toward action regarding the problem.

•Start a small, positive ripple of change and let it grow by itself.

•Look at what is going well, instead of what is going wrong with your relationship. It's much easier to build on what is already there than to tear something down and start all over.

Power Disparities in Romantic Relationships

By far, the most common source of problems in a relationship involves the distribution of power. In a good relationship, ideally there is a balance of power. Unfortunately, this ideal is not always realized, and neither party is happy with the unequal power. The powerless, disenfranchised partner feels cheated and resentful, and, whether aware of it or not, usually seeks ways to even the score. The powerful partner gets resentful because he or she has too much responsibility and carries a disproportionate share of the load.

In a relationship with a power disparity, no one wins. Yet the struggle for power underlies virtually every relationship quarrel. There are two common relationship patterns in which power is the key issue.

One involves the dependent partner who needs his partner to do things, but tries to regain the power lost to dependency by criticizing the way those things are done.

IN DEALING WITH A DEPENDENT PARTNER WHO IS RELENTLESSLY CRITICAL:

•Agree in words, but not in action, with criticism.

•Don't explain or defend yourself.

•Interpret your partner's critical message to mean you can stop doing whatever was criticized: "You're right, I am a terrible cook. I'll let you eat prepared frozen food more." Your partner will either stop in his tracks or—even better—refute the criticism himself.

The second power problem is the most common problem we see in troubled relationships. It involves one partner having control in multiple areas—money, decision-making, social life, conversation topics—such that the relationship begins to resemble that of a parent and child, with the powerful partner treating the other like a child. Even when the person in the powerful role, such as a parent, can be very kind and nurturing, the powerless partner can easily feel inferior, helpless, trapped—as well as resentful. Any attempts to speak out against the arrangement will usually sound like the helpless protestations of a child.

IN DEALING WITH A DOMINEERING PARTNER WHO PLAYS A PARENTAL ROLE:

•Do what you want to do—act independently of your partner's expectations.

> **The ideas that one person can produce meaningful change in a relationship, and that a small change will lead to a ripple of other changes, are not part of conventional wisdom.**

If criticized, agree you were "wrong" or "misguided," but continue to do what you believe is best.

•Use "constructive payback," in which criticism from your partner is met with your "inadvertent" mistakes and "forgetfulness" (being late, stupid, inefficient) that bother your partner and make your partner's life more difficult. This indirectly expresses your anger and resentment and lets your partner know that he or she can't get away with being abusive.

Communication Problems

Three common communication patterns often make individuals unhappy. The first is lack of communication, in which one partner feels distress concerning the other's unwillingness or inability to talk about things. Unlike most other problems, the roles in this pattern consistently divide along gender lines; most often, the male partner is seen as relatively silent and the female partner distressed about it.

IN DEALING WITH AN UNCOMMUNICATIVE PARTNER:

•Do something that's a noticeable change from your previous strategies. Become less available for conversation and do not try hard to initiate or maintain discussion. Cut it short when it does start. This not only removes but reverses all pressure on the male partner. And it gives the female partner more control. The entire pattern is changing, and the power shifts.

•Interpret silence in a positive way: "We are so close we don't always have to be talking." "I feel good when you're quiet because I know that means everything is all right between us." This negates any power your partner may be expressing through silence.

•Focus less on the relationship and more on satisfying yourself. When you do things for yourself, you need less from others in the way of attention and assurance.

A second common communication problem involves a pattern in which one partner is consistently sad or negative—and verbalizes it—and the other is distressed by the complaints and frustrated in his or her attempts to help. Ordinarily, the complaint has at least some basis in fact—a life circumstance has given the person cause to feel depressed or pessimistic. Unfortunately, most people faced with a chronic complainer become cheerleaders; they assume that encouragement and information of a positive nature will help. But the complainer interprets the cheerleading as lack of understanding. Another losing strategy is ignoring the complaining so that the gates of negativism are never opened. Both strategies wind up intensifying the problem.

IN DEALING WITH A
CHRONIC COMPLAINER:

•Accept, agree, and encourage the complainer's position.

•Encourage complaining rather than trying to avoid it.

•Honestly express any negative opinions you have on the topic being complained about. (Do not express any positive opinions.) Initiate topics of complaint at every opportunity. This gives the complainer the freedom of choice to discuss other issues and positive feelings.

A third communication problem is an accuser-denyer pattern that frequently evolves when one partner accuses the other of lying. Lying may—or may not—actually be involved.

IN DEALING WITH AN ACCUSER:

•Don't explain or defend. This extremely simple solution is effective because the situation doesn't escalate—it's hard to argue with someone who doesn't argue back—and you do not appear guilty by reason of protesting too much. Accusations are often made to get an argument started; if one partner does not go for the bait, the accusation strategy stops working and is eventually dropped.

•Go one step further and reflect the insecurity of the accuser. "You're afraid that I'm having an affair." "You're concerned that you're not attractive to me anymore." "You're feeling insecure about my love for you."

Sex and Jealousy

Key aspects of couples' sex lives have little to do with what happens in bed. Jealousy and trust issues in a relationship are a prime example. Both involve one partner' suspecting that the other isn't be-

ing completely loyal or truthful. And in both, the partner who is the object of the jealous feelings or mistrust cannot remove the problem. Many different real or imagined actions can destroy trust, and jealousy certainly isn't the always the result of a real indiscretion. But sometimes it is.

An affair is a very difficult occurrence for a relationship to survive. It is much like surviving the death of a loved one; the relationship as it was before is forever lost. As in coming to grips with a death, the partner who must accept the "loss" needs to grieve, experience, and express the entire range of emotions associated with the affair.

Unfortunately, the partner who had the affair rarely facilitates this grieving process, Rather he or she tries to handle the situation with minimization, avoidance, and indignation, believing that the subject will die if ignored. "It was only sex, not love." "It's over, let's get on with our lives." "It meant nothing to me."

This strategy usually backfires because the other partner, already feeling hurt and angry at the betrayal, now feels dismissed and misunderstood—and brings up the affair even more. Already feeling defensive through guilt, the partner who had the affair gets more defensive ("How long do I have to go on like this?") The mistaken belief that the issue of the affair should be resolved quickly allows this partner to feel wronged, leading greater distance between partners.

IN DEALING WITH A JEALOUS PARTNER:

• Encourage the partner who feels betrayed to express jealous feelings, and listen nondefensively. This allows the affair to be treated as significant; the betrayed partner has no need to emphasize how important and painful an issue it is. And by encouraging discussion of the affair, the agenda of the person who feels betrayed is given priority. This restores some of the

lost power and control without necessitating a prolonged power struggle.

•Initiate at every opportunity discussion of actions or situation that provoke jealousy.

•Keep an exceptionally detailed diary of all your daily activities and recite it at length to your partner every day—in a matter-of-fact fashion. This breaks the questioning-defensiveness cycle. The information overload makes it less likely that accusations of giving partial or incomplete data will be made.

Of all the issues that are related to what happens in the bedroom, sexual frequency is the one about which we hear the most complaints. Usually, one partner decides that there is a problem—usually the partner who wants more sex. He or she begins by stating the problem and directly requesting more frequent sex. The verbal response from the partner is usually encouraging ("Okay, let's try to get together more often"), but the behavior frequently remains the same. At this point, the partner who feels deprived pulls out all the stops—adult movies, sexy clothing, candlelight dinners. The partner being pursued feels pressured and backs away further. The pursuer feels unloved and rejected, and may accuse his or her partner of being involved with someone else.

IN DEALING WITH A SEXUALLY
DISINTERESTED PARTNER:

•Remove all pressure to have sex, but increase nonsexual affection.

•Increase the time spent together in mutually enjoyable, nonsexual activities. This helps put sex back in a healthy perspective by focusing on the enjoyable parts of a relationship.

•Become less available for sex, rather than always being ready and eager. This reduces perceived pressure and frees your partner to accept the role of pursuer.

Inside the Heart of Marital

Violence

Why is it that *people* are more likely to be *assaulted,* even *killed,* in their own homes at the hands of *someone they love*?

Hara Estroff Marano

There must be some mistake. I am standing in a small, dingy, windowless chamber fitted with what appear to be two old wooden electric chairs cast off a grade B movie set. They are even electrically rigged, the wires running down under the cheap carpet and across the hall to a console hidden in a closet-size space. I have flown 3,000 miles and hiked across the huge University of Washington campus to . . . This? I was expecting something flashier, some tangible sign of the drama playing in here when the research is in session.

"This much I will tell you," one of its proprietors, psychologist Neil Jacobson, Ph.D., had said conspiratorially months before, "anger has nothing to do with it." He was talking about domestic violence—specifically, the latest "hard" evidence from this laboratory, where he is recording every physiologic flicker of violently distressed couples as they light into topics that, at other times and places, generally lead to blows.

In the scheme of things, this is not a politically correct thing to do (focusing on the couple relationship is seen by some as implying that women somehow collaborate in their own abuse). It is possibly even a dangerous thing to do. But it appears to contradict the little anyone really knows about spouse abuse—that anger is to batterers what acrylics are to painters.

It is hard to believe that this dreary little room is one of the major fronts in a revolution now unfolding in thinking about and looking at why men batter the women they love. It is part of a seismic

shift in the whole field of psychology— a new awareness that all behavior unfolds in a specific context, and it is necessary to understand the context in order to understand the behavior.

For decades, the puzzle of spouse abuse has been summed up in the question, "Why do they stay?" As if that were all there is to it—the manufacture of victims of a gender hierarchy that encourages men to demonstrate their dominance. But the question is misogynistic; it fails to grapple with a very obvious fact: that between batterer and batteree there is a relationship, and a very powerful one. It has a dynamic that stubbornly defies what is well known at the nation's 1,300 shelters for abused women: the vast majority of battered women return to their abusers. If intellectual curiosity is not enough of a reason, then certainly protecting women requires that their marriages finally be probed.

Researchers and clinicians (many of them hard-core feminists) now peering into the very heart of domestic violence find, even to their own surprise, that it is far more complex, and far less dark, than most had imagined. In a turnabout that might just as well serve as a symbol of all else that is now being learned, the crucial question turns out not to be "Why do they (the women) stay? Rather, it is what makes them (the men) so vulnerable, so dependent?"

Violence may indeed reflect patriarchy run amok and men may indeed

use violence to exert power and control over women. But there's a dirty little secret in the world of domestic violence: It almost always arises from feelings of *powerlessness*. Men experience their own use of force as a loss of control. Abusers do not enjoy being abusive.

"These men give women *too much* power—to take care of all their needs, to solve their loneliness, for example. They expect women to be their psychic nurses," reports family therapist Virginia Goldner, Ph.D. This is just one of the many paradoxes one must now entertain about domestic violence to see it clearly.

In the whole new picture of domestic violence that is emerging, spouse abuse looks a lot like a very strange onion— the product of many forces operating and interacting at many levels between an individual and his environment. There are intimations of influences at the biological level, including disturbances in the activity of the neurotransmitter serotonin, high levels of testosterone production prompting men to aggression, possibly frank brain damage from head injury. There are elements that work at the cognitive level, like a propensity to misread social cues and attribute hostile intent to others. There are defects in interpersonal skills, like a lack of ability to deescalate the conflict that is inevitable in relationships. There are intrapsychic deficits—a hypersensitivity to abandonment, inability to control negative emotions, and poor impulse control. And,

From *Psychology Today*, November/December 1993, pp. 48-53, 76-78, 91. © 1993 by Sussex Publishers, Inc. Reprinted by permission.

of course, there are general cultural contributors like the traditional role structure of marriage. Just when one thing is true at one level, its opposite appears to be true at another.

Among the many provocative findings shaping a new, more holistic view of domestic violence:

• Apart from the coercion, the relationship between batterer and partner has a positive side. It is typically a highly romantic and deeply loving relationship. Both are drawn by the fantasy and reality of having found acceptance for the first time in their lives and feel their relationship is "special," a unique haven from an outside world. "They are Hansel and Gretel," says Goldner, a faculty member at New York's Ackerman Institute for Family Therapy.

• Not every interaction, not even every argument, in an abusive marriage is violent. Some issues turn out to be uniquely troublesome in these relationships. Violent men seem to have deficits in processing social information in specific situations—typically, they negatively misinterpret their wives' behavior when, for example, she pays attention to anyone else. Such situations induce an inner panic because they hint at rejection.

"These men are very dependent on their wives," explains Amy Holtzworth-Munroe, Ph.D., a psychologist at Indiana University. "They constantly want their wives' attention. If they sense signs of rejection, they experience it as a real threat. Violence is related to jealousy and security of attachment. If they think their partners might leave, they become violent."

• But all batterers are not alike. For Neil Jacobson, family psychologist and behaviorist, studies in which he conducts blow-by-blow analyses of arguments turn up at least one "very scary" group of men—about 20 percent of batterers—for whom violence does not seem to be the result of rage at all. He calls them "autonomic athletes." Unlike other people, and unlike the majority of batterers, they do not show any signs of nervous system arousal in situations of conflict—their heart rates go down even when engaging in the clashes that give rise to abuse.

"There is a disconnection between their physiology and their behavior—they are inwardly calm but outwardly contemptuous, belligerent, demeaning, verbally abusive. This dissociation of

physiology from emotion is extraordinary—no one's ever seen such a thing before. We think it may be a clue to the disorder of battering. It may be due to some traumatic experience in early childhood. Most of these men all witnessed high levels of violence among their parents."

• Without deflecting responsibility for male violence, it is possible that batterers are also somehow biologically different. "I started from a straight feminist perspective," reports family therapist Gillian Walker, M.S.W., also at the Ackerman Institute. "I've had to broaden the lens as I go. I'm struck by how many of these men are learning-disabled. Or how often they had their heads pounded into the ground as kids."

One psychologist finds that head injury increases by sixfold the likelihood a man is to physically abuse his partner. It is the most significant predictor there is.

• The stereotype of battered wives as fragile, passive, placating, docile, and self-deprecating does not do justice to their actual role in relationships. Women prove to be the more functional members of these couples. What's more, during confrontations, they reciprocate anger and contempt tit for tat and don't back down. They do not act as if they fear being beaten later. But no matter what they try, once the violence starts, nothing they do can stop it. "The wives are beaten," says Seattle's Jacobson, "but not beaten into submission."

• Most women in battering relationships are themselves violent, a fact that has proved very politically troublesome to victims' advocates. But Jacobson's studies provide powerful proof that their violence occurs only in response to their partners' attacks. Fear turns out to be the telltale emotion. "Only the husband's violence produces fear in a partner," reports Jacobson. "He has the unique capability to subjugate his partner by battering. That's why I can't believe in husband abuse."

It's hard to make sense of statistics about domestic violence. Advocates of all stripes lob statistics that verge on the hysterical—it is increasing, it always increases, and violence always escalates in a relationship: Today's pushes are tomorrow's punches. However, the need to stop domestic violence is not diminished by what the research community accepts as fact: The incidence of domestic violence is *not* increasing. It

has always been high; only an idealized view of the family has prevented us from seeing it until recently. There is no central reporting mechanism on spouse abuse, but two respectable national surveys suggest it *decreased* slightly between 1975 and 1985.

No matter how long domestic abuse has thrived behind closed doors—and it thrives on isolation and privacy as well as on patriarchal attitudes, rigid gender arrangements, acceptance of aggression in other contexts, economic hardship, and other potent stressors—it is increasingly less tolerated today. Rising public and professional interest could make it a watershed issue in American society. It could wind up as the proving ground for a new way of thinking about many complex social problems, where we accept, finally, that major problems almost always have a social context but that doesn't mean they have a social cause. As Virginia Goldner and colleagues at the Ackerman Institute are proving, it is indeed possible to explain, even treat, abusive behavior while regarding it as inexcusable and holding perpetrators fully responsible for their actions.

G oldner and Gillian Walker inhabit a very sharp edge in psychotherapy. They are developing a "feminist/systemic approach to the conjoint therapy of battering." In other words, they believe battering can best be stopped by seeing couples and helping them reconstruct the relationship—without letting batterers get away with a damn thing. The emphasis is on *feminist* and *conjoint,* because in traditional feminist circles, the two are incompatible. In fact, in some states where advocates have had a strong hand in shaping legislation—California, Colorado, Massachusetts among them—conjoint therapy is illegal for spouse abuse.

They jumped in because there are many battered women who want to keep the relationship, albeit without the violence. "How can the victims of violence who have elected conjoint treatment speak and enjoy justice when perpetrators' truths are judged equal?" as systemic thinking requires, Goldner asks. But she's a respected feminist who, after much soul-searching, rejected the polarities of either/or thinking about domestic violence in favor of "the more difficult, but more hopeful, stance of both/and." She has reconciled herself to "recognizing the value of competing and contradictory perspectives." As any good family therapist knows—as does any honest married soul—all relationships inherently involve competing perspectives.

Goldner's absolute requirement is that abuse must stop before therapy can begin, and the men must take complete responsibility for the battering—something they are always trying to foist off on their partners.

Goldner and Walker begin by telling a couple, "We are experts in working with this problem and in determining who this therapy is suitable for. We are saying, by implication, 'We're not yet in the role of therapists, we're consultants, evaluating you to see whether you're suitable to be our clients.' This isn't a trick; we devised it as a way to avoid getting involved in unsuitable cases. But it unexpectedly proved a powerful therapeutic tool. Couples know we're the court of last resort, we're experienced, and we're as good as it gets. They feel they are on trial. They want to pass the test."

The test is that the violence must stop, unconditionally, and there must be a bond, a loving side to the relationship. Of course they secure the woman's safety, which may mean having her live for a time at a shelter.

"What distinguishes my work is that I am looking at key features of the romantic relationship between violent men and their partners. It is an open secret that partners go back to each other. The women can't really explain why they stay with someone who hurts them," says Goldner—until the therapists point out that there is also a loving side to the relationship. This is itself an important step in the therapy; it strips away the shame women feel about being in an abusive relationship. That, in turn, helps restore a woman's dignity, and nullifies the binding power of what has been experienced until now as a secret alliance. The woman is then free to begin fighting for new terms in the relationship.

Others have described a honeymoon phase after the violence, a redemptive moment both partners experience as a bond. But Goldner feels the partners are drawn more by the fantasy and reality of having found acceptance. "Each feels the other knows them more profoundly and accepts them better than anyone before."

That, of course, is a commentary on what went on before. "Almost all the men we've treated come from families where there was physical violence. The women don't necessarily come from violent households but from families where they were unmothered. The unmothered girl and the abused boy are two lost souls who don't trust the world outside. The paradox is they only feel safe together." This romanticism works until real life enters. Say, he wants sex and she doesn't.

In their therapy, Goldner and Walker have developed a line of relentless questioning from multiple angles that separates the "many strands of meaning, memory, and feeling" that they find "packed" into the explosive moment. "When a man says 'I just saw black' or 'I felt a fire in my veins,' the specific conflicts are unavailable to him. But they are there."

Repeated inquiries about his life story capture the violence in slow motion. This technique gets the men to see not only that they have made a choice to hit, but they are full of conflicts that center on deep ambivalences about gender roles. These men are themselves victims of "gendered premises of masculinity." They are engaged in constant denial of "feminine" vulnerabilities they try to hide even from themselves.

"Indeed," Goldner has written, "in remembering the escalation that precedes the violent moment, the men often describe an internal struggle between unmanly feelings and macho feelings occurring in rapid-fire alternation." Only by unpacking a man's globalized experience of rage, unraveling the sequence of steps that end in violence, can he begin to see the issues that ignite his fury and begin to take charge of his reactivity.

"We see that some large vulnerability activates them into the abusive rage. There is a deep disturbance in the person, and he believes it is the female's job to soothe him, to keep him at bay. He sees her job as to make him feel powerful, to attend to him, to meet all his needs, when he wants. If not, that's when there is violence.

"These men hate it when their wives go out with friends. Anything that separates her from him means he has to deal with the large, empty space in his interior. We insist that she has to have a life of her own and that he will survive. We pull them apart psychologically. We address his psychological experience, that she has too much power, too much power to hurt him. We'll tell him, 'You're relying too much on her. You need to take care of yourself. As long as you give her the power to solve your loneliness, you're giving her too much power and you'll hit her. You must solve that alone."

Seven years into the Gender and Violence Project, Goldner and Co. think they've got a form of therapy down pat that reliably gets the violence to stop yet gives couples what they want—each other, but not at the cost of their selves. They see a couple three or four times on a consultation basis, in which time the violence is teased apart until the men can grasp what they have done—and what they have done to their partner. Then the couples are seen about six times in a treatment mode. Of all the couples they have seen (they have worked intensively with about 30) there has been only one instance of hitting that occurred after treatment started. "And that was during a six-week hiatus in treatment over the holidays," Goldner is quick to point out.

But there are questions whether this therapy model is usable by others. Goldner has an unmistakable presence that may help deter violence in the couples she treats. Still, she is now trying to teach what she does to another set of therapists. If she succeeds, "We will be able to send this therapy out to other mental-health centers."

While Goldner's work is dazzlingly insightful, to say nothing of intellectually demanding, researchers leap to suggest the possibility of flaws in her observations. She doesn't use comparison groups; as a result, elements that appear to be linked to violence could in fact be due to extreme marital distress, a typical feature of violent relationships.

Indiana's Amy Holtzworth-Munroe is also looking closely, though scientifically scrupulously, at the men in violent couples. She measures them against two comparison groups—one of men in couples who report similar levels of conflict and distress but do not resort to violence, and one of happy couples. Still, there is remarkable resonance in the findings.

Whatever else leads a man to violence, it operates only in certain *specific* situations, says the Indiana psychologist. In her research, she asks men what they would say or do in response to certain problematic marital situations presented by audiotape. These test the skills people use to decode social information and generate appropriate responses.

A competent response is "one that would solve the current problem and make problems of the same type less likely in the future." Like negotiating mutually agreeable compromises and explaining thoughts and feelings. Threatening statements or behaviors, name-calling, and sarcasm lead the list of "incompetent" responses.

Only the maritally violent men provide incompetent responses to situations involving jealousy—"at a social gathering, your wife is talking to another man and they are smiling and laughing." Or "you receive a phone call from a man who asks for your wife, says he is her friend, but will not leave a name or number."

In such situations, violent men consistently misinterpret their wife's actions as having been done *with hostile intent*. This is an extraordinarily important piece of information to have, not just because it points to a distinguishing flaw in these men. But because attributing hostile intent to a wife's behavior—to anyone's behavior—gives men a way to justify violence. It becomes the grease for the machinery by which they try to shift blame: "She was trying to hurt me/provoke me...."

The violent men also do not generate competent responses in situations that represent rejection or abandonment from the wife—a vignette, say, in which she is not interested in her husband's sexual advances or wants to spend time with friends. Nor do they do well in situations where a wife challenges or embarrasses her husband— she questions his judgment or wants him to cancel plans with friends.

"The data show that violent men repeatedly go into abusive relationships," says Holtzworth-Munroe. "That's not so true for the women. The husband is the problem. What we're finding is that we have to fix these men at the individual level as well as at the societal and couple level. These men do not have the social skills to participate in the culture."

She has proof their problems carry over to nonmarital situations as well. When the maritally violent men listen to vignettes of assorted nonmarital situations—involving bosses, coworkers, and friends—the same deficits in social skills show up. "They have a general deficit, although the marital situations are more arousing."

Holtzworth-Munroe sees the rejection–jealousy issue as one of the keys to domestic violence. "These men appear to be more dependent on their wives. If they sense signs of rejection, they experience it as a real threat. We are now applying measures of attachment. Violent men are more preoccupied with the marital relationship

It's possible to treat abusive behavior while deeming it inexcusable and holding perpetrators responsible.

than other men. They have a narrower focus on their wife. They have few outside friends. They especially rely on their wives for comfort. If they think she might leave, they become violent.

"My work implies that these men have screwed-up relationships with their own parents. They lack the ability to trust, something that comes out of secure early attachment" to a parent or other responsive caregiver. As a result, they fear loss, misinterpret neutral situations as threatening, see hostile intent when it doesn't exist.

There is a certain urgency to itemizing those situations that put men at greatest risk for violent responses. "We need to know where to focus our energy," says Holtzworth-Munroe. "It's clear from the evidence that most treatments don't help. Probably they are applied too late, after violence is a set behavioral pattern. Once violence is used, it becomes reinforced—because it works. The men get what they want, though they may feel bad about doing it."

Neil Jacobson's study of the marriages in which domestic violence takes place is entirely without precedent. It is the first study to include people with severe levels of physical violence, numbering 57 such couples. It also employs two comparison groups: 32 couples who have never used physical violence but whose marriages are equally unhappy, and 22 couples who are happily married.

What's more, he is looking directly at the couples during their arguments. He has them attempt to work out two problems they identify as troublesome. They do this for an intense 15 minutes while tethered to the aforementioned electric chairs by wires that monitor their physiology. Overhead videocameras record every word, every nuance of facial affect, voice tone, posture, and gesture.

Marital violence, Jacobson finds, is not just an extreme form of argument. It's something of a different genre altogether. The batterers look different from other men. They do things other men don't do. In arguments they are highly emotionally aggressive—they are belligerent, contemptuous, demeaning. They lack any empathy for their partners. And in some ways, their wives are different, too.

Just as the Eskimos allegedly have 28 words for "snow," Jacobson feels that "anger" doesn't do justice to this emotion. "Anger is common in unhappy couples. We find there are specific facets of anger and they differentiate the violent from the nonviolent."

In his atlas of anger, there's garden-variety anger, a pure expression of affect with no attempt to control, as in "That really pisses me off!" There's belligerence, a taunting attempt to produce a negative response in another: "What are you gonna do about my drinking?! You don't like it, huh? Well, what are you gonna do about it?" There's contempt, full of demeaning and insulting remarks. There's disgust. And critical disapproval. There's demandingness and control, with hostile affect and tone.

"Anger is shared by both partners in violent relationships," says Jacobson. "Even the provocative types of anger. They taunt. They demean. They hurl contempt at each other even in nonviolent arguments."

The wives of domestic violence, for their part, are very, very feisty. Once an argument is started, they don't back down. They greet negative statements with negative responses—what psychologists call negative reciprocity. Like their husbands, they don't deescalate an argument if one gets started. "These women don't look anything like the passive trauma victims others have described," Jacobson reported at the recent convention of the American Psychological Association. "This is a more flattering portrait of the victims of wife abuse. They look courageous."

That, however, is the view from outside. Internally, things are not always what they seem, Jacobson discovered in a series of studies conducted with John M. Gottman, Ph.D. The wives of violent men are highly aroused physiologically. Their heart rate shoots up, just as one would expect of someone engaged in angry conflict. But, much to Jacobson's surprise, among the violent men, heart rates actually *go down* during discussion of conflicts.

In the normal response to conflict, the autonomic nervous system is activated.

The cardiovascular system turns on. Heart rate goes up. In a subgroup of the violent men—12 of 57—there is an extraordinary divergence between behavior and physiology. Behaviorally, they are full of anger—belligerent, dominating, verbally abusive. But internally they are exceedingly calm. Those who are the most calm physiologically are the most belligerent and contemptuous, and the most abusive verbally. They are also most likely to be violent outside the marriage as well as in it; many have arrest records. And they are most likely to have a family history of violence.

These men are not sensation-seeking, engaging in explosive behavior to get aroused; they are not underaroused to begin with. "They are gaining autonomic control before striking in an emotionally aggressive manner," says Jacobson. "They are like pythons. These men are scary."

Jacobson regards the disconnection between the physiological and emotional as a clue to a core defect in batterers. "It may be due to the early trauma of being around a violent environment. That could occur through some early, emotionally traumatic experience, or it could be a consequence of being violent. Or it may be the result of head trauma." At the hands of people whose loving is supposed to be protective.

Jacobson has spotlighted a way that violence—violence: a behavior!—can ricochet from generation to generation as assertively as a rogue gene. It's possible that these men are so deeply, irrevocably, wounded, changed by experience, that they are even beyond the help of therapy. "Not every problem that exists is appropriate for psychotherapy," notes Jacobson.

The deceleration in heart rate in the face of a stressful situation also suggests that for some men, violence may not be a problem of impulse control at all, which is the traditional view. Rather, Jacobson speculates that the batterers are deliberately, manipulatively controlling what goes on in the marital interaction. "The only other known state in which there is a deceleration in heart rate is focused attention. These men look like they are being very attentive and focused."

In domestic violence, says Jacobson, "Women are fighting for survival and men are fighting for control."

Equally startling to Jacobson was the discovery that heart rate went down, too, among a subgroup of men in distressed but nonviolent marriages. These men, however, were also more emotionally aggressive than the other nonviolent men. "We suspect that there may be some continuity from verbal to physical abuse. It looks like we're tapping into an underlying substrate of aggression that may predict who becomes violent over time."

Two-year follow-up evaluations should reveal whether the nonviolent dissociators become physically violent with time, as the psychologist predicts.

It is an axiom of family relations that women are the barometers of relationship distress. Normally in unhappy marriages, couples develop a communication pattern in which the woman tries to engage her partner while he retreats. She is seeking change. In this demand/withdraw pattern, the demand role signifies dissatisfaction. In violent relationships, there is a switch of roles and the husband shares the dissatisfied role. When wives are the dissatisfied partner, they get angry. When husbands are dissatisfied, the implications are different. They get violent.

How is it that the portrait Jacobson paints of battered wives—feisty, angry, returning negative statements, and extremely aroused internally—can differ so sharply from the conventional one of women silenced into a pathetic state of helplessness as a result of posttraumatic stress?

Jacobson also sees helplessness among battered wives but thinks it reflects their emotional responsiveness. "Usually you see people who are angry *or* psychologically distressed. These women are angry *and* distressed. They are verbally and emotionally aggressive. But they are also defensive, frightened, and sad. *All* their negative affects are heightened simultaneously." The helplessness these women feel, he believes, comes as a result of physical trauma and the threat of trauma, and it is manifested by the activation of all of their negative emotions at the same time; it's confusing and debilitating. Plus the fact that once violence starts, nothing they do, even withdrawing, stops the physical abuse. In fact, attempts to withdraw may even provoke an escalation of the violence.

When psychologist Alan Rosenbaum, Ph.D., arrived several years ago at the University of Massachusetts Medical Center to run the domestic violence research and treatment program, he was required to take a medical history in all abuse cases. Before long, he noticed a distinct pattern. Among a surprising number of the cases of marital injury he was recording an early history of head injury.

Rosenbaum looked at 31 consecutive admissions to the marital violence program. In 19 of them—61 percent—there was in fact a history of significant head injury: loss of consciousness, a diagnosed concussion, or postconcussion symptoms.

That was enough to warrant a grant for a more rigorous study. When the results were tabulated, abusive men were significantly more likely to have had head injury—53 percent, versus 25 percent among nonviolent men from unhappy marriages and 16 percent in the happily married.

"Head injury increases the chance of marital aggression by a factor of six. That makes it the most significant predictor of marital violence that there is," Rosenbaum says. He's now following the fate of two groups of men—one with a history of head injury, the other with orthopedic injury. And he'll be measuring the incidence of marital violence in both groups over the next two years.

At the same time, Rosenbaum is exploring the possibility that, among domestically violent men, there is some defect in the regulation of the brain chemical serotonin. A neurotransmitter widely dispersed in the brain, serotonin is thought to influence much of mental life. There is evidence to suggest that high levels of serotonin correlate with dominant behavior, while low serotonin levels are implicated in anxiety, general aggression, as well as impulsive behavior.

Psychologist Roland Maiuro, Ph.D., of the University of Washington, head of one of country's leading domestic violence clinics, has been giving batterers a drug known to influence serotonin-sensitive paths—Paxil, first cousin of Prozac. "It seems to enhance the resiliency of these men," Maiuro reports. "They're less reactive. When confronted with the same 'provocations,' they're not activating as much. But they still need to work on cognitive and behavioral repertoires. As we say, there are no skills in pills."

A controlled study of the effect of Paxil on domestically violent men is about to get under way.

"Right now, this is not a very politically correct model of domestic violence," Rosenbaum offers. "But I'm not suggesting that marital violence is caused by biologic factors. We have to look at causes at several levels and see whether there are factors that make some men unable to regulate their impulses, that increase the likelihood of an aggressive response to any kind of negative stimulus, such as stress.

"Marital aggression is very complex. We can't say there is one factor. No one factor applies to 100 percent of men. People become aggressive for a variety of reasons. These are some."

After He Hits Her

This study examines the interactional dynamics following woman battering, and specifically addresses the question of whether, as time goes on, male batterers are less likely to offer accounts or aligning actions (i.e., apologies, excuses, justifications, and dismissals) for acts of violence, and whether female victims are less likely to honor the men's accounts. Based on in-depth interviews with 50 white women who had come to a battered women's shelter, the study finds that abusers generally are not likely to stop accounting for their violent behavior but that shelter victims are progressively less likely to honor the accounts. It also is found that, as time goes on, men are more likely to blame their victims for the battering. Similarities and differences between these findings and the research results used to support Walker's (1979, 1984) cycle theory of violence are discussed. Implications for practitioners working with batterers and victims are outlined.

Jane H. Wolf-Smith and Ralph LaRossa

Jane H. Wolf-Smith is an Associate Professor in the Department of Social Sciences, Gainesville College, Gainesville, GA 30503. Ralph LaRossa is a Professor in the Department of Sociology, Georgia State University, Atlanta, GA 30303.

For some time now, researchers and activists in the battered women's movement have realized that "acts of violence" are not discrete acts of physical aggression but are patterns of oppression, occurring over time and including events leading up to as well as following the use of force, itself. Thus, for example, in what may be the most widely cited theory of the pattern or cycle of violence, there is said to be at least three phases—the tension building phase, the acute battering phase, and the loving contrition phase—which ensnare women in a web of punishment and deceit (see Walker, 1979, 1984).

While much has been written about the structural and situational factors which precipitate violence toward women and, as more victims come forward, an all-too-vivid picture of both the range and severity of force in intimate relationships is being acquired, little still is known about

The authors wish to thank the women who participated in the study for their willingness to share their experiences; the staff of the battered women's shelter for their cooperation in arranging the interviews; and Phillip W. Davis and Paula L. Dressel for their comments on earlier versions of this article.

Key Words: cycle theory of violence, family violence, victimization of women.

what happens immediately after the incident—that is, "after he hits her."

Drawing on in-depth interviews with 50 white women who had been abused by their husbands or male companions, and who had come to a battered women's shelter for refuge, this study examines the interactional dynamics following acts of abuse, giving special attention to both the "acts of contrition" (and other verbal strategies) that men use and the kinds of responses that women give to these strategies. The research combines a theoretically informed approach to the concept of contrition with a methodological focus on the sequence of abuse. That is, from the beginning, the intent was to place "acts of contrition" within the class of theoretical concepts variously referred to as "techniques of neutralization" (Sykes & Matza, 1957), "remedial interchanges" (Goffman, 1971), "accounts" (Scott & Lyman, 1968), or "aligning actions" (Stokes & Hewitt, 1976); and, from the beginning, the goal was to examine whether the verbal strategies that batterers used the first time were different from the verbal strategies used later on.

The interest in whether men "repented" in different ways as time went on was sparked by the finding, reported in several previous studies, that men are likely to repent after the first incident of abuse but *increasingly less likely* to repent after subsequent incidents (see Dobash & Dobash, 1984; Ferraro & Johnson, 1983; Walker, 1984). What this means in terms of the cycle theory of violence is that,

after a while, men choose to "delete" the third phase.

If, indeed, abusive men are less contrite as time goes on, this would indicate a shift in their perception of their violent acts. The fact that they would repent for their behavior the first time would indicate some acknowledgment on their part that what they did would be met with disapproval. Their lesser tendency to repent after the 2nd, 10th, or 50th time would indicate that they had begun to "normalize" their violent behavior (i.e., see their violence within the bounds of social acceptability).

The logic here is that deviance and repentance go hand in hand. If individuals feel that they have done something wrong, they often will repent for their apparent misconduct. If, on the other hand, they feel that they are acting correctly, they will not repent. Students, for example, often will talk about why they were late for class, but rarely, if ever, talk about why they were on time (Goffman, 1971; Scott & Lyman, 1968; Stokes & Hewitt, 1976; Sykes & Matza, 1957).

Stopping violence requires an all-out effort to cancel the hitting license. If what happens in abusive relationships is that the license is not only not cancelled but actually renewed and possibly upgraded (i.e., defined as more "normal" than before), battered women and their advocates need to know this. Understanding the part that "acts of contrition" play in the cycle of abuse thus will go a long way toward helping victims of abuse.

From *Family Relations*, Vol. 41, No. 3, July 1992, pp. 324-329. © 1992 by The National Council on Family Relations, 3989 Central Avenue, NE, Suite 550, Minneapolis, MN 55421. Reprinted by permission.

Theoretical Rationale

A Typology of Aligning Actions

From a symbolic interactionist point of view, an act of contrition is *one* example of an *aligning action,* offered in the hope of mending, if only temporarily, a break between socially established norms and misconduct (Stokes & Hewitt, 1976). By offering aligning actions, social actors give neutral or positive meanings to behaviors that are "out of line." If, in turn, the aligning actions are "honored" by the offended party or parties (i.e., if others give the impression that they attach the same neutral or positive meanings to the apparent misconduct), then the aligning actions have the effect of "containing" or "minimizing" what otherwise might have been viewed as a relationship-threatening set of events.

When aligning actions are offered after deviant behavior, they are referred to as *accounts* (Scott & Lyman, 1968). When they are offered before a misdeed—or in the anticipation of a misdeed—they are referred to as *disclaimers* (Hewitt & Stokes, 1975). Given the interest here on what happens "afterward," the focus is on how men account rather than disclaim abusive behavior.

According to Hunter (1984), ex post facto aligning actions generally fall into four categories. Applied to woman battering, what differentiates the four categories is whether or not the batterer (a) makes the case that the violence in question deserves to be viewed as a negative act, and/or (b) says that he is responsible for the violence.

The first category is an apology. An *apology* signifies the batterer's acceptance of both the negative evaluation of the act and responsibility for the act, itself. Regret is also evident in this aligning action: "I know I shouldn't have slapped you. I'm sorry." Apologies are apparently what Walker (1979, 1984) was referring to when she talked about a "loving contrition phase" in her cycle theory of violence.

> In [the loving contrition] phase, the batterer constantly behaves in a charming and loving manner. He is usually sorry for his actions in the previous phases, and he conveys contriteness to the battered woman. He begs her forgiveness and promises her that he will never do it again. (Walker, 1979, p. 65)

> The batterer may apologize profusely, try to assist his victim, show kindness and remorse, and shower her with gifts and promises. (Walker, 1984, p. 96)

Being contrite or apologizing, however, is not the only account available to abusers. Other "third phase" strategies include the dismissal, the excuse, and the justification.

The *dismissal* is the opposite of an apology. Its intent is to invalidate both responsibility for the act and the negative evaluation of the act: "You pushed me to the limit—besides, you need to know who's boss around here."

Then there is the excuse. When using an *excuse,* the batterer accepts the negative evaluation of the act, but denies responsibility for the act: "That was a lousy thing to do—but I've been under a lot of pressure from my boss."

Finally, there is the justification. With the *justification,* the batterer accepts responsibility for the act but denies its negative evaluation: "I felt I had to do something to keep you from making a stupid decision."

A number of researchers have recognized that efforts on the part of both abusers and victims to account for abusive incidents can include more than apologies or acts of contrition. In one of the earliest studies of violence in the home, Gelles (1974) identified a variety of meanings that abusers gave to their violent acts to "explain" why they were violent—from "She asked for it" (an excuse) to "I tried to knock her to her senses" (a justification). Similarly, Ferraro and Johnson (1983), focusing not on the abusers but on the victims, described how women "rationalized" being abused, saying things like "I asked for it" (an excuse), "He's sick" (also an excuse), and "He didn't injure me" (a justification). Ferraro and Johnson (1983) also demonstrate how these accounts prevented the women from seeking help. Along the same lines, Mills (1985) described the "techniques of neutralization" that battered women use "to help them tolerate violent marriages." Mills (1985) found that one way that women "managed the violence" directed toward them was they used "justifications" (e.g., "compared to others, it seems my problems are small") to "minimiz[e] the significance of their victimization" (p. 109). Finally, Ptacek (1988), in a study of abusive men, discovered that he could classify the bulk of the men's accounts into either excuses or justifications. He also found that the men were more likely to excuse than to justify their behavior.

Drawing on Hunter's (1984) typology and following in the footsteps of Gelles (1974), Ferraro and Johnson (1983), Mills (1985), and Ptacek (1988), this study set out to determine not only whether abusers apologized for hitting their wives but also whether they dismissed, excused, and justified their violent behavior. Because of the interest, too, in whether men stopped using aligning actions as time went on (and with repeated incidents of abuse), the study also was designed to plot the chronological sequence of accounts.

A Typology of Honoring Stances

One might suppose that a victim has only two choices when her abuser offers to apologize for, or explain, his behavior: she can reject the aligning action or she can honor it. During the preinterview stage of the study, however, it was deduced that there are at least four honoring stances that a victim may take in response to an aligning action (or set of aligning actions). The four stances are: reject, pseudohonor, ambivalently honor, and wholeheartedly honor.

When the victim *rejects* the aligning action, she makes it clear by her verbal and nonverbal behavior that the aligning action is not acceptable, and consequently not effective in smoothing the disruption caused by the abuse.

With *pseudohonor,* the victim pretends to honor the account, with both verbal and nonverbal behavior indicating acceptance, but in self-interaction and in subsequent interaction with others she does not accept the aligning action as legitimate.

When the victim *ambivalently honors* the aligning action, there is some degree of hesitation before she acknowledges its legitimacy. Her honoring stance is characterized by uncertainty, in which she is tempted to honor the account but also doubts its legitimacy.

Finally, a *wholehearted honoring* of the aligning action occurs when the victim, without hesitation, gives it legitimacy. She readily accepts whatever account is issued and fully believes its validity.

The question of whether accounts are rejected has also been the subject of several inquiries. Ferraro and Johnson (1983), for example, talked about the shifts in events and perceptions that lead women to begin to reject their abusers' rationalizations; and Giles-Sims (1983) noted how the women in her study seemed to be willing to "forgive and forget" the first abusive incident but not the most recent. As far as it is known, however, no one has developed a typology of honoring stances like the one described above and applied it to abusive situations. In order to have a clear sense of the interactional dynamics in relationships, it is important to recognize the variety of accounts that men employ *and* the variety of honoring stances that women use in response.

To summarize, the object of this study was to examine the verbal strategies that abusive men use to neutralize or negate their violent actions and the honoring stances that women take to parry these accounts. A central concern of the project from the beginning was whether aligning actions and honoring stances change over time.

Methodology

Sample

The 50 women in the sample were all residents of a battered women's shelter located approximately 50 miles from a major urban area. Hypothesizing that communication patterns after abusive behavior might vary across racial lines, and feeling that an adequate analysis of racial variation would require a much larger sample, the decision was made (due to restrictions on time and other resources) to limit the interviewees to white victims.

The average age of the women in the study was 28 years. While the variation in educational levels was from less than 8 years of education to college graduate, the average number of years completed was 11.5. About one fourth of the women were employed outside the home. Seventy-eight percent were married to their abusers, 20% were cohabiting, and 2% were dating the abuser. The average length of the relationship was 6.5 years. Ninety-eight percent of the sample had children, the average number being 2.4. The average family income for this sample was $17,585.

As reported by the women, the average age of the abusers was 30 years. The average number of years of education completed was 10.7. The majority of the abusers were employed in blue-collar jobs involving manual labor.

Interviews

The interviews were conducted by the first author over a 2-year period, beginning in the fall of 1986 and ending in the fall of 1988. The interviews lasted from 1 to 2 hours, with the average interview lasting an hour and a half. In all but one case the women were interviewed during their stay in the shelter. With the women's consent, the interviews were tape-recorded, and eventually transcribed. The 50 interviews resulted in 1,500 pages of transcripts.

In order to gain an interpretive understanding of the women's point of view, the women were encouraged to talk at length and in-depth about what they thought and how they felt about the abuse in their relationships. All were asked to report on three separate incidents of abuse—the first, the most recent, and a middle incident. For the middle incident, the victims were asked to select an abusive incident that occurred about halfway between the first and the most recent—one that "stood out" to them for some reason. The women were especially encouraged to talk about what happened *after* an abusive incident, particularly what the batterers did or said. However, the women were not specifically asked whether the batterers apologized, excused, justified, or dismissed their behavior, nor were they specifically asked whether they honored any accounts offered. When the women happened to mention an aligning action, they were asked to repeat, to the best of their recollection, what the batterer said and what they had said and felt in response. Thus, every effort was made *not to solicit* aligning actions or honoring stances.

Analysis

To classify the women's comments into one category or another, the constant comparative method of qualitative analysis was used (Glaser & Strauss, 1967). As the transcripts were read and reviewed, notations were made in the margins about categories suggested by particular sections of the transcript. Often a single passage was coded in two or more categories. Once the entire transcript was reviewed, selected passages were cut from the transcript and placed in the appropriate files. As additional transcripts were reviewed, incidents that were similar to previously noted ones were filed with them. During this time the files themselves were reviewed. Incidents were compared with other incidents within the same category, and common properties were noted. Gradually, particular categories with their own properties began to emerge. It was then possible to compare newly discovered incidents with the properties of the category, rather than with just similar incidents (see also Lofland & Lofland, 1984; Strauss & Corbin, 1990).

Changes in the nature of aligning actions and in the nature honoring stances were examined both cross-sectionally and developmentally. The cross-sectional analysis involved an examination of distributions across the three time periods, looking at the sample as a whole (N = 50). The developmental analysis involved (a) an examination of the patterns of change in aligning actions as reported by 31 (of the 50) women who provided information on aligning actions on at least two of three incidents; and (b) an examination of patterns of change in honoring stances as reported by 23 (of the 50) women who provided information

on honoring stances on at least two of three incidents. The developmental analysis, in other words, is an analysis of change within specific relationships. Sometimes, the women were not specific about when a particular aligning action or honoring stance was used. When this was the case, the women's descriptions of events were classified under a "general" category.

Limitations

There are several limitations to the study which should be considered when interpreting the results. First, the sample was limited to 50 white shelter residents. The experience of white women may be unlike that of other groups, and battered women who come to shelters may be different from other battered women in important ways. A second limitation is that female victims, rather than male batterers, were asked about the batterers' accounts. Essentially, then, the women provided "second-hand" information about the accounts employed. Third, the women were asked about interactions surrounding abusive incidents that had occurred, for most, years earlier. Ability to recall these early incidents of abuse varied from one respondent to the next, with some clearly recalling the first incident and others remembering little about it. Additionally, subsequent events may have altered the victims' perception and interpretation of these earlier incidents. Fourth, the interviewing strategy employed may have resulted in the women's failure to report both aligning actions and honoring stances surrounding abusive incidents. In an attempt to let the victims "tell their story," the women were not specifically asked whether abusers offered accounts for their behavior or, if offered, whether they were honored. Therefore, it is possible that accounts and honoring stances were employed but not reported by the women because the women were not asked about them.

Aligning Actions Following Woman Battering

Altogether, 139 aligning actions were discussed by the 50 victims. Table 1 presents the cross-sectional analysis of these accounts. As can be seen, 68% of all aligning actions issued after the first incident involved an apology only, while 67% after the middle incident and 42% after the last incident involved an apology only.

Here, for example, is how one victim, a 38-year-old mother of two, described how her husband apologized for his abuse:

Yeah, once I kind of calmed down

Table 1.
Aligning Actions Offered by Batterers After the First, Middle, and Last Incidents of Abuse: Cross-Sectional Analysis (N = 139)

	First		Middle		Last		General		Total	
	Percent	Number	Percent	Number	Percent	Number	Percent	Number	Percent	Number
Apology	68	21	67	14	42	13	30	17	47	65
With excuse	26	8	14	3	29	9	5	3	17	23
Excuse	6	2	14	3	16	5	50	28	27	38
Justification	0	0	5	1	3	1	13	7	6	9
With apology	0	0	0	0	6	2	0	0	1	2
With excuse	0	0	0	0	3	1	2	1	1	2
Dismissal	0	0	0	0	0	0	0	0	0	0
Total	100	31	100	21	100	31	100	56	100	139

Note. Percentages may not add up to 100% due to rounding.

and kind of regrouped. I went back in and when I did he was sitting on the chair, sort of mopey looking. And I walked in and I just stood there and he just jumps up and runs over and starts apologizing and hugging and crying and said he never meant to hit me and he'd never do it again.

Noteworthy is the fact that the percentages for the use of the apology (and only the apology) are very similar to the percentages that Walker (1984) reported. In Walker's (1984) study, apologies dropped from 69% after the first incident to 63% after the middle incident and to 42% after the last incident. At first glance, it thus seems that the results of this study are in accord with Walker's. However, when the categories that include the use of an apology (Apology Only, Apology with Excuse, Justification with Apology) are *combined*, a pattern different from the pattern Walker reported is uncovered. Used alone or in combination with other types of aligning actions, apologies were said to have been offered 94% of the time after the first incident, 81% of the time after the middle incident, and 77% of the time after the last incident.

A similar finding emerges in the developmental analysis. Only 32% of the women (i.e., 10 of the 31 women for whom there was enough information to carry out a developmental analysis) reported that their mates continued to use an apology (and only an apology) across the three incidents. However, when the categories that involve the continued use of the apology, (Apology Only, From Apology to Apology with Excuse, From Apology with Excuse to Apology, From Apology to Apology with Justification, From Apology with Excuse to Apology with Justification) are *combined*, it is found that 74% of individual abusers continued to use apologies with repeated incidents of abuse.

Quite often, in other words, men would offer a *mixture* of aligning actions, blending their apologies with other, more "self-preservative" accounts. One woman, for example, a 30-year-old mother of two

reported how her husband used an apology with an excuse:

There was never an "I'm sorry" for what happened. I mean he hugged and kissed me the next day and told me he was sorry but it wasn't like "I'm sorry, sorry," it was just, "Well you shouldn't have asked for that can opener. You shouldn't have been over there talking to those men." And I'm saying, "Well, all I did was ask for a can opener. I wasn't carrying on a conversation with them."

Another victim, a 21-year-old mother of one, echoed a similar theme of mixed accounts:

I had got [the baby] asleep while he was gone and he come in and laid in my lap and said, "Baby, I'm sorry." He said, "I don't believe I did that." He said, "I am sorry." And then in the next breath he said, "But you shouldn't have been up there [at your mother's house]." And then he turned and said, "I'm sorry, but they shouldn't have said that." He'd say he was sorry and then he'd say, "But …"

Interestingly enough, none of the aligning actions described by the women could be classified as a dismissal. Possibly, batterers will resort to a dismissal rarely and only when they feel that an excuse or justification will not be honored.

Walker's (1984) findings led her to conclude that "over time in a battering relationship … loving contrite behavior declines" (p. 97). Assuming that by "loving contrite behavior" Walker meant apologetic acts, this study failed to replicate Walker's results; according to the women interviewed for this project, while the singular use of the apology declined over time, the apology in conjunction with other aligning actions continued throughout the battering relationship.

Noteworthy, too, is what the interviews reveal about the use of the excuse. An excuse, again, is an account whereby the batterer admits that the abuse is bad

but denies responsibility. For example, a 2l-year-old mother of three reported:

He'll say things like, "If you wouldn't run your smart mouth, I wouldn't do this." And he'll say stuff like, "I don't want to do it, you make me do it." Sometimes you could just say something wrong and not even think you had bothered anybody and he'd just fuss you out or cuss you out, but he just says, "You don't know when to shut your mouth, you just go on and on." He always blames it on me, it's never his fault.

And a 25-year-old mother of four stated:

Like I'd say, "Why do you hit me all the time?" [He'd say] "Shut up, you don't need to ask. If you'd done what I asked in the first place, you never would have gotten it." So it was always like my fault. I asked him to hit me. In a sense, that's what he was saying. She deliberately did this, you know, so that's why she got it.

In Table 1, it can be seen that 6% of all aligning actions used after the first abusive incident involved the excuse alone, while 14% and 16% after the middle and last incident respectively, involved the excuse alone. Not much of a difference. However, when the categories are *combined*, a clearer picture of change emerges. Collapsing all categories that involve the excuse, either used alone or in combination with other aligning actions (Excuses Only, Apology with Excuse, and Justification with Excuse), it is found that 32% of all aligning actions after the first incident involved the use of an excuse, while 28% and 48% involved the use of an excuse after the middle and last incident, respectively. In other words, excuses, although they may be used in combination with other aligning actions, are most likely to be used after the last incident of abuse.

A somewhat similar pattern regarding the use of the excuse emerged in the developmental analysis. Although apologies were the most common account to be used across the three incidents (see

3. RELATIONSHIP MAINTENANCE: Potential Crisis Situations

Table 2.
Honoring Stances Taken by Victims After the First, Middle, and Last Incidents of Abuse: Cross-Sectional Analysis (N = 100)

	First		Middle		Last		General		Total	
	Percent	Number	Percent	Number	Percent	Number	Percent	Number	Percent	Number
Rejection	0	0	0	0	50	13	7	2	15	15
Pseudo	3	1	6	1	42	11	29	8	21	21
Ambivalent	27	8	29	5	4	1	25	7	21	21
Wholehearted	69	20	65	11	4	1	39	11	43	43
Total	100	29	100	17	100	26	100	28	100	100

Note. Percentages may not add up to 100% due to rounding.

Table 1), in 13% of the cases (i.e., 4 of 31), batterers were said to move from an apology to an excuse; and in 23% of the cases (i.e., 7 of 31), batterers were said to move from an apology to an apology with an excuse.

The Honoring of Aligning Actions

Changes in honoring stances were analyzed in the same two ways that changes in the use of aligning actions were analyzed (i.e., cross-sectionally and developmentally). The typology of honoring stances developed prior to the interviews and described earlier (i.e., reject, pseudohonor, ambivalently honor, and wholeheartedly honor) was the coding scheme employed.

Examining the first column in Table 2, it can be seen that 20 of the 29 women who provided information on honoring stances after the first incident wholeheartedly honored the aligning actions offered. A 21-year-old mother of one, for example, said that she genuinely thought her husband's accounts were valid:

I believe he was sorry he did it. He just can't control himself. I believe he does it before he realizes it and sometimes he doesn't even remember doing it the next morning. He'll look at me and say, "I did it again, didn't I?" And I'd say, "Yeah." And he didn't remember doing it. It's just out of his memory. I think in his heart he's really sorry for doing it. He just can't help it.

Eight of the 29 women, however, were unsure, or ambivalent, about what their response should be. A 25-year-old mother of one, for example, talked of the difficulty she had trying to decide whether to honor her husband's accounts:

It was very easy for him. Crying, bawling, and I can't stand to see a man cry and he knows it, too. "I swear I'll never do it again. Things are going to be different, I promise. I won't touch you." Just a bunch of lies. Just totally convincing me and knowing better. Me sitting there telling myself "I know this isn't right."

My second wind [*sic*] was I know this isn't right, but there was something else that won over what I thought was right. My heart would say, "Okay, I'll give him another chance. It might just be true this time." And then there was this other thing inside me saying, "You idiot." I always had like two things fighting inside of me. There was one that knew better and then there was the one that let itself be guided by strings.

These findings, which show that women are likely to wholeheartedly or ambivalently honor their mates' accounts after the first incident of abuse, are consistent with the results of prior research. Giles-Sims (1983), who interviewed 31 battered women who had sought help from a battered women's shelter, asked the women whether they had been willing to "forgive and forget" the first abusive incident. The vast majority—93%—said yes. Most of the women also said that they perceived the first abusive incident as an isolated one, and they did not expect it to happen again.

Looking at the second column in Table 2, it can be seen that 17 incidents of honoring were described after the middle incident of abuse. Of these, 65% were wholehearted honoring, 29% were ambivalent honoring, and 6% were pseudohonoring. There were no rejections. These percentages are similar to those found after the first abusive incident, and illustrate that as the battering progressed, the women were *still* likely to honor the aligning actions.

The real shift in honoring stances occurred after the last incident of abuse. Only a small fraction wholeheartedly or ambivalently honored the aligning actions then. However, 42% of the women who provided information pseudohonored their mate's accounts, and 50% flat out rejected them. Thus, if the categories of pseudohonoring and rejection are *combined*, it can be said that 92% of the women did not honor the account offered, whether or not they conveyed this to the batterer. Here is how one victim, for example, a 24-year-old mother of three, described her use of the pseudohonoring stance:

When he would first apologize to me, I would try to act like I was forgiving him, or he would get mad again. He would like come up and hug me, and I would try to act like I believed him, but I would be thinking, "I just hate you, and I'm leaving you, just wait 'til I can get out of here."

And here is how another, a 35-year-old mother of two, described how she moved to flat out reject her husband's accounts:

He came to the door and he was weeping. I don't mean crying just a little bit, I mean weeping, saying, "Please don't take my kids away, they're the only persons I've got, and I've missed you'all," and all that kind of stuff. And I felt so sorry for him, I just, you know. [He said] "Let me kiss you and hug you … I am so sorry. It just got out of hand." But I just can't take that anymore. I've heard it too much, I guess.

The developmental analysis again supported the cross-sectional analysis. Eighty-seven percent of the women (i.e., 20 of the 23 for whom there was enough information to carry out a developmental analysis) shifted from honoring stances which more or less accepted the accounts issued by the abusers (wholehearted or ambivalent honoring) to honoring stances which questioned the accounts (pseudohonor or rejection).

These findings, which show that women who come to a shelter are likely to question their mates' accounts, are also consistent with other studies. Giles-Sims (1983) found that only 18% of her sample were willing to "forgive and forget" the last incident of abuse; and Ferraro and Johnson (1983) found that battered women who decide to go to a shelter generally do so only after they have rejected the rationalizations for abuse.

Implications

For counselors, therapists, and social workers who are working with abusive men and/or abused women, this study—like other recent studies on the "phenomenology" of abuse (e.g., Andrews &

Brewin, 1990; Herbert, Silver, & Ellard, 1991)—helps clarify how batterers and victims "give meaning to" and (from their point of view) "cope with" domestic violence.

If one focuses exclusively on the apology, as Walker (1984) did, the findings from this study are very similar to hers. However, if one looks at the full range of accounts that abusers use, the findings differ. According to the women interviewed in this study, the third phase in the cycle of violence is not bypassed with repeated abuse, as Walker (1984) suggested; rather the third phase is *modified* to include other types of accounts. In other words, the "content" of the stage may change, but its "form" (the offering of accounts) remains essentially the same.

This shift in the type of aligning actions is significant because of the message it conveys. In an apology, the abuser accepts responsibility and implies that what he did was wrong. When the abuser moves to the use of the excuse either alone or in combination with other accounts, he is attempting to deny responsibility for his behavior. Something else—stress, financial problems, alcohol or drug abuse, or the victim's behavior—is "causing" the abuse. Not only the batterer but also the victim may be distracted by these excuses, believing that the abuse will stop if the avowed "causes" could be eliminated (e.g., "If I/he would stop drinking, the violence would stop"). Ultimately, however, these accounts serve to perpetuate the abuse because they prevent the abuser from coming to grips with the fact that *he* is responsible for his violent behavior. Ultimately, they enable the abuser to continue *both* his violent behavior *and* his relationship with his victim.

Counselors, therapists, and social workers can help abusers and victims understand how accounts perpetuate domestic violence. Exposing the accounts for what they are—verbal strategies designed to minimize the violence—is the first step in eliminating their use and their power. It is important also for professional helpers to reject the accounts that abusers offer. Honoring apologies, excuses, and justifications leads the batterer to believe that his abusive behavior is acceptable "in some situations" and "under certain conditions." The hitting license must be *cancelled,* not qualified. The repudiation of the battering must be foremost in the practitioner's mind.

All the battered women in this study left their abusive relationships, at least temporarily. The process of getting out of an abusive relationship is a complex one, both emotionally and physically. Many women leave these relationships and return to them, often more than once (Pagelow, 1984). The honoring stance that a woman adopts can help counselors, therapists, and social workers determine whether a woman is emotionally ready to leave. The women in this study sought help from a shelter after the "last" abusive incident, an incident in which 92% (of those reporting a honoring stance) rejected or pseudohonored an account offered by the batterer. These women clearly did not believe that the abuser was sorry, that something or someone else was to blame, or that it would not happen again. Victims who honor accounts, much like the women in Ferraro and Johnson's (1983) study who offered rationalizations for the abuse which they suffered, may still believe that the abuser is sorry, that it will not happen again, and that he will change. Accounts offered by abusers and honored by victims thus serve the same purpose as victim rationalizations—that is, they prevent women from seeking aid.

Finally, it is important to emphasize that while counselors, therapists, and social workers have an obligation to help victims gain insight into their abuse, they also have an obligation to be nonjudgmental of whatever decision a woman makes about her abusive relationship. A number of women in this study talked about the loss of support they experienced from significant others when they made decisions to stay with or return to their abusers. Victims of male battering face difficult choices—choices about what to say to their abusers, choices about whether to stay. Respecting the choices that women make is an integral part of the counseling/therapeutic process. Victims must always know that there are people ready and willing to listen to them and assist them.

REFERENCES

Andrews, B., & Brewin, C. R. (1990). Attributions of blame for marital violence: A study of antecedents and consequences. *Journal of Marriage and the Family, 52,* 757-767.

Dobash, R. E., & Dobash, R. P. (1984). The nature and antecedent of violent events. *British Journal of Criminology, 24,* 269-288.

Ferraro, K. J., & Johnson, J. M. (1983). How women experience battering: The process of victimization. *Social Problems, 30,* 325-339.

Gelles, R. J. (1974). *The violent home: A study of physical aggression between husbands and wives.* Beverly Hills, CA: Sage.

Giles-Sims, J. (1983). *Wife battering: A systems theory approach.* New York: Guilford.

Glaser, B. G., & Strauss, A. (1967). *The discovery of grounded theory.* Chicago: Aldine.

Goffman, E. (1971). *Relations in public: Microstudies of the public order.* New York: Basic Books.

Herbert, T. B., Silver, R. C., & Ellard, J. H. (1991). Coping with an abusive relationship: I. How and why do women stay? *Journal of Marriage and the Family, 53,* 311-325.

Hewitt, J. P., & Stokes, R. (1975). Disclaimers. *American Sociological Review, 40,* 1-11.

Hunter, C. H. (1984). Aligning actions: Types and distributions. *Symbolic Interaction, 7,* 155-174.

Lofland, J., & Lofland, L. H. (1984). *Analyzing social settings: A guide to qualitative research and analysis.* Belmont, CA: Wadsworth.

Mills, T. (1985). The assault on the self: Stages in coping with battering husbands. *Qualitative Sociology, 8,* 103-123.

Pagelow, M. D. (1984). *Family violence.* New York: Praeger.

Ptacek, J. (1988). Why do men batter their wives? In K. Yllo & M. Bograd (Eds.), *Feminist perspectives on wife abuse* (pp. 133-157). Newbury Park, CA: Sage.

Scott, M. B., & Lyman, S. M. (1968). Accounts. *American Sociological Review, 33,* 46-62.

Stokes, R., & Hewitt, J. P. (1976). Aligning actions. *American Sociological Review, 41,* 838-849.

Strauss, A., & Corbin, J. (1990). *Basics of qualitative research: Grounded theory procedures and techniques.* Newbury Park, CA: Sage.

Sykes, G. M., & Matza, D. (1957). Techniques of neutralization: A theory of delinquency. *American Sociological Review, 22,* 667-670.

Walker, L. E. (1979). *The battered woman.* New York: Harper & Row.

Walker, L. E. (1984). *The battered woman syndrome.* New York: Springer.

The crisis of the
absent father

A quarter of U.S. children have little or no contact with their dads, and the social and emotional consequences are devastating.

RICHARD LOUV

Richard Louv, *Connecting columnist for* Parents *Magazine, is the author of* Father Love *(Pocket), from which this article has been excerpted.*

In a counselor's office at a Wisconsin high school, boys and girls discuss their largely absent fathers. One girl says that her father has barely said a word to her for two years. Another says that after her parents' divorce, her father "had the right to see me every weekend and stopped it, without explaining why." She has not seen her father in ten years.

"My dad's nobody to me," says one boy. "I've never once sat down and eaten dinner with him. But we've got pictures of me and my dad; we were real close when I was young."

According to the school counselor, the students' stories are typical not just of troubled kids but also of overachievers, the brittle students so eager to please. Asked to describe their vision of a "good" father, the teens are blunt:

"You can't stay out partying till five in the morning. If you're a father, you've got to be there to tuck your kid in and tell him bedtime stories at eight-thirty at night."

"The father of my kids is going to do stuff with them. He's not going to run away."

"If things don't work out between us, I don't care if he leaves me, as long as he doesn't leave the kids."

Is the United States in danger of becoming a fatherless society, shorn of its male parents not by war or disease but by choice? A look at the statistics of family life suggests that the answer may be yes.

How often fathers see— or don't see—their kids.

Increasingly, fatherhood has become a volunteer commitment. In 1990 more than one in four of all births was to an unmarried woman, a fivefold increase in 30 years, according to the Census Bureau. Today nearly a quarter of children born in this country live in female-headed households. More than half of all children in the United States can expect to live in such households before they turn 18.

Being raised by a single mother does not automatically deprive a child of a father, but 40 percent of kids who live in female-headed households haven't seen their fathers in at least a year. Of the remaining 60 percent, only a fifth sleep even one night a month in their father's home. Even fewer see their father at least once a week, according to a study by Frank F. Furstenberg Jr. and Kathleen Mullan Harris, both of the University of Pennsylvania.

Men between the ages of 20 and 49 spend an average of only seven years living in a house with young children, a decline of nearly 50 percent in three decades. What accounts for the high drop-out rate from fatherhood among U.S. men?

In many of my interviews around the country, fathers spoke in vague terms about their impact on their kids. They understood that fathering was important, but they often had a difficult time pinning down just what is important about it; they often struggled for words.

Our culture isn't much help. It suffers a kind of paternal amnesia, a masculine stumble. It seems to have forgotten the importance of fathering and to have divorced manhood from fatherhood. Too many men—and women—view fatherhood as a confusion, a burden, a list of chores and vague expectations. Fatherlessness itself is not the main problem; there are plenty of fathers. The problem is the loss of father love.

In its deeper dimensions, father love is nurturing, community building, and spiritually powerful. But at its most fundamental level, father love is expressed through a man's daily involvement with his family.

As mothers have moved into the work force, the logistics of raising children have become increasingly difficult. Clearly, fathers who share the work, pain, and love equally are needed more than ever.

Why does research focus on the mother-child bond?

The media, social scientists, psychologists, and pediatricians, however, have given little attention to the necessary role that fathers must play in their children's lives. For instance, most past research on child care and development has focused on infant-mother attachment. Among psychologists, the generally accepted theory is that children with a secure attachment to their mothers, especially during infancy, are more likely to feel confident and have good relationships with teachers and peers. But until very recently, the father's role as a nurturer was viewed by many researchers as secondary to the mother's.

Similarly, most research on infant health has focused on the behavior of the expectant mother. But what is the impact of the expectant father? The father's support of the mother may play a larger role in an infant's health than factors such as maternal income and educational attainment. For example, the mortality rate of infants born to college-educated but unmarried women is higher than for infants born to married high school dropouts.

Most single mothers work full-time, earn no more than

Fatherless-ness is not the problem; loss of father love is.

$18,000 a year, and receive little child support. Half of children being raised by single mothers live in poverty, compared with 8 percent of those from two-parent families. But the cost of raising children without fathers is more than economic.

A rise in academic and behavior problems.

Children from divorced families (who usually live with their mothers), on average, score lower on reading and math tests. Children living with a single mother are twice as likely as children living with two parents to drop out of high school. Other long-range studies have shown that elementary school children from divorced families are absent more; are more anxious, hostile, and withdrawn; and are less popular with their peers than their classmates from intact families are. Almost twice as many high-achievers come from two-parent homes as come from one-parent homes, according to a study conducted by the National Association of Elementary School Principals.

Children from single-parent homes are more than twice as likely as children from two-parent families to suffer emotional and behavioral problems, according to a National Center for Health Statistics study. Moreover, the most reliable predictor of juvenile crime is not in-

come or race but family structure. Seventy percent of imprisoned U.S. minors have spent at least part of their lives without fathers.

It is true that many of these outcomes would be different if society offered more financial and emotional support to single mothers. But an equally important goal, one that is more important in the long run, is the improvement of the quality of fathering.

The vast majority of current fatherhood programs are directed toward poor parents, a reflection of society's prejudice that fathering is problematic mainly for the poor. This, of course, is not true. Some of the most interesting fatherhood programs, however, are now serving primarily poor teenage fathers.

Fifteen percent of kids don't even know who their fathers are.

Charles Augustus Ballard—president of the National Institute for Responsible Fatherhood and Family Development, a Cleveland group that works with teenage fathers—once asked a group of 15 boys how many

Married, single, or divorced, a man is enriched by fatherhood.

were fathers. Only two raised their hands. When he asked how many had

babies, 14 hands went up.

"They just don't think like fathers," Ballard says. "They don't connect pregnancy with marriage or husbanding or fatherhood." At least 65 percent of his clients never had meaningful relationships with their fathers. Ballard is currently organizing similar programs in 17 other U.S. cities.

Many young fathers, however, *are* eager to help their children. The institute has offered vocational services, counseling, and prenatal and parenthood classes to nearly 2,000 teenage fathers and prospective fathers. In the 11 years since the program was started, more than eight in ten participants have reported daily contact with their children; 74 percent say that they have contributed to their children's financial support. Progress is possible.

What is needed across the country is an ongoing effort to support and nurture good fatherhood, not only for low-income and teen parents but for fathers at all economic and age levels. Schools, churches, YMCAs, and businesses should offer more fatherhood courses. Some hospitals, for example, now offer classes to promote the bond between father and infant. Paul Lewis, creator of a fatherhood curriculum known as Dads University, says, "I tell men, 'Do it for your kids.' Most men, including noncustodial fathers, want to do what's right for their

kids but need help learning what the right thing is."

Needed: tougher laws on responsibility.

Beyond education programs, however, other policy changes are needed. Marriage must be encouraged; divorce laws must be reformed; and mediation to help divorcing parents resolve their child-rearing differences should be widely available. Today, dissolving a business contract is much more difficult to do in the United States than dissolving a marriage. No other contract may be breached as easily. Our laws should discourage separation by creating a braking mechanism, a waiting period of

Why children need fathers

Despite the paucity of studies on fatherhood, considerable evidence does exist attesting to the influence of nurturing fathers on their children.

● Children with involved fathers are more nurturing themselves and are much more likely to raise pets than other kids are, according to Yale Child Study Center psychiatrist Kyle Pruett, M.D. "I believe that these kids will find it easier to nurture their own children," notes Pruett.

● A 26-year study shows that paternal involvement was the single strongest parent-related factor in the development of empathy. "The father's influence was quite astonishing," says psychologist Richard Koestner, Ph.D., of Montreal's McGill University. Fathers who spend time alone with their children more than twice a week—giving baths, meals, and basic care—reared the most compassionate adults.

● Boys with strong, warm, nurturing fathers are more socially competent, more persistent at solving problems, and more self-directed, according to Norma Radin, M.S.W., Ph.D., a social-work professor at the University of Michigan, in Ann Arbor. —R.L.

nine months before a divorce becomes final.

The Progressive Policy Institute, an offshoot of the Democratic Leadership Council, proposes that a "children first" principle should govern all divorces involving children. The judge's main task would be to piece together the best possible agreement to meet the needs of the children and their physical guardian.

Another theory gaining currency espouses eliminating Aid to Families With Dependent Children (AFDC), the nation's largest welfare program (created 58 years ago to support widowed women and their children), and replacing it with a system to support families that include fathers. Current AFDC rules prevent a woman from receiving full benefits if the father is at home and has an employment record or works more than 100 hours a month.

Child-support laws and collection techniques must be radically reformed. To help assure that fathers pay their child support, the Social Security number of both parents should appear on a child's birth certificate.

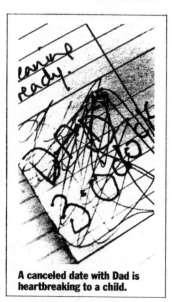

A canceled date with Dad is heartbreaking to a child.

From the time of each child's birth, absent parents should be expected to contribute a portion of their income to that child's support. Payments should be

---

The Murphy Brown problem

Ten days before Dan Quayle gave his speech declaring that the TV sitcom *Murphy Brown* mocked the importance of fathers, there was an op-ed piece in *The Washington Post* titled, "What Is Murphy Brown Saying?" The author was Barbara Dafoe Whitehead, a Democrat and research associate with the Institute for American Values. Here's what she had to say:

• "Childbirth is a time-tested way to boost ratings...but *Murphy Brown* will break new ground." The show, she wrote, reflects the dangerous but increasingly popular notion that fathers are expendable.

• Murphy Brown bears almost no resemblance to most real-life unmarried mothers, who are usually teenagers, desperately poor, and poorly educated. Despite the low odds that a single mother's child will receive enough positive parental contact, Whitehead wrote, "this idea [of not needing men] plays into powerful male fantasies of sexual freedom and escape from responsibility. . . ."

• A TV-dominated culture that encourages these fantasies is in for big trouble. Fathers should not be thrown out with the bathwater. (Indeed, the National Commission on Children had worked for two years to hammer out a 1991 bipartisan report emphasizing the need for government to encourage two-parent households.)

Clearly Whitehead had some useful criticism of the *Murphy Brown* scenario. Unfortunately Dan Quayle polarized the debate, reclaiming the family-values political turf for the Republicans.

"This was a step backward," says Whitehead. "In recent years we were finally creating some common ground between liberals and conservatives." The issue of family values was politicized and trivialized by politicians and by the media. —R.L.

---

collected by employers (just as Social Security taxes are today) and sent to the federal government, which would then send the money directly to the custodial parent. Failure to pay would be comparable to tax evasion.

Society tends to view change as something that happens either at a personal level or through national legislation. But James Levine, director of The Families and Work Institute's Fatherhood Project, a research and consulting group on fatherhood, sees a vast area for change between these two extremes. Levine maintains that unless the institutions that have a direct impact on families' lives—businesses, hospitals, churches, synagogues, social-service agencies, and schools—are transformed, neither personal change nor national legislation will accomplish much.

Levine points out a cultural resistance to fatherhood within business institutions as an example. "No matter how many hours he puts in at work, a father who is worried about his children is unlikely to be fully productive," he says. We do not tend to think of fathers as worried working parents. Before such assumptions can be challenged, they must be the topic of open, and probably organized, conversation within company walls.

Even those institutions whose mission it is to care for and help children must examine their own attitudes toward fathers. Levine, for example, has found some of the strongest resistance to paternal involvement among women who work with and for children. "When we discussed their resistance to fathers, they would say, 'Yes, we know we should get fathers more involved,' but they were making little effort to do that," Levine says.

Most men want to do what's right for their children.

"Their ambivalence is emblematic of the attitude among many helping institutions—hospitals, mental-health organizations, schools," he continues. "My point is not to blame women. We must give voice to these feelings as the first step toward making men and women equal partners in caring for their children."

Each family also must identify and challenge its own cultural prejudices about fatherhood. For example, when a man does take family leave or decides to be a part- or full-time dad, he may encounter subtle or not so subtle messages from relatives, such as, "Aren't you working? Don't you have a job yet?" The father may also send out mixed messages. He may say that he wants to do more at home but may also find the pressure to be the breadwinner a useful excuse to dodge his own responsibilities.

The truth, however politically untidy, is that men will not move back into the family until our culture reconnects masculinity and fatherhood, until men come to see fathering—not just paternity—as the fullest expression of manhood. Married, single, or divorced, a man is enriched by fatherhood, and a child's life is better for it. The good news, the great good news, is that an enormous payoff awaits society—and individual men and their families—as men move deeper into the dimensions of fatherhood. That movement has already begun.

How Kids Grieve

When someone dies, children need adults to help them cope with a range of complicated issues; truth and simplicity are key.

Jennifer Cadoff

Jennifer Cadoff is a free-lance writer specializing in health and family issues and is the mother of two preschoolers.

Two years ago my brother-in-law died unexpectedly of a pulmonary embolism. He was just 40, and he left behind two young children and his wife, my husband's sister. Our family was dazed with shock and grief, barely able to function. How could we explain to our three-year-old daughter what had happened, when just days before she had been tumbling around our living room with her cousins and Uncle Emil?

I must have stumbled through some sort of explanation, although I can't recall the words I used. I do remember thinking that I was doing it all wrong. Everything I said seemed false or incomplete or too frightening for a toddler.

I now know I wasn't alone in feeling this way. Death, according to several experts, has replaced sex as the topic parents have the hardest time discussing with their children.

"How do we tell the kids?"

"The main thing is to keep it simple, and the younger the child, the simpler your explanation should be," says John Schowalter, M.D., professor of pediatrics and psychiatry at the Yale Child Study Center, in New Haven, Connecticut.

"It's important to use the correct vocabulary," adds Helen Fitzgerald, coordinator of The Grief Program at the Mount Vernon Center for Community Mental Health, in Alexandria, Virginia. "Avoid 'she expired' or 'we lost him.' Use the real words: 'dead,' 'funeral,' 'cancer,' 'heart attack,' or 'AIDS.' " You might say, for example, "Grandma had a very bad heart attack and died."

Encourage their questions.

After telling your child the facts, as briefly and honestly as possible, it's best to turn the floor over to her. Ask whether there is anything she wants to know. Don't be concerned if she does not respond right away. "As is true with sex and other emotionally charged areas, the discussion often works best if you give your child time to think and then to ask questions. Make it clear that she's free to come back to you later," says Schowalter.

Although parents tend to think that they should "be strong" when they deliver the bad news—so as not to frighten or upset their child—experts agree that crying in front of your child is both normal and healthy.

"We should allow ourselves to be human. This is not easy to do. We can tell our children that we hurt a great deal when someone dies. Even if we can't find the right words, we can say that we aren't thinking as clearly as we would like because of our sadness," suggests Phyllis Silverman, Ph.D., an associate in social welfare in the Department of Psychiatry at Massachusetts General Hospital, in Boston, and principal investigator in an ongoing study of child bereavement. "Younger children may not be able to understand the full range of feelings and emotions that adults or older children have. With an older child, it may be possible to share some of the feelings you have and to invite her into a dialogue. Together, then, both parent and child can develop a better understanding of what's happening."

John W. James, who founded the Grief Recovery Institute in Los Angeles in 1981 after a son died, wholeheartedly agrees. "The most helpful thing adults can do for children is to be emotionally honest about their own feelings," he says. It's not always easy to be emotionally honest, however, because most of us have been coached since childhood to keep a stiff upper lip and to go to our rooms to cry. "A child who sees this immediately thinks there must be something wrong with crying," James continues. "If, on the other hand, we could just stand in the kitchen and cry, our children could come up and ask, 'What's wrong?' We could then say, 'Grandpa just died and I'm very sad.' Then you have the beginnings of an emotionally honest conversation about grief."

"Mommy, what's 'dead'?"

After stumbling through telling my daughter that Uncle Emil had died, I

A child's simplest questions can be the hardest to answer.

learned that children's simplest questions can be the hardest to answer. Rebecca's was "Mommy, what's 'dead'?" I hesitantly said something about not breathing and hearts not beating—feeling, once again, hopelessly inadequate for this terrible task.

"I think that's all you need to say," Silverman affirms. " 'Dead' is when all functions stop—you don't breathe, you can't see."

Grief counselor Helen Fitzgerald describes a simple yet powerful game she used with one group of five- to twelve-year-olds. "I started by saying, 'I'm alive, I can stomp my feet,' " she says. "The kids got into this immediately, saying things like, 'I'm alive, I can cross my eyes,' and even some gross and silly things like, 'I'm alive, I can pick my nose.' Then, after we'd gone around the room, I said, 'When all of that is gone, that is what "dead" is, at least as we know it here on this earth.' It got really quiet for a few minutes. They weren't upset; they were just letting it sink in."

"Is she in heaven?"

Whether or not religious beliefs enter into the dis-

cussion with your child is entirely up to you.

"Parents should simply tell their children what they believe," says Elizabeth Weller, M.D., director of child and adolescent psychiatry at Ohio State University, in Columbus. "You shouldn't tell children about life after death if you don't believe in it yourself. It's also fine to simply say, 'Some people believe this and some people believe that, but I don't really know what happens.' "

That's the approach Phyllis Silverman took with her own child. "When my son was five, he asked what happens after people die," she recalls. "I told him that I didn't really know, that some people believe nothing happens—the body returns to nature and nourishes the soil and we live on in people's memories. Some people believe we go to heaven, and they see heaven in a very concrete way. And others simply believe that in some way the spirit lives on. My son thought for a while, then said, 'I think I believe that somehow your soul lives on.' And that was the end of it. That was all he needed to hear."

Fitzgerald, who has a new book out called *The Grieving Child* (Fireside), adds one caveat: "I think we have to be careful about such comments as 'God

loved her so much he took her'—as if God goes around zapping people and they're gone." Schowalter agrees: "It can be confusing. If you've been told that Grandpa has gone to heaven and that heaven is a wonderful place, then why are all of these people crying?" Of course, Grandpa is still missed in *this* life, and it may help to explain that to your child.

When can children really understand death?

Children ask questions; parents try to answer. But just how old does a child have to be for the reality of death to truly sink in?

John Schowalter says, "People argue about this, but it's probably somewhere around age ten that death is understood to be irreversible." Of course, there are no hard-and-fast rules. "There are some five-year-olds who will not have a hard time grasping death in its true sense—that death is a one-way trip, that you go and never come back," says Weller. Adds Silverman, "I do think kids understand much earlier than we realize, especially if they've had an experience with an actual death. This doesn't mean that ten minutes later they won't ask, 'When's Papa coming back?' but I think that's a kind of reality testing."

How much it hurts.

How deeply a child will be affected by a death depends on several factors other than age.

Losing a grandmother who lives down the street, a close school friend, or a cousin who plays with the child every weekend is likely to be felt deeply.

On the other hand, if the child has not had a significant relationship with the person who died, she may not feel the loss intensely, notes John James.

Older children, however, may have a strong reaction to the death of a relative they weren't close to. They may feel sadness that the chance to know that person, and to have that person know them, is gone.

Children's secret fears.

A few months after the death of her great-grandmother, and about a year after her Uncle Emil died, my daughter, Rebecca, dropped a bombshell. "Is it almost time for Daddy to die?" she asked quite matter-of-factly as I drove her to nursery school one sunny spring day.

"What? Good grief—of course not!" I sputtered.

Had I said the right thing? How could I promise my child that our family would be spared, when tragedy had struck so close to home?

"You might have said, 'Daddy is very healthy, and he and I will do everything we can to stay that way. We are probably going to live a long time, until you are all grown up,' " says Helen Fitzgerald. "You could say it's rare that someone as young as Uncle Emil dies."

Weller suggests pointing out that "not all daddies

What Not to Say and Why

"Grandpa just went to sleep."	"God took Grandma because he loved her so much."	"Uncle Pete has gone on a very long trip."	"Now that Grandma is gone, you'll have to take care of Grandpa."
Sleep, darkness, and death are inextricably linked for many of us. If a child thinks that Grandpa died by going to sleep, she may become afraid of bedtime herself.	Saying this may make your child think that she didn't love Grandma enough—that if she had, Grandma would not have died.	If you say this, children, who tend to be quite literal, will wonder why Uncle Pete didn't say good-bye to them and when he'll be back.	This is too much responsibility for a child to handle. Children cannot take care of adults; adults take care of children.

die" and mentioning some friends whose families are intact. She adds that it's very common for children to worry that someone close to them, of the same sex and age as the deceased, will also die.

There are several other fears that these experts say are common after a death has occurred:

● A child may worry that somehow she made the person die. "You have to give a lot of reassurance that thoughts and words don't kill," says Fitzgerald. If a child has thought about getting rid of a pesky cousin—or told her grandfather in a fit of anger that she wished he were dead—and that person dies soon afterward, the child may hold herself responsible.

● Death, darkness, and sleep also seem to be universally linked. "Darkness is a time when children fear someone's going to come get them—and anthropomorphically speaking, death does come and get you," says Schowalter.

● "Since death might be thought of as the ultimate punishment, the idea of death as retribution for bad actions or thoughts is very

common," adds Schowalter. A child may, then, ask what the dead person did wrong or whether he was bad. The child may worry that he's going to die too—since all kids know they've done some pretty bad things in their time.

● Older children worry about their own deaths, Weller comments. She recommends saying something like, "It is true that someday everybody will die. But usually death is due to the aging process or a serious illness, and you are still very young and healthy."

Helping children handle complicated feelings.

How can we know if a child is harboring one or another of these fears?

Sometimes it's obvious. "Often if a child does not master the process of understanding this complicated issue, he will bring the subject up over and over again," says Weller. "The parents might think, 'Oh my god, is this child obsessed?' But he is just trying to make sense of what happened."

Other children will suddenly start playing funeral, hospital, or car crash. "This

doesn't mean they are cruel or that they are having fun with a subject that causes the rest of us pain," says Weller. "Play is the work of childhood. Through it all, they try to understand and master what we teach them."

Talking is often a good way for children to sort through issues they don't understand, although some

You can say, "I don't know what happens when someone dies."

children just aren't comfortable talking about feelings. "The easiest way to help your child to talk is for you to go first," suggests John James. You might start by saying, "I really feel bad that I never told Grandpa how much fun I had when we went to that basketball game together," and then ask, "Is there anything *you* wish you had said—or hadn't said—to him?" Having your child write a letter to his grandfather and then read it either at the grave or to a photograph of him can help lay this type of nagging regret to rest.

Helen Fitzgerald suggests getting younger children to draw "something they wish they'd done differently. If something's making a child feel bad and she can't get it out, it becomes a deep, dark secret."

Books can help too. One that Fitzgerald uses in her kids' bereavement groups is *The Tenth Good Thing About Barney* (Aladdin Books), about a child who counts the reasons he loved his dead cat. "I read that a lot," she says, "and then I ask the children to think of ten things about the person who died, but I do tell them that the things don't all have to be good. Not all memories are happy. It's a relief for children to know that it's okay to remember the not so great stuff too." (For more on reading see "Books About Death.")

What about the funeral?

Funerals are an important way of paying respect and saying good-bye to someone when he dies—what experts term a "conclusionary ritual." But how can a parent know whether this ceremony will be good for a child or too frightening and upsetting?

"There's a wide diversity of opinion about this," says John Schowalter. "In studies I've done, I've found that children under nine or ten tended to be quite disturbed about funerals—but only if they were forced to go. It is my feeling that the decision should be left to them. If your child doesn't want to go, she should not be made to feel that she is abandoning anyone or doing something wrong."

If your child does want to go, she needs to know what she's getting into. You need to tell her, briefly, what's going to happen—whether there will be a casket present, for example, and whether it will be open or closed. Be sure to tell her that people will be crying—even Mom and Dad—because they're sad. Then answer any questions, keeping it simple, advises Fitzgerald. Also let your child know that she can leave the service at any time if she needs to.

Taking your child to the burial is even more problematic, according to Schowalter: "For the child who is not really sure that dead people are going to *stay* dead—and again, this tends to mean younger than age ten or so—seeing someone put in the ground in a box and covered with dirt is a lot to handle."

Cremation can seem awfully frightening, although Fitzgerald comments that the children she has counseled have no particular trouble with the concept—as long as it's presented sen-

Books About Death

There are many children's books about death. Here are a few.
Goodbye, Max, words and pictures by Holly Keller (Greenwillow, $12.95; ages three and up).

Remember the Butterflies, words and pictures by Anna Grossnickle Hines (Dutton, $12.95; ages four to seven).
The Tenth Good Thing

About Barney, by Judith Viorst, illustrated by Erik Blegvad (Aladdin, $3.95; ages four to eight).
Everett Anderson's Goodbye, by Lucille Clifton, illustrated by Ann Grifalconi (Henry Holt, $5.95; ages four to eight).
How It Feels When a Parent Dies, words and photographs by Jill Krementz (Knopf, $10; ages nine and up).

—Sarah Hutter

sitively and simply, with additional details provided only as asked for. If a young child is attending only a memorial service, you may not need to broach the topic at all. Older children, and those who are exposed to the planning of a cremation, tend to be interested in how it's done ("in a large kiln, lined with fireproof bricks so that intense heat causes the body to become ashes"); what the ashes look like afterward ("light-gray flour, about the size of a five-pound bag"); and what will be done with them.

If a child decides against going to the funeral, then later regrets her decision, reassure her that at the time, she made the best decision. "You might then arrange a special ceremony," suggests Fitzgerald. This could be something as simple as a poem read at church, or flowers and a letter taken to the grave.

Sometimes a simple ceremony of the child's own devising can be particularly fitting. Fitzgerald mentions one that the children in her group came up with: "Yesterday each of them wrote a message on a silver helium balloon to the person who had died. We picked a spot in the parking lot, under a tree, and planned a very simple ceremony. We all held the string, counted to three, and, as we let the balloon go, said together, 'We sure hope this gets to you!' We watched the balloon until we could no longer see it." Of course, she says, "we had talked about how the balloon couldn't *really* get to the people we wrote to, but also how doing stuff like this makes us feel better anyway. And it did."

AND THE FEMALE AGENDA

Most female mammals are anything but subtle when it comes to telling males it's time for sex. Not humans. For good evolutionary reasons, women have found it's much better to keep men in the dark.

Jared Diamond

SCENE ONE: A dimly lit bedroom; a handsome man lies in bed. A beautiful young women, in nightgown, enters. A diamond wedding ring flashes virtuously on her left hand; her right clutches a small blue strip of paper. She bends, kissing the man's ear.

She: "Darling! It's time!"

Scene Two: Same bedroom, same couple making love; details obscured by dim lighting. Camera shifts to a calendar being flipped by a graceful hand wearing the same diamond wedding ring.

Scene Three: Same couple, blissfully holding smiling baby.

He: "Darling! I'm so glad Ovustick told us when it was exactly the right time!"

Last Frame: Close-up of same graceful hand, clutching same small blue strip of paper. Caption reads: OVUSTICK.

HOME URINE TEST TO DETECT OVULATION.

If baboons could understand our TV ads, they'd find that one especially hilarious. Neither a male nor a female baboon needs a hormonal test kit to detect the female's ovulation, the sole time when her ovary releases an egg and she can be fertilized. Instead, the skin around the female's vagina swells and turns bright pink. She gives off a distinctive smell. And in case a dumb male still misses the point, she also crouches in front of him and presents her hindquarters. Most other female animals are similar, advertising ovulation with equally bold visual signals, odors, or behaviors.

We consider female baboons with bright pink hindquarters an oddity. In fact, though, we humans are the odd ones—our scarcely detectable ovulations make us members of a small minority in the mammalian world. Granted, quite a few other primates—the group of mammals that includes monkeys, apes, and us—also conceal their ovulations. However, even among primates, baboon-style advertisement remains the majority practice. Human males, in contrast, have no means of detecting when their partners can be fertilized; nor did the women themselves until modern, scientific times.

We're also unusual in our continuous practice of sex, which is a direct consequence of our concealed ovulations. Most other animals confine sex to a brief period of estrus around the advertised time of ovulation. At estrus, a female baboon emerges from a month of sexual abstinence to copulate up to 100 times. A female Barbary macaque does it on an average of every

17 minutes, distributing her favors at least once to every adult male in her troop. Monogamous gibbon couples go several years without sex, until the female weans her most recent infant and comes into estrus again. The gibbons relapse into abstinence as soon as the female becomes pregnant.

We humans, though, practice sex on any day of the month. Hence most human copulations involve women who are unable to conceive at that moment. Not only do we have sex at the "wrong" time of the cycle, but we continue to have sex during pregnancy and after menopause, when we know for sure that fertilization is impossible.

Human sex does seem a monumental waste of effort from a "biological" point of view. After all, most other animals are sensibly stingy of copulatory effort, and for a simple reason—sex is expensive. Just count the ways: for males, sperm production is metabolically costly, so much so that mutant worms with few sperm live longer than normal sperm-producing worms. Sex takes time that could otherwise be devoted to finding food. During the sex act itself, couples locked in embrace risk being surprised and killed by a predator or enemy. Finally, fights between males competing for a female often result in serious injury to the female as well as to the males.

So why don't human females behave the way most other animals do and give clear ovulatory signals that would let us restrict sex to moments when it could do us some good?

By now, you may have decided that I'm a prime example of an ivory-tower scientist searching unnecessarily for problems to explain. I can hear several million of you protesting, "There's no problem to explain, except why Jared Diamond is such an idiot. You don't understand why we have sex all the time? Because it's fun, of course!" Unfortunately, that answer isn't enough to satisfy scientists. Humans' concealed ovulations and unceasing receptivity must have evolved for good reasons, and ones that go beyond fun. While engaged in sex, animals, too, look as if they're having fun, to judge by their intense involvement. And with respect to *Homo sapiens*, the species unique in its self-consciousness, it's especially paradoxical that a female as smart and aware as a human should be unconscious of her own ovulation, when female animals as dumb as cows are aware of it.

In speculating about the reasons for our concealed ovulations, scientists tend to focus their attention on another of our unusual features: the helpless condition of our infants, which makes lots of parental care necessary for many years. The young of most mammals start to get their own food as soon as they're weaned and become fully independent soon afterward. Hence most female mammals can and do rear their young without any assistance from the father, whom the mother never sees again after copulation. For humans, though, most food is acquired by means of complex technologies

JUST IMAGINE WHAT MARRIED LIFE WOULD BE LIKE IF WOMEN DID ADVERTISE THEIR OVULATIONS, LIKE FEMALE BABOONS WITH BRIGHT PINK DERRIERES.

far beyond the dexterity or mental ability of a toddler. As a result, our children have to have food brought to them for over a decade after weaning, and that job is much easier for two parents than for one. Even today, it's hard for a single human mother to rear kids unassisted. It was undoubtedly much harder for our prehistoric ancestors.

Consider the dilemma facing an ovulating cavewoman who has just been fertilized. In many other mammal species, the male would promptly go off in search of another ovulating female. For the cavewoman, though, that would seriously jeopardize her child's survival. She's much better off if that man sticks around. But what can she do? Her brilliant solution: remain sexually receptive all the time! Keep him satisfied by copulating whenever he wants! In that way, he'll hang around, have no need to look for new sex partners, and will even share his daily hunting bag of meat.

That in essence is the theory that was formerly popular among anthropologists—among male anthropologists, anyway. Alas for that theory, there are numerous male animals that require no such sexual bribes to induce them to remain with their mate and offspring. I already mentioned that gibbons, seeming paragons of monogamous devotion, go years without sex. Male songbirds cooperate assiduously with their mates in feeding the nestlings, although sex ceases after fertilization. Even male gorillas with a harem of several females get only a few

sexual opportunities each year because their mates are usually nursing or out of estrus. Clearly, these females don't have to offer the sop of constant sex.

But there's a crucial difference between our human couples and those abstinent couples of other animal species. Gibbons, most songbirds, and gorillas live dispersed over the landscape, with each couple or harem occupying its separate territory. That means few encounters with potential extramarital sex partners. Perhaps the most distinctive feature of traditional human society is that it consists of mated couples living within large groups of other couples, with whom we have to cooperate. A father and mother must work together for years to rear their helpless children, despite being frequently tempted by other fertile adults nearby. The specter of marital disruption by extramarital sex, with its potentially disastrous consequences for parental cooperation in child-rearing, is pervasive in human societies. Somehow we evolved concealed ovulation and constant receptivity to make possible our unique combination of marriage, co-parenting, and adulterous temptation. How does that combination work?

More than a dozen new theories have emerged as possible explanations. From this plethora of possibilities, two—the father-at-home theory and the many-fathers theory—have survived as most plausible. Yet they are virtually opposite.

The father-at-home theory was developed by University of Michigan biologist Richard Alexander and graduate student Katharine

Noonan. To understand it, imagine what married life would be like if women did advertise their ovulations, like female baboons with bright pink derrieres. A husband would infallibly recognize the day on which his wife was ovulating. On that day he would stay home and assiduously make love, in order to fertilize her and pass on his genes. On all other days he would realize from his wife's pallid derriere that lovemaking with her was useless. He would instead wander off in search of other, unguarded pink-hued ladies so he could pass on even more of his genes. He'd feel secure in leaving his wife at home because he'd know she wasn't sexually receptive to men and couldn't be fertilized anyway.

The results of those advertised ovulations would be awful. Fathers wouldn't be at home to help rear the kids, mothers couldn't do the job unassisted, and babies would die in droves. That would be bad for both mothers and fathers because neither would succeed in propagating their genes.

Now let's picture the reverse scenario, in which a husband has no clue to his wife's fertile days. He then has to stay at home and make love with her on as many days of the month as possible if he wants to have much chance of fertilizing her. Another motive for him to stay around is to guard her against other men, since she might prove to be fertile on any day he's away. Besides, now he has less reason to wander, since he has no way of identifying when other women are fertile. The heartwarming outcome: fathers hang around and share baby care, and babies survive. That's good for both mothers and fathers, who have now succeeded in transmitting their genes. In effect, both gain: the woman, by recruiting an active co-parent; the man, because he acquires confidence that the kid he is helping to rear really carries his genes.

Competing with the father-at-home theory is the many-fathers theory, developed by anthropologist Sarah Hrdy of the University of California at Davis. Anthropologists have long recognized that infanticide used to be common in many human societies. Until field studies by Hrdy and others, though, zoologists had no appreciation for how often it occurs among other animals as well. Infanticide is especially likely to be committed by males against infants of females with whom they have never copulated—for example, by intruding males that have supplanted resident males and acquired their harem. The usurper "knows" that the infants killed are not his own. (Of course, animals don't carry out such subtle reasoning consciously; they evolved to behave that way instinctively.) The species in which infanticide has been documented now include our closest animal relatives, chimpanzees and gorillas, in addition to a wide range of other species from lions to African hunting dogs.

Naturally, infanticide horrifies us. But on reflection, one can see that the murderer gains a grisly genetic advantage. A female is unlikely to ovulate as long as she is nursing an infant. By killing the infant, the murderous intruder terminates

the mother's lactation and stimulates her to resume estrous cycles. In most cases, the murderer proceeds to fertilize the bereaved mother, who then bears an infant carrying the murderer's own genes.

Infanticide is a serious evolutionary problem for these animal mothers, who lose their genetic investment in their murdered offspring. This problem would appear to be exacerbated if the female has only a brief, conspicuously advertised estrus. A dominant male could easily monopolize her during that time. All other males would consequently know that the resulting infant was sired by their rival,

NATURALLY, INFANTICIDE HORRIFIES US. BUT ON REFLECTION, ONE CAN SEE THAT THE MURDERER GAINS A GRISLY GENETIC ADVANTAGE.

and they'd have no compunctions about killing the infant.

Suppose, though, that the female has concealed ovulations and constant sexual receptivity. She can exploit these advantages to copulate with many males— even if she has to do it sneakily, when her consort isn't looking. (Hrdy, by the way, argues that the human female's capacity for repeated orgasms may have evolved to provide her with further motivation to do so.)

According to Hrdy's scenario, no male can be confident of his paternity, but many males recognize that they might have sired the mother's infant. If such a male later succeeds in driving out the mother's consort and taking her over, he avoids killing her infant because it could be his own. He might even help the infant with protection and other forms of paternal care. The mother's concealed ovulation will also serve to decrease fighting between males within her own troop, because any single copulation is unlikely to result in conception and hence is no longer worth fighting over.

In short, where Alexander and Noonan view concealed ovulation as clarifying paternity and reinforcing monogamy, Hrdy sees it as confusing paternity and effectively undoing monogamy. Which theory is correct?

To find the answer, we turn to the comparative method, a technique often used by evolutionary biologists. By comparing primate species, we can learn which mating habits are shared by those species with concealed ovulation but absent from those with advertised ovulation. As we shall see, the reproductive biology of each species represents the outcome of an experiment, performed by nature, on the benefits and drawbacks of concealing ovulation.

This comparison was recently conducted by Swedish biologists Birgitta Sillén-Tullberg and Anders Møller. First they tabulated the visible signs of ovulation for 68 species of higher primates (monkeys and apes). They found that some species, including baboons and our close relatives the chimpanzees, advertise ovulation conspicuously. Others, including our close relative the gorilla, exhibit slight signs. But nearly half resemble humans in lacking visible signs. Those species include vervets, marmosets, and spider monkeys, as well as one ape, the orangutan. Thus, while concealed ovulation is still exceptional among mammals in general, it nevertheless occurs in a significant minority of higher primates.

Next, the same 68 species were categorized according to their mating system. Some, including marmosets and gibbons, turn out to be monogamous. More, such as gorillas, have harems of females controlled by a single adult male. Humans are represented in both categories, with some societies being routinely monogamous and others having female harems. But most higher primate species, including chimpanzees, have a promiscuous system in which females routinely associate and copulate with multiple males.

Sillén-Tullberg and Møller then examined whether there was any tendency for more or less conspicuous ovulations to be associated with some particular mating system. Based on a naive reading of our two competing theories, concealed ovulation should be a feature of monogamous species if the father-at-home theory is correct, but of promiscuous species if the many-fathers theory holds. In fact, almost all monogamous primate species analyzed prove to have concealed ovulation. Not a single monogamous primate species has boldly advertised ovulations, which instead are mostly confined to promiscuous species. That seems to be strong support for the father-at-home theory.

But the fit of predictions to theory is only a half-fit, because the reverse correlations don't hold up. Yes, most monogamous species have concealed ovulation, yet perpetually pallid derrieres are in turn no guarantee of monogamy. Out of 32 species that hide their ovulations, 22 aren't monogamous but promiscuous or live in harems. So regardless of what caused concealed ovulation to evolve in the first place, it can evidently be maintained under varied mating systems.

Similarly, while most species with boldly advertised ovulations are promiscuous, promiscuity doesn't require flashing a bright pink behind once a month. In fact, most promiscuous primates either have concealed ovulation or only slight signs. Harem-holding species can have any type of ovulatory signal: invisible, slightly visible, or conspicuous.

These complexities warn us that concealed ovulation will prove to serve different functions according to the particular mating system with which it coexists. To identify these changes of function, Sillén-Tullberg and Møller got the bright idea of studying the family tree of living primate species. Their underlying rationale was that some modern species that are very closely related, and thus presumably derived from a recent common ancestor, differ in mating system or in strength of ovulatory signals. This implies recent evolutionary changes, and the two researchers hoped to identify the points where those changes had taken place.

Here's an example of how the reasoning works. Comparisons of DNA show that humans, chimps, and gorillas are still about 98 percent genetically identical. Measurements of how rapidly such gene changes accumulate, plus discoveries of dated ape and protohuman fossils, show that humans, chimps, and gorillas all stem from an ancestral "missing link" that lived around 9 million years ago. Yet those three modern descendants now exhibit all three types of ovulatory signal: concealed ovulation in humans, slight signals in gorillas, bold advertisement in chimps. This means that only one of those three descendants can be like the missing link, and the other two must have evolved different signals.

A strong hint of the problem's resolution is that many living species of primitive primates—creatures like tarsiers and lemurs—have slight signs of ovulation. The simplest interpretation, then, is that the missing link inherited slight signs from a primitive ancestor, and that gorillas in turn inherited their slight signs unchanged from the missing link.

WHAT IT BOILS DOWN TO IS THAT CONCEALED OVULATION HAS REPEATEDLY CHANGED AND REVERSED ITS FUNCTION DURING PRIMATE EVOLUTIONARY HISTORY.

Within the last 9 million years, though, humans must have lost even those slight signs to develop our present concealed ovulation, while chimps, in contrast, went on to evolve bolder signs.

Identical reasoning can be applied to other branches of the primate family tree, to infer the ovulatory signals of other now-vanished ancestors and the subsequent changes in their descendants. As it turns out, signal switching has been rampant in primate history. There have been several independent origins of bold advertisement (including the example in chimps); many independent origins of concealed ovulation (including humans and orangutans); and several reappearances of slight signs of ovulation, either from concealed ovulation (as in some howler monkeys or from bold advertisement (as in many macaques).

All right, so that's how we can deduce past changes in ovulatory signals. When we now turn our attention to mating systems, we can use exactly the same procedure. Again, we discover that humans and chimps evolved in opposite directions, just as they did in their ovulatory signals. Studies of living primitive primate behavior suggest that ancestral primates of 60 million years ago mated promiscuously, and that our missing link of 9 million years ago had already switched to single-male harems. Yet if we look at humans, chimps, and gorillas as they are today, we find all three types of mating system represented. Thus, while gorillas may just have retained the harems of their missing link ancestor, chimps must have reinvented promiscuity and humans invented monogamy.

Overall, it appears that monogamy has evolved independently many times in higher primates: in us, in gibbons, and in numerous groups of monkeys. Harems also seem to have evolved many times, including in the missing link. Chimps and a few monkeys apparently reinvented promiscuity,

after their recent ancestors had given up promiscuity for harems.

Thus Sillén-Tullberg and Møller have reconstructed both the type of mating system and the ovulatory signal that probably coexisted in numerous primates of the remote past. Now, finally, we can put all this information together to examine what the mating system was at each of the points in our family tree when concealed ovulation evolved.

Here's what one learns. In considering those ancestral species that did have ovulatory signals and that went on to lose those signals and evolve concealed ovulation, only one was monogamous. The rest of them were promiscuous or harem-holding—one species being the human ancestor that arose from the harem-holding missing link. We thus conclude that promiscuity or harems, not monogamy, are the mating systems associated with concealed ovulation. This conclusion is as predicted by Hrdy's many-fathers theory. It doesn't agree with the father-at-home theory.

But we can also ask the reverse question: What were the ovulatory signals prevailing at each point in our family tree when monogamy evolved? We find that monogamy never evolved in species with bold advertisement of ovulation. Instead, monogamy has usually arisen in species that already had concealed ovulation, and sometimes in species that had slight ovulatory signals. This conclusion agrees with predictions of Alexander and Noonan's father-at-home theory.

How can these two apparently opposite conclusions be reconciled? Recall that Sillén-Tullberg and Møller found that almost all monogamous primates today have concealed ovulation. That result must have arisen in two steps. First, concealed ovulation arose, in a promiscuous or harem-holding species. Then, with concealed ovulation already present, the species switched to monogamy.

Perhaps, by now, you're finding our sexual history confusing. We started out with an apparently simple question deserving a simple answer: Why do we hide our ovulations and have sex on any day of the month? Instead of a simple answer, you're being told that the answer is more complex and involves two steps.

What it boils down to is that concealed ovulation has repeatedly changed and actually reversed its function during primate evolutionary history. That is, both the father-at-home and the many-fathers explanations are valid, but they operated at different times in our evolutionary history. Concealed ovulation arose at a time when our ancestors were still promiscuous or living in harems. At such times, it let the ancestral woman distribute her sexual favors to many males, none of whom could swear that he was the father of her baby but each of whom knew that he might be. As a result, none of those potentially murderous males wanted to harm the baby, and some may actually have protected or helped feed it. Once the woman had evolved concealed ovulation for that purpose, she then used it to pick a good man, to entice or force him to stay at home with her, and to get him to provide lots of help for her baby.

On reflection, we shouldn't be surprised at this shift of function. Such shifts are very common in evolutionary biology. Natural selection doesn't proceed in a straight line toward a distant perceived goal, in the way that an engineer consciously designs a new product. Instead, some feature that serves one function in an animal begins to serve some other function as well, gets modified as a result, and may even lose the original function. The consequence is frequent reinventions of similar adaptations, and frequent losses, shifts, or even reversals of function as living things evolve.

One of the most familiar examples involves vertebrate limbs. The fins of ancestral fishes, used for swimming, evolved into the legs of ancestral reptiles, birds, and mammals, used for running or hopping on land. The front legs of certain ancestral mammals and reptile-birds then evolved into the wings of bats and modern birds respectively, to be used for flying. Bird wings and mammal legs then evolved independently into the flippers of penguins and whales respectively, thereby reverting to a swimming function and effectively reinventing the fins of fish. At least two groups of fish descendants independently lost their limbs, to become snakes and legless lizards. In essentially the same way, features of reproductive biology—such as concealed ovulation, boldly advertised ovulation, monogamy, harems, and promiscuity—have repeatedly changed function and been transmuted, reinvented, or lost.

Think of all this the next time you are having sex for fun. Chances are it will be at a nonfertile time of the ovulatory cycle and while you're enjoying the security of a lasting monogamous relationship. At such a time, reflect on how your bliss is made paradoxically possible by precisely those features of your physiology that distinguished your remote ancestors, condemned to harems or promiscuity. Ironically, those wretched ancestors had sex only on rare days of ovulation, when they discharged the biological imperative to fertilize, robbed of leisurely pleasure by their desperate need for swift results.

SEXUAL DESIRE

Whether it's dull appetite or ravenous hunger, millions of Americans are unhappy with their intimate lives

She won't look at him. Keeps staring out the window, even though there's nothing to see but the black Minnesota night and a car speeding past, headlights sliding along the glass. "I thought it would just go away," the petite woman says finally, in a small, tired voice. "That it was just a phase I was going through. I would make excuses."

The muffled thuds and shouts of playing children drift from the basement. Her wiry husband, seated on the Early American sofa, is a machinist in his late 30s. She is a homemaker. And all that matters now is that they haven't had sex in eight months. "He'd start a little foreplay. I'd say 'No. Just leave me alone!' "

"Boy, would that put me away," says her husband, his bearded face stony above a red T-shirt. "I was already feeling hurt. I'd roll over and go to sleep."

"Sometimes, every three to four months, I'd force myself," she confesses. "Grit my teeth and get through it."

Neither partner looks at the other, and a hesitant hush hovers over the room. Finally, the husband turns to psychologist Eli Coleman, who runs a sex-therapy clinic in nearby Minneapolis. "There's just one thing I want to know," he says, frowning. "Is this a common situation?"

Common? Try epidemic. The problem under discussion is sexual desire, an instinct that should flow as freely and unself-consciously between two loving humans as the urge for a fine meal or a good night's sleep. This is a story about what happens when desire goes askew. It is a tale of people who typically are articulate, competent and to all appearances quite ordinary, yet they cannot enjoy one of humankind's most basic pleasures. Madonna may be falling out of her bustier on MTV, Prince may be singing the joys of masturbation on FM and the latest sex-and-gore thriller may be packing them in at the Cineplex, but in the bedroom, an estimated 1 in 5 Americans—some 38 million adults—don't want sex at all. As many as 9 million more, meanwhile, suffer almost uncontrollable sexual desire, compulsively masturbating or prowling a surreal landscape of massage parlors and rumpled beds in a frenzied quest for loveless sex.

To be sure, sexual-desire disorders date back a lot further than "The Devil and Miss Jones," or even Don Juan. What's new is that such complaints now constitute the No. 1 problem bringing clients to sex therapists. Women without orgasms and men who ejaculated prematurely once dominated the practice; now—because of the pioneering research of Dr. William Masters and Virginia Johnson in the 1960s—people with such common conditions seek do-it-yourself solutions. "The simpler cases can go out and get self-help books," says Dr. Constance Moore, head of the Human Sexuality Program at Houston's Baylor College of Medicine. "Today, sex therapists are seeing the more complicated problems."

No one is sure whether the onslaught of Americans seeking help reflects a real rise in desire disorders or whether such problems are simply more visible. In the 1960s, public expectations of sex began to shift in profound ways. Thanks to the birth-control pill, women could for the first time in history separate sex from the fear of pregnancy. Suddenly, it was not only OK for women to enjoy sex—it was *de rigueur*. The 1953 Kinsey report that as many as 29 percent of single women were sexually unresponsive now seemed as old-fashioned as stiff petticoats and white gloves.

At the same time, new cultural messages glorified casual sex. More than 80 percent of women and 90 percent of men now engage in premarital intercourse, compared with 50 percent of women and 80 percent of men in the 1920s. And from seductive Calvin Klein–jeans ads to the estimated 176 monthly sex scenes on prime-time TV, free sex has emerged as the presumptive symbol of the good life. Sexual health has become a right.

And so they come for help: A man who, after pursuing his bride-to-be for months, shuts down sexually on his wedding night in their $200-a-day bridal suite. A school administrator with five boyfriends who sandwiches frenzied appointments for sex between dashes to office and supermarket. They are farmers and salesmen, consultants and lawyers, homemakers and clerks. In the sanitized confines of therapists' offices, they haltingly reveal their secrets—it's hard, after all, to confess even to a best friend that one masturbates five times a day or hasn't slept with one's spouse in a year. Eyes downcast, voices leaden, they evoke the anguish of abusive fathers, of religiously suffocating mothers, of families where sex, if discussed at all, was shameful and dirty and where dad sometimes slipped into bed with the kids.

What unites them is fear. As children, they learned that caring too much for others was risky. As adults, they found they could control their fear by controlling sex. Instead of an intimate and loving act, sex became a tool to manipulate those who might get too close. And while no one can properly distinguish why some people channel childhood anxieties into food or booze while others fasten on sex, it may be that what eating disorders were to the '80s, desire disorders will be in the '90s: the designer disease of the decade, the newest symptom of American loneliness and alienation. "Sex isn't just sex," explains Raul C. Schiavi, head of the Human Sexuality Program at Mount Sinai Medical Center. "It's an avenue to express many more needs: intimacy, support, self-esteem or whatever."

Given that baggage, it's no wonder that the treatments for sex problems are neither identical nor tidy. In the past three years, researchers have discovered that antidepressants like Prozac can markedly improve symptoms in sexual compulsives. But for victims of low desire, the results are sketchier. The quest for an aphrodisiac, of course, is ancient: King Tut gulped licorice root before romancing his queen, and other love potions, from powdered rhinoceros horn to bees' wings, have proved just as disappointing. But for most cases, treatment involves counseling and therapy, beginning with an attempt to define when things went wrong.

WHAT IS NORMAL?

At first it was fun: feverish kisses in his red Chevy, giggly nights of passion in the apartment. But then came marriage, two kids, and suddenly her husband's hands on her flesh felt like tentacles, and the sight of him approaching made her body stiffen with revulsion. Then the disagreements began, hurtful scenes ending with each of them lying wedged against opposite sides of the bed, praying for sleep. "I didn't know what to do— look in the yellow pages?" recalls Karen, 35, a clerk-cashier in suburban Minneapolis. Her husband didn't know, either. "We finally got a phone number from our family doctor," he says. "It was three more months before we called."*

It wasn't so long ago that low sexual desire was considered a good thing—at least in women. Madame Bovary scandalized 19th-century France with her extramarital fling in Gustave Flaubert's novel. And no one ever said that the remote Estella of Dickens's "Great Expectations" had a low-desire problem. Indeed, from Eve's seduction of Adam, women's sexuality outside of procreation was often considered evil, and early Christian thinkers were just as unsparing toward men—a philosophy that found particularly fertile ground in the New World. As recently as 1907, Dr. John Harvey Kellogg developed his popular corn flakes in an unsuccessful effort to curb desire.

Nor were men and women always physically able to enjoy sex. In late 17th-century England, for instance,

*Like many desire disorder victims quoted here, Karen is a client of the University of Minnesota's Program in Human Sexuality. All names and identifications have been changed.

people suffered from long bouts of crippling illness, not to mention bad breath from poor dentistry, running sores, ulcers and skin diseases. Without antibiotics, women endured repeated vaginal and urinary tract infections that made sex painful.

Then came marriage, two children, and suddenly her husband's hands felt like tentacles. His approach made her stiffen with revulsion.

In fact, the idea of "normal" sexual appetite is such a 20th-century artifice that few experts are comfortable defining it. Clinically, hypoactive sexual desire means having sexual urges, fantasies and/or activity less than twice a month. But even that is the loosest of definitions, since if both partners are happy, once a month may be as "proper" as once a day. "I make the diagnosis [of HSD] if there's been a definite change in desire," says sexologist Moore, "and if it's causing the patient some distress." In Karen's case, the distress was acute: Each night she huddled on her side of the bed, tormenting herself with guilt and dread that her marriage was slipping away.

More typically, though, it's the patient's *partner* who is in distress. Consider Tom, 35, a Midwestern advertising executive whose wife has HSD. "I would try to ignore it as long as I could," he says. "Then she'd give in [and have sex]. But she'd lie limp, waiting for me to get it over with. She could have been downtown. I felt terrible afterward, very guilty."

Prodded by their mates, victims of desire disorders often show up for therapy complaining of impotence or lack of orgasm. But in the mid-1970s, therapists began to notice that the real problem was often that, as in Karen's case, they didn't truly *want* to have sex. In her groundbreaking 1979 work, "Disorders of Sexual Desire," Dr. Helen Singer Kaplan found that unlike sexual arousal, desire exists primarily in the mind. As a result, Kaplan concluded, HSD stems not from a lack of ability to perform but from a lack of motivation. Even so, the fact that HSD may be "all in your mind" doesn't make living with it any easier. "The most important part of sex," Kaplan says, "is the emotional, subjective part. Without that, mechanical function is not gratifying."

Therapists have found that HSD appears to be about twice as prevalent in women as in men. While no national samples are available, one 1978 study of 100 nonclinical American couples found that 35 percent of the women reported lack of sexual interest, compared with 16 percent of the men. But despite this gap, the causes of HSD for both men and women are the same, and the problem usually begins with the emotions.

CAUSES OF LOW DESIRE

The memories started coming after two years in therapy: gauzy, not quite distinct, yet so haunting that tears slowly squeezed from her eyes right in front of the therapist. Jeanine was 8 years old, lying in bed in her Wisconsin home, watching the door creak open. Suddenly, her father was silently over her, breathing heavily. She never told anybody. How could she? There were crucifixes in every room of the house, and her father led the family in the rosary nightly during Lent. Her mother once lectured her on how little girls who "touched themselves" must confess to the priest. Years later, after she got married, Jeanine never had an orgasm with her husband, Tom. Later, she shut down altogether. She and Tom last had sex 4 ¹/₂ years ago.

The roots of desire disorders often lie between the "Sesame Street" years and junior high. Some adults, like Jeanine, report having been sexually abused as children; for others, the abuse was more emotional. John Money, who has pioneered treatments for deviate sexuality at Johns Hopkins University, says children raised in homes where sex is viewed as evil and harmless activities like "playing doctor" are cruelly punished are likely to grow up with warped sexual identities. "In girls, often you extinguish the lust completely, so that they can never have an orgasm, and marriage becomes a dreary business where you put up with sex to serve the maternal instinct," says Money. "In boys, sex gets redirected into abnormal channels."

Jeanine was 8 years old, lying in bed, watching the door creak open. Suddenly, her father was silently on her, breathing heavily.

Not surprisingly, women like Jeanine, who learn as children not to trust those closest to them, often have trouble melding passion and intimacy. Although victims of low desire may be drawn to hit-and-run encounters with strangers, when they get close to a partner, it's too dangerous to let themselves go sexually. Many men suffer from Freud's famous "Madonna-whore complex," whereby a man endows his partner with the "Madonna-like" qualities of his mother. "You find a sudden cessation of interest in sex right after the wedding, even on the night the engagement was announced," says Harold Lief, professor emeritus of psychiatry at the University of Pennsylvania. "These men can't lust after someone they love, or vice versa."

Then there are the tangled cases, where the core problem is not so much historical as personal: The husband and wife detest each other. Marital difficulties, say Lief and other therapists, underlie as many as half of desire disorder cases. Often the problem stems from suppressed anger. "If a couple comes into my office," says Kaplan, "and they fight about where they're gonna sit, and the only question is who's gonna complain about the other more, I know why they're not having sex."

Childbirth, stress and depression can also precipitate low sexual desire. But only in a minority of cases— roughly 15 percent—are the causes medical, such as hormone deficiencies or diseases like diabetes. Some antidepressants and antihypertensives can also squelch desire. The good news is that such problems usually have a medical solution, sparing patients lengthy hours on an analyst's couch. But the story is not so simple for most HSD sufferers.

TREATMENT FOR HSD

"I just can't do this," Karen announced, midway through the first "homework" session. The kids were asleep in the next room, and the suburban Minneapolis woman and her husband, Bruce, lay naked on the bed. For 15 minutes, according to their therapist, Bruce was to gently explore her breasts and genitals, while she told him what felt good. But as she guided his hand across her rigid body, it might have been made of marble: She felt nothing. Devastated she thought: "This is a waste of time. Nothing's going to change." Later, she told Bruce, "I don't want to go back to therapy." He replied: "We have no choice. We've got to go back."

Reversing low desire takes time. "I went into therapy thinking I'd get an instant fix," says Karen, who has seen a psychologist for a year but still has not had intercourse with her husband. Many therapists estimate the cure rate for low desire is 50 percent at best, and can take months or years of therapy. Nor do desire disorders lend themselves to any standard formula. "It's not a cookbook," says Kaplan. "We work out a different program for each."

Take Jeanine, the Wisconsin woman who was abused by her father. At first, her therapist assigned a set of widely used "homework" exercises based on the work of Masters and Johnson. The program aims to demystify the sex act by having couples practice mutual, noncoital "pleasuring" at first. Therapists emphasize that the practice is not strictly mechanical—a loving atmosphere is considered crucial. In Jeanine's case, the exercises helped her experience the first orgasm of her life by masturbating. And while sex with her husband hasn't yet improved, she has begun in therapy to deal with long-suppressed memories of childhood sexual abuse.

It would be a lot simpler, of course, if scientists could somehow find that elusive "sex pill"—a notion that might not be as farfetched as it seems. Researchers know desire is triggered in the brain by the male hormone testosterone, with the help of chemicals like dopamine that act as "messengers" between nerve cells in the brain. In recent years, doctors have begun using testosterone to stimulate desire in menopausal women, as well as in men with low hormone levels. And the pharmaceutical giant Eli Lilly & Co. has had promising preliminary results with drugs that affect dopamine; the results of a full-scale study are due out next year. But for now, drugs hold far more promise for treating people who have too much desire, not too little.

WHEN SEX BECOMES COMPULSIVE

Gary's pattern was always the same: first, the unbearable anxiety, never feeling good enough to handle the latest stress at his architect's job. Then, the familiar response—a furtive scanning of newspaper ads, a drive to a strip show, two straight Scotches to catch a buzz, and finally a massage parlor. He would park about a block away, slip off his wedding ring and dart through the door, where $100 bought a massage, sex and momentary relief. Afterward, he'd sit naked on the edge of the bed, his thoughts roiling in disgust: "I must be sick . . . I can't change." But a few days later, the anxiety would begin again and he'd pore over the ads.

Too *much* sex? For many Americans, especially young men, the notion sounds like an oxymoron. In fact, the downside of sexual compulsiveness has been largely overshadowed throughout history by a romanticized view of the rake, from Casanova to basketball legend Wilt Chamberlain, with his claims of 20,000 affairs. Compulsive sexual behavior is perhaps easiest to define by what it is not: It does not include someone who masturbates occasionally, periodically rents an X-rated video or engages in a limited period of promiscuity following the breakup of a relationship. As best therapists can tell, those prey to CSB alternate between profound anxiety and all-embracing self-loathing.

But these are not perverts in raincoats. Gary, the architect described above, wears a well-cut tweed sports jacket and speaks in measured tones. "I was two different people," he says quietly, seated in a psychologist's office in Minneapolis. "Most people who knew my wife and me would say we were a good couple. But when I was home I wasn't really there. I felt like a dirty person, rotten." Indeed, one hallmark of compulsive sexual behavior is secrecy: Gary's wife didn't find out about his clandestine visits to porn shops and prostitutes until she discovered a phone bill listing multiple calls to a "900" sex line.

After $100 bought a massage, sex and momentary relief, he'd sit naked on the bed, his thoughts roiling in disgust: "I must be sick."

So secret are their escapades that CSB victims have never even been counted, and experts' figures—they estimate roughly 5 percent of the adult American population—are the merest guess. But if the figures are flimsy, the portrait is precise. To the sexual compulsive, sex is not about love or intimacy or even pleasure. It is mainly about relief. "These are highly anxious people who respond to

stress by attempting to 'medicate' their pain through sex," says Eli Coleman, director of the University of Minnesota's Program in Human Sexuality, and a pioneer in treating CSB. Just as the obsessive compulsive washes his hands 100 times in a row, the sexual compulsive turns to a vast erotic menu that might include compulsive masturbation, feverish cruising and anonymous sex, frenzied multiple affairs or insatiable demands within a relationship.

A small proportion of CSB victims cross the criminal divide into hard-core deviations: voyeurism, obscene phone calls, pedophilia, exhibitionism and others. But the majority prefer ordinary sex—taken to an extreme. What they share is an overwhelming sense of powerlessness. Like the alcoholic, the sexual compulsive is so intent on diverting his pain that he often doesn't even *see* a choice. "If I saw a prostitute on the street, that was it," says Jeff, 36, a public-relations executive from St. Paul, Minn. "It was impossible to not do it."

THE CAUSES OF CSB

His parents were strict Catholics who said the rosary every night and sent their 11 kids to parochial school. The messages about sex began early. Once, at age 12, Jeff overheard his 19-year-old sister tell his father. "Sex is fun." His father shouted. "Don't you ever say that!" Jeff's mother didn't even like hugging and protested loudly on the rare occasions that her husband kissed her in front of the children. As for the nuns, Sister Frances told Jeff's third-grade class: "One should never be naked for longer than necessary." The little boy worried that he had condemned his soul to hell by dawdling in the bathroom. "The message was: 'Lord I am not worthy,' " says Jeff, who became hooked as an adult on compulsive phone sex, masturbation and prostitutes. "I took all of it to heart."

Though he has never cheated on his wife, Karl has spent much of his adult life obsessing about sex: fantasizing, masturbating, demanding sex.

Certainly most people survive strict religious upbringing without becoming "Fantasy Hotline" junkies. Yet over and over, as CSB victims have recounted their stories, therapists have seen a disturbing pattern: As children, these men and women learned that sex was anything but a loving, natural experience. Their parents were rarely able to nurture them or allow them to express feelings in healthy ways. In some cases, they simply neglected the kids: Jeff remembers going weeks without a bath and wearing his clothes to bed. Other parents expected their kids to toe some unattainable line of perfection. "My dad yelled at me, taunted me," says Kevin, 32, a professional from the Midwest who started cruising for anonymous sex in public bathrooms at 16. "Sometimes, he would shake me or choke me. He called me Sissie, told me I was worthless, a mess."

In recent years, family therapist Patrick Carnes—author of the 1983 book "Out of the Shadows"—has gained thousands of followers for his claim that CSB is not an anxiety-based disorder but an addiction, much like alcoholism. It is a spiritual disease, he believes, as well as an emotional and physical one, and his plan for recovery involves belief in a higher power. But while the addiction model has spawned four popular nationwide AA-style support groups, many researchers are skeptical, maintaining that it's impossible to be "addicted" to sex since there is no addictive substance involved. Both the chemical and spiritual explanations, they maintain, grossly oversimplify a complex phenomenon. "It's also sex-negative and moralistic," argues Howard Ruppel of the Society for the Scientific Study of Sex. "They confuse normal activity like masturbating with addiction."

TREATMENT OF CSB

Karl is a Wisconsin farmer, a beefy guy of 42 with sharp blue eyes and hands as big as pie plates. "If I went into town here and told them I was a sexual compulsive," he says, "they'd probably shoot me dead." Instead, he went once a week for group therapy. Though he has never cheated on his wife, Karl has spent months obsessing about sex: fantasizing, masturbating, demanding sex two or three times a day. When he eventually sought help, his therapist prescribed the antidepressant Prozac, which immediately "seemed to take the edge off" his craving. The deeper work came in therapy, where Karl found it was safe to talk—even laugh—about his "problem"; no one condemned or ridiculed him, the way his father had. The turning point came when a group member agreed to role-play Karl's dad and Karl shouted back, finally venting his rage at the way his father always put him down. When his dad died, Karl sat by the coffin at the funeral home and told him haltingly that he knew he'd done the best he could. And then he wept.

"It is so inspiring watching people recover—because they do," says Minneapolis psychologist Anne J. McBean. "I can see someone in my office who's an utter wreck, depressed, anxious, and I know that two years later, the same person is going to be sitting here saying, 'I can't believe it—I've got my life back.'"

For years, psychiatrists treated sex offenders with anti-androgens, compounds that partly block the action of the male sex hormones. But because such drugs have potential side effects and are not government-approved for treating CSB, therapists considered them unsuitable for widespread use. In 1989, when Judith L. Rapoport published groundbreaking studies on obsessive compulsive disorders, researchers who had been attempting to link sexual compulsivity with OCD got a boost. Rapoport and others found that drugs that affect the brain chemical serotonin seem to help many people reduce their obsessive-compulsive behaviors, such as constant hand washing.

Sexologists like Coleman have applied the same principle to CSB. In small studies and clinical trials, they tested the effects of both lithium carbonate, which is also used to treat manic depression, and Prozac, which enhances serotonin activity in the brain. Both drugs, they found had some success interrupting the compulsive sexual cycle.

But drugs are only half of the answer. By the time CSB victims seek help, they need therapy as well. Typically, sexual compulsives are largely disconnected from the childhood loneliness and shame that drive their behavior. After Karl, the farmer, saw his farm sold at auction a few years ago, he began obsessing about sex constantly—even driving his pickup or feeding the hogs. In fact, one of the first aims of therapy—once medication had relieved his compulsive symptoms—was to bring back for Karl memories of his father's intolerance, so that he could begin to release them. Within two years of entering therapy, Karl was virtually cured.

Ultimately, the problem with treating both extremes of sexual desire is that researchers still struggle with their own ignorance. The most comprehensive national survey of American sexual behavior is still the Kinsey report, completed nearly 40 years ago. Such studies are expensive and inevitably controversial. Just in the past year, for instance, the Bush administration, under pressure from conservatives, has derailed two planned surveys of American sexual practices. Yet in the absence of such research, knowledge about HSD and CSB is based largely on privately funded studies requiring heroic extrapolations from small samples. Key research—studying the areas of the brain that control sexual behavior or the effects of drugs on desire—awaits funding. "We have almost no information about how people form their sexual habits," says psychologist Elizabeth Allgeier, co-author of "Sexual Interactions," a widely used college text. "If we don't know how it develops, we can't change it."

Still, for millions of Americans it is reassuring to know that no one is doomed to a life of torment by sex. At the very least, educating and encouraging adults to have more enlightened sexual attitudes might enable children to grow up with healthier feelings toward sex. Psychologist John Money says that sexually repressive attitudes now force "at least 50 percent of the nation [to] get 57 cents to the dollar on their sex lives." When Americans are less imprisoned by public expectations and a private sense of sexual shame, perhaps more couples will earn their full satisfaction.

The American Academy of Clinical Sexologists (202-462-2122) and the American Association of Sex Educators, Counselors and Therapists (send an SASE with $2 to 435 North Michigan Ave., Suite 1717, Chicago, IL 60611) will provide names of qualified local sex therapists.

Lynn Rosellini

Beyond Betrayal: Life After

INFIDELITY

Frank Pittman III, M.D.

Hour after hour, day after day in my office I see men and women who have been screwing around. They lead secret lives, as they hide themselves from their marriages. They go through wrenching divorces, inflicting pain on their children and their children's children. Or they make desperate, tearful, sweaty efforts at holding on to the shreds of a life they've betrayed. They tell me they have gone through all of this for a quick thrill or a furtive moment of romance. Sometimes they tell me they don't remember making the decision that tore apart their life: "It just happened." Sometimes they don't even know they are being unfaithful. (I tell them: "If you don't know whether what you are doing is an infidelity or not, ask your spouse.") From the outside looking in, it is insane. How could anyone risk everything in life on the turn of a screw? Infidelity was not something people did much in my family, so I always found it strange and noteworthy when people did it in my practice. After almost 30 years of cleaning up the mess after other people's affairs, I wrote a book describing everything about infidelity I'd seen in my practice. The book was *Private Lies: Infidelity and the Betrayal of Intimacy* (Norton). I thought it might help. Even if the tragedy of AIDS and the humiliation of prominent politicians hadn't stopped it, surely people could not continue screwing around after reading about the absurd destructiveness of it. As you know, people have *not* stopped having affairs. But many of them feel the need

to write or call or drop by and talk to me about it. When I wrote *Private Lies*, I thought I knew everything there was to know about infidelity. But I know now that there is even more.

CCIDENTAL INFIDELITY

All affairs are not alike. The thousands of affairs I've seen seem to fall into four broad categories. Most first affairs are cases of *accidental infidelity*, unintended and uncharacteristic acts of carelessness that really did "just happen." Someone will get drunk, will get caught up in the moment, will just be having a bad day. It can happen to anyone, though some people are more accident prone than others, and some situations are accident zones.

Many a young man has started his career as a philanderer quite accidentally when he is traveling out of town on a new job with a philandering boss who chooses one of a pair of women and expects the young fellow to entertain the other. The most startling dynamic behind accidental infidelity is misplaced politeness, the feeling that it would be rude to turn down a needy friend's sexual advances. In the debonair gallantry of the moment, the brazen discourtesy to the marriage partner is overlooked altogether.

Both men and women can slip up and have accidental affairs, though the most accident-prone are those who drink, those who travel, those who don't get asked much, those who don't feel very tightly married, those whose running buddies

screw around, and those who are afraid to run from a challenge. Most are men.

After an accidental infidelity, there is clearly the sense that one's life and marriage have changed. The choices are:

1. To decide that infidelity was a stupid thing to do, to confess it or not to do so, but to resolve to take better precautions in the future;

2. To decide you wouldn't have done such a thing unless your husband or wife had let you down, put the blame on your mate, and go home and pick your marriage to death;

3. To notice that lightning did not strike you dead, decide this would be a safe and inexpensive hobby to take up, and do it some more;

4. To decide that you would not have done such a thing if you were married to the right person, determine that this was "meant to be," and declare yourself in love with the stranger in the bed.

ROMANTIC INFIDELITY

Surely the craziest and most destructive form of infidelity is the temporary insanity of *falling in love*. You do this, not when you meet somebody wonderful (wonderful people don't screw around with married people) but when you are going through a crisis in your own life, can't continuing living your life, and aren't quite ready for suicide yet. An affair with someone grossly inappropriate—someone decades younger or older, someone dependent or dominating, someone with problems even bigger than your own—is so crazily stimulating that it's like a drug that can lift you out of your depression and enable you to feel things again. Of course, between moments of ecstasy, you are more depressed, increasingly alone and alienated in your life, and increasingly hooked on the affair partner. Ideal romance partners are damsels or "dumsels" in distress, people without a life but with a lot of problems, people with bad reality testing and little concern with understanding reality better.

Romantic affairs lead to a great many

divorces, suicides, homicides, heart attacks, and strokes, but not to very many successful remarriages. No matter how many sacrifices you make to keep the love alive, no matter how many sacrifices your family and children make for this crazy relationship, it will gradually burn itself out when there is nothing more to sacrifice to it. Then you must face not only the wreckage of several lives, but the original depression from which the affair was an insane flight into escape.

People are most likely to get into these

romantic affairs at the turning points of life: when their parents die or their children grow up; when they suffer health crises or are under pressure to give up an addiction; when they achieve an unexpected level of job success or job failure; or when their first child is born—any situation in which they must face a lot of reality and grow up. The better the marriage, the saner and more sensible the spouse, the more alienated the romantic is likely to feel. Romantic affairs happen in good marriages even more often than in bad ones.

MYTHS OF INFIDELITY

The people who are running from bed to bed creating disasters for themselves and everyone else don't seem to know what they are doing. They just don't get it. But why should they? There is a mythology about infidelity that shows up in the popular press and even in the mental health literature that is guaranteed to mislead people and make dangerous situations even worse. Some of these myths are:

1. Everybody is unfaithful; it is normal, expectable behavior. Mozart, in his comic opera *Cosi Fan Tutti,* insisted that women all do it, but a far more common belief is that men all do it: "Higgamous, hoggamous, woman's monogamous; hoggamous, higgamous, man is polygamous." In Nora Ephron's movie, *Heartburn,* Meryl Streep's husband has left her for another woman. She turns to her father for solace, but he dismisses her complaint as the way of all male flesh: "If you want monogamy, marry a swan."

We don't know how many people are unfaithful; if people will lie to their own husband or wife, they surely aren't going to be honest with poll takers. We can guess that one-half of married men and one-third of married women have dropped their drawers away from home at least once. That's a lot of infidelity.

Still, most people are faithful most of the time. Without the expectation of fidelity, intimacy becomes awkward and marriage adversarial. People who expect their partner to betray them are likely to beat them to the draw, and to make both of them miserable in the meantime.

Most species of birds and animals in which the male serves some useful function other than sperm donation are inherently monogamous. Humans, like other nest builders, are monogamous by nature, but imperfectly so. We can be trained out of it, though even in polygamous and promiscuous cultures people show their

true colors when they fall blindly and crazily in love. And we have an escape clause: nature mercifully permits us to survive our mates and mate again. But if we slip up and take a new mate while the old mate is still alive, it is likely to destroy the pair bonding with our previous mate and create great instinctual disorientation—which is part of the tragedy of infidelity.

2. Affairs are good for you; an affair may even revive a dull marriage. Back at the height of the sexual revolution, the *Playboy* philosophy and its *Cosmopolitan* counterpart urged infidelity as a way to keep men manly, women womanly, and marriage vital. Lately, in such books as Annette Lawson's *Adultery* and Dalma Heyn's *The Erotic Silence of the American Wife,* women have been encouraged to act out their sexual fantasies as a blow for equal rights.

It is true that if an affair is blatant enough and if all hell breaks loose, the crisis of infidelity can shake up the most petrified marriage. Of course, any crisis can serve the same detonation function, and burning the house down might be a safer, cheaper, and more readily forgivable attention-getter.

However utopian the theories, the reality is that infidelity, whether it is furtive or blatant, will blow hell out of a marriage. In 30 odd years of practice, I have encountered only a handful of established first marriages that ended in divorce without someone being unfaithful, often with the infidelity kept secret throughout the divorce process and even for years afterwards. Infidelity is the *sine qua non* of divorce.

3. People have affairs because they aren't in love with their marriage partner. People tell me this, and they even remember it this way. But on closer examination it routinely turns out that the marriage was fine before the affair happened, and the decision that they were not in love

with their marriage partner was an effort to explain and justify the affair.

Being in love does not protect people from lust. Screwing around on your loved one is not a very loving thing to do, and it may be downright hostile. Every marriage is a thick stew of emotions ranging from lust to disgust, desperate love to homicidal rage. It would be idiotic to reduce such a wonderfully rich emotional diet to a question ("love me?" or "love me not?") so simplistic that it is best asked of the petals of daisies. Nonetheless, people do ask themselves such questions, and they answer them.

Falling out of love is no reason to betray your mate. If people are experiencing a deficiency in their ability to love their partner, it is not clear how something so hateful as betraying him or her would restore it.

4. People have affairs because they are oversexed. Affairs are about secrets. The infidelity is not necessarily in the sex, but in the dishonesty.

Swingers have sex openly, without dishonesty and therefore without betrayal (though with a lot of scary bugs.) More cautious infidels might have chaste but furtive lunches and secret telephone calls with ex-spouses or former affair partners—nothing to sate the sexual tension, but just enough to prevent a marital reconciliation or intimacy in the marriage.

Affairs generally involve sex, at least enough to create a secret that seals the conspiratorial alliance of the affair, and makes the relationship tense, dangerous, and thus exciting. Most affairs consist of a little bad sex and hours on the telephone. I once saw a case in which the couple had attempted sex once 30 years before and had limited the intimacy in their respective marriages while they maintained their sad, secret love with quiet lunches, pondering the crucial question of whether or not he had gotten it all the way in on that immortal autumn evening in 1958.

Every marriage is a thick stew of emotions ranging from lust to disgust.

Both genders seem equally capable of falling into the temporary insanity of romantic affairs, though women are more likely to reframe anything they do as having been done for love. Women in love are far more aware of what they are doing and what the dangers might be. Men in love can be extraordinarily incautious and willing to give up everything. Men in love lose their heads—at least for a while.

MARITAL ARRANGEMENTS

All marriages are imperfect, and probably a disappointment in one way or another, which is a piece of reality, not a license to mess around with the neighbors. There are some marriages that fail to provide a modicum of warmth, sex, sanity, companionship, money. There are awful marriages people can't get all the way into and can't get all the way out of, divorces people won't call off and can't go through, marriages that won't die and won't recover. Often people in such marriages make a *marital arrangement* by calling in marital aides to keep them company while they avoid living their life. Such practical affairs help them keep the marriage steady but

In general, monogamous couples have a lot more sex than the people who are screwing around.

5. Affairs are ultimately the fault of the cuckold. Patriarchal custom assumes that when a man screws around it must be because of his wife's aesthetic, sexual, or emotional deficiencies. She failed him in some way. And feminist theory has assured us that if a wife screws around it must be because men are such assholes. Many people believe that screwing around is a normal response to an imperfect marriage and is, by definition, the marriage partner's fault. Friends and relatives, bartenders, therapists, and hairdressers, often reveal their own gender prejudices and distrust of marriage, monogamy, intimacy, and honesty, when they encourage the infidel to put the blame on the cuckold rather than on him- or herself.

One trick for avoiding personal blame and responsibility is to blame the marriage itself (too early, too late, too soon after some event) or some unchangeable characteristic of the partner (too old, too tall, too ethnic, too smart, too experienced, too inexperienced.) This is both a cop-out and a dead end.

One marriage partner can make the other miserable, but can't make the other unfaithful. (The cuckold is usually not even there when the affair is taking place). Civilization and marriage require that people behave appropriately however they feel, and that they take full responsibility for their actions. "My wife drove me to it with her nagging"; "I can't help what I do because of what my father did to me"; "She came on to me and her skirt was very short"; "I must be a sex addict"; et cetera. Baloney! If people really can't control their sexual behavior, they should not be permitted to run around loose.

There is no point in holding the cuckold responsible for the infidel's sexual behavior unless the cuckold has total control over the sexual equipment that has run off the road. Only the driver is responsible.

6. It is best to pretend not to know. There are people who avoid unpleasantness and would rather watch the house burn down than bother anyone by yelling "Fire!" Silence fuels the affair, which can thrive only in secrecy. Adulterous marriages begin their repair only when the secret is out in the open, and the infidel does not need to hide any longer. Of course, it also helps to end the affair.

A corollary is the belief that infidels must deny their affairs interminably and do all that is possible to drive cuckolds to such disorientation that they will doubt their own sanity rather than doubt their partner's fidelity. In actuality, the continued lying and denial is usually the most unforgivable aspect of the infidelity.

One man was in the habit of jogging each evening, but his wife noticed that his running clothes had stopped stinking. Suspicious, she followed him—to his secretary's apartment. She burst in and confronted her husband who was standing naked in the secretary's closet. She demanded: "What are you doing here?" He responded: "You do not see me here. You have gone crazy and are imagining this." She almost believed him, and remains to this day angrier about *that* than about the affair itself. Once an affair is known or even suspected, there is no safety in denial, but there is hope in admission.

I recently treated a woman whose physician husband divorced her 20 years ago after a few years of marriage, telling her that she had an odor that was making him sick, and he had developed an allergy to her. She felt so bad about herself she never remarried.

I suspected there was more to the story, and sent her back to ask him whether he had been unfaithful to her. He confessed that he had been, but had tried to shield her from hurt by convincing her that he had been faithful and true but that she was repulsive. She feels much worse about him now, but much better about herself. She now feels free to date.

7. After an affair, divorce is inevitable. Essentially all first-time divorces occur in the wake of an affair. With therapy though, most adulterous marriages can be saved, and may even be stronger and more intimate than they were before the crisis. I have rarely seen a cuckold go all the way through with a divorce after a first affair that is now over. Of course, each subsequent affair lowers the odds drastically.

It doesn't happen the way it does in the movies. The indignant cuckold does scream and yell and carry on and threaten all manner of awful things—which should not be surprising since his or her life has just been torn asunder. But he or she quickly calms down and begins the effort to salvage the marriage, to pull the errant infidel from the arms of the dreaded affairee.

When a divorce occurs, it is because the infidel can not escape the affair in time or cannot face going back into a marriage in which he or she is now known and understood and can no longer pose as the chaste virgin or white knight spotless and beyond criticism. A recent *New Yorker* cartoon showed a forlorn man at a bar complaining: "My wife understands me."

Appropriate guilt is always helpful, though it must come from inside rather than from a raging, nasty spouse; anger is a lousy seduction technique for anyone except terminal weirdos. Guilt is good for you. Shame, however, makes people run away and hide.

The prognosis after an affair is not grim, and those who have strayed have not lost all their value. The sadder but wiser infidel may be both more careful and more grateful in the future.

distant. They thus encapsulate the marital deficiency, so the infidel can neither establish a life without the problems nor solve them. Affairs can wreck a good marriage, but can help stabilize a bad one.

People who get into marital arrangements are not necessarily the innocent victims of defective relationships. Some set out to keep their marriages defective and distant. I have seen men who have kept the same mistress through several marriages, arranging their marriages to serve some practical purpose while keeping their romance safely encapsulated elsewhere. The men considered it a victory over marriage; the exploited wives were outraged.

I encountered one woman who had long been involved with a married man. She got tired of waiting for him to get a divorce and married someone else. She didn't tell her husband about her affair, and she didn't tell her affairee about her marriage. She somehow thought they would never find out about one another. After a few exhausting and confusing weeks, the men met and confronted her. She cheerfully told them she loved them both and the arrangement seemed the sensible way to have her cake and eat it too. She couldn't understand why both the men felt cheated and deprived by her efforts to sacrifice their lives to satisfy her skittishness about total commitment.

Some of these arrangements can get quite complicated. One woman supported her house-husband and their kids by living as the mistress of an older married man, who spent his afternoons and weekend days with her and his evenings at home with his own children and his sexually boring wife. People averse to conflict might prefer such arrangements to therapy, or any other effort to actually solve the problems of the marriage.

Unhappily married people of either gender can establish marital arrangements to help them through the night. But men are more likely to focus on the practicality of the arrangement and diminish awareness of any threat to the stability of the marriage, while women are more likely to romanticize the arrangement and convince themselves it is leading toward an eventual union with the romantic partner. Networks of couples may spend their lives halfway through someone's divorce, usually with a guilt-ridden man reluctant to completely leave a marriage he has betrayed and even deserted, and a woman, no matter how hard she protests to the contrary, eternally hopeful for a wedding in the future.

Philandering

Philandering is a predominantly male activity. Philanderers take up infidelity as a hobby. Philanderers are likely to have a rigid and concrete concept of gender; they worship masculinity, and while they may be greatly attracted to women, they are mostly interested in having the woman affirm their masculinity. They don't really like women, and they certainly don't want an equal, intimate relationship with a member of the gender they insist is inferior, but far too powerful. They see women as dangerous, since women have the ability to assess a man's worth, to measure him and find him wanting, to determine whether he is man enough.

These men may or may not like sex, but they use it compulsively to affirm their masculinity and overcome both their homophobia and their fear of women. They can be cruel, abusive, and even violent to women who try to get control of them and stop the philandering they consider crucial to their masculinity. Their life is centered around displays of masculinity, however they define it, trying to impress women with their physical strength, competitive victories, seductive skills, mastery of all situations, power, wealth, and, if necessary, violence. Some of them are quite charming and have no trouble finding women eager to be abused by them.

Gay men can philander too, and the dynamics are the same for gay philanderers as for straight ones: the obvious avoidance of female sexual control, but also the preoccupation with masculinity and the use of rampant sexuality for both reassurance and the measurement of manhood. When men have paid such an enormous social and interpersonal price for their preferred sexuality, they are likely to wrap an enormous amount of their identity around their sexuality and express that sexuality extensively.

Philanderers may be the sons of philanderers, or they may have learned their ideas about marriage and gender from their ethnic group or inadvertently from their religion. Somewhere they have gotten the idea that their masculinity is their most valuable attribute and it requires them to protect themselves from coming under female control. These guys may consider themselves quite principled and honorable, and they may follow the rules to the letter in their dealings with other men. But in their world women have no rights.

To men they may seem normal, but women experience them as narcissistic or even sociopathic. They think they are normal, that they are doing what every other real man would do if he weren't such a wimp. The notions of marital fidelity, of gender equality, of honesty and intimacy between husbands and wives seem quite foreign from what they learned growing up. The gender equality of monogamy may not feel compatible to men steeped in patriarchal beliefs in men being gods and women being ribs. Monogamous sexuality is difficult for men who worship Madonnas for their sexlessness and berate Eves for their seductiveness.

Philanderers' sexuality is fueled by anger and fear, and while they may be considered "sex addicts" they are really "gender compulsives," desperately doing whatever they think will make them look and feel most masculine. They put notches on their belts in hopes it will make their penises grow bigger. If they can get a woman to die for them, like opera composer Giacomo Puccini did in real life and in most of his operas, they feel like a real man.

Female Philanderers

There are female philanderers too, and they too are usually the daughters or ex-wives of philanderers. They are angry at men, because they believe all men screw around as their father or ex-husband did. A female philanderer is not likely to stay married for very long, since that would require her to make peace with a man, and as a woman to carry more than her share of the burden of marriage. Marriage grounds people in reality rather than transporting them into fantasy, so marriage is too loving, too demanding, too realistic, and not romantic enough for them.

I hear stories of female philanderers, such as Maria Riva's description of her mother, Marlene Dietrich. They appear to have insatiable sexual appetites but, on closer examination, they don't like sex much, they do like power over men, and underneath the philandering anger, they are plaintively seeking love.

Straying wives are rarely philanderers, but single women who mess around with married men are quite likely to be. Female philanderers prefer to raid other people's marriages, breaking up relationships, doing as much damage as possible, and then dancing off reaffirmed. Like male philanderers, female philanderers put their victims through all of this just to give themselves a sense of gender power.

Spider Woman

There are women who, by nature romantics, don't quite want to escape their own life and die for love. Instead they'd rather have some guy wreck his life for them. These women have been so recently betrayed by unfaithful men that the wound is still raw and they are out for revenge. A woman who angrily pursues married men is a "spider woman"—she requires human sacrifice to restore her sense of power.

When she is sucking the blood from other people's marriages, she feels some relief from the pain of having her own marriage betrayed. She simply requires that a man love her enough to sacrifice his life for her. She may be particularly attracted to happy marriages, clearly envious of the woman whose husband is faithful and loving to her. Sometimes it isn't clear whether she wants to replace the happy wife or just make her miserable.

The women who are least squeamish and most likely to wreak havoc on other people's marriages are victims of some sort of abuse, so angry that they don't feel bound by the usual rules or obligations, so desperate that they cling to any source of security, and so miserable that they don't bother to think a bit of the end of it.

Josephine Hart's novel *Damage,* and the recent Louis Malle film version of it, describe such a woman. She seduces her fiancee's depressed father, and after the fiancee discovers the affair and kills himself, she waltzes off from the wreckage of all the lives. She explains that her father disappeared long ago, her mother had been married four or five times, and her brother committed suicide when she left his bed and began to date other boys. She described herself as damaged, and says, "Damaged people are dangerous. They know they can survive."

Bette was a spider woman. She came to see me only once, with her married affair partner Alvin, a man I had been seeing with his wife Agnes. But I kept up with her through the many people whose lives she touched. Bette's father had run off and left her and her mother when she was just a child, and her stepfather had exposed himself to her. Most recently Bette's man-

All marriages are imperfect, a disappointment in one way or another.

ic husband Burt had run off with a stripper, Claudia, and had briefly married her before he crashed and went into a psychiatric hospital.

While Burt was with Claudia, the enraged Bette promptly latched on to Alvin, a laid-back philanderer who had been married to Agnes for decades and had been screwing around casually most of that time. Bette was determined that Alvin was going to divorce Agnes and marry her, desert his children, and raise her now-fatherless kids. The normally cheerful Alvin, who had done a good job for a lifetime of pleasing every woman he met and avoiding getting trapped by any of them, couldn't seem to escape Bette, but he certainly had no desire to leave Agnes. He grew increasingly depressed and suicidal. He felt better after he told the long-suffering Agnes, but he still couldn't move in any direction. Over the next couple of years, Bette and Alvin took turns threatening suicide, while Agnes tended her garden, raised her children, ran her business, and waited for the increasingly disoriented and pathetic Alvin to come to his senses.

Agnes finally became sufficiently alarmed about her husband's deterioration that she decided the only way she could save his life was to divorce him. She did, and Alvin promptly dumped Bette. He could not forgive her for what she had made him do to dear, sweet Agnes. He lost no time in taking up with Darlene, with whom he had been flirting for some time, but who wouldn't go out with a married man. Agnes felt relief, and the comfort of a good settlement, but Bette was once again abandoned and desperate.

She called Alvin hourly, alternately threatening suicide, reciting erotic poetry, and offering to fix him dinner. She phoned bomb threats to Darlene's office. Bette called me to tell me what a sociopathic jerk

Alvin was to betray her with another woman after all she had done in helping him through his divorce. She wrote sisterly notes to Agnes, offering the comfort of friendship to help one another through the awful experience of being betrayed by this terrible man. At no point did Bette consider that she had done anything wrong. She was now, as she had been all her life, a victim of men, who not only use and abuse women, but won't lay down their lives to rescue them on cue.

EMOTIONALLY RETARDED MEN IN LOVE

About the only people more dangerous than philandering men going through life with an open fly and romantic damsels going through life in perennial distress, are emotionally retarded men in love. When such men go through a difficult transition in life, they hunker down and ignore all emotions. Their brain chemistry gets depressed, but they don't know how to feel it as depression. Their loved ones try to keep from bothering them, try to keep things calm and serene—and isolate them further.

An emotionally retarded man may go for a time without feeling pleasure, pain, or anything else, until a strange woman jerks him back into awareness of something intense enough for him to feel it—perhaps sexual fireworks, or the boyish heroics of rescuing her, or perhaps just fascination with her constantly changing moods and never-ending emotional crises.

With her, he can pull out of his depression briefly, but he sinks back even deeper into it when he is not with her. He is getting addicted to her, but he doesn't know that. He only feels the absence of joy and love and life with his serenely cautious wife

Once an affair is known or even suspected, there's no safety in denial but there is hope in admission.

and kids, and the awareness of life with this new woman. It doesn't work for him to leave home to be with her, as she too would grow stale and irritating if she were around full time.

What he needs is not a crazier woman to sacrifice his life for, but treatment for his depression. However, since the best home remedies for depression are sex, exercise, joy, and triumph, the dangerous damsel may be providing one or more of them in a big enough dose to make him feel a lot better. He may feel pretty good until he gets the bill, and sees how much of his life and the lives of his loved ones this treatment is costing. Marriages that start this way, stepping over the bodies of loved ones as the giddy couple walks down the aisle, are not likely to last long.

Howard had been faithful to Harriett for 16 years. He had been happy with her. She made him feel loved, which no one else had ever tried to do. Howard devoted himself to doing the right thing. He always did what he was supposed to do and he never complained. In fact he said very little at all.

Howard worked at Harriett's father's store, a stylish and expensive men's clothiers. He had worked there in high school and returned after college. He'd never had another job. He had felt like a son to his father-in-law. But when the old man retired, he bypassed the stalwart, loyal Howard and made his own wastrel son manager.

Howard also took care of his own elderly parents who lived next door. His father died, and left a nice little estate to his mother, who then gave much of it to his younger brother, who had gotten into trouble with gambling and extravagance.

Howard felt betrayed, and sank into a depression. He talked of quitting his job and moving away. Harriett pointed out the impracticality of that for the kids. She reminded him of all the good qualities of his mother and her father.

Howard didn't bring it up again. Instead, he began to talk to Maxine, one of the tailors at the store, a tired middle-aged woman who shared Howard's disillusionment with the world. One day, Maxine called frightened because she smelled gas in her trailer and her third ex-husband had threatened to hurt her. She needed for Howard to come out and see if he could smell anything dangerous. He did, and somehow ended up in bed with Maxine. He felt in love. He knew it was crazy but he couldn't get along without her. He bailed her out of the frequent disasters in her life. They began to plot their getaway, which consumed his attention for months.

Harriett noticed the change in Howard, but thought he was just mourning his father's death. They continued to get along well, sex was as good as ever, and they enjoyed the same things they had always enjoyed. It was a shock to her when he told her he was moving out, that he didn't love her anymore, and that it had nothing whatever to do with Maxine, who would be leaving with him.

Harriett went into a rage and hit him. The children went berserk. The younger daughter cried inconsolably, the older one

Most affairs consist of a little bad sex and a lot of telephoning.

became bulimic, the son quit school and refused to leave his room. I saw the family a few times, but Howard would not turn back. He left with Maxine, and would not return my phone calls. The kids were carrying on so on the telephone, Howard stopped calling them for a few months, not wanting to upset them. Meanwhile he and Maxine, who had left her kids behind as well, borrowed some money from his mother and moved to the coast where they bought into a marina—the only thing they had in common was the pleasure of fishing.

A year later, Harriett and the kids were still in therapy but they were getting along pretty well without him. Harriett was running the clothing store. Howard decided he missed his children and invited them to go fishing with him and Maxine. It surprised him when they still refused to speak to him. He called me and complained to me that his depression was a great deal worse. The marina was doing badly. He and Maxine weren't getting along very well. He missed his children and cried a lot, and she told him his preoccupation with his children was a betrayal of her. He blamed Harriett for fussing at him when she found out about Maxine. He believed she turned the children against him. He couldn't understand why anyone would be mad with him; he couldn't help who he loves and who he doesn't love.

 EN AND WOMEN WHO CHEAT

Howard's failure to understand the complex emotional consequences of his affair is typically male, just as Bette's insistence that her affair partner live up to her romantic fantasies is typically female. Any gender-based generalization is both irritating and inaccurate, but some behaviors are typical. Men tend to attach too little significance to affairs, ignoring their horrifying power to disorient and disrupt lives, while women tend to attach too much significance, assuming that the emotions are so powerful they must be "real" and therefore concrete, permanent, and stable enough to risk a life for.

A man, especially a philandering man, may feel comfortable having sex with a woman if it is clear that he is not in love with her. Even when a man understands that a rule has been broken and he expects consequences of some sort, he routinely underestimates the extent and range and duration of the reactions to his betrayal. Men may agree that the sex is wrong, but may believe that the lying is a noble effort to protect the family. A man may reason that outside sex is wrong because there is a rule against it, without understanding that his lying establishes an adversarial relationship with his mate and is the greater offense. Men are often surprised at the intensity of their betrayed mate's anger, and then even more surprised when she is willing to take him back. Men rarely appreciate the devastating long-range impact of their infidelities, or even their divorces, on their children.

Routinely, a man will tell me that he assured himself that he loved his wife before he hopped into a strange bed, that the women there with him means nothing, that it is just a meaningless roll in the hay. A woman is more likely to tell me that at the sound of the zipper she quickly ascertained that she was not as much in love with her husband as she should have been, and the man there in bed with her was the true love of her life.

A woman seems likely to be less concerned with the letter of the law than with the emotional coherence of her life. It may be okay to screw a man if she "loves" him, whatever the status of his or her marriage, and it is certainly appropriate to lie to a man who believes he has a claim on you, but whom you don't love.

Women may be more concerned with the impact of their affairs on their children than they are with the effect on their mate, whom they have already devalued and discounted in anticipation of the affair. Of course, a woman is likely to feel the children would be in support of her affair, and thus may involve them in relaying her messages, keeping her secrets, and telling her lies. This can be mind-blowingly seductive and confusing to the kids. Sharing the secret of one parent's affair, and hiding it from the other parent, has essentially the same emotional impact as incest.

Some conventional wisdom about gender differences in infidelity is true.

More men than women do have affairs, but it seemed to me that before the AIDS epidemic, the rate for men was dropping (philandering has not been considered cute since the Kennedy's went out of power) and the rate for women was rising (women who assumed that all men were screwing around saw their own screwing around as a blow for equal rights.) In recent years, promiscuity seems suicidal so only the suicidal—that is, the romantics—are on the streets after dark.

Men are able to approach sex more casually than women, a factor not only of the patriarchal double standard but also of the difference between having genitals on the outside and having them on the inside. Getting laid for all the wrong reasons is a lot less dangerous than falling in love with all the wrong people.

Men who get caught screwing around are more likely to be honest about the sex than women. Men will confess the full sexual details, even if they are vague about the emotions. Women on the other hand will confess to total consuming love and suicidal desire to die with some man, while insisting no sex ever took place. I would believe that if I'd ever seen a man describe the affair as so consumingly intense from the waist up and so chaste from the waist down. I assume these women are lying to me about what they know they did or did not do, while I assume that the men really are honest about the genital ups and downs—and honestly confused about the emotional ones.

Women are more likely to discuss their love affairs with their women friends. Philandering men may turn their sex lives into a spectator sport but romantic men tend to keep their love life private from their men friends, and often just withdraw from their friends during the romance.

On the other hand, women are not more romantic than men. Men in love are every bit as foolish and a lot more naive than women in love. They go crazier and risk more. They are far more likely to sacrifice or abandon their children to prove their love to some recent affairee. They are more likely to isolate themselves from everyone except their affair partner, and turn their thinking and feeling over to her, applying her romantic ways of thinking (or not thinking) to the dilemmas of his increasingly chaotic life.

Men are just as forgiving as women of their mates' affairs. They might claim ahead of time that they would never tolerate it, but when push comes to shove, cuckolded men are every bit as likely as cuckolded women to fight like tigers to hold on to a marriage that has been betrayed. Cuckolded men may react violently at first, though cuckolded women do so as well, and I've seen more cases of women who shot and wounded or killed errant husbands. (The shootings occur not when the affair is stopped and confessed, but when it is continued and denied.)

Betrayed men, like betrayed women, hunker down and do whatever they have to do to hold their marriage together. A few men and women go into a rage and refuse to turn back, and then spend a lifetime nursing the narcissistic injury, but that unusual occurrence is no more common for men than for women. Marriage can survive either a husband's infidelity or a wife's, if it is stopped, brought into the open, and dealt with.

I have cleaned up from more affairs than a squad of motel chambermaids. Infidelity is a very messy hobby. It is not an effective way to find a new mate or a new life.

It is not a safe treatment for depression, boredom, imperfect marriage, or inadequate gender splendor. And it certainly does not impress the rest of us. It does not work for women any better than it does for men. It does excite the senses and the imaginations of those who merely hear the tales of lives and deaths for love, who melt at the sound of liebestods or country songs of love gone wrong.

I think I've gotten more from infidelity as an observer than all the participants I've seen. Infidelity is a spectator sport like shark feeding or bull fighting—that is, great for those innocent bystanders who are careful not to get their feet, or whatever, wet. For the greatest enjoyment of infidelity, I recommend you observe from a safe physical and emotional distance and avoid any suicidal impulse to become a participant.

Relationships in Transition

- **From Marriage to Family (Articles 22–25)**
- **Parenting (Articles 26–31)**
- **Divorce and Remarriage (Articles 32–36)**
- **Later Years (Articles 37–40)**

> The art of living does not consist in preserving and clinging to a particular mood of happiness, but in allowing happiness to change its form without being disappointed by the change; for happiness, like a child, must be allowed to grow up.
>
> —Morgan

This section focuses on transitions in marriage and family situations. Although contemporary family life affords individuals considerable latitude in defining their positions within the family, there remain some commonly experienced transitions in marriage and family. Individuals and relationships are affected by parenting, divorce, death, remarriage, and aging.

Contrary to tradition, children are no longer an automatic part of the life plan for many contemporary married couples. Over several decades there has been a remarkable change in childbearing patterns among American women. Compared to the mothers of an earlier generation, who tended to marry young and have many children, today's women are marrying later, waiting much longer to have children, and choosing, in some instances, to have no children at all. Today, some women and a few men are choosing parenthood without marriage or a partner.

Parenthood has become more of a choice than an automatic life script. Delaying parenthood is a common choice for a variety of women and couples. There are many reasons to delay childbearing: advanced education for women provides them with more job opportunities, the availability of contraceptives allows for better reproductive control, and the recent economic pinch forces some women to choose between work and children. However, the choice of delaying childbearing is not without risks. Many couples who delayed childbearing in their twenties and thirties are finding that they are having difficulty conceiving. Even as reproductive technology advances, infertility and the "biological clock" are real specters for this generation of women and couples. Yet for those who do choose parenthood, whether via traditional or nontraditional paths, a myriad of decades-old parenting problems, as well as others new at the end of this century, pose threats to idyllic dreams.

The first subsection opens with "Ultrasound: An Amazing Look at Life," an article describing a now fairly commonplace application of sound-wave technology that can monitor fetal development. The next two articles focus on aspects of pregnancy and childbirth and discuss two very different trends in childbirth practices: home births and unnecessary cesarean births. Both provide important information needed by women and couples who strive to make informed choices. The final subsection article, "She Died Because of a Law," reminds us that even today's childbearing choices may be life and death choices.

We expect that becoming parents will bring many pleasurable moments and joys, and it does. However, parents also must cope with hard work, hard choices, worry, pain, exhaustion, and frustration. The six articles in the next subsection deal with the full range of parenting experiences. The first article deals with a situation that every parent hopes will never happen: their child is choking. Simple instructions and clear diagrams cover what can be done to save the child's live. The article "20 Sanity Savers" consolidates the wisdom of experts—professionals and parenting survivors—on how to juggle jobs, marriage, and kids. The next two articles focus on child care, giving assistance and advice to parents struggling to find, afford, and manage safe and quality care for their children. The final two articles in this subsection focus on fathers and fathering. The first describes the Responsive Fathers program and its efforts to teach unwed fathers how to fulfill legal, financial, and emotional responsibilities for their children. "Father Figures" looks at what fatherhood means today, illustrating changes and rising involvement, as well as differences among fathers and between fathers and mothers.

Divorce and remarriage are considered in the next subsection. People may enter marriage with unrealistic goals and expectations. When they are unable to achieve them instantly, they often give up and separate or divorce. The effects of divorce on the partners, the children involved, and society itself are discussed in the articles chosen for this subsection. The first two articles focus on divorce. "Family Values: The Bargain Breaks" looks at causes and effects of divorce—the breaking of the marital bargain—finding devastating effects for men, women, children, and society. "Will the Kids Ever Adjust to Our Divorce?" illustrates the problems associated with parents not acknowledging and dealing with their and their children's feelings about the divorce. The next three articles cover a variety of remarriage issues. The "Second Time Around" illustrates the often-complicated money, time, and loyalty issues involved when two families are joined by remarriage. In "The Myths and Misconceptions of the Stepmother Identity," readers have an opportunity to examine the way our culture has set up stepmothers and families with an impossible evil/angelic dichotomy. The final subsection article presents an innovative program designed to improve the odds for remarriages: "Remarriage Education: The Personal Reflections Program."

Unit 4

The maturing family is the focus of the final subsection of this unit. As many baby boomers age, and life expectancy continues to climb, the number of people over age 50 increases, as does the number of years a couple or family has together after their parenting phase. The articles in this subsection provide readers the opportunity to confront our culture's youth-centered biases, as well as our own denial and avoidance that we, too, will be old someday. The first two articles address divorce-related issues for the over-50 age group that are often neglected. "What Women Want Men to Know about Menopause" should be required reading for everyone, so as to dispel the myths and remove the shroud of mystery and embarrassment from this normal aging process. The final article, "The Grandparent Bond: Why Kids Need It," illustrates the valuable, even crucial, roles these oldest family members can play in today's families.

Looking Ahead: Challenge Questions

Have you decided whether or not to have children? Are there any circumstances under which you would do so without a spouse?

What do you expect parenthood to be like? Have you ever talked with your parents or other parents about their expectations, their experiences, and the differences between the two?

When you become a parent, do you expect to share equally child-care responsibilities with your mate? How will household responsibilities be allocated? How will you as a couple support yourselves? Do you expect to use substitute child care on a part-time or full-time basis so that both you and your spouse can work? What if these ideals cannot happen?

In what ways do you see mothering and fathering roles as different? Should these differences be changed? If so, how, why and when do you think they will happen?

Are your parents divorced or do you know friends whose parents are? How have you, or they, been affected?

Is your family, or that of a friend you know fairly well, a remarried or blended family? If so, how have you, or they, been affected?

What are your images regarding menopause? Your thoughts? Your fears? Have you ever talked about the topic of menopause with anyone? When and how did it go?

How can today's families take advantage of the important and positive roles grandparents can play?

Ultrasound

An Amazing Look at Life

For many expectant parents, the thrill of seeing the tiny fetus confirms that their baby is really on the way.

Fay Stevenson-Smith, M.D.
with Dena K. Salmon

Fay Stevenson-Smith, M.D., *is an obstetrician-gynecologist in private practice in Norwalk, Connecticut.* **Dena K. Salmon,** *a contributing editor to* Parents *Magazine, lives in Montclair, New Jersey.*

My patient Maggie was about eight weeks into her third pregnancy. Her first two pregnancies had ended in first-trimester miscarriages, so when she started spot bleeding again, she panicked. Many women who experience spotting go on to have a perfectly normal pregnancy and baby, but given Maggie's history, I was concerned. We scheduled an ultrasound examination for the following day.

Maggie admitted that she was dreading the exam, fearing it would confirm that there was something wrong. But the exam brought relief, amazement, and joy. The sonogram showed that her baby was the right size for its gestational age and had a strong, healthy heartbeat. In addition, seeing a picture of the tiny fetus made her baby seem real to her. "It's like a miracle—I can really see a tiny baby!" Maggie said.

Ultrasound technology, first developed roughly 30 years ago, has revolutionized the way in which a pregnancy can be evaluated and followed.

The health of the fetus can be monitored much earlier.

Before ultrasound, doctors judged fetal age, size, and health by the mother's observations and by feeling the size and shape of the uterus and baby. To ascertain whether the baby was alive and well, the physician would have had to wait until the sixteenth or seventeenth week of pregnancy to hear the baby's heartbeat with a stethoscope or until the mother could feel the baby move within her.

With the advent of ultrasound, however, parents and doctors suddenly had a window through which they could view the fetus and anticipate problems.

Because the majority of pregnancies proceed with no complications, many physicians believe that routine ultrasound exams are unnecessary. The use of ultrasound during pregnancy, however, is on the rise. As of 1991, approximately one-half of all pregnant women in the United States had a sonogram.

Although ultrasound has thus far proved to be a safe procedure, excessive sonograms are costly and unnecessary. Like many obstetricians, I don't offer one during the first trimester unless there is a medical reason to do so, such as diagnosing an ectopic pregnancy or a miscarriage.

During the first trimester, ultrasound is most commonly used in conjunction with amniocentesis—the sonogram helps the doctor determine where to safely inject the needle. Another reason to conduct a first-trimester ultrasound is to see how many weeks old the fetus is if the mother isn't sure of the date of her last period and her doctor can't tell how far along she is.

Usually I recommend waiting until roughly the eighteenth week of pregnancy to conduct an exam, because at that point I can learn a lot more about the baby and its environment.

Ultrasound at this point helps to verify fetal age and gives us some basic information about the develop-

How a Sonogram Is Created

Ultrasound creates a picture of your baby (called a sonogram) from sound waves, which move at a frequency too high to be heard by the human ear. There are two types of ultrasound exams during pregnancy: transabdominal and transvaginal. Each is painless and takes about ten minutes.

For a transabdominal exam, your doctor or ul-

trasound technologist uses a transducer—a wandlike instrument—to scan your abdomen.

Bouncing sound waves form a picture.

The transducer produces and receives sound waves as it passes over the skin's surface. The sound waves bounce off your uterus, ovaries, and the developing baby and are

then converted into an image of your baby that shows up on a TV-like screen. "Real-time" ultrasound (which can be used for both types of exams) combines one still picture after another to show movement.

The only discomfort of a transabdominal ultrasound is that you will most likely be asked to drink several glasses of water an hour be-

fore and not to urinate until after the procedure. The full bladder is a landmark to help your doctor locate the pelvic organs.

A transvaginal exam is used in early pregnancy and works much the same way as a transabdominal, except that the transducer is inserted into the vagina. For this type of exam, a full bladder is not necessary.

ment of the baby's head, spine, heart, abdomen, kidneys, and limbs. Occasionally, if the baby is in the right position, we can also tell if it is a boy or a girl, but doctors have been known to make the wrong call.

Ultrasound can also provide crucial information about the placement of the placenta—an important diagnosis—because abnormal positioning of the placenta may cause bleeding during labor and delivery

and may even necessitate a cesarean delivery. Doctors also use ultrasound to assess the quantity of the amniotic fluid that protects the baby. Finally, this second-trimester exam can be very useful later on as a point of reference if there is a question about the baby's rate of growth.

In the third trimester, an ultrasound exam is usually done if the mother has a medical condition such as hypertension or diabetes.

Premature rupture of the membranes or preterm labor also warrant an ultrasound exam. I'll conduct an ultrasound examination if I suspect that the baby is in a breech position (buttocks or buttocks and feet first) or if it is still in utero well past the due date. I'll also do an ultrasound screening to check on the baby's growth rate, to determine the cause of decreased fetal movement or abnormal heartbeat pattern.

What doctors do when pregnancy is complicated.

In the above circumstances, your doctor may keep tabs on your baby by administering a biophysical profile, which uses ultrasound for a longer period of time (roughly 30 minutes) to assess fetal breathing, fetal heart rate, movement, muscle tone, and quantity of amniotic fluid. The biophysical profile provides a clear picture of the baby's condition.

Recently, in some high-risk pregnancies, doctors have been using a Doppler ultrasound to evaluate, in color, the blood flow through the fetus and from the uterus into the placenta. (The conventional ultrasound procedure does not show blood flow.) Although this procedure is relatively new, it may help determine whether or not the baby is receiving sufficient oxygen in utero.

Ultrasound cannot tell us everything we wish to know about a pregnancy, but it has given parents and doctors a powerful way to improve obstetric care. With its help, pregnancy is no longer a locked box that reveals its secrets only after a baby is born.

HOME DELIVERY

MIDWIFERY WORKS. SO SHOULD MIDWIVES.

Archie Brodsky

Archie Brodsky, a senior research associate at the Harvard Medical School's Program in Psychiatry and the Law, is a former president of Massachusetts Friends of Midwives and co-author of Medical Choices, Medical Chances *and* Home Birth: A Practitioner's Guide to Birth Outside the Hospital. *The author is indebted to Carol Sakala of the Women's Institute for Childbearing Policy for some of the information in this article.*

When Janet Podell became pregnant in 1989, she determined to have "the real thing"—the fully natural, satisfying birth experience that had eluded her when her first two children were born. Although midwives had assisted her in the two unmedicated births, the impersonality, tension, conflict, and pointless restrictions she experienced in the hospital had left her feeling frustrated and violated. Both times, for example, she was separated from the baby and from her husband after the birth. After moving to western Massachusetts, Podell found a pair of midwives to attend her birth at home. What resulted was a qualitatively different experience: She felt as if she had really given birth under her own power, in an atmosphere of loving support.

As Podell later recalled in *The Midwife Advocate*, the newsletter of Massachusetts Friends of Midwives: "I came away from my hospital births with a sense of helplessness. I came away from my home birth feeling that I had learned deep and amazing lessons about my own strength and resilience, about trusting my body and my instincts. . . . What would happen in this fearful society of ours if all the mothers who gave birth had such an experience?"

Podell is one of many American women who have chosen to give birth outside of a hospital during the last 10 to 15 years. Disillusioned with the routine intrusiveness of conventional hospital obstetrics, they have voted with their feet by giving birth at home with the help of family, friends, and supportive attendants. Some of these women, inspired by the rediscovery of birth as a natural and social event, have become midwives themselves, learning their trade by working with more experienced midwives or with sympathetic physicians.

This social movement, until recently marginalized by organized medicine as a softheaded counterculture rebellion, is now finding common ground with mainstream economic and public-health concerns: the rapid escalation of health-care costs; the loss of obstetricians resulting from the epidemic of malpractice suits; and the high rate of infant mortality among the inner-city poor. Midwifery works, people want it, and it provides an answer to some urgent policy questions. But although midwifery has made progress in recent years, a variety of laws and regulations still prevent midwives from offering their services to everyone who could benefit from them.

By confining midwives to the role of obstetrical handmaidens, the law prevents them from making their full contribution to those who want it.

The advantages of midwifery depend on a more thoroughgoing change than just plugging in one type of practitioner in place of another. If the law confines midwives to the role of obstetrical handmaidens working exclusively in hospitals under the direction of physicians, it will prevent them from making their full contribution. For the word *midwifery* really stands for a fundamentally different model of maternity care: different people doing different things, often in a different place.

Midwives reject the view that giving birth is a medical procedure like having a gall bladder removed. Instead, they understand it as a natural process that ordinarily does not require drugs, surgery, or high-tech equipment. Obstetricians, whose skills and techniques are best reserved for complicated births, are in most cases not well prepared to attend normal births. They know how to intervene but not how to support without intervening.

The high-tech, interventionist approach of obstetricians is illustrated by the widespread use of electronic fetal monitoring. EFM—which records fetal heart tones and the pressure of uterine contractions, either through electrodes passed through the birth canal and attached to the baby's scalp or through a transducer placed on the mother's abdomen—may have a legitimate rationale in high-risk births. But from the beginning it was marketed indiscriminately to physicians hungry for precise diagnostic information.

As a result, by the mid-1970s most U.S. hospitals had adopted EFM for routine use, without any controlled studies showing it to be more effective than traditional, noninvasive methods of listening to the baby's heart. Now studies published in the last two years in such prestigious publications as the British journal *The Lancet* and *The New England Journal of Medicine* have shown that, in the absence of specific indications for its use, EFM not only has no demonstrated benefit in reducing childhood disabilities but may even be dangerous.

EFM plays a major role in the futile cycle of defensive obstetrics brought on by malpractice hysteria. For legal protection the physician uses the monitor so he can show, if anything goes wrong, that he "did all he could." But with the monitor readings a matter of record, his actions will be further scrutinized to see if he once again "did all he could" in response to an abnormal reading.

Alarmist reactions to insignificant variations in monitor readings contribute to the current 24-percent cesarean-section rate in the United States (a rate twice as high as the World Health Organization recommends). Indeed, any medical intervention in childbirth tends to necessitate further intervention by disrupting the normal physiology of labor and by immobilizing, enervating, disabling, and dispiriting the mother.

A midwife strives to avoid such intervention. Rather than "deliver" the baby, she brings out the birthing woman's own physical and emotional strength—resources left untapped or suppressed by standard obstetrical practices. This is more than touchy-feely rhetoric. It translates into concrete clinical expertise: an appreciation of the variations of normal labor, of the way some problems can correct themselves with time, of the influence of emotional support and a sense of well-being during labor, and of many nonchemical, noninvasive means of encouraging progress.

An obstetrician's highly specialized knowledge represents only a narrow segment of the whole range of knowledge relevant to childbirth. A midwife draws upon a traditional body of knowledge that guides her both in forming a supportive bond with a pregnant woman and in shaping a positive experience of—and attitude toward—birth. In addition to emphasizing prenatal education and preparation, she comes to know the woman, her environment, and the way she lives, and thus can better understand her reactions and assist her during labor.

Podell writes: "The midwives gave me all the room I needed, but they were never distant; they were always right there, offering energy, a sip of juice, a word of encouragement. Their presence comforted me and gave me confidence. One thing I didn't understand. . . . Without internal exams, how could they tell how the labor was progressing? . . . They said my body would know what to do and when. And to my very great surprise, they were right."

Instead of pain medication, midwives use noninvasive methods, physical as well as psychological, to help women cope with pain. The midwifery model in its pure form does not allow the use of anesthetic or analgesic drugs in normal births, since these medications interfere with the natural process of labor. Home-birth attendants avoid the use of such drugs entirely, since the safety of a home birth depends on supporting the natural process and not creating added risks. In hospitals, on the other hand, nurse-midwives sometimes make pragmatic compromises, giving pain medication to women who want it in order to make other benefits of midwifery available to them.

Any medical intervention in childbirth tends to necessitate further intervention by disrupting the normal physiology of labor.

It should always be a woman's right to choose between midwifery and obstetrics for whatever reasons matter to her, including her preferences regarding pain medication. At the same time, as the midwifery model comes to be more widely known and better understood, more women may approach the pain of childbearing in a positive way, as Podell did: "The labor was short, intense, and sweet. It wasn't any less painful than the others, but I tried to put all my concentration on welcoming the pain, on assenting to open up. Away from the interference of the hospital, comfortable in my own familiar house, I felt a lovely sense of freedom. I wasn't anybody's patient. I was myself, doing a task I had really been preparing for since childhood."

The beneficial effects of the laboring woman's sense of well-being, comfort, and control are enhanced in the home or (to a lesser degree) in the home-like setting of a midwife-run birth center. In the words of the prominent Dutch obstetrician G. J. Kloosterman: "The advantages of home confinements are that in her own home the expectant mother is not considered a patient, but a woman, fulfilling a natural and highly personal task. She is the real center around which everything (and everybody) revolves. The midwife or doctor and the maternity aide nurse are all her guests, there to assist her. This setting reinforces her self-respect and self-confidence."

This endorsement of home birth runs counter to the prejudices of most Americans, who have been led to believe that the best outcomes occur when childbirth is managed by obstetricians in hospitals where medical technology is readily available and where there is little hesitation about using it. This view equates safety with active technological intervention carried out by highly specialized personnel in an institutional setting.

Proponents of this position offer three main arguments. First, they cite the decline in maternal and infant mortality that coincided with the shift to medicalized, institutionalized childbirth in this century. But such a sweeping historical comparison is meaningless because it disregards many other changes that occurred at the same time: better nutrition, sanitation, and personal hygiene; fewer large families and closely spaced children; the development of antibiotics; and improvements in diagnosis, risk assessment, and instrumentation. Contemporaneous comparisons, such as one conducted by the New York Academy of Medicine from 1930 to 1932, have almost invariably shown that midwife-attended or home births have outcomes as good as or better than physician-attended or hospital births.

British statistician Marjorie Tew, in her 1990 book *Safer Childbirth? A Critical History of Maternity Care*, uses data from the special British birth surveys of 1958 and 1970 to make detailed comparisons—regional, historical, and individual—of the outcomes of home vs. hospital birth and of high-intervention vs. low-intervention birth in populations closely matched for risk factors. Tew concludes that increased hospitalization and obstetrical intervention cannot be credited with improving the safety of childbirth. To her, in fact, the weight of the evidence suggests that these changes have done more harm than good.

Second, opponents of midwifery argue that mortality statistics show babies are at greater risk if they are born outside a hospital. This fallacious comparison, first made in a 1978 press release by the American College of Obstetricians and Gynecologists, rests on raw statewide figures showing that the risk to a baby's life was two to five times greater in an out-of-hospital birth. But the "out-of-hospital" category included not only intentional home births, but also late miscarriages, premature and precipitous births, and unplanned home births. Such undifferentiated data say nothing about the safety of planned, properly attended home births.

Finally, when forced to confront the lack of statistical evidence in their favor, proponents of orthodox obstetrics say, "OK, so the differences in safety are too small to show up in the data. But even one unnecessary infant death is too many—especially if it's yours." This argument, while highly effective in inducing fear and guilt in parents, fails to take into account the countervailing risks of medicalized birth, such as infections resulting from hospital sepsis or from unnecessary surgical procedures and the many complications that can result from interfering with the progress of labor.

Opponents of midwifery also ignore a large body of evidence that low-intervention maternity care by midwives results in outcomes as good as or better than those of hospital births. Since 1925, for example, the Frontier Nursing Service in Kentucky has provided outstanding maternity care to a poor, geographically remote population. The service, whose midwives attended nearly all births at home (sometimes on horseback) until the late 1960s, has compiled an outcome record that compares favorably with that of mainstream America.

In a remarkable real-life experiment in Madera County, California, neonatal mortality dropped from 24 to 10 per 1,000 when nurse-midwives were introduced into a poor agricultural area in 1960. Pressure from the state medical association ended the program in 1963. Midwives were replaced by obstetricians, whereupon neonatal mortality rose to 32 per 1,000. The number of women receiving no prenatal care doubled.

Midwifery programs are having an important impact among the urban poor as well. With one-third of its largely black and Hispanic clients classified as high-risk, the North Central Bronx Hospital midwifery service has the lowest cesarean-section rate in New York City and lower-than-average rates of low birth weight and perinatal and neonatal mortality. In a well-controlled study involving low-income women in a Houston hospital, published in 1991 in *The Journal of the American Medical Association*, the continuous companionship of a *doula*—a woman trained to provide labor support—shortened the duration of labor, cut the cesarean-section rate in half, and reduced the need for other interventions along with the incidence of maternal fever and prolonged infant hospitalization. And the *doula* provides only part of a midwife's comprehensive skills and services.

Two years ago the National Birth Center Study reported on birth outcomes for nearly 12,000 women admitted to freestanding birth centers in the United States, three-fourths of them operated by midwives. In this largely low-risk population, the low overall perinatal-neonatal mortality rate of 1.3 per 1,000 was comparable to that of low-risk hospital births. Moreover, it was achieved with minimal intervention (most notably, a 4.4-percent cesarean-section rate), low morbidity, and high levels of satisfaction. Similar findings were obtained in a review of more than 3,000 out-of-hospital (mainly home) births attended by licensed direct-entry midwives in Arizona between 1978 and 1985.

Further evidence comes from Holland, where the national health-care system deliberately reversed a trend toward American-style hospital births a decade ago. In a study published recently in the British journal *Midwifery*, researchers who analyzed all Dutch births in 1986 found that, at all risk levels after 32 weeks' gestation, perinatal mortality was "much lower under the noninterventionist care of midwives than under the interventionist management of obstetricians." And this is in a country with an ethnically diverse population (including guest workers).

Studies also find that midwifery is much less expensive than conventional obstetrics. The cost-effectiveness of the midwifery model follows from its reliance on natural processes and settings rather than on expensive technology. In one of the first demonstrations of the cost-saving potential of midwifery, Blue Cross/Blue Shield estimated that its costs for a birth in the Maternity Center Association's Childbearing Center in Manhattan in 1976–77 averaged only 37.6 percent of the cost of an uncomplicated birth in a nearby hospital (including both hospital and physician charges). As documented in a report prepared for the Federal Trade Commission, Blue Cross/Blue Shield's decision (against formidable opposition) to authorize reimbursement for the center was a major breakthrough in making the freestanding birth center a viable concept in the United States.

Since then, this initial indication of the savings to be achieved through broader application of the midwifery model has been borne out by other research, most notably a Health Insurance Association of America (HIAA) study published in 1989. These savings can be realized in a number of ways:

Lower fees. According to the HIAA study, the average physician's fee for a normal pregnancy and birth is $1,492, while a midwife's fee averages $994. A midwife's fee typically covers more time spent before, during, and after the birth and includes comprehensive services that otherwise would require a team of providers.

Lower site-related costs. According to the HIAA study, a normal birth involving a one-day stay in a birth center costs $2,111, compared with $3,233 for a one-day hospital stay. (These figures include practitioners' fees.) Since the average length of stay in a hospital is longer than in a birth center, the difference in practice is even greater. Thus, the average hospital cost for a normal vaginal delivery is $2,842 in addition to the physician's fee of $1,492, for a total of $4,334.

In a home birth there are no site-related expenses. In Australia, for example, an estimate published in the journal *Family Physician* indicated that insurers and families might save A$83 million a year if 30 percent of births took place at home. Of course, the cost of maintaining hospital backup for cases requiring transfer must be factored into the overall costs of out-of-hospital birth services. But such on-call auxiliary services require only a fraction of the institutional resources routinely used and paid for under the present system.

Reduced use of technology. Midwives rely much less on technical procedures that entail material costs, increased practitioners' fees, and (often) longer hospital stays. A birth by cesarean section costs an average of $7,186, compared to $4,334 for a vaginal birth in a hospital. Since midwife-attended births have a cesarean-section rate 50 percent to 70 percent lower than physician-attended births in comparable populations with equivalent out-

comes, the savings to be realized from this aspect of the midwifery model are enormous. If all of New York state's hospitals operated in the manner of the North Central Bronx midwifery service, the reduction in cesareans alone might save nearly $150 million annually. Ending the indiscriminate use of other specialized procedures, such as electronic fetal monitoring, ultrasound, IVs, and episiotomy, would also save money.

As of 1987, 71 percent of obstetrician-gynecologists had been named in one or more liability claims, compared with 10 percent of nurse-midwives.

Lower training costs. The Congressional Office of Technology Assessment calculated that the cost of training a certified nurse-midwife in 1985 averaged $16,800, compared with $86,100 to train a general physician, let alone an obstetrician. Since midwifery training is more appropriate for a large majority of births, there is great potential for savings here.

Lower liability costs. As of 1987, 71 percent of obstetrician-gynecologists had been named in one or more liability claims, compared with 10 percent of nurse-midwives. Direct-entry midwives (those not trained and regulated by the nursing profession) are even more rarely sued. Why these disparities? First, obstetricians deal with more complicated cases with a greater likelihood of a tragic outcome. Second, obstetricians have deeper pockets. (Like physicians, certified nurse-midwives—registered nurses with additional training in midwifery—have malpractice insurance; direct-entry midwives generally do not, except in states where they are licensed.)

Third, and perhaps most important, people who choose a midwife (especially a direct-entry midwife) commit themselves to sharing the risks and responsibilities of birth. Rather than expect a guaranteed perfect outcome, they participate with an understanding of nature's uncertainties. The midwife actively encourages this informed participation. And because she established a relationship of trust, full and open communication, and emotional support, the midwife does not leave her clients feeling abandoned and resentful in the event of a tragic outcome.

Lower health-care costs after birth. The costs of childbirth pale beside those of taking care of premature and sick infants and children. According to the HIAA survey, it costs nearly $1,000 a day to keep a baby in a neonatal intensive care unit; a 30-day stay can cost $30,000. Hospitals that bear these often uncompensated costs should heed the documented success of midwifery programs, over a range of settings and income levels, in reducing the incidence of low birth weight, which is directly associated with prematurity. To the extent that midwives' emphasis on a healthy environment during pregnancy can reduce the short- and long-term effects of malnutrition, smoking, heavy drinking, and drug use on maternal and child health—in some cases preventing lifelong disability—the contribution of midwives to reducing health-care costs may be incalculable.

In the case of midwifery, the evidence is overwhelming that better care can cost less. Indeed, the American system of obstetrics is so inappropriate and inefficient that only as a protected monopoly could it have gained and held its dominant position. It could not have survived, and cannot now survive, in a free market. But the monopoly is well entrenched by law.

Direct-entry midwives are legal in some states, illegal in others. In a plurality of states their legal status is uncertain. But if a state's medical-practice act includes childbirth among the conditions exclusively reserved for medicine, then direct-entry midwifery is presumed to be illegal. And in the Catch-22 of midwifery regulation, some states (such as Rhode Island) won't let midwives practice without a license but won't license them either.

This patchwork of laws resulted in part from deliberate efforts by organized medicine to create a protected monopoly and in part from an unconscious societal assumption that midwifery had disappeared. During the past few decades, midwifery has been allowed back in a limited role in the form of certified nurse-midwives. CNMs practice legally in every state, but their scope of practice—indeed, their ability to practice at all—is often severely restricted when physicians withhold the requisite institutional or logistical support.

Direct-entry midwives are often prosecuted for practicing either medicine or midwifery without a license. Sometimes these prosecutions help clarify the legal status of midwives. In 1990, after charges were brought against a Pennsylvania midwife who attended Amish clients, a judge ruled that state law did not prohibit the unlicensed practice of "lay" midwifery. But in Illinois in 1991 a court decision calling for clarification of the state's medical-practice act led to legislation that included childbirth within the scope of the act. Midwives have also suffered setbacks in Southern states such as Alabama, where public-health departments have forcibly retired the experienced "granny" midwives who often were the only providers of maternity care for the rural or urban poor. In Arkansas, public outcry over such action persuaded the legislature to legalize direct-entry midwifery. In Georgia, however, recently issued regulations have made the practice of direct-entry midwifery a felony.

A decade ago in REASON, Sarah Foster documented the various tactics that the medical establishment uses to intimidate and exclude midwives ("Up Against the Birth Monopoly," September 1982). In one of the more prominent cases to have occurred since then, a local obstetrician pilloried nurse-midwife Debby Sweeney in front of her students at the Medical College of Georgia School of Nursing in 1986, falsely charging that she was practicing

medicine illegally and endangering her patients. The obstetrician's group practice prevented Sweeney from continuing to teach in one of the hospitals affiliated with the college, complaining that they "could not allow their patients to be exposed to students who are being instructed by one who advocates the home delivery concept." Sweeney had run afoul of the medical establishment by advertising her home-birth practice.

In the Catch-22 of midwifery regulation, some states won't let midwives practice without a license but won't license them either.

Such anticompetitive tactics thus far have limited the availability of qualified attendants for out-of-hospital births and deprived women and families of information about birth options. Unless a woman happens to know someone who knows the local midwife, she may see and hear only horror stories about home birth.

Reform is coming, however. Many prestigious institutions are calling for more widespread adoption of midwifery or a low-intervention approach to childbirth. These include the World Health Organization, the European Economic Community, the Institute of Medicine, the Office of Technology Assessment, the General Accounting Office, the American Public Health Association, and the National Commission to Prevent Infant Mortality. The strongest advocacy has come from the women's health movement. A detailed position paper issued jointly in 1990 by the Women's Institute for Childbearing Policy, the National Women's Health Network, the National Black Women's Health Project, and the Boston Women's Health Book Collective argues for a midwifery-based maternity care system that favors out-of-hospital birth settings.

The great stone face of the birth monopoly is visibly cracking. Hospitals hit hard by the loss of obstetricians are advertising for midwives. HMOs, after considerable resistance, are incorporating midwifery services. Boston will be joining New York, San Diego, and other localities in setting up a public out-of-hospital birth center for low-income women. At the federal level, direct reimbursement for midwives has been mandated for the armed services, Civilian Health and Medical Programs of Uniformed Services (CHAMPUS), and Medicaid. One by one, state governments are authorizing limited prescription privileges for certified nurse-midwives and licensed direct-entry midwives. They are also beginning to remove the statutory and regulatory barriers to direct third-party reimbursement for midwives.

In a major breakthrough, Ontario recently recognized midwifery as an independent, self-regulating profession authorized to practice in the home, birth center, or hospital. Ontario's action set a precedent for Canada, which had made no provision for midwifery in its national health-care system. In the United States, legislative efforts continue in New York, California, and other states to legalize midwifery as an independent profession.

Licensing clearly is preferable to illegality; however, in states where midwives currently are unregulated, midwives and their supporters are divided over whether it is better to be licensed or to continue on a laissez-faire basis. Midwives who oppose licensing consider midwifery a "spiritual art," in the words of Ohio midwife Kimberly French, that cannot be regulated by uniform standards as medicine is. "Would we be willing to give up certain aspects of our craft in exchange for certification, such as handling breech births, vaginal births after cesareans, and twins?" asks French in the periodical *Friends of Homebirth*. "What about the woman who is left with no other option but a cesarean if we, as midwives, were restricted . . . by law?"

Furthermore, opponents of licensing are reluctant to exclude midwives who might not meet the formal criteria established by the law. "I feel strongly," writes Maine midwife Jill Breen in *The Midwife Advocate*, "that there always will and should be a place for the apprentice-trained midwife, the community-called midwife, the non-medically-oriented midwife."

With few exceptions, midwives who support licensing do so not to protect their hard-won turf or to save the public from unqualified practitioners, but because they are weary of their denigrated status as "lay practitioners."

They are interested not so much in excluding others as in including themselves in the professional health-care system. Longtime Oregon midwifery advocate Alan Solares, whose arguments against licensing were influential a decade ago, has now changed his position. He addresses the concerns of many midwives today who feel that "they cannot fairly compete in a health-care system based increasingly on third-party payment."

Implicit in Solares's argument is the assumption that, in today's highly professionalized society, the benefits of third-party reimbursement, public visibility and trust, and secure hospital backup cannot be obtained without some concession to "professional standards" and "consumer protection." For this reason, most people on both sides of the debate would welcome a system of voluntary certification such as New Hampshire's, which sets standards for certification but does not bar uncertified midwives from practicing as long as they do not claim to be certified. But this is not a likely prospect in many states.

For now, midwives and others who seek to open up the health-care market will continue to face rear-guard obstacles such as unequal access to reimbursement, regulatory mechanisms that place competing practitioners under the control of physicians, an information monopoly that can frustrate informed choice even when more overt restraints are halted, and a long accumulation of prejudice against nontechnological alternatives to conventional health care. The hardest obstacle, however, may well be a certain faintheartedness in the American public, an ingrained reliance on "consumer protection" even at the expense of consumer choice.

Unnecessary Cesarean Sections:

Halting a National Epidemic

Public Citizen's Health Research Group released its third report on unnecessary cesarean sections, entitled *Unnecessary Cesarean Sections: Halting a National Epidemic* on May 12, 1992. The report disclosed that, for the first time, the national rate of cesarean births actually decreased. Based on 2.8 million deliveries in 1990 and 2.6 million in 1989, there was a statistically significant decrease in the proportion of deliveries done by cesarean section, from 23.0 percent in 1989 to 22.7 percent in 1990. The national c-section rate had almost quintupled in 18 years — from 5.5 percent in 1970 to 24.7 percent in 1988 (according to data based on a much smaller number of deliveries from the National Center for Health Statistics - NCHS). Now, based on the Health Research Group's much larger sample (more than two-thirds of all deliveries in the U.S.), the cesarean epidemic seems to have turned the corner. If hopes are realized the decline will continue until the rate reaches 12 percent, or about one-half the 23.5 percent reported by NCHS for 1990 (the most recent year for which finalized data is available).

HRG's latest report represents the most comprehensive source of information on hospital and state cesarean section rates available. It includes cesarean rates for 2,657 hospitals in 34 states and statewide data for 47 states and the District of Columbia (every state except Colorado, Oklahoma and South Dakota). Here are some highlights:

❏ *The five highest statewide cesarean rates* were for Arkansas (27.1 percent in 1989 and 27.8 percent in 1990), Louisiana (27.3 percent in 1990), New Jersey (27.0 percent in 1989), and the District of Columbia (26.6 percent in 1990).

❏ *The five lowest statewide cesarean rates* were for Minnesota (17.6 percent in 1990), Wisconsin (17.5 percent in both 1989 and 1990), and Alaska (15.3 percent in 1990 and 15.2 percent in 1989).

❏ *The 10 hospitals with the highest cesarean rates* were — Abrom Kaplan Memorial Hospital, Louisiana (57.5 percent); Williamson Appalachian Regional Hospital, Kentucky (55.4 percent); Southern Baptist Hospital, Louisiana (50.3 percent); Bunkie General Hospital, Louisiana (50.0 percent); Bogalusa Community Medical Center, Louisiana (49.8 percent); Tyrone Hospital, Pennsylvania (49.4 percent); Highland Hospital, Louisiana (48.4 percent); Hialeah Hospital, Florida (48.3 percent); University of Connecticut Health Center — John Dempsey, Connecticut (46.9 percent); and Mt. Sinai Medical Center, Florida (46.6 percent).

(It is noteworthy that five of the 10 hospitals with the highest c-section rates were in Louisiana which ranked third among states with abnormally high rates.)

Despite a significant decrease in the national c-section rate from 1989 to 1990, cesarean section continues to be the most frequently performed major surgical operation in the U.S., and the most frequently performed unnecessary surgery. It is

> *Cesarean section continues to be the most frequently performed major surgical operation in the U.S., and the most frequently performed unnecessary surgery*

unconscionable that every day thousands of needless cesareans are performed, squandering millions of scarce health care dollars (to say nothing of putting women unnecessarily at risk) while nearly 40 million Americans lack access to care they really do need. Moreover, the HRG report clearly shows that most

From *Health Letter,* Vol. 8, No. 6, June 1992, pp. 1-6. *Health Letter,* Public Citizen Health Research Group, 2000 P Street, NW, Washington, DC 20036.

U.S. physicians, hospitals, and insurers continue to ignore more than 10 years of evidence undeniably showing that American women are undergoing an onslaught of unnecessary and dangerous surgery.

Not only does recent research clearly demonstrate that c-section rates are too high, but there is little doubt that an optimal, much lower rate could be achieved while preserving or even improving maternal and infant health. Public Citizen Health Research Group agrees with rates proposed by Dr. Edward Quilligan, Dean of the School of Medicine at the University of California at Irvine and editor of the *American Journal of Obstetrics and Gynecology.* Dr. Quilligan has set targets of 7.8 to 17.5 percent for hospitals, the lower number for those serving low-risk patients and the higher number for those serving high-risk patients, with a range of 12 to 14 percent for states and the country as a whole.

These numbers represent conservative goals well above rates already achieved in hospitals with comprehensive programs designed to prevent unnecessary cesareans, as discussed later in our story. Using the conservative target rate of 12 percent, we estimate that 480,520 of the 982,000 cesareans performed in 1990 (48.9 percent) were unnecessary — more than 1,300 *a day* — and cost the economy more than $1.3 billion.

Four diagnoses have been associated with the recent explosive growth of cesarean section use and accounted for about seven-eighths of all cesareans done in 1989: *repeat cesareans,* 35.6 percent of all cesareans; *dystocia* (abnormal progress of labor), 28.9 percent; *breech position,* 12.3 percent; and *fetal distress,* 9.9 percent.

Growth in the rate of automatic repeat cesarean sections has started to slow recently as "VBAC" (vaginal birth after cesarean) has gained popularity. VBAC, which accounted for 12.6 percent of all births in 1988, rose to 18.5 (an increase of 46 percent) in 1989 and to 20.4 percent (a further 10 percent increase) in 1990. Though the 1988-89 increase

was substantial, the VBAC rates for both 1989 and 1990 were still far too low. Approximately 80 to 90 percent of all women with a cesarean history should be candidates for VBAC.

The 20 percent VBAC rate in 1990 suggests that most hospitals and doctors are still not heeding important new recommendations by the American College of Obstetricians and Gynecologists (ACOG). In October 1988 ACOG revised its guidelines on vaginal (normal) delivery, scrapping the outdated philosophy of "once a cesarean, always a cesarean." ACOG's revised guidelines recommend that, in the absence of medical complications of pregnancy, all women with previous cesarean sections be encouraged to attempt VBAC. These recommendations were based on studies demonstrating VBAC's safety and success.

Many other studies have demonstrated that indiscriminate use of fetal monitoring increases the cesarean rate without added benefit for infants, while the availability of non-invasive tests to identify *real*

Using the conservative target rate of 12 percent, we estimate that 480,520 of the 982,000 cesareans performed in 1990 (48.9 percent) were unnecessary

---

fetal distress has improved. Improvements in management of dystocia and in the appropriate management of breech babies have also been made, although ideal strategies in these areas remain unclear. Unfortunately, it seems that most of these advances have not been integrated into most physicians' practice patterns.

The good news is that a growing number of initiatives in various places around the country are doing their part to stop this epidemic.

❑ Cesarean reduction programs at several U.S. hospitals have successfully reduced c-section rates while maintaining or even improving infant and maternal health. St. Luke's Hospital in Denver, Mt. Sinai Medical Center in Chicago, University Medical Center in Jacksonville, West Paces Ferry Hospital in Atlanta, North Central Bronx Hospital in New York City (where all primary care for birthing women is provided by certified nurse midwives), and the Kaiser Permanente health maintenance organization's hospitals in southern California have developed strategies aimed at preventing unnecessary cesareans and other interventions, as well as improving women's overall childbirth experiences.

❑ Consumer groups are working to make information on cesarean rates routinely available to women and their partners. In 1985, through the work of C/SEC (Cesarean Support, Education, and Concern) and other organizations, the Massachusetts legislature passed a bill (Chapter 714) mandating that hospitals provide consumers with hospital cesarean rates and other important maternity information. This bill served as a model for the maternity information bill eventually passed by New York state in 1989 (S.2803-j), thanks to the work of ICAN (International Cesarean Awareness Network), the New York Public Interest Research Group (NYPIRG), and the National Women's Health Network of New York, as well as other groups. Several state data agencies, including those in Illinois, Iowa, Maryland, Massachusetts, Nevada, and Vermont, also publish brochures or reports containing this vital information.

❑ Cesarean support/education groups around the country, such as ICAN, formerly the Cesarean Prevention Movement, have grown tremendously in membership and activism. Many of these groups publish newsletters, hold conferences, produce their own educational materials, and work toward preventing unnecessary cesarean surgery in their area.

❏ A handful of Blue Cross/Blue Shield programs around the country, including those in Illinois, Kansas, Minnesota, North Carolina, Pennsylvania, and Rhode Island, now reimburse physicians at the same rate for vaginal delivery as for cesarean.

❏ As reported in *Health Letter* (vol. 7, no. 6), an exciting new study conducted at Jefferson Davis Hospital in Houston found that the reassurance and support during labor and delivery from trained companions (called *doulas*, a Greek word) who know about childbirth from personal experience

---

Reassurance and support during labor and delivery from trained companions dramatically reduced the use of obstetrical interventions

---

dramatically reduced the use of obstetrical interventions such as epidural anesthesia, forceps, and cesarean delivery (confirming ancient wisdom that childbirth educators and

midwives have known all along). This study verified the importance of a supportive atmosphere that responds to a woman's many emotional and social needs during childbirth.

❏ A new-format United States Standard Birth Certificate introduced in 1989 will permit virtually every state to monitor indications for cesarean section and cesarean rates, as well as other obstetrical procedures. Disseminating such information to the public, however, will continue to be a major challenge.

Questions for the Doctor

Below are questions pregnant women should ask their obstetricians about obstetrical interventions, including cesarean section, and other issues that may affect their childbirth experience. Also included is information on a number of organizations around the country that work on childbirth issues, including cesarean section (see page 133). We encourage women and their partners to contact such organizations if they have pregnancy or childbirth-related questions.

1. *What is your c-section rate?* (Ideally, doctors with high-risk practices should have rates of no more than 17 percent, and doctors with low-risk practices should have rates under 10 percent. If possible, try to avoid doctors with cesarean rates above the national rate of approximately 24 percent.)

2. *Do you offer "trial of labor" (attempted vaginal delivery) to women who have had a previous c-section? If so, what percentage of them deliver vaginally?* (Ideally, approximately 80-90 percent of women with a prior cesarean should

be encouraged to undergo a trial of labor, and approximately 60 percent to 90 percent of these women should be able to deliver vaginally, meaning that 50-80 percent of women with prior cesareans could subsequently have a normal delivery.)

3. *Do you consider an independent second opinion for elective c-sections good medical practice?* (If your doctor gets angry or defensive when you ask questions, including this one, consider changing physicians — if you have that option.)

4. *How do you monitor labor of low-risk patients? Of high-risk patients? Do you routinely use electronic fetal monitoring (EFM) to monitor certain groups of patients? Do you use fetal blood sampling or fetal stimulation tests to confirm fetal distress indicated by EFM?* (Routine use of EFM may only be useful for high-risk patients. At least one other test should be used to confirm fetal distress unless a serious emergency is noted.)

5. *If a patient presents with a fetus in breech position, do you attempt to turn the fetus manually to a head-first position* (called "external cephalic version") *after 37 weeks?*

6. *Are you concerned about the high c-section rate in this country (or at this hospital)? Do you follow policies designed to reduce this rate?*

Not all of these questions may pertain to every woman's situation, but women have a right to ask their obstetricians these and any other questions they wish. Effective communication is an important part of the doctor-patient relationship, especially if women intend to negotiate for limitation of obstetrical interventions, including cesarean section.

Cesarean Section Rates for 47 States and the District of Columbia

State	Year	Total Cesareans	Total Births or Deliveries	Cesarean Rate
Alabama	1989	15,901	61,913	25.7%
	1990	16,443	63,420	25.9%
Alaska	1989	1,773	11,659	15.2%
	1990	1,813	11,883	15.3%

(continued)

State	Year	Total Cesareans	Total Births or Deliveries	Cesarean Rate
Arizona	1990	11,802	59,280	19.9%
Arkansas	1989	9,378	34,616	27.1%
	1990	9,819	35,300	27.8%
California	1989	126,504	551,625	22.9%
	1990	127,105	592.817	21.4%
Connecticut	1990	10,828	49,431	21.9%
Delaware	1989	2,791	10,492	26.6%
	1990	2,800	11,073	25.3%
District of Columbia	1989	2,895	11,567	25.0%
	1990	3,139	11,802	26.6%
Florida	1990	44,254	167,603	26.4%
Georgia	1989	25,566	110,272	23.2%
	1990	25,808	115,833	22.3%
Hawaii	1990	4,162	20,218	20.6%
Idaho	1990	3,113	16,491	18.9%
Illinois	1989	39,626	181,018	21.9%
Indiana	1989	17,532	82,834	21.2%
Iowa	1989	4,440	22,007	20.2%
Kansas	1989	8,963	37,817	23.7%
	1990	8,865	37,965	23.4%
Kentucky	1989	12,393	52,409	23.6%
	1990	12,623	53,108	23.8%
Louisiana	1990	19,635	72,046	27.3%
Maine	1990	3,576	16,080	22.2%
Maryland	1990	16,990	69,671	24.4%
Massachusetts	1989	21,285	92,836	22.9%
Michigan	1989	33,860	148,164	22.9%
	1990	33,744	153,080	22.0%
Minnesota	1989	12,005	66,509	18.1%
	1990	11,962	67,798	17.6%
Mississippi	1990	11,266	42,915	26.3%
Missouri	1990	18,793	80,608	23.3%
Montana	1989	2,308	11,148	20.7%
	1990	2,323	11,118	20.9%
Nebraska	1990	4.738	24,184	19.6%
Nevada	1989	3,828	16,761	22.8%
New Hampshire	1989	3,665	16,681	22.0%
	1990*	1,874	8,448	22.2%
New Jersey	1989	31,617	117,075	27.0%
New Mexico	1989	5,033	26,934	18.7%
	1990	4,982	26,980	18.5%
New York	1989	68,397	290,771	23.5%
	1990	70,494	298,702	23.6%
North Carolina	1990	24,044	104,347	23.0%
North Dakota	1990	1,927	9,980	19.3%

(continued)

4. RELATIONSHIPS IN TRANSITION: Marriage to Family

State	Year	Total Cesareans	Total Births or Deliveries	Cesarean Rate
Ohio	1989	40,160	164,894	24.4%
Oregon	1989	7,920	37,756	21.0%
Pennsylvania	1989	38,424	167,234	23.0%
	1990	37,437	171,053	21.9%
Rhode Island	1989	3,166	15,237	20.8%
	1990	3,144	15,737	20.0%
South Carolina**	1989/90**	11,547	50,583	22.8%
Tennessee	1989	18,840	77,119	24.4%
	1990	18,372	74,870	24.5%
Texas	1989	52,919	204,318	25.9%
Utah	1989	6,516	35,377	18.4%
	1990	6,686	37,295	17.9%
Vermont	1989	1,517	7,948	19.1%
	1990	1,518	7,817	19.4%
Virginia	1989*	12,040	50,021	24.1%
	1990	23,313	96,626	24.1%
Washington	1990*	6,996	33,280	21.0%
West Virginia	1989	5,014	19,716	25.4%
	1990	5,251	19,964	26.3%
Wisconsin	1989	12,212	69,828	17.5%
	1990	12,791	73,080	17.5%
Wyoming	1989	1,200	6,484	18.5%
	1990	1,283	6,544	19.6%

* indicates data for a 6-month period
** indicates data for a fiscal year

The Cutting Edge

The 16 Hospitals with the Highest Cesarean Section Rate
45 Percent and Over

State	Name of Facility	Total Births or Deliveries	Cesarean Rate
Louisiana	Abrom Kaplan Mem. Hosp.	120	57.5%
Kentucky	Williamson App. Regional Hosp.	101	55.4%
Louisiana	* Southern Baptist Hosp.	1,913	50.3%
Louisiana	Bunkie General Hosp.	62	50.0%
Louisiana	Bogalusa Community Med. Ctr.	251	49.8%
Pennsylvania	Tyrone Hosp.	77	49.4%
Louisiana	Highland Hosp.	395	48.4%
Florida	Hialeah Hosp.	1,890	48.3%
Connecticut	U. of CT Health Ctr. — John Dempsey	407	46.9%
Florida	Mt. Sinai Med. Ctr.	1,244	46.6%

(continued)

The 16 Hospitals with the Highest Cesarean Section Rate
45 Percent and Over (Continued)

State	Name of Facility	Total Births or Deliveries	Cesarean Rate
Louisiana	* Lakeside Hosp.	2,899	46.5%
Louisiana	St. Anne Hosp.	353	46.5%
Louisiana	St. Tammany Parish Hosp.	285	46.3%
New Jersey	St. James Hosp.	576	46.2%
New York	Carthage Area Hosp.	266	45.9%
New York	Victory Mem. Hosp.	924	45.6%

* indicates this facility has a neonatal intensive care unit (nicu).
Data are for either 1989 or 1990.

What You Can Do

Contact the following helpful organizations.

Cesarean Section Support Groups:
International Cesarean Awareness Network (ICAN, formerly the Cesarean Prevention Movement, CPM)
PO Box 152
Syracuse, NY 13210
Telephone (315) 424-1942
This group publishes a newsletter and has approximately 80 chapters across the country.

Cesarean Support, Education, and Concern (C/SEC)
22 Forest Road
Framingham, MA 01701
Telephone: (508) 877-8266
This group no longer publishes a newsletter, but back copies of its letter are still available, and the group will continue responding to mail and phone calls, directing women to resources and groups in their area.

Childbirth Educators:
American Society of Psychoprophylaxis in Obstetrics (ASPO/Lamaze)
1840 Wilson Blvd., Suite 204
Arlington, VA 22201
Telephone: (703) 524-7802

International Childbirth Education Association (ICEA)
PO Box 20048
Minneapolis, MN 55420-0048
Telephone: (612) 854-8660

Certified Nurse-Midwives:
The American College of Nurse-Midwives (ACNM)
1522 K Street NW, Suite 1120
Washington, DC 20005
Telephone: (202) 347-5445

Midwives Alliance of North America (MANA)
30 South Main
Concord, NH 03301
Telephone: (603) 225-9586

Consortium for Nurse-Midwifery, Inc. (CNMI)
1911 West 233rd St.
Torrance, CA 90501
Telephone: (213) 539-9801
Information about nurse-midwifery in California

"She Died Because of a Law"

A mother denounces parental consent

Rochelle Sharpe

Rochelle Sharpe is a national reporter at Gannett News Service, covering social issues. She was the first to break the story of Rebecca Bell nationally.

At the age of 46, Karen Bell was flying on an airplane by herself for the first time in her life. She looked at the speech her husband had written for her and decided she could not deliver it.

Karen wasn't sure what she wanted to say to the National Women's Political Caucus about laws requiring parental consent for abortion, but she knew that speech just didn't sound like her. So when she finally talked to the crowd, she merely described how she felt about the law that destroyed her family: "My life was over when my little girl died."

Karen explained how her daughter became the first teenager in the nation known to die because of a parental consent law. She described 17-year-old Rebecca's desire to keep her pregnancy secret, her futile attempts to get a legal abortion near her home in Indianapolis, Indiana, and her death from an abortion-related infection. By the time Karen was finished, women were wiping tears from their eyes; many approached her to discuss how they could work together to defeat parental consent legislation—an area of the reproductive rights struggle that even some pro-choice activists seem willing to compromise.

Karen's life as a full-time housewife had ended, but her work as an activist had just begun. Although she does not always enjoy her new role, she is committed to it. And she is unusually effective because her story is so genuine. She can do what seems impossible in the debate on abortion: she can change people's minds.

"She made an impact on me," said Ginger Barr, a Republican legislator in Kansas who was wavering on parental consent until she heard Karen Bell and her husband testify at a committee hearing. "Everybody was just spellbound," she said. The committee eventually voted down three parental notification and consent bills by a 12 to 8 margin.

In Albany, New York, the Bells had a similar effect, galvanizing four aides to Governor Mario Cuomo into a sympathetic group. Karen's question to them was intensely personal: "Do you remember the first time you were in love?" Then she described her daughter's first boyfriend and showed pictures of the smiling, blond-haired girl. "My little girl was my life and she died because of a law I didn't know existed." Lobbyists try to explain to her the power and impact she brings to the abortion debate, but she scoffs and says, "Oh, no, I'm just a mom. That's all I know how to do."

All Karen Bell ever wanted was to be a good mother. For years, she lived in a Leave It to Beaver world; when she wasn't playing hostess, Karen often volunteered as a teacher's aide for special education students and baby-sat at a local church during Bible study meetings. She never read the newspaper. Until last year, she had never heard of the National Organization for Women. She lived in a quiet neighborhood near the Indianapolis Motor Speedway until she married her husband, William, when she was 24. After the wedding, the couple moved into a house three doors away from her parents, and started a family. Once her son, Bill, and Rebecca had been born, she thought, "We've got the perfect family."

In Karen's view, she and her daughter were like best friends, talking about everything—including sex. They almost always got along until Rebecca met her first boyfriend. After that, their relationship was strained. Before long, Karen heard through a family friend that Rebecca feared she was pregnant and that she was using

 From *Ms.*, July/August 1990, pp. 80-81. © 1990 by Rochelle Sharpe. Reprinted by permission.

drugs as well. Mortified, she rushed her daughter to Planned Parenthood for pregnancy tests, which proved negative. Later, she and her husband put Rebecca in a detoxification center to rid her of her new drug habit.

"Becky, I don't want to go through this again," William Bell recalls telling his daughter while she was recovering. Neither he nor his wife realized the impact of that statement; Rebecca repeatedly told her best friend she would be thrown out of the house if she got into trouble again. And Karen had no idea that Rebecca resumed seeing her boyfriend and became pregnant.

Rebecca tried to deal with her unwanted pregnancy by herself. She returned to Planned Parenthood and asked for an abortion, only to be told she would need her parents' consent. She talked with a friend about driving to an abortion clinic in Kentucky, where parental consent wasn't required, but she kept postponing the trip.

Karen still has no idea what Rebecca did to end her pregnancy. All she remembers of her daughter's last week of life is that a mysterious illness began to afflict her one Saturday night. In hindsight, Karen believes her daughter had someone try to induce an illegal abortion that night. But at the time, she believed Rebecca's story that she had the flu—a likely scenario since relatives were just recovering from it. The illness, however, was really pneumonia, triggered by the infection in her womb.

All the while, Karen couldn't understand why Rebecca would go to the bathroom and mutter, "Nothing's happening." By the following Friday, she was puzzled when her daughter reported with glee that she had started her period, an event Rebecca usually dreaded since she got such bad cramps. Now, Karen realizes, her daughter was awaiting the onset of a miscarriage.

Once the bleeding began, Rebecca agreed to go to a doctor, but it was too late. Neither Karen nor her husband learned about the pregnancy until they talked to a doctor who emerged from their daughter's room saying, "I don't know whether we're going to be able to save the baby." Only after Karen opened her daughter's purse did she discover a list of abortion clinics outside of Indiana that did not require parental consent.

When she and her husband were planning their daughter's funeral, they decided they did not want abortion mentioned during the service at all. But the minister convinced them they might help other teenage girls by discussing Rebecca's pregnancy in the eulogy.

At the funeral, Karen "felt kind of ashamed. I kind of held my head down, wondering, 'Oh, what are they thinking?'" But before long she was glad the minister had told the teenagers that she would help anyone afraid to talk to her parents. "At least fifteen kids came to tell me about their abortions," she said. One girl left a note on Rebecca's grave: "I did exactly what you did, Becky, but I lived."

For more than a year Karen grieved, and did not speak publicly of her daughter's death. It wasn't until she heard from Rebecca's teacher that Indiana NOW was circulating a flier about her daughter's death that Karen began to understand why Rebecca died. When a TV reporter called, she discovered that Indiana had a parental consent law. Then she started getting mad. Before long, the Bells agreed to talk to reporters and state legislators. They decided to help pro-choice groups make documentaries and commercials about parental consent.

Karen usually makes public appearances with her husband, letting him do most of the talking. "I always get up and tell the story of Becky. I can't go out and quote statistics. He's the toughie and I'm the big fluffie." She believes public speaking has helped them both. It has transformed her husband, she says, making him act more alive because he feels he is avenging Rebecca's death. And for her part, she says, "I feel happy when I speak because I feel like I have my daughter with me."

At times the public appearances are scary for Karen, who still is happiest staying at home. But she says: "Nothing really frightens me anymore. Nothing can hurt me now because I hurt the most when my little girl died."

Although most people are supportive, she occasionally meets someone who wants to debate abortion. She's learned to give a terse reply: "If you're against abortion, then don't have one. But don't take it away from me or anyone else." Karen respects feminist organizations now, but says she has little desire to become politically active in them—except to speak out against parental consent. "I don't want to make a career out of this," she says. "I don't like this world, if you want to know the truth. I just want what was, but it can never be.

"Now, if I can help somebody or some family, I'll do it."

When your child is choking

Tear out and keep these steps handy. They may save your child's life.

For infants under one year:

If the infant is coughing forcefully, allow him to continue to cough, but watch him carefully. If he does not stop coughing in a few minutes, or if he coughs weakly, makes a high-pitched sound while coughing, or cannot cry or cough, call 911 or the local emergency number for help (see "How to Call for Help," next page). Then begin the following rescue efforts:

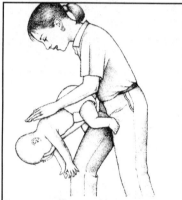

1 With the infant lying face-down on your forearm, support his head with one hand and use the heel of your other hand to deliver five back blows between his shoulder blades.

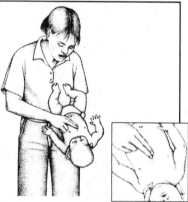

2 Position the infant faceup on your forearm. Place two or three fingers on the breastbone just below an imaginary line between the nipples, and give five quick chest thrusts by pushing down about one inch. Repeat back blows (step 1) and chest thrusts until the object is coughed up, the infant begins to breathe on his own, or he loses consciousness. (If he starts breathing well, he should still be checked by a doctor.)

TEXT COURTESY OF THE AMERICAN NATIONAL RED CROSS, 1993; ILLUSTRATIONS, JEAN GARDNER

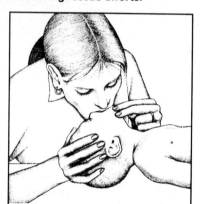

3 If the infant is unresponsive or has stopped breathing, tilt his head back and seal your lips tightly around his mouth and nose. Give two slow breaths. Each time, breathe about one to one and a half seconds until you see the chest rise; pause between breaths to let the air flow back out.

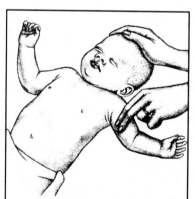

4 If the infant's chest rises, his airway is open. Check for a pulse on the inside of the upper arm, between the infant's elbow and shoulder. If a pulse is present but the baby is still not breathing, give one slow breath every three seconds. Do this for about one minute (20 breaths). Recheck pulse and breathing about once a minute. Continue rescue breathing efforts as long as a pulse is present but the infant is not breathing.

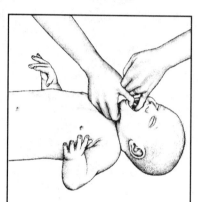

5 If the infant's chest does not rise as you give breaths, retilt his head, lift his chin, and try to give two breaths again. (Repeat step 3.) If the breaths still do not go in, give five back blows and five chest thrusts. (Repeat steps 1 and 2.) Lift the baby's jaw and tongue and check for the object; if you see it, sweep it out with your finger. Then give two more breaths. Repeat back blows, chest thrusts, and breaths until the air goes in.

6 If the infant is not breathing and has no pulse, you need to start cardiopulmonary resuscitation (CPR). Begin by placing the infant on his back on a hard surface, such as the floor or a table. Position two fingers on the breastbone and push down about one inch on the chest five times, counting "one and two and three and four and five" to keep a regular rhythm. Give one slow breath. Repeat cycles of five compressions and one breath for about one minute (about 12 cycles). Recheck pulse and breathing for about five seconds. If there is still no pulse, repeat sets of five compressions and one breath until a pulse returns or help arrives.

Be a lifesaver

The best way to be prepared for an emergency is to take a first-aid course in which you practice on mannequins. First-aid courses are intended to enable you to act more confidently in an emergency. For more information contact your local chapter of the American Red Cross.

From *Parents* Emergency Medical Card, October, 1993, pp. 251-252. © 1993 by Gruner & Jahr USA Publishing. Reprinted from *Parents* magazine by permission.

For children ages one through eight:

If the child is coughing forcefully, encourage him to continue coughing. If he does not stop coughing or does not cough up the object within a few minutes, call for help. If the child is coughing weakly, is making a high-pitched sound, or can't speak, breathe, or cough, begin these rescue efforts:

1 Place the thumb side of your fist against the middle of the child's abdomen just above the navel. Grasp fist with your other hand. Give quick upward abdominal thrusts (Heimlich maneuver). Repeat until object is coughed up or the child loses consciousness. (If the child starts breathing well, he should still be checked by a doctor.)

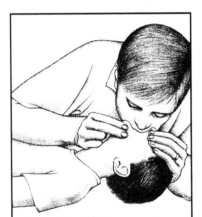

2 If the child is unconscious and is not breathing, tilt his head back, lift the chin, and pinch his nose shut. Give two slow breaths. Breath in until the child's chest gently rises.

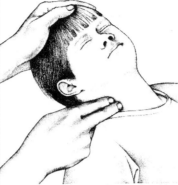

3 Check for a pulse at the side of the neck. If a pulse is present but the child is still not breathing, give one slow breath about every three seconds. Do this for about one minute (20 breaths); then call for help if you haven't already done so. Recheck pulse and breathing about every minute. Continue rescue breathing efforts as long as a pulse is present but the child is not breathing.

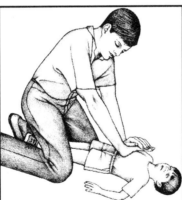

4 If the child's chest does not rise and fall as you give breaths, retilt his head and give two slow breaths again. If the air still won't go in, place the heel of one hand against the middle of the abdomen just above the child's navel. Place the other hand on top of the first. Give up to five abdominal thrusts. Lift the jaw and tongue and check for the object; if you see it, sweep it out with your finger. Then tilt the child's head back and give two breaths again. Repeat breaths, thrusts, and sweeps until breaths go in or the child starts to breath on his own. If child does start breathing on his own, monitor his breathing until the emergency personnel arrive.

How to call for help

Dial 911 or the local emergency number. Then give this information:

- Location, including street address, city or town, cross streets or landmarks

- Telephone number from which the call is being made

- Your name

- What happened

- How many people are injured or ill

- Condition of victim(s)

- Help (first aid) being given

- Finally, *do not hang up* the phone until the person who is helping you has hung up.

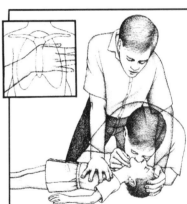

5 If the child is still not breathing and has no pulse after you have been checking for about five to ten seconds, begin CPR. Kneel beside the child's chest. Keep one hand on his head, tilting it back, and the other hand on the breastbone in the middle of the child's chest. Then push the chest down and let up five times. Each compression should be about an inch and a half; five compressions should take about three seconds. Give one slow breath. Repeat cycles of five compressions and one breath for one minute (about 12 cycles). Recheck pulse and breathing for five seconds. If there is still no pulse, continue sets of five compressions and one breath until the child starts breathing or emergency personnel arrive. Recheck the child's pulse and breathing every few minutes.

Common choking hazards

- Balloons
- Chunks of meat
- Chunks of peanut butter
- Coins
- Grapes
- Hard candy
- Hot dogs
- Marbles
- Nuts
- Pen caps
- Popcorn
- Raisins
- Raw carrots
- Raw celery
- Raw cherries
- Small toy parts

20 sanity savers

If your attempts to get more done aren't working, heed the wise advice of parents who've been there.

KAREN LEVINE

Karen Levine, a contributing editor of Parents *Magazine and the mother of two sons, is the author of several books on work and family life.*

Since the best survival tips for working parents come from other folks in the same boat, I asked a group of working couples with young children to pass on some pearls of wisdom to families like their own. Here are some fail-safe tactics that they have tried:

1 Get clothes ready ahead of time.

Barbarann Finocchiaro, an executive secretary at the *Boston Globe* and the mother of a two-year old, lays out her clothing for the week in ensembles on Sunday night. As a result, her mornings go remarkably smoothly, considering that her husband, who delivers fruit and produce, leaves by 4:30 AM and isn't around to help get their daughter ready.

2 Make a place for everything.

A few winters ago, my own family would spend mornings searching for hats, gloves, mittens, and scarves. Last winter we bought four hanging wall baskets—one for each family member. We hung the baskets right near our coat hooks, and putting hats and gloves where they belonged quickly became routine. The baskets—which could work for any number of things besides gloves and mittens—saved us time and cut down on clutter. Other families also suggest using toy bins, shoe bags, and strategically placed pencil holders.

3 Stay flexible about responsibilities.

Ira Zimbler—a clinical social worker and the father of Ezra, four, and Sarah, seven—says that he and his wife, Becky, a fifth-grade teacher, avoid having "assigned chores." "We both spend time with the kids, and we both cook, clean, and do all of the stuff involved with daily maintenance," Ira explains. "When you do the same thing all the time, you risk burnout and resentment. And if there are things you never do, you might panic when you're suddenly called upon to do them," he adds.

4 Avoid running time-consuming errands.

Michele Granger, a children's-book author and special-education teacher, is the mother of two school-age children. She recommends doing as much of your shopping as possible by mail. "I'd much rather thumb through a catalog than waste time dragging around to different stores," says Michele. This same philosophy carries over to paying bills and banking. Call your bank and ask whether you can do your banking by phone or computer.

5 Buy white socks for the children.

A father of four offered a priceless tip to all parents—regardless of whether you work outside the home. "Only buy white socks," he said. In addition to saving sorting and pairing time, this simple hint makes it easier for young children to dress themselves.

6 Consider getting cleaning help.

Pamela Lappies—editorial director of Book Creations, a book-production company, and the mother of Daniel, nine, and Cristian, seven—has someone come in every other week for three hours to clean her house. "It's well worth the 30 dollars," says Pamela. "I still spend lots of time straightening up, but I'm willing to let some things slide, knowing that within two weeks, someone will help clean it up."

7 Cook ahead for the entire week.

Barbarann Finocchiaro is a weekend cook. "I prepare a week's worth of meals and put them in the freezer or refrigerator. During the week, my husband gets home from work earlier than I do. He takes things out of the refrigerator and gets it all going so that by the time I come home, dinner is ready to eat."

8 Divide up helping with the kids' schoolwork.

Ken Schuman, a New Jersey real-estate developer, and his wife, an editor, keep tabs on their son's schoolwork according to their particular interests. "My wife has him read to her and plays word games with him,

From *Parents,* October 1993, pp. 34, 36-37, 39. © 1993 by Gruner & Jahr USA Publishing. Reprinted from *Parents* magazine by permission.

and I give him fun math problems to do," says Ken. "When I come home at night, I know exactly what my role is, and so does she," he adds. "It helps keep things from falling through the cracks."

9 Keep the mess behind closed doors.

Eileen Young, academic adviser at Regents College, in Albany, New York, and the mother of three, discovered "the great value of keeping doors shut." As she says, "I know that the mess is still there, but it doesn't bother me as much if I don't have to look at it."

10 Ask your child to lend a hand.

Jim Burbine, a newspaper-circulation manager, often includes his four-year-old daughter in the planning when he and his wife, a recovery-room nurse, are expecting a particularly busy workweek. "If we know that we have early-morning meetings, we sit down with our daughter the night before and explain that we have to be out of the house very early the next day, so we need her to get dressed and go through her morning routine without any reminders. Jacqueline always rises to the occasion, and it makes a big difference."

11 Allow time alone in the morning.

Most parents who work outside the home recommend getting up at least an hour earlier and using the solitary time for exercise, meditation, and even a quiet cup of coffee. Alan Gelb, a free-lance writer and father of two, spends 20 minutes on a cross-country machine every morning before his family gets up. "I feel energized by my workout," says Alan. "It's sort of my

warm-up for the day. I'm ready to cope with the morning by the time my children come into the kitchen to eat breakfast."

12 Help your children help themselves.

In our family, we set aside one low shelf in the pantry and another in the refrigerator for items that our children ask for most frequently. We also bought small, manageable pitchers for milk and juice that we always keep filled and well within everyone's reach. In addition to saving ourselves time, my husband and I are helping to increase our children's independence and self-esteem.

13 Don't sweat the housework.

Lighten up on your standards of what constitutes a clean house. My own mother, who was a full-time homemaker, used to do things like vacuum every day and turn our mattresses once a week. My husband and I, on the other hand, congratulate ourselves on offering up clean sheets every two weeks. Do we feel guilty? Rarely. It helps to remember, however, that very few families in which both parents work have houses as clean as the ones they grew up in.

14 Limit your kids' choices.

Kathy Engel, mother of two and president of Riptide Communications, a New York City consulting firm, used to ask her six-year-old daughter what she wanted to wear every morning. "Now I suggest one outfit and one alternative," Engel says, "and Ella seems glad to choose between them." This same philosophy is equally efficient when it

comes to choices of food, books, and activities. "Would you like an apple or some grapes?" is much more effective than "What would you like to eat?"

15 Rethink how you define dinner.

Donna Douglass, vice-president of the Time Management Center, in Marietta, Georgia, and mother of seven, says that her priority is spending time with her kids. "We sit down to dinner together every night," she says, "but sometimes that dinner consists of frozen waffles, leftovers, yogurt, or fruit."

16 Let the kids help with the laundry.

Pamela Lappies has made laundry gathering a part of her family's morning routine. "When the boys come down for breakfast every day, they bring their dirty clothing with them and drop it right in the laundry room," she says. "This way the laundry is where it's supposed to be when I get the time to do it, and the kids' clothes aren't left all around the house for me to have to pick up."

17 Encourage play dates for the kids.

Janice Patterson, an interior decorator and the mother of a seven-year-old son, touts the value of play dates. "This may be particularly true if you have an only child," she says, "but when Chris has a friend over, they have a great time playing, and that gives me a chance to get lots done without feeling guilty."

18 Make a date with your spouse.

For parents who work outside the home, finding adults-only time together

generally requires planning. Ann Pleshette Murphy, *Parents* Magazine editor-in-chief, and her husband phone each other from their offices—with calendars in hand—to schedule a lunch date or time together after work.

19 Create a strong support network.

Working parents agree that they need all the help they can get. The Finocchiaros have dinner twice a week with their parents, which strengthens family ties and also frees them from two nights of shopping and cooking. Ira Zimbler's family gets together with a group of friends every Sunday night for a potluck dinner. "We really offer each other a kind of Sunday-night support that energizes us for the rest of the week," Ira says.

20 Always maintain a sense of humor.

Whenever I'm feeling really overwhelmed, I think back, with a smile, to the birthday card that my mother sent me just a few years ago. The front of the card said, "My daughter, she's a wife, mother, worker, cook, housecleaner, chauffeur, and volunteer." When I opened up the card, I found the punch line: "My daughter, she's a basket case!"

A basket case or a balancing act? I like to think of it as the latter. And I like to think that the more time I spend on that tightrope—holding a briefcase in one hand and a baby bottle in the other—the more skilled I become. It helps, however, to know that there is a strong net below to catch me when I slip—a net woven of friends, contacts, and others from whose experiences I can draw insight and support.

WHO'S MINDING AMERICA'S KIDS

For millions of them, it's someone other than parents during working hours. Finding quality care at reasonable cost is never easy, but some companies are helping workers.

Susan Caminiti

KATHY SPIVACK has her schedule down to a science. While her son, Jeffrey, was in kindergarten this past spring, the divorced mother from Closter, New Jersey, arranged her work as an executive with Tupperware so she could drop him at school at 9 A.M. and pick him up at 3 P.M.—except on Tuesdays and Thursdays, when Jeffrey's school ended at 11:30. For those days Spivack enrolled him in the Jack in the Box Early Learning Center, which bused him from school to its premises, where he played until three. Cost: $214 a month. Now that school is out for the summer, Jeffrey attends an all-day camp near home. Spivack has again arranged her work so she can drop him off in the morning and pick him up in the afternoon. She considers herself lucky when it comes to care for Jeffrey, yet still says, "If there is just one little flaw, if one thing changes in my routine with him, it can screw up everything else for the rest of the day."

Spivack's child care setup is notable not because it is the best or worst, but rather because it is so typical. It will become more so. The National Association for the Education of Young Children in Washington, D.C., estimates that some 80,000 day care centers look after four million preschool children and a million school-age children. Another 3.1 million are in family day care, also called neighborhood day care, mainly homes of nonrelatives. American children are increasingly likely to live with just one

REPORTER ASSOCIATE *Tricia Welsh*

TIME OFF FOR NEW MOMS
Guaranteed by law

	Maximum weeks allowed	Percent of salary replaced
Sweden*	51	90%
France	16-38	84%
Italy	20	80%
Britain	18	90%
Canada	15	60%
Germany	14	100%
Japan	14	60%
Netherlands	7	100%
U.S.	NONE	NONE

*For both parents combined.

FORTUNE CHART / SOURCE: SOCIAL SECURITY ADMINISTRATION

parent. In two-parent families, the odds are great that both parents work. The bottom line is that out of choice or necessity, ever more kids are being looked after by someone other than parents—or by no one at all—for much of the day.

The prospect worries many: parents, kids, assorted experts. Probably every parent has heard at least one horror story of a day care provider who allows children to sit zombielike in front of the TV all day, or who leaves infants crying in their cribs. The recent hit movie *The Hand That Rocks the Cradle* unsettled parents with the story of a maniacal nanny who nearly destroys a family after moving in to care for the children. Lurid fantasies aside, research suggests that while day care isn't always as good as parental minding, with luck it isn't bad. Besides, what alternative do working parents have?

Corporations, seeing their own interest in helping employees and customers han-

dle child care, have stepped forward with some practical answers. Dayton Hudson, the $16-billion-a-year retailer that owns the Target and Mervyn's chains, ran 50 million special advertising inserts in July 12 newspapers to tell parents in which of their stores they could meet representatives of local nonprofit child care resource and referral agencies. The Minneapolis company has also hooked up with local social service agencies to train and accredit care givers who open their homes to care for other people's children. The program, called Family-to-Family, reaches 25 communities in 16 states and has trained more than 5,000 care givers.

Sometimes knowing what *not* to offer working parents can be just as helpful. In September, Time Warner (parent of FORTUNE's publisher) will open an emergency drop-in child care center in the lobby of the Time & Life Building in Manhattan. The center, able to accommodate 30 kids, will offer short-term care for parents whose regular child care arrangements have gone awry. Work-family programs director Karol Rose says the company has for years considered setting up a full-time child care center. She explains: "We decided on an emergency center when we discovered that parents weren't as interested in taking their children into Manhattan with them every day as they were in having an option to fall back on if their own child care arrangements fell through."

Small companies have a harder time being as generous as giant ones when it comes to child care. But the Child Care Action Campaign, a national nonprofit educational organization, has published a report, "Not Too Small to Care," that shows how 29 small businesses found imaginative child care solutions—from worker flex-time to on-site care.

Every company with more than 50 employees would be required to give workers up to 12 weeks of unpaid leave to care for a new or ill family member under the Family and Medical Leave Act, which Congress has passed. President Bush vows to veto it, as he has done before, citing the burden to already heavily laden small business. But, as the table shows, the U.S. is the only major industrialized country without a parental leave law.*

Child care costs vary widely. Family day care usually ranges from $35 (in the South) to $150 a week. Care in centers is steeper, and infant care, the most expensive, can cost $35 to $200 a week. A full-time sitter in your home will run even more.

And what are you getting for your money? That is sometimes hard to know. Conscientious parents will investigate any provider thoroughly. To help, the National Association for the Education of Young Children and the National Association for Family Day Care began voluntary accreditation programs several years ago. To become accredited, child care providers must meet standards for safety, nutrition, the learning environment, and interaction between themselves and the children. NAEYC, which deals only with day care centers and schools, has accredited 2,500. The National Association for Family Day Care has accredited only 300 in-home providers, partly because many of these informal care givers don't know the program exists.

To lower costs and improve quality, some parents are getting deeply involved in their kids' care. The Cambridgeport Children's Center in Cambridge, Massachusetts, is a nonprofit center with 33 children, 15 months to 5 years old, of varying racial and economic backgrounds. Parents pay $155 to $180 a week, depending on the child's age and hours at the center; it is open from 8 A.M. to 5:30 P.M. State subsidies cover most of the cost for 11 kids. Parents are involved in every aspect of the center, from fund raising and monthly dinner meetings to discuss programs, to shopping for the snacks the children eat each day. Twice a year they get together to repaint the center and take care of any other maintenance that needs doing. Says director Marcia Boston: "These parents realize if they want a good atmosphere for their children, they are going to have to get involved themselves."

Finding and paying for high-quality child care is difficult for dual-income middle-class families; for low-income households whose kids are more likely to be at risk, it is especially tough. The YWCA has organized two innovative programs to

*Since this article was written, President Bill Clinton signed the Family and Medical Leave Act into law, effective August 1993. *Ed.*

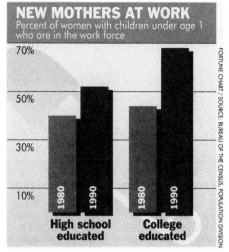

NEW MOTHERS AT WORK
Percent of women with children under age 1 who are in the work force

High school educated — 1980, 1990
College educated — 1980, 1990

FORTUNE CHART / SOURCE: BUREAU OF THE CENSUS, POPULATION DIVISION

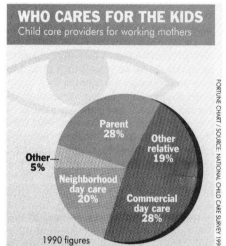

WHO CARES FOR THE KIDS
Child care providers for working mothers

Parent 28%
Other relative 19%
Other 5%
Neighborhood day care 20%
Commercial day care 28%

1990 figures

FORTUNE CHART / SOURCE: NATIONAL CHILD CARE SURVEY 1990

help. The Family Support Network in New Britain, Connecticut, offers temporary child care for families in crisis. Tracey Madden-Hennessey, director of children and youth services for the Y, says the program started in 1984 to help parents whose troubles went beyond child care. "We found that people who are laid off or in the middle of some other family problems often need a bridge to get to what their next step should be," says Madden-Hennessey. "We didn't design this to be a permanent child care arrangement, but it does give parents a place for their children and lets them catch their breath as they figure out their lives."

The cost is based on a family's ability to pay, with a maximum fee of $10 a week. Last year 183 families from New Britain's predominately blue-collar community used the center, where about 30 child care workers offer books, blocks, painting, and other activities. Any child under 5 is welcome, and in extreme cases the center will pay the carfare to bring the child to the center and back home again.

Though the program's promotional materials nowhere mention child abuse, for fear of scaring parents away, Madden-Hennessey views the Family Support Network as a means of preventing such abuse. "When parents are stressed out in other parts of their life, it could lead to abuse of the kids," she says. "A lot of the people who come here are single parents who don't have a big support network of other family members to help them out. We think that by giving parents an option for their children, we can avoid any chance of abuse."

PERHAPS NO GROUP of children falls through the child care cracks as easily as those from homeless shelters. That's why three years ago the Baltimore YWCA helped start the Ark Day Care Center. While studying homelessness with other

groups in the area, YWCA associate executive director Dorothy Critcher says the organization realized the acute need for care for children in emergency shelters. "Too often parents in shelters had no choice but to bring their kids along with them on the bus while they went looking for housing or jobs," she says.

The Ark's program is designed for children ages 3 to 5 and includes the type of curriculum found in most day care centers—painting, playing in groups, and storytelling. Parents pay nothing; the center's $120,000 annual operating budget comes mainly from local donations.

To make sure the program reaches as many eligible children as possible, a small bus owned by the YWCA makes the rounds from shelter to shelter, picking up children at 8 A.M. and dropping them off around 3:30 P.M. "In the beginning parents were very fearful of putting their kids on the bus," says Critcher. "I think they felt we were going to take them away for good. But now that word has spread about the program, we don't have a problem." Though the Ark promotes workshops that help parents play and communicate better with their children, Critcher admits attendance is low. "A lot of these parents are very young," she says, "and while they care about their children, when you're facing a crisis such as homelessness, you're not exactly thinking about coming in to watch your children play."

Then there's the child care solution that costs nothing and requires no charity: leaving kids home alone. According to a 1990 study by the Urban Institute, 3.4 million children between 5 and 12, 12% of the total, take care of themselves either before or after school. These are the so-called latchkey kids.

A look at children in self-care is disturbing. A study done in April by the American Academy of Pediatrics showed that latchkey children were more socially isolated than other children since they were not allowed to play outside or have a friend visit their home as often. The study also showed that children in the care of older brothers or sisters ranked themselves lower in self-worth, social acceptance, and physical appearance. Other studies by the academy indicate that latchkey kids were about twice as likely as supervised children to smoke, drink alcohol, and use marijuana.

A parent's group in Boston is battling the problem of after-school care head-on. Parents United for Child Care, made up of low- to middle-income families, formed in 1987 to improve the care available to members' children. One of the first issues the group took on was the lack of before- and after-school programs for children from 5 to 14. In May 1989 the group gathered data from 1,650 families with elementary school children at a wide range of ten Boston public schools and six parochial schools.

The survey showed that 75% of working parents could not be home every day after school, and 24% had to leave for work in the morning before their children left for school. Yet only 14% of the children were in any kind of formal after-school program each day. Perhaps the most shocking finding was that nearly 50% of the working mothers in the survey claimed they could not call their children from work or receive calls from their kids, even in an emergency. "Clearly there was a desperate shortage of services," says Parents United director Elaine Fersh. "And telling these people, many of whom are single parents, that the solution was to be home with their children, was no solution at all."

Since the study was released, Parents United for Child Care has worked with the principals at over a dozen Boston elementary schools to start before- and after-school programs. The group is also working with other neighborhood organizations, such as churches and community centers, to set up similar programs.

New England Telephone in Boston is tackling the problem of latchkey children from another direction. Since spring it has offered employees an on-site workshop that teaches parents and their children about safe and effective self-care. The course, designed by the Center on Work and Family at Boston University, runs for two hours one night a week for five consecutive weeks and covers subjects such as after-school schedules, how to deal with peer pressure, and home and neighborhood safety. The program requires that families tour their house to teach children what to do if the toilet overflows (turn off the valve underneath), where the electrical switch box is, and how to use a fire extinguisher.

Fran Trainor, a repair service assistant with New England Telephone, participated in the program with her 12-year-old daughter, Michelle. Trainor's job, which has been part time since her daughter was a baby, is scheduled to become full time this fall. "I was a little apprehensive at first, but Michelle really liked the program, and I think we both got a lot out of it," says Trainor. "One of the most important things it taught both of us is that there has to be good communication between the parent and child and a schedule of what the child is expected to do before the parent gets home. Just because I'm not there doesn't mean Michelle is going to sit in front of the TV all afternoon."

Family care, day care centers, self-care: It comes down to a lot of not-quite-satisfying choices for parents who want to do their best for their kids but can't be home when their children aren't in school. It's also plenty of work: choosing care, keeping close tabs on it, maybe helping run a care center, paying for it. No way is it easy, and for many parents, especially single ones, it can't end until the child is nearly grown. Smart employers can help. But nothing will change the hard, basic principle of child care, sometimes forgotten: The kids' welfare comes first, and vigilant parents are its best protector.

CHILD CARE:
What Do Families Really Want?

Parents are hard-pressed to find facilities that are accessible, affordable, and reliable.

Michael Schwartz

Mr. Schwartz is director, Center for Social Policy, Free Congress Research and Education Foundation, Washington, D.C.

WHEN PARENTS seek substitute care for their children, there are three fundamental considerations they weigh—accessibility, affordability, and reliability. The first two seem to be fairly obvious. A substitute caregiver must be accessible: near home and work. Any arrangement that entails substantial added commuting time is not practical. Similarly, the cost of child care must not take up such a large portion of a family's disposable income that it seriously would diminish the benefits of working.

These two factors so closely are related that they could be combined under affordability. If a family can afford to pay, accessible child care will be available. The market of providers is so flexible that it is potentially infinite. The Department of Labor concluded in 1988 that there is no lack of child care. There may be temporary, localized shortages, but the market has proved to be highly responsive to these situations. Where a need appears, someone inevitably and quickly moves to fill it.

The question of reliability is more problematic. When parents hire a babysitter for even one night, they want to be confident their offspring will be safe and secure. This concern is even greater when it is a matter of entering into an arrangement for substitute care on a regular basis over a long period of time.

What constitutes reliability is a highly individualized judgment. Most parents probably have experienced child care arrangements they found unsatisfactory for some reason, and have shopped around for a better one. The factors they weigh in making a judgment about the reliability of a substitute caregiver could be extremely varied.

Parents may be concerned about the meals their youngsters are served or the kind of entertainment offered to them, as well as the ages and behavior of the other children being cared for. The physical environment in which their kids are placed may be uppermost in their minds. In many cases, it may be a personal response to the substitute caregiver. If they find one they like, who inspires confidence and builds a positive relationship with their children, other, more easily measured factors may pale in significance.

Government is incapable of making these personal judgments. What it can do, and does, to address the reliability of child care is to establish certain minimum standards for commercial child care. This is reasonable because there are some objective, measurable conditions the state has a right to demand of those who offer a service on the market.

Yet, it must be admitted that a regulatory standard is a clumsy instrument for guaranteeing a satisfaction that depends so heavily on intangible factors. People will have various conceptions of what is acceptable, desirable, and ideal. Most of all, they will have different ideas about who is trustworthy. The main task of regulation is to protect children from foreseeable threats to their health and safety. As regulation goes beyond that point, it becomes a matter of replacing the personal judgment of parents with the abstract decisions of regulators not directly involved in the relationship.

Currently, Congress is considering legislation that would establish certain minimum regulatory standards for virtually all commercial child care providers. It is very important, in this connection, to bear in mind that the issue is not whether there should be regulatory standards, but whether they should be set at the state or Federal level. Each of the 50 states already has a set of regulatory standards they have determined are best suited to their particular circumstances and conditions.

Are Federal standards needed?

The question, then, is whether Federal law, in the interest of increasing the reliability of child care, should replace the standards set by the states with more stringent ones. This is ill-advised for several reasons.

In the first place, there is no evidence that the existing standards in any state are inadequate. Many of the tragedies that have occurred to youngsters while they were

Elaine M. Ward

under the care of parental substitutes have resulted from unforeseeable accidents. Some have involved instances in which local regulatory standards were violated. Far more often, they have resulted from circumstances in which children were placed in situations beyond the reach of state regulation, frequently without adult supervision at all. In no instance has it been shown that a child has suffered harm because a state regulation was so lax that it placed his or her health and safety in danger.

The argument has been made that there are Federal standards for airline and consumer product safety and environmental pollution, so they should exist for child care as well. This analogy, however, fails in at least three ways:

● The safety of airplanes or the flammability of pajamas can be measured objectively, scientifically, and precisely. The reliability of child care is not amenable to this sort of laboratory analysis.

● It neither would be practical nor in the public interest to have 50 different sets of safety standards for products that are sold throughout the country. However, child care is not an interstate industry. It is a highly localized neighborhood business.

● There already are standards in all 50 states that—on the record, at least—are adequate to ensure the health and safety of

change would not fall evenly on the entire all children covered by them. Thus, there is no reason to substitute the judgments of Federal regulators for those of the millions of consumers, providers, and state and local authorities who have established the existing standards.

A second significant consideration when weighing the advisability of Federal child care standards is that there is a trade-off between regulatory standards and the cost and availability of child care. The more stringent standards become, the more expensive it is for providers to meet them, and the more they must charge their clients. Those states with stricter regulatory standards tend to have a relatively smaller proportion of children cared for in a state-regulated setting, compared to the ones with more relaxed standards.

The states have had to strike a balance between maximizing standards at the cost of affordability and accessibility, or maximizing affordability and accessibility by placing fewer demands on child care providers. Connecticut, for example, has chosen to pursue the former course; Florida, the latter. Both of these decisions are honest attempts to serve the public good. It must be noted, however, that a far larger proportion of the children of Florida who are in substitute care are in regulated settings than in Connecticut.

Imposing stricter standards through Federal intervention will have at least two consequences. It will raise the cost of regulated child care in the affected states and prompt more providers and consumers to seek out arrangements that escape regulation, leaving a higher number of youngsters in unregulated care settings.

The industry trade journal, *Child Care Review,* conducted a study to assess the impact of Federal minimum standards on a single aspect of child care—staff-child ratios. It concluded that, if proposals pending before Congress become law, the cost of child care to consumers would increase by an average of $350 a year, and one-fifth of the licensed providers would go out of business, leaving more than 750,000 fewer places for children in licensed centers.

The impact of this single regulatory country. Some states would be unaffected, while others would suffer catastrophic dislocations in the child care market. In Arizona, for instance, parents would have to pay almost $750 a year more for licensed care. In South Carolina, the increase would be over $1,300. In Florida, more than 150,000 youngsters would be displaced from licensed care, while 250,000 places would disappear in Texas.

In those states that have chosen to emphasize accessibility and affordability by imposing lighter regulatory burdens on providers, licensed child care is plentiful and cheap. The system is working for families of modest means. Under Federal regulation, it would not, and they and their children would be hurt by strict standards.

Consumer choice is the key

In the final analysis, even the most stringent standards do not guarantee reliability because trust can not be imposed by regulation. What is far more effective than regulation is consumer choice. Where competition exists, consumers can ensure satisfaction by taking their business elsewhere if they lose confidence in a child care provider.

In order for the market to work this way, consumers must have the financial means to exercise choice. The family that can not afford more than $30 a week has very limited options. One that can spend $60 will have more choices open. Those who can pay $150 will have no problem finding care that meets their requirements. The problem is that there are a lot more families in the $30 than the $150 bracket.

Families of modest means have little choice except to take what is available at the price, and often that is not entirely to their liking. One mitigating circumstance is that churches—particularly in low-income neighborhoods which for-profit providers would not find attractive—have been generous in establishing child care programs at below-market cost. This has cushioned the hardship of meager resources for thousands of families in a way they find highly satisfactory. In addition, the natural solidarities of extended families and neighborhoods have enabled families of modest means to find reliable child care at

low cost. Yet, despite these bright spots, the one element that assures parental choice and gives them real leverage over the reliability of child care is their ability to pay.

For this reason, it would make more sense to commit the resources of the Federal government toward strengthening the financial position of consumers instead of restructuring the child care industry. Putting money into the hands of parents obviously addresses the question of affordability, but also addresses the other two issues. When parents are able to pay for child care, providers emerge. Child care becomes accessible where it may not have been before. When parents have the means to choose among providers, they are able to demand standards of reliability they find satisfactory.

The current dependent care credit in the tax code is a well-intentioned effort to attain this objective. However, for a number of reasons, it fails to aid most of those families who are most in need of help. The main weakness is that it is keyed to spending money for child care; in general, the more one can afford to spend, the larger the credit. Families of modest means would find it more in their interest to spend as little as possible for child care and forgo the benefits of the tax credit, rather than take fuller advantage of the credit by spending more.

The way out of this dilemma is to break the link between receiving the credit and spending money for substitute care. There are many parents who rely on nonmonetary child care in exchange for some other service they can provide the substitute caregiver; who adjust their working hours—often sacrificing additional income and leisure time in the process—to ensure

the presence of one parent at home all the time; or work at home and care for their offspring simultaneously.

Not everyone is in a position to do this, but those who do should not be penalized by the denial of a benefit they would qualify for if they hired someone else to watch their children. They often are people who place the welfare of their kids above short-term economic gain. In general, their children are better off because of the sacrifices their parents make. In effect, they are reducing the burden on the child care industry, thereby helping to keep accessibility up and costs down for those families who do patronize commercial providers.

The equitable approach to this is to issue an income supplement to families with young children in the form of a refundable tax credit. It should be scaled inversely to income, so that those with the greatest need would receive the most assistance. It need not be offered to families who earn significantly more than the median income, since that would amount to a transfer of income from the less to the more affluent. Clearly, budgetary considerations will determine the size of this credit and the number of families who will be eligible for it, but Federal resources should be stretched as far as possible to strengthen the economic position of families with children.

This solution goes directly to the heart of the child care dilemma—financial security. The only reason parents have to seek out substitute caregivers is so they can be free to earn enough money to support their kids. Enhancing the income of families with children will do more to help improve the quality of life for youngsters, and do so more effectively, than any other step that can be taken by government.

FATHERS AND FAMILIES
Forging Ties That Bind

*New programs are teaching young unwed fathers how
to take legal, financial, and emotional
responsibilities for their children.*

Theodora Lurie

Ms. Lurie is a senior writer, Ford Foundation, New York. This article is based on a Ford Foundation Report.

KEVIN HILL'S 1985 sedan is falling apart, door handles held together with tape, springs pushing through torn upholstery. It's a far cry from the red and white Stingray Corvette he tooled around in when he was dealing drugs at age 13, but Hill [not his real name] slides into the driver's seat with a show of pride. It is not the best car he has owned, but it's the first one he ever bought with money earned legally. Having worked two jobs to scrape together the down payment, Hill sees the car as a sign that he finally is turning his life around.

Now 21, Hill has a past of drugs, gangs, and jail. For the first time, he can imagine a different future. "I always dreamt about making it, having a family, going to school, and right now it's finally starting to come together."

An unmarried father, Hill has a two-year-old daughter whom he makes a point of seeing every day. An 11th-grade dropout, he recently earned a General Equivalency Diploma (GED), enrolled in a community college, and began working as a technician at the University of Pennsylvania Medical School.

Hill measures his accomplishments against grim statistics. Scores of his former buddies have met violent deaths. Two of his older brothers were killed in gang wars and one is in jail for shooting a policeman. Two sisters had babies before they were 14. "Out of 15 kids, I'm the only one in my family to get a high school degree and the first one to go to college. When I found out I passed the GED test, I started crying, and when I told my mom she cried with me. She said, 'I know you can do it. I know you're going to make it.' "

Hill gives credit for his new direction to the Responsive Fathers Program at the Philadelphia Children's Network. One of a growing number across the country that

offer counseling and job-seeking assistance to young unwed fathers, the program provides intensive individual guidance to some 45 participants ranging in age from 16 to 26. It is one of six sites—the others are Cleveland, Ohio; Fresno, Calif.; Racine, Wis.; St. Petersburg, Fla.; and Annapolis, Md.—participating in a national demonstration project sponsored by Public/Private Ventures (P/PV), a nonprofit public policy organization that designs and evaluates programs for disadvantaged youth.

Partially funded by the Ford Foundation with grants totaling $588,500, the project's goal is to determine the most effective ways to help young unwed fathers take legal, financial, and emotional responsibility for their children. It is part of a broader Ford Foundation effort to support research and pilot projects that explore ways to improve the employment opportunities of unwed mothers and fathers of children on welfare.

The soaring rate of out-of-wedlock births has brought a corresponding rise in the number of poor single-parent families dependent on welfare. According to Federal data, 26% of all babies in the U.S. are born to an unwed mother, four times the rate of a generation ago. Nearly half of all families headed by single mothers live in poverty. Studies show that never-married mothers are far more likely than divorced ones to become chronically dependent on welfare, in part because they receive so little child support. Just 24% of never-married single mothers nationwide had court orders for child-support payments from fathers in 1989, compared to 72% of divorced or separated mothers.

Most efforts to address this situation have focused on helping unwed mothers move from welfare to work and getting absent fathers to pay child support. However, in cases where the fathers are inner-city young men with a poor education, spotty work experience, and few job prospects, child-support enforcement is difficult. Programs like the one at P/PV are testing new ways to help these men meet their support obligations. The P/PV project specifically has targeted younger unwed fathers. "We want to build on the pride they feel when their baby has just been born," explains Nigel Vann, a P/PV program officer. "That's the moment when these guys are most involved with their kids and most likely to want to talk about fatherhood issues. It's harder to re-engage fathers once their children are older."

Research findings are challenging the stereotype of young unwed fathers as irresponsible "baby-making machines" who refuse to help care for their kids. In fact, many want to be good parents, but face daunting obstacles.

Needed skills

As Bernardine Watson, P/PV vice president and director of field operations, indicates, "Most of the men we're working with are not disconnected from their children. They'll buy them clothes and food, take them to the doctor, contribute money when they can. Their problem is that they are very poorly equipped for the labor market."

Although teenage mothers long have had access to social-assistance programs, little effort has been made to help unwed fathers get the education, training, and jobs they need if they are to become steady providers. "We have to be advocates for these young men because the system is not geared to helping them be successful," notes Thomas J. Henry, director of the Philadelphia project. Inflexible child-support laws and a cumbersome, often unfriendly government bureaucracy can discourage unmarried fathers from taking legal responsibility for their offspring.

"If a young man formally acknowledges paternity or is named the father by the child's mother, he is expected to start making child-support payments immediately. But in many cases these young men lack the skills to command more than the minimum wage and have only sporadic employment."

Many experts agree that the short-term training programs available to some unwed fathers offer quick-fix solutions that do not prepare them to become self-sufficient. If they take the two to three years needed to learn new skills, they fall behind in support payments and could end up owing the state tens of thousands of dollars or face jail for nonpayment. As a result, some men who do acknowledge paternity take dead-end jobs just to keep up with their payments. Many others try to avoid getting caught in the system altogether.

At the Responsive Fathers Program, Tom Henry and case manager Greg Patton put in long days trying to make that system more sensitive to the difficulties faced by unwed fathers. "We're trying to motivate these young men to change their lives and become responsible parents, but the systems we're dealing with seem designed to alienate them," Patton maintains.

Appearing in family court can be a frustrating and sometimes humiliating experience, particularly for fathers of children on welfare. They often are made to wait for hours and then grilled in front of others about their private lives. Although couples who can afford a lawyer are likely to get a customized child-support agreement, poor unwed fathers can be ordered to pay an amount that does not take into account their fluctuating employment history. Without an attorney to explain how they can file for a reduction of payments if they lose their job or inform them of their visitation rights, many end up feeling overwhelmed and powerless to get ahead.

Henry and Patton have met with family court officers to explore ways to improve procedures, but helping unwed fathers get fair treatment in the child-support system is only part of the program. Before they can become good fathers, these young men—most of whom received little or no fathering themselves—need guidance in dealing with feelings of anger, confusion, and low self-esteem. "Our biggest challenge is to make them aware of their responsibilities, to show them how to negotiate the system and not to quit when they feel frustrated," Henry explains.

Most participants join in the hope of getting a job or vocational training, but Henry has had a hard time persuading training and employment programs to give these men a chance. Many are high school dropouts with no steady work experience. Some have arrest records or a past of drug dealing and substance abuse. Most come from single-parent homes and have received little encouragement to break the cycle of fatherless families and welfare dependency.

So far, with the project's help, six participants have earned or are working on a GED, nine are attending community college, and 19 have found jobs. Henry is trying to get several into programs that would train them to be electricians, barbers, printers, and radiology technicians.

Several of the other sites participating in the project have had more success linking young men to training and employment, mainly because of closer ties to other service providers and access to Federal funds for job training and placement. In Fresno, Cleveland, and Racine, participants are expected to attend four to eight weeks of intensive daily classes to prepare them generally for employment, followed by skills training and job placement. Established in 1990, the Philadelphia Children's Network is a newer organization and it still is building its links to local employers. It also is working with the city's Private Industry Council, a Federally funded agency that provides job training mostly to single mothers on welfare, to design similar programs for unemployed young men.

A changed life

The Philadelphia program is having a profound effect on the lives of some participants. Kevin Hill learned about the program from a flyer left on his car window. He admits he was skeptical, even combative, when he went to check it out. His past experience had made him wary of "anything that sounded positive." His earliest memories are of working in the tobacco and corn fields of North Carolina with his sharecropper grandparents. When he was seven, his mother moved the family to an inner-city neighborhood of West Philadelphia, where she struggled to support her children with low-paying factory jobs. He barely knew his father. "My father is the only person I hate," Hill says. "He would come around just long enough to get my mother pregnant and then disappear."

Despite his mother's best efforts, Hill got caught up in the street culture of violence and fast money. "I did what I had to do to survive. When you live in the ghetto, there's no one to lean on but other ghetto people, and all they've got is drugs and guns." The men he looked up to were the ones with "the big cars, the women, money, and jewelry."

Hill seemed destined to follow in their footsteps. At the age of 11, he shot a teenager in the chest for hitting his sister. At 12, he joined a gang and began stealing cars. By 13, he was selling and snorting cocaine, earning up to $1,000 a day. That is when his mother put him out of the house and Hill got an apartment with a friend.

Between 14 and 18, he was in and out of detention centers. "When I was dealing drugs, I used to try to give my mother money, but she always refused to take it because she knew it was wrong. It's because of her that I got stronger. When I got out of jail this last time and found Tom Henry, I said for once I'm going to make it right, make her proud of me."

Henry was unlike any male adult Hill ever had known. "When I met Tom, I thought, this guy ain't real. I'd never seen any guy like him—don't get high, all clean in a suit and stuff, telling me I can do this and I can be that."

Hill now has a goal—to become a registered nurse, a dream he nurtured secretly for years. Even when he was running with gangs and dealing drugs, Hill would sneak off to watch the daytime soap opera "General Hospital" because one of the characters was a male nurse. When he confided this ambition to Henry, Hill was encouraged to go to college to make his dream come true. Hill recalls feeling he would never be able to get that far.

As he does with all the young men in the program, Henry encouraged, prodded, pestered, got tough, and paved the way for Hill to take the necessary steps. Although he spent two months studying for the GED exam, Hill froze when he sat down to take it. He was given another appointment, but never showed up. Henry scheduled a third try, and this time Hill took the test and passed, scoring so well in placement exams for community college that he was put in an accelerated mathematics class. "I never had no one in my corner until I met Tom," Hill indicates. "People would tell me I could do things, but they were always the wrong things."

The support Henry and Patton provide has no office hours. Patton wears a beeper so the young men can reach him at any time. He has gotten calls in the middle of the night, once to help a group member see his newborn son at the hospital (his girlfriend's mother was trying to keep him away), another time to bring a participant carfare to go to work the next day, in other instances to assist in sorting out personal problems or mediate in disputes with girlfriends. Henry has driven to the men's homes in the morning to make sure they go to job interviews, take their GED exams, or just get to work on time.

"If you're not willing to commit fully to these young men, then you should not be involved in a program like this," maintains Henry, who believes it will take two to three years to get the young fathers on the right track so they can take care of their families. Adds Patton: "Every program they've ever seen looks good on paper but doesn't follow through. This is the first time they have people who are really there for them. When they're wrong, we tell them, and when they're right, we back them 100%."

Although this kind of mentoring is bringing good results, the staff is careful not to claim success too soon. Henry and Patton are powerful role models, but they feel locked in a constant struggle with competing influences. "We're dealing with these young men once a week, and then they have all the other days to fall back into the negative things that are in their community and reinforced by their peers," Henry notes. "I might tell a young man to stop selling drugs and promise to get him a job, but then if three weeks go by and I can't deliver on that promise, he still needs money to live. So he says, 'I tried your way and it didn't work, so what are you talking about?'"

Married to his high school sweetheart for 27 years and the father of two grown children, Henry has been active in community youth projects for more than two decades. Both he and Patton know what it is like to be a teenage father unprepared for the pressures of parenthood. "In each of the young men I see a little bit of myself," says Patton, who still remembers the terror he felt at 15 when his girlfiend got pregnant. Henry and his future wife were 18 when she had their first child. "I didn't know how to deal with it, so I went into the military to get away."

Their own experiences help them connect with the pain and frustration vented by the young men in weekly discussion groups. For many participants, these sessions are the best part of the program. Held at the downtown office of the Philadelphia Children's Network, the Tuesday night meetings deal with male-female relationships, child rearing, decision-making, racism, how to control anger, and what it means to take responsibility for your life. For inner-city youths accustomed to showing the world a "cool" facade, having a place where they can let down their emotional guard is liberating.

Rick Shaw, 26, has five children, whose ages range from three months to five years. His oldest lives with her mother, Shaw's former girlfriend. He plans to marry the mother of his youngest four. He heard about the group from friends who felt it was helping them change their lives. "I thought it was a lot of bull," he recalls, but he finally decided to check out an evening session. "Everything they were talking about was something I could relate to. Then I started talking, letting out things that I had always wanted to talk about but could never express before. When I left I was smiling."

The young men use the group meetings to grapple with basic issues of identity. One 22-year-old with a troubled past feels the sessions are changing his self-image. "With this program, I've learned so much about being a man because I was no man before, even though I thought I was. I might have been earning a lot of money, but I was dumb to life. Now I'm finally beginning to set a good example for my son."

Shaw feels he's on the right road. A high school graduate who works sporadically in construction, he had been unemployed for eight months when he entered the program. "Being out of work was getting to me. My kids needed Pampers and stuff and I wasn't able to give it to them." With help from Henry, Shaw applied to enter a training program in building maintenance and hopes eventually to become a carpenter. Meanwhile, once a week he makes the round of downtown companies to fill out job applications. "I've been to the bottom and I knew I was going to do what was necessary to get out. This program is part of that. It teaches you to respect yourself and others, how to get a job and take care of your family."

Shaw already can see improvements in his home life. "My girlfriend and I used to fight a lot and sometimes it would get out of hand. But Tom [Henry] is teaching me how to control my anger. I still have a way to go, but I try to talk things out now. My girl says she really sees a change in me."

Domestic tensions have been eased by changes in Shaw's lifestyle. Before entering the program, most of his days and evenings were spent hanging out with his friends and playing basketball. "I used to think I didn't have to tell my girlfriend where I was going or when I'd be back. If I was out with my friends and I'd say I'm going home to my girl now, they'd say, 'Already? Who runs the show, you or your girl?,' so I'd stay out longer. Now, when I tell her I'm coming back at nine o'clock, I'm home by nine o'clock."

Shaw also spends more time with his children, playing with them at home, taking them on outings to the mall and the movies. "I want to live as a family and that's starting to happen." His only regret is that he didn't have all his children with the same mother, because he doesn't get to see his oldest daughter as often as he would like. "She's my heart," he says. "But every time I go over to visit, her mom will start an argument."

Changing the image

Many of the men feel held back by negative stereotypes of inner-city black youth. Henry challenges them to take positive steps to alter that image. "You have the power to make people respect you," he tells the young men, "and the only way to do that is to stop messing around and start growing."

For Hill, that process already has begun. At least three times a week, he picks up his daughter at day care after work, helps feed and put her to bed, then goes to study in the library until eight p.m., when his classes begin at community college. No longer living with his child's mother, Hill maintains that he has learned not to let the strains between them interfere with his relationship with his daughter. "My main thing is I got to take care of my little girl. That's something decent, something special in my life."

Henry would like to expand the program to include the mothers of the children. "If we're ever going to put the family back together, we've got to look at this holistically. It's not enough to work just with the father because when he starts to grow, his partner can feel threatened. We've got to help the young women grow at the same time."

P/PV has extended the initial 18-month term of the project for another year and is analyzing the experience of all six sites to determine what changes in policies covering child support and employment training would enable these fathers to pursue the education and job opportunities they need to become good providers. It also will examine the long-term benefits of the intensive individual support they receive and try to track what happens once they leave the program. "We're seeing that many of the young men really do need a lot more support than is available in traditional programs," says P/PV's Bernardine Watson. "It's important to have a dedicated staff who can relate to them and gain their trust.

But the hope is that once they receive a solid preparation they will be able to make good use of what they have learned and become less reliant on the case managers."

Whatever the future brings, Kevin Hill has no doubts about what the program has meant to him. "If I hadn't started coming here, I'd be dead or in jail by now. When I entered the program, I was uneducated, I was a criminal; I had no job, no money. I had a family, but it wasn't really a family. Now I got a job, I'm going to college, and I have a family so strong nobody's going to break it up."

FATHER FIGURES

SUMMARY   The facts on fathers aren't what you might expect. Fathers have rising standards for their own behavior, and minority fathers give more care to their tots. Non-Hispanic white fathers read to young children often, but they are also more likely to yell at older children. Absentee fathers' visits may be more like playtime than true parenting. This survey gives a valuable first look at what fatherhood means today.

Linda Jacobsen
and
Brad Edmondson

Linda Jacobsen is research director and Brad Edmondson is editor-in-chief of American Demographics.

Every man with children sometimes wonders how he rates as a father. At the top of the scale are Super Dads: good providers who also praise their children's accomplishments, read bedtime stories, and change diapers. The patron saint of Super Dads is Cliff Huxtable of "The Cosby Show." He stands in stark opposition to the worst-performing fathers: Deadbeat Dads, who don't help with child care, don't pay child support, and might never see their kids at all. Deadbeat Dads are defined mostly by government officials and other experts who claim loudly and often that absentee fathers are wreaking havoc with children's lives.

The reality of fatherhood in America is more complex than either of these two extremes. The good father, like the good mother, is a role in transition.

A generation ago, fathers were expected to be good providers, but they weren't expected to nurture their kids. Since then, the number of both Super Dads and Deadbeat Dads has grown, while old-fashioned breadwinning fathers are going the way of full-time homemakers.

In most households, men are still the primary providers for the family. But their share of family income is steadily declining. And as their economic power declines, the old model of fatherhood falls away. Thanks to wives' rising incomes, fathers in the 1990s "have been freed to participate more fully in the family," writes sociologist Frank Furstenberg. In some cases, of course, "they have also been freed from family responsibilities altogether."

To get at the truth about fathers, we consulted the National Survey of Families and Households (NSFH) and other sources. We wanted to know how married and absentee fathers are doing: how often they give physical care to their children, play with them at home, take them on outings, read to them, help with homework, praise them, yell at them, and pay child support to custodial mothers.*

We found that a father's age, education, race, and other demographic factors can offer clues to his performance on the Super Dad-Deadbeat Dad scale. But our findings weren't always in line with conventional wisdom. For example:

• Black and Hispanic married fathers are just as involved with their children as are non-Hispanic white married fathers;
• College-educated married fathers spend less time caring for their preschoolers than do less-educated fathers; and
• A solid majority of ever-married absentee fathers pay some child support.

Most fathers say that their children come first. Yet fathers also play the roles of workers, husbands, ex-husbands, consumers, and individuals. [F]ind out how much time today's fathers actually devote to their children.

---

* See "Behind the Numbers." Single-father families comprise less than 2 percent of all U.S. households, so we did not include them in this analysis.

Rising Standards

The talk about Super Dads is more than just hype. Many surveys show that married men are setting higher standards for themselves when it comes to child-rearing. In 1993, 65 percent of married men agree that "when making important family decisions, consideration of the children should come first," according to DDB Needham's Life Style Study. Just 48 percent agreed with this statement in 1977.

The share grew to 60 percent by 1982, remained stable until 1989, then headed up again. The data support the view that men become more family-conscious during recessions.

The idea that a bleak economy strengthens family values may explain why men aged 18 to 44, who came of age in an era of economic fits and starts, are more likely than men aged 45 and older to agree that "children should come first." But older men are more likely than younger ones to agree that "children are the most important thing in a mar-

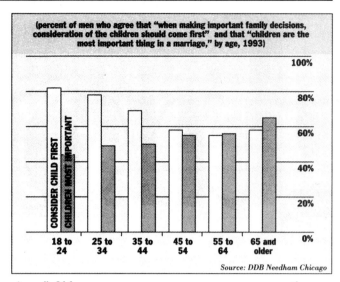

(percent of men who agree that "when making important family decisions, consideration of the children should come first" and that "children are the most important thing in a marriage," by age, 1993)

Source: DDB Needham Chicago

riage." Older men may see children as more important in an abstract sense, while younger men may see them as more of a day-to-day personal responsibility.

Time for Tots

On a good day, full-time working parents may have one hour before work and three hours after work to share with their children. This precious time must contain all of the daily chores of child care. When the NSFH queried married men with a child younger than 5 in 1987-88, 95 percent said they do some child-care chores every day. But there is still room for improvement. Only 30 percent of the fathers with working wives did three or more hours of daily child care, compared with 74 percent of employed married mothers.

More than one-fourth (28 percent) of married fathers with a preschooler say they do three or more hours of child-care chores a day. These highly involved fathers are real-life Super Dads, but their

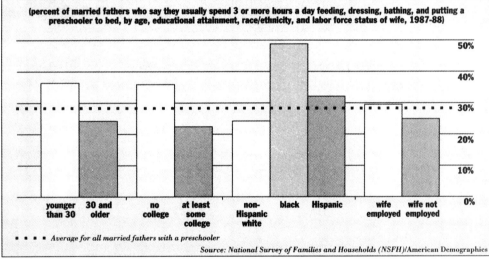

(percent of married fathers who say they usually spend 3 or more hours a day feeding, dressing, bathing, and putting a preschooler to bed, by age, educational attainment, race/ethnicity, and labor force status of wife, 1987-88)

• • • • Average for all married fathers with a preschooler

Source: National Survey of Families and Households (NSFH)/American Demographics

demographics resemble those of Cliff Huxtable in only one respect. Black and Hispanic married fathers are more likely than non-Hispanic white married fathers to spend three or more hours a day caring for preschoolers. But unlike Cliff, highly involved fathers are a downscale group, dominated by married men in their 20s and men who did not go to college.

Young, downscale, and minority men are often blamed for the rapid increase in absentee fathers. But these same men, at least those committed to a marriage, are more involved as fathers to young children for several reasons. First, young adults are more likely than older adults to believe that both spouses should share equally in homemaking and child-rearing. Second, young men are more likely than older men to find themselves unemployed while their wives are working, because both unemployment rates and women's labor force participation are highest among the young.

Finally, couples with two lower-paying jobs often stagger their work hours to cut down on the need for day care. In 1985, one in six two-income couples with a preschool child worked hours that did not overlap at all, according to demographer Harriet Presser.

Having Fun

Once parents finish with work, housework, and physical child care, there isn't much time left for fun. Most married fathers go on outings such as the park, zoo, or movies with their children less than once a week. This pattern is relatively stable across age, education, and race/ethnicity categories. It holds true for fathers with preschoolers and those whose oldest child is aged 5 to 18. Some variations exist: college-educated married fathers are more likely than average to go on outings at least once a week, for example, and black and Hispanic married fathers are more likely to go out "almost every day." The strong

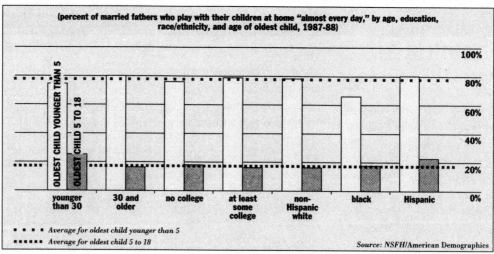

(percent of married fathers who play with their children at home "almost every day," by age, education, race/ethnicity, and age of oldest child, 1987-88)

• • • • Average for oldest child younger than 5
▪▪▪▪▪ Average for oldest child 5 to 18

Source: NSFH/American Demographics

showing among minorities may be partly due to their higher unemployment rates. Also, because rates of nonmarital childbearing are high among blacks, married black fathers may be a select, highly committed group.

Most married fathers play with preschoolers often, but as children get older, fathers play less. Most married men whose oldest child is aged 5 to 18 play with their children at home at least once a week, but only 17 percent play with their children at home almost every day. Young fathers in their 20s are most likely to play with their school-aged children every day, probably because the kids are still young enough to need and want lots of playtime with parents. Hispanic fathers are also more likely than average to be highly involved with older children.

Setting an Example

A well-rounded father is a playmate, but also a coach, a teacher, and a disciplinarian. To a surprising extent, demographics can predict how often fathers play these roles.

Did you ever wonder why children from white, college-educated families do better in school? One probable reason is that 36 percent of college-educated fathers of preschoolers read to their children almost every day, compared with 17 percent of less-educated fathers. Also, 31 percent of non-Hispanic white fathers of preschoolers read to their children every day, compared with 5 percent for blacks

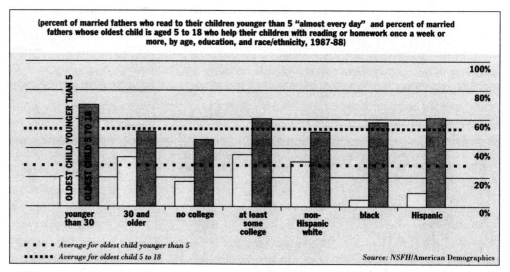

(percent of married fathers who read to their children younger than 5 "almost every day" and percent of married fathers whose oldest child is aged 5 to 18 who help their children with reading or homework once a week or more, by age, education, and race/ethnicity, 1987-88)

• • • • Average for oldest child younger than 5
▪▪▪▪▪ Average for oldest child 5 to 18

Source: NSFH/American Demographics

and 10 percent for Hispanics.

Minority mothers are much more likely than minority fathers to read to their preschoolers almost every day. But minority children are read to much less often by both parents than are non-Hispanic white children.

Most fathers whose oldest child is school-aged say they read or help with homework at least once a week. College-educated fathers are more likely than average to help school-aged children with homework. But black and Hispanic fathers help with homework more often than do non-Hispanic whites, and younger fathers help more often than do older ones. Perhaps fathers who read to young children regularly might not need to help with homework as often when their children go to school.

Do fathers grow more stern

and distant as their children get older? Perhaps. It is a fact that as children age, fathers praise less and yell more. Eighty-two percent of fathers whose oldest child is a preschooler say they praise their children "very often," but only 53 percent of fathers whose oldest is school-aged praise kids that frequently. And 57 percent of fathers whose oldest is school-aged yell at their children "sometimes" or "very often," compared with 47 percent of fathers whose oldest is a preschooler.

College-educated fathers are more likely than average to praise children in both age groups, but they are just as likely as other fathers to yell. Older fathers are much more likely than younger fathers to praise young children often, but not school-aged children. Younger fathers are more likely to raise their voice than older fathers.

Paternal encouragement and discipline differ most by race and ethnicity. Non-Hispanic white married fathers whose oldest child is school-aged are more likely than comparable minority fathers to yell at their children "sometimes" or "very often." Black married fathers are less likely than average to praise their preschoolers and more likely than average to yell at them. But Hispanic married fathers say they are much more likely than other fathers to withhold both praise and anger. Hispanic fathers appear to have a more traditional fathering style: they are willing but somewhat distant playmates.

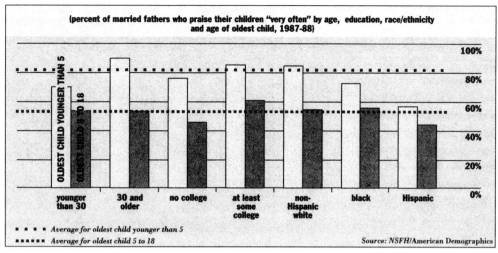

(percent of married fathers who praise their children "very often" by age, education, race/ethnicity and age of oldest child, 1987-88)

- - - Average for oldest child younger than 5
■■■■ Average for oldest child 5 to 18

Source: NSFH/American Demographics

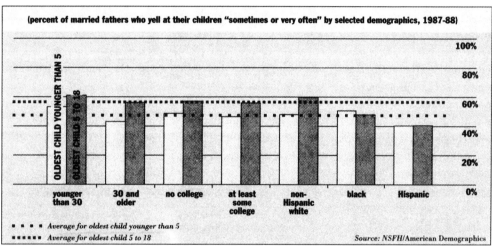

(percent of married fathers who yell at their children "sometimes or very often" by selected demographics, 1987-88)

- - - Average for oldest child younger than 5
■■■■ Average for oldest child 5 to 18

Source: NSFH/American Demographics

ABSENTEE FATHERS

Keeping in Touch

You've probably heard that increasing divorce and nonmarital childbearing will force about half of today's American children to live in a single-mother family for at least part of their childhood. The often-overlooked corollary is that a growing share of fathers will live apart from their children. And the confusion that married men harbor about fatherhood pales in comparison with the anxiety of noncustodial dads.

In 1987-88, 14 percent of all fathers reported having a biological or adopted child who did not live with them at least half of the time. This proportion is 27 percent among black fathers and 21 percent among Hispanic fathers.*

One of the hallmarks of a good father is spending time with children. But more than

To reduce the legal and social ambiguities surrounding nonmarital childbearing, this analysis is restricted to ever-married absentee fathers.

one-fourth of absentee dads reported seeing their children less than once a month in the previous year, and one-fifth did not see them at all. Slightly more than one-quarter of ever-married absentee fathers see their children at least once a week.

Younger fathers are more likely to never see their children, and they are less likely to see them at least once a week. College-educated dads are more likely than the average absentee father to see their children less than once a month. Hispanic fathers have the highest proportion of men who never see their children, and of men who see them at least once a week.

Perhaps the strongest predictor of how often an absentee father sees his children is whether he is married or has other children living with him. Almost 30 percent of currently married fathers never see their children who live in other households, compared with 13 percent of unmarried dads. Only 17 percent of married absentee fathers make weekly visits to their children, compared with nearly 40 percent of unmarried dads.

These patterns add up to what many sociologists call "serial parenting"—that is, men are active parents only to the children who live with them,

characteristic	none	one to several times a year	one to several times each month	one or more times a week
AVERAGE FOR ALL ABSENTEE FATHERS	21.0%	27.0%	20.8%	27.3%
AGE				
Younger than 30	25.1	26.6	22.1	25.1
30 or older	20.4	27.1	20.7	27.6
EDUCATION				
No college	21.7	23.2	24.2	27.3
At least some college	20.0	32.2	16.5	27.2
RACE				
Non-Hispanic white	21.1	28.5	20.3	26.8
Black	18.7	25.9	21.6	27.6
Hispanic	26.0	15.1	24.5	30.6
MARITAL STATUS				
Married	28.5	32.6	19.4	17.1
Not married	13.2	21.2	22.3	37.9
PRESENCE OF CHILDREN				
Children in current household	26.9	33.4	20.6	17.1
No children in current household	16.5	22.2	21.0	35.0

(percent distribution of number of times during the past year that absentee fathers report visiting their child, by age, education, race/ethnicity, marital status, and presence of other children in current household, 1987-88)

Note: Rows may not sum to 100 percent due to a small percentage who refused to answer. Limited to ever-married absentee fathers.

Source: NSFH/American Demographics

whether they are biological or step-children. The share of absentee fathers who never see their children born in a previous marriage increases from 4 percent within 2 years of parental separation to 31 percent by 11 or more years since the break-up, according to sociologist Judith Seltzer at the University of Wisconsin.

Many other factors reduce visitation frequency, including a father's geographic distance from his children, legal agreements, and payment of child support. Angry custodial mothers also erect barriers to separate absentee fathers from their children. This adds up to frustration for fathers. Custodial mothers are more satisfied with absentee fathers' contact with children than are fathers themselves, according to the NSFH. Only 57 percent of absentee fathers are very or somewhat satisfied, compared with 67 percent of custodial mothers.

Admission Fees

Absentee fathers are often pilloried in media accounts of men who don't pay child support. But two-thirds of ever-married absentee fathers made at least one child-support payment in 1986-87, according to the NSFH.* This figure rises above 70 percent among col-

The NSFH asks about any support paid in the previous year, which is one reason why its estimates are higher than those reported in studies that only include legally mandated support.

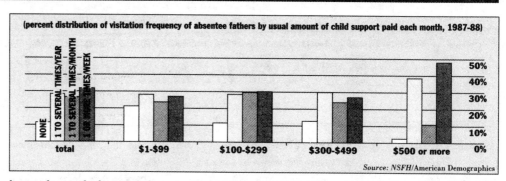

(percent distribution of visitation frequency of absentee fathers by usual amount of child support paid each month, 1987-88)

Source: NSFH/American Demographics

lege-educated absentee fathers, but drops to 60 and 57 percent among black and Hispanic dads, respectively.

Sixty-five percent of ever-married absentee fathers have a legal agreement with their children's mother to pay child support. This proportion drops to 43 percent among minority absentee fathers, compared with 74 percent of non-Hispanic whites.

Child-support payments may be the rule among absentee fathers, but the total amount paid is small. Two-thirds of absentee fathers usually pay less than $300 each month. This share rises to around three-fourths among blacks and Hispanics. Less than 12 percent of non-Hispanic white fathers say they pay $500 or more a month, and 4 percent of minority fathers pay this much. Child support is clearly a sensitive issue: almost 10 percent of absentee fathers refused to disclose the amount they pay each month.

Child-support payments are positively related to visitation. Only 3 percent of fathers who pay at least $500 a month never see their children, compared with 21 percent of those who pay less than $100 a month. Nearly half of fathers in the highest payment bracket report weekly visits, compared with one-fourth of fathers in the lowest bracket. This may happen because custodial mothers who receive more child support are more generous about letting fathers see their children. It may also be that highly committed absentee fathers simply want to both support their children financially and visit them frequently. In contrast to visitation, custodial mothers are less happy than absentee fathers with support payments. Less than half of custodial mothers are very or somewhat satisfied with the amount of child support absentee fathers pay, compared with more than three-fourths of the fathers themselves.

Quality Time

Even the most highly involved absentee fathers must struggle to maintain the closeness and involvement with children that residential fathers take for granted. Many absentee fathers are not Deadbeat Dads—they're Disney Dads.

John is a successful lawyer. Every weekend that his children come to stay at his city apartment, he plans fun outings. They spend little time at his apartment and almost always eat out. Disney Dads are not teachers, coaches, or disciplinarians—they are playmates.

In direct contrast are absentee fathers like Bill, an audio technician. When his children come to visit, he concentrates on making them feel like family members in their second home. Although he also likes to take them on outings, Bill's kids spend most of their visits doing the kinds of things intact families do—yard work, preparing meals together, and schoolwork.

Among ever-married absentee fathers who saw their children at least once a month in the past year, 62 percent took them on at least one outing a month. More than one-fourth reported weekly recreational outings. Older, college-educated, and Hispanic fathers are most likely to go on weekly outings, while monthly outings are most frequent among younger, college-educated, or non-Hispanic white fathers.

Of the absentee dads who see their children at least once a month, 38 percent talk, play, or work on projects together one or more times a week. Non-Hispanic white dads are more likely than minority fathers to talk or play with their children both monthly and weekly. Seventy-two percent of college-educated absentee fathers say they talk or play with their children once a month or more, compared with 59 percent of less-educated fathers.

Most absentee fathers cannot be classified exclusively as Disney Dads. Many who take their children on frequent outings also spend time talking, playing, or working on a project together.

Changes in fatherhood have important consequences for everyone in the family, whether they live together or not. Fathers closer to the Super Dad end of the scale enjoy the positive benefits of close relationships with their children, even as they share the stress of combining work and family long faced by working mothers.

Although absentee fathers may fare better in the short run than the mothers and children they leave behind, those at the Deadbeat end of the scale may end up as lonely, poor old men. And if the number of Deadbeat Dads continues to grow, businesses may face an increasing number of requests to garnish employees' wages as child-support enforcement toughens.

While most divorced men and women say they do not regret their decision to split up, research in the last decade has made it abundantly clear that children are damaged by a divorce. This is why policymakers urge more involvement by absentee dads, both financial and social.

A recent study by University of Pennsylvania sociologist Valarie King finds that children's academic achievement rises with the level of financial support they get from absentee fathers. Yet all absentee dads, from active to Deadbeat, are more likely to have children who suffer from behavioral problems, low self-worth, poverty, and impaired scholastic performance. King's and other research indicates that the trauma of divorce may do long-term damage to children, even if both parents remain highly involved in their lives.

Behind the Numbers The 1987-88 National Survey of Families and Households (NSFH) is a national probability sample of 13,017 U.S. adults aged 19 and older, with double samples of minority groups, single parents, step-parents, cohabiting couples, and recently married persons. We report weighted frequencies, which correct for these different probabilities of sample selection. Our analysis examines two groups: married-couple families with dependent children and ever-married absentee fathers with dependent children who live elsewhere. Because the absentee fathers are ever-married, a substantial proportion, but not all, of their children were born in a previous marriage. The results for absentee fathers must therefore be interpreted with caution for two reasons: first, nonresponse rates in the NSFH are much higher among never-married, separated, and divorced men; and second, the numbers of black and Hispanic absentee fathers are small. However, the NSFH is the only national study that obtains reports from absentee fathers themselves. For more information about the study or to get a copy of the data tape, contact the Center for Demography and Ecology at the University of Wisconsin-Madison at (608) 262-2182.

Family Values: The bargain breaks

Marriage is a bargain between men and women. That bargain is increasingly broken by divorce. The sufferers are men, women and children

ONCE the rock on which society was founded, marriage is being increasingly chiselled away. All over the industrial world, more couples are choosing to live together and even to start a family without marrying. More of those who do marry subsequently divorce. This article examines these trends. It argues that women increasingly see marriage as a bad bargain; but that divorce may not be a better one.

First, the trends. Men and women are marrying later. In the 12 countries of the EC the mean age of marriage for women is now just over 25, two years older than in the late 1970s. In the United States by the end of the 1980s, the age of marriage for American women stood at a 20th-century high. To some extent, the decline in marriage has been offset by a rise in cohabitation. The prevalence of cohabitation varies enormously. In northern Europe people tend to live together for long periods. In America such partnerships are shorter. In Italy people hardly ever cohabit.

Births out of wedlock are not always births to women living alone. In Sweden more than half of all births are to unwed mothers, but perhaps three-quarters of these are to women living in "consensual unions"—ie, stable partnerships. Such households are also common in Britain, where 30% of all births are out of wedlock, but much rarer in America, where one in four births of all babies (and 60-65% of black babies) is to a single mother.

People enter marriage later; they leave it earlier. By far the highest **divorce** rate in the industrial world is that of the United States. On current rates, about half of all American marriages will be dissolved. In Europe, if present rates continue, two out of every five marriages in Britain, Denmark and Sweden will end in divorce, but only one in ten in some southern European countries. "Even in Japan," says John Ermisch, professor of economics at Glasgow University and au-

thor of a recent book on lone parenthood*, "on present trends one marriage in five will eventually end in divorce."

In many countries the divorce rate picked up in the 1960s and accelerated in the 1970s. In the United States the rate doubled between 1966 and 1976. Now it shows signs of levelling off in several countries, including the United States and Sweden (it has fallen in both), Britain and Holland.

More births out of wedlock and more divorce mean more children spending at least part of their youth in **one-parent families**. In the United States a quarter of all families with children are headed by one parent; in Britain, one in five; in Sweden and Denmark, one family in seven. Divorce is the main reason. In the United States, half of all children are likely to witness the break-up of their parents' marriage; in Britain, a quarter; in Norway, a third.

Breaking up

Does a common cause lie behind these changes in the importance of marriage, and particularly in the increase in divorce? Some see a pervasive cultural change, an erosion of morality that has accompanied the decline of religious belief and the rise of materialism. Others point to changes in the laws which have made divorces easier to obtain. Still others see a link with the rise in women's employment.

A change in attitudes to divorce has certainly taken place. In 1945 and again in 1966, national samples of Americans were asked if they thought the divorce laws in their states were too strict or not strict enough. In both years, the most popular response was "not strict enough". But at some point after 1968, a sharp change in attitudes took place. In 1968 and 1974, a sample of Americans was asked whether divorce should be made easier or more difficult. Between the two sample years, the number replying "easier" rose by 15%, while the num-

ber who said "more difficult" declined by 21%. Since then, the proportion who thought divorce should be more difficult has been increasing once again; by 1989 it accounted for a majority of Americans.

But what people believe and what they do may be quite different. Andrew Cherlin, author of a riveting book† on American marriage, draws attention to a group of young mothers who were interviewed several times between 1962 and 1977. At first, half the women agreed with the sentiment: "When there are children in the family, parents should stay together even if they don't get along." But the women who agreed were almost as likely as those who disagreed to divorce in the following 15 years.

Changes in attitudes may have accompanied or followed the rise in divorce, rather than caused it. The same may well be true of changes in the law, although each time a divorce law is made more permissive, the divorce rate tends to rise a little. But for underlying causes it may be wiser to look at the job market rather than the courts.

Since the end of the second world war, the proportion of women in paid employment has risen dramatically in every industrial country. Increasingly, women now go out to work even while their children are toddlers. Almost two-thirds of all women in the OECD have paid work, and in Sweden the proportion (four out of five) is almost as high as for men.

The expanding employment of women is a theme that runs through many of the changes occurring in the family. Gary Becker, professor of economics at Chicago University and winner of the 1992 Nobel prize for economics, has encouraged people to think of the economic forces that influ-

....

* "Lone Parenthood: an Economic Analysis". National Institute of Economic and Social Research
† "Marriage, Divorce, Remarriage". Harvard University Press

ence people to get married and have children. He believes they are as powerful as the forces that govern decisions to buy a new car or change jobs. The better the opportunities for women to earn, the greater the costs of giving up work to have children, and so the later women are likely to start their families and the fewer children they are likely to have. "Children are cheaper during recessions," Mr Becker observed when he gave his presidential address to the American Economics Association.

Mr Becker was by no means the first to point out that women's employment might affect marriage. Back in 1919 one Arthur W. Calhoun argued that "the fact of women's access to industry must be a prime factor in opening to her the possibility of separation from husband." A number of studies, mainly of American women in the 1970s, have shown that married women with jobs are more likely to divorce or separate than those who stay home.

Mr Ermisch, whose book analyses the economic forces behind the break-up of marriages in Britain, establishes that the more time British women spend in paid work, the more likely their marriage is to end in divorce. Of course, it is unlikely that the mere act of getting a job makes women unhappy in their marriages—although, as Mr Ermisch puts it, "Their employment may provide better opportunities for meeting another partner who compares favourably with their present one." But women with an income may worry less about the poverty that generally comes with divorce; and those in unhappy marriages may see employment as an insurance policy.

Fathers don't do the ironing

Once women earn, one of the oldest advantages of marriage is undermined: economic support. Another, sex, is safely available without marriage, thanks to effective contraception. As a result, couples—or rather, wives—are likely to care more about the other potential benefits of marriage, such as emotional support or help in the home.

The extra emphasis on marriage as an emotional partnership may make it more vulnerable. That men and women expect different things from marriage has been the stuff of good novels for many years, but the differences are now minutely picked over by sociologists. Penny Mansfield, a member of One plus One, a British research group, has been studying a group of 65 London couples who married in 1979. Interviewed in the sixth year of their marriage, each partner was asked to describe a range of social and family relationships, and then to say to whom they felt closest. Several husbands (but no wives) were baffled by the question. "I don't know what you mean, 'feel closest to'," said one. "People of most importance in my life? Who I'd be most worried by if something happened to them?"

The gap between expectation and reality grows wider once children arrive. The sort of partnership advocated by romantic magazines is hugely time-consuming. Finding space for all those candle-lit dinners and meaningful conversations is difficult enough when both partners have jobs; it is harder still when they have children as well. True, husbands—at least in the United States and Britain—boast to sociologists like Miss Mansfield that they play a bigger part in running the house than their fathers did. Sadly, as Kathleen Kiernan, of the Family Policy Studies Centre in London, points out in the latest issue of *British Social Attitudes*, reality is usually different.

She has looked at couples where both partners are employed, and compared men who disagree with the statement, "A husband's job is to earn money; a wife's job is to look after the home and family", with men who agree. The "egalitarian" men are more likely than the fogeys to share household tasks. But whereas half share the shopping and the evening's washing up, only a third share the cleaning or preparation of the evening meal, and only 12% share the washing and ironing. The proportion of couples who think such tasks should be shared has increased since 1984, but the practice has hardly changed.

Washing up the evening dishes seems to be, she reports, "an idiosyncrasy of the British male, or a success story for the British female." Seven out of ten British men do at least some of the washing up, compared with an EC average of four out of ten. Maybe this foible of British husbands explains the extraordinary reluctance of their wives to acquire automatic dishwashers. In 1990 only 12% of British households owned dishwashers; 20% had a home computer and 50% a microwave.

Men seem to be more willing to help with looking after children than with household chores. Miss Mansfield, drawing on British and American research, argues that "men who become involved with their children often do so because their partner is working. They tend to have better relationships with both their children and their wives. Indeed, women seem to find it very sexy when men care for their children. It creates a new bond in the marriage."

But if the husbands do not help much in the home, and the job market beckons, some women may wonder what they gain from being married. The costs of divorce may then seem smaller than the costs of staying in an unsatisfactory marriage. The trouble with that siren song is the evidence that divorce is bad for people: for men, for women and, above all, for children.

Married people tend to be healthier people. At every age, as a recent study of Britain by One plus One records, men and women are more likely to die prematurely if they are single, divorced or widowed than if they are married. These differences partly reflect the lower incomes of those who are not married. But whatever adjustments are made, it is clear that people suffer physically from not being married—and, incidentally, men suffer more than women.

Wanting out

As ever, some of the links may run both ways. For example, among both sexes, the divorced are the group most likely to be admitted to mental hospitals. This may simply prove that the unstable make difficult partners. Similarly, in Britain divorced men are the heaviest drinkers. But alcoholics may be less likely to marry and more likely to be thrown out by their partners than those who drink moderately.

Divorce also affects living standards. Men may actually see their disposable incomes rise, especially if they pay little or no child support. Official American figures for 1989 found that 41% of all divorced and separated women living with children under 21 received nothing from their former husbands; the rest received on average just over $3,000 a year.

The predictable upshot is that women and children are poorer. A study of American families who have been interviewed each year since 1968 finds that separated and divorced women suffer an average fall of about 30% in their incomes the year after their marriage breaks up. Worst hurt are middle-class wives who have stayed at home. But 31% of all wives whose incomes were above average when they were married found that their living standards fell by more than half in the first year after their marriages collapsed.

To cope with poverty, divorced mothers go out to work. Their working patterns are different from those of their married sisters. In most countries (but not in Britain), they are more likely to have paid work. Even so, they make up a large and growing proportion of the poor in most industrial countries. It may be a struggle to bring up a family on a single male wage with the free childcare that a stay-at-home wife can provide; it is harder still to raise children on a single female wage, especially if they are young enough to need to be looked after.

Moreover, the poverty does not end when the children grow up. For a women, divorce often means losing pension rights, as well as income; in the next century, some of society's poorest people will be elderly women whose marriages broke up in middle age, especially if they had stayed at home to care for the children. The problem could be particularly severe in Britain, where pension rights are rarely divided at divorce.

Heather Joshi, a British economist, has estimated that the lifetime earnings of a married mother of two may be little over a quarter of those of a similarly qualified married man. Marriage, she points out, is often a bargain: the husband can earn more because the wife gives up employment opportunities to care for the home. The labour

4. RELATIONSHIPS IN TRANSITION: Divorce and Remarriage

market is employing the couple, not the husband alone. Pensions legislation, she argues, should recognise that reality.

Divorce makes men unhealthy and women poor. But it also seems to be worse for children than was once thought. Oddly, the long-term effects of divorce on children is an area where little research has been done, and most of the evidence comes from the United States and Britain. It would be helpful to know whether the effects are the same in, for example, Sweden, where lone parents are less poor and single-parenthood seems to be more socially acceptable.

Children suffer

A dramatic account of the effects of divorce on children has come from work by an American, Judith Wallerstein, who studied 131 children from 60 recently separated families at a counselling centre in Marin County, California. She paints a dismal picture. Ten years after their parents' divorce, the boys were "unhappy and lonely"; they and the girls found it hard to form relationships with the opposite sex. Unfortunately, her study was confined to problem families; and as no control group of children in intact families was monitored, it is impossible to know how many of these young Hamlets would have been miserable anyway.

More convincing than such impressionistic research is the work conducted in America and Britain on surveys of random groups of children as they grow up. In the United States, Sara McLanahan has shown that children who grow up in single-parent families are more likely to drop out of school, marry during their teens, have a child before marrying and experience a breakdown of their own marriages. Some of these consequences—perhaps half, she estimates—are related to the poverty of single-parent families. But the rest do indeed seem to be the other consequences of divorce.

Similar results have been found from surveys of British children born in a single week in 1946 and 1958. One study, by Ms Kiernan, found that girls brought up by lone parents were twice as likely to leave home by the age of 18 as the daughters of intact homes—and three times as likely to be cohabiting by the age of 20 and almost three times as likely to have a birth out of wedlock. Boys seemed to be slightly less affected than girls, but were more likely than their sisters to leave school by the age of 16 if they came from a one-parent family. Martin Richards, a Cambridge psychologist, has looked at the children born in 1958 and concludes that the chance of a child going to university is halved by a parental divorce. All these effects, incidentally, are either weaker or nonexistent when a father has died.

Mr Richards also notices another effect. When their mother remarries, the children of a divorce may no longer be poor. But the other effects of divorce are either unchanged or even strengthened. In particular, girls who live in stepfamilies are much more likely to leave school at 16, to leave home because of friction and to be married by the age of 20 than even girls whose divorced mothers do not remarry. And boys in stepfamilies are particularly likely to leave home early because of a quarrel, and to set up home early. "In surveys," he reports sadly, "teenagers from divorced homes say sensible, cautious things about forming relationships; yet they do exactly the opposite. They seem to have a great need for affection, and when they find a relationship, they jump into it."

Many of these effects may be the result not of the divorce, which is easy to record, but of the thunderous atmosphere of a rocky marriage. An important study of children on both sides of the Atlantic appeared in *Science* in June 1991, by Mr Cherlin, Ms Kiernan and five other authors. It argued that "a substantial portion of what is usually considered the effect of divorce on children is visible before the parents separate." For boys in particular, most of the effects usually ascribed to divorce seem to appear before the parents actually break up.

Ask Mr Cherlin what he thinks today about the effects of divorce, and he responds thus: "Divorce is bad for children, but not for all children equally. It is very bad for a small group of children, and moderately bad for many more. If the marriage is truly filled with conflict, it may be better to have a divorce. But here in the United States, many marriages that could limp along end because people are bored. I'm not sure that children are harmed in such marriages."

"Will the kids ever adjust to our divorce?"

Mandy is wetting her bed, and Chad's nightmares are getting worse.

JANE MARKS

Jane Marks is the author of We Have a Problem: A Parent's Sourcebook *(American Psychiatric Press, Inc.).*

"I wasn't eager to move," said Vicky Edwards, 30. "I felt that the children would do better in familiar surroundings, but my friends who had been through divorce insisted that a fresh start was what we needed. I agreed that we'd all go nuts if we stayed in the house, with everything there to remind us that Peter was no longer living with us.

"He had moved out and was staying at a hotel until he found a permanent place. But his job required so much traveling that he probably wouldn't get around to finding an apartment anytime soon.

"So I spent lunch hours combing the ads until I found a nice, cozy house in the same school district. I longed for our old life back, but I talked up our new place to the children.

"Six-year-old Chad and four-year-old Mandy seemed excited. I let them help pick out new rugs and curtains for their rooms, and I had them stay at my mother's while I turned the chaos that was created by the move into an inviting new home.

"Once we were moved in, the kids seemed to adjust, which helped me put my own frustration and anger about the divorce on the back burner. After all, this was a time to be wholeheartedly positive. How else would we ever get through this?

"But then Peter called and wanted to see the kids, and all of our progress seemed to crumble. We hadn't ironed out a visitation agreement because Peter was out of town so often. Instead he would call when he was around. After only a day with him, the children were wild!

" 'I want to go back to my

After the kids spent a day with their father, all of our progress seemed to crumble.

daddy,' Mandy sobbed, refusing to be consoled. Chad chased the cat until he knocked over a new lamp, breaking it beyond repair.

" 'Now, calm down, you two,' I begged, gamely ignoring the lamp and concentrating on my children. I called a family conference, which was something I'd started when we moved.

" 'I miss my climbing tree,' Chad said.

" 'And I don't like the flushy thing on the toilet here,' Mandy chimed in. 'It's different.'

" 'It works the same way as any other,' I told her.

" 'No, it doesn't,' she said firmly, shaking her head.

" 'Look,' I said, 'we'll be okay here. It just takes time to get used to a new place.' I put them to bed and cleaned up the lamp—and then I turned on the TV. But Peter was all I could think of. Hurt and furious that he had rejected me for another woman, I burst into tears. I missed him so! Would that ever change?

"I felt a little better in the morning. But Chad asked me to call Peter and find out when he'd come again. I said, 'Daddy will come when he's able to.' Chad didn't ask again, and Peter didn't call. I was relieved because in his absence, the children were more themselves, although sometimes they seemed so sad. For instance, one morning Chad woke up crying.

" 'I dreamed that my turtle got stolen,' he sobbed. He was feeling cheated—and it broke my heart.

"And the next day, Mandy said, 'Daddy left because I had an accident,' referring to an incident in which she had wet her bed.

" 'Oh, honey, that's not true!' I said.

" 'Yes, it is,' she insisted.

"And her bed-wetting was becoming more frequent. I asked her if she was afraid that I, too, would leave her, and Mandy nodded.

" 'That will never, never happen,' I promised.

"But later that evening, when I was feeling so down that I almost didn't want to answer the phone, something wonderful happened: It was Sheila, my cousin, who had moved away after college. We'd been out of touch for a few years, but now her voice was so welcome. Her firm had transferred her back to our town.

" 'So, you're here? For good? Can you come over tomorrow night?'

" 'Yes,' Sheila said, and how her presence chased the blues away!

"The children laughed their heads off at Sheila's funny stories of our antics as kids. Mandy wouldn't even let me take her to bed until she'd gotten Sheila to promise that she would come back again—with more 'Mommy' stories.

" 'They're super kids,' Sheila declared.

" 'Well, you certainly saved the day around here,' I told her gratefully.

"It was almost like magic. Every time Sheila came over, the kids were playful. But many other days, they were sad and lonesome.

" 'I hate it when you have to work at night and we have to have a baby-sitter,' Chad complained on the phone as I struggled to finish my work. 'Mandy will wet her bed again,' he added just before he hung up. I was concerned about that—and the nightmares Chad was having.

" 'One parent just isn't enough for two kids,' I thought grimly as I drove home. But what was the solution? Peter was barely there, which was fine with me, but it still left a hole.

"Then suddenly I had a thought: Sheila! Who said it had to be a parent? Maybe the children only needed another regular, caring adult in residence. Sheila was still in a hotel, and she was lonely too. The kids loved her, and vice versa. If she took the extra bedroom, there would be more stability and fun, and four in the house would feel more like a family. Plus, if I had to work late, Sheila would be there to relieve the baby-sitter."

A solution to combat the children's loneliness.

"Excited, I called Sheila as soon as I got home. She thought it sounded great.

" 'Yay!' Chad and Mandy were excited when I told them that Sheila had agreed to come and live with us. 'When? When?' they wanted to know.

" 'Next Saturday!' I answered happily.

"On Saturday I made a special dinner, while the children bickered companionably over whose drawing of Sheila was better on the Welcome poster that I'd made for them to decorate.

"At seven I heard the doorbell. 'She's here!' I sang out. It rang a second time, and then a third time.

" 'Yo, Chad! I thought you were supposed to be the greeting guy,' I called. But as I headed for the door, I saw Chad in the bathroom. Why had he chosen that moment to clean his turtle's tank? And why was Mandy upstairs watching TV?

"Sheila gave them each a hug, but they seemed shy. At supper the children were unusually quiet, but during dessert, they giggled.

" 'What's up?' I asked.

" 'Nothing!' They got silly. Chad made monster faces. Laughing, Mandy spilled her milk. I gave the two of them a look.

" 'They're just excited,' Sheila said, excusing their strange behavior. Perhaps she was right. Life had been quiet with just the three of us, and now they had an audience. But the shock came after supper, when Sheila went up to her room. I heard her yell, and I ran up. There was Sheila, wordlessly pointing to her pillow, where the children had placed a large, dead cricket.

" 'It was a joke,' Mandy offered weakly.

" 'How could you do that?' Hadn't Sheila mentioned more than once how much she hated bugs?

"Fortunately Sheila was forgiving. But things have not been okay. It's been a week now, but the kids treat Sheila like a servant, not a friend. Most of the time they ignore her. Mandy still wets her bed, and Chad's nightmares are getting worse.

"Last night I called a family conference, but the kids were reluctant to talk.

"Sheila said, 'I'm not so sure this is working.'

"Is it my imagination—or is everything falling apart here? I feel that I need to talk to somebody."

The counselor replies.

Ruth M. Stirtzinger, M.D., is a psychiatrist affiliated with the Clarke Institute of Psychiatry, in Toronto, Canada. Stirtzinger has recently published findings on children's reactions to their parents' divorce.

"I could see that Vicky was a caring mother who was alert to symptoms that indicated her children were having a problem.

"Bed-wetting, I told her, is not uncommon, but Mandy's slips could also represent something important.

As for Chad's nightmares, I assured Vicky that children and adults have them from time to time; but the frequency of Chad's—and their themes of loss and abandonment—might also indicate real fears that he had for himself and his family.

" 'You're not neurotic,' I said to her. 'Let's look at what we can do.'

" 'I've instituted family meetings,' Vicky began.

" 'That's fine,' I said. 'It's good to have a time when all of you can talk about problems. It sounds, however, as if your kids are feeling things that they don't know how to explain.'

"I asked Vicky how she was feeling about the divorce from Peter.

" 'I'm a mess!' Vicky admitted. 'But I'm working it out alone and not burdening the kids with my feelings.'

" 'You know, kids often know much more than we give them credit for,' I said gently. 'I strongly suspect that Chad and Mandy are taking cues from you. Part of grieving is accepting what has happened. If your children feel that you haven't accepted the loss and aren't dealing with it, they could be dragging their feet on your behalf.'

> **"Your mistake wasn't in moving but, rather, in trying to plug up the kids' loneliness."**

" 'I can't believe that! I've been trying so hard to do everything right, but I guess it's all for nothing.'

" 'Oh, no!' I said. 'You're doing a whole lot of things right. I'm just asking you to consider your own unresolved state of mourning and the fact that it has to affect your children.'

" 'Was it a mistake to move to a new house?' she

asked. 'I let other people convince me that it was best, but now I wonder. Mandy still can't seem to adjust to the toilet.'

" 'Moving from the family home after divorce—or staying—brings up different issues,' I said. 'Staying in the family home may feel better, but it can also delay the healing process, since denying the big change that has taken place is then easier.

" 'On the other hand, staying in the family home can make children feel more secure about boundaries and how to behave. Perhaps your children miss those boundaries—which may have had something to do with Chad's breaking the lamp and even what Mandy experienced about the toilet and wetting her bed.

" 'There are pros and cons,' I continued. 'If you've made a mistake, I don't think it was in moving but in trying to plug up the children's loneliness by bringing Sheila in too quickly.'

" 'Do you think that was the wrong thing to do?'

" 'Your intent was very good. I can see how hard you've tried to do everything right. But as much as you saw Sheila as a resource for the kids, they may see her as a rival: a new person at home, someone they have to share you with.'

" 'But that's ridiculous!' Vicky said.

" 'I agree,' I said. 'But children can often have irrational ideas.'

" 'That's true,' Vicky said.

" 'Perhaps they feel that having Sheila in the house will make it impossible for Peter to return,' I said. 'It might be best for Sheila not to be part of the household at this point. She can still be with your family often, but that's different. Again, it's a matter of boundaries. The children need to know who really is their immediate family and who isn't.'

" 'It's so confusing,' Vicky sighed. 'The kids see parents who loved each other not loving anymore. It must make them wonder whether any love can last.'

"I asked Vicky if the children did much talking about their father.

" 'Oh, no,' she said. 'It's out of sight, out of mind. And they're definitely calmer when he isn't around.'

" 'Have you asked them how they're feeling about him—or whether they miss him?' I asked.

" 'No!' Vicky waved my question away. 'I'm still so mad at Peter. I don't want to convey my own discomfort to the kids, so I don't talk to them about him—at all, if I can help it.'

"I praised Vicky's sensitivity, but I told her that however 'messy' she thought her feelings were, it was still better to be up-front about them than to try to hide them from her children. Vicky looked perplexed.

"I said, 'They will feel less confused if you let them separate their feelings about Peter from yours.' I advised Vicky to tell the children,

'Even if I'm feeling mad at your father, I want you to be able to tell me what you're feeling about him.' "

Exploring the children's feelings about their dad.
"This first session helped. Vicky went home and followed my suggestions. Sheila was understanding and even relieved, and she and Vicky agreed to shelve the new living arrangement.

" 'I guess I was so busy trying to make things perfect for the kids, I wasn't even giving them a chance to grieve,' Vicky admitted.

"The children were also relieved—especially when it was made clear to them that nobody was angry or blamed them. Now they were free to like Sheila again.

"When Vicky invited the children to talk about Peter, they hung back at first; but when they saw that she was sincere, a lot of their fears and feelings came out.

" 'Is Dad okay?' they asked. 'Is he lonely?'

"Vicky wasn't sure how to respond, so I scheduled a session for her and the children together. I learned that Mandy and Chad were not only worried about their dad but also scared of upsetting their mom. Vicky was devastated to hear that, but the children felt better.

"Next, I wanted to see the children with their father.

" 'I don't think he'll come,' Vicky predicted, but Peter did come, surprised and pleased to learn that he was essential to his children and that they had been really upset by his absence.

" 'I certainly hadn't gotten that message,' he said. 'I guess I felt guilty about the divorce, and when they never called me, I assumed that they were angry at me.'

"The next and final session was for the whole family, and certain plans were made: Peter and Vicky agreed to work out a schedule so that the children would know exactly when they'd see their father. They were also given permission to call him anytime.

"Finally I told Peter and Vicky privately that since they would be in closer contact, it would be a good idea for them to get some separation counseling to help them deal with uncomfortable issues.

"Peter and Vicky agreed, understanding now that Chad and Mandy needed both parents, even if only one lived at home. Divorce is always difficult, but parents and children can withstand even the most devastating changes if everyone is free to acknowledge his or her own deep feelings, whatever they are."

love may be more comfortable, but it's also more complicated . . .

THE SECOND TIME AROUND

John Manners

They met the way they might have in their twenties. The woman came into the bar with a date. The man on the other side of the room looked up and couldn't look away.

"My date was restless," she recalls today. "He didn't like the band. He wanted to leave. But my girlfriend wanted to stay. I told him he could go, and he left."

Across the room, the man was watching. "I saw the guy leave and not come back," he remembers, smiling. "I wanted to ask her to dance, but she was so pretty I figured I'd ask the friend first. Then on my way over I decided, 'What the hell.' I asked her, and she said yes." Eight months later, she said yes again, and four months after that, "I do"—and they went off to live in a brand-new house on a hill.

Like any love story, an account of the meeting and February 1992 marriage of Gloria Schmidt and Bob Soleim has familiar elements of pulp romance. But these St. Paul newlyweds are not starry-eyed youngsters. Both Gloria, 48, and Bob, 49, have been married before, and, like most of the 1.7 million Americans a year who remarry, both brought to the altar their own children and as-

sets, commitments and obligations— the complex emotional and financial baggage of adult life.

Kids are astonished to see their parents acting young again. "I mean, that's my mom!" says Gloria's daughter Justine.

For so-called blended families like the Soleims, the challenge is not just to see that the kids get along but also that the new partners' finances are joined so that no one feels cheated or left out. "Deciding who gets x and who needs y can seem a little complicated," says Bob. "But this is a marriage, not a divorce. Good will goes a long way."

The Soleims' good will has to cover some substantial x's and y's. When his 24-year first marriage ended in divorce two years ago, Bob gave up his half of a $92,000 home but retained his interest in John G. Kinnard & Co., the Minneapolis brokerage where he works as sales manager. He owns 68,400 Kinnard shares recently valued at $359,100 and $96,000 worth of warrants for 32,000 addi-

tional shares. He also has $65,400 in the firm's 401(k) and pension plans.

Gloria too brings sizable assets to the table. Though she was widowed 16 years ago and raised three children on a secretary's salary that never topped $27,500, she has $90,000 in 9% CDs that start maturing in 1998 and another $50,000 in cash and stocks acquired after selling her house for $104,000 last year and paying off mortgage and fees of $54,000. Add in the couple's $61,000 equity in their newly built $273,000 home, and Bob and Gloria have a net worth of $822,700—nearly 10 times the median for their age.

Along with these assets, however, come responsibilities. Bob's mother, Edna Soleim, 78, of nearby Hastings, Minn. is in declining health and may have to move in with them within two or three years. And though two of their four children seem firmly launched—Bob's only child Rob, 24, as a broker at Kinnard and Gloria's son Andrew, 23, as an accountant with a local medical-technology company—the other two still need help. Gloria's eldest, Justine, 27, is living at home while she finishes an M.B.A. at the University of Minnesota (her employer, another medtech firm, pays most of her $3,000-a-year tuition). And though Jason,

19, plans to move to a dorm when he enrolls as a U of M freshman this month, Bob will foot the $7,700-a-year tab.

With kids and Bob's mother in mind, the Soleims designed their new 4,200-square-foot home to accommodate as many as three long-term guests. And though Gloria left her job before the wedding and does not plan to return to work, Bob's commission-based income—$205,000 last year—should cover both their bills and the children's.

Family members on both sides and of all ages lay claim to the time and resources of the two newlyweds.

Still to be completed, however, is the dividing of inheritances. "When Gloria accepted my proposal," says Bob, "I called the kids together and told them Gloria's assets would go to her children eventually and mine would go to Rob. Any assets we built together would be split evenly among them. And then," he adds with a chuckle, "I said if we lived long enough, we intended to spend every penny." The kids took it good-naturedly: "I'd do the same," says Andrew.

Four months after the wedding, Bob took a first step toward fulfilling these promises: He took out a $500,000 term life policy from Manufacturer's Life (annual premium: $2,190), naming his bride as sole beneficiary. The policy, Bob reasons, will protect Gloria and also make up for the fact that he plans to execute a will leaving his interest in Kinnard—now worth about $455,100—to his son Rob. "I look on the Kinnard stock as something like my share in a family business," he says.

Bob's father did the same thing a generation ago, handing on his dry-cleaning business in Hastings to Bob's older brother Skip, the only one of

the four siblings who wanted it. Bob went off to St. Olaf College in Northfield, Minn., returning after graduation long enough to marry a hometown girl and join the Air Force. Rob was born in '68, after Bob completed 241 combat missions in Vietnam as a forward air controller in a slow-moving propeller plane. "We were fired on every night and hit dozens of times," he says. "I can't imagine how I survived."

When Bob quit the military in 1970, the family moved back to Hastings and Bob went to work as an insurance salesman, his wife as a secretary. Rob remembers his parents at the time as "independent, career-minded people." Over the years, though, that independence evolved into distance. When Rob entered the U of M in 1985, his mother rented an apartment in Minneapolis. In January 1990, she moved to New York and, a year later, the couple agreed to seek a divorce on grounds of incompatibility. One month after that, in February 1991, Bob met Gloria.

Gloria had grown up poor in St. Paul. Her father, the son of Egyptian and Lebanese immigrants, headed west when she was 12, winding up as a special-effects technician in Hollywood. Her mother, of Norwegian ancestry, stayed put and married twice more. Gloria quit college after six months in 1963 to marry an ex-Marine who was studying to become a teacher. By 1972, they had saved enough to put $5,000 down on a $29,000 house, the same one Gloria recently sold.

Five years later, when their kids were 11, seven and three, the couple were driving home from a friend's house one night when a pickup truck crossed a 30-foot-wide highway median and plowed into their 1974 Pinto. Gloria's husband, who was driving, was killed instantly. She spent two weeks in the hospital with head, neck and chest injuries while her mother took care of the kids. "The boys were too young to dwell on their father's death for long," says Gloria, "but Justine took it very

hard. She kept a diary and would brood over it every day." Fortunately, financial strains were eased by a $110,000 insurance settlement and $1,200 a month from Social Security. Together with Gloria's paycheck, this supported the family and formed the core of her current assets.

The young widow had no shortage of suitors. She turned down five marriage proposals over the years, three after first saying yes. "I just changed my mind," she says. "I hated being single, but being married to the wrong person would have been worse."

Gloria and her children warmed quickly to Bob. "He's real stable," explained Justine, "and Mom's very happy with him. It's embarrassing to see how they act with each other. I mean, that's my mom!"

Building a new life together—not to mention a new home—takes lots of planning and careful attention to small details.

Two months after their marriage Bob and Gloria borrowed $180,000 on a 15-year mortgage at a fixed 8.5% (monthly payment: $1,800) to pay for their new four-bedroom home. "Both of us had always dreamed of custom building a house," says Bob, "and with mothers and grown kids to accommodate, we needed the space." They covered the balance of the $273,000 tab with $61,000 in cash and a $32,000 home-equity loan (it's a 15-year, variable-rate note that costs them roughly $300 a month at the current interest rate of 8%).

Now they're sharing the financial chores. Bob handles most of the saving and investing; he salted away close to $28,000—14% of his income—last year, dividing it between his 401(k), his company pension plan (both invested in Putnam Voyager, a growth-stock fund) and Kinnard stock. Gloria, meanwhile, manages

Time to diversify

With 55% of their net worth in Kinnard brokerage stock, the Soleims are quite vulnerable to a price slide.

INCOME

Mortgage and home-equity loans	$212,000
Salaries and commissions	205,000
Sale of Gloria's house	104,000
Savings withdrawal and stock sale	56,000
TOTAL	**$577,000**

OUTGO

Payment for the new house	$273,000
Taxes	72,900
Retirement plan and stock purchases	66,700
Gloria's mortgage and house-sale fees	54,000
Decorating and landscaping	26,000
Wedding, honeymoon and vacation	25,800
Insurance and car expenses	17,700
Mortgage payments	14,500
Food, clothing, utilities	14,400
Miscellaneous	12,000
TOTAL	**$577,000**

ASSETS

Kinnard stock and warrants	$455,100
New home	273,000
CDs and money-market funds	115,900
Other stock and savings accounts	73,800
Bob's 401(k) and pension	65,400
Cars and personal property	51,500
TOTAL	**$1,034,700**

LIABILITIES

Mortgage on new home	$180,000
Home-equity loan	32,000
TOTAL	**$212,000**
NET WORTH	**$822,700**

By early December, Bob and Gloria had set up their wills, post-nup and QTIP, as Kaplan recommended, and had sunk $26,000 into decorating and landscaping. "You know how it is with a new house," said Bob with a sigh. "Your old curtains never fit, so you've got to get new ones. The old rugs are the wrong color; the old shades are too wide. But with Jason moving out in January and Justine graduating and moving away sometime next summer, Gloria and I look forward to finally spending some time alone."

their new joint checking account—a job for which she's well qualified by her passion for order (the blouses in her closet, for example, are organized by style—long-sleeved, short-sleeved, sleeveless—as well as by fabric). Yet both Gloria and Bob keep separate checking accounts too, "because everybody needs something of their own," says Bob. In fact, Gloria has two—a new one under the name Gloria Soleim, and her old one, under Gloria Schmidt, that saw her through 15 tough years of single motherhood. "Why do I keep it?" she says. "I guess because it's the last shred of me from my former life."

THE ADVICE

Draw up a comprehensive estate plan. The usual first step in ensuring that children of a blended family inherit what their parents intend is for the couple to draft a prenuptial agreement stipulating how their assets will be divided. Since the Soleims didn't do so before the wedding, Minneapolis attorney Sidney Kaplan recommended they now prepare wills spelling out their inheritance wishes. Then they should jointly execute what amounts to a "post-nup"—a document in which each endorses the other's will and waives the normal spousal share of the other's estate (usually about half in Minnesota, as in most states).

The post-nup is especially important because of Bob's wish to give Rob his Kinnard stock, which makes up 72% of his net worth and 55% of the couple's combined wealth. "If Bob were hit by a bus tomorrow, any competent lawyer would advise Glo-

ria to go after her spousal share—which would have to include some of that stock," says Kaplan. Nobody thinks Gloria would do that, of course, but all agree the post-nup is a prudent step. Lawyers' fees for the two wills and the post-nup will run at least $1,000, he said.

Set up a QTIP. Kaplan also suggested that the Soleims establish a QTIP, or qualified terminable interest property trust, as part of their wills. In it, both spouses stipulate that, when one dies, a predetermined part of the deceased's assets will be held in trust for specified beneficiaries, managed by the survivor and a co-trustee. The survivor gets the income from the trust and may even dip into its principal (with the co-trustee's approval) to keep up his or her standard of living. But he or she may not change the beneficiaries, who receive the full assets of the trust—often free of federal estate taxes—after the second spouse dies. Cost for the QTIP: another $1,500 or more.

Diversify your retirement funds. Judith Brown, president of her own financial planning firm and a former head of Kinnard's planning division, cautioned Bob against putting so much of his wealth in the stock of a single firm—especially one that also provides his salary and benefits. She recommended that he cut his Kinnard holdings to no more than half his portfolio and reinvest the money in blue-chip stocks or in state- and federal-tax-free Minnesota municipal bonds—perhaps through a fund like Putnam's **Minnesota Tax Exempt II** (4.75% load; recent yield: 6.49%).

Give each other a little financial space. Finally, Brown endorsed the newlyweds' approach to household money management and urged them to maintain separate credit cards as well. "You've both lived independently for a long time now," she said. "The last thing you want when you're starting a marriage is to worry about everyday money matters."

THE MYTHS AND MISCONCEPTIONS OF THE STEPMOTHER IDENTITY

DESCRIPTIONS AND PRESCRIPTIONS FOR IDENTITY MANAGEMENT*

There are two cross-cultural and trans-historical myths associated with stepmotherhood: the evil stepmother myth and the myth of instant love. The tenacity of these myths has served to stigmatize stepmothers. This paper describes the myths associated with stepmothers, details how these myths affect stepmother life, reveals dilemmas in identity management for stepmothers, and indicates identity management strategies stepmothers might utilize.

Marianne Dainton

Marianne Dainton is a doctoral student at Ohio State University, Department of Communication, 319 Neil Hall, Columbus, OH 43210.

In America there are a multitude of family forms, one of which is the stepfamily. Statistics indicate that currently 16% of all married couples in this country have at least one stepchild (Moorman & Hernandez, 1989). Moreover, current predictions are that 35% to 40% of children born in the 1980s will spend time in a stepparent family before they are young adults (Coleman & Ganong, 1990a).

Although researchers are increasingly turning their attention to the stepfamily form, there are many areas of stepfamily life that have not received adequate attention (Coleman & Ganong, 1990a). One such area is the effect of myths about stepfamily relations on stepfamily members. A focus upon myths is salient to the study of stepfamilies in general, and stepmothers in particular, because of the prevalence of myths concerning step-relations. For example, at least three of the Brothers Grimm's fairy tales—"Hansel and Gretel," "Cinderella," and "Snow White"—revolve

around the actions of an evil stepmother. These stories may appear innocuous enough, unless of course you happen to be a stepmother or a stepchild. "Fairies do not exist, and witches do not exist, but stepmothers do exist, and therefore certain fairy tales are harmful rather than helpful to large segments of the population" (Visher & Visher, 1979, p. 6).

The myths associated with stepmotherhood may constrain stepmothers' identity management. Identity management refers to efforts on the part of stepmothers to foster preferred perceptions about themselves. Accordingly, this article examines some of the impediments to the identity management strategies enacted by stepmothers. Specifically, throughout the course of this article the myths and misconceptions of stepmotherhood will be identified, the implications of these myths for stepmothers will be discussed, issues of identity will be elaborated, and, finally, some initial steps toward identity management strategies for stepmothers will be detailed.

STEPMOTHER MYTHS

The term *myth* is popularly conceived to be analogous to "falsehood." Indeed, myths often contain false and/or negative information. Scholars, however, define myth as a recurring theme or character type that incorporates infor-

mation about cultural standards (Birenbaum, 1988). Thus, myths represent a way of viewing the world that embodies a culture's beliefs, regardless of whether these beliefs are accurate.

According to Bruner (1960), myths can be characterized by two components. The first component is an externalization, which Bruner describes as a "corpus of images and identities" (p. 280). This externalization provides a cultural explanation of the way the world works. The second component is an internalization. Bruner argues that a myth can only exist to the extent that cultural members internalize personal identities based upon the externalized corpus of ideas propagated by the myth.

Regarding stepmotherhood, there are two generic myths that are simultaneously cross-cultural and transhistorical (Schulman, 1972). The first of the myths is that of the *evil stepmother,* a myth propagated through fiction of all forms. The second myth is that of *instant love,* wherein a stepmother is expected to immediately assimilate into a family and to love the children as if they were her own. Each will be discussed in turn.

Myth #1: The Evil Stepmother

The myth of the evil stepmother has a strong and inveterate legacy; the negative connotations of the term *step* were firmly in place as early as 1400 (Wald,

*The author would like to thank Patrick McKenry and Dirk Scheerhorn for editorial comments, and three anonymous reviewers for their valuable suggestions.

Key Words: identity management, myths, stepmothers, stigma.

1981). Moreover, scholars have identified the existence of evil stepmother folktales in virtually every part of the world. In fact, Smith (1953) identifies 345 versions of the "Cinderella" story alone, revealing the evil stepmother myth as a global phenomenon.

Although evil stepmothers appear in all genres of fiction, the evil stepmother is particularly prevalent in fairy tales (Wald, 1981). In an analysis of fairy tales, one researcher found that the most frequent representations of evil included bears, wolves, giants and ogres, witches, and stepmothers (Sutton-Smith, 1971, cited in Wald, 1981). Thus, fairy tales suggest that stepmothers are the equivalent of wild animals and supernatural beings—entities that children have very little chance of facing in real life—in their wicked treatment of children.

Myth #2: Instant Love

The second myth is instant love (Schulman, 1972; Visher & Visher, 1988; Wald, 1981). This myth is based upon cultural standards about mothering (Visher & Visher, 1988), and the resulting societal expectations about stepmothers' assimilation into the family. Specifically, the myth maintains that remarriage in and of itself creates an instant family, that stepmothers should (and will) automatically love their stepchildren, and that stepchildren will automatically love their stepmother. Further, because of this love, mothering is assumed to come naturally and easily.

In reality, none of the above necessarily happens. Counselors working with stepmothers suggest that many women are surprised and dismayed when they don't feel immediate love for their stepchildren (Lofas & Sova, 1985). Moreover, stepchildren are often afraid, unsure, and uncomfortable with the changes in the family, and may express these feelings by being surly and resentful. As a result, many stepmothers experience a great deal of ambivalence regarding their stepchildren (Ambert, 1986).

The Prevalence of These Myths Today

Despite the increasing number of stepfamilies in America today, the myths identified above show no signs of losing strength. In a series of research efforts, one group of researchers found that the role of stepmother elicited more negative connotations than any other family position (Bryan, Coleman, Ganong, & Bryan, 1986; Ganong & Coleman, 1983). Specifically, stepmothers were perceived as less affectionate, good, fair, kind, loving, happy, and likable, and more cruel, hateful, unfair, and unloving. More recently, researchers have determined that these negative perceptions still stand, although there is little difference in the perceptions of stepmothers and stepfathers (Fluitt & Paradise, 1991; Ganong, Coleman, & Kennedy, 1990). Similarly, clinicians assert that the myth of instant love has yet to be replaced by more realistic expectations (Visher & Visher, 1988).

Individually, these myths negatively affect the experiences of stepmothers. For example, both clinical and empirical evidence reveals that stepmothers identify the wicked stepmother myth as directly contributing to the stress they experience in adapting to the stepmother role (Duberman, 1973; Hughes, 1991; Visher & Visher, 1979). Further, counselors have identified the unrealistic expectations associated with the myth of instant love as a possible cause of stress for stepmothers in general, and have suggested that such expectations may actively interfere with the family integration that the myth promises (Visher & Visher, 1988).

Ironically, these myths provide external images of the stepmother that are at polar extremes; one myth depicts stepmothers as unrealistically evil, the other as unrealistically loving and competent. Together, these contradictory images may contribute to identity management difficulties, as stepmothers must struggle with internalizing two conflicting sets of ultimately unrealistic expectations. Clearly, taking on the mantle of stepmother includes not only taking on the responsibility of a family, but taking on a host of potential identity management challenges (Hughes, 1991; Visher & Visher, 1979, 1988).

THE CONCEPT OF IDENTITY

Before discussing the identity issues associated with stepmotherhood, some fundamental issues surrounding the concept of identity itself must be addressed. In so doing, some critical distinctions between key terms need to be made. Finally, a framework for understanding identity management must be constructed.

First, *identity* can be defined as an individual's self-concept (McCall & Simmons, 1978). Thus, an individual's identity involves beliefs about whom he or she is, and how he or she should be perceived and treated in social life (Schlenker, 1980). Although our identities are frequently manifested in the roles that we enact, the notion of identity is broader than that of roles. Definitionally, *roles* are expectations held about the occupant of a social status or a position in a social system, while *identity* is a constellation of all of the roles an individual performs (McCall & Simmons, 1978).

The same distinction can be made between role performance and identity management. A *role performance* (also known as *role enactment*) is the individual's day-to-day behavior associated with a given role (McCall & Simmons, 1978). *Identity management,* on the other hand, is a broader concept; it is an individual's efforts to foster perceptions (usually positive) relevant to his or her self-concept. Similar terms include *self-presentation* (Goffman, 1959) and *impression management* (Schlenker, 1980).

The definitions above imply that an identity is chosen. This is not always the case. McCall and Simmons (1978) assert that individuals do not entirely have discretion in the roles they will enact, and hence in the perceptions others will have of them. For example, most stepmothers do not choose the stepmother persona; it is thrust upon them when they choose to marry a man with children. Identity management for stepmothers, then, is not simply the process of maintaining preferred perceptions, but of preventing unwanted perceptions associated with preconceived evaluations of a given social role.

To clarify, McCall and Simmons argue that each role identity has two elements: the *conventional* and the *idiosyncratic*. The conventional aspect of a role identity consists of social stereotypes. These stereotypes might be captured in myths such as the myths associated with stepmotherhood. The idiosyncratic elements of a role identity, on the other hand, are those characteristics an individual modifies and elaborates within the given role.

IDENTITY DILEMMAS

Generally, identities are inferred by appearance and actions (McCall & Simmons, 1978). In the case of stepmothers, however, the perceptions associated with stepmotherhood are not conveyed by appearance or actions, but are label-bound. Accordingly, stepmothers fulfill the requirements of being a stigmatized group. *Stigmas* are products of definitional processes in which a defining attribute (such as being a stepmother) eclipses other aspects of the stigmatized person, including individual personalities and abilities (Ainlay, Coleman, & Becker, 1986; Stafford & Scott, 1986). Thus stigmas are categorizations that often involve negative affect (Jones et al., 1984).

Goffman (1963) posits that stigmatization is the result of the relationship between a particular attribute and a stereotype about that attribute. "Society establishes the means of categorizing persons and the complement of attributes felt to be ordinary and natural for members of each of these categories" (Goffman, 1963, p. 2). Ironically, the "ordinary and natural" attributes that society has established for stepmothers (through myths) are that they are inherently wicked, yet capable of providing instant love. It is the very fact that stepmothers are characterized in such an extraordinary manner that causes their stigmatization.

Further, Goffman (1963) argues that there are two primary types of stigmas: the *discredited* and the *discreditable.* Discredited individuals are those in which the stigma is immediately apparent (e.g., those with physical deformities). Discreditable individuals are those whose stigma is not known or immediately perceivable. The fact that stepmothers' stigma is not visually apparent would lead one to believe that they have a discreditable stigma. That is, despite fairy tales' depiction of stepmothers as evil hags, real stepmothers look just like real mothers. Their stigma is not immediately apparent.

However, with different audiences stepmothers are sometimes discredited and sometimes discreditable. For example, members of the stepfamily are aware of a woman's stepmother status, so in their eyes she is discredited. In the general public, however, a stepmother remains merely discreditable. This contradiction brings up one of the major problems stepmothers have with identity management; part of the dilemma of managing a stepmother identity is the public/private dichotomy. Stepmothers believe that they are judged based on stepmother myths in both the public and private arenas of social life (Hughes, 1991). Because of this, stepmothers may find themselves with the paradox of having inconsistent identity management strategies become necessary to manage the same identity.

Goffman (1963) has identified two broad classes of identity management strategies. *Corrective practices* are what people do after their preferred identity is threatened. According to Goffman, it is likely that discredited individuals will be forced to engage in corrective strategies. *Preventative strategies,* on the other hand, are behaviors an individual uses to avoid negative perceptions. In general, the discreditable will rely on preventative strategies.

In order to determine which class of strategies to enact, a stepmother must consider a contextual matrix. That is, stepmothers must consider where they

are and who their audience is in order to select the appropriate identity management techniques (McCall & Simmons, 1978). This matrix might look like the one in Figure 1.

As the matrix shows, stepmothers face competing concerns when selecting identity strategies: *who* and *where.* Within each of these superordinate categories is a dichotomy. For example, when considering who, a stepmother might be in the company of her family or she may be in the company of some generalized others. When considering *where,* she might be in private (e.g., at home) or in public (e.g., a restaurant).

Taking each quadrant of the grid in turn, the following issues are stressed. First, the upper left quadrant is one in which there is little inconsistency. Here, stepmothers are with their family in private. Given that they are already discredited in this forum (i.e., their stigma is known), it is likely that they will utilize corrective identity management strategies in this case. Such strategies might include assertive techniques described by Jones and Pittman (1980) like *exemplification* (projecting integrity), *self-promotion* (showing competence in mothering), or *ingratiation* (being helpful and positive).

Similarly, there is probably little quandary about strategy selection when in the others/public quadrant; here, the stepmother is discreditable (her stigma is not known). Accordingly, it is likely a stepmother would select what Goffman (1963) describes as preventative strategies, such as *passing* (behaving in a way consistent with a nonstigmatized identity without specifically claiming to be nonstigmatized) or using *disidentifiers* (behaviors deliberately used to indicate a nonstigmatized identity, e.g., saying "my son" instead of "my stepson").

The two remaining quadrants might cause psychological tension between

competing identity management options, however. For example, in the family/public quadrant, an initial reaction might be to use preventative strategies. After all, other patrons of a restaurant have little need to know that the normal family seated next to them might in fact be a stepfamily. However, if a stepmother selects such strategies she is neither accomplishing her goal of overcoming negative perceptions within the family, nor is she safe from intentional or unintentional unmasking. The last quadrant, others/private, is liable to involve a very different sort of tension. An example of such a situation is holding a professional gathering at home. Given that the interaction is at home, her stigma is already known among family members who may be present. Therefore, corrective strategies might seem appropriate. However, because she is also with nonintimate others, preventative strategies might be preferred. Here, the tension reflects a pull towards actively managing existing negative stereotypes within the family, and at the same time preventing others from learning of the stigma.

Confounding contextual constraints are the ways in which expectations based upon stepmother myths affect our identity management. That is, people might interpret a stepmother's behavior as negative (even if by objective measures it is not) simply because stepmothers' behaviors are expected to be negative (Coleman & Ganong, 1987a; for a discussion about how this process might work, see Darley & Gross, 1983). A dilemma that stepmothers face, then, is whether they should use corrective strategies at all, since any efforts to actively repair others' perceptions might be interpreted unfavorably. She is stuck in a "damned if you do, damned if you don't" situation.

A final identity management dilemma stepmothers face is related to the

Figure 1. *Matrix for Stepmothers' Identity Management Strategies*

Who

		Family	Others
Private		Corrective	???
Public		???	Preventative

(Where)

extent to which they play an active parenting role. That is, in attempting to fulfill the stepparent role, stepmothers are in a double bind. On one hand, they are expected to love the child as if he or she were their own, but on the other hand, they are often sanctioned against adopting a bona fide parental role (Visher & Visher, 1979). Thus, becoming a stepmother requires a careful balancing act, wherein a woman must regulate perceptions of involvement without being perceived as overinvolved or uncaring.

The dilemma described above is complicated by the ambiguity associated with the stepmother role. According to Cherlin (1978), remarriage represents an "incomplete institution" because there are few norms or rules to define expected behavior in stepfamily life. Cherlin posits that this ambiguity causes stress on family members. There is recent evidence for this hypothesis; in a review of the literature, Fine and Schwebel (1991) identified role ambiguity as the core difficulty in stepfamilies.

Role ambiguity involves four types of uncertainty: (a) uncertainty about the scope of one's responsibilities; (b) uncertainty about the particular behaviors needed to fulfill one's responsibilities; (c) uncertainty about whose expectations for role behavior must be met; and (d) uncertainty about the effects of one's actions on the well-being of oneself and others (King & King, 1990). This uncertainty is a function of the difference between stepfamily roles and biological family roles, and the difference between effective stepfamily functioning and effective biological family functioning (Coleman & Ganong, 1987b). There are two primary differences: (a) the degree of clarity about which behavior is appropriate for a given role, and (b) the degree to which the role is either ascribed or achieved (Walker & Messinger, 1979).

IDENTITY MANAGEMENT STRATEGIES

Given the dilemmas of identity management outlined above, the selection of specific strategies may be complex, if not overwhelming, to a stepmother. However, research has provided some preliminary answers as to which strategies stepmothers are likely to use, whether such strategies are likely to work, and which strategies are not often used but might be beneficial given the specific identity problems stepmothers face.

First, because the nature of the stigma of being a stepmother is not immediately apparent to those who don't know a woman's stepmother status, an identi-

ty strategy frequently selected for the general public is one of concealment (e.g., Duberman, 1975; Jones et al., 1984).

> For many women who have chosen to become stepmothers, the realization that they are part of a minority group comes as a bit of a shock. But by masquerading as a natural mother, altering her true identity in order to fit into a society and to be accepted as part of a "normal" family, a stepmother acts like any member of a minority group who is striving to conform. (Morrison, Thompson-Guppy, & Bell, 1986, p. 17)

Concealment is an example of a preventative strategy (Goffman, 1963). Despite the frequency of use of this strategy, however, some counselors have suggested that concealment is ineffective as a long-term solution (Morrison et al., 1986).

A more proactive strategy for public identity management is what Jones et al. (1984) call *confrontation and breaking through*. This strategy involves acknowledging one's stepmother status and working to frame the identity in a constructive and commendable context. Recall McCall and Simmon's (1978) distinction between the conventional and idiosyncratic elements of identity. Based on this distinction, one way to accomplish confrontation and breaking through might be to foster the idiosyncratic elements of the stepmother identity, while simultaneously diminishing the conventional elements. However, due to the strength of the myths of stepmotherhood, such efforts might be construed negatively. As Coleman and Ganong (1987a) noted, people's expectations of negative behavior might lead them to perceive even idiosyncratic elements negatively.

Moving from individual identity management efforts to societal efforts to change the stigma of stepmotherhood, one controversial public strategy that has been suggested is to change the label. If the term *stepfamily* engenders negative reactions, some authors contend we should just change the name to one without such negative connotations (see Coleman & Ganong, 1987a, for a summary of the debate). This can be classified as a corrective strategy. Alternatives to stepfamily include *blended* or *reconstituted family*. What the associated changes in the name of *stepmother* would be is unclear. Other scholars believe that changing the terminology would be confusing (Wald, 1981) or insulting (Lofas & Sova, 1985), or would only add to the mystification (Hughes, 1991).

There have also been some specific strategies identified to overcome the

myths within the stepfamily itself. Based on empirical evidence, Cissna, Cox, and Bochner (1990) assert that an effective way to overcome myths about stepmotherhood involves two steps. First, they claim, the remarried partners must establish the solidarity of the marriage in children's minds. Then, they say, the partners should use this solidarity to establish the credibility of the stepparent as a valid parental authority. Such efforts are clearly corrective in nature, and take into account overly negative expectations due to the evil stepmother myth as well as overly positive expectations due to the myth of instant love.

Taking quite a different approach, Salwen (1990) proposes that stepmothers might remove themselves from the parenting role altogether by insisting that the biological father take on all parenting responsibilities. This does not mean that stepmothers cannot be supportive or nurturing to their stepchildren. However, Salwen argues that by avoiding the parental role, stepmothers simultaneously avoid the negative expectations associated with the role. They are therefore free to work on positive, nonparental relationships with their stepchildren that are not weighted down by preconceived, unfavorable perceptions. Again, such a strategy is an effort to achieve a middle ground between the two myths.

A similar, but perhaps less radical, approach to identity dilemmas within the stepfamily is to focus on alternative role enactment. Furstenberg and Spanier (1984) posit that the stepparent role is ambiguous, as there is no single prescribed role for stepparents (see the section on role ambiguity above). Thus, they should feel free to try on various roles until they find one that fits (see also Walker & Messinger, 1979). Alternative roles a stepmother can don to ease her interactions with stepchildren include *primary mother* (which works only if the biological mother is physically and/or psychologically dead to the child), *other mother,* and *friend* (Draughon, 1975).

Related to alternative roles in managing identity, simply finding a name that a child is comfortable calling the stepmother might assist in the individualization of a stepmother's identity (Visher & Visher, 1988). Very often, a child avoids finding a name for his or her stepmother, referring to her simply as "you" or "she." By insisting on a name, the stepmother moves out of the realm of the group of all stepmothers (a stigmatized group) to personhood (Maglin & Schniedewind, 1989). Possible names include the stepmother's own first name, a mutually agreed upon nickname, or a variation of mother not used for the biological mother (Wald, 1981).

Finally, while not directly related to the problems of stepmothers, Crocker and Lutsky (1986) have identified three strategies for changing cognitions about stigmas. First is the *sociocultural* approach, which emphasizes a change in socialization practices. In the case of stepmothers in particular, this might involve replacing evil stepmother fairy tales with stories with more positive messages. Second is the *motivational* approach. This involves redefining group boundaries to allow the stigmatized persons to become part of the normal population. For example, the category of *mothers* might be expanded to include stepmothers. Lastly, Crocker and Lutsky identify *cognitive* approaches to changing stigmas. This involves proving the stereotype wrong. In global terms this might mean a public relations campaign of sorts for stepmothers. More specifically, however, it might involve allowing a stepmother's positive actions within the stepfamily to prove the myth wrong (i.e., replacing conventional elements of identity with idiosyncratic elements).

IMPLICATIONS FOR RESEARCH

There are several directions for future research. First, Goffman's theoretical differentiation between corrective and preventative identity management strategies needs to be operationalized. Specific research questions might be "What communicative behaviors serve corrective functions?" and "What communicative behaviors serve preventative functions?"

Second, because our knowledge of the identity management strategies stepmothers actually use is quite limited, it would be of interest to identify the specific identity management strategies stepmothers select, when they select them, and why. In addition, future research should strive to fill in the empty squares of the identity matrix detailed by Figure 1. That is, research should focus upon what identity management strategies women select when in a private setting with nonfamily members, and, perhaps more interestingly, what they do when they are with family members in a public situation. Moreover, researchers should ascertain whether the theoretical predictions of strategies that have been identified are correct.

More important than merely identifying what women do, however, is to identify what actually works. A repertoire of strategies is useless unless they actually assist a stepmother in overcoming the negative perceptions associated with stepmotherhood. Thus, critical research questions include: "What specific identity management strategies work to overcome negative public perceptions?" and "What strategies work to overcome negative perceptions within the family?"

IMPLICATIONS FOR PRACTICE

The issues raised here also have several implications for educators and counselors working with stepfamilies. Most importantly, practitioners can enact two global strategies to ameliorate the identity management difficulties stepmothers face. The first strategy is to assist individual stepmothers in overcoming some of the myths and misconceptions associated with this family role. Ideally, this assistance would take place before the formation of the stepfamily. By presenting future stepmothers—and all stepfamily members—with the reality of stepmother life before the remarriage, the frustrations associated with the myths of the evil stepmother and of instant love might be avoided. A first step in such counseling might be the completion of the Personal Reflections Program (Kaplan & Hennon, 1992).

More realistically, however, this assistance will likely be sought after the identity management difficulties have been encountered. In this case, practitioners might offer some of the strategies described in the previous section on identity management. In addition, referral to organizations proffering support to stepmothers and stepfamilies might be warranted. Finally, preliminary evidence suggests that the use of fiction can assist stepfamilies and stepfamily members in counseling (Coleman & Ganong, 1990b).

The second strategy is to actively work to diffuse these myths and misconceptions on a societal level. This paper points to the need for greater attention to the messages we are sending children about stepmothers. Family life educators and primary school educators might be especially important in normalizing the stepfamily experience (Crosbie-Burnett & Skyles, 1989). Family life educators can assist in debunking the myths by informing the public about the realities of stepmothers and stepfamily life. Similarly, primary school educators might be recruited to assist in this information campaign. Through programs such as the Classroom Guidance Program discussed by Crosbie-Burnett and Pulvino (1990), by selecting texts and children's literature that include normal stepfamilies, and by incorporating stepfamily roles in everyday classroom discussions, grade school teachers might make great strides in overcoming the evil stepmother myth.

CONCLUSION

The stepmother role is a stressful one that is particularly challenging in terms of identity management. Stepmothers must combat the firmly entrenched myths of the wicked stepmother and of instant love. Despite the fact that the stepfamily form is becoming increasingly more common, empirical and clinical evidence suggests that stepmother myths show little sign of changing (Bryan et al., 1986; Ganong & Coleman, 1983; Fluitt & Paradise, 1991). Thus, identity issues will remain salient for stepmothers for some time to come. Accordingly, researchers and practitioners must incorporate the concept of identity when considering the experiences of stepmothers.

REFERENCES

Ainlay, S. C., Coleman, L. M., & Becker, G. (1986). Stigma reconsidered. In S. C. Ainlay, G. Becker, & L. M. Coleman (Eds.), *The dilemma of difference: A multidisciplinary view of stigma* (pp. 1-13). New York: Plenum Press.

Ambert, A. (1986). Being a stepparent: Live-in and visiting stepchildren. *Journal of Marriage and the Family, 48,* 795-804.

Birenbaum, H. (1988). *Myth and mind.* Lanham, MD: University Press.

Bruner, J. S. (1960). Myth and identity. In H. A. Murray (Ed.), *Myth and mythmaking* (pp. 276-287). Boston: Beacon Press.

Bryan, H., Coleman, M., Ganong, L., & Bryan, L. (1986). Person perception: Family structure as a cue for stereotyping. *Journal of Marriage and the Family, 48,* 169-174.

Cherlin, A. (1978). Remarriage as an incomplete institution. *American Journal of Sociology, 86,* 634-650.

Cissna, K. N., Cox, D. E., & Bochner, A. P. (1990). The dialectic of marital and parental relationships within the stepfamily. *Communication Monographs, 57,* 44-61.

Coleman, M., & Ganong, L. (1987a). The cultural stereotyping of stepfamilies. In K. Pasley & M. Ihinger-Tallman (Eds.), *Remarriage and stepparenting: Current research and theory* (pp. 19-41). New York: Guilford.

Coleman, M., & Ganong, L. (1987b). Marital conflict in stepfamilies: Effects on children. *Youth and Society, 19,* 151-172.

Coleman, M., & Ganong, L. H. (1990a). Remarriage and stepfamily research in the 1980s: Increased interest in an old family form. *Journal of Marriage and the Family, 52,* 925-940.

Coleman, M., & Ganong, L. H. (1990b). The uses of juvenile fiction and self-help books with stepfamilies. *Journal of Counseling and Development, 68,* 327-331.

Crocker, J., & Lutsky, N. (1986). Stigma and the dynamics of social cognition. In S. C. Ainlay, G. Becker, & L. M. Coleman (Eds.), *The dilemma of difference: A multidisciplinary view of stigma* (pp. 95-122). New York: Plenum Press.

Crosbie-Burnett, M., & Pulvino, C. J. (1990). Children in nontraditional families: A classroom guidance program. *School Counselor, 37,* 286-293.

Crosbie-Burnett, M., & Skyles, A. (1989). Stepchildren in schools and colleges: Recommendations for educational policy changes. *Family Relations, 38,* 59-64.

Darley, J., & Gross, P. H. (1983). A hypothesis confirming bias in labeling effects. *Journal of Personality and Social Psychology, 44,* 20-33.

Draughon, M. (1975). Stepmother's model of identification in relation to mourning in the child. *Psychological Reports, 36,* 183-189.

Duberman, L. (1973). Step-kin relationships. *Journal of Marriage and the Family, 35,* 283-292.

Duberman, L. (1975). *The reconstituted family: A study of remarried couples and their children.* Chicago, IL: Nelson-Hall.

Fine, M. A., & Schwebel, A. I. (1991). Stepparent stress: A cognitive perspective. *Journal of Divorce and Remarriage, 17,* 1-15.

Fluitt, M. S., & Paradise, L. V. (1991). The relationship of current family structures to young adults' perceptions of stepparents. *Journal of Divorce and Remarriage, 15,* 159-174.

Furstenberg, F. F., Jr., & Spanier, G. (1984). *Recycling the family: Remarriage after divorce.* Beverly Hills, CA: Sage.

Ganong, L., & Coleman, M. (1983). Stepparent: A pejorative term? *Psychological Reports, 52,* 919-922.

Ganong, L., Coleman, M., & Kennedy, G. (1990). The effects of using alternate labels in denoting stepparent or stepfamily status. *Journal of Social Behavior and Personality, 5,* 453-463.

Goffman, E. (1959). *The presentation of self in everyday life.* New York: Doubleday Anchor.

Goffman, E. (1963). *Stigma: Notes on the management of spoiled identity.* New York: Simon & Schuster.

Hughes, C. (1991). *Stepparents: Wicked or wonderful?* Brookfield, VT: Gower Publishing Co.

Jones, E. E., Farina, A., Hastorf, A. H., Markus, H., Miller, D. T., & Scott, R. A. (1984). *Social stigma: The psychology of of marked relationships.* New York: W. H. Freeman.

Jones, E. E., & Pittman, T. S. (1980). Toward a general theory of strategic self-presentation. In H. Suls (Ed.), *Psychological perspectives on the self.* Hillsdale, NJ: Lawrence Erlbaum Associates.

Kaplan, L., & Hennon, C. B. (1992). Remarriage education: The Personal Reflections Program. *Family Relations, 41,* 127-134.

King, L. A., & King, D. W. (1990). Role conflict and role ambiguity: A critical assessment of construct validity. *Psychological Bulletin, 107,* 48-64.

Lofas, J., & Sova, D. B. (1985). *Stepparenting.* New York: Zebra Books.

Maglin, N. B., & Schniedewind, N. (1989). Women and stepfamilies. Philadelphia: Temple University Press.

McCall, G. J., & Simmons, J. L. (1978). *Identities and interactions* (rev. ed.). New York: The Free Press.

Moorman, J. E., & Hernandez, D. J. (1989). Married-couple families with step, adopted, and biological children. *Demography, 26,* 267-277.

Morrison, K., Thompson-Guppy, A., & Bell, P. (1986). *Stepmothers: Exploring the myth.* Ottawa, Canada: Canadian Council on Social Development.

Salwen, L. V. (1990). The myth of the wicked stepmother. *Women and Therapy, 10,* 117-125.

Schlenker, B. R. (1980). *Impression management: The self-concept, social identity, and interpersonal relations.* Monterey, CA: Brooks/Cole.

Schulman, G. L. (1972). Myths that intrude on the adaptation of the stepfamily. *Social Casework, 53,* 131-139.

Smith, W. C. (1953). *The stepchild.* Chicago, IL: University of Chicago Press.

Stafford, M. C., & Scott, R. R. (1986). Stigma, deviance, and social control: Some conceptual issues. In S. C. Ainlay, G. Becker, & L. M. Coleman (Eds.), *The dilemma of difference: A multidisciplinary view of stigma* (pp. 77-91). New York: Plenum Press.

Visher, E. B., & Visher, J. S. (1979). *Stepfamilies: Myths and realities.* Secaucus, NJ: Citadel.

Visher, E. B., & Visher, J. S. (1988). *Old loyalties, new ties: Therapeutic strategies with stepfamilies.* New York: Brunner/Mazel.

Wald, E. (1981). *The remarried family: Challenge and promise.* New York: Family Services Association of America.

Walker, K. N., & Messinger, L. (1979). Remarriage after divorce: Dissolution and reconstruction of family boundaries. *Family Process, 18,* 185-192.

Remarriage Education:

The Personal Reflections Program

Lori Kaplan and Charles B. Hennon

Lori Kaplan is a doctoral student at the University of Minnesota, Department of Family Social Science, 290 McNeal Hall, 1985 Buford Avenue, St. Paul, MN 55108. Charles B. Hennon, is Professor and Associate Director of the Family and Child Studies Center, Miami University, Oxford, OH 45056.

"Personal Reflections" is a program developed for remarriage education. The premise of the program is that those contemplating or entering remarriage should examine certain issues, especially making explicit each partners' expectations for how family roles should be played. The program is designed to help couples learn about role expectations and potential role strain and stress resulting from a remarriage situation. A brief synopsis of the theoretical orientation is presented, as well as a discussion concerning the implementation and evaluation of such a program.

Many myths surround the formation and existence of stepfamilies in U.S. society (Coleman & Ganong, 1985; Visher & Visher, 1979). These myths can lead remarrying individuals to hold unrealistic expectations of what their new family life may be, which subsequently can cause stress. It has been noted that there is a lack of readily available and quality assistance for remarriage and stepfamily preparation and that few family professionals have been trained for working with stepfamilies (Ganong & Coleman, 1989). Education about stepfamily life, as well as normal stepfamily development, is required (Papernow, 1984). The "Personal Reflections" pro-

gram can help meet this need through assisting individuals in the identification of potential unrealistic role expectations for stepfamily and remarried life. It can also help individuals begin to address these issues, through reflection, self-insight, and consequential communication, before the issues expand into role strain (the felt difficulty in enacting a role, Burr, Leigh, Day, & Constantine, 1979).

This article will provide an overview of the theoretical background and guidelines for conducting a Personal Reflections remarriage education program, as well as raise some evaluation issues. An educational packet is available (see Kaplan & Hennon, 1990b, 1990c). The packet contains a discussion of the theoretical foundation as well as the goals, objectives, and step-by-step guidelines for implementing the program (including exercises and worksheets).

The pedagogical model used for Personal Reflections is based on the premise that individuals can and should be aware of their past performances in various roles. Other theoretical and programming premises include: that situated identities and concerted actions are more easily obtained by a remarrying couple if the partners share a joint vision of the future; that people regulate their actions based upon self-identities of who they are and who they want to be; that people assess their pasts and evaluate their futures in order to give meaning to present interactions; and that past and future role performance can be brought to awareness, expectations for roles can be critically evaluated, and these expectations can be shared with self (internal dialogue) and partner.

People are seen as possessing a "self" which helps regulate their actions

(Stone, 1962). Another basic premise is that humans assess situations, speculate about the implications for self and others, take the role of others in order to conduct concerted action, and engage in a process of asking and answering "what if..?" questions before engaging in social actions (Deutscher, 1970). Grounded in symbolic interactionism, the program includes exercises that emphasize bringing to awareness and sharing self and partner's expectations for playing roles within the structure of a remarriage and/or stepfamily (Hennon, 1985). The program model is an extension and refinement of earlier intervention lines (Cole & Hennon, 1980a, 1980b; Hennon, 1980, 1985; Hennon & Cole, 1981) and is rooted in theoretical and empirical work in the areas of the social self, family roles, stress, and remarriage. The program assists individuals in reflecting upon past and current role enactments, as well as possible role selection or accumulation in the future. The sharing of this information between partners can help to reduce ambiguity about how remarriage roles should be played. Reducing ambiguity should also reduce stress.

The program is structured around the joint expectations held by a remarrying couple for playing nine family roles, with consideration of changes that may take place. The premise for Personal Reflections is that if individuals are (a) provided with information about roles, role expectations, the hows and whys of potential or real role strain and/or stress, and are guided through the use of personal reflection and introspective analysis, then (b) they can be empowered to take positive steps to negotiate interpersonal contracts or scripts that allow for maximum role satisfaction and a higher quality of remarried life. The program is thus based on a

This document is #19-91 of the Family and Child Studies Center manuscript series, Miami University, Oxford, OH 45056, and authorship is equally shared.

Key Words: family life education, family roles, remarriage, stepfamilies.

rationalistic view of humans, as people who can make decisions that can further their self-interest in solitary and joint action. Aspects of both compensatory and medical helping models (Brickman et al., 1982; Hennon & Arcus, in press) guided the development of the program.

How Prevalent is the Need for Remarriage Education?

Review of the remarriage and stepfamily literature indicates directions for intervention, particularly of an educational nature. Understanding that the dynamics, experiences, and expectations in a remarriage are not the same as in a first marriage (Duberman, 1975; Giles-Sims, 1987; Giles-Sims & Crosbie-Burnett, 1989; Visher & Visher, 1979) must be emphasized (Coleman & Ganong, 1985). As noted by Ganong and Coleman (1989), "remarriages ... are faced with complexity and complications beyond the typical stresses and strains facing any married couple" (p. 28).

Acknowledgment of the difference between natural and stepchildren is necessary (Miller, 1985), including parent-child relationship difficulties following a remarriage (Cherlin, 1978; Clingempeel, 1981; Coleman & Ganong, 1990; Kurdek & Fine, 1991). As noted by various researchers, ambiguity and disagreements concerning issues such as stepchildren, discipline, and finances are major stepfamily stressors (Coleman & Ganong, 1990; Lown & Dolan, 1988; Nelson & Levant, 1991), though they are often not discussed by remarrying couples (Ganong & Coleman, 1989). Developing new sets of meaning for relationships is necessary between former spouses, between former and current spouses, between stepparents and stepchildren, between step- and half-siblings, with extended kin, and with the new spouse (Ahrons & Rodgers, 1987), because all of these relationships contribute to the final level of reorganization in a binuclear family (Kurdek & Fine, 1991; Rodgers, 1987). And according to Ahrons and Rodgers (1987), clarification of roles, rules, and expectations are important for a successful remarriage and stepfamily.

Several scholars (e.g., Bachrach, 1983; Cherlin & McCarthy, 1985; Hobart, 1988; Miller & Moorman, 1989) note the necessity of obtaining more information about stepfamilies as they are becoming a more common family type. As stepfamilies become more common, society will more clearly define roles for the family members (Miller & Moorman, 1989). In the meantime, role-making is a necessity; each remarried individual must engage in developing roles for both her/himself and the partner. Clinicians and family life educators can help to inform the public about realities of remarried and stepfamily life, as well as characteristics of the remarried and/or blended family system (Pill, 1990). Just the fact that many people are remarrying and yet redivorcing (Cherlin, 1981; Glick, 1989; Martin & Bumpass, 1989; National Center for Health Statistics, 1989; Norton & Moorman, 1987) indicates the necessity for remarriage education. Preventative rather than remedial programs are called for (Ganong & Coleman, 1989; Hennon & Arcus, in press).

Theoretical Framework

Three theoretical streams are tapped to develop the conceptual foundation for the Personal Reflections program (Kaplan & Hennon, 1990b). First is the conceptualization of the family as an interactive system of positions which are composed of various role sets. Second is the understanding that family roles are multidimensional and that expectations develop for role performance along each of nine dimensions. Role congruency, crystallization, and expectations become important concepts for explaining remarriage and stepfamily role satisfaction. Third is the symbolic interactionism conceptualization of vocabularies of motives, which are the accounts and disclaimers that people offer to explain role behavior (e.g., the language used to explain their motives). These vocabularies become part of the self-identity and thus theoretically influence role choice, role-making, and role-playing.

Family Positions and Roles

Ahrons and Rodgers (1987) believe that stepfamily members may bring clashing expectations and beliefs into the new family unit due to different experiences and family histories. Thus, with varying experiences and expectations from the past, there is opportunity for disagreement over issues pertaining to roles in the new family unit. According to Miller (1985), a common reason given for problems in stepfamilies is the failure to plan and prepare for the new marriage and new family relationships (positions and roles). A redefinition of family identities, boundaries, and expectations is needed for a successful remarriage (Pasley & Ihinger-Tallman, 1982). For this reason, Personal Reflections advocates discussion of these issues in advance of remarrying. This can be accomplished through the process of self-insight into past and current role enactments, as well as possible role selection or accumulation in the future (Hennon, 1985).

Individuals entering remarriage face many new expectations for behavior. Many times these expectations conflict in that the expectations one holds for how she/he should act, think, feel, are ambiguous or in conflict with the expectations held by one's partner. (Expectations can also be in conflict with those held by children and others, but for simplicity, this program focuses on the couple as the unit of analysis.) Often this conflict is not recognized until "after the fact"; that is, when action is expected but it is unclear what to do, or one is challenged to account for why her/his behavior is inadequate, deviant, or excessive. Each individual engages in the processes of role selection, role negotiation, and role-making (Aldous, 1974) to organize behaviors and allocate resources around the tasks associated with the positions she/he holds in the family system (Goebel & Hennon, 1983).

Families can be conceptualized as social systems composed of positions such as wife/mother and son/brother. Each position is composed of a set of interrelated roles, which in turn are composed of a set of interrelated norms (usually referred to as expectations in this article), duties, rights, and responsibilities (Bates, 1956; Nye, 1974). The same nominal role can be found in a variety of different positions (e.g., the provider role can be played by the incumbants of both the positions of stepmother and father). A role can be defined as the behavior enacted by people due to their holding specific positions as well as the cognate attitudes, emotions, and cognitions. These cognitions include perceptions, attributions, expectations, assumptions, and standards (Fine & Kurdek, in press). Roles are dynamic and processual, and conceptually capture the interpersonally shared expectations for behavior (cf. Burr et al., 1979). In this sense, the term is used to define the normative aspect of roles—expectations in people's minds of what individuals in a position should or should not be doing, feeling, thinking—rather than the mere presence of some identifiable behavior (Nye, 1974). However, it is acknowledged that people can role-make. That is, individuals can create new lines of action and are not simply "robot-like," responding only in pre-programmed ways. These role expectations refer to interactional processes that are dynamic, on-going action sequences involving people.

Changes of expectations or performance in any of these roles can lead to somatic, psychological, or social stress for the individual. As an individual experiences family developmental changes (such as marriage, divorce, and remarriage), her/his role set and role expectations change. Remarriage implies the addition of roles, and any time roles are added to a role set, stress can result. In other words, role strain becomes an inevitable, normal, and expected consequence of multiple roles (Tiedje et al., 1990) and role change.

Role Expectations and Dimensions

Nine family roles which comprise the positions of wife/mother and husband/father have been conceptualized (cf. Goebel & Hennon, 1983; Hennon, 1985; Nye, 1974, 1976) (also, of course, wife/stepmother and/or husband/stepfather). The instrumental roles (the basic maintenance of a household and/or family) include (a) provider, (b) housekeeper, and (c) child rearer. The expressive roles (human emotions and feelings) include (d) recreational, (e) sexual, (f) therapeutic, (g) child socializer, (h) self-maintenance, and (i) kinship. According to Scanzoni and Scanzoni (1976), both instrumental and expressive roles are important for marital cohesion and satisfaction.

The set of rights and responsibilities of each role carries expectations encompassing several possible dimensions. These include (a) location, (b) timing, (c) degree of commitment, (d) standard of task completion, (e) allocation of resources, (f) degree of instrumentality/expressiveness, (g) degree of interpersonal specificity, and (h) responsibility (Hennon & Brubaker, 1983; Hennon & Cole, 1981; Kaplan & Hennon, 1990b). Therefore, while there are nine possible roles one can play, there are also eight dimensions influencing each role. In addition, both self and "the other" have expectations for each role formatted by the parameters of the various dimensions as played by self and other.

Congruency between how each role is expected to be played and how it is actually played leads to crystallization of the role. How well the role is performed relative to these expectations indicates role competence (Hennon & Cole, 1981; Nye, 1974). The more crystallized the role, the more likely the possibility (given appropriate motivation, resources, and skills) of competent role performance, and thus less the likelihood of role strain and stress. Turner (1970) argues that it is not the inadequacy of the performance relative to agreed upon parameters that leads to marital strife, but rather it is that partners disagree as to the expectations for role performance. He also indicates that partners regard each other more favorably when role consensus (crystallization) is high. As noted by Li and Caldwell (1987), it is more important that there

is intracouple agreement as to role expectations than if there is simple conformity to societal norms. Personal Reflections does not advocate directly for the improvement of performance, but rather the negotiation of expectations. For example, the program is not designed to specifically address "How to improve communication skills," but rather "What are the expectations about communicating?" The family life educator can guide remarrying couples to resources on improving skills in needed areas, or provide these as part of, or in addition to, the Personal Reflections program.

Vocabularies of Motives

Once people choose to play roles in certain ways, they then verbalize motives and produce accounts to explain unanticipated or untoward behavior (Scott & Lyman, 1968). That is, when behavior does not match self or other's expectations, people provide accounts to explain this deviance. *Disclaimers* are statements that precede the negative act, and are devices to "ward off and defeat in advance doubts and negative typifications which may result from intended conduct" (Hewitt & Stokes, 1975, p. 3). *Accounts* are statements that are offered after the fact; that is, to explain behavior that has already taken place. Both disclaimers and accounts are motives that are verbalized (sometimes only to the self) when others (or self) challenge actions as being unexpected, inappropriate, deviant (Mills, 1940), or unduly idiosyncratic (Zurcher, 1979). Language is thus used to explain behavior. Statements are typically made when a person has, in some way, violated normative expectations. These explanations, as well as expectations, are learned. According to Mills (1940), along with rules and norms of action for various situations, vocabularies of motives appropriate to these situations are also learned.

Over time, each individual's vocabularies of motives become autonomous from their original development. Also over time, aspects of these vocabularies become internalized as part of the valued self-identity (self-as-object). Hence, an individual's actions and related motives become defining features of the self, influencing further role selection and enactment. For example, if in a previous marriage a parent was chided for not spending enough time with the children, this parent, in all likelihood, produced some vocabulary of motives to explain this behavior. Over time, this vocabulary could become part of his/her self-identity. It thus could influence role performance because the parent may see him/herself as career-oriented, distant, or unable to establish

communication with children. This internalization could carry over and affect role performances and expectations in a remarriage and/or stepfamily. Personal Reflections allows people to reflect upon the vocabularies they have developed and why. With this personal insight, choices can be made concerning role selection and performance.

Summary

With the realization that there are so many dimensions upon which people hold role expectations, it is not surprising that role strain, stress, and conflict occur. The probabilities of two people holding perfectly congruent expectations on every dimension for every role is minute. The ability of people to role-play correctly and to take the role of the other is also problematic. Role-taking is the cognitive construction of the roles of the other people with whom a person engages in some social transaction. This is done for the purpose of articulating their lines of action with one's own. Turner (1956) notes that not only does the person recognize and accommodate the expectations held by others, but does so in a manner which affords some personal uniqueness in role enactments. Role-taking also becomes role-making. Taking the role of the other and role-playing may not be done accurately unless individuals have a fairly precise sense of others' expectations for their own behavior. In many situations, approximations to the standards are all that are needed. In other situations, the tolerance for error is smaller.

It is assumed that individuals can make choices as to whether they wish to adhere to role expectations. When expectations are discussed and negotiated, couples may be able to reach a shared reality. In this way, possible unintended violations of expectations can be avoided. Personal Reflections is a program which emphasizes and provides the means for remarrying couples to identify, communicate, and perhaps negotiate their expectations.

A brief synopsis of the theoretical orientation behind Personal Reflections has been presented. A more detailed presentation is included in the packet developed by Kaplan and Hennon (1990b). Understanding this background material is essential for the family life educator who conducts such programs. The following section reviews the program.

Family Life Education Using Personal Reflections

The Personal Reflections technique encourages self-insight about remarriage and stepfamily roles. Self-insight (and communicating this insight) is sought to facilitate role crystallization, thereby reducing role strain. Focus is placed on attaining as much congruence as possible regarding the expectations of both partners for the new marriage. Once this is achieved, couples can change their orientation from expectations for roles to actual performance of roles. It is predicted that the greater the shared definition of norms for remarriage and/or stepfamily roles, the greater will be the individual feelings of well-being, the extent of satisfaction with role performance, and the degree of dyadic adjustment and remarriage satisfaction.

Family life educators can help people to gain insight, gather information, see what options are available, assess trade-offs, live with ambiguity, and explore both change and coping strategies relative to the stressor of remarriage role performance. The educator must also be supportive of attempts to change behavior. He/She can help to develop resources needed to manage the stress brought on by role changes during the remarrying process. As argued by Visher and Visher (1988), finding out the belief systems and expectations of the stepfamily and helping its members to relinquish unrealistic ones, seems helpful.

Program Goals and Objectives

Several goals and objectives are identified for Personal Reflections. It should be noted, however, that the educator can specify specific or different goals and objectives, and thus place different emphases on what is appropriate to teach, highlight, or evaluate. One of the characteristics of the program is its flexibility, allowing each educator to fashion the program to match local contingencies.

Goals

Personal Reflections is based upon theoretical understanding and uses structures to help participants:

1. Establish and maintain "enabled families"; that is, those succeeding as systems in meeting family and individual goals and environmental demands, overcoming difficulties, and sustaining themselves over time (Constantine, 1986).

2. Understand and negotiate incongruencies in role expectations.

3. Become more satisfied with role performances in the remarriage and/or stepfamily.

4. Understand the role of "self" in choosing how to play re-marital roles.

5. Enhance their senses of personal mastery (locus of control).

6. Enhance their feelings of well-being.

Objectives

Participants attending the Personal Reflections program will be able:

1. To define nine family roles.

2. To understand behavior as being role-related and that various expectations for behavior exist.

3. To identify the eight possible role expectation dimensions.

4. To articulate how "self" influences behavior.

5. To discuss the use of vocabularies of motive (including disclaimers and accounts).

6. To identify expectations for their own role performances.

7. To identify expectations for their partners' role performances.

8. To identify discrepancies between their own and their partners' expectations for role behavior.

9. To decide which, if any, discrepancies are to be discussed with their partners.

10. To successfully negotiate these discrepancies in role expectations.

Implementing the Personal Reflections Program

The following presentation is based on a workshop conducted at Pennsylvania State University, entitled, "Strengthening Remarriage: Using the Personal Reflections Technique" (Kaplan & Hennon, 1990a). The Personal Reflections program is designed to meet three times, preferably one time per week, for a total of approximately 8 hours (with the first meeting lasting longer than the others). This type of family life education workshop should ideally be taught to both partners, as preparation for remarriage. However, it can also be used with those who are already remarried.

The educator's role includes (a) providing structure for the group; (b) educating individuals about role changes, strain, and stress; (c) encouraging and guiding self-reflection and awareness of role expectations and dissonance in these expectations; (d) providing resource materials; and (e) advising individuals about other community resources. The educator should develop an atmosphere conducive to workshop participants gaining self-insight through personal reflection. Participants are to be encouraged to communicate with their partners concerning the revealed differences among role expectations. This introspection and communication is useful for negotiating the role scripts most compatible for meeting individual and family goals. Consideration should be given by participants to past and present enactment of the roles, as well as short- and long-term projections for the future.

The educator seeks to empower people toward achievement of a level of role performance satisfying to those concerned. In line with a compensatory helping model (Brickman et al., 1982), remarrying persons carry much of the burden for their own insight and identification of role expectations, how congruent these are with their partners' expectations, and how to negotiate differences. Personal Reflections provides the structure for reflecting about the remarriage and what the partners desire. Those involved in the remarriage process can acquire insight, identify causes of real or potential role strain, decide if these should be discussed with their partners, and if so, decide whether differences should be negotiated. As a result, participants might enhance their senses of self-esteem and feelings of having mastery over at least this aspect of their lives.

The following is an outline of the steps to be followed in a program. Complete instructions are included in the program packet (Kaplan & Hennon, 1990c). These steps are presented here in the same chronologic order as in the program's format.

1. *Introduction.* The family life educator should introduce her/himself and provide an overview of the program. It should be stressed that participants are not required to say anything they do not want to reveal and that the focus is on helping people learn to better understand what they expect from themselves and from their spouses in the new marriages. The educator should emphasize that these expectations will be determined through self-insight and reflecting upon how the participants acted in the past, as well as the expectations held for how they and their partners will behave in the future. The educator should also emphasize that in a remarriage, people play a variety of different roles, that expectations develop for how these roles are to be played, and when expectations are violated, people often feel disturbed and upset, which can be stressful. If people do not know how to play the roles (do not know the expectations), or are simply unable to play them, they may feel ambiguity, distress, and/or uncertainty, which can also be stressful (King & King, 1990). Thus, participants should be informed that the workshop is to help those remarrying to more clearly understand their own, and their partners', expectations for how each will play a vari-

ety of different roles in their new marriages. This can reduce stress and help provide for a better quality of remarried life.

2. *The importance of remarriage scripts.* As a teaching metaphor, the educator may describe the following: As Shakespeare wrote in *As You Like It,* "All the world's a stage, and all the men and women merely players: they have their exits and entrances; and one man in his time plays many parts..." *(Oxford Dictionary of Quotations,* 1979). Remarriage can be seen as a stage; certain props and background help set the stage for how individuals are to act in remarriages. The props and the backdrop are cultural expectations for how marriages are to be conducted, laws governing such issues as child support, alimony payments, or visitation rights, and even physical objects such as the size of the house or apartment, the kind of furniture, and how it is located.

It can be explained that people then play out their scripts. The scripts are what people are expected to do, relative to other people in the remarriage drama, and are usually written in such a way that people have choices as to how to act. Following the script requires understanding clues from the other actors; in this case, the children and spouse and others who are involved with the remarriage. The scripts, however, may contain implied expectations for behavior; the trick is in knowing exactly what is expected and making it more explicit. Scripts must be learned through interacting with others, and there is much room for error. People, therefore, do not always act out the play in the way that they, or their co-actors, would like to see it directed. If people can more clearly set the props and the background, and if they can more clearly write the scripts and discuss them, then the probability of having a well-directed and well-performed play may increase. The purpose of this program is to help people write these scripts so that the remarriage drama can be better performed.

3. *Roles in the remarriage drama.* The family life educator should give an overview of the nine family roles. Participants can be told that within the remarriage drama, there are certain positions that the actors take. In this case, focus is on the positions of the wife/mother and/or stepmother, and husband/father and/or stepfather. Although these are the positions that the actors hold, they will play many roles that are part of these positions. The educator can develop the context of each role, giving many examples. It can also be emphasized that role strain can occur when a person is required to try to play different roles at the same

time. An explanation about each role carrying expectations encompassing eight dimensions (an overview can be provided and the learning aids included in the packet employed) should also be given. The educator should stress that conflict can arise as to which dimensions are most important to different people, in different situations. An understanding of how the role dimensions will influence the remarriage is important. [Examples can be taken from the theoretical background section of the packet, and/or constructed by the program director. Participants can also be asked to provide some examples for these various roles in terms of what kinds of behaviors go along with playing the roles.]

After presenting appropriate background information, the educator and participants can jointly work toward developing an analytical understanding of one role (e.g., housekeeper). During a group session (and using the appropriate educational aids), the educator can help individuals to reflect upon how the role was played during the participants' past marriages. Discussion can include how well each individual thought the role was played by both self and partner, allowing participants to focus on *past* experiences. The next step is to assess participants' understanding of how the role is *currently* being played. This allows participants to express fears, inadequacies, reflect upon their vocabularies of motives, what they do or do not like about how the role is being played, what strain this may be creating, and how this role impacts with other roles. Such discussions allow participants to gain insight into their current situations and to examine why strain and/or stress is felt.

The next step is projecting how the individual would like the role to be organized in the *near future* (a few months from the present time, or a year or two away). A discussion can ensue as to how each individual can organize his/her life and about available resources to achieve these goals. The process can continue with each person outlining how she/he wishes the role to be played in a more *distant future* (perhaps 5 years from the present time). The participants and educator can address how the individual and couple plan to obtain these goals: What kind of planning is needed? What resources are available? What new skills need to be acquired? Where can one obtain these skills? What types of support, help, or education are needed?

4. *Expectations for roles.* There are certain expectations as to how to play each of the nine family roles. Participants can use the Discussion Stimulators Worksheets contained in the program packet

to begin thinking about expectations of each role. These worksheets provide examples of possible role expectations and are designed to aid participants in thinking about their own expectations for the nine roles. For instance, expectations for the provider role may include whether one spouse is more responsible for playing this role than the other, as well as how much time should be devoted to this role. Expectations for the child rearer role, on the other hand, may include which spouse stays home when a child is sick, and how often ex-spouses will be consulted concerning child rearing.

Each individual can be led to understand that these expectations are held both by oneself as well as by other people for how the individual will play his/her own roles. Further, one person may never know exactly what the other person wants from him/her in terms of how to play a role. This is why communicating such information to the partner can help clarify expectations and help the person more closely approximate a match between the partner's expectations and his/her own.

5. *Roles can become problematic.* Discussion can ensue regarding the concept of role overlap and resulting stress. In some cases, though rare, there may be no overlap of roles. Other times, however, there may be some overlap. There are other occasions in which much role overlap will occur. In some circumstances people may be asked to play many (e.g., child rearer, housekeeper, and provider) or all roles at once (a seemingly impossible task). Specific examples can clarify these concepts. The expectations for which role should be salient, and when, can become clearer for the participating couples.

6. *When role expectations are not met.* The educator can explain that people violate expectations for roles because they do not always understand how to play the role (the concept of role strain can be explained and used here) or because situational constraints demand that they play the role otherwise. When expectations are violated and individuals are called upon to account for them, they tend to provide excuses for why they acted the way they did. This is done to align themselves with what is expected so others will think well of them; individuals want their self identities to be good and to feel good about themselves. Over time these vocabularies of motives may become expectations for behavior. These become part of the role expectations; this is why people act as they do.

Given that marriage involves conflicting expectations and interests (Sprey, 1979), especially those that end in divorce (White, 1990), participants have had ample opportunities in their previous marriages to develop accounts, excuses, and disclaimers for their role performances. Participants can be asked for examples of vocabularies of motives used in the past to explain untold or challenged behavior. Illustrations of behaviors can be provided by the participants, and they can be asked to reflect upon what kinds of motives they have used to account for the way they behaved. Spanking a child or yelling at a stepchild might be explained with a vocabulary such as, "Discipline is for his/her own good." Or spending more money on one's own child than on a stepchild could be explained with a motive such as, "But Becky really needed new shoes more than Debbie."

7. *Validating one's self-identity.* The "Who am I?" questionnaire from the program packet might be administered, which allows people to get a sense of how they see themselves. The educator should review with participants the viewpoint that people have a self and are able to discuss, label, talk about, and give it an identity. The second point to be stressed is that who the participants are (positions and roles), who they think of (significant others), and how they see themselves (self-identity) affect the way they will act in the remarriage. For example, if they see themselves as good parents, they may act differently than if they see themselves as parents who do not seem to handle tense situations well.

It may be stressed that individuals often have internal conversations with themselves—about what they are going to do, what they did, and why they did it. These conversations may be to align behaviors with whom individuals are, versus the constraints and demands imposed upon them in a particular situation. For example, if an individual finds out that a child has been misbehaving in school, she/he may have an internal conversation before talking to the child about the behavior. This helps the parent play the role of child socializer, in this case. The individual thinks about what is expected from the child in terms of being a student, or acting up, or representing the family, and also thinks about what kind of parent she/he is. Is she/he a parent who is going to yell at the child? Does the parent even care if the child misbehaves? Is the individual going to allow the child to explain his/her behavior first? Is she/he going to take the teacher's word without asking the child about it? How severe of a punishment is going to be given, if any? Will rewards be offered if the child changes the behavior? These and possible other notions may be considered internally. What actually happens then is an interplay between how the parent perceives the self as a child socializer, how the child acts in the situation, and the interactions between the parent and child. As a result, a line of action is played out; a drama is performed.

Sometimes when these dramas begin, the anticipated outcome may not be reached because of the demands of the situation. The clearer the expectations, the easier the performance often becomes—especially, if the expectations are congruent.

8. *The importance of congruent expectations.* The family life educator can explain the importance of congruency of expectations. Participants can be encouraged to think about both the incongruity and congruency of expectations they hold, and expectations their partners hold, for playing various roles in the remarried family. For example, to demonstrate how roles can be congruent or divergent, the Expectations Worksheets (contained in the packet) can be used. Individuals can be encouraged to personally reflect upon their own behaviors and the expectations they have for acting out the various roles within a remarriage. They may reflect upon what they have done in the past, or what they might do in the future if they violate these expectations. Also, participants may reflect upon and think about the expectations they hold for their partners and what they think their partners hold for them. Individuals can choose one role and then list the following: (a) the expectations that they hold for their own behavior for playing that role; (b) the expectations they assume their partners have for them to play the same role; (c) what they assume are their spouses' own expectations; and (d) their expectations for how their spouses can play the role.

As a homework assignment, participants can take the sheets home and discuss differences that have been revealed as to the expectations for how to play the role. During the program, it is important for the educator to encourage participants to think about (a) the role and what it encompasses, (b) the various dimensions, and (c) the expectations they have and all the various aspects in terms of what is to be done and what is not to be done. When the couples write down their expectations, they may not list all expectations. This is because there are probably more expectations than will be initially recognizable, or because people will not know the expectations until they are violated and called to attention. This exercise is to stimulate a discussion between the partners as to the expectations of roles, which will hopefully carry over to other situations where partners can discuss and clarify their expectations.

9. *Sharing differences with partner.* During the second meeting, people can be given a chance to talk about what they experienced when they discussed the differences that were revealed with their spouse. Examples can be given of major differences not known about, differences not resolvable, and differences that were easily resolved. Sometimes participants will note that having different expectations was a real revelation and these differences, once revealed and made clear, could be easily negotiated.

10. *Learning to negotiate.* Couples can be encouraged by the family life educator to negotiate the expectations, especially any differences that are revealed. Negotiation is important for families to be able to reach a state of satisfaction, happiness, and a high quality of life. Some negotiation skills and knowledge may be taught as well, such as effective communication, whether people have to reach a state of consensus or not, how compromises can be reached, and the idea of zero-sum versus nonzero-sum games. This can help people understand that if they can negotiate their differences and their expectations for the remarriage, they may be able to have a much more satisfying remarriage. For the rest of this meeting, another role might be selected and the expectations for that role be listed on the expectation worksheets. The homework assignment is for the participants to go over the expectations for the second role, as well as choosing and discussing expectations for any third role.

11. *Wrap up and questions.* The third program meeting offers another opportunity to talk about (a) how people negotiated, (b) how they revealed differences in their expectations, and (c) anything else that may have come up during conversations about the remarriage and the expectations for it. This workshop time might also be used to go over two additional roles; participants may select any two from the list of nine roles and fill out their expectations.

12. *Review.* The program can close with a review of the following: family roles, role dimensions, expectations for these dimensions, how there can be conflict about these dimensions, that disagreements on these expectations can create role strain, that role strain can lead to stress, and that stress can lead to unsatisfactory remarriages. Therefore, the clearer the expectations for how to play the roles, the less ambiguity, the less role strain, the less stress. It can be mentioned that this is not a cure-all for remarriages, but is one way to help people understand the expectations that everyone has so they can make choices as to how to live out the remarriage drama. As part of the wrap-up, it can be suggested that people think about (a) their identity,

(b) that their identity will help them make choices as to how they want to play out the remarriage drama, and (c) that people have vocabularies of motives which modify this self-identity when the present self is seen as different from the self of the past. How individuals perceive themselves will affect the nature of the role performances they play, which will affect the kinds of identities they have, both in terms of how they see themselves as well as how others see them. It can also be mentioned that all marriages have conflict. The difference is that in satisfactory marriages, conflict seems to be managed; individuals can negotiate because they have a set of rules governing how to negotiate.

Who Can Benefit from this Education?

Information presented through Personal Reflections is potentially useful to all remarried couples, as well as those contemplating remarriage. However, outreach is only effective when individuals are aware of such services. It is the responsibility of family life educators to contact groups, organizations, and community agencies/services to address the need for remarriage education (Ganong & Coleman, 1989; Hennon & Arcus, in press; Wilke, Kenkel, & Brown, 1984).

Recruitment for participants can occur through religious organizations, community groups, professional service and fraternal organizations, Cooperative Extension professionals, family counselors and therapists, and local mental health organizations. Personal Reflections can be offered either as a single effort to address remarriage, or parallel to larger attempts to address family life. Instead of a series of meetings, a one-time presentation of the program can be conducted. Another possibility for education based on this program is through extension publications or the mass media. And finally, this program can be used to assist individuals through self-help materials.

Evaluation

Evaluation of Personal Reflections is encouraged. Evaluation can take different forms and use different methodologies, depending upon the particular interests of the family life educator and the constraints imposed within the immediate environment. This section will discuss some points to consider when conducting an evaluation of the Personal Reflections program.

1. Depending upon the particular goals and objectives of the program emphasized, different evaluation strategies can be employed. The evaluation methodology and objectives can differ depending upon whether the program contained couples or just one partner, and if the participants are anticipating remarriage or are already remarried.

2. Whether the evaluation should be specific or global is the decision of the family life educator. For example, is it important to understand whether the program seemed to have some influence on participants' overall re-marital satisfaction, or the congruence of re-marital role expectations?

3. Depending upon the evaluator's goals, an evaluation instrument may be constructed to tap the amount of agreement achieved by partners as to their role expectations, both before and after participating in the program. Such an investigator-constructed instrument can tap more closely the expected results due to the material actually covered in a specific program. Information about such instruments can also be obtained from the authors of Personal Reflections.

Standardized instruments can also be used to gauge such things as dyadic satisfaction, self-esteem, family cohesion and adaptability, and other important concepts. Some standardized instruments that can be used include the Kansas Family Life Satisfaction Scale, the Marital Comparison Level Index, the Dyadic Adjustment Scale, the Family Adaptability and Cohesion Evaluation Scales (FACES-III), the Locke-Wallace Marital Adjustment Test, the Tennessee Self-Concept Scale, the Inventory of Family Feelings, the Self-Esteem Inventory, the Role Consensus Index, and the "Who Does What?" Scale. For more information on these and other measurement instruments, see Robinson and Shaver (1973), and Touliatos, Perlmutter, and Straus (1990). Mentioning these scales should not be taken to mean that the authors of Personal Reflections believe that one short educational program such as this will have major and long-lasting impact, but rather that these scales can help educators ascertain in what areas impact is noted (positive or negative), and can be used to refine existing as well as develop innovative programming (Hennon & Arcus, in press).

Depending upon one's purposes and needs, more or less sophisticated evaluation designs can be incorporated. For example, control groups or repeated measures can be utilized. Comparison with other types of education programs may be attempted (see for example, Larson, Anderson, & Morgan, 1984; Lown, McFadden, & Crossman, 1989; Nelson & Levant, 1991). Also, potential gender differences in degree of role ambiguity as well as in parenting and marital satisfaction (Kurdek & Fine, 1991), and how this might be affected by educational intervention can be assessed. Hennon and Arcus (in press) can be consulted for a more detailed discussion of family life education evaluation issues and designs.

It is also suggested that participants provide feedback concerning the presentation of the program. Participants' suggestions for how to clarify parts of the program, whether it should be shortened or lengthened, whether participants should take more or less of an active role, and the usefulness of the various homework or in-session assignments have been used to refine the program. Both types of evaluation data can help the educator gauge the effectiveness of the intervention, as well as fine-tune it to make it more efficient.

Summary

Personal Reflections can be offered through a variety of methodologies. The choice of program emphasis will vary. Regardless of the exact structure of the program offered however, the need for education for remarrying couples is evident. Development and implementation of this form of family life education is necessary simply due to the vast number of persons in remarriage and stepfamily situations (Glick, 1989; Moorman & Hernandez, 1989). A premise of this program is that clarifying expectations is an important step towards role competency. At least if the expectations are clear, then inadequate performance or role strain is not due to cloudy expectations. With clear expectations, many disagreements and disappointments can be avoided. Personal Reflections is designed not only to help alleviate the role strain and stress produced from these family structures, but also to help improve the quality of remarried life for the individuals involved.

REFERENCES

Ahrons, C., & Rodgers, R. (1987). *Divorced families: A multidisciplinary developmental view.* New York: Norton.

Aldous, J. (1974). The making of family roles and family change. *The Family Coordinator,* 23, 231-235.

Bachrach, C. (1983). Children in families: Characteristics of biological, step-, and adopted children. *Journal of Marriage and the Family,* 45, 171-179.

Bates, F. (1956). Position, role, and status: A reformulation of concepts. *Social Forces,* 34, 313-321.

Brickman, P., Rabinowitz, V. C., Karuza, J., Jr., Coates, D., Cohn, E., & Kidder, L. (1982). Models of helping and coping. *American Psychologist,* 37, 368-384.

Burr, W., Leigh, G., Day, R., & Constantine, J. (1979). Symbolic interaction and the family. In W. Burr, R. Hill, F. I. Nye, & I. Reiss (Eds.), *Contemporary theories about the family: Volume 2. General theories/theoretical orientations* (pp. 42-111). New York: Free Press.

Cherlin, A. (1978). Remarriage as an incomplete institution. *American Journal of Sociology,* 84, 634-650.

Cherlin, A. (1981). *Marriage, divorce, and remarriage.* Cambridge, MA: Harvard University Press.

Cherlin, A., & McCarthy, J. (1985). Remarried couple households: Data from the June 1980 current population survey. *Journal of Marriage and the Family,* 47, 23-30.

4. RELATIONSHIPS IN TRANSITION: Divorce and Remarriage

Clingempeel, W. G. (1981). Quasi-kin relationships and marital quality in stepfather families. *Journal of Personality and Social Psychology,* **41,** 890-901.

Cole, C., & Hennon, C. (1980a, May). *Blue collar split-shift families and stress: Sources of role strain and stress management strategies.* Workshop and paper presented at the annual meeting of the Groves Conference on Marriage and the Family, Gatlinburg, TN.

Cole, C., & Hennon, C. (1980b, November). *The split-shift marriage syndrome.* Paper presented at the annual meeting of the American Association of Marriage and Family Therapists, in conjunction with First International Meeting, Toronto, Canada.

Coleman, M., & Ganong, L. (1985). Remarriage myths: Implications for the helping professions. *Journal of Counseling and Development,* **64,** 116-120.

Coleman, M., & Ganong, L. (1990). Remarriage and stepfamily research in the 1980s: Increased interest in an old family form. *Journal of Marriage and the Family,* **52,** 925-940.

Constantine, L. (1986). *Family paradigms: The practice of theory in family therapy.* New York: Guilford.

Deutscher, I. (1970). Buchenwald, Mai Lai, and Charles Van Doren: Social psychology as explanation. *The Sociological Quarterly,* **11,** 533-540.

Duberman, L. (1975). *The reconstituted family: A study of remarried couples and their children.* Chicago, IL: Nelson Hall.

Fine, M. A., & Kurdek, L. A. (in press). A multidimensional cognitive-developmental model of stepfamily adjustment. In K. Pasley & M. Ihinger-Tallman (Eds.), *Remarriage and stepparenting: Research theory, and practice.* New York: Praeger.

Ganong, L., & Coleman, M. (1989). Preparing for remarriage: Anticipating the issues, seeking solutions. *Family Relations,* **38,** 28-33.

Giles-Sims, J. (1987). Social exchange in remarried families. In K. Pasley & M. Ihinger-Tallman (Eds.), *Remarriage and stepparenting: Current research and theory* (pp. 141-163). New York: Guilford.

Giles-Sims, J., & Crosbie-Burnett, M. (1989). Stepfamily research: Implications for policy, clinical interventions, and further research. *Family Relations,* **38,** 19-23.

Glick, P. (1989). Remarried families, stepfamilies, and stepchildren: A brief demographic profile. *Family Relations,* **38,** 24-27.

Goebel, K., & Hennon, C. (1983). Mother's time on meal preparation, expenditures for meals away from home, and shared meals: Effects of mother's employment and age of younger child. *Home Economics Research Journal,* **12,** 169-188.

Hennon, C. (1980, October). *Journey through divorce: Personal reflections.* Paper presented at the annual meeting of the National Council on Family Relations, Portland, OR.

Hennon, C. (1985). Family life education during divorce: A theoretical model for developing programs using the personal relationships technique. In R. Williams, H. Lingren, G. Rowe, S. Van Zandt, P. Lee, & N. Stinnett (Eds.), *Family strengths 6: Enhancement of interaction* (pp. 277-290). University of Nebraska: Center for Family Strengths.

Hennon, C., & Arcus, M. (in press). Lifespan family life education. In T. Brubaker (Ed.), *Family relationships: Current and future directions.* Newbury Park, CA: Sage.

Hennon, C., & Brubaker, T. (1983, June). *Responsibility for household tasks: Does wife's employment make a difference?* Paper presented at pre-conference workshop "Work and Family," American Home Economics Association, Milwaukee, WI.

Hennon, C., & Cole, C. (1981). Role strain and stress in split-shift relationships. *Alternative Lifestyles: Changing Patterns in Marriage, Family and Intimacy,* **4,** 142-155.

Hewitt, J., & Stokes, R. (1975). Disclaimers. *American Sociological Review,* **40,** 1-11.

Hobart, C. (1988). Perception of parent-child relationships in first married and remarried families. *Family Relations,* **37,** 175-182.

Kaplan, L., & Hennon, C. (1990a, April). *Strengthening remarriage: Using the Personal Reflections technique.* Celebrate the Family Conference, University Park, PA.

Kaplan, L., & Hennon, C. (1990b). *A social psychology of remarriage: A theoretical foundation for Personal Reflections* (Manuscript #1-90). Unpublished manuscript, Miami University, Family and Child Studies Center, Oxford, OH.

Kaplan, L., & Hennon, C. (1990c). *Family life education using Personal Reflections: Model implementation* (Manuscript #2-90). Unpublished manuscript, Miami University, Family and Child Studies Center, Oxford, OH.

King, L., & King, D. (1990). Role conflict and role ambiguity: A critical assessment of construct validity. *Psychological Bulletin,* **107,** 48-64.

Kurdek, L., & Fine, M. (1991). Cognitive correlates of satisfaction for mothers and stepfathers in stepfather families. *Journal of Marriage and the Family,* **53,** 565-572.

Larson, J., Anderson, J., & Morgan, A. (1984). *Effective stepparenting.* New York: Family Service America.

Li, J., & Caldwell, R. (1987). Magnitude and directional effects of marital sex-role incongruence on marital adjustment. *Journal of Family Issues,* **8,** 97-110.

Lown, J., & Dolan, E. (1988). Financial challenges in remarriage. *Lifestyles: Family and Economic Issues,* **9,** 73-88.

Lown, J., McFadden, J., & Crossman, S. (1989). Family life education for remarriage: Focus on financial management. *Family Relations,* **38,** 40-45.

Martin, T., & Bumpass, L. (1989). Recent trends in marital disruption. *Demography,* **26,** 37-51.

Miller, A. (1985). Guidelines for stepparenting. *Psychotherapy in Private Practice,* **3(2),** 99-109.

Miller, L., & Moorman, J. (1989). Married-couple families with children. In U. S. Bureau of the Census, *Studies in marriage and the family* (pp. 27-36) (Current Population Reports, Series P-23, Number 162). Washington, DC: U. S. Government Printing Office.

Mills, C. W. (1940). Situated actions and vocabularies of motive. *American Sociological Review,* **5,** 904-913.

Moorman, J., & Hernandez, D. (1989). Married-couple families with step, adopted, and biological children. *Demography,* **26,** 267-277.

National Center for Health Statistics. (1989). *Remarriages and subsequent divorces: United States* (Vital and Health Statistics, Series 21, No. 45). Washington, DC: U. S. Government Printing Office.

Nelson, W., & Levant, R. (1991). An evaluation of a skills training program for parents in stepfamilies. *Family Relations,* **40,** 291-296.

Norton, A., & Moorman, J. (1987). Current trends in marriage and divorce among American women. *Journal of Marriage and the Family,* **49,** 3-14.

Nye, F. I. (1974). Emerging and declining family roles. *Journal of Marriage and the Family,* **36,** 238-245.

Nye, F. I. (1976). *Role structure and analysis of the family.* Beverly Hills, CA: Sage.

Oxford Dictionary of Quotations (3rd ed.). (1979). Oxford, England: Oxford University Press.

Papernow, P. (1984). The stepfamily cycle: An experiential model of stepfamily development. *Family Relations,* **33,** 355-363.

Pasley, K., & Ihinger-Tallman, M. (1982). Stress in remarried families. *Family Perspective,* **16,** 181-190.

Pill, C. (1990). Stepfamilies: Redefining the family. *Family Relations,* **39,** 186-193.

Robinson, J., & Shaver, P. (1973). *Measures of social psychological attitudes.* Ann Arbor: University of Michigan, Institute for Social Research, Survey Research Center.

Rodgers, R. (1987). Postmarital reorganization of family relationships: A propositional theory. In D. Perlman & S. Duck (Eds.), *Intimate relationships: Development, dynamics, and deterioration* (pp. 239-268). Beverly Hills, CA: Sage.

Scanzoni, L., & Scanzoni, J. (1976). *Men, women, and change.* New York: McGraw-Hill.

Scott, M., & Lyman, S. (1968). Accounts. *American Sociological Review,* **33,** 46-62.

Sprey, J. (1979). Conflict theory and the study of marriage and the family. In W. Burr, R. Hill, F. I. Nye, & I. Reiss (Eds.), *Contemporary theories about the family: Volume 2. General theories/theoretical orientations* (pp. 130-159). New York: Free Press.

Stone, G. (1962). Appearance and the self. In A. M. Rose (Ed.), *Human behavior and social processes: An interactionist approach* (pp. 86-118). Boston: Houghton-Mifflin.

Tiedje, L., Wortman, C., Downey, G., Emmons, C., Biernat, M., & Lang, E. (1990). Women with multiple roles: Role-compatibility perceptions, satisfaction, and mental health. *Journal of Marriage and the Family,* **52,** 63-72.

Touliatos, J., Perlmutter, B., & Straus, M. (1990). *Handbook of family measurement techniques.* Newbury Park, CA: Sage.

Turner, R. (1956). Role-taking, role standpoint, and reference group behavior. *American Journal of Sociology,* **61,** 316-328.

Turner, R. (1970). *Family interaction.* New York: John Wiley.

Visher, E., & Visher, J. (1979). *Stepfamilies: A guide to working with stepparents and stepchildren.* New York: Brunner/Mazel.

Visher, E., & Visher, J. (1988). *Old loyalties, new ties: Therapeutic strategies with stepfamilies.* New York: Brunner/Mazel.

White, L. (1990). Determinants of divorce: A review of research in the eighties. *Journal of Marriage and the Family,* **52,** 904-912.

Wilke, S., Kenkel, M., & Brown, R. (1984). Rural clergy's attitudes and activities in primary prevention. *Journal of Rural Community Psychology,* **5,** 15-34.

Zurcher, L. (1979). Role selection: The influence of internalized vocabularies of motive. *Symbolic Interaction,* **2(2),** 45-62.

After my son's divorce

Her grandchildren were the light of her life. Would the breakup of her son's marriage change all that?

Doris Willens

Doris Willens, a writer and lyricist, is the author of Lonesome Traveler: The Life of Lee Hays, *recently published by the University of Nebraska Press.*

" This won't make any difference to the relationship between you and the children."

My oldest son had just informed me that he and his wife had split.

"If anything," he rushed on, into the vacuum of my stunned silence, "they will need your love even more."

Amazingly (it seemed afterward), I hadn't seen the breakup coming. Perhaps I'd filtered out disturbing incidents, needing to hang on to my image of a happy family. I had raised my three sons alone after the early death of my husband. When the oldest finished school, married, and produced my first grandchild, I'd reveled in the satisfaction of having made it through. The mantle had been passed; my oldest son had fulfilled the requirements for leader of the clan. We had a strong, new foundation…and now it seemed shattered.

Knowing that one in two marriages ends in divorce doesn't help. Knowing that tens of thousands of grandparents are devastated by similar announcements doesn't help. Each failure is its own individual calamity.

Would this *really* not make any difference in my relationship with the children? Especially to five-year-old Benjamin. (Elizabeth, just two, hadn't yet developed any attitude toward Grandma other than emulating Ben to make sure that she didn't miss out on anything.)

At Benjamin's birth, I had been swept away by an unexpectedly overwhelming love for a baby who was mine only by line extension. The feeling grew every time I saw him.

I remembered a joyous Thanksgiving dinner for 20-odd people when Benjamin was ten months old. Uncles and aunts and cousins, a great-grandmother, parents, and friends. He never took his eyes off me. The bond between us was intense, almost mystical.

My youngest son graduated from college before Ben's first birthday, and I could at last do what I'd longed to do—give up my office job and work on freelance assignments. The move happily coincided with Ben's wonder-filled early years.

Thus I had time to sing him all of the folk songs I knew, and read him the stories that my own children had loved. We'd add new verses to the songs and change the names in the stories to his and those of his family. For a while his favorite color was red and his favorite number was two. We'd spend hours finding red numeral twos in the Yellow Pages of the telephone book, hailing each one with glee. I've had great affection for the Yellow Pages ever since.

The connection between us grew over time.

Ben didn't much like going to sleep, and when I stayed over I'd solemnly make him promise not to shut his eyes all night. He'd laugh and make me promise the same. We'd tiptoe to the kitchen for a midnight snack. (We still called it a midnight snack when his sleeping habits improved and we did our snacking at 8:00 PM.) Neither of us ever did see the dawn come up.

There had been terrifying moments too. Benjamin was only three weeks old when a high fever caused the doctor to rush him into the pediatric ward and start pumping antibiotics into him. At eight months Benjamin was back in Lenox Hill Hospital, screaming in terror under a steam-filled plastic tent during a bad attack of croup. Sharing the nursing duties during these life-threatening episodes left me feeling that I'd helped to bring him through danger, intensifying our bond.

I had, idiotically, supposed that life would be clear sailing once my own children were safely grown up. Francis Bacon's famous words needed updating and paraphrasing: "She that hath children and grandchildren hath given hostages to fortune."

And now? As the story unfolded, I understood that my son had worked for months to try to keep the marriage together. Having failed in that, he worked equally hard to hold the children's lives together in some replica of a "normal" family. The continuation of my once-a-week visits was encouraged.

Now there were two homes and fewer visits.

The children would live with their mother during the week and with their father on weekends. This in itself had an air of normalcy because my son's job involved late hours and frequent travel, and on weekends he had always taken

keeping grandparents involved

"Grandparents can offer children a safe haven during a rocky period, when kids need more continuity and support than ever," says Helen Q. Kivnick, Ph.D., professor of social work at the University of Minnesota. Some things for divorcing parents to keep in mind:
● Divorce does not have to mean cutting ties with your spouse's family. If you had a good relationship with your in-laws, continuing it can be reassuring to the children.
● Even if you are not close to your in-laws, or have reason to dislike them, try to put aside your feelings for your children's sake.
● Avoid making derogatory remarks about your spouse's family in front of the children. This way they will be able to see their grandparents without feeling guilty or that they are choosing sides.
● Children's questions such as "Do you hate Grandma?" may really mean "Am I going to lose Grandma?" You might answer, "Grandma and I may not always get along, but she loves you and will always be there for you."
● Try to keep the children's routines with their grandparents as close to normal as possible. Children who are used to seeing their grandparents on a regular basis should be allowed to continue the visits.
—Kate Jackson Kelly

care of the children so that his wife could work on her academic projects.

But now Ben and Elizabeth bounced between their two residences. My visits were not the same. The only games that Benjamin proposed (and Elizabeth gaily seconded) tended to put me in the role of the mother and them in the role of my offspring— whether in the form of puppies, kittens, or babies. My mind boggled. I played guardedly; Ben played feverishly. These were not hidden games. Benjamin continued as the baby (or puppy or kitten) when his mother came to pick him up. If the children across the street rang the bell, they were invited to join the litter. Benjamin never spoke to me of his parents' break-up, but he surely was acting out a longing for safety.

The first year was the hardest. We're not a let-it-all-hang-out family. We talked about jobs and schools, about Ben's musical gift and Elizabeth's pranks. Everyone worked hard to remain civil. But I could see that Benjamin's particular attachment to me worried his mother. His relationship with her, not with me,

would be the constant in his life. I let my once-a-week overnight visits slacken into once every other week, then once every three weeks. After months of this, his mother seemed reassured that I was just a grandmother, not a threat.

Life goes on. Benjamin and Elizabeth and I are having midnight snacks at 8:00 PM again, once or twice a month. We're playing word and math games now. We spent two weeks together last summer with their father, two uncles, pregnant aunt, girl cousin, and large dog. We had a hilarious good time, despite the two girls' getting chicken pox.

So the bond is there, but of course it's different. Anything, in the way of geography or emotions or new spouses, can happen at any time. An old Irish woman once told a childless friend of mine that "what never made you laugh can never make you cry."

Maybe. But I wouldn't exchange the heartbreak for the memory of all our love and laughter.

Divorce After 50: When Breaking Up Is Better— When It's Not

Elise W. Snyder, M.D.

ELISE W. SNYDER, M.D., a psychoanalyst in private practice, is clinical associate professor of psychiatry at Yale University School of Medicine.

"I don't believe she wants a divorce after 37 years! I can't imagine life without her."

"I've given up my life for him, moved 14 times when he was transferred, and *now* he wants to leave."

"We've had a good working relationship, but that's all it's ever been—with the kids grown and gone, we're finally calling it quits."

Not long ago, divorce after 50 would have been unthinkable. Over 50 was old: too old to want something new and too late to bother. Now, a new generation, living longer, has an opportunity for second careers, travel, education and rich personal relationships. What does that mean for the institution of marriage?

Although the overall divorce *rate* (the percentage of married people divorcing each year) has been stable or decreasing slightly in the past several years, the *number* of people in their 50s and 60s who seek a divorce is rising—because there are now more of us than ever before. Still, fewer older people divorce than younger ones. One reason is that many unsatisfactory marriages have already ended. Those still married at this age are, in some sense, survivors of the marital wars. Also, men and women now over 50 grew up at a time when divorce was considered shameful, always a sign of failure, never a sign of growth. But current statistical trends indicate that, in coming years, older people may be even more willing to end unsatisfactory relationships.

Is divorce the right answer? The word *right* implies a moral judgment that I, as a psychiatrist, cannot make for another person. The reasons that individuals of any age divorce are complex and partially unrecognized, as are the reasons they marry and stay together. We all have wishes and fears that are in conflict with each other. We want to experience pleasure, to be responsible, to care for others, to be cared for, to succeed; we fear loss, rejection, guilt, shame. People tend to consider divorce when, realistically or not, they believe their marriage interferes with important wishes or aggravates deep fears. If a marriage cannot expand to fit the needs of its two members, then they should consider the possibility of leaving it. I do not believe that age is a deterrent to growth or that older people have any less capacity for or right to happiness than younger ones. In fact, they may have more.

Consider a couple I'll call Philip and Madeline. Philip, a professor, became infatuated with one of his graduate students and asked for a divorce. This young woman resembled Madeline when Philip first married her: naive, dependent, impressed with his intellect and sophistication. Soon after Philip confessed the affair, Madeline came to see me. She needed to explore and work through her feelings of rejection and betrayal. "He always treated me with contempt," she said. "All he wanted from me was caretaking. When I was young, he prevented me from pursuing my own professional interests, and now he's threatened by my recent success in real estate. He's thinking of marrying this student because she gives him the admiration he so desperately needs."

That certainly described what had gone on between them from Madeline's perspective, but was it accurate? During therapy, she realized that her subservience had actually hidden *her* contempt for *him*. "He's just a child, I'll let him have his way" and "I have to do everything for him because he can't really manage" were her guiding beliefs. But beneath her contempt was envy. She had been afraid to pursue a profession of her own, preferring to bask in his successes. Often she would describe his achievements as her own: "When *we* published that paper on . . ." or "I was so happy when *we* won that prize for . . ." In therapy, she began to realize how the marriage had served her needs. It

Divorce is often an external solution to avoid confronting internal upheaval

provided a haven from her fears of competing in the intellectual world; it was an arena in which she could secretly take over her husband's accomplishments while at the same time subtly putting him down. Their interaction justified her feelings of being a victim and of being morally superior.

Eight months later, Philip, on his side of the marital divide (and perhaps as a result of Madeline's changes), offered to go into therapy himself. According to Madeline, it had begun to dawn on him that a woman's unquestioning devotion was no substitute for mature self-esteem. Despite his many successes, he had never been able to feel like a grown-up unless some woman was gazing admiringly at him. It is still not clear at this point, either to me or to Philip and Madeline, whether each of them can develop emotionally within their marriage. They are both struggling to work through the lifelong difficulties around which they built their relationship. Despite their efforts and their desire to change, the long-standing patterns of the marriage may ultimately obstruct their attempts to mature as individuals.

People often become aware that a relationship is stagnant just at the time they are experiencing the emotional and physical changes that characterize the years after 50. Psychologically these years closely resemble adolescence, when, emerging from childhood's stability, teenagers face choices in all arenas of life. Almost nothing is fixed or decided; even their bodies become unfamiliar. Over-50s are emerging from the years when they pursued professional, marital and child-rearing goals they had set for themselves at the end of adolescence. Once again, everything is up for grabs; it's a time of high anxiety.

During any period of dramatic *internal* upheaval, we tend to seize on radical and *external* solutions to avoid confronting the anxiety engendered by inner change. Divorce is often this kind of external solution. It may facilitate growth or, as with Philip and Madeline, it may be an attempt to reproduce the past after one partner upsets the marital balance. Madeline first upset it by becoming a success in business, and Philip upset it further by deciding to leave. It's too soon to tell whether their marriage will survive these onslaughts, but they do have a chance for a future together. That's not always true.

Another couple—I'll call them Rich and Miranda—married when Miranda got pregnant in her senior year of high school. Their commitment to the family kept them together while their children were growing up. But when the nest was truly empty, the emptiness of their marriage came into focus. In confidence, Rich explained how he felt: "I've been faithful for more than 30 years to a woman who just isn't interested in sex. Now that we're in our 50s, she feels that she doesn't have to accommodate my needs any more. And she's right. She's paid her dues . . . but I have, too. I want a woman I can love physically, a woman who can feel and express her passion for me."

Miranda, however, wanted to hold on to what she had. "It's hard enough for me now that my children are gone. They were the center of my life. I used to be actively miserable with Rich, but now we have a truce and I'm willing to settle for that. I know I could manage financially if we split up. Still, the idea of being alone terrifies me."

Although Rich and Miranda agreed about the financial consequences of divorce, they differed with respect to the emotional consequences. Rich seemed willing to change, to take his chances with an unknown future, but for Miranda the dangers outweighed the opportunities. Was Rich the victim of Miranda's lovelessness or was Miranda the victim of Rich's desire for sexual fulfillment?

I thought that neither of them was any more mature than they had been as high-school seniors. Back then, Miranda had acquiesced to Rich's desires because she wanted a boyfriend and feared he would leave if she refused. She had felt no sexual desire and resented sex throughout the marriage. "I never refused him, though. I didn't want to give him a reason to be unfaithful." Rich was not unlike the boy he had been at 18: He wanted a woman who would go to bed with him. His capacity for a mature relationship was as underdeveloped as Miranda's sexuality. Both of them had stopped developing emotionally. In this situation, there is no happy ending.

Other marriages have a greater potential for change and growth. Corinne and George, as I'll call them, were a two-career family. George had already retired when Corinne was finally made CEO of a company where she'd been an executive for 30 years. Suddenly she was busier than ever, working late and making frequent trips. George, who had expected her to take early retirement, felt disappointed and hurt. After several bitter arguments, George acknowledged that Corinne really wasn't ready to retire. And this caught him unprepared. He had admirably fulfilled the ambitions and responsibilities of his professional life—but he had never taken care of anything outside of work. Corinne had found their friends, arranged their vacations, even chosen their hobbies.

George now discovered that he could do by himself many things he had hoped they would do together. Indeed, he was able to fulfill one lifelong dream that Corinne had not shared: He went to the rain forests of Africa and Brazil, where he nurtured his interest in photography—and developed a reputation as a photographer of endangered species.

Before George retired, Corinne had maintained a low profile at work, partly because she was one of the few women in her industry and partly because she had put George's work first. Now she felt her time had come. Her guilt about continuing to work diminished, as did her fears of appearing competitive with men and especially with George. She felt freed to be more outspoken and direct. With George, Corinne now found common cause in working together on ecological matters. Her company, previously oblivious to environmental concerns, began to clean up its act under her leadership. Each of them found that changing direction to suit their new interests and responsibilities did not destroy their marriage but, on the contrary, strengthened their relationship.

A good marriage provides us with a haven of continuity and stability in a world that is often changing and difficult. Within such a haven, individuals have the space and encouragement to grow and mature. When a marriage has been deeply flawed or incompatible from the beginning, when one or both of its members have become irremediably rigid, or when the marriage itself has become so fixed that no change is possible, the result is often divorce—or unrelenting misery. If a marriage is stalled, professional help may be necessary to jump-start its continued growth or to help make the decision to end it. But divorce is not a solution in itself; for it to work, it should be a means to continued growth and development.

What Women Want Men To Know About Menopause

Claire Safran

Award-winning journalist CLAIRE SAFRAN has written about health matters and social issues for numerous publications, including READER'S DIGEST, REDBOOK, GOOD HOUSE-KEEPING and TV GUIDE.

Do you remember puberty? The surging hormones? The growing pains? The mood swings? The mysterious changes in mind and body? Menopause is the other end of all that, the inevitable time when raging hormones turn into aging hormones.

It happens to men, too, but at a creeping pace. It hits women harder, faster, more dramatically. Like puberty, menopause has a sure cure—time. Like puberty, it's the start of a new stage of life, one that women want to make the most of.

"But unlike puberty," says my friend Rosalie, silver-lining it, "this time you don't get zits."

She'd like to say all of the above, and more, to her husband, but so far she hasn't. Menopause may be out of the closet, no longer hushed by taboos. But in my straw poll of women, taken sometimes over coffee, sometimes over the phone, I hear that most wives are still reticent with their husbands, saying as little as possible about all of this. Each has her own reasons.

"Because I can just see him turning pale. I can hear him saying, 'Menopause? *Uh-oh!*'" says one. "Because it's about getting older, and neither of us is ready for that," ad-

mits another. "Because it's something you do in private, like flossing your teeth," ventures yet another. "Because it scares the pants off him," a friend in east Texas declares. She has heard that his mother went "crazy" during menopause, crying all the time, weeping even while she vacuumed. "I've been telling him for 30 years that I'm not his mother. But you know how men are."

My own explanation is "because it's no big deal," but many of my friends disagree with that. They complain of hot flashes and night seats, joint pains and vaginal dryness. They worry about osteoporosis, bladder problems, losing their memories and their minds. They aren't imagining it, as some men think. And they aren't playing Camille.

Menopause is unpredictable, changing from woman to woman, which is why it makes so many of us edgy and frustrated. "You never know what's going to happen," my friend Jane complains. "*Or when.*" Usually it begins sometime between ages 45 and 55, when a woman's level of estrogen goes into free-fall, sending confusing signals to the body, stirring up different symptoms in different women, turning regular menstrual periods into irregular ones. Eventually a woman has her last period. But it can take two years—or more—for ovulation to cease. The range of what is "normal" in menopause is as

wide as a politician's promise, and as shifty.

It's a *process* rather than an event, and according to Marian Boyle, R.N., research coordinator at the North American Menopause Society (NAMS), "You're never really over it." The overt symptoms tend to fade after a couple of years, though a small number of women have hot flashes for 10 years or longer. The silent symptoms—the inexorable aging process, the loss of estrogen's natural protection against osteoporosis and heart disease—go on forever.

Each woman has her own experience of menopause, and there's no way of forecasting whether it's going to be smooth sailing or a rough passage. As for me, I'm one of the lucky 10 to 15 percent of women who don't even realize they're menopausal until they come across the unused box of tampons in the closet. But that doesn't mean I'm home free. Menopause is an unmistakable signal that I'm getting older, and in a society that treasures youth, that feels like a felony. So I spend a lot of time thinking about what the rest of the world, especially my husband, thinks of me.

The majority of women (from 75 to 80 percent, depending on which study you read) have one or more menopausal symptoms that are in-

 From *New Choices*, March 1993, pp. 14-17.

convenient but manageable. "Don't call them 'symptoms.' Call them 'signs' or 'complaints,' " urges Mara Taub of the Santa Fe Health Education Project. "A big part of the problem with menopause is that people think of it as a disease rather than a natural event."

A minority of women, only 5 to 15 percent, have symptoms severe enough to cause them to see a doctor. For them, menopause does feel like a major disease, an assault on every system of the body, including the brain. A woman in Baltimore, for example, remembers sitting at her desk in tears and terror. She trains people to use the computer, but suddenly she couldn't remember how to log on.

Husbands, of course, know more about menopause than what their wives tell them. And that worries some of us. Menopause is the new media buzz. It's on *Oprah*. It's on the cover of *Newsweek*. It's on the *New York Times* best-seller list, with *The Silent Passage*, by Gail Sheehy—a book that, in part, is one woman's lamentation about getting older—and *The Change*, by Germaine Greer, which celebrates this time in women's lives.

Most of the media blitz is scary stuff—worst-case scenarios—as if menopause were something conjured up for a Stephen King novel. It's true that a minority of women do go through the private hell that Sheehy writes about, with symptoms severe enough to stop normal life in its tracks. Yet even for these women, most symptoms can be tamed by hormone-replacement therapy, usually a combination of estrogen and progestin. The question of hormones, though, is what drives a lot of women crazy during menopause. Should we or shouldn't we? Most of us have more questions about hormones than our busy doctors have time to answer.

A fter her first few hot flashes, for instance, my friend Joanne went to see her doctor. Ten minutes later, with little talk of risks versus benefits, with no mention of other things she might try—like a change of diet, exercise or layered clothing— she walked out with a prescription for hormones.

Like many wives, Joanne knows about every aspirin that her husband swallows. But he hasn't a clue that she's taking these potent, still controversial pills. Maybe she needs them. And maybe not. Maybe husbands ought to get more involved in their wives' health. And maybe, as the women's health movement urges, some doctors need to think more about normalizing menopause and less about medicating it.

At the 1992 NAMS conference, the doctors wondered aloud why "only" 20 percent of the eligible women (those without specific contraindications, such as a history of breast cancer or gallstones) take hormones. By the end of one year, an estimated 40 percent of these women stop taking them, often because they dislike the menstrual-like monthly bleeding that the pills cause. For some women, the side effects of the hormone pills—"like having PMS all over again," as one woman put it—are worse than the menopausal symptoms they are supposed to cure. But for others, especially the minority who experience the worst symptoms, hormone replacement is the only thing that makes life bearable.

"What's a few hot flashes?" asks my friend Doris, who is among the fortunate group of women who are not hit hard. Like many feminists, she's going public with hers, talking about them not just to her husband but to the men at work. At office meetings, she fans herself with a piece of paper. "Oops," she says with a laugh. "I'm having a hot flash." The intense heat is gone after a minute or two, but she wants the men around the table to see that a menopausal woman can still function, still be creative, still not miss a beat.

Among ourselves, women are debating whether to say even more to the men at work. Should we talk about the more severe symptoms? Should we tell them that some of us are going to have bad days, just as some men have bad days? Will they understand? Or will they use our hormones against us?

"It depends," women tell me, "on the man." As the baby boomers move toward menopause, there may be more and more men in the workplace who accept menopause as an ordinary fact of life, who respond to it with understanding and a sense of humor, the way my friend Janet's husband does. Menopause, he's discovered, has a few small advantages on the home front. On chilly winter mornings, he and Janet used to argue over whose turn it was to leave their warm bed to turn up the thermostat. These days, it's always her turn. "Just wait for the next hot flash," he tells her. "And then make a dash for it."

The bedroom may be the place where women most need a man's understanding about menopause. If a woman is having night sweats, she may feel too sticky to be touched. If she's having hot flashes, one may arrive at just the wrong, intimate moment. Her interest in sex may dim. Still, at that 1992 NAMS conference, the mostly male doctors heard a report documenting something women have been whispering about for years: Menopausal women in new relationships stay eager for sex and often find it better than ever. That could be a hint to old established husbands to bring something more creative and experimental to the bedroom.

For most women, though, menopause is just a sexual blip. According to Bernice Neugarten, Ph.D., a University of Chicago behavioral scientist who has conducted studies on the subject, the great majority of women say it does little or nothing to change their sexuality or their feelings about themselves.

Next to hot flashes, the most common symptom is vaginal dryness, which can make sex uncomfortable. Yet for most women this problem is easily handled with creams and water-soluble jellies that are now available. A Colorado wife talks of incorporating the use of the jelly into her lovemaking. "It's a turn-on for both of us," she reports.

With the drop in estrogen, women also experience a rise in FSH (follicle-stimulating hormone), and that can lower the libido. It's the same thing that makes women lose interest in sex just after a pregnancy. Then and now, if husbands will be patient, it's a passing phase.

Menopause is not just about women's plumbing; it's about feelings and emotions, a time when strange thoughts can turn us unexpectedly sad. My friend Kathy, for example, who long ago chose to be child-free, now finds herself mourning the children she never wanted in the first place, "because it's no longer my choice," she says with a sigh. Many women are happy to see the end of a monthly period, "the curse," as some called it. But my neighbor Amy used to call it "a visit from my friend." As she explains, "I miss the regularity of it."

In menopause, as the body's familiar rhythms go out of whack, many women feel out of control, irritable and confused. Those mood swings, up one day and down the next, may be the first thing a husband notices. Suddenly, his wife acts as if she has permanent PMS. She's quicker to cry, faster to fight.

"If he dismisses it, that makes it worse," says Janine O'Leary Cobb, a woman who quit her job as a sociology professor to research her own menopausal problems and then started a newsletter on the topic, *A Friend Indeed*, out of Montreal, Canada. "In her 20s, the last thing a woman wanted to hear was, 'Oh, it's that time of the month.' In her 50s, the last thing she wants to hear is, 'Oh, it's that time of life.'"

At any time of life, it's the trivial things that can drive a woman wild. "There are little things that have bothered me for years, says my friend Sandy. "The way he leaves his socks on the floor. The way he talks about my sister. I used to ignore them. I was busy; I didn't want to quibble in front of the children. But now we're alone, and I don't want to put up with those socks for the next 30 years. So I speak up. And he's surprised. Menopause is like a second glass of wine; it loosens my tongue."

Sandy wants what most menopausal women want: sympathy, support and a sense of humor about the absurdity of it all. "We need to be able to talk with our men about this," says Davi Birnbaum, chair of the Midlife Women's Health Committee of the National Women's Health Network in Washington, D.C. "And communication may be easier now, even for couples who haven't shared their feelings before. The fears of aging are much closer to the surface than the fears of youth."

The irony of menopause is that, just as women are getting over it, men are suddenly able to understand it. In older men, prostate problems are common, and the latest treatment involves female hormones. Guess what they bring on? How's that for a hot flash?

The grandparent bond: why kids need it

Children thrive on the simple undemanding love of a grandparent. And the benefits are mutual.

Noelle Fintushel

Noelle Fintushel is coauthor of A Grief Out of Season: When Your Parents Divorce in Your Adult Years *(Little, Brown).*

*t*he other morning my six-year-old daughter, Ariel, and I were curled up in the porch swing together. A warm breeze was blowing, and to me it was one of life's Perfect Moments... but I've learned that I don't always measure up to Ariel's standards. She touched my cheek and told me, "I wish your face was as soft as Grandma Rose's. I love to stroke her wrinkly cheeks, and I especially love her white hair."

Later that day I called my mother-in-law. "Ariel thinks you're beautiful!" I told her.

Rose laughed. "That's our little secret," she said.

It's something we know intuitively, and recent studies have confirmed it: The bond between grandparents and grandchildren is unique and precious. At a time of her life when Rose might have succumbed to negative images of "little old ladies," she can bask in the glow of her granddaugh-

ter's admiration and affection. What she offers Ariel in return is hard to define: More than anything, Rose sends her the message, "I'm so lucky to have you."

Of course, I feel that way about my daughter too. It's just that through all the static of everyday life, the message sometimes gets a little blurred. "The bond between a child and a grandparent is the purest, least psychologically complicated form of human love," says Arthur Kornhaber, M.D., author of *Between Parents and Grandparents* (St. Martin's Press). Kornhaber, who is engaged in a long-term study of children, parents, and grandparents in the United States, explains, "Since grandparents are usually not directly responsible for grandchildren, their egos are not as mixed up with them, and their love is less conditional."

Grandparents, according to Kornhaber, can offer an emotional safety net when parents falter. They pass on traditions in the form of stories, songs, games, skills, and crafts. Kornhaber adds that grandparents, as if all this were not enough, have another "magic ingredient"

that parents lack: time. What many grandchildren appreciate most is the relaxed rhythm of life at Grandma and Grandpa's.

Not surprisingly, Kornhaber has found that children who are close to at least one grandparent reap many benefits: They are more emotionally secure than children who have no such ties; they have more positive feelings about old people and the process of aging; and they have an enriched understanding of the world because of what their grandparents taught them about other times and ways of living.

As for grandparents themselves, they testify repeatedly to having a profound attachment to their grandchildren. Indeed, Kornhaber and the other researchers report that grandparents often get quite emotional when trying to describe their feelings for their grandchildren. Grandchildren are their link to the future, their living legacy, their

chance to experience a love that is freer and more playful than the love they were able to feel as parents.

Distance and divorce can weaken the ties.

As gratifying as a close grandparent-grandchild relationship is, a large percentage of grandparents seem to be missing out on it. Of the 300 grandparents in the United States initially studied by Kornhaber and his colleagues, only 15 percent were intimately involved with their grandchildren, seeing them at least once a week.

In a study published in 1986, Andrew J. Cherlin and Frank F. Furstenberg Jr., authors of *The New American Grandparent* (Basic Books), found that 29 percent of the grandparents they interviewed had little or no contact with their grandchildren. Why? Geographical distance ranked among the most important factors: Grandparents reported having closer ties to grandchildren who lived

Grandparents offer an emotional safety net when parents falter.

no more than 100 miles away. It appears that phone calls tend to strengthen ties that are already close rather than compensate for physical distance. These findings suggest—despite what we tell ourselves about the magic of air travel and long-distance communication—that the tremendous mobility of our society weakens the grandparent-grandchild bond.

High divorce rates also affect intergenerational ties. Although grandparents sometimes become closer to grandchildren in the wake of a daughter's divorce, the relationship seems to grow more distant in the case of a son's divorce. At the same time, the increased divorce rate among older couples has an effect on their involvement as grandparents.

"If my parents had stayed together, I know my father would have been a good grandfather," a friend told me wistfully. "But now he's married to a woman with three children at home, and he just doesn't have the time or the energy."

How much should grandparents be involved?
According to Cherlin and Furstenberg, the "new American grandparent" must perform a balancing act. The majority of grandparents the authors studied wanted to feel close to their grandchildren but didn't want to interfere. Often they assumed a passive role, waiting for clear signals that their presence or involvement was desired.

Whether or not grandparents were close to their grandchildren depended to a significant degree on whether they had a good relationship with the children's mother. And they tended to feel most confident about, and gratified by, their role as grandparents when the grandchildren were small. A common remark was, "I'd love to see more of my grandchildren,

but now that they've gotten older, they're just so busy."

The reality is that this country's adults—both young and old—are pulled by somewhat contradictory feelings about extended family: We value close kinships, but we also value independence. Balancing autonomy and family connectedness is not always easy, as my friend Teresa found.

Teresa, the mother of four-year-old twin girls, works part-time. Her husband is in graduate school, so money is tight. Teresa relies on her mother-in-law, Ruth, for child care and financial support. "I'm very grateful to my mother-in-law," Teresa says. "Without her help, I couldn't afford to work, and she's very generous in other ways too. Still—and I feel guilty for saying this—sometimes I resent her. Peter and I have so little time together, and she is always expecting us to come to her house. We're there once a week for dinner and on Sundays after church."

The economic pressures of recent years have created similar strains for many families, and the double bind

that Teresa feels is not uncommon. But for Teresa, as for other parents, her conflict with her mother-in-law has as much to do with a clash of attitudes as with overinvolvement: "Though I consider myself to be religious, she is almost fanatical. She's always giving the girls religious instruction. Sometimes I even feel that I'm competing with her for the souls of my children."

Perhaps the most common complaint about grandparents is that they are too indulgent with the children. One mother told me, "When my daughter comes home from her grandma's, it takes a while for the 'princess' treatment to wear off." Some parents—particularly those whose children spend a lot of time with a very doting grandparent—worry that they will take second place in their child's affections.

Other parents find that grandparents are too old-fashioned and strict with the children, too materialistic, or too concerned with the children's appearance. Often the clash of values erupts when gifts are given,

leaving a parent feeling misunderstood and discounted. Sylvia, the mother of three, showed me with horror the huge plastic guns that her children had just received from their grandparents. "Don't they notice anything about the way we live?" she asked. "My children don't even have squirt guns!"

Often, of course, we take personally comments and actions that are not intended that way. "Many conflicts between the generations are really the result of changing beliefs about child rearing," says Angela Stewart, Ph.D., a psychologist in Rochester, New York.

Conflicts often arise when grandparents seem to favor one set of grandchildren over another. Although it's only natural for grandparents to feel closer to the grandchildren who live nearby, this needn't become a source of hurt feelings. Grandparents who are sensitive and diplomatic can find ways to make out-of-town grandchildren feel special. (My own grandmother used to tell me, "You're special *because* I don't get to see you very

Solving the thorniest problems
getting through to each other

even the most ingrained conflicts between parents and grandparents can be resolved by the use of problem-solving techniques, according to Vicki Lewin, of Goodman Counseling and Mediation Associates, in Rochester, New York. Lewin recommends these basic strategies to help you work through your differences:
● Agree to the ground rules. Pick a time and place that's comfortable for all of you, when the

children will not be around. Agree that you will not resort to name-calling or blaming each other and that you will try to stick to the issue at hand.
● Let each person speak without interruption. Be specific, and use very clear "I" statements to clarify the issue. A declaration like "You don't respect our way of bringing up the children!" is too general and overwhelming. A more workable complaint is "It really upsets me

when you let the children watch violent programs on television. I worry that they'll become numb to violence."
● Check for mutual understanding. Our own anxiety and defensiveness can make it easy to misunderstand or even not hear another's message. After one of you states her position, it's helpful if the other repeats it in her own words.
● Brainstorm. Ask yourselves what you can do to change the situation, and try to

make both positions part of the solution. If Grandma relies on television to occupy the children when she's tired, perhaps Mom and Dad can supply some non-violent videos. Or maybe Grandma can teach the children some other, more old-fashioned amusements.
● Agree on a trial solution, and give yourselves an opportunity to renegotiate. Saying "Let's try this for a week and see how we feel" helps defuse the situation. —N.F.

often!") Even the little things—like writing letters, keeping a scrapbook to preserve photographs and mementos of visits, and creating a few rituals that are reserved for the out-of-town grandchildren—can go a long way toward righting the balance.

A far more painful situation is created when grandparents' lack of closeness to one set of grandchildren arises from a troubled history between the parents and the grandparents. This was the case with my friend Lucia, who had always felt like a misfit in her family. When Lucia and her husband separated, it seemed to confirm her parents' view that she "always made a mess of her life." They are very wrapped up in their son's family, but they ignore Lucia and her daughter, even though they live in the same town. Understandably, Lucia feels hurt and bitter—all the more so because she is a struggling single mother and feels that her daughter would benefit greatly from closer family ties.

"It is common for unresolved problems to resurface when we become parents," says Stewart. "As adults, it is often easier to see ourselves as advocates for our children than to acknowledge our own pain. Not only does this prevent us from really healing those old wounds, but it also places an unfair burden on our children."

Issues between you and your parents can affect your children, too.

How can you tell where your own conflicts end and the true needs of your children begin? First, focus on the issue that is uppermost in your mind, such as, "My mother is too indulgent with the children" or "My father forgot their birthdays this year." Do you find yourself obsessing about the problem? Does thinking about it bring up feelings you associate with the past?

"If you continue to be upset and angry," says Stewart, "and if your distress is keeping you from finding a solution to the problem, then it's likely that you have your own unresolved issues to work through."

My friend Teresa, who felt overwhelmed by her mother-in-law, was able to unravel the complex knot of her own feelings. When she looked more closely at their relationship, she realized that it brought back long-buried childhood memories. The "inner cringing" that she felt around Ruth was very much what she had felt with her authoritarian father.

"Just seeing this was a big step for me," Teresa said. "Once I realized I was partly responsible for re-creating my childhood scenario, I saw that it was important for me to take some initiative."

Teresa started with a manageable issue: family gatherings. "I explained to Ruth that because of Peter's busy schedule, we weren't going to get together every week and that sometimes I'd like them to visit us. At first she was a bit hurt, but when I explained to her that it was important for me to not always be on the receiving end, she seemed to understand."

Eventually, when Teresa felt that this first step had been successful, she turned to the more difficult issue of religion: "I felt that I owed Ruth something because of all she does for us—but my daughters' souls were not on the list! I told her that I knew the example of her devotion would always be an inspiration to the children, but that as their parents, Peter and I wanted to be the ones to give them religious instruction. I let her know that I really did appreciate her concern and generosity. Bit by bit, things have smoothed out."

"It's wonderful when people can work things out for themselves," says Stewart. In the case of someone like Lucia, however, for whom feelings of jealousy

and parental rejection were so painful and long-standing, Stewart believes that there is "no substitute for the deep work and supportive relationship that can take place in therapy." Whatever the family situation may be, parents can benefit from having a clear understanding of how the roles that are played by parents and grandparents differ.

As Arthur Kornhaber suggests, the relationship between grandparents and grandchildren is naturally simpler and more relaxed than the relationship between parents and their children. Grandparents, because they are not the primary caretakers, can be less concerned with the children's performance and achievements; they can be more indulgent and may unintentionally subvert your day-to-day rules.

When parents worry that their children's grandparents are spoiling them, they can take comfort in the thought that it is natural for grandparents to provide an emotional haven for their grandchildren. Parents should not be overly concerned that their children will suffer from the inconsistencies between home and Grandma's house.

"So long as the child has not been harmed and does not appear anxious, parents should relax," says Stewart. "You may notice a little entry-exit difficulty for the first few hours, so on the way home from Grandma's, you can prepare your children for the transition by saying something like, 'Now, remember, at our house bedtime is at eight.' Most children can make the adjustment."

When grandparents provide child care.

Of course, if grandparents will be taking on a major role in daily child care, the situation is different and needs to be more structured. Problems arise when parents and grandparents drift into such arrangements without a clear understanding of each other's needs and expectations.

In fact, the task is much like that of parents who share custody of their children: To promote a harmonious life for the children, both parties will have to compromise on some issues. For parents this means giving up a certain degree of control. For grandparents the situation demands a special flexibility. As Kornhaber has written, "The trick for a grandparent in this situation is to be able to switch back to an advisory role when the parent returns to full duty."

Another situation that demands great flexibility is when a grandparent's mental or physical health irrevocably declines. So long as possible, it's important that the contact between grandparent and grandchildren continue. Visits may need to be drastically limited, and even then, some children may complain that it's too distressing to see their grandparent so unwell. At such times, reminding them of how important they are to their grandparent may alleviate their sense of grief and helplessness.

Indeed, Kornhaber says, "When loving grandparents are involved in family life, it's good for everyone. Children are supplied with a closeness second only in emotional strength to the parent-child connection, giving a feeling of security not only to the young and old but also to the parents. And our research shows that being a grandparent assures a meaningful and fulfilling old age."

In the moment that my daughter stroked my cheek and told me that my skin wasn't quite up to par, I received a glimpse of the special love between Ariel and her grandmother—and a gift for myself as well. Suddenly I wasn't so afraid of growing old and wrinkled. I saw that one day, if I was really lucky, I just might qualify to be someone's superlatively soft and cuddly grandmother.

New Styles and the Future

- **Emerging Patterns (Articles 41–45)**
- **Focus: It's Time for Happiness (Articles 46–50)**

Your family is what you've got. . . . It's your limits and your possibilities. Sometimes you'll get so far away from it you'll think you're outside its influence forever, then before you figure out what's happening, it will be right beside you, pulling the strings. Some people get crushed by their families. Others are saved by them.

—Peter Collier

Most people would agree that families will remain powerful in the lives of those within them. Change within social institutions is often viewed with fear and apprehension. A person who questions the meaningfulness, appropriateness, and workability of the traditional, lifelong, monogamous marriage in today's society is liable to be judged as an enemy of family, home, children, and even the American way of life.

Family values are more than buzzwords for election-year candidates. Though Americans continue to talk often about families and their importance, arguments about what the family should be seem stronger today than in most years past. Behind these lines of conflict, today's families do go on. Today's families are best described by their variation and efforts to adapt to the changes that appear today to be the only constant in human life.

Society, in general, and the institutions of marriage and family are likely to continue rapid change through the last years of the twentieth century. These changes can precipitate crisis or progress, for, as family sociologist Hard Christensen suggests, changes and innovations often lead to a great many contradictions, and negotiating these contradictions becomes the task of living. Strong and successful families of tomorrow will have to find ways to enjoy the benefits, cope with the problems, and grow.

This section concerns two areas that are important when considering present and future relationships. The first subsection deals with emerging patterns and opens with "Terms of Endearment," which presents a case for more flexible marriage laws. Next, "The New Family: Investing in Human Capital" explores ways we as a society need to support today's families. "The New Family Values" posits the emerging family values of the 1990s as "striking a balance" between the family primary of the 1950s and the individualism of the 1980s. The final two articles in the subsection focus on single-parent families. "Stop the World So I Can Get Off for a While" examines the levels and sources of stress experienced by low-income mothers of young children. "Single Parents and Damaged Children: The Fruits of the Sexual Revolution" ties many of the American family's (and society's) current woes to the sexual revolution of the 1960s and 1970s and the subsequent rise in teenage out-of-wedlock parenting.

The final subsection of *Annual Editions: Marriage and Family 94/95* does something we often challenge newspapers, television, news programs, and even our friends and family members to do: focus on the positive. It contains five articles that describe the strengths of today's families and provides a glimpse of an assortment of healthy, happy American families. We hope you come away from them feeling strengthened, encouraged, warmed, and hopeful about our shared future.

Looking Ahead: Challenge Questions

What would you include in a marital contract of rights and responsibilities? Do you feel couples should be allowed to divorce if one partner does not want to? Why or why not?

If you were given the power to propose three governmental programs to support today's families, what would they be?

If it were possible to return to the family of the 1950s (for example, the Cleavers and Nelsons of television fame), would you do it? Why or why not?

Given today's state of marriage and family (and after reading these articles), what decisions have you made about marriage? Family?

When you look around at families you know, what impresses you about them? What makes you hopeful for your and their future?

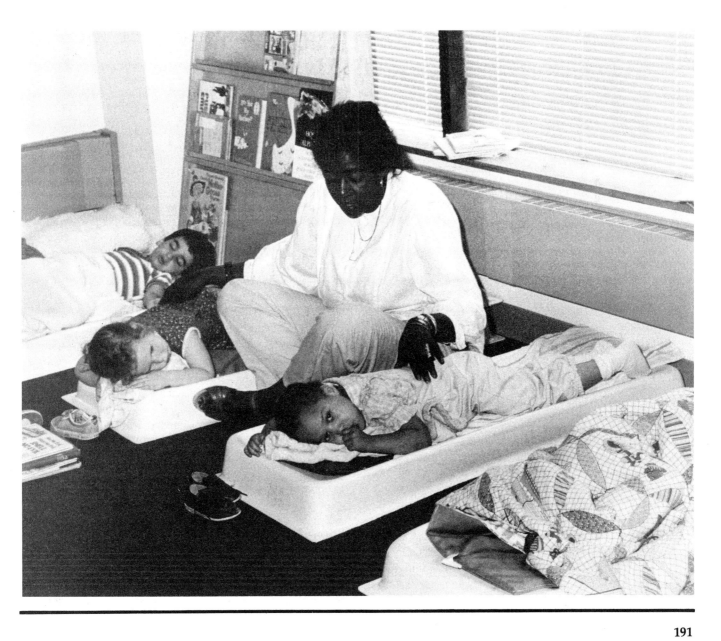

Terms of Endearment

Can More-Flexible Marriage Laws Save the American Family?

Allen M. Parkman

Allen M. Parkman, an economist and lawyer at the University of New Mexico, is the author of No-Fault Divorce: What Went Wrong? *(Westview Press).*

Few situations have ever been as idyllic as the traditional family portrayed in the 1950s television series *Father Knows Best.* So it's natural for politicians, especially those of a conservative bent, to glorify the family of an earlier era and call for its reestablishment. Last year's Murphy Brown–inspired controversy about "family values" reflected the power of this theme.

Certainly families of the kind depicted in *Father Knows Best* have declined in recent decades. The proportion of American adults who are married is falling, the share of children born to unwed mothers has soared, and most Americans under age 18 will spend part of their childhoods living with only one parent. A look at a few statistics confirms the move away from traditional marriage and family patterns:

- The percentage of households consisting of married couples fell from 79 percent in 1950 to 55 percent in 1991.
- Non-family households—mostly people who live alone— grew from 10 percent to 30 percent of households during the same period.
- Between 1956 and 1990, the median age at first marriage rose from 20.1 to 24 for women and from 22.5 to 26 for men.
- Since 1950, the percentage of American families headed by women has nearly doubled, to 17 percent.
- Thirty-one percent of one-parent families are now headed by never-married women, in contrast to 6.5 percent in 1970.

During the last year's presidential campaign, candidates responded to these changes with a variety of polemics and proposed solutions. But the debate ignored one of the most important factors behind the decline of the American family: government regulation of marriage and divorce. In particular, the shift to no-fault divorce is a major reason family life has become less attractive to many Americans. Under the no-fault divorce laws of most states, one spouse may unilaterally dissolve a marriage. These laws have reduced the incentives for spouses to commit themselves to their relationship and have caused many other people to either delay or forgo marriage.

Decrying these developments, some conservatives have called for a return to the old, fault-based divorce regime, under which marriages were harder to dissolve. But that system was abandoned because many people were dissatisfied with it, just as many are dissatisfied with current marriage laws. Rather than

The state should allow couples embarking upon marriage the freedom to arrange whatever contract best suits their individual needs and desires.

adopt a different one-size-fits-all solution, the government should give couples embarking upon marriage the freedom to make whatever arrangements best suit their needs and desires. This could be accomplished if the states simply extended to marriage agreements the same latitude as commercial contracts.

The government's role in regulating marriage has moral and religious roots, but it is also an attempt to stop individuals from imposing costs on other members of society. Children born out of wedlock can be a burden on others, since they are more likely to need outside support, whether private charity or public welfare. This problem was magnified in a world of limited contraceptives and low incomes. Government therefore established penalties for sex outside of marriage. Richard Posner, a federal appeals-court judge and law-and-economics scholar, argues that the history of public policy toward sex since the beginning of the Christian era is a history of efforts to confine sexual activity to marriage.

In additional to the stick of government penalties, the carrot of economic incentives has tended to encourage marriage. Economist and Nobel laureate Gary Becker argues that marriage is reinforced not only by romance and sexual attraction but also by the extra goods and services that married couples and their children can enjoy.

Some of these benefits come simply from sharing a household. People who live together can increase their welfare through both specialization and joint consumption. For example, one person can do the shopping while the other does the cooking, instead of each performing both activities. Not only do they economize on their time, they become more proficient at each activity. In addition, sharing goods and services can reduce total expenses. For instance, two people who are willing to watch the same television programs can get by with one television set rather than two.

These examples of specialization and joint consumption explain why people live together, not necessarily why they marry. The economic logic behind marriage is based on forms of specialization that involve long-term costs. There are few long-term costs when roommates assume roles as shopper and cook. If the arrangement ends, neither party is worse off than he would have been had he never entered the relationship in the first place. But if one person specializes in earning an income and the other specializes in domestic work, the second person can find herself worse off if the arrangement is dissolved than she would have been had she never been married.

Couples often arrive at this breadwinner/homemaker arrangement after deciding to have children. It usually costs more for both parents to assume equal shares of child rearing than for one to assume primary responsibility. Say the mother is a corporate lawyer, a job that requires her to be at a particular place for specific hours, with occasional, unanticipated overtime. She could find a more-flexible job, but only at the cost of a substantial reduction in her income. Meanwhile, the father is a free-lance writer, a job that pays according to how much work he produces and allows him to set his own hours. Under those circumstances, it probably makes sense for the father to assume the main child-rearing responsibility.

But the domestic efforts of the father, especially the child rearing, tend to occur during the early part of the relationship. The contribution of the income-earning parent, on the other hand, tends to increase over time. If the relationship is eventually dissolved, the mother, who has specialized in income earning during the marriage, would lose the services provided by the father, who worked at home, but these services may have limited value after the children have left. Meanwhile, the parent who has worked at home has skills with limited market value; he suffers long-term costs because he decided to specialize in domestic work.

Because of this potential asymmetry, most couples who want children marry with the understanding that it is a long-term arrangement. While marriage has many similarities to a commercial contract, the state has regulated it heavily, usually under the rationale of protecting children. In past centuries, because people married when they were older and had shorter life expectancies, children were dependent on their parents for most of their parents' lives. In addition, few men—the main source of income—were able to support more than one family, so marriage had to be a permanent relationship. To protect the children, the parties had to recognize that a marriage would be difficult or impossible to dissolve.

Between 1602 and 1857, for example, only 317 divorces were granted in England, and they were all based on private acts of Parliament. Conditions were less strict in the United States, but divorce was still difficult. The Constitution gave the states

jurisdiction over marriage and divorce, and some had established grounds for divorce from the very beginning. When divorce was permitted, the grounds were based on the fault of a spouse: desertion, adultery, or cruelty. Because of the federal system, people could move from a state with strict grounds to one with liberal grounds if they wanted to end their marriage.

Until recently, the marriage laws corresponded pretty well with the preferences of most people. But conditions have changed. With improved forms of contraception, people can have active sex lives without fear of pregnancy. Higher incomes have enabled one person to support more than one family. Increased social tolerance has allowed homosexual couples to establish open relationships.

As the earnings and opportunities available to men and women have become more similar, the gains from specialization during marriage have dropped. When women had few alternatives to marriage, marriage could mean a substantial increase in their welfare. In the absence of domestic labor-saving devises and convenient, ready-made food, men also could increase their welfare through marriage. In both cases, the growth of alternatives reduced the gains from marriage.

As the earnings and opportunities available to men and women have become more similar, the gains from specialization during marriage have dropped.

Higher earnings for women also mean that children tend to cost more, since women who assume the child-rearing role often have to sacrifice or limit their employment. The increased cost of raising children has further reduced the desirability of marriage. (Most couples who choose to live together without marrying do not have children.)

With these changes, some people discovered after marriage that they were not realizing the gains they had anticipated. Reflecting this reevaluation, the divorce rate rose from 1.6 per 1,000 people in 1920 to 3.5 per 1,000 population in 1970. Since fault grounds for divorce did not conform to these individuals' preferences, they took steps to get around the laws.

Increasingly, divorces were uncontested. Parties who wanted a divorce used fabricated testimony, usually "proving" cruelty, to establish the necessary legal grounds. Since the plaintiff in such divorce cases had to be the innocent party, the defendant was usually the person who wanted the divorce and who obtained the cooperation of the other party by promising compensation. In effect, the divorce was based on mutual consent. The requirement of mutual consent for divorce provided some protection for spouses who had specialized in domestic work during marriage.

Individuals forced to fabricate testimony to establish the grounds for divorce suffered embarrassment and inconvenience (as well as the risk of perjury charges). In addition, some legal scholars found the fault grounds for divorce hypocritical. As a result, a movement developed to change the grounds for divorce from fault to no-fault. Between 1969 and 1985, all the states enacted laws that either replaced the fault grounds for divorce with no-fault grounds (such as "incompatibility" or irretrievable breakdown") or added no-fault grounds to the existing fault grounds. While some states required agreement on the no-fault grounds, in most states divorce became effectively unilateral.

No-fault divorce was promoted by people, such as divorced men and career women, who did not appreciate the advantages of marriage as an arrangement that could be dissolved only with mutual consent. The people who were willing to assume more-specialized roles during marriage and therefore wanted it to be a long-term arrangement were conspicuously absent from the debate. Instead of requiring mutual consent of the parties, divorce is now based on the preferences of one party, subject to the legal requirement for a property settlement, alimony, and child support and custody.

No-fault divorce was promoted by people who did not appreciate the advantages of dissolving marriage only with mutual consent.

These laws are extremely unfair to spouses who specialize in domestic work during marriage. Property settlements tend to recognize only physical assets such as houses and cars and financial assets such as stocks and bonds. Largely ignored is the most valuable asset affected by marriage—the parties' income-earning capacities. The person who worked at home will receive little compensation for a career that was sacrificed or restricted to raise a family. Courts once attempted to correct for the financial situation of these people through alimony, but increasingly alimony is designed for a limited period of rehabilitation. The problems that custodial parents have had in collecting child support are legend.

No-fault divorce laws have made it more likely that a given divorce will produce more costs than benefits. The mutual-consent divorces that occurred under the fault-based system required the divorcing spouse to compensate the divorced spouse so that they both felt better off than they would have been had the marriage continued. Hence their combined welfare improved. But under no-fault divorce, the net gain to the divorcing spouse may not exceed the net cost to the divorced spouse and the children. Hence divorce can reduce the total well-being of everyone involved.

Women gradually noticed the adverse effects of no-fault divorce. Married women became aware that divorced women and their children were being treated very poorly at divorce. With limited negotiating power, divorced women were receiving financial settlements lower than what they would have received under the old system. As a result, married women became less willing to specialize in domestic work, recognizing that they needed to maintain or increase their marketable skills during marriage. This aware-

ness contributed to the rise in the labor-force participation rate of married women and to the increase in the number of married women continuing their education during marriage.

These decisions can reduce the welfare of families. With the protection provided by fault divorce, married women often sacrificed employment and education opportunities because the services they provided at home were worth more to the family than the income they lost. This changed with no-fault divorce. Although the whole family still shared the current income loss, if the marriage ended the woman might have to bear the burden of the future income loss alone. With no assurance that the law would take into account the sacrifice involved in specialization, women became less willing to work primarily at home, even when it was in the best interest of their families. Because the government controlled the grounds for divorce, a couple could not create a contract that adequately protected the spouse who chose to specialize in domestic work.

The current no-fault divorce laws do not meet the needs of individuals who want a relationship in which the party who specializes in domestic work receives adequate compensation if the marriage ends. The "marriage contract" provided by law permits unilateral divorce subject to financial and custodial arrangements that can be very unfair to at least one of the parties and the children.

The problem is the limits on the right of individuals to draft their own marriage contracts. The laws treat marriage agreements and commercial agreements differently. When individuals find that the laws governing a particular commercial contract do not serve their best interests, they have broad latitude to draft an agreement that circumvents the laws. For example, the Uniform Commercial Code provides that delivery of a good will be within a "reasonable" time *unless the parties specify another time.* The law has not traditionally given parties to a marriage agreement similar freedom. They may not alter the basic agreement prescribed by the state.

Family life would be improved if the law gave individuals the chance to draft their own marriage contracts, subject to protection for children.

Many of the conditions of a marriage contract, especially the grounds for divorce, cannot be altered by the parties. So even if a couple wants to make their marriage a long-term commitment that can be dissolved only with mutual consent, they are not able to do so. The states have always maintained the exclusive right to prescribe the grounds for divorce. While the parties were given some discretion about financial and custodial arrangements at divorce under the fault system, the courts were unwilling to permit people to make those arrangements at marriage. The courts were antagonistic to premarital agreements because of fears that they would encourage divorce and that no contract could adequately deal with all the circumstances that might confront the parties in a long marriage.

Premarital agreements are coming into wider use because of changes in marital patterns. By the early 1980s, men and women over 30 years of age accounted for 41 percent and 32 percent, respectively, of new marriages. Not only are these people older and therefore more aware of the potential problems associated with marriage, they also bring more assets to their marriages. The increasing divorce rate also means more and more people are marrying repeatedly. In about 45 percent of marriages, at least one party has been married before.

Many courts now uphold premarital agreements, especially when strict standards of fairness are met or for a second marriage. The courts ask whether there was a fair disclosure of the parties' wealth at the time of the contract, how the provisions of the contract compare with the legal support obligations they would replace, and whether enforcement of the contract would make one spouse a burden on society. Courts tend to look more kindly on agreements concerning property settlements than agreements affecting support obligations. Premarital agreements that seek to define or waive support obligations and other essential duties of marriage are likely to be declared invalid. So there is still substantial doubt about the enforceability of premarital agreements.

Many people in the United States would benefit from the more predictable enforcement of premarital and postmarital contracts. The states could enact marriage and divorce laws that are similar to the Uniform Commercial Code, establishing standards that apply except when the parties specify otherwise. For example, no-fault grounds for divorce might be appropriate during the period early in the marriage when the parties are becoming more familiar. When the importance of long-term assurances increases, such as when a child is conceived, the grounds could change to mutual consent. In their contracts, couples who wanted a traditional marriage might choose to make mutual consent the only basis for divorce. Couples who anticipated careers that would not be affected by children might provide for unilateral divorce. Marriage contracts would allow for homosexual as well as heterosexual relationships.

Because of sentimentality and uncertainty about the future, people find it difficult to draft premarital agreements. Even if they consider a premarital agreement, they may be discouraged because the states control the grounds for divorce, the most obvious condition that they might want to set for themselves. If the government gave spouses control over the grounds for divorce, they might be more likely to consider the other aspects of divorce over which they would like a binding agreement.

We like predictability, and the law often provides it. But predictability does not require uniformity. Rather than dictating a take-it-or-leave-it arrangement, the law should give individuals the opportunity to draft their own marriage contracts, subject to protection for third parties such as children. The result would be an improvement in the quality of family life.

THE NEW FAMILY
INVESTING IN HUMAN CAPITAL

DAVID A. HAMBURG

*Mr. Hamburg is president of the
Carnegie Corporation of New York.*

The dramatic changes in the American family can be highlighted by comparing its structure and function as it was in 1960 with what it had become in 1990. Until 1960 most Americans shared a common set of beliefs about family life. Family should consist of a husband and wife living together with their children. The father should be the head of the family, earn the family's income, and give his name to his wife and children. The mother's main tasks were to support and facilitate her husband's, guide her children's development, look after the home, and set a moral tone for the family. Marriage was an enduring obligation for better or worse. The husband and wife jointly coped with stresses. Sexual activity was to be kept within the marriage, especially for women. As parents, they had an overriding responsibility for the well-being of their children during the early years—until their children entered school, they were almost solely responsible. Even later, it was the parents who had the primary duty of guiding their children's education and discipline. Of course, even in 1960, families recognized the difficulty of converting these ideals into reality. Still, they devoted immense effort to approximating them in practice.

Over the past three decades these ideals, although they are still recognizable, have been drastically modified across all social classes. Women have joined the paid labor force in great numbers stimulated both by economic need and a new belief in their capabilities and right to pursue opportunities. Americans in 1992 are far more likely than in earlier times to postpone marriage. Single-parent families—typically consisting of a mother with no adult male and very often no other adult person present—have become common. Today at least half of all marriages end in divorce. Most adults no longer believe that couples should stay married because divorce might harm their children.

Survey research shows a great decrease in the proportion of women favoring large families, an upsurge in their assertiveness about meeting personal needs, and an attempt by women to balance their needs with those of their children and the men in their lives. A clear and increasing majority of women believe that both husband and wife should be able to work, should have roughly similar opportunities, and should share household responsibilities and the tasks of child rearing. A majority of mothers of preschool children now work outside the home. A growing minority of young married women, often highly educated and career oriented, are choosing not to have any children and have little interest in children's issues—yet one more indication of the dramatic transformation of American families that has been taking place in recent decades.

While the rate of pregnancy among adult women has declined since 1970, that among American adolescents, especially girls under age fifteen, is one of the highest among technically advanced nations. Teenagers account for two-thirds of all out-of-wedlock births. There are 1.3 million children now living with teenage mothers only about half of whom are married. Six million children under the age of five are living with mothers who were adolescents when they gave birth.

Childbearing in adolescence has been a common feature of human history. But traditional societies provided relatively stable employment and had reliable networks of social support and cultural guidance for young parents. For such adolescents to set up a household apart from either family was rare in pre-industrial societies. Even rarer was the single-parent family. Rarest of all was a socially isolated, very young mother largely lacking an effective network of social support.

It is startling to realize that today, whether through their parents' divorce or never having been married, most American children spend part of their childhood in a single-parent family. The increase in the proportion of children living

From *Current,* July/August 1993, pp. 4-12. Originally "The American Family Transformed," from *Society,* January/February 1993, pp. 60-69. © 1993 by Transaction Publishers, Inc. Reprinted by permission.

with just one parent (usually the mother) has strongly affected large numbers of white, black, and Hispanic children. Female-headed families with children are much more likely to be poor than are married-couple families with children, regardless of race. By conservative estimates, one-fifth of young American children are raised in poverty, many by their mothers alone. Black families with children are more likely to be poor than white families with children, regardless of family type.

By the time they reach age sixteen, close to half the children of married parents will have seen their parents divorce. For nearly half of these, it will be five years or more before their mothers remarry. Close to half of all white children whose parents remarry will see the second marriage dissolve during their adolescence. Black women not only marry less often and experience more marital disruption but they also remarry more slowly and less often than do white women. Generally, as compared with other countries, the United States exhibits a pattern of attachments and disruptions in marriage that is certainly stressful for developing children and adolescents.

Divorce and remarriage create a complex set of new relationships, resulting in many different family configurations. About two-thirds of the children in step-families will have full siblings plus either half- or step-siblings. Many children will have multiple sets of grandparents. On the other hand, children of single mothers or mothers who do not remarry will have a more restricted set of active family relationships than children with two parents.

CHILD CARE In the United States especially, but in many other nations too, mothers of children under three are the fastest-growing segment of the labor market, so child care arrangements at the preschool level are of enormous practical significance. Even though remarriage after a divorce is common, there are still complicated problems of handling child care responsibilities in blended families. For parents who have never been married, the strain is probably greatest. They have all the responsibility as head of household and the least help available. About two-thirds of single mothers with preschool children are employed, most of them full time. No matter how poor they may be, they must find some kind of arrangement for care of their very young children. More often than not, this means a child care center or other home that can take them in.

Child care is thus increasingly moving outside the home, with children's development often placed in the hands of strangers and near-strangers. As late as 1985 only 14 percent of preschool children were cared for in an organized child care facility. This figure has doubled in the last five years. By 1990 half of all children of working parents were either being cared for in a center or in another home. In 1985, 25 percent of working mothers with children under five used a child care facility as the primary form of care, compared with 13 percent in 1977. This transformation was unforeseen, unplanned, and is still poorly understood. With rapid, far-reaching social changes, it is not surprising that public opinion surveys find that many American parents are deeply troubled about raising their children, and two-thirds say they are less willing to make sacrifices for their young than their parents were. Neither they nor the nation's social institutions have had much time to adjust to the new conditions.

HOW PARENTS ARE COPING

Young people moving toward parenthood today face more rapidly changing circumstances and a wider spectrum of life choices than ever before. But choices and decisions as well as transitions can be burdens, even as they offer attractive opportunities and privileges. Young couples today often agonize over decisions taken for granted as recently as a generation ago. Should they get married? If yes, should they wait until one or both have a steady job? What about the fateful decision to have children?

Once married, it is very likely that both husband and wife will be in the paid labor force, and with the advent of the baby, they will have to renegotiate their relationship. How will they divide up the baby-care chores? What sort of parental leaves, if any, will either take? How will they handle the housework? How can they balance work and family life? If the mother takes off from work for a while, when is it sensible to go back, and how can she make the transition in the best interests of the child? Can they afford quality child care? If not, what alternatives are there?

Some studies have been done on the efforts of parents to balance their various interests and responsibilities in new ways. The results show that this is a complicated process that is in its earliest stages. Sociologist Arlie Hochschild of the University of California, the coauthor of *The Second Shift: Working Parents and the Revolution at Home*, has conducted systematic research that illuminates the tension between work and family. She describes the tremendous penalty women pay whether they choose to work at home or to have a paid job. The housewife pays the cost of remaining outside what is today the mainstream of society; the working woman pays the cost in time and energy for family commitments. The evidence clearly indicates that men are sharing very little of the burden of raising children and care of the home. Hence, as Hochschild points out, women are coming home from a paid job to work "a second shift." Most men devote long hours to their jobs. Even if they want to be helpful at home, their institutional settings usually do not make it easy for them to do so.

There is no reason to believe that this phenomenon of the two-parent working family is a transient one. Indeed, a variety of economic and psychological factors reinforce the persistence of the pattern as a financial necessity. The actual and proportionate costs of child raising today are much higher than they were in the 1950s and 1960s. In many families, both husband and wife must have an earned income if the family is to attain or maintain a middle-class standard of living. This is now much harder than it used to be. In the past few decades the shift from a manufacturing to a service-based economy has brought a decline in wages for many people. The industries that have declined in the United States in relation to foreign competition are precisely the ones that historically provided relatively high-earning positions for men, especially those who did not go on to higher education. On the other hand, the new growth in the American economy has been mainly in the sectors that are major employers of women, where the pay is less. One effect of this is that parents have a great deal less leisure time than they used to have and not enough time perhaps for their children.

NEW REALITIES

For all the attractive features of technological progress and economic success, the recent changes have served to attenuate human relationships in the family. Concerns have grown about the effects of the changing family patterns—single-parent families as well as working mothers, and remote fathers—on their availability for intimate, sensitive parenting of young children. The change in the frequency and quality of contact between children and their adult relatives is remarkable.

Not only are mothers home much less, fathers do not seem to spend more time at home to compensate. Only about 5 percent of all American children see a grandparent regularly, a much lower level than in the past. Children spend a huge chunk of time during their years of most rapid growth and development in out-of-home settings or looking after themselves, which often means gazing at the mixture of reality and fantasy presented by television. Adolescents increasingly drift into a separate "teen culture" that is often lacking in adult leadership, mentorship, and support, and is sometimes manifested in violence-prone gangs.

Such attenuation in family relationships is most vividly reflected in rising indicators of adverse outcomes for infants, children, and adolescents. Over the past several decades, the largely unrecognized tragedy of moderately severe child neglect has been accompanied by more visible, flagrant child neglect. This is most

obvious in the growing number of adolescents—even pre-teens—who have babies and then walk away from them. Adolescent mothers are often less responsive to the needs of the infant than are older mothers. They also tend to have more babies in rapid succession than older mothers, placing their infants at greater biological and behavioral risk. Children of adolescent mothers tend to have more cognitive, emotional, behavioral, and health problems at all stages of development than do children of fully adult mothers.

But insidious problems have arisen in a much *POVERTY* wider portion of the society. Not only are more children growing up in poverty than was the case a decade or two ago, but they are increasingly mired in persistent, intractable poverty with no hope of escape. They lack constructive social support networks that would promote their education and health. They have very few models of competence. They are bereft of visible economic opportunity.

The fate of these young people is not merely a tragedy for them, it affects the entire nation. A growing fraction of our potential work force consists of seriously disadvantaged people who will have little if any prospect of acquiring the skills necessary to revitalize the economy. If we cannot bring ourselves to feel compassion for these young people on a personal level, we must at least recognize that our economy and our society will suffer along with them.

As society puts greater emphasis on options, freedom, and new horizons—an accentuation of the longstanding American emphasis on individuality—one side effect clearly is a sharp increase in the divorce rate. Conventional wisdom on this issue had it that if the parents handled the situation with enough sensitivity, the effect of divorce on the children would be minimal. And this certainly can be the case. But practically speaking, divorcing couples find it exceedingly difficult to handle such situations over a long enough period of time and to protect their children from the psychological and economic fallout of divorce.

Studies of divorcing families reveal several recurrent themes. Marital separation commonly involves major emotional distress for children and disruption in the parent-child relationship. Single parents, try as they will, tend to diminish parenting for several years after the break-up. Improvement occurs gradually and is enhanced by the formation of a close, dependable new relationship. Over the years, the non-custodial parent's involvement with the child tends to fade. The effects of marital disruption vary with the age of the children involved. Children aged six to eight react with grief, fear, and intense longing for reconciliation. Those aged nine to twelve tend to be openly angry. They are inclined to reject a stepparent. At both ages, the children's behavior at home and at school often deteriorates. The tranquil passage through middle childhood is altogether disrupted by drastic family changes.

The economic impact of divorce on children is often profound. Most children of divorce end up living with their mother. Since women do not earn as much as men on average, and absent parents frequently fail to provide child support, children growing up in single-parent households headed by women are likely to fall into poverty. In one study of divorce during the 1970s, poverty rates for children rose from 12 percent before divorce to 27 percent after divorce. The 1987 poverty rate among female-headed families with children was 46 percent, compared with 8 percent among married-couple families.

In addition to having fewer financial resources, single parents may be less able to supervise their adolescent children. There is evidence that an adolescent living in a single-parent family and having little parental supervision will be susceptible to delinquent behavior and substance abuse. Of course, some single parents do in fact maintain adequate supervision and overcome many difficulties, but on the average the situation is not conducive to successful child rearing.

FAMILY SUPPORT

While all these remarkable changes of the last three decades were increasingly jeopardizing healthy child development, the nation took little notice. Until a few years ago, political, business, and professional leaders had very little to say about the problems of children and youths. Presidents tended to pass the responsibility to the states and the private sector. State leaders often passed responsibility to the federal government or to the cities. One arcane, but important, manifestation of this neglect has been the low priority given to research and science policy for this field. As a result, the nature of this new generation of problems has been poorly understood, emerging trends have been insufficiently recognized. Authority was substituted for evidence, and ideology for analysis.

All this is now changing. While the government has thus far provided little encouragement or incentive for employers to help parents balance their work and family responsibilities, the debate is growing among decision makers over what measures would strengthen today's families—family leave for new mothers and fathers, job sharing, part-time work, flexible schedules, and the like. Within the scientific and professional communities, a remarkable degree of consensus is emerging concerning conditions that influence child and adolescent development and how parents can cope with the changes within themselves and in the world around them. Much has become known about ways to prevent the damage being done to children.

SUPPORT PROGRAMS There has been an upsurge in programs. Community organizations, churches, schools, and youth service organizations provide child care, support, and guidance for parents and their young. Successful interventions have taken many forms in programs in many cities. They include home visits, parent-child centers, child and family resource programs, school-based and school-linked services, life-skills training, mentoring, self-help programs, and other supports. These programs have found ways of compensating for a damaging social environment by creating conditions that can build on the strengths and resiliency of those caught in difficult circumstances.

Sadly enough, the emerging consensus and the positive results of some interventions are not widely understood by the general public or, for that matter, by many policymakers in public and private sectors. It is crucial now to have a well-informed, wide-ranging public discussion and to link experts with open-minded policymakers in an ongoing process of formulating constructive policy options. No single approach to families and children can be a panacea; many different approaches are needed to span the years of early childhood, when main growth and development occur, and continuing through middle childhood and adolescence. Social neglect is no answer to the crisis families face.

During their years of growth and development, children need dependable attachment, protection, guidance, stimulation, nurturance, and ways of coping with adversity. Infants, in particular, need caregivers who can promote attachment and thereby form the fundamental basis for decent human relationships throughout the child's life. Similarly, early adolescents need to connect with people who can facilitate the momentous transition to adulthood gradually, with sensitivity and understanding. Despite the radical transformations of recent times, such people are usually within the child's immediate family. If not, they exist in the extended family. But if these caregivers cannot give a child what it needs to thrive, we must make an explicit effort to connect the child with people outside the family who have the attributes and skills, and also the durability, to promote healthy child development.

PRENATAL CARE

Early prenatal care for both parents is fundamental in helping families with children in the crucial formative years. The essential components of prenatal care are medical care, health education, and social support services. Good prenatal care dramatically improves the chances that a woman will bear a healthy baby. Those who do not have access to such services suffer higher rates of infant mortality or may give birth to premature or low-birthweight babies. Yet, one-quarter of all pregnant women in the United States now receive insufficient or no prenatal care.

We can prevent nutritional deficiencies by educating expectant mothers and by providing supplementary nutrition and primary health care. This integrated approach has been demonstrated to work well in the federal Women, Infants, and Children Food Supplementation Program. Through prenatal care, pregnant women can also be informed and provided necessary support and skills to help them stop smoking, minimize alcohol consumption, and avoid drugs if they are to have a healthy baby. The educational component of prenatal care can be expanded beyond pregnancy to include a constructive examination of options for the life course. Such a thrust can lead to job training, formal schooling, or other education likely to improve prospects for the future of the mother and her new family.

A major facilitating factor is the ready availability of a dependable person who can provide social support for health and education through the months of pregnancy and beyond. In one intriguing set of innovations, pregnant girls are connected with "resource mothers." These are women living in the same neighborhood as the adolescent mother. They have assimilated life's experiences in a constructive way, have successfully raised their own children, and have learned a lot that can be useful regarding life skills most relevant for the young mother. They convey what they have learned about the problems facing the young mother and in general provide sympathetic, sustained attention as well as gateways to community resources.

"RESOURCE MOTHERS"

Such examples highlight the value of social support for health and education throughout childhood and adolescence. It is vital that national, state, and local policymakers recognize the importance of prenatal care for all women. They need to understand that it will be much less expensive to society in the long run than is medical care for low birthweight and otherwise unhealthy babies, particularly those born to poor women. Intervention helps two generations at once and can have lifelong significance not only for the children but for their young parents as well.

PREVENTIVE CARE

Well-baby care oriented toward prevention of lifelong damage is vital not only for child health but for building parental competence. Immediately after delivery, the pediatrician assesses the newborn's health and informs the parents. In addition to providing immunizations during infancy, pediatricians also monitor children's growth carefully to detect nutritional problems and treat infectious diseases. Pediatricians nowadays provide well-informed guidance and emotional support to help families attain healthy lifestyles. They foster attachment between mother and baby and help prepare her for coping with unpredictable difficulties with her infant. They answer parents' questions and anticipate questions about growth and development. They provide other vital services, for example, early treatment of ear infections and correction of vision deficits so that hearing and visual impairments do not interfere with learning.

As the infant becomes a toddler, the pediatrician or other primary care provider, in addition to assessing the child's health and growth, can check the child for injuries or signs of neglect and abuse. They can help guide parents in providing safe play areas, dealing with difficult behavior, and easing the child's transition to out-of-home care and preschool. Since pediatricians are often in short supply, particularly in poor city neighborhoods and remote rural areas, it is essential to enlist the aid of pediatric nurse practitioners, home visitors, parent support groups, and primary prevention program directors. Neighborhood health centers have proved to be effective in reaching low-income children with preventive services, but they are not widespread.

More policymakers are seeing the wisdom of such preventive care for children, but greater progress has to be made on the most critical fronts: immunization, low birthweight, child abuse, and health education. Still not widely understood is the fact that the major health hazards for American children no longer stem from disease but from injuries—both accidental or unintentional and intentional. Injuries account for half of all deaths of children and are an increasing source of long-term disability and serious health problems for children and adolescents. Intentional injury and neglect—child abuse—is a very unpleasant subject, but it is slowly being faced as a national problem. Abused children are likely to suffer severe psychological and sexual problems later in life, and all too commonly perpetuate violent behavior in the way they treat their own children. The risk of child mistreatment is increased when parents endure a high level of stress, such as unemployment and social isolation.

Despite the limited amount of research that has been done in this area, preventive efforts have been launched that aim mainly at preventing repeated abuse in families rather than preventing the first incident. These interventions include parent education about child development and parenting behavior, counseling, parent self-help support groups, crisis centers, and protective day care, home visitor programs, and programs to promote stronger early attachment between mother and infant. Such preventive efforts are a good deal less costly than paying for problems of seriously neglected and abused children later on. They deserve vigorous exploration and research.

As child rearing moves beyond the home, the quality of custodial care becomes crucial. The vast majority of responsible parents are eager to ensure that the care their children get will facilitate their healthy development. Just as they want a competent doctor to foster their children's health, so too, they want a capable caregiver. Yet, the more I have probed this issue, the more I have become impressed with how difficult it is to meet this need. There is little precedent for outside-the-home care on such a vast scale as is now emerging in the United States. The crucial factor in quality of care is the nature and behavior of the caregiver. As the demand for child caregivers has surged, those trying to provide it have frantically sought to recruit more child care workers. Even with the best of intentions, this field has been characterized by low pay, low respect, minimal training, minimal supervision, and extremely variable quality. Although most child-care workers try very hard to do a decent job, the plain fact is that many of them do not stay with any one group of children very long. This in itself puts a child's development in jeopardy; it is especially damaging for young children, for whom long-term caretaking relationships are crucial.

At present most professionals recommend that parents defer day care beyond infancy if possible. But in the absence of policies for paid maternity leave, the trend seems to lean increasingly toward day care for infants. Many clinicians and researchers are working to develop effective models and standards of dependable day care that will promote normal, vigorous child development. At present the issue of what constitutes high-quality care and how it can be accomplished in practice is still unresolved. We can learn some lessons from other nations that have addressed this problem seriously. We need a better sense of how powerful institutions might help to fulfill the potential of this extraordinary movement. While there is an emerging consensus on what can be achieved, we do not yet know how to respond to this great challenge.

One of the most important research findings shows that the children who benefit most from child care are those who come from relatively poor families. Perhaps the rich experiences at the center provide such children with opportunities they might be missing at home. Can we extract the essential ingredients and heighten the efficiency of these good effects, so that they may become standard practice?

High-quality child care and preschool education in the mode of Head Start has proven valuable for children age four and now is being offered to those age three. Overall, individuals who have been in good early education programs have better achievement scores in elementary school, are less likely to be classified as needing special education, have higher rates of high school completion and college attendance, and lower pregnancy and crime rates than comparable students who were not in preschool programs.

The lessons of Head Start have wide applicability. Such valuable early stimulation, encouragement, instruction, and health care provided in quality preschool programs (all with substantial family involvement) can be incorporated into a variety of child care settings. Early education should not be seen as a one-time event akin to immunization but as an important component of a constructive series of developmental experiences throughout childhood and adolescence.

PARENTAL COMPETENCE

One of the most important and recurring themes in the research on early intervention is the potential value of teaching young parents to deal effectively with their children. Ideally, such education should begin before the baby is born. Thus, as indicated, a good prenatal care regimen would involve not only obstetrical, nutritional, and other measures that would protect mother and infant throughout pregnancy, labor, and delivery but also some basic preparation for both parents regarding their tasks as parents and their own life course; in the case of poor parents at least, this would include connection with opportunities to develop occupational skills.

Because the first few years of a child's life are a critical period of development, physical, emotional, and psychological, the family's capacity to nurture—or its failure to do so—has the most profound effect on a child's growth. Research findings strongly support the centrality of a loving, dependable relationship for a good start in life. This does not mean that only one person matters to that child or that the biological mother must be that person. Certainly, a baby can form secure attachments with other caregivers and with siblings. But research evidence indicates the great importance of one central caregiver who creates a sustaining, loving relationship with the infant. Expectant or new mothers or other adults in the consistent caregiving role can be taught effective parenting techniques including those that foster attachment.

As their children grow, parents can be helped by programs that promote verbal interaction among family members and the verbal responsiveness of adults to children. Numerous studies confirm that the mother's responsiveness strengthens her child's learning and sense of self-sufficiency and thereby opens doors to development that would otherwise be closed. Parents can also be helped to understand that there is an optimal range for the intensity and variety of stimulation for a child's healthy development. The great challenge is to devise on a broader scale family-centered interventions that will enhance children's cognitive development and emotional resiliency despite the problems of chronic poverty and relative social isolation.

SOCIAL SUPPORTS

As parent education programs spread, it is essential to avoid the extremes of dogmatism on the one hand and vague, wishful, uninformative approaches on the other. We have to look to the scientific and scholarly community as well as experienced practitioners in relevant fields to devise a standard of reference for prospective and actual parents to use.

Studies in a variety of contexts show that social supports for families (that are eroded, disintegrated, or otherwise weakened under circumstances of persistent poverty and social depreciation) can buffer the effects of stressful life transitions for both parents and children. We can no longer take for granted the supportive systems that were built into human experience over millions of years. Even the most successful, capable parents cannot teach their children the wide array of skills needed for today's complex, rapidly changing society. Increasingly, we must consider crucial skills for education and health that have a strong bearing on survival and the quality of life in contemporary American society.

Institutions and organizations beyond the family can provide the social support necessary for strengthening the family and/or offering surrogates for parents, older siblings, or an extended family. Examples of such interventions are in communities across the country, in churches, schools, agencies, and minority-run organizations. They build constructive networks for families that serve parents and attract youngsters in ways that foster their health, their education, and their capacity to be accepted rather than rejected by the mainstream society.

Whereas parent education efforts have historically focused on the child, family support efforts view the entire family as one unit. Their goals are to augment parents' knowledge of a skill in child rearing, to enhance their skills in coping with the child and other family matters, to help families gain access to services and community resources, to facilitate the development of informal support networks among parents, and to organize to counteract dangerous trends in the community. Most of these programs are served by para-professionals who are members of the community, although professionals are also involved.

Social supports for adolescent mothers are particularly vital, especially for those who are poor and socially isolated. Such programs not only teach parenting skills and ensure the provision of health and educational services, they help mothers stay in school and acquire skills for gainful employment. Evaluations of some interventions show that young mothers improve their diets, smoke less, and generally take better care of themselves and their babies than those who do not have such services; they also have fewer children.

FAMILIES WITH ADOLESCENTS

Compared to families with young children, families with adolescents have been neglected. Even for the affluent sector, little work has been done on strengthening support networks for families during the stresses of the great transition from childhood to adulthood. Still less attention has gone into strengthening networks for families who live in poverty or culturally different situations. Although adolescents are moving toward independence, they are still intimately bound up with the family, which is much more important to them than is evident. This is especially true in early adolescence. For that reason, we need to pay attention to the ways in which family relationships can be utilized to help adolescents weather the conditions of contemporary life. This is a difficult time for parents, too. Their own marital relationships, their own coping skills, are often in transition. They may need help in renegotiating family relationships at this time.

Stephen Small has identified for the Carnegie Council on Adolescent Development forty-one programs to help families strengthen their capacity to tackle problems associated with adolescent development. Most of these programs center on curricula developed for this purpose and made available for use by local organizations. Some of the more promising ones are initiated and maintained by voluntary youth-serving organizations such as the Boys Clubs of America, the 4-H Clubs, and the Parent-Teacher Association. One of Small's strongest recommendations is for a network through which parents can obtain social support from other parents—sharing experience, pooling information and coping strategies. A mutual-aid ethic among parents who have a common concern for the well-being of their developing adolescents and yet bring diverse experiences to the encounter can be helpful.

LIFE SKILLS TRAINING

Adolescents have to navigate through a mine field of risks to their healthy education and development. They need attention from adults who can be positive role models, mentors, and sources of accurate information on important topics. They need to understand the biological changes of puberty and the immediate and long-term health consequences of lifestyle choices. They need to learn interpersonal and communication skills, self regulation, decision making, and problem solving. Today there are few guidelines for behavior available to children or even to adults. Many of the messages they receive are conflicting or ambiguous. Clearly, our adolescents need life skills training—the formal teaching of requisite skills for surviving, living with others, and succeeding in a complex society.

Formal education can provide or at least supplement the life skills training that historically was built into the informal processes of family and kin relationships. Successful school programs are typically administered by agencies outside of the schools. Many use some variant of social skills training and use peers in their interventions. Across the nation, most communities have programs outside the schools that offer youngsters recreation or teach them skills. Youth agencies, such as Girls, Inc., serve about 25 million young people annually and thus are in regular contact with almost as many children as are the schools. Their aim is to help teens acquire social skills, develop a constructive personal identity, and build a dependable basis for earned respect. Their strengths are that they are free to experiment, they reach children early, and they typically work in small groups with ten to fifteen young people at a time. Effective programs tend to respond to more than one serious problem or risk factor and try to create incentives for dealing with them that adolescents perceive as relevant to their own lives.

Based on the lessons of experience with all such approaches that work for families and children, it should be possible in the foreseeable future to design interventions that go beyond what has been possible up to now. First, we can use our experience from the programs so far undertaken, ascertain which are the most effective and which need the most attention, and construct informed models for future interventions. With so much at stake, terrible suffering, grievous loss of talent and life, we can surely find ways to make these programs available on a much wider scale.

STRENGTHENING DISADVANTAGED FAMILIES

Democratic societies are being challenged as never before to give all children, regardless of social background, the opportunity to participate in the modern technical world. This means preparing them to qualify for modern employment opportunities; to achieve at least a decent minimum of literacy in science and technology as part of everyone's educational heritage; to make lifelong learning a reality so that people can adjust their knowledge and skills to technical change; and to foster a scientific attitude useful both in general problem solving throughout society and in understanding scientific

aspects of the major issues on which an informed citizenry must decide.

Traditionally, America's technologically educated work force, which has by and large been very efficient by world standards, has come from a small fraction of the white, male, college-educated population. We have skimmed the cream of a very preferred, fortunate group, while blacks, Hispanics, American Indians, and even women have historically been under-represented in the fields that require technical competence. Even if we were not interested in rectifying historical injustices, we must consider that the traditional white male source of scientists and engineers has become inadequate at the very time when more technically trained people are needed. This brings the country to a point where equity intersects with economic vitality, democratic civility, and military security. Because of this intersection, there are now broader and more urgent reasons than ever before to support an unprecedented effort in the education of disadvantaged minority children. What must motivate us is not only decency but also national interest.

In the immediate years ahead, the number of young people in the United States will be smaller than in recent decades. Fewer young people will enter the work force. By the year 2000, about one-third of these young people will be black or Hispanic, the groups now at the bottom of the educational and economic ladder. Already, in the 1990s, racial and ethnic minorities constitute the majority of primary and secondary school students in twenty-three of the twenty-five largest American cities. In another eight years, they will be the majority in fifty-three cities.

While the lives of individual members of minority groups have greatly improved since the 1960s, many of the millions remaining in the inner cities have been relegated to marginal status in our society. They are the poorest and least-educated Americans and are served by the least-adequate health care in the nation. As in past generations, those who can escape severely damaged environments do so, leaving behind those who have come of age on the streets, without stable adult models and constructive support systems and often without parents.

For the majority of American schoolchildren to be excluded from the mainstream of education and worthwhile jobs in the next century would be a personal loss and a tragic waste of human resources that will weaken the country's economic and social foundations. Increasingly, this injustice threatens our democratic foundations as well as the economic vitality of the United States. Plain national interest demands that minority students be educated equally with majority students, particularly in the science-based fields. The country can no longer endure the drain of talent that has been the norm up to now. The entire sequence of developmentally useful interventions must be applied in a concerted effort to poor and disadvantaged communities. There is much that can be achieved if we think of our entire population as a large extended family, tied by history to a shared destiny, and requiring a strong ethic of mutual aid.

WEIGHING COST

The biology of our species makes necessary a huge parental investment in order to achieve the fulfillment of each child's potential. This means far more than an economic investment. It is a continuing, relentless, recurrent demand for investment of time, energy, thought, consideration, and sensitivity. It is an investment in patience, understanding, and coping. It requires persistence, determination, commitment, and resiliency. The awareness of such a large investment, however vaguely formulated, is inhibiting many young people from undertaking childrearing now that the choice is more readily available to them. Others have gone ahead and started families, only to find they are unprepared for the challenge.

If they cannot or will not give their children what they need, then others must do so. But who? In general, parents have responded that they are willing to do a good deal of what is necessary but cannot do all of it. Therefore, we have seen the rise of institutions that provide parent-equivalent functions. We are in mid-passage in this process; no one can say with justifiable confidence what the consequences will be for the generation of children in crisis.

In almost all cases, the expenditures for optimal child and adolescent development are not simply add-ons but can be at least partly achieved by wiser use of existing funds. Huge amounts are already spent for these purposes. Much of this current spending could be greatly improved and redirected by some of the measures suggested here. To replace inadequate interventions would

in some cases cost less and in other cases cost more than we are now spending. This sort of analysis must largely be done on a case-by-case, place-by-place basis. What is likely is that the total economic and social costs of present child-relevant activities could be greatly reduced.

We are all paying heavily for the neglect of our children—however inadvertently and regretfully. These costs have many facets: economic inefficiency, loss of productivity, lack of skill, high health care costs, growing prison costs, and a badly ripped social fabric. In one way or another, we pay. The vital investments outlined have to be viewed as the responsibility, not only of the family, but of the entire society—not just the federal government but other levels of government; not just business but labor; not just light-skinned people but dark-skinned ones as well; not just the rich but the middle class and the poor. We are all in this huge leaking boat together. We will all have to pay and reason and care and work together. Our habitual short-term view will not suffice. There are many useful, constructive steps to be taken but no quick fix, no magic bullet, no easy way will do. We will not get rich quick on the backs of our children.

We have to move beyond the easy and pervasive recourse of passing the buck. It is the responsibility of every individual, every institution and organization, of every business, and all levels of government. We cannot lose sight of the fact that wise investment in human capital is the most fundamental and productive investment any society can make. Constructive development of our children is more important than oil or minerals, office buildings or factories, roads or weapons. The central fact is that all of these and much more depend in the long run on the quality of human resources and the decency of human relations. If these deteriorate, all else declines.

Forty-three percent of employed women age 26 to 45 expect to reduce their job commitments in the next five years, according to the Gallup Poll.
—*American Demographics*
Dec. 1991

The new family values

Striking a balance between '50s family values and '80s individualism

Stanford economist Victor Fuchs found that parental time available to children fell appreciably—10 hours less per week—between 1960 and 1986.
—*When the Bough Breaks: The Cost of Neglecting Our Children* (Sylvia Ann Hewlett, Basic Books/HarperCollins, 1991)

BARBARA DAFOE WHITEHEAD · FAMILY AFFAIRS

The Institute for American Values—a non-partisan family policy research organization—has been getting calls from reporters who ask a question that goes something like this: "Are the values of the '80s giving way to a new set of values? Is there a new zeitgeist out there?"

Clearly, there is plenty of evidence to prompt such a question. Michael Milken and Leona Helmsley were sent to jail. The economy stalled. The word *yuppie* is fading from our vocabulary. So is the word *superwoman*. The baby boom generation is settling down and getting grayer, and the divorce rate has leveled off. There were 4.2 million births in 1990, the highest number since 1964 (and high figures held up in 1991, with 4.1 million births that year). The AIDS epidemic has altered our sense of the nature and meaning of sexual freedom, and the divorce revolution has hurt women and children in ways we never fully anticipated.

I won't pretend to know what deep changes might be taking place in the polity or the economy. But I do believe that, within the culture, a shift *is* beginning to take place. It is a shift away from an ethos of expressive individualism and toward an ethos of family obligation and commitment. It is a shift away from the assertion of individual rights—what Harvard University law professor and family law expert Mary Ann Glendon calls "rights talk"—and toward a recognition of individual responsibility. It is a shift away from a preoccupation with adult needs and toward a greater attention to children's needs. It is a shift away from a calculus of happiness based on individual fulfillment and toward a calculus of happiness based on the well-being of the family as a whole. This emergent cultural ethos is what Institute for American Values board member David Blankenhorn and I have called the new familism.

Many forces might be contributing to this shift, but I believe one of the most important is the changing life cycle of large numbers of the baby boom generation—particularly those who hold professional and managerial jobs and are in the upper third of the generation's socioeconomic scale.

During the '70s and '80s, there was a nice fit between the life stage of many baby boomers and the values of expressive individualism. Singlehood on the one hand. Individual freedom on the other hand. Career development on the one hand. An absorption with the self on the other.

Today, a critical mass of baby boomers has reached a new stage in the life cycle. They've married. They are becoming parents. And they're discovering that the values that served them in singlehood no longer serve them in parenthood. This is not to say that individualism is no longer a dominant force in American society. It certainly is. Nor is it to say that all is well with American families. Much of the current evidence would argue otherwise. Nor do I mean to suggest that this shift is now pervasive. It is not. It is concentrated in the middle class. But I do believe that we are entering a period when there is not only a growing recognition of the limits of expressive individualism, but also an increasing commitment to family life.

To provide a rough framework for my discussion, I've divided the past 50 years into three distinct cultural periods. The first is the period of what we might call traditional familism, the period extending from the mid-1940s to the mid-1960s. Demographically, this period of family life was characterized by the overwhelming dominance of married couples with children, by high birth rates, low divorce rates, and a high degree of marital stability. Economically, it was marked by a robust economy, a rising standard of living, and an expanding middle class. Culturally, it was defined by individual conformity to social norms, the ideology of separate spheres for men and women, and the idealization of family life.

The second period might be called the period of individualism, extending from the mid-1960s to the mid-1980s. It was characterized by greater demographic diversity, a decline in birth rates, accelerating divorce rates, individual and social experimentation, the breakdown of the separate spheres ideology, the creation of a singles "lifestyle," the idealization of career and work life, and the search for meaning in life through self-expression.

The third period is the period we are now entering: the period of the new familism. Demographically, it features a leveling off of the divorce rate, a leveling off of participation in the work force among women, and

the highest number of births since 1964. Socially, it is a lot less uptight than the first period but a little more uptight than the second period. Culturally, it is shifting away from expressive individualism and a fascination with self toward greater attachments to family and commitment to others.

Let me illustrate these three cultural periods with a newspaper story about a high-powered female attor-

---

There's a shift away from expressive individualism and toward family commitment.

---

ney who decided to leave her full-time job as a trial lawyer because her younger child was emotionally distressed at being left with a babysitter so frequently. The woman didn't want to give up her professional work, so she became president of Greater Boston Legal Services, continued her *pro bono* work for the Boston Bar Association, and ran for the board in her town. Her husband left his partnership at a law firm and took a judgeship that gave him more manageable hours. Both parents

---

The long haul

Parenting is a 25-year commitment

MY SON JOSH CALLED ME COLLECT FROM junior college during his first year away from home. "Mom, want to hear the talk on AIDS that I'll be presenting for my final exam?" he asked. "I need your opinion on how it sounds. I want an A in speech."

I could have answered, "C'mon Josh…you're 19…you're independent…I don't need to worry about your schoolwork anymore, especially on my long-distance phone bill."

Instead, I said, "Yes, let's hear it…make the beginning stronger… those facts are fascinating…the ending is great…you're speaking a little fast." I gave the needed advice, the strokes of support—to a young man, my son, striving toward adulthood.

When I had my babies in the '60s I didn't realize that I would still be parenting in the late '80s. I thought my mother role would end when my children reached 16; they

would get their drivers' licenses and speed away toward total independence. I was wrong.

As children grow older, they still need parental guidance. Between the ages of 16 and 25, they make numerous important decisions. With your help, they will solve their problems "on their own." I'm talking about big issues: sex, drugs, alcohol, the military, college, jobs, marriage, money. If you believe in concerned parenting, you will have your hands full during your children's late teens and early twenties.

Certain types of failures are not worth experiencing. Too many jobs lost, courses flunked, and dollars wasted can add up to a sense of disappointment with life. If you can help your children to develop a positive mental attitude, they will avoid the stresses that plague so many teens and adults today. Watch your language—the messages you send. Give your teens

strokes and tell them how beautiful, smart, and successful they are.

Growing up entails too many new decisions and new responsibilities for any teen to handle alone. You will not want to suffocate them and make decisions for them, but neither will you want to cut them so loose that they flounder and fail to reach their own highest goals.

In our family, I have discovered that parenting is a 25-year commitment. I never suspected that it would last quite this long, but I am thrilled to stay active. Children do not change into adults overnight. It is a long, slow process in which we parents continue to play a meaningful part.

—*Geeta Dardick*
Mothering

This article was excerpted from *Mothering* (Winter 1987). Geeta Dardick has written for many national publications including *The Christian Science Monitor, Readers Digest,* and *Family Circle.* Her book *Home Butchering and Meat Preservation* was published by Tab Books, Blue Summit, PA.

agree that their family life is better and that their children are happier. The mother says her decision produced the most satisfying arrangement for her although she might return to a law firm when her children are older.

In the period of traditional familism, this woman probably would not have had a law degree in the first place, much less the opportunity to create a flexible and satisfying arrangement of family and work responsibilities. Her husband probably would not have resigned his law partnership to spend more time with his daughters.

In the period of individualism, the woman might have faced severe criticism and experienced great self-doubt had she decided to leave a highly successful career to raise her daughters. Her decision would have been condemned as selling out her sisters or giving in to the male power structure. And, of course, her contributions to the community, through her *pro bono* work, would have been considered a waste of her time and talent.

In the period of the new familism, both parents give up something in their work lives in order to foster their family lives. The woman makes the larger concession, but it is one she actively elects and clearly sees as temporary. She does not give up her professional life, although she does give up some money to get greater control of her time. She makes this choice based on a vision of what she sees as a complete life, rather than a life defined by traditional male models of career and success.

Interestingly, there is very little "rights talk" by either the women or the men interviewed in this story. They describe their work and family arrangements in language that seems to place the happiness and well-being of the family before their individual desires or ambitions.

It would be foolish to make too much of one story clipped from the pages of the *Boston Globe*. But it is worth considering for several reasons. First, arrangements like the ones described in the *Globe* article are increasingly common. Several recent surveys suggest that a growing number of men and women want to devote more time to their children. A number of the experts and scholars we polled also say that they see evidence that women are revising their career plans in order to raise young children. In addition, my own field research with middle-income parents of young children confirms this trend. These parents' job decisions are heavily influenced by a consideration of how best they can maximize the time they spend with their children. Many choose tag-team arrangements with a spouse, weekend work, or second- or third-shift work over traditional nine-to-five work schedules.

The new familism is strongest in the baby boom generation. This is a huge generation. This generation invented singlehood as a "lifestyle." It cohabited and delayed marriage and childbearing in record numbers. But now this generation has settled down into family life.

Particularly influential are the baby boomers in the upper third of the generation's socioeconomic scale.

These are the relatively affluent professionals and managers—the people that Ralph Whitehead calls "bright collars" and Robert Reich calls "symbolic analysts." A decade ago, they were some of the most committed exponents of careerism and expressive individualism. The self was their subject. Today, family life is becoming their subject. Where they used to paint self-portraits, they're now painting murals.

These members of the baby boom generation have a disproportionate impact on the media culture. They are screenwriters, advertising executives, journalists, movie directors, ministers in megachurches, novelists, book editors, and television producers. Since much of our culture today is a media culture, they have an

To enter parenthood is to cross a cultural divide from the domain of the self to the domain of civil society.

enormous influence on what values and behaviors are depicted, what values and behaviors are affirmed and celebrated, and what roles are held up as models.

A majority of the baby boomers—roughly 45 million—are now parents. Becoming a parent is a defining individual and social event. Across time and across cultures, it is nearly universally understood as a radical and transformative experience. It makes you settle down, think ahead, become less selfish.

Becoming a parent also changes your relationship to the larger society. Raising children is a social task. It requires the support and participation of many adults in non-contractual, non-exchange relationships. Consequently, it is hard to be socially isolated when you are engaged in raising children. Parenthood inevitably leads one beyond the spheres of both the home and the workplace and out into the neighborhood and community.

Parenthood also changes your view of the workplace. Throughout the '70 and '80s, we saw an idealization of the workplace that very much paralleled the idealization of family in the '50s. Work life replaced family life as the realm of self-fulfillment and intimacy. Careers replaced children as the central focus for adult time and energy. Today, as the baby boom generation becomes involved in parenthood, we see a reassessment of work life, particularly among baby boomers and especially among baby boom mothers. More and more parents of young children are realizing that work life and family life conflict, that time is scarcer than money, and that time and attention are the chief currency of family life and the well-being of children.

Parenthood also changes your view of what makes for happiness. We all know people who are single-minded in their pursuit of career, who profess no interest, much less affection, for children—until they have one of their own. The love most adults feel for a newborn child is totally irrational. There is no way to describe it in the language of choice, the language of individual self-interest, or the language of cost-benefit.

5. NEW STYLES AND THE FUTURE: Emerging Patterns

The cultural challenge to the traditional familism of the 1940s to '60s left many people—especially well-educated baby boomers—wary about any discussion of parenthood, much less a celebration of the pleasures of raising children. Some of this wariness grew out of a still powerful and often expressed fear that *any* recognition of the pleasures of raising children might somehow backfire and work against women—might put them back into what Betty Friedan once called the comfortable concentration camp of the home.

Consequently, what remains unspoken, at least at the level of elite discourse, is that children bring joy as well as sorrow, rewards as well as sacrifice, into adult lives. Experience speaks eloquently of these pleasures. It is no small thing to have so many adults finally experiencing firsthand the pleasures of loving and caring for a child.

Finally, parenthood changes your view of the culture. Parents are responsible for transmitting values to children, and many parents today report that the culture, particularly the mass media, promotes values that assault and undermine their efforts. As Christopher Lasch puts it, "To see the modern world from the point of view of a parent is to see it in the worst possible light."

In focus groups I've conducted, parents consistently point to a culture that celebrates sex, violence, and materialism and call it a hostile force in their lives and the lives of their children. This anger at the state of our culture is not confined to prudes and straight arrows. It cuts across traditional ideological lines and seems to be intrinsically connected to the responsibilities of parenthood. Indeed, it is possible that, in the coming decade, the strongest and most effective moral critique of our culture will be offered not by people who avoided the individualism of an earlier era, but by those who lived it; not by conservative politicians, but by the former champions of sex, drugs, and rock 'n' roll.

In short, to enter parenthood is to cross a cultural divide. On one side is the individual and the domain of the self. On the other side is the family and the domain of the civil society. For individual parents, this life passage requires a willingness to set aside individual desires in order to serve the insistent needs of children. For the generation as a whole, this cultural passage may lead to a shift of social energies from the self to the larger society.

If a new familistic ethos is emerging, it is good news for children. There are many positive aspects to the social and cultural changes of the past 25 years. Greater choice for adults. Greater freedom and opportunities for women. Greater tolerance for difference and diversity. But, overall, the period has not been positive for children. The most compelling reason for welcoming and fostering the new familism is that, by doing so, we may be able to make life better for children.

Any meaningful effort to strengthen family life must come to terms with the culture and with the cultural sources of family well-being. This is not to deny the importance of family-friendly public policies or workplace policies. Nor is it to say that economic, political, and technological forces do not affect the family for better or worse. They certainly do.

But the principal source of family decline over the past three decades has been cultural. It has to do with the ascendancy of a set of values that have been destructive of commitment, obligation, responsibility, and sacrifice—and particularly destructive of the claims of children on adult attention and commitment.

The family has weakened because, quite simply, many Americans have changed their minds. They changed their minds about staying together for the sake of the children; about the necessity of putting children's needs before their own; about marriage as a lifelong commitment; and about what it means to be unmarried and pregnant. And many American men changed their minds about the obligations of a father and husband.

At the moment, we have a political conversation about the family that's giving rise to public policy solutions. We have an economic conversation about the family that's giving rise to workplace solutions. We do not yet have an equivalent cultural conversation about the family that's giving rise to cultural solutions. Let us begin. That, it seems to me, is where an opportunity for leadership lies in the decade ahead.

Excerpted with permission from the Institute for American Values quarterly publication Family Affairs *(Summer 1992). Subscriptions: $25/yr. (4 issues) from Institute for American Values, 1841 Broadway, Suite 211, New York, NY 10023. Back issues available from same address.*

"STOP THE WORLD SO I CAN GET OFF FOR A WHILE"

SOURCES OF DAILY STRESS IN THE LIVES OF LOW-INCOME SINGLE MOTHERS OF YOUNG CHILDREN*

▼

This research examines daily stressors in the lives of 52 low-income single mothers of preschool-age children. Mothers recorded daily events that they perceived as stressful for a period of 2 weeks, and described how they attempted to cope with each episode. The majority of events that were recorded involved stressful interactions with children, particularly incidents of child misbehavior. Stressful exchanges involving other adults were also frequently recorded, as were financial stressors. The diary records reveal substantial inter- and intraindividual variability in coping strategies and in the types of barriers that mothers faced in attempting to implement these strategies. Thus, the diaries provide a useful means of examining sources of perceived stress in the daily lives of these women.

Sheryl L. Olson and Victoria Banyard**

**Sheryl Olson is Assistant Professor, Department of Psychology, University of Michigan, 580 Union Drive, Ann Arbor, MI 48109. Victoria Banyard is a doctoral candidate in clinical psychology at the University of Michigan.

It is difficult to imagine a more demanding life task than parenting young children alone under conditions of poverty. Yet, this is becoming an increasingly common situation for millions of women in the United States. One of the most startling demographic changes in recent decades has been the rapid increase in single-parent families (Garfinkel & McClanahan, 1986; Norton & Glick, 1986). The number of single-parent families with children under age 18 rose from 3.8 million in 1970 to 9.7 million in 1990 (U.S. Bureau of Census, 1990), and all signs point to a continuation of this trend (Bumpass, 1984; Norton & Glick, 1986). The vast majority of these families are headed by women, and lone mothers with dependent children are the poorest of all demographic groups. For example, about 60% of children living in mother-only families are impoverished, compared with only 11% in two-parent families (Kamerman & Kahn, 1988).

Irrespective of income level, single mothers experience higher rates of life stress than their married counterparts (McLanahan, 1983; McLanahan, Wedemeyer, & Adelberg, 1981; Weintraub & Wolf, 1983). Financial stressors are the most salient source of emotional distress

*Portions of this article were presented in an invited paper at the May 1989 meetings of Midwestern Psychological Association, Chicago, IL. Research was supported by funds from a Faculty Research Award at the University of Maine and from the Department of Psychology, University of Michigan. We gratefully acknowledge the assistance of Barbara Haylock, Beth Beck, Jeri Sawall, Francesca Kleinsmith, Usha Tummala, and Melissa McDaniels in data collection. We also thank Sandra Graham-Bermann for helpful comments on an earlier draft. Most importantly, we thank the mothers who participated.

Key Words: poverty, single mothers, stress.

for single mothers (Brandwein, Brown, & Fox, 1974; Colletta, 1979, 1983; Compas & Williams, 1990; Pett, 1982; Quinn & Allen, 1989; Richards, 1989), and those who are poor are at extremely high risk for anxiety, depression, and health problems (Belle, 1982a, 1984, 1990; Guttentag, Salassin, & Belle, 1980; Hall, Williams, & Greenberg, 1985; McAdoo, 1986; McGrath, Keita, Strickland, & Russo, 1990; Pearlin & Johnson, 1977). Moreover, the chronic strains of poverty combined with the task overload involved in single parenting (e.g., Weiss, 1979; Weitzman, 1985) markedly increase these women's vulnerability to new life stressors (Belle, 1984; Turner & Noh, 1983). Feelings of hopelessness and despair are common and understandable reactions to this vicious cycle (Belle, 1982a, 1990; Richards, 1989).

Despite their high prevalence and elevated risk status within the general population, single mothers in poverty comprise a significantly underresearched group (Belle, 1990; Zelkowitz, 1987). It is essential to understand the types of stressors that these parents experience, and to identify factors associated with effective coping under conditions of such chronic and pervasive strain. Although impoverished women experience much higher rates of stressful life changes than others (Brown, Bhrolchain, & Harris, 1975; Dohrewend, 1973; Makosky, 1982), discrete stressful life events are relatively poor predictors of their mental health status (Dohrewend, 1973; Makosky, 1982; Radloff, 1975). Rather, much of the strain of single parenthood and poverty derives from chronically distressing conditions inherent in daily life (Brown et al., 1975; Makosky, 1982; Peters & Massey, 1983). For example, in one study of urban low-income mothers, psychological distress was more strongly

related to the presence of oppressive life conditions than to stressful life events, even though a high proportion of negative life events was reported (Makosky, 1982). According to these respondents, the most emotionally distressing conditions involved ongoing problems of money, parenting, inadequate and/or dangerous living arrangements, and intimate relationships. Thus, in order to achieve a window on the stressful experiences of impoverished single parents, "slices" of daily life must be assessed.

The purpose of the present study was to examine daily stressors in the lives of low-income single mothers of young children. The main objective was to document the types of emotionally distressing experiences that were most salient in the day-to-day lives of these women. The authors wished to achieve a prospective assessment of these stressors, and one that was sensitive to the mothers' subjective evaluations of difficult life situations. Thus, mothers were asked to keep daily journal records of stressful experiences for a 2-week period. The second goal is to document the types of strategies mothers used in attempting to cope with these distressing events, as well as their evaluations of the efficacy of these problem solving efforts. In doing so, we hoped to learn more about the experiences of mothers who perceived that they coped effectively despite high levels of life stress, a topic that has been neglected in research on single parenting (cf. Gongla & Thompson, 1987).

METHOD

Subjects

Subjects were 52 low-income single mothers of young children (mean age =

4.9 years, 53% male), recruited through fliers sent to their children's preschool centers. In order to be eligible for participation, mothers had to be at least 20 years old and single for one year or more. Thirty-one mothers were recruited through Head Start preschools in small, rural Northeastern communities, and 21 through preschool programs serving low-income families in and around a midsize Midwestern college community. Participation rates ranged from 51% to 80% in the different centers. Mothers ranged in age from 24 to 40 years and had been single parents for an average of 4 years (range = 1 to 11 years). The number of minor children in their households ranged from 1 to 5 (*M* = 2). Of the 52 mothers, 39 had been married and divorced at least once before, whereas 13 had never been married. All but 2 had completed high school. Seven had completed college, and 2 had taken some graduate classes. Most of the mothers (96%) were white, reflecting the extremely low rates of racial variability in their home communities. The majority of women (63%) were unemployed, and 80% had incomes which fell below national poverty levels. Mothers were paid $25.00 for their participation.

Procedure

As part of a larger project on stress and coping in the lives of low-income single parents, mothers kept daily journals of stressful events for a period of 2 weeks. Mothers were asked to record all daily events that they considered stressful, and to briefly describe them. Next, they were asked to list the types of emotional reactions they experienced in relation to the event, and to rate the intensity of these reactions on a 10-point scale (10 = the most intense level of affect). Finally, they were asked to record how they tried to handle each problem and (if applicable) to describe the outcomes of their coping efforts.

No suggestions were given concerning the types of events mothers might record, as we wished to describe their independent perceptions of daily stressors. However, as a shaping exercise during the task explanation, mothers were asked to use the diary format to describe a stressful event that occurred during the past week. Each mother was called after one week to see how the records were progressing, and whether she had questions concerning procedures. Most mothers clearly understood the task, and few (< 3%) had procedural questions during the one-week follow-up call.

Content analyses revealed that mothers' diary responses fell into the fol-

lowing domains: a) Stressful interactions involving one's own children subdivided into noncompliance, irritating behaviors, temper tantrums, rule violations, conflicts with sibs, making messes, demanding attention, slow in getting ready for outings, illness, school problems, parent-child conflict, and stressful interactions with child care providers (see descriptions and examples below); b) stressful encounters with other adults, subdivided according to the type of relationship (friends and acquaintances, relatives, ex-husbands); c) financial stressors; d) work stressors; e) household stressors; and f) negative affective states such as depression and anxiety. All records were coded independently by two individuals. Intercoder reliability, calculated using the percentage of agreement statistic (*N* of agreements/*N* of agreements + *N* of disagreements), averaged .95 across categories (range = .92-.99).

The types of problem-solving strategies mothers reported in relation to child, interpersonal, and financial stressors were also content analyzed (see Tables 1-3 for content codes). Intercoder reliability (percentage of agreement, based on all records) averaged .93 across categories (range = .91-.95).

Finally, mothers' perceptions of the effectiveness of their coping efforts were rated on a 3-point scale: 1 = *clearly successful* (desired outcome achieved, and/or mother uses positive descriptors such as "good" or "excellent" to describe outcome of coping efforts); 2 = *fair outcome* (partial success in achieving goals, and/or mother uses words such as "fair" or "OK" to describe outcome); and 3 = *unsuccessful* (desired outcome not achieved, and/or mother uses negative descriptors such as "bad" or "poor" to describe outcome). Intercoder reliability, calculated for all diary entries, was .89.

RESULTS

Categories of Daily Stress

A total of 473 stressful daily events were recorded (range = 5-31 events per record). Frequency analyses revealed that the majority (56%) involved child-related stressors. Interpersonal stressors involving adults comprised the next most frequently cited category (21%), followed by financial stressors (8%), household stressors (5%), work stressors (4%), negative emotional states (4%), personal illness (1%), and ecological stressors (1%). These different categories of daily stress are discussed below.

Child-related stressors. Stressful interactions with children accounted for the highest proportion of stressful daily events reported by the mothers. Because child-related stressors comprised a heterogeneous group of events, they were in turn broken into subcategories. Not surprisingly, most of these stressful encounters (50%) involved negative or challenging behaviors on the part of the child. These included noncompliance ("fought with kids again to clean up their room"; "my youngest refused to take his nap"; "the kids refused to come home for dinner"), irritating behaviors ("the kids ran in and out all day and made a lot of noise"; "my son interrupted my conversation with another adult"; "my daughter began whining during her nap"), defiance ("my child sassed me"; "my daughter was very defiant and rebellious today"), temper tantrums, and rule violations ("my 4-year-old daughter went to the neighbors without asking first"; "my son stole a toy from the store while we were grocery shopping"). Remaining child stressors involved conflicts with siblings (12%), making messes (10%), demanding attention (9%), slow in getting ready for outings (7%), illness (7%), school failure and/or misbehavior (3%), and stressful interactions with child care providers (2%).

Interpersonal relationships with adults. The second most populous category of daily stressors involved interactions with other adults. As with the child-related stressors, these events were quite heterogeneous in nature, and were therefore divided into subcategories. Stressful interactions with friends and acquaintances accounted for 44% of these entries, and included experiences such as conflicts with boyfriends, crises in friends' lives (e.g., divorce, abusive treatment, legal problems), and having friends make difficult or time-consuming demands. The next most frequently cited source of interpersonal stress (37%) involved interactions with relatives. Family crises such as death, illness, and divorce were commonly cited, as were conflicts with and impositions on the part of family members. As an example of the latter, one mother of four young children reported that her brother's behavior was a constant source of stress in her daily life: "My brother comes over every night for supper. Most of the time he fights with my kids. He eats enough for three to four people and acts like this is a restaurant where he can eat anytime he feels like it and won't clean up after himself. I tell him repeatedly to rinse his plate and put it in the sink when he's done, and repeatedly he just leaves his plate wherever. He won't even offer to clean the table if I'm sick." Finally, the remaining entries involved stressful interactions with ex-husbands and focused primarily on conflicts over child support and visitation.

Financial stressors. Financial stressors comprised the third most frequently cited source of daily stress, accounting for 8% of the total entries. The most common examples involved not having enough money to buy food or supplies for the family or to cover incoming bills (e.g., "I always find at least five notices of nonpayment of bills each week in my mailbox").

Household stressors. Stressors involving day-to-day management of the household comprised 5% of the journal entries. Typical examples included having a messy house, or having household appliances break down.

Work stressors. Although most mothers did not work outside their homes, employment-related stressors accounted for 4% of the total entries. Conflicts with bosses and co-workers were the most commonly cited work stressors. In addition, some mothers reported that they were reprimanded by their supervisors for staying at home when their children were ill, and that they felt helpless in response to this "double bind" situation.

Negative affect. Many mothers reported that negative emotional states were a significant source of stress. These included depressive thoughts ("I feel old, ugly, and depressed. I'm resolved to be an old maid"), anxiety over the children's welfare ("I worry constantly about my kids' happiness—I hope they are resilient enough"), or feelings of being overwhelmed by fatigue and stress ("I have times of confidence, but the same feelings of exhaustion and despair come back again").

Other stressors. Other stressors involved personal illness (1% of entries) and concerns about the ecological situation of the family (1%). The relative rarity of concerns about housing adequacy and neighborhood safety most probably reflects the fact that respondents lived in small rural and college communities, as opposed to large urban areas.

Coping Responses

The diary records provided rich information concerning mothers' self-perceived attempts to cope with the many sources of chronic stress in their lives. Typical strategies that mothers reported were analyzed separately in relation to child, interpersonal, and financial stressors, the three most frequently cited sources of daily stress. As shown in Table 1, the most commonly

Table 1.
Coping Responses to Child Stressors

Type of Response	Percent of Total
Threaten punishment or punish	27
Explain/reason	20
Issue command	15
Direct action	14
Provide attention, play, nurturance	7
Give child a choice	4
Self-talk	3
Ignore	2
Ask another adult for help	2
Distract self	2
Relax	1
Compromise	1
Give in to child's demands	1
Do nothing	1

reported response to child stressors involved threatening punishment or actually punishing the child. Although not all punitive action involved physical punishment, the following entries were typical: "S. refuses to take his nap and I am getting tired of running up and down the stairs and spanking him." Another mother wrote: "My oldest kept calling his brother names and being rotten to him. I felt furious, and slapped him." Talking (explaining/reasoning) with the child, commanding the child, or taking direct action (e.g., transporting a sick child to the doctor) were also frequently reported. Strategies such as giving the child a choice, ignoring irritating behavior, compromising, or soliciting help from others were rarely used. Although coping responses are listed separately for the sake of clarity, mothers often reported using multiple strategies in stressful interactions with their children, particularly when misbehavior was involved. For example, one mother wrote that she felt stressed by her children's fighting with one another ("I'm angry—sick of it—NERVES!"). She stated that she punished them in their room, tried to talk things out, ignored their tattling, then took them outside for a walk. In response to her children's persistent refusals to clean their room, another mother wrote that she "yelled, screamed, threatened to hold camp

Table 2.
Coping Responses to Interpersonal Stressors

Type of Response	Percent of Total
Talk/explain	16
Offer emotional/material support	16
Confront	16
Self-talk	14
Enlist other's help	7
Refuse request	6
Take direct action	6
Distract self	6
Relax	5
Do nothing	4
Ignore	3

against them, then went in with a garbage bag and started picking up everything." Similarly, in response to a public temper tantrum, a mother wrote that she "reasoned, counted to five, threatened loss of privileges, and finally gave in" to her child's demands.

Mothers' coping responses in relation to interpersonal stressors are shown in Table 2. The most commonly cited strategies involved having a discussion with the other adult, offering emotional or material support, and engaging in "self-talk" (supportive inner speech).

Finally, as shown in Table 3, the most frequent response to financial stressors was to take some kind of direct action. Strategies such as careful budgeting, calling creditors to make special arrangements, "stretching" resources as much as possible, and attempting to generate small amounts of subsistence funds pervaded these records. Mothers also frequently relied upon the assistance of others, such as friends, relatives, and caseworkers. Finally, cognitive coping strategies ("self-talk") were also frequently reported as means of handling financial stressors (e.g., "I am trying"; "Calm down—just try to get through another day"; "Must have FAITH everything will be OK. I must believe it").

There was considerable variability between mothers in their approaches to problem solving and perceptions of coping efficacy. In some cases, the diaries revealed remarkable resilience in the face of nearly insurmountable obstacles. For example, P.D., the mother of three children under the age of 6, contributed the following entry: Under the column for stressful situations she simply wrote, "Have no money left." She also stated that she felt intensely angry and frustrated about this. However, when asked how she attempted to handle this situation, she wrote: "The children and I left the house at 8:30 a.m., packed a picnic lunch, and spent the day looking for cans and bottles. . . . We didn't find too many cans and bottles, but had a really good time together." Later, she wrote that she tried to make dinner for her family with "mostly nothing" to cook, and again described feeling angry and

Table 3.
Coping Responses to Financial Stressors

Type of Response	Percent of Total
Take direct action	44
Help from others	26
Self-talk	21
Do nothing	7
Distract self	1

frustrated. Her response: "I made the best dinner I could with what I had. I remembered the fun we had earlier, and felt a little better. I hoped that tomorrow would be better."

Similarly, N.S., a mother of five, reported very high levels of daily stress but managed to handle it to her satisfaction. For example, she recorded the following stressful event sequence, which occurred after an unusually difficult workday: "The boys are at home fighting, constantly yelling 'Mama' and tattling while I am trying to do some paperwork. My little girl is tired and fussy." She wrote that she "felt like screaming," and rated her level of negative affect 8 out of 10. Her responses, however, were thoughtful and effective: "I took the squirt guns away from the boys and warned that one more ungodly scream of 'Mama' would earn them some time out. Took a few minutes to quiet and soothe B. (the 5-year old). Laid her down on the sofa with her favorite blanket and turned on TV to *Sesame Street* for her. Put paperwork away and enjoyed a quiet cup of coffee." Midway through this mother's diary, however, she experienced the loss of her car: "The mechanic looked at my car today—motor is gone! NO CAR!! I have no credit for a loan—am laid off from work—no savings—$15.00 to my name. I desperately need a car." She wrote that she felt "Trapped—panicky-depressed" (all 8 out of 10), "DESPERATE" (10 out of 10), and added "I feel like the knot I tied in the end of my rope is about to let go. I am so upset over everything! Would like someone to stop the world so I can get off for awhile." Although she coped by trying to reassure herself that there were people she could borrow from and that "things will be OK," she concluded by stating that "the same feelings of despair come back again." This sequence clearly illustrates how severe financial stressors can become "contagious" in relation to other oppressive conditions (Makosky, 1982), threatening to overwhelm the coping abilities of even the most resilient individuals.

In addition to revealing inter- and intraindividual variability in coping behavior, the diary records showed that there are many environmental barriers to effective coping in the lives of these women. "Environmental barriers" are situations which resist coping efforts of any kind. An extended example from the diary of R.T., a mother of four small children, is illustrative: (a) "I'm getting the youngest child ready for school, company came, I'm getting lunch for the other three, and a friend tells me she can't take me grocery shopping. (b) I

found another ride—she said she'd be there in 15 minutes. It took 1-1/2 hours and she brought three kids with her who are absolute terrors. (c) I went grocery shopping, finally, on a tight budget. The prices were unreal. I tried to stick as close to my budget as I could, but still spent more than I could really afford. (d) I'm unloading groceries and bringing them into the house—the neighborhood kids swarmed all over like flies on garbage—ripped off some of my stuff, dumped bags all over the yard trying to get at things. Someone HELP! I felt like I was going crazy! I told their mothers and asked them to please keep their kids away for a few minutes. The mothers just laughed and went back to whatever they were doing."

Demographic Correlates of Perceptions of Stress, Distress, and Coping Efficacy

Although all mothers in the sample were poor and single, they showed variability in other demographic background characteristics. Therefore, we asked whether these characteristics might help to differentiate individual mothers in relation to their perceptions of daily stress, distress, and coping effectiveness. Maternal age, work status (working outside the home vs. full-time homemaker), prior marital status (never married vs. divorced), age at first marriage, family size (number of dependent children in household), and educational level were correlated with each mother's total number of stress entries, mean negative affect ratings (summed across all entries), and proportion of stress event entries rated as successfully handled. Only maternal age was significantly correlated with the percentage of successful coping episodes: Older mothers reported relatively fewer successes than younger mothers, $r = -.25$, $p < .05$. Both the total number of daily stress entries and mean negative affect ratings were significantly correlated with employment status. Working mothers reported more stressful events ($r = .29$, $p < .05$), but experienced less distress in relation to these events than mothers who remained at home full-time ($r = .29$, $p < .05$). There were no other significant demographic correlates of mothers' perceptions of stress, distress, and coping effectiveness.

Some child characteristics were also significantly correlated with mothers' reports of stress and distress. Mothers of preschool-age boys tended to report more daily stressors ($r = .27$, $p < .05$) and failures in coping with child misbehavior ($r = .33$, $p < .01$) than mothers of

girls. In addition, the ages of the children were related to mothers' ratings of emotional distress: Those with younger children tended to report higher mean negative affect levels in response to child stressors ($r = .32$, $p < .01$) than those with older children.

DISCUSSION

There has been little research on quality of life in impoverished, mother-headed families, despite the increasing salience of these families in our society (cf., Belle, 1990). Further, much of the existing research on single-parent families has reflected biases and misassumptions about this family form that pervade society at large. For example, single-parent families have been viewed as "symptoms" of societal decay and as pathogenic influences upon child adjustment, with low-income, female-headed single-parent families portrayed as the most pathogenic (see critiques by Blechman, 1982; Brandwein et al., 1974; Gongla & Thompson, 1987; Mednick, 1987). Moreover, single-parent status has been primarily treated as a transitional family structure, although it is a relatively stable adaptation for many families and one that does not always result from marital disruption (Mednick, 1987; Smith, 1980). Finally, little attention has been given to the experiential world of the single-parent, or to the socioenvironmental context of the single-parent family system (Gongla & Thompson, 1987).

Collectively, these biases and misassumptions add up to a "single parent uniformity myth," or an undifferentiated (and unjustifiably negative) view of single-parent family life. It is likely that public policy has been shaped by the same biases that have affected research. As Sprey (1967) has emphasized, treating single-parent status as an "independent variable" is conceptually and methodologically untenable given that the life circumstances of single-parent families vary so widely.

This study focused on the subgroup of single parents most highly at risk for succumbing to the negative effects of chronic life stress: impoverished mothers of young children. Clearly, single mothers in poverty face multiple stresses and strains in their daily lives and possess fewer resources than others for efficient and effective coping (cf., Dill & Feld, 1982). Although the risk potential of this group has been amply demonstrated, much can be learned by examining how these mothers experience stress in their daily lives and by identifying individuals who manage to cope effectively despite conditions of intense and chronic strain. The respondents of this study comprised a group of mothers for whom single-parent status was a relatively stable adaptation. A diary method was used to examine stressful experiences in their daily lives.

Interactions with children were the most pervasive source of stress and distress in the daily lives of these mothers. Of the many different types of child stressors that were reported, incidents of misbehavior such as noncompliance, defiance, and rule infractions were most salient. These stresses, and the emotional distress associated with them, were most acute for mothers of young boys, a finding that is consistent with previous research on the long-term adaptation of single-parent families (e.g., Hetherington, Cox, & Cox, 1985). Although individual mothers varied considerably in their responses to child stressors, nearly half of these responses involved punitive or power assertive behaviors such as yelling, commanding, threatening punishment, or actually punishing the child.

These findings converge with those of Makosky (1982), who reported that parenting stresses were rated among the most highly distressing conditions of daily life by low-income mothers. Similarly, Crnic and Greenberg (1990) analyzed parents' ratings of the frequency and intensity of daily "hassles" with their young children. They found that minor parenting hassles were an important source of daily stress in the lives of their low-risk families and provided a critical context for assessing strain in parent-child relationships. For example, the rated intensity of minor parenting stresses was an excellent predictor of both child maladjustment and symptoms of emotional distress in mothers. Moreover, a substantial body of research has shown that high maternal stress is associated with irritable and restrictive parenting (e.g., Colletta, 1983; Hetherington, Cox, & Cox, 1978; Longfellow, Zelkowitz, & Saunders, 1982; Patterson, 1983; Weissman & Paykel, 1974; Zelkowitz, 1987). Such interactions have been related to elevated rates of behavioral maladjustment in children (McLoyd, 1990), which in turn intensify stress on already overtaxed caregiving systems (Hetherington et al., 1978; Patterson, 1980, 1983).

However, although all respondents had very high levels of stress in their lives, they varied widely in the frequency with which they reported stressful encounters with their children and in their coping behaviors. There were many incidents of calm, firm, and nurturant responses to stressful child behaviors, even when mothers reported experiencing high levels of emotional distress (e.g., intense anger) in relation to these behaviors. Analyzing individual and socioenvironmental factors which contribute to resilient parenting under conditions of chronic and severe stress is a critical direction for further research.

Social interactions with other adults (friends, relatives, ex-husbands) were the next most frequently cited source of daily stress. Functional social networks are necessary to the survival of disadvantaged single mothers (Stack, 1974). Thus, in describing their strategies for handling severe and often unexpected financial stressors, the respondents frequently reported receiving direct aid from friends and relatives. However, the diary records clearly illustrated the "double edged" nature of social network ties described by Belle (1982b), in that women frequently reported feeling concerned about others in their lives or distressed by their behavior. Moreover, offering emotional or material support to friends and relatives was one of the most commonly reported responses to these concerns. In her ethnography of poor, black, urban mothers, Stack (1974) also found that social network ties exacted high emotional costs, and Milardo (1987) and Riley and Eckenrode (1986) reported that low-income women with extensive social network ties tend to give more support than they receive in return.

In summary, these data indicate that the social networks of disadvantaged single mothers are important contexts of daily stress and support. In further research, more refined analyses of individual-network transactions should be conducted in relation to the stress-reducing and stress-exacerbating qualities of network ties. For example, social support networks don't just "happen" to people—they are actively constructed. Individual characteristics and environmental barriers may strongly affect one's ability to obtain support and use it effectively. These considerations imply that social support is not a static entity, but rather, a dynamic set of relationship systems. The critical question for researchers is not "Does social support mediate stress?", but rather, "What is the nature of the exchange?"

Somewhat surprisingly, financial stressors accounted for only 8% of the total diary entries. This finding may be an artifact of the methodology, in that money stressors so pervaded the lives of these women that only crises such as eviction notices, threats to shut off heat in the dead of winter, or having little or no food stood out as particularly noteworthy. Both Makosky (1982) and Richards (1989), using different methods, found that financial strains were perceived as the most emotionally distressing life conditions by low-income mothers. However, consistent with other research on the coping behaviors of impoverished women (Dill & Feld, 1982; McAdoo, 1986; Richards, 1989; Stack, 1974), the present respondents coped very actively with these potent stressors, using self-reliant strategies in the majority of cases.

Maternal work status and age were also found to correlate with mothers' experiences of daily stress. To a modest degree, older mothers reported fewer successful coping episodes than their younger counterparts, a finding that could reflect age-mediated differences in energy levels or in the appraisal of coping outcomes. The relationship between maternal work status and perceived stress and distress is interesting, in that it suggests that working outside the home may confer a slight protective advantage to these mothers. However, there were relatively few significant demographic correlates of daily stress measures overall, and these relationships were quite small. Thus, further research should focus upon other characteristics of these mothers' lives and backgrounds (e.g., family history; personality characteristics; social network) which may predict individual differences in coping behavior.

As a means of examining sources of perceived stress in daily life, the diary records proved quite useful. Although the types of daily events that were perceived as stressful tended to be similar, mothers varied a great deal in their responses to these stressors. Moreover, the concept of coping could not be easily encapsulated into individual "styles" which remained temporally or situationally consistent. For example, because the diary records extended over a period of 2 weeks and included multiple daily event sequences, they revealed considerable intraindividual variability in coping behavior. The authors strongly suspect that even within an economically disadvantaged sample such as this one, financial "microcrises" may play an important role in explaining this intraindividual variability, heightening one's vulnerability to feelings of hopelessness and despair and to episodes of irritable parenting.

Similarly, the records revealed that in many cases there were environmental barriers which resisted even the most persistent and constructive coping efforts. As currently conceptualized, coping involves a series of exchange events between person and environment (e.g., Lazarus & Folkman, 1984). During the last decade, the understanding of individual characteristics that mediate stressful experiences (cf. Eckenrode, 1983; Henderson, 1992; Sarason et al., 1991) has increased. However, the idea that environmental context factors *continue* to play an important role in coping is not well understood, nor is much known about linkages between individual characteristics and contextual factors. Thus, greater research emphasis should be placed on the study of environmental barriers to coping and on understanding the dynamic interplay between characteristics of individual mothers and their social networks.

Although our diary assessment method has many advantages for understanding experiential contexts of daily stress, it also has some significant limitations. First, this method requires substantial amounts of time and effort on the part of respondents. Initially, we felt concerned that our respondents might perceive the diary as an intrusive and troublesome imposition upon their already overstressed lives. Fortunately, this was not the case. Only one mother mentioned that completing this task was stressful, and she went on to describe how the experience of keeping the diary led her to seek constructive help from a counselor. Many other mothers spontaneously told us that they enjoyed the journal because it helped them to achieve some objectivity on their life situations. Also, several mothers mentioned that this was the first time that anyone had ever considered their life experiences to be valuable.

On the negative side, mothers varied in verbal facility and in the motivation/ability to record their experiences in writing. When we received a sparse record, we had no idea whether that mother perceived little stress in her daily life (an unlikely interpretation, given the nature of the sample), or whether she simply did not record these experiences. Indeed, one mother turned in a very sparse diary and commented that she had experienced few recent stresses. When she sat down to talk with an interviewer, however, she described many different current stressful life events and conditions. Clearly, these records should be supplemented with other means of assessing daily stressors, such as rating scales or checklists (cf. Crnic & Greenberg, 1990; Kanner, Coyne, Schaefer, & Lazarus, 1981; Makosky, 1982).

We also caution that these results are not generalizable to racially diverse or urban populations of economically

disadvantaged single parents. One third of female-headed, single-parent families are nonwhite (U.S. Bureau of Census, 1990). Women of color are not only overrepresented among single parents in poverty, but they also face a unique constellation of stressors related to racial discrimination. Describing this type of life condition as "mundane extreme environmental stress," Peters and Massey (1983) have discussed the importance of recognizing the impact of both a global atmosphere of institutionalized racial oppression as well as chronic, racially related stressors in the daily lives of minority families. Such stress is not merely added on to the burdens of single parenthood documented in the present study, but creates a qualitatively different experience altogether. Further inquiry will benefit from the careful study of African-American and Hispanic women's experiences.

In addition, over 80% of impoverished single parents live in metropolitan areas (U.S. Bureau of Census, 1990). Inner-city women face a variety of stressors that differ from those of the present denizens of small rural and midsize college communities, including grossly inadequate housing and dangerous neighborhoods. It is also possible that urban environments provide resources that were not as readily available to the respondents of this study, such as public transportation and increased access to social service programs. These considerations again highlight the immense sources of variability in the lives of single mothers. They are a heterogeneous group, and social service delivery to these women (as well as a more general understanding of single parenthood) will undoubtedly be improved by placing differences among women in the spotlight.

IMPLICATIONS FOR PRACTICE

These findings have implications for supportive interventions with poor, single mothers of young children. Caregiving issues were the most salient sources of stress and concern in the daily lives of these women, even though they received part- or full-time day care for their preschool-age children. Consistent with the goals of the emergent family support movement (e.g., Weissbourd & Kagan, 1989), finding ways to relieve this strain is of paramount importance. Providing additional child care resources and helping parents to restructure interactions with their young children so as to mitigate the frequency of coercive parent-child interactions, are two obvious foci for supportive intervention.

Less obvious, perhaps, is ensuring that mothers receive adequate emotional support by helping them to mobilize and sustain supportive relationships with other adults.

More concretely, the act of keeping a daily stress diary could be a useful adjunct to counseling. As Makosky (1982) has noted, there is a "contagion" of stressors in the lives of multiply and chronically stressed individuals such as impoverished single mothers (i.e., different stressors potentiate or exacerbate others in continuous succession). It is easy to see how mothers might feel overwhelmed by this tidal wave of stressors, particularly when they lack the material resources needed for efficient problem resolution. In this regard, keeping a daily diary may help these mothers gain some objectivity on their life situations and become more aware of persistent "trouble spots" in their daily experience, or, conversely, of situations that they handle quite effectively. For example, one mother offered the following unsolicited observation of how the process of keeping the daily diary led her to reevaluate her life: "Every time I sit down to write about my feelings . . . I find myself having a hard time as to what my feelings are and if they are right or wrong. I am going to seek some counseling . . . seems like I have been missing alot for years and years. Maybe I'll be a new person." The diary records could also help mothers achieve insight into the types of coping strategies that seem optimally effective in different situations.

Clearly, the most important changes in the life situations of poor, single mothers must be made on a macrosystemic level (e.g., through the provision of greater material resources, child care, health care, and educational opportunities). Unfortunately, these changes have not been forthcoming, and the ranks of poor, single mothers are expanding. Perhaps the greatest risk to these mothers' well-being (and to the well-being of their children) is adopting an attitude of helplessness. The daily diary is one of many tools which may help empower such mothers to achieve constructive attitudes toward coping with the many sources of stress in their lives.

CONCLUSION

In conclusion, low-income single mothers of young children are exposed to high levels of daily stress. Depression and hopelessness seem understandable responses to such life situations. However, this study found substantial variability between mothers in their approaches to difficult life situations and in their perceptions of coping efficacy. This article thus presents several challenges to future researchers. Not only must an attempt be made to explain this variability in further research, but the methodological repertoire needs to be expanded. Qualitative methods which capture the diversity of stressful experiences inherent in the daily lives of single parents should supplement the more standard stress event inventories. Through such a combination of methods, movement away from stereotypes and toward a more accurate documentation of these women's lives will be accomplished.

REFERENCES

Belle, D. (Ed.). (1982a). *Lives in stress: Women and depression.* Beverly Hills, CA: Sage.

Belle, D. (1982b). Social ties and social support. In D. Belle (Ed.), *Lives in stress: Women and depression* (pp. 133-144). Beverly Hills, CA: Sage.

Belle, D. (1984). Inequality and mental health: Low-income and minority women. In L. Walker (Ed.), *Women and mental health policy* (pp. 135-150). Beverly Hills, CA: Sage.

Belle, D. (1990). Poverty and women's mental health. *American Psychologist, 45,* 385-389.

Blechman, E. (1982). Are children with one parent at risk? A methodological critique. *Journal of Marriage and the Family, 44,* 179-195.

Brandwein, B., Brown, C., & Fox, E. (1974). Women and children last: The social situation of divorced mothers and their children. *Journal of Marriage and the Family, 36,* 498-514.

Brown, G., Bhrolchain, M., & Harris, T. (1975). Social class and psychiatric disturbance among women in an urban population. *Sociology, 9,* 225-254.

Bumpass, L. (1984). Children and marital disruption: A replication and update. *Demography, 21,* 71-82.

Colletta, N. (1979). Support systems after divorce: Incidence and impact. *Journal of Marriage and the Family, 41,* 837-846.

Colletta, N. D. (1983). Stressful lives: The situation of divorced mothers and their children. *Journal of Divorce, 6,* 19-31.

Compas, B. E., & Williams, R. A. (1990). Stress, coping, and adjustment in mothers and young adolescents in single and two-parent families. *American Journal of Community Psychology, 18,* 525-545.

Crnic, K. A., & Greenberg, M. T. (1990). Minor parenting stresses with young children. *Child Development, 61,* 1628-1632.

Dill, D., & Feld, E. (1982). The challenge of coping. In D. Belle (Ed.), *Lives in stress: Women and depression* (pp. 145-161). Beverly Hills, CA: Sage.

Dohrewend, B. S. (1973). Social class and stressful life events. *Journal of Personality and Social Psychology, 28,* 225-235.

Eckenrode, J. (1983). The mobilization of social supports: Some individual constraints. *American Journal of Community Psychology, 11,* 509-528.

Garfinkel, I., & McClanahan, S. (1986). *Single mothers and their children: A new American dilemma.* Washington, DC: The Urban Institute Press.

Gongla, P. A., & Thompson, E. H. (1987). Single parent families. In M. B. Sussman & S. K. Steinmetz (Eds.), *Handbook of marriage and the family* (pp. 397-418). New York: Plenum Press.

Guttentag, M., Salassin, S., & Belle, D. (1980). *The mental health of women.* New York: Academic Press.

Hall, L. A., Williams, C. A., & Greenberg, R. S. (1985). Supports, stressors, and depressive symptoms in low-income mothers of young children. *American Journal of Public Health, 75,* 518-522.

Henderson, A. S. (1992). Social support and depression. In H. O. F. Veiel & U. Baumann (Eds.), *The meaning and measurement of social support* (pp. 85-91). New York: Hemisphere.

Hetherington, E. M., Cox, M., & Cox, R. (1978). The development of children in mother-headed families. In H. Hoffman & D. Reiss (Eds.), *The American family: Dying or developing?* (pp. 117-145). New York: Plenum.

Hetherington, E. M., Cox, M., & Cox, R. (1985). Long-term effects of divorce and remarriage on the adjustment of children. *Journal of the American Academy of Psychiatry, 24,* 518-530.

Kamerman, S. B., & Kahn, A. J. (1988). *Mothers alone: Strategies for a time of change.* Dover, MA: Auburn House.

Kanner, A. D., Coyne, J. C., Schaefer, C., & Lazarus, R. S. (1981). Comparisons of two modes of stress measurement: Daily hassles and uplifts versus major life events. *Journal of Behavioral Medicine, 4,* 1-39.

Lazarus, R., & Folkman, S. (1984). *Stress, appraisal, & coping.* New York: Springer.

Longfellow, C., Zelkowitz, P., & Saunders, E. (1982). The quality of mother-child relationships. In D. Belle (Ed.), *Lives in stress: Women and depression* (pp. 163-176). Beverly Hills, CA: Sage.

Makosky, V. P. (1982). Sources of stress: Events or conditions? In D. Belle (Ed.), *Lives in stress: Women and depression* (pp. 35-53). Beverly Hills, CA: Sage.

McAdoo, H. (1986). Strategies used by black single mothers against stress. In M. Simms & J. Malveaux (Eds.), *Slipping through the cracks: The status of black women* (pp. 153-166). New Brunswick, NJ: Transaction Books.

McGrath, E., Keita, G. P., Strickland, B. R., & Russo, F. R. (1990). *Women and depression: Risk factors and treatment issues.* Washington, DC: American Psychological Association.

McLanahan, S. (1983). Family structure and stress: A longitudinal comparison of two-parent and female-headed families. *Journal of Marriage and the Family, 45,* 347-357.

McLanahan, S., Wedemeyer, N., & Adelberg, N. (1981). Network structure, social support, and psychological well-being in the single parent family. *Journal of Marriage and the Family, 43,* 601-612.

McLoyd, V. (1990). The impact of economic hardship on black families and children: Psychological distress, parenting, and socioemotional development. *Child Development, 61,* 311-346.

Mednick, M. T. (1987). Single mothers: A review and critique of current research. *Applied Social Psychology Annual, 7,* 184-201.

Milardo, R. (1987). Changes in social networks of women and men following divorce: A review. *Journal of Family Issues, 8,* 78-96.

Norton, A. J., & Glick, P. C. (1986). One-parent families: A social and economic profile. *Family Relations, 35,* 9-17.

Patterson, G. (1980). Mothers: The unacknowledged victims. *Monographs of the Society for Research in Child Development, 45,* No. 186.

Patterson, G. (1983). Stress: A change agent for family process. In N. Garmezy & M. Rutter (Eds.), *Stress, coping, and development in children* (pp. 235-264). Baltimore, MD: Johns Hopkins Press.

Pearlin, L., & Johnson, J. (1977). Marital status, life-strains, and depression. *American Sociological Review, 42,* 704-715.

Peters, M., & Massey, G. (1983). Mundane extreme environmental stress in family stress theories: The case of black families in white America. *Marriage and Family Review, 6,* 193-218.

Pett, M. (1982). Predictors of satisfactory social adjustment of divorced single parents. *Journal of Divorce, 5,* 1-17.

Quinn, P., & Allen, K. R. (1989). Facing challenges and making compromises: How single mothers endure. *Family Relations, 38,* 390-395.

Radloff, L. (1975). Sex differences in depression: The effects of occupation and marital status. *Sex Roles, 1,* 249-266.

Richards, L. N. (1989). The precarious survival and hard-won satisfactions of white single-parent families. *Family Relations, 38,* 396-403.

Riley, D., & Eckenrode, J. (1986). Social ties: Subgroup differences in costs and benefits. *Journal of Personality and Social Psychology, 51,* 770-778.

Sarason, B. R., Pierce, G. R., Shearin, E. N., Sarason, I. G., Waltz, J. A., & Poppe, L. (1991). Perceived support and working models of self and actual others. *Journal of Personality and Social Psychology, 60,* 273-287.

Smith, M. (1980). The social consequences of single parenthood: A longitudinal perspective. *Family Relations, 29,* 75-81.

Sprey, J. (1967). The study of single parenthood: Some methodological considerations. *Family Coordinator, 16,* 29-34.

Stack, C. (1974). *All our kin: Strategies for survival in a black community.* New York: Harper & Row.

Turner, R., & Noh, S. (1983). Class and psychological vulnerability among women: The significance of social support and personal control. *Journal of Health and Social Behavior, 24,* 2-15.

U.S. Bureau of Census, (1990). Household and family characteristics. *Current Population Reports,* Series P-20, No. 447. Washington, DC: U.S. Government Printing Office.

Weintraub, M., & Wolf, B. (1983). Effects of stress and social supports on mother-child interactions in single and two-parent families. *Child Development, 54,* 1297-1311.

Weiss, R. (1979). *Going it alone: The family life and social situation of the single parent.* New York: Basic Books.

Weissbourd, B., & Kagan, S. (1989). Family support programs: Catalysts for change. *American Journal of Orthopsychiatry, 59,* 20-31.

Weissman, M. M., & Paykel, E. S. (1974). *The depressed woman: A study of social relationships.* Chicago: University of Chicago Press.

Weitzman, L. J. (1985). *The divorce revolution.* New York: Basic Books.

Zelkowitz, P. (1987). Social support and aggressive behavior in young children. *Family Relations, 36,* 129-134.

SINGLE PARENTS AND DAMAGED CHILDREN

The Fruits of the Sexual Revolution

Lloyd Eby and Charles A. Donovan

Lloyd Eby is assistant senior editor of The World & I. *Charles A. Donovan is senior policy consultant at the Family Research Council, Washington, D.C. Research assistance was provided by Diane Falk, Jayne Turconi, and Mark Petersen.*

Vice President Dan Quayle was right. Murphy Brown—the unmarried TV character who became pregnant on the show—was a bad role model for women, legitimizing and glamorizing single motherhood. But Quayle did not go on to raise or discuss the more difficult problems. Should Murphy Brown have had an abortion? Should she have taken more precautions with contraception so she didn't get pregnant? As she was unmarried, was it wrong for her to have sex? Should she have given up the baby for adoption?

The social science evidence now available shows conclusively that children suffer when they grow up in any family situation other than an intact two-parent family formed by their biological father and mother who are married to each other. As recently as 1960, the biological two-parent family was the norm; in that year, about 75 percent of children in the United States lived with both of their biological parents, who had been married only once, to one another. By 1991 this percentage had declined to about 56 percent. Now, if the darker forecasts are accurate, fewer than 50 percent of children can expect to live continuously throughout their childhood in such families.[1]

The costs of this ever-increasing decline in families and family support of children are huge: to the children, to the larger society, and to the nation. An increasing number of our children, largely from single-parent homes, are unable to participate constructively and ethically in our economic, political, and social life, although many children from single-parent families nonetheless do succeed in life. Costs include immense and ever-increasing welfare rolls; remedial and repeated education; anomie, crime, and lawlessness; high and increasing rates of teen suicide; dealing with unemployable people; and the financial, spiritual, and civic costs of all kinds of social pathologies. All these impose very great financial expenditures as well as enormous psychic and civic burdens. Indeed, it may not be too much to say that family breakdown— with its attendant pathologies and their costs—is our country's most serious social and economic problem, threatening to overwhelm us and even threatening our very democracy and the society on which it rests, unless somehow curbed.

When it was published in 1962, Anthony Burgess' *A Clockwork Orange* seemed overwrought in its depiction of the anomie, violence, pathology, and nihilism of some young people. Today, Burgess' fiction appears to have been remarkably prescient; the murders, rapes, thefts, assaults, burnings and lootings, and other crimes and damages committed by feral and often emotionless youths now surpass his depictions. These developments are very closely linked to the rise in family breakdown and single parenthood.

Today, more than half of all children will live for some period in a single-parent home, either as a result of being born to an unwed mother or as a result of divorce, and the number of such children continues to increase. Some of those children will find themselves having one or more stepparents—even successive series of different stepparents—through the marriage of their previously single parent or parents. But stepfamilies themselves are more prone to divorce, and in general stepparents do not care for or bond as well with children as do biological parents. Increasingly, children are living not with their biological parents but with their grandparents, in foster homes, or in other quasi-family situations. Of course, many children will survive all these troubles and traumas and become fulfilled and productive adults, and many single parents, foster parents, and stepparents cope very well and perform heroically. But those cases increasingly are being overshadowed by the number and severity of other ones. All the children who survive and flourish in these circumstances will do so because they somehow found a way through or around the difficulties, not because of them.

The Murphy Brown character's wealth, prominent social position, education, career success, management skills, race, and mature age with its attendant relative emotional stability will protect her and her child from some of the worst consequences of unmarried pregnancy and of growing up with a single parent: poverty, lack of educational opportunity and social standing, and the burdens and chaos resulting from having too much responsibility too young. The same holds for the hundreds of real-life actresses, princesses, and other prominent and successful women who have recently—often publicly and defiantly, sometimes quietly or even secretly—borne children out of wedlock. But even in these cases not all is well; children who grow up in single-parent families invariably suffer. The greatest suffering and deprivation, however—for both mothers and children—comes about from unmarried teenage pregnancy.

PREGNANCY OF UNMARRIED TEENAGERS

Today, the United States has a very high and increasing rate of pregnancies to unmarried teenage girls, a much higher rate than any other country in the developed world. In 1950 there were 56,000 births to unmarried teenage girls aged 15 to 19 years, and the birthrate was 12.6 births per thousand such teenagers. In 1960 there were 87,000 such births, and the rate had climbed to 15.3. Between 1961 and 1962 the rate fell slightly, although the number of such births continued to rise. From that date on, the rate has continued to rise every year, and the rate of increase itself has risen—the problem is accelerating. In 1970 there were 190,000 births to unmarried teenage mothers aged 15 to 19, and the rate of such births was 22.4 per thousand unmarried teenagers. In 1980 the figures were 263,000 births and a rate of 27.6. In 1990—the last year for which reliable statistics are available—the rate was 42.5 and the number of births was nearly 350,000—361,000 if we include those children born to girls under 15.

In 1990, 4,158,212 babies were born in the United States to all women. This means that of all births in 1990, about 8.7 percent—or one out of every twelve—was born to an unmarried teenager between 15 and 19 years of age.[2] One birth in twelve may seem relatively insignificant, but the total is for births to unmarried teenagers of all races, compared to

PRÉCIS

Attitudes changed in America after the post-1950s social-sexual revolution. Unmarried people came to view having sex as normal and right. Avoidance of divorce for the sake of the children gave way to favoring the happiness of adults as individuals. The taboo against birth out of wedlock eventually disappeared. So ever-more children are being born to unmarried women and growing up in single-parent families. The worst consequences—for both children and parent—occur from births to unmarried teenagers.

The costs—financial and nonfinancial—of the decline of families and family support of children are very high: Ever-increasing welfare rolls. Poor mothers who cannot escape poverty for themselves or their children. An increasing number of our children, largely from single-parent homes, who are lost to our economic, political, and social life. All kinds of social pathologies. Can our society and democracy survive these threats?

Previous attempts to deal with the problem have emphasized technological solutions—various forms of contraception, especially the pill and condoms. But teenagers are poor users of contraception. Rates and virulence of sexually transmitted diseases are rising.

What is to be done about all this? Perhaps we should return to teaching and emphasizing abstinence.

all births to all women, of whatever age or race, married or unmarried. If the statistics are broken down by race and restricted to unmarried women, a strong trend appears. Of all births to white women of all ages, the percentage of births to unmarried women in 1990 was 20.35 percent. For all births to women of all races, 28.0 percent were to unmarried women. Of all births to black women of all ages,

66.5 percent were to unmarried women.

The figures for nonmarital births to girls age 15 to 19 are even more bracing. For white teens, 56.4 percent of births were nonmarital in 1990; for black teens, 91.97 percent. Overall, 67.1 percent of teen births in 1990 were nonmarital—a mirror image of the situation as recently as 1970, when 70 percent of *all* teen births were to married women.

5. NEW STYLES AND THE FUTURE: Emerging Patterns

If anything, current figures may be worse: More than half the white teens giving birth are unmarried, and among young black mothers fewer than one in ten is married. In short, hardly any births to black teenagers are to married women, and two-thirds of births to all black women are to unmarried women. Each year, one in ten black teenagers will give birth. Nearly half will become unmarried mothers before the end of their teenage years—and many will have more than one child. Another conclusion is that in the United States a large number of children of all races—and the vast majority of black children—are growing up as children of single mothers, that is, as *fatherless* children.

TEENAGE GIRLS AND ABORTION

The figures given above are for live births, not conception rates. To compute conception rates, we need to include the figures for the number of pregnancies terminated through abortion, plus the number of pregnancies that result in miscarriages. The number of miscarriages is unknown but is estimated to be equal to 20 percent of births plus 10 percent of abortions. The number of pregnancies to unmarried teenagers that are terminated through abortion is quite large. Of the 1,590,750 abortions performed in the United States in 1988, 1,314,060, or 82.6 percent, were performed on unmarried women (of all women age 15–44, not just teenagers, and including separated, divorced, and never-married women).[3] Although statistics given by different authorities vary, conservative figures indicate that about 1,033,730 women under 20 became pregnant in 1988, and 40 percent of each age level in that group chose abortion.[4] In any case, we can conclude that a large number of teenage girls are choosing to end their pregnancies through abortion, and that abortion is being used as a last-ditch form of birth control for many teenage girls, establishing a pattern that, after more than two decades of abortion on demand nationwide, is reverberating throughout the cohort of women in their 20s.

Moreover, many counselors and other people concerned with the welfare of teenagers—or, less charitably, with burgeoning welfare rolls—advocate abortion and encourage unmarried pregnant girls to seek abortions.

CAUSES OF TEENAGE PREGNANCY

As Barbara Dafoe Whitehead has noted, a great change in the "social metric" occurred in post-1950s America, from an overarching emphasis on adults sacrificing themselves to achieve child well-being to a concern for adult individual self-fulfillment without regard to whether that is good for children.[5] The attitude that divorce was to be avoided for the sake of the children was exchanged for an attitude that what makes parents happy as individuals is what counts. The ancient taboo against birth out of wedlock was given up. Hugh Hefner's *Playboy* ethic and aesthetic (first issue, December 1953) sanctioned and encouraged young males in their pursuit of unattached sex, and Helen Gurley Brown's *Sex and the Single Girl*, published in 1962, proclaimed loudly that it was not only OK for single women to engage in sex but that they were entitled to it, as an issue of equality. These changes amounted to a great cultural shift, away from the attitude that sex should be restricted to married couples, toward an attitude that proclaimed sex as both good and necessary. The new attitude paid far less attention to marriage, in many cases actually disdaining it. Hollywood and the mass media took up these trends, so that today they are firmly ensconced in American popular culture.

What hardly anyone was willing to see at the time, however, was how children were being affected by these changes. Teenagers—girls especially—became ensnared in a dilemma: Are they adults or children? If they are adults, then they should be able—even encouraged, at least according to one kind of thinking—to participate in all the supposed pleasures of adulthood, including unmarried sex. But if they do engage in sex, then many of the girls will become pregnant. But they are not really adults; they are adolescents, even though their bodies have become sexually mature. The media and the popular culture, however, continually push them toward being sexually active. If the adults who are concerned for their welfare were to claim that it was wrong or misguided for them to be engaging in sex, this would tend to commit those adults to questioning whether the cultural shift is indeed good and beneficial, something very few people who are active in the mass and dominant culture—the universities and the media,

including TV, metropolitan newspapers, movies, the magazines, and so on—have been willing to do, until very recently anyway. Those who do question this cultural shift—for example, Dan Quayle—almost always are attacked as meanspirited, stupid, unrealistic religious bigots who want to "turn back the clock" to some supposed past golden era, as old fogies who are unwilling to accept the facts of contemporary life.

One result is widespread and rising amounts of sexual activity among teenagers at younger and younger ages. In 1982, 30.1 percent of women 15–17 years old reported that they were sexually experienced. By 1988 the figure had risen to 37.5 percent. Among unmarried women 18–19 years old, 59.7 percent reported that they were sexually experienced in 1982, and by 1988, 72 percent of such women reported sexual experience. This increased activity is coupled with a rising rate and number of teenage pregnancies. These changes have occurred across all races and social classes, but the most disruptive and devastating effects have been among those who were the poorest and most vulnerable. For them, the allure of sexual freedom broke the threads of cultural and moral cohesion that were the real safety net between temporary poverty and chronic destitution.

THE COSTS OF UNMARRIED PREGNANCY AND FATHERLESSNESS

Teenage pregnancy has costs to the mothers, to the children, and to the larger society and nation. In 1987, more than $19 billion in public funds was spent for income maintenance, health care, and nutrition for support of families begun by teenagers. Babies born to teenagers have a high risk of being born with low birth weight, and low birth weight requires initial hospital care averaging $20,000 per infant. The total lifetime medical costs for each low birth-weight infant average $400,000. For all adolescents (married and unmarried) giving birth, 46 percent go on welfare within four years, and 73 percent of unmarried teenagers giving birth go on welfare within four years.[6] The costs of welfare are extremely high, especially for state budgets. The total state budget for Michigan in 1992, for example, was about $30 billion, and one-third of this—$10 billion—went to the state's social service (welfare) program. Michigan's plight is similar to that of other states—it has neither the lowest nor the highest such expenditure. Moreover, members of these single-parent–headed, welfare-receiving families are at very high risk of remaining poor and ill educated throughout their lives. When married women go on welfare, they tend to get off welfare within a few years. When unmarried women go on welfare, they tend to remain there permanently. We now have the phenomenon in every state of large numbers of families, made up of unmarried women and their children, being on welfare for three or more generations, with no end in sight.

Has anyone ever heard of a child who is happy because he does not know his father? Being a child of a single mother is a handicap, regardless of the wealth, maturity, or social status of that mother.[7]

Numerous studies of child development have shown that growing up as the child of a single parent is linked with lower levels of academic achievement (having to repeat grades in school or receiving lower marks and class standing); increased levels of depression, stress, and aggression; a decrease in some indicators for physical health; higher incidences of needing the services of mental health professionals; and other emotional and behavioral problems.[8] All these effects are linked with lifetime poverty, poor achievement, susceptibility to suicide, likelihood of committing crimes and being arrested, and other pathologies. One such study, based on data from the 1988 National Health Interview Survey, concludes as follows:

> Data ... revealed an excess risk of negative health and performance indicators among children who did not live with both biological parents. These findings are consistent with the hypotheses that children are adversely affected ... by the relative lack of attention, supervision, and opposite-sex role models provided by single parents, regardless of marital status.[9]

THE ATTACK ON FATHERHOOD

While the cultural shift Whitehead describes was occurring, fatherhood was coming under attack.

Among other things, these attacks included feminist rhetoric, the claim that fathers are distant and brutal and repressive, based on the observation that some fathers abuse and otherwise mistreat their children and wives, and the observable fact that some children without fathers grow up quite well and become very good and productive adults. "A woman without a man is like a fish without a bicycle," defiantly proclaimed one feminist slogan. But fathers do have a crucial role in rearing children. The small boy with a bicycle wants a father to help him learn to ride it, and both boys and girls usually like their fathers to take them fishing.

Children need two parents, playing into the daily dramas of discipline, self-sacrifice, sincerity, and complementarity. Historically, fathers have given and enforced rules of behavior and provided role models of proper male behavior for both girls and boys. Traditionally, fathers have been very concerned with the sexual virtue of their daughters. Fathers know the attitudes and intentions of teenage boys, having once been teens themselves, and therefore are uniquely able both to guide their daughters and to check out and enforce rules on boyfriends. This does not mean that mothers do not or cannot perform these tasks and roles, but they are handicapped doing it alone. Fathers are vital, and their place cannot be taken by a single mother, however able, resolute, and resourceful she may be. Having fathers as guardians, disciplinarians, and role models is necessary to help teenagers navigate those most difficult experiences and years.

Today, increasing numbers of children, even preteens, are becoming involved in acts of violence and crime, including drug usage and drug dealing, assault, robbery, burglary, theft, carjacking, and shootings and murders, often for seemingly the most trivial of reasons. On the street, a disrespectful look, or an en-

vied pair of sneakers, can provoke a bullet. ("I shot him cause he 'dissed' me.") The costs of this are immense. For all of us—rich and poor, of whatever race—our sense of civic order, safety, and well-being is increasingly threatened, if it has not already collapsed. The monetary

---

It may not be too much to say that family breakdown—with its attendant pathologies and their costs—is our country's most serious social and economic problem.

---

price is enormous; public costs include the expenses of law enforcement, prisons, and other expenditures of crime fighting. Private costs include insurance, security systems, repairing the damages, and the forced exodus of people as they flee our cities in an attempt to find a safe area. A majority of the young people who are responsible for these crimes, with their attendant costs, are products of what once was unashamedly acknowledged as "broken homes."

The criminal and other destructive activities of these teenagers tend to make them into poor or unsuitable prospective marriage partners. Female children of single mothers are more likely to engage in early premarital sex, thus leading to increasing rates of unmarried pregnancy at younger and younger ages. Male children of single mothers are less and less able to become responsible fathers and marriage partners. So we can conclude that unmarried parenthood is feeding on itself, contributing to its own rise.

As already stated, women who are single parents tend to be poorer, more prone to being on welfare, less educationally advantaged, less able to handle careers and work, and more beleaguered in every way than their married sisters. These conclusions hold true for the vast majority of cases, even though there are many instances of such women performing notably and heroically. Single mothers are understandably less likely to be able to accumulate any appreciable amount of savings, purchase homes, afford higher education for themselves and their children, or finance a start-up of any business or profession for themselves or their offspring. In fact, if they are on welfare—Aid to Families with Dependent Children (AFDC)—they are forbidden by the rules to have any significant savings. Some economists have gone so far as to suggest that increasing rates of single motherhood point toward the economic demise of a nation. All these effects are especially pronounced and accentuated for women who become mothers as single teenagers. So the cost of teenage pregnancy to all—to the parents, to the children, to the society, and to the nation—is very high and rising.

PREVENTION OF TEENAGE PREGNANCY

It is estimated that 41 percent of unintended pregnancies among teenagers could be avoided if all sexually active teenagers used contraception. But one-fourth of such teenagers use no contraceptive method or an ineffective one. Half of all teenage pregnancies occur within six months of first sexual intercourse, and more than 20 percent of all initial premarital pregnancies occur in the first month after the initiation of sex. But the use of contraception requires planning, and planned initiation of sexual intercourse among teens is rare. Only 17 percent of women and 25 percent of men report having planned their first intercourse. The contraceptives most widely used by teenagers are the pill and condoms.[10]

Nature equips humans with two differing timetables for maturity; physical and sexual maturity comes first, and emotional and psychological maturity appears later. Teenagers, particularly younger ones, are poorly equipped with the ability to foresee the consequences of their acts and plan accordingly. Teens tend to see themselves as invulnerable to risks. Moreover, this is a time of life when peer pressure and media pressure for engaging in sex are especially acute.

There is reliable but anecdotal evidence that, at least for many inner-city and other poor unmarried teenage girls, their pregnancies are not actually unplanned but actively desired. These studies conclude that the girls are not ignorant about contraception; they do not use it because they actually yearn for babies. Their emotional and psychological immaturity, however, does not allow them to know or understand the real consequences of motherhood, especially teenage motherhood. This is the phenomenon

commonly called "babies having babies." Typically, a poor girl who has a baby while unmarried is especially vulnerable to becoming pregnant again while still in her teens.

The primary goal of teenage pregnancy prevention programs since 1970 has been to educate teenagers about the risks of pregnancy and to get them to use contraceptives; this sometimes has been derided as "throwing condoms at the problem." But teenagers typically do not go to see the school nurse or to a health clinic until after they have become sexually active; girls often go for the first time because they think they may be pregnant.

The received approach to the problem of teenage pregnancy has been "technological," in that it has relied on providing teenagers with the technology for avoiding pregnancy, or, once pregnant, with abortions as a technological solution to the pregnancy. But rising rates of teenage pregnancy, abortion, and births to teenage mothers show that these technological solutions have been anything but effective. Advanced as the "realistic" answer to the out-of-wedlock pregnancy problem, these interventions have come athwart the reality of failure statistics. Abortion has reduced the overall adolescent birthrate, but the unmarried adolescent birthrate has gone up dramatically since 1970. Adolescents have become slightly more efficient users of contraception in recent years, but they remain dramatically less so than the adult married population. Moreover, the slight increase in efficiency has been overwhelmed by three factors that are not unrelated to contraceptive availability itself: (a) an increase in the percentage of adolescents in each age cohort having sex; (b) a decrease in the age of the first reported sexual experience; and (c) increases in the frequency of intercourse and the number of sexual partners among adolescents. In this environment, more intense contraceptive use and increased pregnancy rates coexist and may be mutually reinforcing.

All this says nothing about sexually transmitted disease (STD). Increased sexual activity is correlated with rising rates of these diseases in teenagers. Regular, conscientious, and proper use of condoms lowers the incidence of such disease transmission, but we know that teenagers often fail to use them and that, even with conscientious use, condoms sometimes fail. There is no lowering of the risk of sexually transmitted disease through use of oral contraceptives.

This is the fruit of the newfound sexual freedom among adolescents. Not surprisingly, these dismal outcomes are tempting a new generation of advocates to discard freedom when it comes to the latest generation of contraceptive devices.

NORPLANT AND TEENAGE GIRLS

The failure of free-choice use of the pill or condoms to reduce the rates of pregnancy in teenage girls has led to proposals for recommending or requiring Norplant as a contraceptive for teenage girls—particularly for girls who already have a baby. The best technical argument for Norplant is that it removes the diligence factor for those adolescents who receive the implant. Those pregnancies to teenage girls that resulted because they "forgot" to take the pill or because a condom was not readily available will not occur, advocates say, with Norplant. Once inserted in the woman's upper arm, Norplant works automatically, so it would lower the threshold of conscientiousness that adolescents need to practice contraception diligently.

By similar reasoning, however, Norplant will lower adolescent conscientiousness about avoiding sexual encounters on the grounds that pregnancy might result. The conclusion is that, although Norplant arguably would be effective in reducing the number of pregnancies, it may well promote a rise in sexually transmitted diseases.

Norplant advocates recommend continued use of condoms to avert this result, but this raises the diligence problem again. If diligence was not an effective strategy for contraception, will it be so for disease? AIDS infection and syphilis are on the rise, as is antibiotic-resistant gonorrhea. This rise has occurred even in a time when there has been a slight increase in contraceptive efficiency among adolescents. But condom use itself is no guarantee against disease. As one expert notes, "The inescapable fact is that, during one act of intercourse, condoms *may* protect against STD, but for frequent, repeated acts of intercourse over months and years, *they will not*."[11]

Increases also are occurring in other significant venereal diseases, such as chlamydia (which can cause sterility), herpes, and HPV (human papilloma virus). This last is associated with precancerous conditions, from which invasive cancer can develop. So, even if Norplant turns out to reduce the incidence of teenage pregnancy, it may well lead to even more serious problems involving spread of an impressive and growing array of sexually transmissible diseases.

The most recent news on STDs is especially grim. A study released by the Alan Guttmacher Institute on March 21, 1993, reaches the conclusion that 56 million Americans—one in five—are infected with a sexually transmitted viral disease. These diseases can be controlled but not cured. The study estimates that even more Americans are likely to contract an STD during their lifetimes. The greatest effect will be on women and people under the age of 25. According to the study, each year 100,000 to 150,000 women become infertile as a result of STDs. Teenagers and blacks are disproportionately affected by STDs because these people are more likely to be unmarried and thus to have multiple sexual partners. Moreover, teenagers who begin sexual activity earlier are more likely to have more partners. About one in nine women aged 15 to 44 are treated for pelvic inflammatory disease (PID) during their reproductive lifetimes, according to the report, and, if current trends continue, one-half of all women who were 15 in 1970 will have had a PID by the year 2000.[12]

The contraceptive debate of the 1970s occurred in a completely different environment from today's—medically, morally, and socially. Medically, with HIV, the stakes now are significantly higher, even if heterosexual transmission remains relatively uncommon. Morally and socially, the sex education and contraception movements of the 1970s competed against established mores that militated against teen sexual experimentation, but these movements did not compete against an alternative institutional and educational approach, namely abstinence education. Today, the generation that

lived through the '70s is debating the policies of the '90s. Experience of what has happened in this field in the ensuing three decades does not lend much respect or hope for any "magic bullet" approach such as is epitomized by free-choice use of Norplant. In today's debate, advocates of the technological approach embodied in Norplant are battling against advocates of an abstinence-based approach who are armed with texts, studies, and curricula of their own. Veterans of the sexual revolution can be found in both camps, leading to a much more realistic—and interesting—public policy debate, with neither side having a monopoly on scientific opinion.

WHAT IS TO BE DONE?

Patterns of teenage pregnancy, abortion, and out-of-wedlock childbearing, although stabilizing somewhat in the 1980s, continue to worsen. After a trial of two decades, national pregnancy policies have failed to reduce pregnancy rates, have succeeded in lowering birthrates only through a sharp concomitant rise in abortions among adolescents, and have coincided with an unprecedented increase in teenage sexual activity. A generation or more of young people—especially inner-city blacks, but others too, of all races—is being lost to productive adulthood and citizenship and is imposing huge and ever-increasing costs—financial, social, and medical—on the larger society and nation. These costs are so great that they threaten to overwhelm us. Can civil liberties, democracy, civil order, and the rule of law survive these present conditions? For the sake of the next generation of American children, it is time for a generous dose of domestic "new thinking" about one of the nation's most intractable social problems.

If all unmarried women of childbear-

ing age for whom it is not medically contraindicated were forced to use it, Norplant would be one solution, but forced imposition is ethically objectionable as well as impossible in a democratic society. Can voluntary use of this method, or any other contraceptive, significantly lower this rising tide of births to single women, with the enormous and ever-rising attendant costs both to children and the nation? So far, voluntary contraceptive methods have failed to curb this problem. Besides, Norplant does not prevent—and may even exacerbate—the spread of venereal disease. Norplant plus condoms has all the problems of teenagers not being sufficiently diligent to practice effective contraception. Perhaps it is time to abandon technological solutions and return to teaching abstinence on moral grounds. Although it sometimes failed, teaching children to abstain was socially, psychologically, and medically far more effective than any of the methods introduced by the sexual revolution—a revolution that was supposed to offer us freedom but that seems instead to have failed us, threatening our livelihoods, our civil order, and perhaps even our liberty itself.

NOTES

1. Deborah A. Dawson, "Family Structure and Children's Health and Well Being: Data from the 1988 National Health Interview Survey on Child Care," *Journal of Marriage and the Family* 53 (August 1991): 573–84.

2. The National Center for Health Statistics, *Vital Statistics of the United States*, annual and *Monthly Vital Statistics Report*, vol. 41, no. 9 supplement, February 25, 1993.

3. Alan Guttmacher Institute, *Abortion Factbook, 1992*.

4. Cited in Center for Population Options, "Adolescents and Abortion Factsheet," February 1993.

5. Barbara Dafoe Whitehead, "Dan Quayle Was Right," *Atlantic Monthly*, April 1993, 47 ff.

6. David A. Hamburg, M.D., *Today's Children: Creating a Future for a Generation in Crisis* (New York: Random House, Times Books, 1992), 198.

7. Margaret Carlson, "Why Quayle Has Half a Point," *Time*, 1 June 1992, 30, 31.

8. Dawson, 573, 574.

9. Dawson, 580.

10. Cited in Center for Population Options, "Adolescent Contraceptive Use Factsheet," June 1990.

11. Joe S. McIlhaney, M.D., *Sexuality and Sexually Transmitted Diseases* (Grand Rapids, Mich.: Baker Book House, 1990), 36. Emphasis in original.

12. Study by Alan Guttmacher Institute, reported in the *New York Times*, 1 April 1993, A1.

A Critique of Pessimistic Views About U.S. Families

Profound social and economic changes in recent decades have contributed to a rising tide of pessimistic assessments of U.S. children and families. Focusing the analysis on the pace of children's development, on families' use of self-care (latchkey) arrangements, and on work-family relations, we demonstrate that the pessimistic views are often inaccurate or exaggerated. We conclude our critique by indicating that system-wide adaptations are needed to meet the challenges brought about by rapid change.

Hyman Rodman and Judy Sidden

Hyman Rodman is Excellence Foundation Professor and Judy Sidden is a doctoral student in the Department of Human Development and Family Studies, University of North Carolina at Greensboro, Greensboro, NC 27412.

Public perceptions about the health or strength of "the U.S. family" move in cycles, and in the late 1980s and early 1990s these perceptions are in the trough of a cycle. We shall point out the sources of this strong shift toward pessimistic views, and we will document the inaccuracies and exaggerations of these views. Although these negative views pertain to many family and child issues, we will focus our discussion on three topics: (a) childhood and parents' expectations about the pace of children's development, (b) self-care (latchkey) children and school-age child care, and (c) work and family relations. In addition, we will briefly discuss the complex social system issues that confront us as we move toward the 21st century.

If there were an Index of Perceived Family Strength analogous to the Index of Consumer Confidence, we suspect that it would show a decline through the 1980s and into the 1990s. Political rhetoric about declining morality often focuses on family failures and media stories about family problems abound. Three recent publications reflect the pessimistic view about U.S. families: *Disturbing the Nest* (Popenoe, 1988), *Rebuilding the Nest* (Blankenhorn, Bayme, & Elshtain, 1990), and *Beyond Rhetoric* (National Commission on Children, 1991). *Disturbing the Nest* focuses its analysis on family decline in Sweden but also deals comparatively with family decline in other advanced societies, including the United States. Although Popenoe clearly states that "family decline" is not necessarily "bad," he nevertheless expresses strong concerns about current family trends that have a negative impact on children. *Rebuilding the Nest* is a collection of essays by prominent social and behavioral scientists who paint a largely negative picture of the current state of the U.S. family. *Beyond Rhetoric* is the final report

of the National Commission on Children, chaired by Senator John D. Rockefeller IV, that portrays the current situation of children and families in pessimistic terms. In all three publications, despite occasional protestations to the contrary, ideological positions lead the authors toward their deeply felt concerns and their pessimistic views.

Before turning to specific topics, several general points need to be introduced. The first is that society in general, and families in particular, are constantly changing within the context of environmental, economic, political, and other changes. These changes may be fast or slow, harmonious or unsettling, and may have a different impact upon different segments of society. Some changes may be difficult to accept because they challenge traditional values or the traditional structure of power (Goldscheider & Waite, 1991). We believe that this is one major reason for some of the pessimistic views about U.S. families.

The second is that changes in one domain reverberate through the system and may require changes in other domains in order to restore a degree of stability and harmony. This involves more than a challenge to traditional values and power structures—it may require new values and new power arrangements. These kinds of changes meet strong resistance from vested interests and can engender conflict, confrontation, and violence. The changes also engender political and scholarly statements that support traditional family arrangements and that use the traditional family as a benchmark in judging alternative arrangements as family decline, social deviation, or moral deterioration (Popenoe, 1988).

The conflicts that accompany change attract media attention, and this leads us to our third general point—the role of the media in reporting the news. Their attention focuses on the most dramatic conflicts, the most violent confrontations, the most negative news. These negative reports capture the headlines and attract the most extensive news coverage. Groups with partisan agendas, unhappy

with some state of affairs, make effective use of the media's penchant for conflict, confrontation, and violence. In this way, public perceptions are often focused on the negative and pessimistic sides of an issue. This has clearly occurred in the 1980s and 1990s and has contributed to pessimistic views about the U.S. family that are sometimes unwarranted and often exaggerated (cf. Demo, 1992). It is not our position that all social and family changes are positive and beneficial. Our objective, rather, is to provide a counterweight to the outpouring of overly pessimistic views about the present state and future prospects for U.S. families.

The Pace of Children's Development

A major criticism of U.S. families focuses on the negative consequences for children's development. For example, there is a widespread belief that the pace of children's development is too rapid, that children are forced to take on too many responsibilities too soon, and that children are robbed of their childhood. An argument certainly can be made for this position and, as we shall document, it has been made by numerous social scientists and popularized by the media. But a stronger argument can be made for the opposite position, namely that U.S. values and U.S. schools create a climate that delays children's development and deprives them of opportunities to take on appropriate responsibilities when they are competent to do so (cf. Gatto, 1991).

Variations in the pace of children's development and their impact on children and families is of longstanding concern. Hess and Handel (1959) pointed out that

> families differ ... in how the parents pace their children through childhood—whether they push, encourage, or restrain.... When we observe that one parent is eager for his child to behave as much like an adult as quickly as possible, whereas another

---

Key Words: family decline, pace of children's development, self-care children, work-family relations.

From *Family Relations*, Vol. 41, No. 4, October 1992, pp. 436-439. © 1992 by The National Council on Family Relations, 3989 Central Avenue, NE, Suite 550, Minneapolis, MN 55421. Reprinted by permission.

regrets his child's loss of babyish ways, it is clear that different personal wishes or aims are operating. (p. 17)

In addition, "different concepts of growth and different time perspectives also operate" (pp. 17-18), stemming from cultural, subcultural, or familial norms about the appropriate pace of development.

The widespread view that family changes over the past two decades are forcing the pace of children's development and robbing children of their childhood is disseminated by several popular scholars and by the media. Elkind, in his popular book *The Hurried Child,* first published in 1981 and revised in 1988, is the chief proponent of this viewpoint, but many others have taken a similar position. Spock (1989) says that

our excessive competitiveness is being passed on to our children. Some parents are now caught up in efforts to produce superkids ... A deplorable and ludicrous example of parents' overzealousness is the desire to have their 2-year-olds taught to read, though no one has shown that this will produce a better reader. Such misplaced pressure is more likely to produce lopsided development and an aversion to school. (p. 106)

Hymowitz (1988) quotes several educators and psychologists who express concern about children who are forced to follow overprogrammed schedules. She is distressed that with such rigidly organized activities "children may be forgetting how to have fun." And her pessimism extends to "fast-track couples eager for a fast track for their kids. They're pushing them sooner and more often into activities they believe will enhance their kids' chances to land at the best schools and later, the best jobs" (p. 41). The media are filled with stories, typically phrased in negative terms, about parents pushing preschoolers to read, kindergartners to use computers, and school-age children to fend for themselves while their parents are at work (Gibbs, 1989; Putka, 1988). Edward Zigler says, "Kids understand that they are being cheated out of childhood" (cited in Gibbs, 1989, p. 61).

In the preface to his revision of *The Hurried Child,* Elkind (1988) expresses deep concern about our overly optimistic conception of children's competence. He argues that children are viewed as more competent than they really are in order to rationalize many economic, educational, and family practices that are highly stressful to children. His pessimistic views about "the hurried child" reflect the current pessimistic U.S. view about children

and families. We argue, however, that a major problem in U.S. society stems from the underestimation of children's competence and a reluctance to provide them with information and opportunities to develop responsibilities and maturity that they are developmentally ready for.

Rodman (1990) discussed several areas in which scholars mistakenly and unfortunately stress children's lack of competence rather than their competence. In the area of sexuality, for example, there is much public and political emphasis on the supposed need to shield children and adolescents from information. We are subject to partisan rhetoric and organized pressure that shrilly argues that sex education will corrupt children and will undercut parental authority (Kasun, 1978). As a result, U.S. children are on a starvation diet when it comes to education on human sexuality. We stress children's lack of competence, and we mistrust their ability to absorb sexual information in a responsible and healthy manner. In consequence, adolescents in the United States engage extensively in sexual behavior and have higher rates of pregnancy, abortion, and illegitimate childbirth than in most other developed societies. In brief, children and adolescents are not trusted to do various things; they do them anyhow; and because of this mistrust they are not provided with the educational information that would enable them to develop their competence to behave in a responsible manner.

Fine and Sandstrom (1988) point out that children are more competent than most adults believe them to be. They cite several studies with findings that document children's competence and "note that these are merely representative studies that demonstrate that children have considerable emotional, social, and cognitive capacities for which we do not always give them credit" (p. 73).

The discussion here about the pace of children's development is necessarily brief. A comprehensive discussion would deal with certain complexities and ambiguities. First, for example, U.S. children may be granted too much responsibility in some areas and not enough responsibility in other areas. Second, our knowledge about the appropriate or normative pace of development is limited. Third, cultural influences on the pace of development have been alluded to but have not been addressed. Fourth, a semantic analysis might demonstrate some overlap between the too-hurried and the too-delayed viewpoints. The essential point, however, is that an overly pessimistic and clearly questionable viewpoint has come to predominate our popular thinking.

Latchkey Children

The use of the term "latchkey children" reflects the negative perception that many individuals hold about children who spend time at home alone or with their siblings while their parents are at work. Some writers have referred to the "latchkey syndrome" as though it is a disease and the media report horror stories about children who are left alone at home (cf. Rodman, 1988). It is because of the negative connotations of "latchkey" that Rodman introduced the term self-care, and a self-care child has been defined as "between the ages of approximately 6 and 13 who spends time at home alone or with a younger sibling on a periodic basis" (Cole & Rodman, 1987, p. 93).

A critical issue about families' use of the self-care arrangement is the impact of the arrangement on children's development. The question is almost always phrased in terms of whether it has harmful effects. Many scientists and journalists have assumed that self-care is necessarily harmful and have deplored the practice (cf. Rodman, 1988). The empirical evidence, however, suggests that these negative views are premature and probably unwarranted. Although the findings are mixed, the weight of the evidence thus far suggests that school-age children in self-care are not significantly different from those in adult care in their adjustment and development. The premature criticism and the negative assumptions about self-care in the 1980s are reminiscent of the negative reactions to "working mothers" and to "day care" in the 1950s and 1960s (cf. Rodman, Pratto, & Nelson, 1985). It is now clear that the impact of mothers' employment, day care, or self-care on children's development are complex issues involving many other variables. Since we have dealt with self-care issues previously, the present discussion will be brief. Once again, however, the major point is that a negative viewpoint about self-care emerged in the absence of empirical evidence, and that the developing empirical evidence now suggests that such negativism is oversimplified and unwarranted.

The self-care issue is clearly related to the pace of children's development. When are children competent enough to care for themselves for an hour after school? How can parents introduce self-care as one way of helping children to develop independence and responsibility? Because of the pervading pessimism about families and children, discussions of these questions are often distorted. Elkind (1988), for example, writes negatively about latchkey children and does not acknowledge that many parents and children choose self-care as their preferred option. He therefore rebukes women's magazines that suggest that the self-care experience may be beneficial for children. "It supposedly teaches them responsibility and self-reliance," he writes mockingly, "and gives them quiet time in which to do their homework. A necessity is thus neatly turned into a virtue!" (p. xvii). Elkind's pessimistic viewpoint may be popular, but it is inaccurate. The great majority of parents chooses self-care carefully and uses it responsibly; in many of these cases it is one of many ways in which parents are teaching their children to be responsible and independent (Cole & Rodman, 1992).

Exaggerated notions about the number of latchkey children in the United States, about the amount of time they spend in self-care, and about negative effects on their development provide grist for the mill of right-wing ideologues (cf. Flynn & Rodman, 1991). Social and economic changes in U.S. society have propelled an increasing percentage of mothers into the labor force in recent decades. This has increased the number of children in self-care arrangements, and the negative views about latchkey children have provided those who are troubled by recent changes with ammunition to assail these changes. In most cases the criticism is directed against mothers who work and thus presumably short-change their children, or against families that are so preoccupied with economic activities that their children are left to fend for themselves. These criticisms overlook the social context in which families operate and to which families must adapt, and they also overlook the many positive social and familial adaptations that are taking place.

Work and Family

Scholarly and journalistic writings are filled with pessimistic views about family decline, the pace of children's development, day care, latchkey children, and divorce trends. These views are often paired with a concern about the dramatic increase in the number of women entering the work force. Debates about these issues, and the thinly disguised threat such debates usually represent for working women, are diversions which mask far more substantive issues facing the nation and its families as we enter the 21st century. Efforts to strengthen or save "the family" are largely nostalgic throwbacks to a time that never was. Social change is happening at a breathtaking pace and alarmists about the family are expressing our collective anxiety about the ambiguities of the present and the unknowns of the future. What is fundamentally at stake is not the decline of the family but the transformation of a social and economic system that has its foundation in the oppression of groups of people based on gender, race, and class. Relationships in the workplace and opportunities for U.S. workers are changing as a result of shifts during the 20th century from either legalized or implicit discrimination to less discriminatory practices.

It is particularly the elimination of bars against women's participation in the marketplace that has had the most profound effect. A recent dip in women's employment (Morin, 1991) has been interpreted by some as an indication that women are rejecting the workplace in favor of the home. While it is certainly true that some women are deciding that the costs of outside employment outweigh the gains, another reasonable explanation for the 1991 dip was the increased unemployment rate across the nation. But more to the point, the issue of whether women as a group will participate in the labor market is a red herring that diverts our attention from the fact that all people, regardless of race or gender, have the right of full access to the labor market and all its perquisites. Given the changes in U.S. society over the past three decades, the question of whether or not women will work is as senseless as the question of whether or not men will work.

The changes in the workplace—especially women's increased participation—have affected marital and intergenerational relations. These profound changes call for family adaptations and threaten vested interests and traditional values. This is the source of much of the pessimism about families. Since we are not going back in time, a key question that individuals and families face is: What is the nature of their relationship with work going to be in the next century? One consequence of women's increased access to the labor market has been a confrontation between the demands of home and work. As the 1980s myth of the superwoman who could do it all has been discarded, women have placed greater demands on their partners for participation in housework and child care. Although women still carry the larger burden of child care (Sanik, 1981, 1990) and especially of housework, men are also being confronted with the conflict between work and home. Because our values often lag behind behavioral changes, many men, like women, feel they cannot be honest at the workplace about the conflicts with home (Shellenberger, 1991). This conflict is often intensified by our sense that work commands more than its fair share of our time and energy. Feeble constructs such as "quality time" have done little to assuage our growing dissatisfaction with the demands of the workplace and with the need to develop a better balance between work and family.

The changing relationships between work and family have contributed to the growth of a new group of second class people, that of day-care and preschool workers. Whereas in the past it was on the shoulders of wives and mothers that the male worker stood, now it is on the shoulders of day-care and preschool workers that dual-earner and dual-career parents stand. And the manifestations of oppression are similar—low wages, low status, and little opportunity for advancement. Poverty, of course, is a continuing problem in U.S. society and during the past two decades the gap between rich and poor has widened. For those in low-paid employment, both parents find it economically necessary to work. In 1990 more than 7.2 million U.S. workers found it necessary to work two or more jobs (Stinson, 1990). While Americans at every level of society are feeling the growing conflict between work and family, the working poor are feeling it most of all. They have fewer alternatives than middle and upper income people when work and family demands are in conflict.

Social and economic changes are challenging Americans to develop innovative relationships between work and family. The challenge of doing so calls forth pessimistic statements about families; criticism of working women, and especially of working mothers, is often ill-concealed by these pessimistic statements. The continuing focus on women's labor force participation as the wellspring of the family's problems is misguided. A nation whose economy is based upon oppression and discrimination cannot sustain itself indefinitely. Neither women nor any minority group will give up gains they have achieved. We must address ourselves more fully to the creative emergence of new relationships between work and family which openly acknowledge the demands of both settings and which give due attention to the needs of nurturing families. This is a joint responsibility of government, employers, unions, and employees, and many positive developments are already under way.

Moving Toward the 21st Century

Although we have chosen to focus our critique on pessimistic views about the pace of children's development, self-care children, and work-family relations, we could have focused on many other family phenomena that are viewed in pessimistic terms. It is important to stress that pessimistic views directed at any one family phenomenon may ignore the larger social system within which families function. The national economy affects employment opportunities for family members, as does the women's movement, the international marketplace, and a host of other factors. Similarly, child care arrangements are interconnected with family and kinship structures, government policies, workplace practices, and cultural values. To focus pessimistically on any one aspect as "the problem" is as futile as using a microscope to view the stars. Thus, to approach the family, or some aspect of the family, with the idea that it is in decline or in trouble and needs fixing is not very useful.

We need to address the total social context within which the family operates and to recognize the revolutionary global, national, and interpersonal changes that are taking place. Our vision of the very nature of family must change. We must recognize that the form of the family is undergoing and will continue to undergo profound changes even as the needs of its members remain. These needs are for nurturance and support, the development and expression of competence and creativity, a sense of belonging and self-worth, and the development of ample physical and emotional health. There is no evidence to suggest that certain specific forms of the family are the only way of meeting these needs.

Family professionals, in their roles as researchers, educators, and practitioners,

have a major part to play within the ongoing changes that are leading us into the 21st century. Perhaps the most significant contribution they can make is to deflect pessimistic evaluations of the family toward an understanding of the complex connections between families and the larger social system. We must help policymakers and the public to broaden their vision, when they are concerned about families, to examine education, health, the economy, government, and a host of other important connections. In the work we do as teachers, writers, and consultants we need to focus more attention on how changes in the wider social and economic system are leading to changes in family composition and organization. Finally, underlying this work, must be a fundamental commitment to promoting interpersonal tolerance and to eliminating injustice and discrimination wherever it exists in the social system.

REFERENCES

Blankenhorn, D., Bayme, S., & Elshtain, J. B. (Eds.). (1990). *Rebuilding the nest: A new commitment to the American family*. Milwaukee: Family Service America.

Cole, C., & Rodman, H. (1987). When school-age children care for themselves: Issues for family life educators and parents. *Family Relations, 36*, 92-96.

Cole, C., & Rodman, H. (1992). *A theoretical model for explaining parents' child care decisions*. Manuscript submitted for publication.

Demo, D. H. (1992). Parent-child relations: Assessing recent changes. *Journal of Marriage and the Family, 54*, 104-117.

Elkind, D. (1988). *The hurried child: Growing up too fast too soon* (rev. ed.). Reading, MA: Addison-Wesley.

Fine, G. A., & Sandstrom, K. L. (1988). *Knowing children: Participant observation with minors*. Beverly Hills, CA: Sage.

Flynn, C. P., & Rodman, H. (1991). Latchkey children and after-school care: A feminist dilemma? In E. A. Anderson & R. C. Hula (Eds.), *The reconstruction of family policy* (pp. 77-89). New York: Greenwood.

Gatto, J. (1991, September/October). Why schools don't educate. *Family Therapy Networker*, pp. 55-59.

Gibbs, N. (1989, April 24). How America has run out of time. *Time*, pp. 58-67.

Goldscheider, F. K., & Waite, L. J. (1991). *New families, no families? The transformation of the American home*. Berkeley: University of California Press.

Hess, R. D., & Handel, G. (1959). *A psychosocial approach to family life*. Chicago: University of Chicago Press.

Hymowitz, C. (1988, September 20). For many kids, playtime isn't freetime. *Wall Street Journal*, p. 41.

Kasun, J. R. (1978). Teenage pregnancy: A reply to zero population growth. *Society, 15*, 9-15.

Morin, R. (1991, July 14). The trend that wasn't: Are moms leaving work? or did the dip deceive? *Washington Post*, p. C1, C4.

National Commission on Children. (1991). *Beyond rhetoric: A new American agenda for children and families*. Final report of the National Commission on Children. Washington, DC: U. S. Government Printing Office.

Popenoe, D. (1988). *Disturbing the nest: Family change and decline in modern societies*. New York: Aldine de Gruyter.

Putka, G. (1988, July 6). Some schools press so hard kids become stressed and fearful. *Wall Street Journal*, pp. 1, 17.

Rodman, H. (1988). From latchkey stereotypes toward self-care realities. In S. K. Steinmetz (Ed.), *Family and support systems across the life span* (pp. 99-104). New York: Plenum.

Rodman, H. (1990). Legal and social dilemmas of adolescent sexuality. In J. Bancroft & J. M. Reinisch (Eds.), *Adolescence and puberty* (pp. 254-266). New York: Oxford University Press.

Rodman, H., Pratto, D. J., & Nelson, R. S. (1985). Child care arrangements and children's functioning: A comparison of self-care and adult-care children. *Developmental Psychology, 21*, 413-418.

Sanik, M. M. (1981). Division of household work: A decade comparison—1967-1977. *Home Economics Journal, 10*, 175-180.

Sanik, M. M. (1990). Parents' time use: A 1967-1986 comparison. *Lifestyles: Family and Economic Issues, 11*, 299-316.

Shellenberger, S. (1991, August 16). Men become evasive about family demands. *Wall Street Journal*, p. B1.

Spock, B. (1989). It's all up to us. *Newsweek* [Special Issue, The 21st Century Family], pp. 106-107.

Stinson, Jr., J. F. (1990). Multiple jobholding up sharply in the 1980s. *Labor Review, 113*, 3-10.

MARRIAGE AND ROMANTIC RELATIONSHIPS

DEFINING INTIMACY IN ROMANTIC RELATIONSHIPS*

▼

Although the ongoing sharing of romantic intimacy is recognized as being health promoting and as a sought-after goal, there has been no consensus in the literature on a definition of the construct. The present paper proposes a multidimensional definition of romantic intimacy that was developed following a review and analysis of published definitions of intimacy. The differences between the constructs of love and intimacy are also discussed, as well as how the present definition may have value to family practitioners.

Barry F. Moss and Andrew I. Schwebel

Barry F. Moss is a Post-doctoral Fellow in Psychology at the University of Washington, Seattle, WA 98105. Andrew I. Schwebel is Professor of Psychology, Ohio State University, 1885 Neil Avenue Mall, Columbus, OH 43210.

The level of intimacy that individuals experience within relationships exerts a profound influence on their social development, personal adjustment, and physical health. Specifically, intimacy plays an integral role in individuals' successful passage through developmental stages, solidification of friendships, attainment of marital happiness, and success in psychotherapeutic encounters (Erikson, 1963; Fisher & Stricker, 1982; Schaefer & Olson, 1981; Sullivan, 1953). Further, individuals in intimate relationships are more resistant to a number of diseases and physically disabling conditions, have a lower rate of mental illness, and are involved in fewer automobile fatalities than others in the general population (Brown, Harris & Copeland, 1977; Lynch, 1977; Traupmann, Eckels, & Hatfield, 1982).

Failure to obtain satisfactory levels of intimacy in a romantic relationship has been identified as the largest category of problem behavior which motivates

*Preparation of this manuscript was supported in part by an Ohio State Graduate Student Research Alumni Award and by a Sigma Xi Grant-in-Aid Research Award.

Key Words: definition, intimacy, love, relationships, romantic.

people to obtain outpatient psychotherapy (Horowitz, 1979) and as the most frequent reason given by couples for their divorce (Waring, 1988). People in intimacy-deficient committed relationships, compared to those in intimacy-providing relationships and those who are single or divorced, experience greater vulnerability to stress-related psychophysiological disorders, depression, and other nonpsychotic emotional illnesses (Medalie & Goldbourt, 1976; Patton & Waring, 1984; Waring, Patton, Neron, & Linker, 1986).

Although individuals could experience intimacy in many kinds of interpersonal relations, in present-day Western societies, intimacy is particularly sought in romantic relationships. In fact, people typically evaluate their romantic relationship in terms of its level of intimacy and, if they find it deficient, may choose to attend relationship enrichment programs designed to help couples reach their intimacy potential (Frankel, 1982; Greenberg & Johnson, 1986).

Although intimacy is of central importance in enduring romantic relationships, practitioners and researchers interested in this topic have to contend with a slow-developing literature (Sexton & Sexton, 1982). In fact, many authors have stressed the need for more perspicacious definitional and investigative efforts (Hinde, 1978; Oden, 1974; Schaefer & Olson, 1981; Tolstedt &

Stokes, 1983; Waring, 1988; Wynne & Wynne, 1986).

TYPES OF DEFINITIONS

The focus of the present paper is on the development of a parsimonious, widely applicable definition of intimacy in romantic relationships by analyzing, integrating, and building upon the definitions of intimacy found in the literature. Such a definition can stimulate research by specifying the nature of intimacy as it manifests itself in romantic relationships, and by identifying the elements that comprise it. It also will have indirect and direct benefits for practitioners. Specifically, practitioners will be able to use it to help clients better understand the concept of intimacy, intimacy-related problems they are experiencing, and steps they can take to attain the level of intimacy they seek.

The present authors conducted an extensive, computer-assisted search of scholarly publications and books for definitions of intimacy and, through this process, found 61 unique definitions. Three types were identified: general, multidimensional, and operational definitions. Respectively, these types described intimacy in global terminology, as a composite of discrete subcomponents, and with behavioral measurement criteria. Each type offered a unique perspective on the construct of intimacy.

From *Family Relations*, Vol. 42, No. 1, January 1993, pp. 31-37. © 1993 by The National Council on Family Relations, 3989 Central Avenue, NE, Suite 550, Minneapolis, MN 55421. Reprinted by permission.

General Definitions

General definitions were usually based on their auhors' personal interpretation of the meaning of intimacy (Billow & Mendelsohn, 1982; Hinde, 1978) or were part of a larger theoretical model (Berne, 1964; Erikson, 1963; Sullivan, 1953). Hinde illustrates the former case, defining intimacy as "the number of different facets of the personality which are revealed to the partner and to what depth" (1978, p. 378). Berne (1964) illustrates the latter case, drawing his definition from Transactional Analysis, "The spontaneous game-free candidness of an aware person" (p. 180).

Most general definitions are vague and lack operational clarity and empirical validation. For example, Eshleman and Clarke (1978) propose that "intimacy . . . refers to any close association or friendship that involves informal warmth, openness, and sharing" (p. 127). Similarly, Nowinski (1988) suggests, "Intimacy means getting close. It means opening up, which means being vulnerable" (p. 49). Although the general definitions are essentially veridical in content and capture the nuances and complexities of the intimacy construct, their global nature leaves open a large array of interpretive and operational possibilities.

Multidimensional Definitions

Multidimensional definitions, although also subjectively derived, are typically based in part on an empirical foundation. Investigators analyzed subjects' statements about the meaning of intimacy and then compiled them into reliably scaled items in accordance with an a priori multidimensional theory (McAdams, 1988; Oden, 1974; Schaefer & Olson, 1981; Waring, McElrath, Lefcoe, & Weisz, 1981).

For example, Oden asked individuals to visually recall a time of fulfilling intimacy and to write down their experiences as clearly and descriptively as possible. Oden analyzed the data generated for common themes and used them to formulate a 12-component definition of intimacy (duration, ecstasy, accountability, negotiability, empathy, congruence, emotive warmth, conflict capability, self-disclosure, letting-be, finitude, and transcendence). Others who derived multidimensional definitions through data collection also developed definitions with a large number of components and a broad conceptual field (McAdams, 1988; Waring, 1988).

Authors also built multidimensional definitions by drawing from existing research findings relevant to the con-

struct of intimacy (Dahms, 1972; Hatfield, 1982; White, Speisman, Jackson, Bartis, & Costos, 1986). For example, Dahms and Hatfield included a physical expressiveness component, citing work (Patterson, 1984) showing the necessity of physical touch for adequate psychological development and the tendency for those involved in close relationships to initiate more physical contact with each other than they would with other individuals. Because of their empirical derivation and the fact that their authors tended to focus on committed couples, the multidimensional definitions are particularly germane to specifying the nature of intimacy in enduring romantic relationships.

Operational Definitions

The operational definitions, which were chiefly derived from pragmatic concerns for behavioral indices of intimacy, can be grouped into three subtypes: behavioral manifestations, self-report measures, and relationship status indicators of intimacy. Examples of measures of these subtypes are: an assessment of the amount of pleasurable stimulation given to another's thighs and buttocks (Davis & Martin, 1978), Jourard Self-Disclosure Questionnaire scores (Carpenter & Freese, 1979), and indices of marital status (Stone, 1973).

Most operational definitions were not developed to be inclusive. One criticism of them is that they view intimacy as being synonymous with other constructs or a limited number of circumscribed behaviors. For example, Carpenter and Freese (1979) and Buhrmester and Furman (1987) equate intimacy with self-disclosure. However, certain disclosures, such as the "no-holding-back" type that often occur prior to

divorce, may function as "attacks" that hurt self-esteem and serve to reduce intimacy (Gilbert, 1976). Other operational definitions measure intimacy in terms of cohesion, marital satisfaction, or amount of direct physical contact (Chelune, Waring, Vosk, Sultan, & Ogden, 1984; Heslin & Boss, 1980).

Identification of Predominant Intimacy Themes

Of the 61 unique definitions of intimacy found in the literature, 31, 10, and 20 were general, multidimensional, and operational definitions, respectively. These definitions, plus three general definitions from the *American Heritage Dictionary* (1992), *Webster's Encyclopedic Unabridged Dictionary* (1989), and *Webster's New World Dictionary* (1989) were evaluated by the authors and the main theme(s) in each recorded. Rather than limiting themes to mutually exclusive categories, all possible themes were recorded. Next, all definitions were reexamined to determine how many times each of the themes had occurred. When this process was completed, the identified themes and the tabulations were reviewed by three judges with family science interests. These individuals, Ph.D.-trained scientist/practitioners in the health and social science fields, agreed that the decisions made in the analysis were sound.

Finally, the authors identified those themes that occurred in at least 50% of any of the three types of definitions (general, multidimensional, operational). Seven such themes were found and are presented in Table 1 and discussed below:

Table 1.
*Themes Found in at Least 50% of the General (GEN), Multidimensional (MLT), or Operational (OPR) Definitions of Intimacy**

GEN Intimacy Theme	GEN #	GEN %
Mutual Interaction/Exchange	27/34	79%
Depth of Affective Awareness/Expressiveness	20/34	59%
Depth of Cognitive Awareness/Expressiveness	18/34	53%
Communication/Self-Disclosure in general	17/34	50%
MLT Intimacy Theme	**MLT #**	**MLT %**
Mutual Interaction/Exchange	10/10	100%
Depth of Affective Awareness/Expressiveness	10/10	100%
Depth of Cognitive Awareness/Expressiveness	9/10	90%
Depth of Physical Awareness/Expressiveness	9/10	90%
Communication/Self-Disclosure in general	8/10	80%
Commitment/Cohesion	6/10	60%
Closeness in general	5/10	50%
OPR Intimacy Theme	**OPR #**	**OPR %**
Mutual Interaction/Exchange	15/20	75%
Depth of Physical Awareness/Expressiveness	12/20	60%
Depth of Cognitive Awareness/Expressiveness	10/20	50%

*GEN refers to 34 general definitions; MLT refers to the 10 multidimensional definitions; OPR to the 20 operational definitions of intimacy.

1) An exchange or mutual interaction (characterizing intimacy as a process that occurs between individuals).

2) In-depth affective awareness-expressiveness (the reception or expression of affect from and to another).

3) In-depth cognitive awareness-expressiveness (the reception or expression of cognitive material from and to another).

4) In-depth physical awareness-expressiveness (the reception or expression of physical acts from or towards another, ranging from interpersonal distance to sexuality).

5) A shared commitment and feeling of cohesion.

6) Communication or self-disclosure (disclosing or communicating information from any content domain to another).

7) A generalized sense of closeness to another.

Examination of Table 1 reveals that the themes of mutuality and of cognitive awareness and expressiveness were included in more than half the definitions of each type. More than half the general and multidimensional definitions also included the themes of affective awareness/expressiveness and communication/self-disclosure. Further, the multidimensional definitions, which focused on committed romantic relationships, also placed emphasis on the themes of physical awareness/expressiveness and commitment/cohesion, both factors which distinguish intimacy in romantic relationships from intimacy in other types of relationships (e.g., friendships, therapist-client relations, etc.).

A FORMAL DEFINITION

Based on the literature and the material summarized in Table 1, the following definition is proposed:

Intimacy in enduring romantic relationships is determined by the level of commitment and positive affective, cognitive, and physical closeness one experiences with a partner in a reciprocal (although not necessarily symmetrical) relationship.

The definition specifies five components of intimacy: a) Commitment; b) Affective Intimacy; c) Cognitive Intimacy; d) Physical Intimacy; and e) Mutuality. Thus, it includes all seven major intimacy themes occurring in the reviewed definitions with the exception of the themes of Closeness, which was thought to be inherent in the themes of Cognitive, Affective, and Physical Intimacy, and Communication/Self-disclosure.

Although the theme of communication or self-disclosure is found in many definitions, there are several reasons for conceptualizing this theme as a facilitator rather than as a component of intimacy. First, self-disclosure occurs in committed romantic relationships devoid of intimacy (Cuber & Harroff, 1965; Gilbert, 1976; Wynne & Wynne, 1986). Second, separating self-disclosure from intimacy facilitates operational clarity (Chelune et al., 1984; Davis, 1973; Gilbert, 1976; Hatfield, 1988). Researchers have found moderate to strong correlations between measures of intimacy and interpersonal communication (Chelune et al., 1984; Schaefer & Olson, 1981) suggesting these two constructs are related yet distinct. Third, marital therapists often conceptualize mutual disclosure exercises as a vehicle to promote intimacy in couples (Gottman, Notarius, Gonso, & Markman, 1976; Greenberg & Johnson, 1986; Guerney, 1977; Waring, 1988).

By restricting the definition to these five themes, an attempt was made to define romantic intimacy parsimoniously, without being too narrow or so general that its operational and empirical testability and its utility in practice would be compromised. In this definition, "level" indicates the amount of intimacy individuals experience in an enduring relationship while "commitment" refers to their desire to permanently remain with the partner. Commitment is viewed as the foundation that provides opportunities for the other intimacy dimensions to develop.

The word "positive" signifies valence (rather than pleasantness). More specifically, "positive" refers to those thoughts, feelings, and physical encounters that attract (as opposed to repel) individuals to the partner. While "affective closeness" refers to the depth of awareness individuals have about their partner's emotional world and the exchanges of emotions they share, (e.g., feelings of caring and compassion), "cognitive closeness" refers to the depth of awareness individuals have of their partner's cognitive world and the exchanges of cognitions they share (e.g., values, goals, and other information). Physical closeness refers to the extent of shared physical encounters (ranging from proximity to sexuality) as well as to the physiological arousal state experienced toward the partner at each level of physical encounter.

The term "reciprocal" refers to the mutual interaction/exchange theme of intimacy, whereas the statement regarding symmetry indicates that partners may differ in the energy they invest in maintaining intimacy and in the value they place on the intimacy achieved. This definition assumes that to experience genuine intimacy, partners must be able to accurately process information about their partner's cognitive, affective, and physical levels.

Although the present definition partitions romantic intimacy into five components to provide descriptive clarity, in actuality, the components are highly interrelated. For example, cognitive factors influence the perception, interpretation, and encoding of emotional experiences in relationships and vice versa. Likewise, emotional and cognitive experiences are linked to neurochemical and autonomic nervous system activity (Hatfield, 1988).

EVALUATION

To evaluate the efficacy of the proposed definition for practice and research, it was examined from three perspectives: 1) How do the levels of the five romantic intimacy components (Commitment, Affective Intimacy, Cognitive Intimacy, Physical Intimacy, and Mutuality) differ in romantic relationships compared to nonintimate relationships and intimate relationships that are not romantic? 2) Do empirical findings support the proposed definition? 3) How does the proposed definition of romantic intimacy differ from definitions of romantic love?

The Levels of Intimacy Themes in Various Relationships

Romantic relationships compared with nonintimate relationships. Davis (1973) categorized relationships in terms of the presence or absence of intimacy. He suggests that strangers, role relations, acquaintances, and enemies comprise a set of basically nonintimate relationships. Davis provided the following definitions: Strangers are those individuals with whom we engage in few reciprocal behaviors; role relations are individuals with whom we engage in only a few narrowly prescribed reciprocal behaviors (such as the behavioral transactions between a bank teller and a customer); acquaintances are individuals we have met and with whom we continue to interact, using only a limited number of prescribed behaviors; and enemies are individuals to whom we obsessively harbor destructive intentions.

Romantic partners, strangers, role relations, acquaintances, and enemies can be differentiated in terms of the level of the five components of romantic intimacy in each relationship. Whereas romantic relationships involve high levels of all five intimacy components, the stranger relationship typically involves a low level of one or two of the components. For example, as strangers pass on the street, their eyes may fleetingly meet and they may both feel attracted (Mutuality, with a positive valence). Role relations and acquaintances, in contrast, are characterized as having some level of Mutuality, Affective Intimacy, and Cognitive Intimacy, but rarely any Physical Intimacy or Commitment. The Mutuality, Affective, and Cognitive Intimacy components can have a positive valence, meaning that people feel attracted and want to share some thoughts or feelings as they interact, or a negative valence, meaning they feel a pull away as they interact and have no desire to transact more than the business at hand.

Finally, enemy relationships, which encompass all five romantic intimacy components, are distinguished from romantic relationships by the valence of the themes. An enemy may readily interact with a partner (Mutuality), know and feel a great deal about a partner (Cognitive and Affective Intimacy), and be committed (Commitment) to continuing the relationship until the opportunity for doing physical harm arises (Physical Intimacy). Although this description may fit some couples, especially some involved in the divorce process (Vaughan, 1986), its primary purpose is to highlight that the essential difference between romantic intimates and enemies is in the valence of the components and not in their presence or absence.

Romantic intimacy compared with other intimate relationships. Intimacy in romantic relationships will be com-

pared with intimacy in three other types of relationships: a) unfamiliar-other, b) therapist-client, and c) friends. Unfamiliar-others are persons who are not well known at the time when intimacy is shared. Further, both parties intend the relationship to be short-term. Examples of such relationships range from a discussion with a passenger occupying an adjacent seat on an airplane to a one-night affair with a person met in a bar. Although the former relationship involves significantly less Physical Intimacy than the latter, both are characterized as having very low levels of Commitment. Although these relationships involve intense but brief sharing along one or more intimacy dimension(s), the low level of Commitment involved limits the levels of Cognitive and Affective Intimacy and makes unfamiliar-other relationships differ sharply from romantic relationships. Further, the Mutuality component of intimacy may also not be well-balanced. Figure 1 shows that, compared to a romantic relationship, the unfamiliar-others relationship has low levels of Mutuality and Commitment and moderately low levels of Cognitive, Affective, and Physical Intimacy.

The therapist-client relationship has been characterized as exceptionally intimate (Fisher & Stricker, 1982). However, in comparison to romantic intimacy, it is limited in terms of Physical Intimacy, Commitment, and the balance of reciprocity (Mutuality) (Billow & Mendelsohn, 1982). Figure 1 represents this relationship, assigning the lowest level of intimacy to Physical Intimacy followed by Mutuality and Commitment and then Cognitive and Affective Intimacy. As also shown in Figure 1, the intimacy exchanged between friends differs from romantic intimacy, primarily in the depth of Physical Intimacy and possibly Commitment experienced between partners, as well as in the capacity to tolerate shifts in Mutuality (Derlega & Winstead, 1986).

Empirical Foundation of Proposed Definition of Romantic Intimacy

Research findings bearing on four aspects of the present definition will be examined next: 1) mutual, positive cognitive closeness; 2) mutual, positive affective closeness; 3) mutual, positive physical closeness; and, 4) commitment.

Mutual, positive cognitive closeness. A considerable body of research suggests that friends, dating partners, and spouses involved in intimate relationships develop deep cognitive understandings of one another, sharing a range of personal information including their values, strengths, weaknesses, hopes, fears, and idiosyncrasies (Altman & Taylor, 1973; Huesmann & Levinger, 1976). The amount of personal information individuals disclose is positively related to how intimate they consider their relationship (Altman & Taylor, 1973; Miller, 1976) and to marital satisfaction (Miller, Corrales, & Wackman, 1975; Hendrick, 1981). Moreover, Waring (1988; Waring & Russell, 1980) demonstrated that increasing the amount of cognitively based information spouses exchanged increased the level of intimacy they experienced.

The valence of the information partners exchange may be more crucial to intimacy than the amount or depth of cognitive disclosure alone (Gilbert, 1976; Tolstedt & Stokes, 1983). While sharing positive information may enhance the level of intimacy, disclosing other information (criticisms, attacks) may reduce the level of intimacy within a marriage or relationship (Strong, 1975).

One enriching aspect of the cognitive exchange process is becoming aware that a partner shares similar attitudes, values, and beliefs. Byrne and Clore (1968) suggest that this discovery is intrinsically rewarding because the

Figure 1. *Level of Romantic Intimacy Components in Four Types of Intimate Relationships*

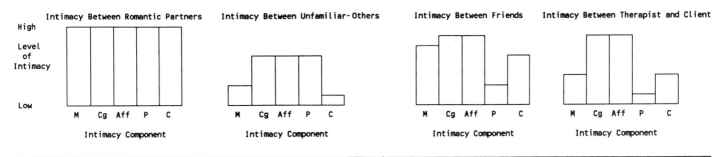

mutual consensus validates each partner's ability to correctly interpret the stimulus world. Married couples, in particular, exhibit greater similarities in beliefs, attitudes, and values than random pairs of spouses and randomly assigned stranger dyads (Byrne & Murnen, 1988). Further, couples exhibiting high levels of belief, attitude, value, and personality similarity have greater levels of relationship satisfaction than couples with less cognitive similarity (Cattell & Nesselroade, 1967; Murstein, 1976).

Finally, several empirically derived scales that measure romantic intimacy found the cognitive aspect of intimacy strongly associated with scales measuring other intimacy components. For example, researchers who have used the Personal Assessment of Intimacy in Relationships Inventory (PAIR; Schaefer & Olson, 1981) and the Waring Intimacy Questionnaire (WIQ; Waring, 1984) found high intercorrelations between intellectual intimacy scales and scales measuring emotional, physical, and commitment aspects of relationships.

Mutual, positive affective closeness. Emotions of a positive valence such as love, a deep sense of caring, and a generalized sense of positive attraction or likability toward the intimate partner have been commonly identified. Levinger and Senn (1967) found that couples reporting high levels of marital satisfaction, in contrast to those reporting lower levels, tended to discuss positive feelings more often than negative feelings. Further, again in contrast to their counterparts, when the more maritally satisfied couples discussed negative feelings, they tended to be more directed toward external events than toward each other.

The Affect Model of Mutual Attraction (Clore & Byrne, 1974) provides one theoretical explanation for the Levinger and Senn (1967) findings. This model asserts that overall attraction to another is based on the proportion of positive and negative feelings aroused by the other. A number of studies have found support for the operation of the Affect Model in intimate relationships such as friendship, serious dating partnerships, and marriage (e.g., Gold, Ryckman, & Mosley, 1984).

Mutual, positive physical closeness. Individuals in romantic relationships are comfortable in close physical proximity (e.g., Allgeier & Byrne, 1973), exhibit extended periods of mutual gaze (e.g., Exline, 1972), and engage in deeper stages of tactile involvement (e.g., Rosenfeld, Kartus, & Ray, 1976). While physiological changes in autonomic nervous system and neurochemical transmitters have been associated with attraction toward an intimate partner (Zillman, 1984), disclosing information considered highly intimate to another can result in physiological changes associated with increased blood pressure, heart rate, and palmar sweating (e.g., Ashworth, Furman, Chaikin, & Derlega, 1976).

Sexual aspects of romantic intimacy have also been studied. Findings indicated that the sexuality subscales of the Intimacy Maturity Scale (IMS; White et. al., 1986), PAIR, and WIQ are significantly correlated with scales assessing cognitive and affective aspects of intimacy, and that the PAIR and IMS sexuality scales are positively correlated with measures of marital adjustment and satisfaction.

Commitment. The more commitment a person feels toward another, the more likely he or she is to focus affective and cognitive attention toward that other individual (Beach & Tesser, 1988). To illustrate, subjects led to believe they would have to date a person assigned to them exclusively for a five-week period exhibited greater attentiveness to a taped presentation of this partner than counterparts who believed they would have only one date (Berscheid, Graziano, Monson, & Dermer, 1976). Increased attention, in turn, can foster polarized feelings regarding that person (Tesser & Leone, 1977). For example, Tesser and Paulhus (1978) found that the amount of time a subject spent thinking about someone he/she had dated was positively related to higher scores on the Rubin Love Scale (1970). Research on cognitive dissonance theory also suggests that once an individual commits to the decision to remain with another, mental processes are activated which can polarize thoughts and feelings about that individual in a positive direction (Brehm & Cohen, 1962).

Commitment is also related to other dimensions of romantic intimacy. The WIQ Cohesion (marital commitment) Subscale and the IMS Commitment Scale correlate significantly with measures of affective, cognitive, and physical aspects of intimacy. Further, studies have found measures of commitment positively associated with scales of marital adjustment and satisfaction (Murstein & MacDonald, 1983; Tolstedt & Stokes, 1983).

Distinguishing Romantic Intimacy from Romantic Love

The construct of love, like intimacy, has been theoretically and operationally defined in varied ways, ranging from the extent of positive reinforcement given to a partner to self-actualization (Brehm, 1985; Foa & Foa, 1980; Maslow, 1954). Many definitions suggest that love is a subset of intimacy or, more precisely, that individuals assess their level of love by subjectively evaluating the extent to which they experience one or more of the five presently described intimacy components.

Several theories of love are multidimensional (Sternberg & Barnes, 1988), including Sternberg's (1986) triangular theory of love, which most closely approximates the presently proposed intimacy paradigm. Sternberg suggests that love is composed of three components: intimacy, passion, and decision/commitment. He defines intimacy in loving relationships as feelings of bondedness, closeness, connectedness; passion as the drives and motivations that lead to arousal in loving relationships; and the decision/commitment component as the decision that one loves another and the subsequent decision of whether to commit to maintaining that love over time.

Although not identical, there is an overlap between Sternberg's three components of love and the five components of intimacy in the present definition. Cognitive and Affective Intimacy approximate Sternberg's intimacy, Physical Intimacy approximates passion, and Commitment and Mutuality approximate the decision/commitment component. However, romantic intimacy as presently defined is a broader concept than love, as defined in Sternberg's theory. A key difference between the two resides in the decision/commitment component. The experience of romantic intimacy with another does not necessarily contribute to an individual's decision that he or she loves another. Instead, the individual continually monitors and evaluates his or her level of intimacy with another and experiences love when he or she decides that the assessed level of the intimate experience matches expectations of what an individual in love experiences. In other words, it is presently argued that love is experienced after an individual makes a subjective assessment of the level of intimacy experienced with another.

Another major difference is that love does not have the same emphasis on mutuality as does intimacy. An individual can feel unrequited love, but there can be no "unrequited intimacy." Although one partner may behave in more intimate ways than the other, there must be an active mutual sharing (Mutuality) on the component dimensions of Cognitive, Affective, and Physical Intimacy, and Commitment for intimacy to exist. To illustrate, after a divorce, one ex-spouse may still love the other, despite the absence of romantic intimacy.

IMPLICATIONS

The proposed definition, which delineates the components of romantic intimacy, may have utility for family practitioners, regardless of the theoretical perspective that guides their work. Practitioners often encounter clients who have only a vague notion of why they are not achieving the intimacy they want in their relationships. These clients may express their problem with statements or questions like: "I just don't know where our relationship went wrong," "My relationship just seems to be boring. Why did we lose our romantic feelings?" or "We just don't seem to care about one another the same way anymore."

Providing clients with a clear definition of intimacy in romantic relationships and an explanation of its components may be an important first step in helping them manage their problems or solve them. Clients with such understandings are empowered in problem-solving in many ways. First, this information provides partners with a common definition of intimacy which, in turn, gives them the potential to communicate more effectively. Second, the definition structures partners' efforts in examining their problems and the relative health of their relationship, leading them to explore the reciprocity in their relationship and how they relate along cognitive, affective, physical, and commitment domains of intimacy. Through this process clients often develop a more profound awareness of both the strengths and weaknesses of their romantic relationship.

In addition to helping practitioners and clients identify areas of difficulty in a relationship's intimacy, the present definition also suggests avenues for effective therapeutic interventions. Specifically, the present definition states that romantic intimacy is strongest when all five components of intimacy (Mutuality, Commitment, and Cognitive, Affective, and Physical Intimacy) are thriving. Therefore, treatment strategies designed to address all five domains are expected to be most efficacious.

A number of strategies have been developed that can be used to foster intimacy and curtail its loss in each of the domains. For example, Frijda (1988) proposed that repeatedly bringing into consciousness pleasant aspects of one's relationship and how it could be (or was) otherwise permits positive cognitive and emotional associations toward a partner to be perpetually reinstated through imagination and recollection. This may minimize general habituation to the partner and strengthen commitment. Byrne and Murnen (1988) suggested that emotional habituation to the partner may be curtailed by using strategies such as continually finding pleasurable intellectual and physical activities to share and by introducing novelty into the relationship.

Finally, besides thinking carefully about the definition of intimacy, pinpointing the nature of their intimacy problems, and engaging in interventions like those described above, clients may be able to benefit from a series of cognitive-behavioral techniques aimed at enhancing their intimacy in all domains. In this connection, Schwebel and Fine (1992) suggest that practitioners, in work with couples and families, can apply behavioral rehearsal, communication enhancement, in vivo assignments, modeling, problem-solving training, role playing, and other interventions from individual cognitive behavioral therapy approaches, along with interventions from behavioral marital therapy (Jacobson & Gurman, 1986) and cognitive-behavioral therapy for families (Epstein, Schlesinger, & Dryden, 1988).

Specifically, Schwebel and Fine (1992) suggest that practitioners can use such interventions both to help clients make health-promoting changes and to guide them in discovering the links between their intimacy-related cognitions and the thoughts, feelings, and behaviors they experience in their relationship. For example, consider spouses who seek assistance because they feel their relationship has became more distant, rather than closer as they had expected, since the birth of their baby. Practitioners can offer these spouses a series of cognitive-behavioral interventions that will enable them to identify the cognitions they hold regarding what family life should be like after a baby is born, to evaluate how realistic their expectations are, and to help them identify discrepancies between these and recognize the impact such discrepancies may have. Following this, practitioners might also assist the spouses in working toward the development of new behaviors and associated cognitions that will provide them with healthy ways to share intimacy as a couple and as a three-person family. In sum, then, practitioners could use cognitive-behavioral interventions to help the spouses come to better understand what has unfolded between them since the baby was born and to take steps to try to build their level of intimacy to a level that suits them at this point in their family's development.

CONCLUSION

Most individuals seek and work to achieve intimacy in their lives. Experiencing intimacy, in turn, has been identified as a factor that helps individuals maintain their physical and mental health. Given its importance in human well-being, intimacy has been relatively understudied. Perhaps this has been caused, at least in part, by the construct's complexity and the difficulties it poses to researchers who wish to quantify it. Because the definition of romantic intimacy developed in this paper is comprehensive, yet parsimonious, it may be of value to researchers as well as to practitioners, who can use it as a tool in assisting clients with problems involving intimacy.

REFERENCES

Allgeier, A. R., & Byrne, D. (1973). Attraction toward the opposite sex as a determinant of physical proximity. *Journal of Social Psychology,* **90,** 213-219.

Altman, I., & Taylor, D. A. (1973). *Social penetration: The development of interpersonal relationships.* New York: Holt.

American heritage dictionary of the English language (third edition). (1992). Boston: Houghton Mifflin.

Ashworth, C., Furman, G., Chaikin, A., & Derlega, V. (1976). Physiological responses to self-disclosure. *Journal of Humanistic Psychology,* **16**(2), 71-80.

Beach, S. H., & Tesser, A. (1988). Love in marriage: A cognitive account. In R. J. Sternberg & M. L. Barnes (Eds.), *The psychology of love* (pp. 330-355). New York: Vali-Ballou Press.

Berne, E. (1964). *Games people play.* New York: Grove Press.

Berscheid, E., Graziano, W., Monson, T., & Dermer, M. (1976). Outcome dependency: Attention, attribution, and attraction. *Journal of Personality and Social Psychology,* **34,** 978-989.

Billow, R. M., & Mendelsohn, R. (1982). Intimacy in the initial interview. In M. Fisher & G. Stricker (Eds.), *Intimacy* (pp. 383-401). New York: Plenum Press.

Brehm, J. W., & Cohen, A. R. (1962). *Explorations in cognitive dissonance.* New York: John Wiley & Sons, Inc.

Brehm, S. S. (1985). *Intimate relationships.* New York: Random House.

Brown, G. W., Harris, T., & Copeland, J. R. (1977). Depression and loss. *British Journal of Psychiatry,* **30,** 1-18.

Buhrmester, D., & Furman, W. (1987). The development of companionship and intimacy. *Child Development,* **58,** 1101-1113.

Byrne, D., & Clore, G. (1968). *A reinforcement model of evaluative responses.* Unpublished manuscript, Purdue University.

Byrne, D., & Murnen, S. K. (1988). Maintaining loving relationships. In R. J. Sternberg & M. L. Barnes (Eds.), *The psychology of love* (pp. 293-310). New York: Vali-Ballou Press.

Carpenter, J., & Freese, J. (1979). Three aspects of self-disclosure as they relate to quality of adjustment. *Journal of Personality Assessment,* **43,** 78-85.

Cattell, R. B., & Nesselroade, J. R. (1967). Likeness and completeness theories examined by Sixteen Personality Factor measures on stably and unstably married couples. *Journal of Personality and Social Psychology,* **7,** 351-361.

Chelune, G. J., Waring, E. M., Vosk, B. N., Sultan, F. E., & Ogden, J. K. (1984). Self-disclosure and its relationship to marital intimacy. *Journal of Clinical Psychology,* **40,** 216-219.

Clore, G. L., & Byrne, D. (1974). A reinforcement-affect model of attraction. In T. L. Huston (Ed.), *Foundations of interpersonal attraction* (pp. 143-170). New York: Academic Press.

5. NEW STYLES AND THE FUTURE: It's Time for Happiness

Cuber, J. F., & Harroff, P. B. (1965). *Sex and the significant Americans: A study of sexual behavior among the affluent.* Baltimore: Penguin Books.

Dahms, A. M. (1972). *Emotional intimacy: Overlooked requirement for survival.* Boulder, Colorado: Pruett Publishing Co.

Davis, D., & Martin, H. (1978). When pleasure begets pleasure: Recipient responsiveness as a determinant of physical pleasuring between heterosexual dating couples and strangers. *Journal of Personality and Social Psychology, 36,* 767-777.

Davis, M. (1973). *Intimate relations.* New York: The Free Press.

Derlega, V. J., & Winstead, B. A. (1986). *Friendship and social interaction.* New York: Springer-Verlag, Inc.

Epstein, N., Schlesinger, S., & Dryden, W. (1988). *Cognitive-behavioral therapy with families.* New York: Brunner/Mazel.

Erikson, E. H. (1963). *Childhood and society.* New York: W. W. Norton.

Eshleman, J. R., & Clarke, J. N. (1978). Intimacy in relating: Love and cohabitation. In J. R. Eshleman & J. N. Clarke (Eds.), *Intimacy, commitments, and marriage: Development of relationships* (p. 127). Boston, MA: Allyn and Bacon, Inc.

Exline, R. (1972). Visual interaction: The glances of power and preference. In J. Cole (Ed.), *Nebraska symposium on motivation, 1971* (pp. 163-206). Lincoln: University of Nebraska Press.

Fisher, M., & Stricker, G. (1982). *Intimacy.* New York: Plenum Press.

Foa, E. B., & Foa, U. G. (1980). Resource theory: Interpersonal behavior as exchange. In K. J. Gergen, M. S. Greenberg, & R. H. Willis (Eds.), *Social exchange: Advances in theory and research* (pp. 77-94). New York: Plenum Press.

Frankel, B. (1982). Intimacy and conjoint marital therapy. In M. Fisher & G. Stricker (Eds.), *Intimacy* (pp. 247-266). New York: Plenum Press.

Frijda, N. H. (1988). The laws of emotion. *American Psychologist, 45*(5), 349-358.

Gilbert, S. J. (1976). Self-disclosure, intimacy, and communication in family. *Family Coordinator, 25,* 221-231.

Gold, J. A., Ryckman, R. M., & Mosley, N. R. (1984). Romantic mood induction and attraction to a dissimilar other: Is love blind? *Personality and Social Psychology Bulletin, 10,* 358-368.

Gottman, J., Notarius, C., Gonso, J., & Markman, H. (1976). *A couple's guide to communication.* Illinois: Research Press Co.

Greenberg, L. F., & Johnson, S. M. (1986). Affect in marital therapy. *Journal of Marital and Family Therapy, 12,* 1-10.

Guerney, B. G. (1977). *Relationship enhancement.* San Francisco, CA: Jossey-Bass, Inc.

Hatfield, E. (1982). Passionate love, companionate love, and intimacy. In M. Fisher & G. Stricker (Eds.), *Intimacy,* (pp. 267-292). New York: Plenum Press.

Hatfield, E. (1988). Passionate and companionate love. In R. J. Sternberg & M. L. Barnes (Eds.), *The psychology of love* (pp. 191-217). New York: Vali-Ballou Press.

Hendrick, S. S. (1981). Self-disclosure and marital satisfaction. *Journal of Personality and Social Psychology, 40,* 1150-1159.

Heslin, R., & Boss, D. (1980). Nonverbal intimacy in airport arrival and departure. *Personality and Social Psychology Bulletin, 6,* 248-252.

Hinde, R. A. (1978). Interpersonal relationships—In quest of a science. *Psychological Medicine, 8,* 373-396.

Horowitz, M. J. (1979). *States of mind: Analysis of change in psychotherapy.* New York: Plenum Publishing.

Huesmann, L. R., & Levinger, G. (1976). Incremental exchange theory: A formal model for progression in dyadic social interaction. In L. Berkowitz & E. Walster (Eds.), *Advances in experimental social psychology,* (pp. 192-229). New York: Academic Press.

Jacobson, N. S, & Gurman, A. S. (1986). *Clinical handbook of marital therapy.* New York: Guilford.

Levinger, G., & Senn, D. J. (1967). Disclosure of feelings in marriage. *Merrill-Palmer Quarterly, 13,* 237-249.

Lynch, J. (1977). *The broken heart.* New York: Basic Books.

Maslow, A. H. (1954). *Motivation and personality.* New York: Harper and Row, Publishers.

McAdams, D. P. (1988). *Power, intimacy, and the life story.* New York: The Guilford Press.

Medalie, J. H., & Goldbourt, U. (1976). Angina pectoris among 10,000 men. *American Journal of Medicine, 60,* 910-921.

Miller, B. (1976). A multivariate developmental model of marital satisfaction. *Journal of Marriage and the Family, 38,* 643-657.

Miller, S., Corrales, R., & Wackman, D. B. (1975). Recent progress in understanding and facilitating marital communication. *Family Coordinator, 24,* 143-152.

Murstein, B. I. (1976). *Who will marry whom?* New York: Springer Publishing Co., Inc.

Murstein, B. I., & MacDonald, M. G. (1983). The relationship of "exchange-orientation" and "commitment" scales to marriage adjustment. *International Journal of Psychology, 18,* 297-311.

Nowinski, J. (1988). *A lifelong love affair: Keeping sexual desire alive in your relationship.* New York: Dodd, Mead & Company, Inc.

Oden, T. C. (1974). *Game free: A guide to the meaning of intimacy.* New York: Harper & Row.

Patterson, M. L. (1984). Intimacy, social control, and nonverbal involvement: A functional approach. In V. J. Derlega (Ed.), *Communication, intimacy, and close relationships* (pp. 105-132). Orlando, FL: Academic Press, Inc.

Patton, D. P., & Waring, E. M. (1984). The quality and quantity of marital intimacy in the marriages of psychiatric patients. *Journal of Sex and Marital Therapy, 10,* 201-206.

Rosenfeld, L. B., Kartus, S., & Ray, C. (1976). Body accessibility revisited. *Journal of Communication, 26,* 27-30.

Rubin, Z. (1970). Measurement of romantic love. *Journal of Personality and Social Psychology, 16,* 265-273.

Schaefer, M. T., & Olson, D. H. (1981). Assessing intimacy: The PAIR inventory. *Journal of Marital and Family Therapy, 7,* 47-60.

Schwebel, A. I., & Fine, M. A. (1992). Cognitive-behavioral family therapy. *Journal of Family Psychotherapy, 3,* 73-91.

Sexton, R. E., & Sexton, V. S. (1982). Intimacy: A historical perspective. In M. Fisher & G. Stricker (Eds.), *Intimacy,* (pp. 1-20). New York: Plenum Press.

Sternberg, R. J. (1986). A triangular theory of love. *Psychological Review, 93,* 119-135.

Sternberg, R. J., & Barnes, M. L. (1988). *The psychology of love.* New Haven and London: Yale University Press.

Stone, W. F. (1973). Patterns of conformity in couples varying in intimacy. *Journal of Personality and Social Psychology, 27*(3), 413-418.

Strong, J. R. (1975). A marital conflict resolution model: Redefining conflict to achieve intimacy. *Journal of Marriage and Family Counseling, 55,* 269-276.

Sullivan, H. S. (1953). *The interpersonal theory of psychiatry.* New York: W. W. Norton.

Tesser, A., & Leone, C. (1977). Cognitive schemas and thought as determinants of attitude change. *Journal of Experimental Social Psychology, 13,* 340-356.

Tesser, A., & Paulhus, D. L. (1978). Toward a causal model of love. *Journal of Personality and Social Psychology, 34,* 1095-1105.

Tolstedt, B. E., & Stokes, J. P. (1983). Relation of verbal, affective, and physical intimacy to marital satisfaction. *Journal of Counseling Psychology, 30,* 573-580.

Traupmann, J., Eckels, E., & Hatfield, E. (1982). Intimacy in older women's lives. *The Gerontologist, 22,* 493-498.

Vaughan, D. (1986). *Uncoupling: Turning point in intimate relationships.* New York: Oxford University Press.

Waring, E. M. (1984). The measurement of marital intimacy. *Journal of Marital and Family Therapy, 10,* 185-192.

Waring, E. M. (1988). *Enhancing marital intimacy through facilitating cognitive self-disclosure.* New York: Brunner/Mazel.

Waring, E. M., McElrath, D., Lefcoe, D., & Weisz, G. (1981). Dimensions of intimacy in marriage. *Psychiatry, 44,* 169-175.

Waring, E. M., Patton, D., Neron, C. A., & Linker, W. (1986). Types of marital intimacy and prevalence of emotional illness. *Canadian Journal of Psychiatry, 31,* 720-726.

Waring, E. M., & Russell, L. (1980). Family structure, marital adjustment, and intimacy in patients referred to a consultation-liaison service. *General Hospital Psychiatry, 3,* 198-203.

Webster's encyclopedic unabridged dictionary of the English language. (1989). Avenel, NJ: Gramercy Books.

Webster's new world dictionary (third college edition). (1989). New York: Simon and Schuster.

White, K. M., Speisman, J. C., Jackson, D., Bartis, S., & Costos, D. (1986). Intimacy maturity and its correlates in young married couples. *Journal of Personality and Social Psychology, 50*(1), 152-162.

Wynne, L. C., & Wynne, A. R. (1986). The quest for intimacy. *Journal of Marital and Family Therapy, 12,* 383-394.

Zillman, D. (1984). *Connections between sex and aggression.* Hillsdale, NJ: Lawrence Erlbaum.

How Our Marriage Was Saved

We tried our best to work things out, but when we stopped talking to each other, I knew it was time to get help.

Ann Campbell

Ann Campbell is the pseudonym of a free-lance writer based in New England.

I hate therapists' offices. I hate the ever-so-readily-available box of tissues, the carefully chosen artwork, the muted colors, the suggestion that one person in the room is a lot better equipped for dealing with life than the other, and that person isn't you. I hate seeing people ahead of me come out with red-rimmed eyes and compensatory smiles; and I hate seeing people waiting to go in after me with their nervous, apologetic, curious faces. I hate making appointments and taking time out of an already frantic schedule to show up for them.

I also hate, however, seeing my relationship with my husband deteriorate before my eyes. And perhaps I am finally mature enough to recognize that sometimes I need to make sacrifices for some higher good.

I asked my husband to start marital therapy with me following one particularly bad morning when, after he went to work, I ended up sitting at the kitchen

13 good reasons to see a marriage counselor

1 We fight a lot.

2 We have trouble communicating; my spouse just doesn't understand.

3 We can't agree on how to raise our child.

4 We need help making a major decision (e.g., whether to have another baby, move, or make a career change).

5 We need help dealing with other family members (e.g., in-laws, stepchildren).

6 We need help dealing with a major crisis (such as illness in the family, birth of a child with special needs, financial loss).

7 We are having conflicts in our sex life.

8 We are drifting apart.

9 I feel suffocated in our marriage.

10 I feel unloved or taken for granted by my spouse.

11 I'm afraid of my spouse.

12 I don't trust my spouse.

13 I'm unhappy being married, but I don't know why.
—Evelyn Bassoff, Ph.D.

table far too long with an empty cup. I couldn't put together what had happened. All I know is that when he left for work, I felt as if he hated me—and he undoubtedly felt that I hated him. And it wasn't a flare-up; our inability to talk to each other had become a pattern.

I had begun seeing a therapist a few weeks earlier in an effort to help me deal with some of the problems I'd been having, especially in my marriage. But it occurred to me that morning that if, in fact, it was the

marriage that needed help, then both people involved needed to work on it. I had an appointment that afternoon, and I called the therapist to see if it was okay for my husband to join me. Then I called him at work to ask him to go with me. He agreed, and it struck me for the first time that he knew as well as I that we were in serious trouble.

We sat in chairs with the therapist between us and told our respective stories. For the first time, each of us had a chance to finish. The presence of the therapist

had us on our best behavior. We may have been dying to burst in and correct or disagree with or belittle what the other said, but we didn't. We heard the other out. That was a new thing, and it felt good.

Powerful feelings were unleashed in a safe place.
I had imagined that the process of marital therapy could be rather sterile and tidy. We would articulate our problems. Then the therapist would propose some kind of compromise that was acceptable to both

of us. Then we would go home and have a better marriage. One, two, three.

Only it didn't work like that. Instead we became exposed, both of us, in a way that was rather terrifying. For example, I was asked at one point to give an instance in which I thought my emotional needs were ignored. I promptly told about a morning when I had awakened full of sadness because of a very powerful dream I'd had. I sat, disturbed and frightened, on the edge of the bed, unable to release myself from the nightmare's hold. My husband was putting on his tie before the mirror above our dresser, and he saw me reflected there out of the corner of his eye. "What's the matter?" he asked. I told him the horrible details of the dream, my voice shaking. He murmured something like, "Hmmm; weird" and left for work.

When the incident happened, I felt a combination of numbness and anger; and I felt foolish for sharing the dream with my husband. But in telling about it in the therapist's office, I found myself feeling only enormous pain, and I burst into tears. "If you had just sat on the bed beside me for just a *moment*," I said. "If you had just made some kind of remark that showed me you understood, if you had just given me some sense that you cared at all..." I reached for the box of tissues and was glad it was there. While I wept, I looked at my husband. And what I saw was that he was not bored or disgusted. What I saw was that he was ashamed and, in that moment, was hurting for me.

Why did that happen there and not at home? I think it happened because having another, objective person present can make you feel safe. It was as though someone was saying, "What she's feeling is not crazy; she has a right to these emotions." There was, in essence, a caring monitor there—for both of us.

We're learning to listen to each other.

When it was my husband's turn to talk, I heard him say more in 15 minutes than I'd heard him say in, literally, years. I began to see things from his point of view. I still didn't agree with much of what he said, but I began to have an idea of what made him say it. What went on at that first session was not pleasant. It was not easy. But it showed us there was a chance for us, and we willingly made an appointment to go back.

We have been going for counseling for six weeks now. Sometimes we fight there, and at those times I feel as though I am shaking inside. But we have felt closer and better about each other at the end of every session we've had. It's as though we're battling each other *for* each other.

We also take therapy seriously and do our "homework." In one instance that meant spending very deliberate, planned time talking: One partner was to speak for a full 15 minutes while the other partner just listened and could not comment on what was said until the next therapy session. The speaker was required to speak only about her- or himself. This exercise showed me things about my husband that I knew nothing about. It revealed his dreams, his fears, his disappointments, his pleasures. When it was my turn to talk, I felt that I didn't have to rush or compensate in some way for my conversational content. He listened to me, and that's all I wanted.

I find that my husband and I have come to rely on these weekly meetings to work things out: the ways we damage each other by not acknowledging, appreciating, or permitting each other's differences; opposing views on how to disci-

Getting a reluctant spouse to go with you

● **Tell your spouse that getting counseling together would mean a great deal to you.**

● **Without accusing, shaming, or blaming, describe your concerns about the marriage and how marital problems are affecting you.**

● **Assure your spouse that you wish to fix the problems, not him or her.**

● **Choose a counselor who is acceptable to both of you; ask whether your spouse would be more comfortable with a man or a woman.**

● **Suggest that your spouse commit to only three sessions and then decide whether to continue; or begin counseling alone with the understanding that your spouse will join in when ready.**

● **If your marriage problems are disabling you and your spouse still rejects counseling, you may need to say, "Unless you work with me on our problems, I will be forced to separate from you." Sometimes ultimatums are necessary to save a marriage. —E.B.**

pline the children; what to do with our money.

A good thing about this therapy is that each of us feels that we have someone on our side. That speaks for the therapist's skill, I suppose. But the best thing is that we have begun to feel that we are all on the side of saving the marriage. There is something that has replaced the nagging sense of despair that I had begun carrying around in my chest. That something is hope.

How to Find a Therapist That You Can Afford

Average fees charged by psychiatrists, psychologists, and social workers for one session range from $62 to $100. Insurance coverage varies. Many policies cover a portion of the fee—usually 50 percent to 80 percent—and there may be an annual cap on payments.

If cost is a factor, talk with the therapist about your financial situation and see whether he or she is willing to work on a sliding scale. Some clinicians don't charge for the first visit.

To find a professional in your area, contact the following:
● American Psychological Association, Public Affairs, 750 First Street N.E., Washington, DC 20002-4242.
● National Association of Social Workers, 750 First Street N.E., Suite 700, Washington, DC 20002; call 202-408-8600.
● American Association for Marriage and Family Therapy, 1100 17th Street N.W., Tenth Floor, Washington, DC 20036; call 1-800-374-2638.

Happy Families

WHO SAYS THEY ALL HAVE TO BE ALIKE?

Susan Chollar

Susan Chollar writes about science and health for a number of national magazines.

It's Thursday evening in Watsonville, a small agricultural town on California's central coast. Cathy Chavez-Miller is fixing dinner for her "blended" family: her husband, Mike, her stepson, Cliff, and her son from her first marriage, Patrick, who spends half his time with his father. "At times it's been a real challenge," she says, "but we really enjoy each other and wouldn't change the way things are." On the opposite coast, it's nighttime in suburban Washington, and mental health therapist Shelly Costello tucks her five-year-old twins Chelsea and Carly into bed. Worn out after 10 hours in day care followed by a rowdy evening at home with Mom, the kids are soon fast asleep. But Shelly, a single parent, must tackle a sinkful of dirty dishes and a couple of loads of laundry before she can call it a day. Her philosophy concerning our oldest social institution: "I don't believe in the rule that a family has to have two parents living together, but I do believe that people have to be happy. As long as a family is happy, it will be a good place for children to grow up."

American families are not what they were 40 years ago when Father Knew Best and every household was presumed to live *The Life of Riley.* Ozzie and Harriet and the Cleavers have long since given way to Murphy Brown and the *Full House* gang, and the traditional two-parent family sometimes seems like an endangered species.

We all know the statistics: Half of all marriages in the U.S. end in divorce, and nearly a third of our children are born out of wedlock. As a result, four out of 10 kids don't live with both of their biological parents; one in four lives in a single-parent home; and almost one in six families includes at least one stepchild.

Critics such as former Vice President Dan Quayle have blamed these demographic changes for everything from the Los Angeles riots and the growing wave of violence among teenage boys to declining scholastic performance. But while social scientists don't deny that American children and parents face greater challenges than ever before, they increasingly question the assumption that broken homes and single-parent families per se are threatening children. Several recent sophisticated studies suggest that growing up under the same roof with both biological parents is less crucial to a child's psychological health than growing up in a stable home.

"The quality of the individuals and relationships in the household matters more than who the particular actors are," says Dr. Frank Mott, a senior research scientist at the Center for Human Resource Research at Ohio State University in Columbus. "If you have a happy home, you'll probably have well-adjusted children." In other words, the atmosphere of the home counts for more than the type of family who inhabits it—even when it comes to "broken" homes.

In 1980 Dr. Paul Amato, an associate professor of sociology at the University of Nebraska in Lincoln, began charting the progress of 2,000 marriages; over the course of his study, 15% ended in divorce. In 1992 he contacted 500 adult children from those failed marriages and measured their psychological and social adjustment. The offspring of the failed unions tended to fall into two distinct groups: Those from marriages in which there had been little external conflict before the divorce were likelier to have personal problems as young adults than those from overtly troubled marriages.

Amato believes that children from seemingly harmonious homes that break up bear the greater scars because, to them, "the divorce means the loss of a stable home. Although the parents were unhappy with the

> **THE STRONGEST PREDICTOR OF SUCCESS IS THE LEVEL OF CONFLICT BETWEEN A MOTHER AND HER CHILD: LESS IS BEST.**

marriage, from the child's perspective it wasn't really that bad."

For children who had lived in homes where there were arguments and perhaps physical violence, however, divorce often meant an end to discord. Therefore, the adult children from such homes tended to have better psychological health—and even stronger social relationships and marriages—than those from homes in which there had been little external conflict before divorce. "To the children," Amato concludes, "the consequences of divorce depend on the quality of the marriage prior to it." He adds: "It might be better for children to be in a well-functioning divorced single-parent family than a nuclear family marked by high levels of conflict."

Research on families headed by single women also suggests that the quality of a home is more important than its cast of characters. Sociologist David Demo, an associate professor of human development and family studies at the University of Missouri in Columbia, examined the emotional health and academic performance of 742 teens from the four most prevalent types of households: intact two-parent, never married single-parent, divorced single-parent and stepfamily.

When Dr. Demo analyzed all his data, he found that the type of family a child belonged to was a surprisingly weak predictor of the child's well-being and achievement. Although teens who resided with both biological parents tended to do better academically and behaviorally, they did only slightly better than those from never-married single-parent families. The most powerful predictor of the young people's adjustment and academic performance was the level of conflict between mother and child: Less is best.

"Dan Quayle argues that families headed by never-married mothers are inherently harmful to children," says Demo, "but the data don't show that. In fact, the never-married [single-parent] family offers a type of continuity that can parallel that of intact two-parent families." He summarizes his research this way: "Families are diverse by race, class, structure and well-being. Some are in trouble, some are doing very well. And some are somewhere in-between."

If some divorces—but not all—cause problems, so do some stepfamilies. Dr. Louise Silverstein, a family therapist and an assistant professor of psychology at Yeshiva University in New York City, observes that research shows relationships are often more difficult in stepfamilies, particularly for girls who find themselves living under the same roof with their mother's new husband. Boys who accompany their mother to a new household seem to fare better, presumably because there is less sexual tension in their relationship with a same-sex stepparent.

Children who deal with strife that continues between parents *after* divorce also often suffer. Silverstein illustrates with a case history: The parents of three-year-old Sean separated in a tangle of bitterness and anger when his mother, Mary Ann, was six months into a second pregnancy her husband, Tom, opposed. When Tom reacted by embarking on an affair with Mary Ann's closest friend, their conflict escalated into screaming matches and even physical violence that showed no sign of abating months after their marriage dissolved. "They were completely out of control," says Silverstein. Unfortunately Sean was his parents' real victim: Over eight months, his once normal behavior deteriorated into frequent tantrums and a severe case of separation anxiety.

Researchers who found that children from broken homes generally don't do as well as those whose parents stayed together may have misinterpreted the causes. Nearly half of single-parent families live in poverty, for example, compared with only 8% of married families. Almost 12 million households are headed by women, whose economic status is slashed by at least a third following divorce; never-married mothers are among the poorest members of our society. In many single-parent homes, low income—not divorce—causes children to live in high-crime neighborhoods and to have more health and academic problems.

Sociologist Nicholas Zill is vice president of the Westat research corporation in Rockville, Md., which explores social issues for the federal government, among other clients. "If you are the classic Murphy Brown type with all the advantages, and you decide to have a child out of marriage," he says, "your child is not necessarily at risk. But if you're a teenager with little education or money, that can be a recipe for disaster."

Assessing the effects of growing up in a household headed by a single woman is clearly not a simple matter. Ohio State's Mott analyzed data about 1,714 youngsters aged five to eight from various socioeconomic backgrounds, to see if a father's absence from the home caused academic and/or behavioral problems. He discovered that those from fatherless homes indeed scored lower on math and reading achievement tests. But additional probing revealed that the children's mothers scored lower on aptitude tests than the married mothers; they also tended to be poorer and were more likely to have dropped out of school. When he compared children in the sample from similar socioeconomic backgrounds, he found that they performed equally well, regardless of a father's presence.

When it came to behavior, the absence of a father didn't correlate with any particular problems among black children. But fatherless white children had significantly more behavioral difficulties than peers who had fathers, even when income and education levels were similar. White girls and white boys from fatherless homes were less sociable and less independent than white children from homes with fathers. In addition, white boys from fatherless homes were also more prone to hyperactivity, peer conflict, anxiety and depression.

Mott offers several suggestions for these race- and gender-based differences. Girls may be less vulnerable than boys in the absence of a father, he says, because they're closer to their mothers. And black children are part of a culture in which single parenting is not only more prevalent but also more accepted. While nearly half of the fatherless black households in Mott's study had never had a paternal presence, 94% of similar white homes had; many more white children had "lost" their fathers due to divorce or other family disruption. "From a child's perspective," says Mott, "never having had a father in the home may be better, at least in a psychological sense, than having had one who left." Along with more accepting attitudes toward families without fathers, many

The '50s: Not So Happy Days

The 1950s are often portrayed as a simple time when fresh-faced children flourished in nuclear families, men ruled their castles with wisdom and benevolence, and women relished their roles as ever-nurturing wives and mothers. Not so, says Stephanie Coontz, a family historian at The Evergreen State College in Olympia, Wash. "The reality of these families was far more painful and complex than the situation-comedy reruns or the expurgated memories of the nostalgic would suggest," she writes in *The Way We Never Were: American Families and the Nostalgia Trap* (Basic Books, 1992, $27). "Contrary to popular opinion, *Leave It to Beaver* was not a documentary." A quarter of Americans, a third of U.S. children and nearly two-thirds of the elderly were desperately poor, making do without food stamps or housing programs. Half of two-parent black families lived in poverty, and 40% of black women with small children had to work outside the home.

Even for families who came closer to the Cleaver mold, life was often not as simple or happy as it appeared. A quarter to a third of '50s marriages eventually ended in divorce. Many who described their unions as "happy" in national polls nonetheless admitted many dissatisfactions with their mates and day-to-day lives. Child and spouse abuse was common, though largely unacknowledged.

For women in particular, the '50s were not what they seemed to be on *Ozzie and Harriet*. (In his new book, *The Fifties*, author David Halberstam argues that the real-life Nelsons—dominated by autocratic, workaholic Ozzie, who stole "the childhood of both his sons and used it for commercial purposes"—were in fact a dysfunctional family.) "It was a period where women felt tremendously trapped," says Coontz. "There were not many permissible alternatives to baking brownies, experimenting with new canned soups and getting rid of stains around the collar." In some states, husbands had legal control over family finances. In 1954, an article in *Esquire* magazine labeled working wives a "menace." Feminist values and lack of interest in childbearing were considered abnormal, if not pathological. Some women unwilling or unable to fulfill their expected domestic roles were subjected to electroshock or confinement to psychiatric institutions. Throughout the '50s, the press reported a growing wave of frustration and resentment among full-time homemakers, whose use of tranquilizers and alcohol skyrocketed.

To those who point to the '50s as an era of conservative sexual values, look again, says Coontz. Birth rates among teenagers reached numbers since unequaled. The percentage of pregnant white brides more than doubled, and the number of babies born out of wedlock and put up for adoption rose 80% between 1944 and 1955. "What we now think of as 1950s sexual morality," writes Coontz, "depended not so much on stricter sexual control as on intensification of the sexual double standard."

Although Coontz's research shines light on the weaknesses of American families from earlier historical periods as well, she denies that family bashing is her goal. "To say that no easy answers are to be found in the past is not to close off further discussion of family problems, but to open it up," she says. "Only when we have a realistic idea of how families have and have not worked in the past can we make informed decisions about how to support families in the present or improve their future prospects."

with boys and girls raised by gay parents also tends to refute the conventional wisdom. After reviewing studies of the children of lesbian mothers, Dr. Charlotte Patterson, an associate professor of psychology at the University of Virginia in Charlottesville, concluded in the October 1992 issue of *Child Development* that there was no evidence that these children's development had been compromised in any significant respect. "Children don't need a father to develop normally," says Silverstein, "and future research on children raised by gay fathers will probably show that they don't need a mother either. What children need are affectionate, nurturing adults—regardless of their gender or biological relationship—who love them."

Considering the very real challenges of growing up in a nontraditional home, family researchers are quick to acknowledge the advantages that the *right kind* of traditional family can confer. If the worst scenario is a family marked by hostility and conflict, "the best situation," says Nebraska's Amato, "is to grow up in a family where there are two adults who get along well and love the child. Two parents can supervise a child better, provide more practical help, discipline and guidance, and serve as effective role models."

What is most promising about the new research, says Missouri's Demo, "is the suggestion that a lot of these changes in traditional family structure are not harmful to children. But what is disturbing is that the studies point out that negative and disruptive events in children's lives do have important effects on their well-being. Those are the real problems—and those are the patterns that are increasing in our society."

One point on which family experts agree is that we should spend our energy on securing a happy future for our children rather than waxing nostalgic about the past. "It is important to look at the realities of how families are actually functioning," says Westat's Zill, "rather than labeling some as inevitably bad and others as inevitably good." Adds Amato: "All of these types of families are here to stay. And by and large, all of them can work quite well. We need to concern ourselves with making sure that each of them works as well as it can."

black communities offer single parents more extended-family support.

This extra help can make the difference between success and failure in families of any color, says Yeshiva's Silverstein, offering another case history as an example: Alice, now a well-adjusted, young white adult, was raised in a household consisting of her mother, grandmother and aunt; the mother was the breadwinner, while the grandmother created a warm, nurturing atmosphere. "The additional adults also acted as an emotional safety net for Alice," Silverstein says. "If she had a fight with her mother, there was always her grandmother or aunt to comfort her. And their presence meant she didn't have to experience her mother's anger or disappointment so intensely."

The newest research conducted

Happy Families Are Not All Alike

They may shatter the Ozzie-and-Harriet stereotype, but today's families still thrive on mutual care and respect.

Roberta Israeloff

Roberta Israeloff is a contributing editor at *Parents* Magazine and the author of *In Confidence: Four Years of Therapy* (Penguin).

When I mentioned at dinner that I was writing a story about happy families, my eleven-year-old son, Ben, piped up, "Are we a happy family?" "What do you think?" I asked. He was silent for what felt like a very long time, and my heart was in my throat.

"I think we are," he finally said, offering a recent example: "Remember when I won the award for the long jump and everyone in the family was excited? That meant a lot to me."

His answer meant a lot to me. Dysfunctional families are in the news so frequently these days—what's not working, who's unhappy—that it was a pleasure to find myself talking to the five "happy" families profiled here. Without exception, the phrase "happy family" made them flinch. "We're not perfect," many told me. No family is. Although the media shamelessly promote happy endings and conflicts that are resolved in 30 minutes, the people I spoke with aspire to a much more realistic type of happiness. "Happy families don't necessarily have a high laughter quotient," says Andrew I. Schwebel, Ph.D., a professor of psychology at The Ohio State University, in Columbus, "but, rather, have learned to accommodate their own needs and meet their own goals."

All the families emphasized the need to be flexible, recognizing, in the words of Teresa Peck, Ph.D., a clinical psychologist in San Francisco, "that the family is like any other organism that grows and changes through time."

Each of these families faces the future with a healthy optimism, tempered by the knowledge that life offers no guarantees. Finally, they wholeheartedly believe that they are doing the best they can. Otherwise, they are a picture of diversity.

The details of small-town family life.

Denise and Greg Brown, both in their early thirties, live in the 100-year-old house in which Denise grew up, in Minneapolis, Kansas, a farm town of 2,000 people. "I always thought I'd be a June Cleaver kind of mom," Denise says. "And having taught third grade for years, I was sure that having a child of my own would be a piece of cake." But her daughter, Jill, now seven, changed Denise's outlook. "She was very colicky," Denise recalls. "She cried and didn't want to be held. And I'd think, 'I don't know the first thing about being a mother.'"

Today Jill has two brothers: five-year-old Nicholas and three-year-old Spencer.

And their mother has since figured out a few things: "Years ago I would plan great activities down to the final detail, and then at the last minute one of the kids wouldn't want to do it, and I'd be so upset. Now I try to plan one thing to do with the kids each day. It doesn't have to be a big deal; sometimes we spend time in the garden or go to the library. And whatever else doesn't happen that day, well, I just let it slide."

Greg seconds this approach. "If the house has to be cleaned, we all pretend we're professionals cleaning someone else's house, and after we finish, we take a coffee break. The kids love it."

Bedtime is also very important in the Brown household—it's an event that Greg doesn't miss even when he's helping neighbors with their wheat harvest. "We want to make bedtime a sweet and relaxing time for the kids so they can go to sleep feeling good about themselves," says Greg, who teaches high school math and coaches football. The Browns, who have been married ten years, apply this rule to themselves as well. "The Bible says, 'Don't let the sun go down on your anger,'" Greg explains. "No matter how bad a fight, we always try to make up before the end of the day."

The ability to resolve conflict this way is a crucial element of a family's happiness, according to Teresa Peck. "If you can take in another person's point of view, even if you don't like it, and say 'I'll think about what you said,' rather than dismiss it, you will have a more resilient family."

Life in a two-mom household.

Sharon Rich, a 35-year-old financial planner, and Nancy Reed, a 39-year-old psychotherapist, have been together for more than thirteen years, living now in a suburb of Boston with their two daughters—four-year-old Mariah and one-year-old Sophie—two cats, and a goldfish. They attribute their success as a family to their compatibility.

"Our differences are our strength," explains Sharon, who gave birth to both girls. "I love to clean and hate to cook, and Nancy is exactly the opposite. Because Nancy is a therapist, she is sensitive to what the kids are thinking and feeling, and can anticipate what they'll need better than I can. I'm more spontaneous. We each value the other's contribution."

Both women have organized their work schedules so that someone is always at home with the girls. "We spend a lot of time not only being together," Sharon says, "but also talking about what happens. We have complaint sessions and include the girls. We made up an 'I Feel Grumpy' song to help Mariah through the terrible twos, and now we all sing it. We don't even hide our fights from them, unless we're arguing about child rearing. We want them to grow up with real expectations of what it means to be a family."

"This is an important goal," says Maria Mancusi, Ph.D., a clinical psychologist in Fairfax Station, Virginia. Although children clearly suffer if there is too much conflict within a family, too little conflict can be equally debilitating. "Nowhere else are feelings as intense as they are within a family," Mancusi explains. "Children need to see that this intensity can be coped with within the context of an enduring relationship." In other words, the next time your daughter screams "I hate you," take heart; she feels secure enough to speak her mind, a sure sign that she is part of a healthy family.

Mariah and Sophie have the same father; as a friend of the family, he is part of this "support team" and visits regularly. "Our biggest fear," Sharon says, "is that our girls may meet with less tolerant people as they grow older. But in some ways, being an unconventional family is also our strength. We made a very

conscious decision to have children—they know how loved and precious they are.

"We have the same hopes for our girls that all other parents have—that they will be happy in love and work, that they know we will welcome whoever they turn out to be," Sharon adds. "Happiness is working with what you have, changing what you can, and accepting the rest with a sense of humor."

A happier family because of divorce.

"Rich and I met in college," recalls Carol Conger, of West Orange, New Jersey. "We were the perfect couple. Rich was simply the sweetest, most accommodating man I had ever met. We followed my mother's and society's plan for happiness: got married right out of college, found jobs, bought a house, and had children."

But then the Congers began fighting. "No one chooses to get divorced," says Carol. "I never wanted the words 'single mother' or 'broken home' to apply to me. For a long time I thought that nothing was worse than separating." But when the fights intensified, Carol realized that she would rather face down her fears of loneliness than expose her children, Emily and Gary, then five and three, to so much domestic conflict.

Rich moved out three years ago. "It was a very painful time," he says. "We both had to work hard after the separation to put the kids' needs ahead of our own. That meant making decisions in their best interest. For example, I asked Carol not to sell the house and move back to south Jersey, where her family lived. Having the kids so far away would have been devastating to me. And we decided together not to sell the house at all but to let the kids continue to live there so they could attend the same school."

Last year, when Rich and his new wife, Helen Ponzi-Conger, decided to buy a house, they found one just three miles away from Carol's so that the children could easily sleep over on a school night. "We also let them design their own bedrooms in the new house. They don't even call it 'Daddy's house,'" Rich says with pride. "They think of it as their house, too."

And how is everyone doing? "Much better," both parents agree. A testament to their mutual trust is the fact that the children have no fixed visitation schedule; instead, Rich and Carol decide each week what will work best for them.

Rich, who works in the financial office of a chemical company, makes sure that he spends "special time" with each of his kids alone, even if it's only a breakfast chat with Emily or shooting hoops with Gary. "I encourage them to talk to me, to get their feelings off their chest," Rich explains. "I want them to know they can always say anything to me."

Treating each child to extra time alone is important, according to Maria Mancusi. "You can't lose sight of each person's needs, even as you are trying to enlist everyone's cooperation," she says.

Carol, who works in a Manhattan insurance office, feels that she is a better parent now: "I find I have more patience for the children, since I have time for myself each week.

"My friendship with Rick never ended," Carol continues. "We both have so much to lose by fighting with each other and so much to gain by working together. And we all have so much to look forward to now. I have a sense of possibility, of potential, that I never had when I was married. Things may be hard any given day, but I know that they can change, and change for the better, just as our family did after the unthinkable happened."

Seeking help when times get tough.

Jill Bradley—the director of Child Care Services for The Chicago Housing Authority—and her husband, Carlos, who owns his own heating and air-conditioning business, agree that in their eighteen-year marriage they've had their ups and downs. Jill recalls two especially tough times—the first when her daughter, Ginneh, now sixteen, was a baby. "Carlos was an involved father; he took care of Ginneh as much as I did. But we had very different child-rearing styles. He was structured and organized, while I tended to be flexible. For a long time I wanted to convert him to

Recipe for Happiness

Are happy families all alike, as Tolstoy claimed in the novel *Anna Karenina?* In many ways the answer is yes. Happy families, whatever their makeup, don't struggle to compare themselves with an idealized version of the American family. Still, they do share certain qualities. Here are a few ingredients commonly

found in today's happy families:
● A healthy sense of humor, which is good for getting through both day-to-day stresses and major life crises.
● Respect for one another's differences; this is essential for the long haul.
● A valuing of one's own level of satisfaction, because happy parents tend to have happy kids.

● Simple kindness, an example for all family members to follow.
● A measure of flexibility, because families change and grow, just as individuals do.
● A dose of optimism, for getting through the rough times.
● Faith in the belief that each member of the family is doing the best that he or she can.

my approach because I thought Ginneh responded better to it, but eventually I learned to butt out and let him work through his own relationship—good and bad—with his daughter."

All this work paid off thirteen years later. "Just as Ginneh was becoming independent, I found out that I was pregnant again," Jill relates. Allena, the Bradley's "bonus baby," now three, "is really the happy beneficiary of all we learned the first time around with Ginneh."

The second difficult period for the Bradleys occurred seven years ago. "I was unhappy at work," remembers Carlos, "and for years I had had a dream of starting my own business. I come from a risk-taking family. Jill, on the other hand, comes from a traditional family, where you worked at a secure job, from nine to five. Not only was she leery about my striking out on my own, but she also wanted to go back to school.

"Usually I'm the peacemaker in the family, the one without strong opinions," Carlos says. "And I felt that I'd always been supportive of her decisions. So this time I just put my foot down and said, 'This is a well-thought-out plan, and I am going through with it.'"

He did, but the Bradleys separated. Within a month,

however, they found their way to couples' counseling. "I tried to step outside myself and get a perspective on our situation," Jill reflects. "I thought, 'Is anyone going to die or suffer physically or emotionally because of this? If not, then let's take a moment and sort this out. Here's what I'm willing to give up and here's what I want. How about you?'"

By talking together this way, the Bradleys reached a resolution they could both live with: Carlos went ahead with his business, Jill returned to school, and they both worked hard to make a new commitment to their marriage.

As Carlos explains, "I had to learn that I could live with the fact that something I did made Jill unhappy, that I could disappoint her. Before that, I had become so conciliatory that I had begun to deny my own important needs."

"Now," says Jill, "we're not afraid to talk. I've learned that if you go into a conversation with an open mind, you just might hear something you didn't expect, and come out with a fresh way of looking at things."

The Bradleys learned, according to Mancusi, that "the family has a life cycle that mirrors an individual's and moves from one stage to the next with attendant growing pains. Families

who keep this in mind have an easier time accepting the rocky intervals."

Carlos agrees: "Our arguments get loud, but we're always honest and fair with each other, and we always have good intentions. We're ready for the next eighteen years."

Committed equally to the marriage and the children.

When I spoke with Margaret McGovern, she and her family—her husband, James, a systems commissioner for a mechanical contractor; seven-year-old Grant; and four-year-old Ashley—had just returned from a camping trip in Yosemite. "We had a great time; we all love camping," she said, "but right now I can't wait to get a baby-sitter so Jim and I can go out alone one night."

The McGoverns are both in their midthirties, and their home is very obviously child-centered. "We don't hide the kids' toys; our refrigerator is covered with their artwork." At the same time, they have never lost sight of the importance of maintaining their ten-year marriage. "We think it's important for the kids to see their parents go out—to a party or the movies, or to dinner with friends," says Margaret. "Children need to see that

life is not all work, that parents can enjoy life too."

Margaret, who worked in advertising until Grant was born, is now a freelance media consultant and works out of her home. Sometimes she questions her decision to stay home, especially when financial worries set in. "But then," she says, "last week I was standing in back of Ashley when she drew her first detailed picture of a whole person—earlobes, eyelashes, the whole thing. I was overwhelmed with feeling, and I thought, 'This is why I'm home.'"

Learning to divide the responsibilities of caring for the children has always been a thorny issue for Margaret and Jim. "I had to learn to stand back and let Jim have a relationship with our kids without interfering," Margaret says. "I may be home with the kids, but that doesn't mean I know them totally. I had to stop filtering their relationships with their dad."

The McGoverns work hard to stay in balance; they feel they've come a long way. "After Grant was born, Jim and I began competing for who had the worst day. Now we try to listen to each other and not interrupt with 'Me too' statements. Family life means always having to give up something," she adds, "but by putting the family first, we've all grown."

Credits/ Acknowledgments

Cover design by Charles Vitelli

1. Historical and Cross-Cultural Patterns

Facing overview—United Nations photo by Kate Bauer.

11— © 1993 The Gifted Line, John Grossman, Inc.

2. Formation of Relationships

Facing overview—Dushkin Publishing Group, Inc., photo by Pamela Carley.

3. Relationship Maintenance

Facing overview—United Nations photo by L. Barns.

4. Relationships in Transition

Facing overview—Dushkin Publishing Group, Inc., photo by Pamela Carley. 144—Elaine M. Ward.

5. New Styles and the Future

Facing overview—*Children Today* photo by Dick Swartz.

PHOTOCOPY THIS PAGE!!!*

ANNUAL EDITIONS ARTICLE REVIEW FORM

■ NAME: _____ DATE: _____

■ TITLE AND NUMBER OF ARTICLE: _____

■ BRIEFLY STATE THE MAIN IDEA OF THIS ARTICLE: _____

_____

_____

_____

_____

■ LIST THREE IMPORTANT FACTS THAT THE AUTHOR USES TO SUPPORT THE MAIN IDEA:

_____

_____

_____

_____

_____

■ WHAT INFORMATION OR IDEAS DISCUSSED IN THIS ARTICLE ARE ALSO DISCUSSED IN YOUR
TEXTBOOK OR OTHER READING YOU HAVE DONE? LIST THE TEXTBOOK CHAPTERS AND PAGE
NUMBERS:

_____

_____

_____

_____

_____

■ LIST ANY EXAMPLES OF BIAS OR FAULTY REASONING THAT YOU FOUND IN THE ARTICLE:

_____

_____

_____

_____

■ LIST ANY NEW TERMS/CONCEPTS THAT WERE DISCUSSED IN THE ARTICLE AND WRITE A
SHORT DEFINITION:

_____

_____

_____

_____

*Your instructor may require you to use this Annual Editions Article Review Form in any number of ways:
for articles that are assigned, for extra credit, as a tool to assist in developing assigned papers, or simply
for your own reference. Even if it is not required, we encourage you to photocopy and use this page;
you'll find that reflecting on the articles will greatly enhance the information from your text.

ANNUAL EDITIONS: MARRIAGE AND FAMILY 94/95
Article Rating Form

Here is an opportunity for you to have direct input into the next revision of this volume. We would like you to rate each of the 50 articles listed below, using the following scale:

1. **Excellent: should definitely be retained**
2. **Above average: should probably be retained**
3. **Below average: should probably be deleted**
4. **Poor: should definitely be deleted**

Your ratings will play a vital part in the next revision. So please mail this prepaid form to us just as soon as you complete it.
Thanks for your help!

Annual Editions revisions depend on two major opinion sources: one is our Advisory Board, listed in the front of this volume, which works with us in scanning the thousands of articles published in the public press each year; the other is you—the person actually using the book. Please help us and the users of the next edition by completing the prepaid article rating form on this page and returning it to us. Thank you.

Rating	Article	Rating	Article
	1. Prophets of Doom		30. Fathers and Families: Forging Ties That Bind
	2. What Is Love?		31. Father Figures
	3. The Right Chemistry		32. Family Values: The Bargain Breaks
	4. Generalized Extended Family Exchange: A Case from the Philippines		33. "Will the Kids Ever Adjust to Our Divorce?"
	5. Sizing Up the Sexes		34. The Second Time Around
	6. Intimacy: The Art of Working Out Your Relationships		35. The Myths and Misconceptions of the Stepmother Identity
	7. The Changing Nature of Relationships on Campus: Impasses and Possibilities		36. Remarriage Education: The Personal Reflections Program
	8. Choosing Mates—The American Way		37. After My Son's Divorce
	9. Love and Mate Selection in the 1990s		38. Divorce after 50: When Breaking Up Is Better—When It's Not
	10. The Mating Game		39. What Women Want Men to Know about Menopause
	11. When Parents Disagree		40. The Grandparent Bond: Why Kids Need It
	12. What's Happening to American Marriage?		41. Terms of Endearment
	13. Receipts from a Marriage		42. The New Family: Investing in Human Capital
	14. Saving Relationships: The Power of the Unpredictable		43. The New Family Values
	15. Inside the Heart of Marital Violence		44. "Stop the World So I Can Get Off for a While"
	16. After He Hits Her		45. Single Parents and Damaged Children: The Fruits of the Sexual Revolution
	17. The Crisis of the Absent Father		46. A Critique of Pessimistic Views about U.S. Families
	18. How Kids Grieve		47. Marriage and Romantic Relationships: Defining Intimacy in Romantic Relationships
	19. Sex and the Female Agenda		
	20. Sexual Desire		48. How Our Marriage Was Saved
	21. Beyond Betrayal: Life after Infidelity		49. Happy Families: Who Says They All Have to Be Alike?
	22. Ultrasound: An Amazing Look at Life		50. Happy Families Are Not All Alike
	23. Home Delivery		
	24. Unnecessary Cesarean Sections: Halting a National Epidemic		
	25. "She Died Because of a Law"		
	26. When Your Child Is Choking		
	27. 20 Sanity Savers		
	28. Who's Minding America's Kids		
	29. Child Care: What Do Families Really Want?		

(Continued on next page)

ABOUT YOU

Name_____ Date_____

Are you a teacher? ☐   Or student? ☐

Your School Name _____

Department _____

Address _____

City_____ State _____ Zip _____

School Telephone #_____

YOUR COMMENTS ARE IMPORTANT TO US!

Please fill in the following information:

For which course did you use this book? _____

Did you use a text with this Annual Edition?   ☐ yes   ☐ no

The title of the text? _____

What are your general reactions to the Annual Editions concept?

Have you read any particular articles recently that you think should be included in the next edition?

Are there any articles you feel should be replaced in the next edition? Why?

Are there other areas that you feel would utilize an Annual Edition?

May we contact you for editorial input?

May we quote you from above?

ANNUAL EDITIONS: MARRIAGE AND FAMILY 94/95

BUSINESS REPLY MAIL

First Class   Permit No. 84   Guilford, CT

Postage will be paid by addressee

The Dushkin Publishing Group, Inc.
Sluice Dock
DPG **Guilford, Connecticut 06437**

No Postage
Necessary
if Mailed
in the
United States